The
Prose Works
of
Alexander Pope

Edited by
Rosemary Cowler

Vol. II: The Major Works, 1725–1744

ARCHON BOOKS
1986

First published in the U.S.A. as an Archon Book, an imprint
of The Shoe String Press, Inc., Hamden, Connecticut 06514
and in the U.K. by Basil Blackwell, Ltd., Oxford OX4 1JF.

Set in Garamond No. 3 by Brevis Press, Bethany, Connecticut.

Designed by Nancy Ovedovitz.

The paper in this book meets the guidelines for performance
and durability of the Committee on Production Guidelines for
Book Longevity of the Council on Library Resources.

Library of Congress Cataloging-in-Publication Data

Pope, Alexander, 1688–1744.
The prose works of Alexander Pope. Vol. II, The
major works, 1725–1744.

Vol. I, The earlier works, 1711–1720, edited by
Norman Ault, originally published: Oxford : B. Blackwell,
1936.
Bibliography: p.
Includes index.
I. Cowler, Rosemary, 1925– . II. Title.
PR3622.C69   1986   828'.508   86–3625
ISBN 0–208–02059–4 (alk. paper)

CONTENTS

[For each of Pope's prose works there are: an introduction (occasionally shared), a note on publication and text, textual variants (located by alphabetical letters in the margins of the text), and annotations (indicated by numbers within the text). The titles here of the works are those of the first editions, normalized, with the original typography reproduced for chapter title pages. The texts themselves carry the titles of the copytext editions.]

FOREWORD

This book brings to a happy close a collective twentieth-century enterprise, making it possible at long last to view on one shelf the entire body of Pope's writings in prose and verse.

The six volumes of the Twickenham edition of the poems appeared between 1938 and 1960; the last four, containing the Homer translations, in 1967—an interval of almost thirty years. Pope's prose has an even more astonishing publishing history. *Prose Works, 1711–1720,* edited by Norman Ault and issued in a beautifully printed edition by Basil Blackwell in 1936, has waited fifty years for its companion, *Prose Works, Volume II, 1725–1744,* edited (and this time fully annotated as well) by Rosemary Cowler. Add Charles Kerby-Miller's 1950 edition of the *Memoirs of Scriblerus* (reissued in 1966) and you have Pope's works complete—or at least you may have if you have lived long enough and been wise enough to buy when the buying was good; for the individual Twickenham volumes are now largely out of print and expensive to obtain, as are the earlier two volumes of his prose. It is a curiosity of modern publishing that in 1986 Pope should be almost as hard to collect, complete, in editions of this century as in those of his own.

One advantage of the twentieth-century editions is that they bring between two covers writings of great interest that were not collected by Pope himself or by any of his later editors, down to and including Elwin and Courthope. In Norman Ault's volume, for instance, such surreptitious ripostes as *The Critical Specimen,* which shows Pope's facility with a comic prose as different from the passionate advocacy of the *Iliad* Preface as that is from the detached ironies of the Preface to the *Works* of 1717. Rosemary Cowler's volume offers even richer resources for comparative prose analysis. In serious vein, but studiously different in tone, the Shakespeare Preface and the Postscript to the *Odyssey.* In satirical and comic vein, but no less unlike, "A Master Key to Popery" and "A Letter to a Noble Lord." It is a pity that in English-speaking countries this form of analysis remains in its infancy.

If one must choose among the three existing modern volumes of the prose, this volume wins on points. It has the two formidable ironic apologias just cited. It has the two centrally important serious pieces of Pope's maturity, the Preface to his Shakespeare and the Postscript to the *Odyssey.* And it has the entire *Peri Bathous,* the best Art of Poetry that the eighteenth century produced. Readers of this volume will be able to follow also the intrigues and deceptions by which Pope accomplished the publication of his letters, which he rightly judged to be a more faithful image of himself than the caricatures of his enemies. His account of the *Method* by which Curll allegedly obtained the 1735 *Letters* and the various prefaces he contributed to the editions which followed make a fascinating even if depressing study of the art of lying, another art of which Pope was unfortunately a master.

Happiest feature of all in the present volume is that the texts have been scrupulously collated, fully annotated, and thoughtfully introduced. What more can a reader ask?

Maynard Mack

ABBREVIATED REFERENCES

Anecdotes = *Observations, Anecdotes, and Characters of Books and Men.* By Joseph Spence. Edited by James M. Osborn. 2 vols. Oxford: Clarendon Press, 1966.

BL = British Library, London.

Boileau = "A Treatise of the Sublime." *The Works of Monsr· Boileau Despreaux.* [Translated by Ozell.] Vol. II [sep. pagination for the Treatise (1–88)]. London, 1711.

Bossu = [René Le Bossu.] *Monsieur Bossu's Treatise of the Epick Poem.* . . . *"Done into* English *from the* French, *with a new Original* Preface *upon the same Subject, by* W. J." London, 1695.

Correspondence = *The Correspondence of Alexander Pope.* Edited by George Sherburn. 5 vols. Oxford: Clarendon Press, 1956.

Curll = Note by Edmund Curll appended to his reprinting of Pope's *Narrative of the Method.* In *Mr. Pope's Literary Correspondence.* Vol. II. London, 1735.

Dennis, *Works* = *The Critical Works of John Dennis.* Edited by Edward Niles Hooker. 2 vols. Baltimore: Johns Hopkins Press, 1939, 1943.

DNB = *Dictionary of National Biography.*

Dryden, *Essays* = *Essays of John Dryden.* Edited by W. P. Ker. 2 vols. Oxford: Clarendon Press, 1900.

Early Career = *The Early Career of Alexander Pope.* By George Sherburn. Oxford: Clarendon Press, 1934.

EC = *The Works of Alexander Pope.* Edited by Whitwell Elwin and William John Courthope. 10 vols. London: John Murray, 1871–89.

E.L.S. = Note by Edna Leake Steeves, ed. *The Art of Sinking in Poetry.* New York: King's Crown Press, 1952.

F.W.B. = Note by F. W. Bateson, ed. "A Master Key to Popery." *Epistles to Several Persons* (TE III ii), Appendix C. London: Methuen, 1961.

Griffith = *Alexander Pope: A Bibliography.* By Reginald Harvey Griffith. 1 vol. in two parts. Austin, Texas: University of Texas Press, 1922, 1927.

Guerinot = *Pamphlet Attacks on Alexander Pope, 1711–1744.* By J. V. Guerinot. London: Methuen, 1969.

J.B. = Note by John Butt, ed. "A Master Key to Popery." In *Pope and His Contemporaries: Essays Presented to George Sherburn.* Edited by James L. Clifford and Louis A. Landa. Oxford: Clarendon Press, 1949.

Johnson, *Lives* = *Lives of the English Poets*. By Samuel Johnson. Edited by George Birbeck Hill. 3 vols. Oxford: Clarendon Press, 1905.

Loeb = Loeb Classical Library. Cambridge: Harvard University Press and London: William Heinemann.

Memoirs = *Memoirs of the Extraordinary Life, Works, and Discoveries of Martinus Scriblerus*. Edited by Charles Kerby-Miller. New Haven: Yale University Press, 1950.

OED = *Oxford English Dictionary.*

Roberts = *Longinus on the Sublime*. Translated by W. Rhys Roberts. 2nd ed. Cambridge: Cambridge University Press, 1907.

Spingarn = *Critical Essays of the Seventeenth Century*. Edited by J. E. Spingarn. 3 vols. Oxford: Clarendon Press, 1908.

Straus = *The Unspeakable Curll*. By Ralph Straus. London: Chapman and Hall, 1927.

TE = *The Twickenham Edition of the Poems of Alexander Pope*. John Butt, gen. ed. 10 vols. London: Methuen, 1938–67. (In general, the latest edition of each volume has been used.)

Teerink/Scouten = *A Bibliography of the Writings of Jonathan Swift*. 2d. ed. By H{erman} Teerink. Edited by Arthur H. Scouten. Philadelphia: University of Pennsylvania Press, 1963.

W. = Note attributed to himself by William Warburton, ed. "A Letter to a Noble Lord." *The Works of Alexander Pope Esq*. Vol. VIII. London, 1751.

Warren = *Alexander Pope as Critic and Humanist*. By Austin Warren. Princeton: Princeton University Press, 1929.

PREFACE

In comparing Pope with Dryden, Dr. Johnson observed that "Poetry was not the sole praise of either, for both excelled likewise in prose. . . ."[1] The parallel is carried out to the conclusion that "Dryden's page is a natural field, rising into inequalities, and diversified by the varied exuberance of abundant vegetation; Pope's is a velvet lawn, shaven by the scythe, and levelled by the roller."[2] If Dr. Johnson's topography is disputable, there is no question about his familiarity with the terrain. And however extravagant we find Spence's report:

> This is the happiness, which of all things I admire in this writer: either in prose, or verse, he has the finest flow that can be imagin'd. I have often heard a very good Critick say, That *whenever he is reading any Prose of Mr. Pope's, he cannot help thinking that he should never have wrote any thing else: and whenever he reads his Verses, he is angry with him, for losing any time from them, for Prose.*[3]

again it is to be remarked how much more aware the eighteenth century was of Pope as a prose writer than we are today, when Pat Rogers' 1975 *Introduction to Pope* can be advertised as treating "for the first time in a book on Pope"[4] his prose—a statement that if somewhat misleading is still evidential. "Little account," Professor Rogers rightly insists, "is generally taken of this side of Pope's career. It deserves closer attention, and offers ample rewards in enjoyment and literary distinction."[5]

True enough. But to bring about this change calls for a modern collection of the prose works, just as it took the Sherburn edition of the letters to educate readers to the man revealed in the correspondence and the Twickenham edition of the poems to initiate the postwar reassessment of the poet. Reinterpreting and revaluating normally depend on reediting. In Pope's case, this involves assembling his many scattered and lesser known pieces as well as the famous ones; establishing a text that offers as accurately as possible what, through whatever revisions, he wanted to say; and supplying such annotations as will unlock topical obscurities, place each piece in an orienting context, and, in the case of the literary criticism, relate his thinking to contemporary theory.

It is in this spirit that the present edition has been prepared. In Pope's chronology, it follows Norman Ault's 1936 (reissued 1968) *The Prose Works of Alexander Pope: Vol. I. The Earlier Works, 1711–1720,* which it supplements and completes; in scholarly style, it follows the Twickenham vol-

umes, which, appearing over the years since Ault's publication, have served
as models for the editing of eighteenth-century literature.[6] With Ault's
volume, this volume, and Charles Kerby-Miller's admirably edited *Memoirs
of the Extraordinary Life, Works, and Discoveries of Martinus Scriblerus* (reissued 1966), readers may now have at hand the body of Pope's prose,
bulwarked of course by the epistolary prose of the Sherburn *Correspondence.*

The collection offered here covers the years from 1725 (for there were
no prose pieces in the four years—a period for Pope of editing and translating—following Ault's final entries of 1720) to Pope's death. It includes
the well-known (if perhaps not actually so well-read) "Postscript" to the
Odyssey and "Preface" to *The Works of Shakespear,* which, with the "Preface"
to the *Iliad,* constitute Pope's chief prose contribution to neoclassical criticism: not, as Austin Warren remarked long ago, "as rich, as stimulating,"
as that of Dryden and Johnson, but yet an important third force, yielding
a "nearer approach to his superiors . . . than contemporary criticism has
yet conceded."[7] And if Pope the "serious" critic is important and valuable,
a further dimension of his thinking comes into view when he takes up his
double-edged satiric quill for his burlesque *Peri Bathous, or The Art of
Sinking in Poetry,* which he admitted to Spence "may be very well worth
reading seriously as an art of rhetoric."[8] In this vein belong also his other
Scriblerian pieces, where we see him—as he wrote to Swift describing
their collaboration in the *Miscellanies*—"walking down hand in hand to
posterity; not in the stiff forms of learned Authors . . . but in a free,
unimportant, natural, easy manner; diverting others just as we diverted
ourselves."[9] His friendship with Swift was to be commemorated in the
publication of their letters, one of the series of epistolary ventures whose
fascinating—if partly discreditable—history can be traced here through
the range of prefaces to the various editions of the letters and *A Narrative
of the Method,* his account of the machinations by which he maneuvered
Curll into publishing the first collected edition.

If we see Pope in various moods and modes in this volume, perhaps
the most unexpected Pope encountered is the author of the *Letter to a Noble
Lord,* an attack on Lord Hervey not published in Pope's lifetime and
hitherto unavailable in a modern printing (and with it, reprinted for the
first time, the related *A Most Proper Reply to a Nobleman's Epistle to a Doctor
of Divinity*). In the *Letter,* a precursor to the famous Sporus portrait, we
find a more "personal"—a touchingly more exposed—Pope, whose usual
creatively distanced mask has for once slipped—one reason, no doubt,
that the piece was not made public and that he saved himself for the
cherished "above-it-all" posture of the *Epistle to Dr. Arbuthnot.* Although
these two documents should figure in any discussion of the depersonali-

zation of Pope's art, it is never with him a simple issue, even less so as the man and the carefully crafted image began to meld, the man Pope was and the man he would be both realized in his friendships and in the moral vision they helped to shape. It seems appropriate then that his very last piece of writing, his last will and testament, be, like his letters, a testimonial to friendship, to that enduring and endearing aspect of his life and career.

To keep this collection of manageable size as well as to avoid unnecessary duplication, some prose pieces have been omitted which are to be found in Twickenham volumes, where they are largely accessible, well documented, and perhaps read more effectively in the poetic context: in TE V, all the critical apparatus to the *Dunciad Variorum*, "Virgilius Restauratus" (works still of debatable authorship)[10] and "Of the Poet Laureate"; in TE III ii, the letter to Lord Burlington prefixed to the *Epistle to Burlington*. (*A Master Key to Popery*, Appendix C of that volume, has however been reprinted here as a satiric piece of separate interest.) Readers may also miss a few selections listed by Griffith but now rejected by more recent scholarship (Pope's life in Giles Jacob's *Historical Account*,[11] four letters in *The St. James's Journal*,[12] and "A True and Faithful Narrative of What pass'd in London . . .[13]) or considered still too questionable to warrant inclusion or further search: *The Honour of Parnassus*,[14] *The Character of Katharine, Late Duchess of Buckinghamshire and Normanby*,[15] and, from *A Collection of Pieces . . . publish'd on Occasion of the Dunciad*, the dedication[16] and the postscript—the latter probably originally a newspaper advertisement and so designated when included as an appendix to the *Dunciad*.[17] Such advertisements, attendant on the publication of Pope's works or responding to those of his attackers[18]—some no doubt actually by Pope; others, although signed, more likely by booksellers—have been left out. Even if authenticated, they add little to the canon.

This edition of Pope's uncollected prose, 1725–1744, was originally undertaken in collaboration with Maynard Mack, who first directed my interest to Pope's critical prose. Although other commitments led him later to turn over to me the entire project, he has continued to be present in it as guide, philosopher, and friend. To him, above all, and others of the Yale English Department of my generation, I owe a period of my life that forged the lines of my subsequent career and generated my most enduring friendships. They were my Scriblerian years.

One of the rewards of research projects such as this is the opportunity of working in some of the great libraries of the world: Sterling Library, Widener and Houghton Libraries, the Bodleian Library, and the British Library. In particular I would acknowledge the special generosity of the superintendents and staff members of the North Library, who have not only given me access to the vast resources of the British Library but bestowed the convenience of a working shelf—all in an environment enriched by the presence of many colleagues in the field. For the hospitality of Crosby Hall, the Chelsea clubhouse of the British Federation of University Women, I am also grateful. There too I have profited from association with fellow academics and with other professional women.

As for individuals, the roster is a long one. Eighteenth-century studies seem to inspire in their followers a unique camaraderie, and the list that follows, incomplete as it is, is a record of that spirit—whether from "Augustans" or not. With special appreciation to Irvin Ehrenpreis, it gives me pleasure to acknowledge the assistance of Richmond Bond, Betty Bostetter, Ann Bowen, Philip Daghlian, Marvin Dilkey, Joyce Fox, Levi Fox, Morris Golden, Bertrand Goldgar, Ann Louise Hentz, G. H. Hoare, Thomas McFarland, Joann Morse, James Osborn, Charles Ryskamp, Ruth Sharvy, David Vieth, William K. Wimsatt, and Samuel Woods, Jr. To the American Council of Learned Societies I am indebted for a grant-in-aid, and to my college, Lake Forest College, I owe a quality of support of my scholarly life that has included but also far exceeded the value of grants and sabbaticals. Finally, to my editors at Archon Books, my appreciation for their care and patience in seeing a difficult text into print.

At the time of my first publication, one chapter of a collection on the familiar letter in the eighteenth century, I wrote to my mother, my only parent then living, that had it been all mine, it would have been all hers. Now I dedicate this volume to the memory of both my parents; it is indeed all theirs.

Notes

1. Johnson, *Lives,* III, 222.

2. Ibid.

3. Joseph Spence, *An Essay on Pope's Odyssey* (London, 1726), pp. 92–93.

4. Pat Rogers, *An Introduction to Pope* (London: Methuen, 1975), back cover notes.

5. Ibid., p. 131.

6. Since my work on this volume was completed before I encountered David Foxon's Lyell lectures (collected in an unpublished, typescript volume in the BL, "Pope and the Early Eighteenth-Century Book Trade," copy. 1975), I have not considered systematically his challenging bibliographic theories, though I have reviewed some of my collations in the light of his arguments for Pope's role in promoting various formats (duodecimo, quarto, and octavo) and in pioneering

changes in typography (away from extensive capitalization and italicization) and for his practice of revising the accidentals of his texts. My observations (and editing procedures, as noted) corroborate some, at least, of his conclusions. Although I had not included accidentals in the listings of textual variants (for beyond capitalization and italicization such changes had not seemed to provide any significant patterns of improvement), I have now added a few covering notes where I could readily do so.

7. Warren, p. 278.

8. *Anecdotes,* I, 57.

9. *Correspondence,* II, 426.

10. See TE V, xxiv–xxvii; *Memoirs,* pp. 267, 269.

11. See Griffith 123 and *Early Career,* pp. 2–3.

12. *Early Career,* pp. 272–73.

13. Gay's authorship has been established; see *Anecdotes,* I, 58.

14. Advertised by Curll, this piece (Griffith 421: "Being a curious Draught and Prospect of Mr. Pope's House and Gardens at Twickenham, with Verses describing the same . . .") has not been located; in the *Grub-Street Journal* of 19 June 1735 (#286) there is the following notice under Domestic News:

> On Thursday Mr. Curll, with a very eminent painter, went to Twickenham, to survey Mr. Pope's house, gardens, statues, and grotto, with the inscriptions thereon, &c. and has ordered draughts thereof to be taken, which will be engraven by the best masters, and publish'd next month without fail. P. [Daily Post Boy].—*This story of the survey is very improbable; and the* taking *of the draughts* seems *altogether* impracticable.

One view of Pope's villa from the river was, however, engraved and published.

15. See Griffith, p. 493.

16. Signed "R. Savage," but often attributed to Pope, the dedication still raises questions of authorship given Savage's close involvement with Pope on the *Dunciad* (see TE V, xxv–vi).

17. TE V, 418.

18. For example, Griffith, piece 137, p. 160.

THE
PREFACE
OF THE
EDITOR.
to
THE
WORKS
OF
SHAKESPEAR.

INTRODUCTION

Despite an approach far removed from the later attitude which holds that "Assuredly, that criticism of Shakespeare will alone be genial which is reverential,"[1] Shakespearian criticism of the late seventeenth and early eighteenth centuries is more positive than is generally acknowledged. Focusing on Rymer's famous disparagement of *Othello*,[2] Dennis's strictures on *Coriolanus*,[3] Gildon's exposition and defense of classical principles of drama,[4] Dryden's criticism of Shakespeare's style,[5] and Pope's consideration of his faults,[6] commentators have too easily concluded that it was a period inimical to the genius of the dramatist, ignoring the fact that these same critics—with Rymer the only real "castigator"—did not fail to recognize Shakespeare's preeminence as they tried also to establish the nature and source of his powers. Pope, as usual, stands among them as one of the finest spokesmen of his age. His Preface to his edition of Shakespeare, praised as "the best and the representative piece of Shakespearean criticism written during the first half of the eighteenth century,"[7] is just such a sane, generous, well-written account as one might expect from him, but is also in the mainstream of judicious commentary reaching from Dryden's "model of encomiastick criticism"[8] to Dr. Johnson—who replied "when a lady . . . talked of his preface to Shakespeare as superior to Pope's: 'I fear not, Madam, the little fellow has done wonders.' "[9]

Pope's inheritance from Dryden is apparent, even if not so exclusively derived as Johnson implies ("In his Preface he expanded with great skill and elegance the character which had been given of Shakespeare by Dryden").[10] In fact, the notes to the present text indicate how much of his material Pope shared with a number of his fellow critics: the organization of his essay suggests that he might have had Dennis's letters "On the Genius and Writings of Shakespear" at hand when he began writing, just as there are scattered passages throughout recalling Rymer, Gildon, Farquhar, Rowe, and Addison. To read Johnson's preface is to recognize that he in turn had his Pope before him.[11]

Although it should not be surprising for anyone acquainted with the Augustan attitude toward originality to find that most of Pope's opinions can be traced in contemporary thought, his Preface does offer an interesting development over the usual point of view. As was suggested, critics at the time were very conscious of what they considered to be Shakespeare's shortcomings. With Dryden it was a matter of acknowledging his extravagances but subordinating them to his achievements; with Gildon it was

3

a question of censuring dangerous "faults" by the tested criterion of the rules. For Dennis it was an immediate issue, as he had just adapted *Coriolanus* and was aware of the errors in historical knowledge which he felt had weakened the original play. Rowe, determined to eulogize, had merely passed over most of the problem points.[12] Only Pope set out to clear Shakespeare of some of the charges levelled at him or at least to extenuate his responsibility.

The transfer of blame from Shakespeare to his groundling audience and a pair of careless opportunistic publishers allows Pope not only to vindicate Shakespeare and evade some teasing inconsistencies in the problem of his learning,[13] but to justify his own efforts as an editor (an issue still controversial).[14] It must be remembered, a point that Pope emphasizes at the outset of his essay, that the Preface was written as an explanation of his editorial policy and not as a general critical estimate—though he makes equally clear that such a criticism "would be the best occasion that any just Writer could take, to form the judgment and taste of our nation," and he cannot resist a little digression on some of his author's Excellencies ("Not that this is the proper place of praising him, but because I would not omit any occasion of doing it").

To find Pope functioning as a critic in a more specific modern sense, one must look beyond the preface to the edition proper, where in notes and in the selection of "beauties" and "interpolations" he demonstrates his taste and judgment.[15] Though Dr. Johnson took a dim view of such editorial signals ("I have never observed that mankind was much delighted or improved by their asterisks, commas, or double commas; of which the only effect is, that they preclude the pleasure of judging for ourselves, teach the young and ignorant to decide without principles; defeat curiosity and discernment, by leaving them less to discover; and at last show the opinion of the critic, without the reasons on which it was founded, and without affording any light by which it may be examined"),[16] it does provide an insight into the Augustan sensibility as projected by a reader of unusual poetic sensitivity. From it we learn of Pope's preference for description, for the nondramatic (possibly paralleling, suggests John Butt, the oratorio-like performance of the stage), and for the sententious.[17] He does not give the attention to the songs that we would give today,[18] is evidently more troubled than we are by matters of decorum, and disapproves (apparently) of homely images[19] and extravagant figures.[20] It is interesting to note, on the other hand, that he is particularly susceptible to pathos and sentiment[21] and that his taste in comedy is closer to our own than his taste in tragedy.[22] Finally, and not surprisingly, there is his enjoyment of the satiric; in fact, Peter Dixon argues that Pope, finding

Shakespeare there "almost an Augustan 'wit,' " used the playwright's words "to define and consolidate his own satiric standpoint."[23]

This examination of a text for shining passages and spurious accretions is based on the procedures of classical scholarship, the chief models that Pope had, and reflects his understanding of the functions of an editor. The spirit of his undertaking has variously been described as that of a literary executor[24] or even a translator.[25] On the one hand, it was a matter of perfecting and purifying a text as the author himself would have done had he seen his work through publication; on the other, of preparing a text for readers who no longer shared with the author a common sensibility, vocabulary, or frame of reference. Language and poetic style had changed greatly in the hundred years between the First Folio and Pope's edition; in some respects, in fact, the language of the eighteenth century was less close than our own to Elizabethan speech.[26] Certainly Dryden had found the situation difficult:

> Yet it must be allowed to the present age, that the tongue in general is so much refined since Shakespeare's time, that many of his words, and more of his phrases, are scarce intelligible. And of those which we understand, some are ungrammatical, others coarse; and his whole style is so pestered with figurative expressions, that it is as affected as it is obscure.[27]

So did Atterbury in Pope's time:

> I have found time to read some parts of Shakespear which I was least acquainted with. I protest to you, in an hundred places I cannot construe him, I dont understand him. The hardest part of Chaucer is more intelligible to me than some of those Scenes, not merely thro the faults of the Edition, but the Obscurity of the Writer; for Obscure he is, & a little (not a little) enclin'd now & then to Bombast whatever Apology you may have contriv'd on that head for him.[28]

Much of this impression, though not all, was owing to the tangle of the text. The state of Shakespeare's text in those days was scarcely calculated to inspire any reader-critic (who in this period might well be an editor too) with unquestioning reverence for the author and his works. Whether he attributed them to Shakespeare's limitations, or to those of his age (so much less refined than the critic's!), or to the hazards of publication, the obstacles to understanding were real. For Dryden the solution was to excavate ("Yet, after all, because the play was Shakespeare's, and that there appeared in some places of it the admirable genius of the author, I undertook to remove that heap of rubbish under which many excellent thoughts lay wholly buried");[29] for Pope the solution was to compare and select. But the total job was too much for any one talent, as the very different achievements of Lewis Theobald and of Pope as Shakespearean editors show.

If Pope had neither the training nor the temperament for the careful investigations into Elizabethan syntax and idiom which were necessary and which characterized Theobald's otherwise uninspired activity, he was a man of taste (he could unhesitatingly reject as spurious the *Double Falshood,* a play ascribed to Shakespeare by Theobald); he was a fine poetic technician; he had a sensible understanding of what had to be done, as Dr. Johnson and most later commentators acknowledge;[30] and he actually accomplished more of that than they have realized. Pope's own hint of his editorial methods, in a letter to Tonson—"I'm resolved to pass the next whole week in London, purposely to get together Parties of my acquaintance ev'ry night, to collate the several Editions of Shakespear's single Plays, 5 of which I have ingaged to this design"[31]—might well suggest the basically shrewd but procedurally haphazard approach of a man who all his life scorned what he considered the pedantry of scholars like Bentley and Theobald. Such certainly was McKerrow's assumption: "The only possible conclusion is that he had no consistent policy in the matter. Probably he collated those plays or those passages of plays, which interested him, *throughout,* and for the rest merely consulted the early texts when it seemed to him that the reading before him [Pope was using as a base Rowe's second edition, taken from the Fourth Folio] was unsatisfactory."[32] Yet John Hart's study of his collations—while still leaving unanswered some questions about his use of the folios—has demonstrated that not only did Pope have a good selection of quartos and folios to work with but that he used them carefully and systematically, although he preserved for a final reading his own independence of judgment. Despite previous critics, Hart concludes, "Pope's errors and failures must be attributed to something else besides a careless putting together of his text."[33]

Granted, then, that although Pope did not live up to all the editorial promises of the Preface (too often allowing himself what Lounsbury called "the unchecked license of editors of English classics before and after his time" in his silent alterations),[34] he did indeed make certain valid contributions as a Shakespearian editor. He rejected the apocryphal plays of the third and fourth folios, established the importance of collating the early texts, added notes of bibliographical interest and made source attributions whenever he could, suggested emendations in readings and line structure some of which have been kept to the present day, and, finally, contributed to Shakespearian criticism and to the history of eighteenth-century aesthetics his preface.

Whether or not one accepts Austin Warren's judgment, that "It is perhaps, all things considered, the best criticism Pope ever wrote,"[35] certainly it is in the best tradition of Pope the poet-critic, as he responds to a sensibility so different from his own. One is reminded that at the highest levels of art and aesthetics, value transcends current taste—even in an age noted, indeed overly noted, for formalizing those standards. Thus in a context neither docile nor doting, Pope very satisfyingly offers us an exuberant recognition of a great poet by a major one as he "drew the publick attention upon his works, which, though often mentioned, had been little read."[36]

Notes

1. S. T. Coleridge, *Lectures and Notes on Shakespeare and Other Dramatists* (London: Oxford University Press, 1931), pp. 49–50.

2. Thomas Rymer, *A Short View of Tragedy* (London, 1693).

3. Dennis, "An Essay on the Genius and Writings of Shakespear," *Works,* II, 1–17.

4. [Charles Gildon], "An Essay on the Art, Rise, and Progress of the Stage," *The Works of Mr. William Shakespear,* VII (London, 1710).

5. Dryden, "An Essay of Dramatic Poesy," "Preface to *An Evening's Love,*" "Defence of the Epilogue; or, An Essay on the Dramatic Poetry of the Last Age," "Preface to *Troilus and Cressida,*" *Essays,* I.

6. "Preface of the Editor," see pp. 13, 14–17, 25.

7. David Nichol Smith, *Shakespeare in the Eighteenth Century* (Oxford: Clarendon Press, 1928), p. 66.

8. ". . . exact without minuteness, and lofty without exaggeration": Johnson, *Lives,* I, 412.

9. [Mrs. Piozzi] *Johnsonian Miscellanies,* ed. G. B. Hill (Oxford: Clarendon Press, 1897), I, 184–85.

10. Johnson, *Lives,* III, 139. But see n. 14, where Peter Seary links Pope more closely to Rymer's views and Theobald to Dryden's.

11. As he himself wryly noted, "Pope's preface every editor has an interest to suppress, but that every reader would demand its insertion." (Johnson, *Lives,* III, 139n.)

12. N. Rowe, "Some Account of the Life, &c. of Mr. William Shakespear," *The Works of Mr. William Shakespear* (London, 1709), I, xvi: "Whatever may have been his Meaning, finding fault is certainly the easiest Task of Knowledge, and commonly those Men of good Judgment, who are likewise of good and gentle Dispositions, abandon this ungrateful Province to the Tyranny of Pedants."

13. See annotation 19 to the text, p. 29.

14. The furor began at once, of course, with Theobald's *Shakespeare Restored* in 1726. Early twentieth-century studies of Pope's scholarship (Lounsbury's and Schmidt's) were critical too of his theory and practice, finding him as an editor careless and unsystematic. In reaction to such attack, James Sutherland, in "The Dull Duty of an Editor" (*Review of English Studies*, 21 [1945], 202–15), tried to understand Pope's position (largely by tracing his satiric comments on verbal criticism through the *Dunciad* and its prose adjuncts), concluding that his and Theobald's assumptions about scholarship were so radically different that their performances would inevitably be so too, with Pope, by Augustan standards, a conservative editor: "he probably resisted the temptation to astonish the world with conjectural emendation far more often than did Theobald." In "Pope as Scholar-Editor" (*Studies in Bibliography*, 23 [1970], 45–59), John A. Hart, in a discussion that reinforces Sutherland's view, examines Pope's practice in word definition and textual collation. His finding is that Pope's achievement as a scholar "was much greater than has previously been thought, although his scholarship was directed to a different end from that of modern editors. He was not interested in collating editions in order to reproduce the historical text of Shakespeare; he wished to examine all the available material so that he could select the 'best' of it for the entertainment and edification of his age" (p. 59). Another recent commentator is less sanguine about Pope as editor and critic. Concerned too to examine the critical postulates of Pope and Theobald in their approaches to Shakespeare, Peter Seary ("Language versus Design in Drama: A Background to the Pope-Theobald Controversy," *University of Toronto Quarterly*, 42 [1972], 40–63) reviews two established but opposed trends in dramatic criticism in the 1720s over which Pope and Theobald were also to divide: the disagreement between Dryden and Rymer on the relative importance of language and design in dramaturgy. He sees in Pope an emphasis on structure over the verbal that, he believes, raised doubts for him about Shakespeare's achievement—with the result, he argues, that many of Pope's statements in the Preface are critically indecisive or ambiguous.

15. Here too, though, he was in part reflecting contemporary sensibility. As Peter Dixon notes in "Pope's Shakespeare" (*Journal of English and Germanic Philology*, 58 [1964]), "Of the passages admired by Pope (there are more than 160 of them) just over half had been admired by one or more of his predecessors" (p. 197).

16. Johnson, "Proposals" for his Edition of Shakespeare [facsimile reproduction] (London: Humphrey Milford, 1923), pp. 7–8.

17. John Butt, *Pope's Taste in Shakespeare* (London: Humphrey Milford, 1936). Pope's index "of the Characters, Sentiments, Speeches, and Descriptions in Shakespear" is significant of his interest, though it must be borne in mind that the work of compilation was probably Fenton's (see *Correspondence*, II, 244).

18. As Warren notes, "From all the plays but two lyrics are marked . . . the

Take, oh take those lips away, from *Measure for Measure,* and the *Fear no more the heat of th' sun* from *Cymbeline.*" (Warren, p. 151.)

19. He excises from *Macbeth*: "Sleep that knits up the ravell'd sleeve of care" and "What, all my chickens, and their dam, / At one fell swoop?"

20. Again to illustrate from *Macbeth,* he omits "Thy multitudinous seas incarnadine," and in the line "Here lay Duncan, / His silver skin lac'd with his golden blood," substitutes "goary" for "golden."

21. He finds many "beauties" of sentiment to mark in *Romeo and Juliet*; and he praises such scenes of pathos as the description of the death of the children in the Tower in *Richard III* and the lament over Imogen in *Cymbeline.*

22. While Pope has many passages to mark in *Troilus and Cressida, Timon of Athens, Julius Caesar,* and *Macbeth,* he cites but relatively few in *Othello* and only two each in *Hamlet* and *King Lear* (and these, like the speech of Polonius to Laertes, scarcely the lines that a modern writer would single out for praise).

23. See Peter Dixon's study "Pope's Shakespeare," pp. 191–203.

24. Smith, *Shakespeare in the Eighteenth Century,* p. 34.

25. John A. Hart, "Alexander Pope's Edition of Shakespeare" (Ph.D. diss., Yale University, 1943), p. 17.

26. T. R. Lounsbury, *The Text of Shakespeare* (New York: Scribner's, 1906), p. 87. Lounsbury had censured Pope for carelessness in word-definition but John Hart defends him: "He defined as many words as he could according to the best authorities of his day; when he failed, the failure may be attributed to the age in which he lived." ("Pope as Scholar-Editor," p.48.)

27. Dryden, "Preface to *Troilus and Cressida,*" *Essays,* I, 203.

28. *Correspondence,* II, 78–79.

29. Dryden, "Preface to *Troilus and Cressida,*" *Essays,* I, 203–04.

30. Dr. Johnson's commentary, "Pope in his edition undoubtedly did many things wrong, and left many things undone; but let him not be defrauded of his due praise: he was the first that knew, at least the first that told, by what helps the text might be improved. If he inspected the early editions negligently, he taught others to be more accurate" (Johnson, *Lives,* III, 139), may be compared with McKerrow's (Ronald B. McKerrow, *The Treatment of Shakespeare's Text by his Earlier Editors, 1709–1768,* Proceedings of the British Academy, No. 19 [London, 1933], p. 19): "Pope with all his shortcomings was the first editor of Shakespeare to make a genuine attempt to collect all the available material and to use it for the construction of what he regarded as the best possible text, and for this I think we may be grateful to him."

31. *Correspondence,* II, 118.

32. McKerrow, *The Treatment of Shakespeare's Text,* p. 22.

33. Hart, "Pope as Scholar-Editor," p. 59.

34. Lounsbury, *The Text of Shakespeare,* p. 109.

35. Warren, p. 148.

36. Johnson, *Lives,* III, 139.

NOTE ON PUBLICATION AND TEXT

The five years that followed the completion of the *Iliad* translation in 1720 saw Pope engaged in a number of projects: there were the editing and publishing of the works of his recently deceased friends Thomas Parnell and John Sheffield, duke of Buckinghamshire, and the more important activity of editing Shakespeare and translating the *Odyssey*. The chronology of these undertakings is at times vague, but correspondence with Bishop Atterbury in the summer of 1721 suggests that by that time, at least, Pope was involved with the Shakespeare;[1] and by fall the public was notified of his intentions and solicited for help.[2] To judge again from his letters, 1722 found him deep at work on the edition,[3] which was finished in 1724, for on 31 October of that year, he wrote to Broome: "Shakespeare is finished. I have just written the preface, and in less than three weeks it will be public."[4] The three weeks, however, stretched into four months, and the six-volume edition in quarto, sponsored by Tonson, did not appear until 12 March 1725. A seventh, supplementary volume of poems with a preface by Dr. Sewell was also issued in 1725, but Pope had no hand in it.

The bibliography of subsequent editions is confused. Theobald's *Shakespeare Restored* (1726) forced Pope to bring out a second edition with some revisions. William Jaggard, in his *Shakespeare Bibliography* (Stratford: Shakespeare Press, 1911), lists—and Griffith follows him—two such 1728 editions: the so-designated "Second Edition," again by Tonson (9 vols., 12mo., with the ninth volume a supplementary one of attributed plays); and a ten-volume Knapton set, which the BL describes accurately as a duplicate of the Tonson with a new title page to Vol. I and with the addition of a second supplementary volume containing the poems. It is a question whether Knapton bought up unsold copies of the Tonson (presumably unsuccessful because of Theobald's ridicule) or Pope himself did, to be sold to or distributed by Knapton.

Jaggard also lists as edited by Pope a 1731 *Works* by Knapton, for which he provides no reference and which I have been unable to locate, and an eight-volume 12mo. 1734–36 *Works* by Tonson, which he cites as the second stage edition, each play with separate title page and pagination. This edition (the BL copy misdated 1635) follows more closely Tonson's first stage edition than Pope's and, in any case, does not carry his Preface; in fact the BL has a separate "index" volume of the set which includes the title pages to all the volumes, Rowe's Life, Shakespeare's will, and *Theo-*

bald's "Preface" (and, interestingly, also a "Table of the Several Editions of Shakespeare's Plays, Collated by the Editor," which lists among the contemporary editions only Rowe's and the Pope-Tonson 1725 quarto and 1728 duodecimo). A nine-volume cr. 8vo. *Works* by Tonson, 1635 [*sic pro* 1735], listed by Jaggard (and hence by Griffith) with BL and Shakespeare Memorial Library references is not to be found in either library. *The Dramatick Works of William Shakespeare,* printed by R. Walker, 1734–35, which Griffith had questioned as being Pope's, does not carry the Preface. Pope's preface was, however, widely reprinted, Warburton, Hanmer, and Johnson including it in their editions; and Warburton collected it with Pope's prose in the 1751 *Works* of the poet.

The present text follows changes in the 1728 revision, but preserves the typography and accidentals of the 1725 edition;[5] and to complete the history of the text, substantive variants in the 1751 printing are noted with the rest.

Key to the Critical Apparatus

1725 = *The Works of Shakespear,* Vol. I, quarto, Griffith 149.
1728 = Vol. I, second edition, duodecimo (Tonson), Griffith 209.
      = Vol. I, duodecimo (Knapton), Griffith 210.
1751 = *Works,* ed. Warburton, Vol. VI, octavo, Griffith 648.

Notes

1. *Correspondence,* II, 78–79 (2 August 1721).
2. *Early Career,* p. 233.
3. *Correspondence,* II, 101, 102, 106, 117, 118, 142. In this last letter, to Mrs. Judith Cowper, he mentions that "the book is about a quarter printed, & the number of Emendations very great."
4. *Correspondence,* II, 270 (31 October [1724]).
5. Reviewing my collations in the light of David Foxon's arguments about Pope's revisions (see n.6, pp. xiv–xv), I do not find here that the changes in accidentals provide conclusive evidence for using the duodecimo as copytext. With Warburton following the quarto closely, there are in the duodecimo five instances of additional capitalization of nouns and one instance of a change to lower case; three instances of italicization, two perhaps for emphasis; four instances of additions of commas and one of deletions, none altering meaning significantly; one semicolon substituted for a colon and one colon for a period; two instances of *ed* for *'d* and one *'till* for *till*; and *playhouses* hyphenated in the duodecimo. The only interesting (but crucial?) modifications are in the duodecimo's substitution of

commas for periods in the series *"Actus tertia. Exit Omnes. Enter three Witches solus"* and in the spellings of the Virgilian passage, where the quarto's (and Warburton's) *Cingito* has been corrected (?) to *Cingite* of the duodecimo, though that has a questionable *laudaret* for the *laudarit* of the quarto and the *laudarît* of 1751. The only other spelling adjustment is *separate* for *seperate*—a current alternative. What one can deduce from all this is questionable, especially in a second edition forced by Theobald's attack.

THE PREFACE OF THE EDITOR.

It is not my design to enter into a Criticism upon this Author; tho' to do it effectually and not superficially, would be the best occasion that any just Writer could take, to form the judgment and taste of our nation. For of all *English* Poets *Shakespear* must be confessed to be the fairest and fullest subject for Criticism, and to afford the most numerous, as well as most conspicuous instances, both of Beauties and Faults of all sorts.[1] But this far exceeds the bounds of a Preface, the business of which is only to give an account of the fate of his Works, and the disadvantages under which they have been transmitted to us. We shall hereby extenuate many faults which are his, and clear him from the imputation of many which are not: A design, which tho' it can be no guide to future Criticks to do him justice in one way, will at least be sufficient to prevent their doing him an injustice in the other.

I cannot however but mention some of his principal and characteristic Excellencies, for which (notwithstanding his defects) he is justly and universally elevated above all other Dramatic Writers.[2] Not that this is the proper place of praising him, but because I would not omit any occasion of doing it.

If ever any Author deserved the name of an *Original,* it was *Shakespear. Homer* himself drew not his art so immediately from the fountains of Nature, it proceeded thro' *Ægyptian* strainers and channels,[3] and came to him not without some tincture of the learning, or some cast of the models, of those before him. The Poetry of *Shakespear* was Inspiration indeed: he is not so much an Imitator, as an Instrument, of Nature;[4] and 'tis not so just to say that he speaks from her, as that she speaks thro' him.[5]

His *Characters* are so much Nature her self, that 'tis a sort of injury to call them by so distant a name as Copies of her. Those of other Poets have a constant resemblance, which shews that they receiv'd them from one another, and were but multiplyers of the same image: each picture like a mock-rainbow is but the reflexion of a reflexion. But every single character in *Shakespear* is as much an Individual, as those in Life itself; it is as impossible to find any two

alike; and such as from their relation or affinity in any respect appear
most to be Twins, will upon comparison be found remarkably dis-
tinct.[6] To this life and variety of Character, we must add the wonderful Preservation of it; which is such throughout his plays, that
had all the Speeches been printed without the very names of the
Persons, I believe one might have apply'd them with certainty to
every speaker.[7]

The *Power* over our *Passions* was never possess'd in a more eminent
degree, or display'd in so different instances. Yet all along, there is
seen no labour, no pains to raise them; no preparation to guide our
guess to the effect, or be perceiv'd to lead toward it: But the heart
swells, and the tears burst out, just at the proper places: We are
surpriz'd, the moment we weep; and yet upon reflection find the
passion so just, that we shou'd be surpriz'd if we had not wept, and
wept at that very moment.[8]

How astonishing is it again, that the passions directly opposite
to these, Laughter and Spleen, are no less at his command! that he
is not more a master of the *Great,* than of the *Ridiculous* in human
nature; of our noblest tendernesses, than of our vainest foibles; of
our strongest emotions, than of our idlest sensations![9]

Nor does he only excell in the Passions: In the coolness of Reflection and Reasoning he is full as admirable. His *Sentiments* are not
only in general the most pertinent and judicious upon every subject;
but by a talent very peculiar, something between Penetration and
Felicity, he hits upon that particular point on which the bent of
each argument turns, or the force of each motive depends.[10] This is
perfectly amazing, from a man of no eduation or experience in those
great and publick scenes of life which are usually the subject of his
thoughts: So that he seems to have known the world by Intuition,
to have look'd thro' humane nature at one glance, and to be the
only Author that gives ground for a very new opinion, That the
Philosopher and even the Man of the world, may be *Born,* as well
as the Poet.[11]

It must be own'd that with all these great excellencies, he has
almost as great defects; and that as he has certainly written better,
so he has perhaps written worse, than any other.[12] But I think I can
in some measure account for these defects, from several causes and
accidents; without which it is hard to imagine that so large and so

enlighten'd a mind could ever have been susceptible of them. That all these Contingencies should unite to his disadvantage seems to me almost as singularly unlucky, as that so many various (nay contrary) Talents should meet in one man, was happy and extraordinary.

It must be allowed that Stage-Poetry of all other, is more particularly levell'd to please the *Populace,* and its success more immediately depending upon the *Common Suffrage.* One cannot therefore wonder, if *Shakespear* having at his first appearance no other aim in his writings than to procure a subsistance, directed his endeavours solely to hit the taste and humour that then prevailed. The Audience was generally composed of the meaner sort of people; and therefore the Images of Life were to be drawn from those of their own rank: accordingly we find, that not our Author's only but almost all the old Comedies have their Scene among *Tradesmen* and *Mechanicks*: And even their Historical Plays strictly follow the common *Old Stories* or *Vulgar Traditions* of that kind of people.[13] In Tragedy, nothing was so sure to *Surprize* and cause *Admiration,* as the most strange, unexpected, and consequently most unnatural, Events and Incidents; the most exaggerated Thoughts; the most verbose and bombast Expression; the most pompous Rhymes, and thundering Versification. In Comedy, nothing was so sure to *please,* as mean buffoonry, vile ribaldry, and unmannerly jests of fools and clowns. Yet even in these, our Author's Wit buoys up, and is born above his subject: his Genius in those low parts is like some Prince of a Romance in the disguise of a Shepherd or Peasant; a certain Greatness and Spirit now and then break out, which manifest his higher extraction and qualities.[14]

It may be added, that not only the common Audience had no notion of the rules of writing, but few even of the better sort piqu'd themselves upon any great degree of knowledge or nicety that way; till *Ben Johnson* getting possession of the Stage, brought critical learning into vogue:[15] And that this was not done without difficulty, may appear from those frequent lessons (and indeed almost Declamations) which he was forced to prefix to his first plays, and put into the mouth of his Actors, the *Grex, Chorus,* &c. to remove the prejudices, and inform the judgment of his hearers. Till then, our Authors had no thoughts of writing on the model of the Ancients: their Tragedies were only Histories in Dialogue; and their Comedies follow'd the thread of any Novel as they found it, no less implicitly than if it had been true History.[16]

To judge therefore of *Shakespear* by *Aristotle's* rules, is like trying a man by the Laws of one Country, who acted under those of another.[17] He writ to the *People*; and writ at first without patronage from the better sort, and therefore without aims of pleasing them: without assistance or advice from the Learned,[18] as without the advantage of education or acquaintance among them: without that knowledge of the best models, the Ancients, to inspire him with an emulation of them;[19] in a word, without any views of Reputation, and of what Poets are pleas'd to call Immortality: Some or all of which have encourag'd the vanity, or animated the ambition, of other writers.

Yet it must be observ'd, that when his performances had merited the protection of his Prince, and when the encouragement of the Court had succeeded to that of the Town;[20] the works of his riper years are manifestly raised above those of his former. The Dates of his plays sufficiently evidence that his productions improved, in proportion to the respect he had for his auditors. And I make no doubt this observation would be found true in every instance, were but Editions extant from which we might learn the exact time when every piece was composed, and whether writ for the Town, or the Court.

Another Cause (and no less strong than the former) may be deduced from our Author's being a *Player,* and forming himself first upon the judgments of that body of men whereof he was a member.[21] They have ever had a Standard to themselves, upon other principles than those of *Aristotle.* As they live by the Majority, they know no rule but that of pleasing the present humour, and complying with the wit in fashion; a consideration which brings all their judgment to a short point. Players are just such judges of what is *right,* as Taylors are of what is *graceful.* And in this view it will be but fair to allow, that most of our Author's faults are less to be ascribed to his wrong judgment as a Poet, than to his right judgment as a Player.[22]

By these men it was thought a praise to *Shakespear,* that he scarce ever *blotted a line.* This they industriously propagated, as appears from what we are told by *Ben Johnson* in his *Discoveries,* and from the preface of *Heminges* and *Condell* to the first folio Edition.[23] But in reality (however it has prevailed) there never was a more groundless report, or to the contrary of which there are more undeniable evidences.[24] As, the Comedy of the *Merry Wives* of *Windsor,* which he entirely new writ; the *History of* Henry *the 6th,* which was first published under the Title of the *Contention of* York *and* Lancaster; and that of *Henry the 5th,* extreamly improved; that of *Hamlet* enlarged to almost as much again as at first, and many others.[25] I believe the common opinion of his want of Learning proceeded from no better ground. This too might be thought a Praise by some;[26] and to this his Errors have as injudiciously been ascribed by others.[27] For 'tis certain, were it true, it could concern but a small part of them; the most are such as are not properly Defects, but Superfoetations: and arise not from want of learning or reading, but from want of thinking or judging: or rather (to be more just to our Author) from a compliance to those wants in others. As to a wrong choice of the subject, a wrong conduct of the incidents, false thoughts, forc'd expressions, &c. if these are not to be ascrib'd to the foresaid accidental reasons, they must be charg'd upon the Poet himself, and there is no help for it. But I think the two Disadvantages which I have mentioned (to be obliged to please the lowest of people, and to keep the worst of company) if the consideration be extended as far as it reasonably may, will appear sufficient to mislead and depress the greatest Genius upon earth. Nay the more A modesty with which such a one is endued, the more he is in danger of submitting and conforming to others, against his own better judgment.

But as to his *Want of Learning,* it may be necessary to say something more: There is certainly a vast difference between *Learning* and *Languages.* How far he was ignorant of the latter, I cannot determine; but 'tis plain he had much Reading at least, if they will not call it Learning. Nor is it any great matter, if a man has Knowledge, whether he has it from one language or from another.[28] Nothing is more evident than that he had a taste of natural Philosophy, Mechanicks, ancient and modern History, Poetical learning and Mythology: We find him very knowing in the customs, rites, and manners of Antiquity. In *Coriolanus* and *Julius Caesar,* not only the Spirit, but Manners, of the *Romans* are exactly drawn; and still a

nicer distinction is shown, between the manners of the *Romans* in
the time of the former, and of the latter. His reading in the ancient
Historians is no less conspicuous, in many references to particular
passages: and the speeches copy'd from *Plutarch* in *Coriolanus* may,
I think, as well be made an instance of his learning, as those copy'd
from *Cicero* in *Catiline,* of *Ben Johnson's*.[29] The manners of other
nations in general, the *Egyptians, Venetians, French,* &c. are drawn
with equal propriety. Whatever object of nature, or branch of science, he either speaks of or describes; it is always with competent,
if not extensive knowledge: his descriptions are still exact; all his
metaphors appropriated, and remarkably drawn from the true nature
and inherent qualities of each subject. When he treats of Ethic or
Politic, we may constantly observe a wonderful justness of distinction, as well as extent of comprehension. No one is more a master
of the Poetical story,[30] or has more frequent allusions to the various
parts of it: Mr. *Waller* (who has been celebrated for this last particular)[31] has not shown more learning this way than *Shakespear.* We
have Translations from *Ovid* published in his name, among those
Poems which pass for his, and for some of which we have undoubted
authority, (being published by himself, and dedicated to his noble
Patron the Earl of *Southampton*:)[32] He appears also to have been
conversant in *Plautus,* from whom he has taken the plot of one of
his plays:[33] he folows the *Greek* Authors, and particularly *Dares Phrygius,*[34] in another:[35] (altho' I will not pretend to say in what language
he read them.) The modern *Italian* writers of Novels he was manifestly acquainted with; and we may conclude him to be no less
conversant with the Ancients of his own country, from the use he
has made of *Chaucer* in *Troilus* and *Cressida,* and in the *Two Noble
Kinsmen,* if that Play be his, as there goes a Tradition it was, (and
A   indeed it has little resemblance of *Fletcher,* and more of our Author's
worst sort than some of those which have been received as genuine.)
    I am inclined to think, this opinion proceeded originally from
the zeal of the Partizans of our Author and *Ben Johnson*; as they
endeavoured to exalt the one at the expence of the other.[36] It is ever
the nature of Parties to be in extremes; and nothing is so probable,
as that because *Ben Johnson* had much the most learning, it was said
on the one hand that *Shakespear* had none at all; and because *Shakespear* had much the most wit and fancy, it was retorted on the other,

that *Johnson* wanted both. Because *Shakespear* borrowed nothing, it was said that *Ben Johnson* borrowed every thing. Because *Johnson* did not write extempore, he was reproached with being a year about every piece; and because *Shakespear* wrote with ease and rapidity, they cryed, he never once made a blot. Nay the spirit of opposition ran so high, that whatever those of the one side objected to the other, was taken at the rebound, and turned into Praises; as injudiciously, as their antagonists before had made them Objections.[37]

Poets are always afraid of Envy; but sure they have as much reason to be afraid of Admiration. They are the *Scylla* and *Charybdis* of Authors; those who escape one, often fall by the other. *Pessimum genus inimicorum Laudantes,* says *Tacitus*:[38] and *Virgil* desires to wear a charm against those who praise a Poet without rule or reason.

> ———*Si ultra placitum laudarit, baccare frontem*
> *Cingito, ne Vati noceat———*[39]

But however this contention might be carried on by the Partizans on either side, I cannot help thinking these two great Poets were good friends, and lived on amicable terms and in offices of society with each other. It is an acknowledged fact, that *Ben Johnson* was introduced upon the Stage, and his first works encouraged, by *Shakespear*.[40] And after his death, that Author writes *To the memory of his beloved Mr.* William Shakespear, which shows as if the friendship had continued thro' life. I cannot for my own part find any thing *Invidious* or *Sparing* in those verses, but wonder Mr. *Dryden* was of that opinion.[41] He exalts him not only above all his Contemporaries, but above *Chaucer* and *Spenser,* whom he will not allow to be great enough to be rank'd with him; and challenges the names of *Sophocles, Euripides,* and *Æschylus,* nay all *Greece* and *Rome* at once, to equal him. And (which is very particular) expresly vindicates him from the imputation of wanting *Art,* not enduring that all his excellencies shou'd be attributed to *Nature.*[42] It is remarkable too, that the praise he gives him in his *Discoveries* seems to proceed from a *personal kindness*; he tells us that he lov'd the man, as well as honoured his memory; celebrates the honesty, openness, and frankness of his temper; and only distinguishes, as he reasonably ought, between the real merit of the Author, and the silly and derogatory applauses of the Players.[43] *Ben Johnson* might indeed be sparing in his Commendations (tho' certainly he is not so in this instance) partly from his own nature,[44] and partly from judgment. For men of judgment think they do any man more service in praising him justly, than lavishly.[45] I say, I would fain believe they were Friends, tho' the violence and ill-breeding of their Followers and Flatterers were enough to give rise to the contrary report. I would hope that it may be with *Parties,* both in Wit and State, as with those Monsters described by the Poets; and that their *Heads* at least may have something humane, tho' their *Bodies* and *Tails* are wild beasts and serpents.

As I believe that what I have mentioned gave rise to the opinion of *Shakespear*'s want of learning; so what has continued it down to us may have been the many blunders and illiteracies of the first Publishers of his works. In these Editions their ignorance shines almost in every page; nothing is more common than *Actus tertia. Exit Omnes. Enter three Witches solus.*[46] Their *French* is as bad as their *Latin,* both in construction and spelling: Their very *Welsh* is false.[47] Nothing is more likely than that those palpable blunders of *Hector*'s quoting *Aristotle,*[48] with others of that gross kind, sprung from the same root. It not being at all credible that these could be the errors of any man who had the least tincture of a School, or the least conversation with such as had. *Ben Johnson* (whom they will not think partial to him) allows him at least to have had *some Latin*; which is utterly inconsistent with mistakes like these. Nay the constant blunders in proper names of persons and places, are such as must have proceeded from a man, who had not so much as read any history, in any language: so could not be *Shakespear*'s.

I shall now lay before the reader some of those almost innumerable Errors, which have risen from one source, the ignorance of the Players, both as his actors, and as his editors. When the nature and kinds of these are enumerated and considered, I dare to say that not *Shakespear* only, but *Aristotle* or *Cicero,* had their works undergone the same fate, might have appear'd to want sense as well as learning.

It is not certain that any one of his Plays was published by himself.[49] During the time of his employment in the Theatre, several of his pieces were printed separately in Quarto. What makes me think that most of these were not publish'd by him, is the excessive carelessness of the press: every page is so scandalously false spelled, and almost all the learned or unusual words so intolerably mangled, that it's plain there either was no Corrector to the press at all, or one totally illiterate. If any were supervised by himself, I should fancy the two parts of *Henry the 4th,* and *Midsummer-Night's Dream* might have been so: because I find no other printed with any exactness; and (contrary to the rest) there is very little variation in all the subsequent editions of them. There are extant two Prefaces, to the first quarto edition of *Troilus* and *Cressida* in 1609, and to that of *Othello*; by which it appears, that the first was publish'd without his knowledge or consent, and even before it was acted, so late as seven or eight years before he died: and that the latter was not printed till after his death.[50] The whole number of genuine plays which we have been able to find printed in his life-time, amounts but to eleven.[51] And of some of these, we meet with two or more editions by different printers, each of which has whole heaps of trash different from the other: which I should fancy was occasion'd, by their being taken from different copies, belonging to different Playhouses.

The folio edition (in which all the plays we now receive as his, were first collected) was published by two Players, *Heming* and *Condell,* in 1623, seven years after his decease. They declare, that all the other editions were stolen and surreptitious, and affirm theirs to be purged from the errors of the former.[52] This is true as to the literal errors, and no other; for in all respects else it is far worse than the Quarto's:

First, because the additions of trifling and bombast passages are in this edition far more numerous. For whatever had been added, since those Quarto's, by the actors, or had stolen from their mouths into the written parts, were from thence conveyed into the printed text, and all stand charged upon the Author. He himself complained of this usage in *Hamlet,* where he wishes that *those who play the Clowns wou'd speak no more than is set down for them.* (Act. 3. Sc. 4.)[53] But as a proof that he could not escape it, in the old editions of *Romeo* and *Juliet* there is no hint of a great number of the mean conceits and ribaldries now to be found there.[54] In others, the low scenes of Mobs, Plebeians and Clowns, are vastly shorter than at present:[55] And I have seen one in particular (which seems to have belonged to the playhouse, by having the parts divided with lines, and the Actors names in the margin) where several of those very passages were added in a written hand, which are since to be found in the folio.[56]

In the next place, a number of beautiful passages which are extant in the first single editions, are omitted in this:[57] as it seems, without any other reason, than their willingness to shorten some scenes: These men (as it was said of *Procrustes*) either lopping, or stretching an Author, to make him just fit for their Stage.

This edition is said to be printed from the *Original Copies*; I believe they meant those which had lain ever since the Author's days in the playhouse, and had from time to time been cut, or added to, arbitrarily.[58] It appears that this edition, as well as the Quarto's, was printed (at least partly) from no better copies than the *Prompter's Book,* or *Piece-meal Parts* written out for the use of the actors: For in some places their very* names are thro' carelessness set down instead of the *Personae Dramatis*: And in others the notes of direction to the *Property-men* for their *Moveables,* and to the *Players* for their *Entries,*** are inserted into the Text, thro' the ignorance of the Transcribers.[59]

The Plays not having been before so much as distinguish'd by *Acts* and *Scenes,* they are in this edition divided according as they play'd them; often where there is no pause in the action,[60] or where they thought fit to make a breach in it, for the sake of Musick, Masques, or Monsters.

Sometimes the scenes are transposed and shuffled backward and forward; a thing which could no otherwise happen, but by their being taken from seperate and piece-meal-written parts.

Many verses are omitted intirely,[61] and others transposed;[62] from whence invincible obscurities have arisen, past the guess of any Commentator to clear up, but just where the accidental glympse of an old edition enlightens us.

Some Characters are confounded and mix'd, or two put into one,

*Much ado about nothing. *Act* 2. *Enter Prince* Leonato, Claudio, *and* Jack Wilson, *instead* of Balthasar. *And in Act* 4. Cowley, *and* Kemp, *constantly thro' a whole Scene.* Edit. Fol. of 1623, and 1632.
 ***Such as,*
—————My Queen is murder'd! *Ring the little Bell*——
—————His nose grew as sharp as a pen, and *a table of Greenfield's,* &c.
A which last words are not in the first quarto edition.

for want of a competent number of actors. Thus in the Quarto edition of *Midsummer-Night's Dream,* Act. 5. *Shakespear* introduces a kind of Master of the Revels called *Philostratus:* all whose part is given to another character (that of *Ægeus*) in the subsequent editions: So also in *Hamlet* and *King Lear.* This too makes it probable that the Prompter's Books were what they call'd the Original Copies.

From liberties of this kind, many speeches also were put into the mouths of wrong persons, where the Author now seems chargeable with making them speak out of character:[63] Or sometimes perhaps for no better reason, than that a governing Player, to have the mouthing of some favourite speech himself, would snatch it from the unworthy lips of an Underling.

Prose from verse they did not know, and they accordingly printed one for the other throughout the volume.[64]

Having been forced to say so much of the Players, I think I ought in justice to remark, that the Judgment, as well as Condition, of that class of people was then far inferior to what it is in our days. As then the best Playhouses were Inns and Taverns (the *Globe,* the *Hope,* the *Red Bull,* the *Fortune,* &c.) so the top of the profession were then meer Players, not Gentlemen of the stage: They were led into the Buttery by the Steward, not plac'd at the Lord's table, or Lady's toilette: and consequently were intirely depriv'd of those advantages they now enjoy, in the familiar conversation of our Nobility, and an intimacy (not to say dearness) with people of the first condition.[65]

From what has been said, there can be no question but had *Shakespear* published his works himself (especially in his latter time, and after his retreat from the stage) we should not only be certain which are genuine; but should find in those that are, the errors lessened by some thousands. If I may judge from all the distinguishing marks of his style, and his manner of thinking and writing, I make no doubt to declare that those wretched plays, *Pericles,*[66]
A *Locrine, Sir John Oldcastle, Yorkshire Tragedy, Lord Cromwell, The Pu-*
B *ritan, London Prodigal,* and a thing call'd the *Double Falshood,*[67] cannot be admitted as his.[68] And I should conjecture of some of the
C others, (particularly *Love's Labour's Lost, The Winter's Tale, Comedy of*
D *Errors,* and *Titus Andronicus*) that only some characters, single scenes, or perhaps a few particular passages, were of his hand. It is very

probable what occasion'd some Plays to be supposed *Shakespear*'s was only this; that they were pieces produced by unknown authors, or fitted up for the Theatre while it was under his administration: and no owner claiming them, they were adjudged to him, as they give Strays to the Lord of the Manor. A mistake, which (one may also observe) it was not for the interest of the House to remove. Yet the Players themselves, *Hemings* and *Condell,* afterwards did *Shakespear* the justice to reject those plays in their edition; tho' they were then printed in his name, in every body's hands, and acted with some applause; (as we learn from what *Ben Johnson* says of *Pericles* in his Ode on the *New Inn.*)[69] That *Titus Andronicus* is one of this class I am the rather induced to believe, by finding the same Author openly express his contempt of it in the *Induction* to *Bartholomew-Fair,* in the year 1614, when *Shakespear* was yet living.[70] And there is no better authority for these latter sort, than for the former, which were equally published in his life-time.

If we give into this opinion, how many low and vicious parts and passages might no longer reflect upon this great Genius, but appear unworthily charged upon him? And even in those which are really his, how many faults may have been unjustly laid to his account from arbitrary Additions, Expunctions, Transpositions of scenes and lines, confusion of Characters and Persons, wrong application of Speeches, corruptions of innumerable Passages by the Ignorance, and wrong Corrections of 'em again by the Impertinence, of his first Editors? From one or other of these considerations, I am verily per-
ʒwaded, that the greatest and grossest part of what are thought his errors would vanish, and leave his character in a light very different from that disadvantageous one, in which it now appears to us.

This is the state in which *Shakespear*'s writings lye at present; for since the above-mentioned Folio Edition, all the rest have implicitly followed it, without having recourse to any of the former, or ever making the comparison between them.[71] It is impossible to repair the Injuries already done him; too much time has elaps'd, and the materials are too few. In what I have done I have rather given a proof of my willingness and desire, than of my ability, to do him justice. I have discharg'd the dull duty of an Editor,[72] to my best judgment, with more labour than I expect thanks, with a religious abhorrence of all Innovation, and without any indulgence to my

A

private sense or conjecture. The method taken in this Edition will show it self. The various Readings are fairly put in the margin, so that every one may compare 'em; and those I have prefer'd into the Text are constantly *ex fide Codicum,* upon authority.[73] The Alterations or Additions which *Shakespear* himself made, are taken notice of as they occur.[74] Some suspected passages which are excessively bad, (and which seem Interpolations by being so inserted that one can intirely omit them without any chasm, or deficience in the context) are degraded to the bottom of the page;[75] with an Asterisk referring to the places of their insertion. The Scenes are mark'd so distinctly that every removal of place is specify'd; which is more necessary in this Author than any other, since he shifts them more frequently: and sometimes without attending to this particular, the reader would have met with obscurities. The more obsolete or unusual words are explained.[76] Some of the most shining passages are distinguish'd by comma's in the margin; and where the beauty lay not in particulars but in the whole, a star is prefix'd to the scene.[77] This seems to me a shorter and less ostentatious method of performing the better half of Criticism (namely the pointing out an Author's excellencies)[78] than to fill a whole paper with citations of fine passages, with *general Applauses,* or *empty Exclamations* at the tail of them. There is also subjoin'd a Catalogue of those first Editions by which the greater part of the various readings and of the corrected passages are authorised, (most of which are such as carry their own evidence along with them.) These Editions now hold the place of Originals, and are the only materials left to repair the deficiencies or restore the corrupted sense of the Author: I can only wish that a greater number of them (if a greater were ever published) may yet be found, by a search more successful than mine, for the better accomplishment of this end.

I will conclude by saying of *Shakespear,* that with all his faults, and with all the irregularity of his *Drama,* one may look upon his works, in comparison of those that are more finish'd and regular, as upon an ancient majestick piece of *Gothick* Architecture, compar'd with a neat Modern building: The latter is more elegant and glaring, but the former is more strong and more solemn. It must be allow'd, that in one of these there are materials enough to make many of the other. It has much the greater variety, and much the nobler apartments; tho' we are often conducted to them by dark, odd, and uncouth passages. Nor does the Whole fail to strike us with greater reverence, tho' many of the Parts are childish, ill-plac'd, and unequal to its grandeur.[79]

Textual Variants

[Page 17: A. a] an *1728.*]

Page 18: A. Author's worst sort] Author *1725, 1751.*

Page 22: A. which . . . edition. *Add. 1728; the entire footnote om. 1751.*

Page 23: A. *Puritan,*] Puritan, and *1725, 1751.*

Page 23: B. and . . . *Falshood, Add. 1728; om. 1751.*

Page 23: C. *Labour's*] Labour *1725.*

Page 23: D. *Comedy of Errors, Add. 1728; om. 1751.*

Page 24: A. those] those eight *1725, 1751.*

Annotations

1. For Pope, as for the Augustans generally and the Renaissance critics before them, the critical task is to discriminate what is from what is not to be admired, for the benefit of both reader and apprentice writer. Cf. Dennis:

> Thus, Sir, have I laid before you a short but impartial Account of the Beauties and Defects of *Shakespear,* with an Intention to make these Letters publick if they are approv'd by you; to teach some People to distinguish between his Beauties and his Defects, that while they imitate the one, they may with Caution avoid the other [there being nothing of more dangerous Contagion to Writers, and especially to young ones, than the Faults of great Masters]. . . . (Dennis, "On the Genius and Writings of Shakespeare," *Works,* II, 17.)

Gildon's defense of classical rules is offered on the same basis: "Thus I shall all along recommend the Beauties of *Shakespear*; but must beg leave to lay down the Rules of the *Drama* least we fall into an Erroneous Imitation of his Faults." ([Charles Gildon], "An Essay on the Art, Rise, and Progress of the Stage," *The Works of Mr. William Shakespear* [London, 1710], VII, xi.)

2. Though the Augustan critics would have been shocked by the nineteenth-century notion that Shakespeare (or any other author) is above criticism, their response to him is generous. Dryden may complain that Shakespeare's writing is "many times flat, insipid; his comic wit degenerating into clenches, his serious swelling into bombast," but in the same passage he acclaims him "the man who of all modern, and perhaps ancient poets, had the largest and most comprehensive

soul" ("An Essay of Dramatic Poesy," Dryden, *Essays*, I, 80, 79). Similarly, Dennis boggles at Shakespeare's cavalier treatment of historical figures, but his objections do not prevent his declaring him "one of the greatest Genius's that the World e'er saw for the Tragick Stage. Tho' he lay under greater Disadvantages than any of his Successors, yet had he greater and more genuine Beauties than the best and greatest of them." (Dennis, "On the Genius and Writings," *Works*, II, 4.) And Gildon takes a like position ("Progress of the Stage," p. v). Pope's praise is particularly strong because it places Shakespeare without qualification above the ancients, an idea elaborated on in his next paragraph.

3. It was generally held that Homer had traveled in Egypt, first home of the arts and sciences, and drawn there much of his knowledge (both Mme Dacier and Parnell make a strong point of this in their biogaphies of him). See also Leonard Welsted, "A Dissertation Concerning the Perfection of the English Language," *Critical Essays of the Eighteenth Century*, ed. W. H. Durham (New Haven: Yale University Press, 1915), p. 361; Sir William Temple, "An Essay upon the Ancient and Modern Learning," Spingarn, III, 32–72; and Sir Richard Blackmore, "An Essay upon Epick Poetry," in *Essays upon Several Subjects* (London, 1716), p. 27.

4. "It is without Controversie, that he had no knowledge of the Writings of the Antient Poets, not only from this Reason, but from his Works themselves, where we find no traces of any thing that looks like an Imitation of 'em . . ." (N. Rowe, "Some Account of the Life, &c. of Mr. William Shakespear," *The Works of Mr. William Shakespear* [London, 1709], I, iii). For comparable statements see Dennis ("On the Genius and Writings," *Works*, II, 4), Gildon ("Progress of the Stage," p. vi) and Addison (*Spectator*, No. 160 [3 September 1711]).

5. ". . . he needed not the spectacles of books to read Nature; he looked inwards, and found her there." (Dryden, "Of Dramatic Poesy," *Essays*, I, 80.)

6. Dennis is cooler: "His Characters are always drawn justly, exactly, graphically. . . . He has for the most part more fairly distinguish'd them than any of his Successors have done. . . ." ("On the Genius and Writings," *Works*, II, 4.) But see Margaret Cavendish, Letter CXXIII, *Sociable Letters* (1664), quoted by D. N. Smith, *Shakespearian Criticism* (London: World Classics, 1923), p. 14— ". . . so Well he hath Express'd in his Playes all Sorts of Persons, as one would think he had been Transformed into every one of those Persons he hath Described. . . ."

7. Gildon's similar comment—"he has not only distinguish'd his principal Persons, but there is scarce a Messenger comes in but is visibly different from all the Rest of the Persons in the Play. So that you need not to mention the Names of the Person, that speaks when you read the Play the Manners of the Persons will sufficiently inform you who it is speaks . . ." ("Progress of the Stage," p. li)—is later echoed in Addison's discussion of Homer's characters: "In short,

there is scarce a speech or action in the *Iliad,* which the reader may not ascribe to the person that speaks or acts, without seeing his name at the head of it" (*Spectator* No. 273 [12 January 1712]), and subsequently in Pope's *Iliad* preface (TE VII, 7–8).

8. "He had so fine a Talent for touching the Passions . . . that they often touch us more without their due Preparations, than those of other Tragick Poets, who have all the Beauty of Design and all the Advantage of Incidents." (Dennis, "On the Genius and Writings," *Works,* II, 4.) ". . . and in his Tragick Vein, he Presents Passions so Naturally, and Misfortunes so Probably, as he Peirces the Souls of his Readers with such a True Sense and Feeling thereof, that it Forces Tears through their Eyes. . . ." (Margaret Cavendish, Letter CXXIII, *Sociable Letters,* quoted by Smith, *Shakespearian Criticism,* pp. 14–15). See also Dryden ("Preface to *Troilus and Cressida, Essays,* I, 224 and "Of Dramatic Poesy," *Essays,* I, 79–80), Gildon ("Progress of the Stage," p. v), Richard Steele (*Tatler* No. 68 [15 September 1709]).

9. "There is no Man has had more of this *vis Comica* ["*Comedy* . . . is an Imitation both of *Action* and *Manners,* but those must both have a great deal of the *Ridiculum* in them . . ."] than our *Shakespear.* . . ." ([Gildon], "Progress of the Stage," p. lix).

10. "His Sentiments for the most part in his best Tragedies, are noble, generous, easie, and natural, and adapted to the Persons who use them." (Dennis, "On the Genius and Writings, *Works,* II, 4.) Pope's responsiveness to these "Sentiments" is reflected in the indexes which follow the text of the plays. In addition to an index of "Manners, Passions, and their external Effects," he has a lengthy "Index of Thoughts, or Sentiments" as well as a "Table of the most considerable [Speeches] in *Shakespear.*"

11. Shakespeare's intuitive, "natural" learning was, of course, a critical commonplace of the time, reiterated by Dryden ("Preface to *All for Love,*" *Essays,* I, 201; "Of Dramatic Poesy," *Essays,* I, 80), by Dennis ("On the Genius and Writings," *Works,* II, 14), and Addison (*Spectator* No. 592 [10 September 1714]).

12. Cf. Dryden's statement in n. 2.

13. "For while the Poet's Success depends so much upon the injudicious Taste of the Managers, and the Whim of the unjudging Town, it is impossible, that this Glorious Art can ever be brought to that Excellence, to which it arriv'd in Greece. . . . In *England* Plays begun at the very Bottom of the People, and mounted by degrees to the State we now see them in, the yet imperfect Diversion of Ladies, and Men of the first Quality." ([Gildon] "Progress of the Stage," p. lxvi). See also Gildon, *A Comparison between the Two Stages* (London, 1702), pp. 148–49. This academic attitude toward the mob contrasts with the view of a professional theater man like Farquhar: "The Rules of English Comedy don't lie in the Compass of *Aristotle,* or his Followers, but in the Pit, Box, and Gal-

leries." (George Farquhar, "A Discourse upon Comedy," *The Works of . . . Mr. George Farquhar,* 2d ed. [London, (1711?)], p. 73.)

14. Shakespeare may be particularly remembering Florizel in *The Winter's Tale.*

15. Dryden had called Jonson "the most learned and judicious writer which any theatre ever had." ". . . something of art was wanting to the Drama, till he came." ("Of Dramatic Poesy" *Essays,* I, 81, 82.)

16. "His [Shakespeare's] Tales were seldom invented, but rather taken either from true History, or Novels and Romances: And he commonly made use of 'em in that Order, with those Incidents, and that extent of Time in which he found 'em in the Authors from whence he borrow'd them." (Rowe, "Some Account of the Life," p. xxvii.)

17. "If one undertook to examine the greatest part of these by those Rules which are establish'd by *Aristotle,* and taken from the model of the *Grecian* Stage, it would be no very hard Task to find a great many Faults: But as *Shakespear* liv'd under a kind of mere Light of Nature, and never had been made acquainted with the Regularity of those written Precepts, so it would be hard to judge him by a Law he knew nothing of." (Rowe, "Some Account of the Life," p. xxvi.) See also Farquhar, "A Discourse upon Comedy," p. 73.

18. ". . . nor had he Friends to consult upon whose Capacity and Integrity he could depend." (Dennis, "On the Genius and Writings," *Works,* II, 15.)

19. Pope is inconsistent on this issue. There is this statement and his earlier recognition of Shakespeare as a great, original mind, one naturally learned (this in the tradition of Dryden); but later he tries to demonstrate that the playwright was well read and informed, even if he could not read the classics directly. He concludes by ascribing the prevailing concept of Shakespeare's ignorance to the myth fostered by Jonson's supporters and to the evidence of the plays, with their wretched inaccuracies. See Preface, pp. 18, 20ff.

20. "Queen *Elizabeth* had several of his Plays Acted before her, and without doubt gave him many gracious Marks of her Favour . . ." (Rowe, "Some Account of the Life," p. viii).

21. "As for Friends, they whom in all likelihood *Shakespear* consulted most, were two or three of his Fellow-Actors, because they had the Care of publishing his Works committed to them." (Dennis, "On the Genius and the Writings," *Works,* II, 15.)

22. Pope's attitude toward actors was biased, partly no doubt by his personal experiences in the theater with the production of *Three Hours after Marriage,* a farce which he wrote in 1717 with Gay and Arbuthnot, but partly too by what had come to be, sometimes with reason, a tradition of mistrust and disapproval. Dennis was much more severe:

. . . Actors are so far from having the great Qualities of extraordinary Men, that they have not the Understanding and Judgment of ordinary Gentlemen; because they have not had their Education. . . . There cannot be a more certain Sign of the Meanness of Actors Capacities, than their being the worst Judges in the World of the very Things about which they are eternally employ'd. And the present Actors, who are the Managers of the Play-House, have given all the World an irrefutable Proof, that they have still less Knowledge of Plays than had any of their Predecessors. . . . Their sordid Love and Greediness of Gain, contributes not a little to the corrupting their Understandings. For when a foolish Play happens to have a good Run, as they call it, their sordid Temper inclines them to believe it good. . . . (Dennis, "The Characters and Conduct of Sir John Edgar," *Works*, II, 184, 185.)

23. *"I remember* the Players have often mentioned it as an honour to *Shakespeare*, that in his writing, what soever he penn'd, hee never blotted out [a] line. My answer hath beene; would he had blotted a thousand:" (Ben Jonson, "Timber," Spingarn, I, 19.) "And what he thought, he vttered with that easiness, that wee haue scarce receiued from him a blot in his papers." (Iohn Heminge and Henrie Condell, "To the Great Variety of Readers" [facsimile ed. of First Folio]).

24. Cf. Pope's statement in his *Imit. Hor.*, Ep. II i—"To Augustus" (1737):

> And fluent Shakespeare scarce effac'd a line.
> Ev'n copious Dryden, wanted, or forgot,
> The last and greatest Art, the Art to blot.
>   (TE IV, 219, ll. 279–81.)

25. There is some exaggeration in these assertions, as David Nichol Smith notes (*Eighteenth Century Essays on Shakespeare* [Glasgow: James MacLehose, 1903], p. 312), but Pope is quite correct insisting that Shakespeare did know how to "blot."

26. "Those who accuse him to have wanted learning, give him the greater commendation. . . ." (Dryden, "Of Dramatic Poesy," *Essays*, I, 80.)

27. " 'Tis my opinion, that if *Shakespear* had had those Advantages of Learning, which the perfect Knowledge of the Antients wou'd have given him, so great a *Genius* as his, wou'd have made him a very dangerous Rival in Fame, to the greatest Poets of Antiquity. . . ." ([Gildon], "Progress of the Stage," p. iii.) See also Dennis, "On the Genius and Writings," *Works*, II, 15. Pope goes further, granting to Shakespeare in his points of excellence a superiority to all other dramatists.

28. "I should be very proud to own my Veneration for Learning, and to acknowledge any Compliment due to the better sort upon that Foundation; but I'm afraid the Learning of the Better Sort is not confin'd to College Studies, for there is such a thing as Reason without Sillogism, Knowledge without *Aristotle*,

and Languages besides *Greek* and *Latin*." (Farquhar, "A Discourse upon Comedy," p. 61.)

29. Pope possibly has in mind Dennis's criticism of *Coriolanus* and *Julius Caesar* ("Essay on the Genius and Writings of Shakespear") for errors in characterization, lapses in decorum, mistakes in history and manners, and a failure to observe the propriety of poetic justice:

> How comes it that he takes *Plutarch*'s Word, who was by Birth a *Graecian*, for the Affairs of *Rome*, rather than that of the *Roman* Historian [Livy], if so be that he had read the latter? Or what Reason can be given for his not reading him, when he wrote upon a *Roman* story, but that in *Shakespear*'s time there was a Translation of *Plutarch*, and there was none of *Livy*? If *Shakespear* was familiarly conversant with the *Roman* Authors, how came he to introduce a Rabble into *Coriolanus*, in which he offended not only against the Dignity of Tragedy, but the Truth of Fact, the Authority of all the *Roman* Writers, the Customs of Ancient *Rome*, and the Majesty of the *Roman* People? By introducing a Rabble into *Julius Caesar*, he only offended the Dignity of Tragedy. (Dennis, *Works*, II, 9).

Pope's views are closer to those of Rowe and Gildon: "Nor are the Manners, proper to the Persons represented, less justly observ'd, in those Characters taken from the *Roman* History; and of this, the Fierceness and Impatience of *Coriolanus*, his Courage and Disdain of the common People, the Virtue and Philosophical Temper of *Brutus*, and the irregular Greatness of Mind in *M. Anthony*, are beautiful Proofs. For the two last especially, you find 'em exactly as they are describ'd by *Plutarch*, from whom certainly *Shakespear* copy'd 'em." (Rowe, "Some Account of the Life," pp. [xxviii], xxx–xxxi.) "The Characters he has in his Plays drawn of the *Romans*, is a Proof, that he was acquainted with their Historians. . . ." ([Gildon], "Progress of the Stage," p. vi.)

30. That is, the mythology of the ancient poets.

31. Although Dryden heralded Waller's Virgilian translations ("Dedication of the Aeneis," *Essays*, II, 222), Dr. Johnson was to write, "He borrows too many of his sentiments and illustrations from the old mythology" (*Lives*, I, 295), but then, Dr. Johnson was wont to be critical of what he called "those dark and dismal regions of mythology."

32. ". . . I think there are many Arguments to prove, that he knew at least, some of the *Latin* Poets, particularly *Ovid*; two of his Epistles being here translated by him" ([Gildon], "Progress of the Stage," p. vi). Both Rowe's and Pope's editions of Shakespeare had a supplementary volume of poetry (added to Rowe's edition in 1710 by Gildon and reprinted in 1725 to complete Pope's edition, in a "revision" by Dr. Sewell), in which *Venus and Adonis* and the *Rape of Lucrece* were included along with Shakespeare's dedication of them to the Earl of Southampton.

Two poems *Amorous Epistles of Paris to Helen* and *Helen to Paris* were also printed, though they were in fact written by Thomas Heywood.

33. Pope seems to speak to Rowe's doubt that Shakespeare had "*Latin* enough" to read *The Menoechmi* "in the original" (Rowe, "Some Account of the Life," p. xv), and to Dennis's conviction that he must have drawn on a translation now lost or had the Latin original read and translated to him "by some learned Friend" ("On the Genius and Writings," *Works,* II, 14). Pope shares Gildon's view, "but that he had read *Plautus* himself, is plain from his *Comedy of Errors,* which is taken visibly from the *Menoechmi* of that Poet. . . ." ([Gildon], "Progress of the Stage," p. vi.)

34. Supposed author of an account of the destruction of Troy and chief source of the medieval Troy legends. By his authority Theobald justifies correcting Pope's text of lines spoken by the Prologue in *Troilus and Cressida*: "I doubt not but the Author ought to be corrected by this Authority [the correcter Editions of *Dares Phrygius*]. . . ." (Lewis Theobald, *Shakespeare Restored* [London, 1726], p. 188.)

35. *Troilus and Cressida.*

36. "It was, and is, a general opinion that Ben Jonson and Shakespeare lived in enmity against one another. Betterton has assured me often that there was nothing to it, and that such a supposition was founded only on the two parties which in their lifetime listed under one, and endeavored to lessen the character of the other mutually." (*Anecdotes,* I, 23.)

37. "*Ben* was naturally Proud and Insolent, and in the Days of his Reputation did so far take upon him the Supremacy in Wit, that he could not but look with an evil Eye upon any one that seem'd to stand in Competition with him. And if at times he has affected to commend him, it has always been with some Reserve, insinuating his Uncorrectness, a careless manner of Writing, and want of Judgment; the Praise of seldom altering or blotting out what he writ, which was given him by the Players who were the first Publishers of his Works after his Death, was what *Johnson* could not bear; he thought it impossible, perhaps, for another Man to strike out the greatest Thoughts in the finest Expression, and to reach those Excellencies of Poetry with the Ease of a first Imagination, which himself with indefinite Labour and Study could but hardly attain to. *Johnson* was certainly a very good Scholar, and in that had the advantage of *Shakespear*; tho' at the same time I believe it must be allow'd, that what Nature gave the latter, was more than a Ballance for what Books had given the former. . . . *Johnson* did indeed take a large liberty, even to the transcribing and translating of whole Scenes together. . . . *Shakespear,* on the other Hand, was beholding to no body farther than the Foundation of the Tale, the Incidents were often his own, and the Writing intirely so." (Rowe, "Some Account of the Life," pp. xiii–xv.)

38. Tacitus, *Agricola* 41: ". . . those worst of enemies, the people who praise you." (Loeb [1946], p. 241.)

39. Virgil, *Eclogues* 7. 27–28: ". . . should he [Codrus] praise me unduly, wreathe my brow with foxglove, lest his evil tongue harm the bard. . . ." (Loeb [1956], p. 51.)

40. "His Acquaintance with *Ben Johnson* began with a remarkable piece of Humanity and good Nature; Mr. *Johnson,* who was at that Time altogether un-known to the World, had offer'd one of his Plays to the Players, in order to have it Acted; and the Persons into whose Hands it was put, after having turn'd it carelessly and superciliously over, were just upon returning it to him with an ill-natur'd Answer, that it would be of no service to their Company, when *Shakespear* luckily cast his Eye upon it, and found something so well in it as to engage him first to read it through, and afterwards to recommend Mr. *Johnson* and his Writings to the Publick." (Rowe, "Some Account of the Life," pp. xii–xiii.)

41. ". . . an insolent, sparing, and invidious panegyric:" (Dryden, "A Dis-course Concerning the Original and Progress of Satire," *Essays,* II, 18.) Spence also refers to this statement of Dryden's and Pope's reservations (*Anecdotes,* I, 29).

42.　　My *Shakespeare,* rise; I will not lodge thee by
　　　　　Chaucer, or *Spencer,* or bid *Beaumont* lye
　　　　A little further, to make thee a roome:
　　　　　Thou art a Moniment, without a tombe. . . .

　　　　·　·　·　·　·　·　·　·　·　·　·　·　·　·　·

　　　　And though thou hadst small *Latine,* and less *Greeke,*
　　　　　From thence to honour thee, I would not seeke
　　　　For names; but call forth thund'ring *Æschilus,*
　　　　　Euripides, and *Sophocles* to us
　　　　. . . to heare thy Buskin tread,
　　　　And shake a Stage: Or, when thy Sockes were on,
　　　　　Leaue thee alone, for the comparison
　　　　Of all, that insolent *Greece,* or haughtie *Rome*
　　　　　Sent forth, or since did from their ashes come.

　　　　·　·　·　·　·　·　·　·　·　·　·　·　·　·　·

　　　　Yet must I not giue Nature all: Thy Art,
　　　　　My gentle *Shakespeare,* must enjoy a part.
　　　　For though the *Poets* matter, Nature be,
　　　　　His Art doth giue the fashion. And, that he,
　　　　Who casts to write a liuing line, must sweat,
　　　　　(Such as thine are) and strike the second heat
　　　　Upon the *Muses* anuile: turne the same
　　　　　(And himselfe with it) that he thinkes to frame;
　　　　Or for the lawrell, he may gaine a scorne,
　　　　　For a good *Poet's* made, as well as borne.

(Jonson, "To the memory of my beloued, the Author Mr. William Shakespeare: And what he hath left us" [facsimile ed. of First Folio; original in reverse italics].)

43. "I had not told posterity this, but for their ignorance who choose that circumstance to commend their friend by wherein he most faulted; And to justifie mine owne candor, for I lov'd the man, and doe honour his memory, on this side Idolatry, as much as any. He was indeed honest, and of an open and free nature, had an excellent *Phantasie,* brave notions, and gentle expressions. . . ." (Jonson, "Timber," Spingarn, I, 19.)

44. See n. 37.

45. While I confesse thy writings to be such,
      As neither *Man,* nor *Muse,* can praise too much.
    'Tis true, and all mens suffrage. But these wayes
      Were not the paths I meant vnto thy praise:
    For seeliest Ignorance on these may light,
      Which, when it sounds at best, but eccho's right;
    Or blinde Affection, which doth ne're aduance
      The truth, but gropes, and vrgeth all by chance. . . .

(Jonson, "To the memory of . . . Mr. William Shakespeare" [facsimile ed. of First Folio; original in reverse italics].)

46. "This blunder [*Enter three Witches solus*] appears to be of Mr. Pope's own invention. It is not to be found in any one of the four folio copies of *Macbeth,* and there is no quarto edition of it extant." (George Steevens, quoted by D. N. Smith, *Eighteenth Century Essays,* p. 313.) I have checked also, without being able to find the reference.

47. Pope seems to have had particularly in mind *Henry V,* III, iv, where, as the Cambridge editors note, Katherine's French "was set right, or nearly so, by successive alterations made by Rowe, Pope, Theobald, Warburton, and Capell." In the same play Pope would encounter Welsh in the dialogue of Fluellen, though just what he considered "bad" Welsh is difficult to determine from his emendations. *The Merry Wives of Windsor* also offers a French and a Welsh character. There Pope has changed the French ("unboyteene verd" becoming, for example, the recognizable "un boitier verd") but the matter of the Welsh is still perplexing. Pope sometimes changes "goot" to "good"; other times he doesn't.

48. Dennis had stressed this as an example of Shakespeare's lack of learning (Dennis, "On the Genius and Writings," *Works,* II, 8)—to which, in *Shakespeare Restored,* Theobald would reply: "I believe this Anachronism of our Poet (and, perhaps, all the Others that he is guilty of,) was the Effect of Poetical License in him, rather than Ignorance." (P. 134.)

49. ". . . *Venus and Adonis,* the only Piece of his Poetry which he ever publish'd

himself, tho' many of his Plays were surrepticiously and lamely Printed in his Life-time." (Rowe, "Some Account of the Life," pp. ix–x.)

50. *"Eternall reader, you haue heere a new play, neuer stal'd with the Stage. . . ."* (Preface to the 1609 Quarto of *Troilus and Cressida*.) References in the Quarto's preface to "this author" and his works are vague and indirect. "To set forth a booke without an Epistle, were like to the old English prouerbe, *A blew coat without a badge,* & the Author being dead, I thought good to take that piece of worke upon mee." (Thomas Walkley, "The Stationer to the Reader," First Quarto of *Othello,* 1622; original in reverse italics.)

51. It is difficult to determine how Pope arrived at this figure. At the end of his edition he lists the quartos which he had available. Those printed before Shakespeare's death are: (1) *A Midsummer Night's Dream,* 1600; (2) the *Merchant of Venice,* 1600; (3) *Loves Labor lost* [sic], 1598; (4) *The Taming of a Shrew,* 1607 (This he may not have considered genuine, for he notes, "I should think it is not written by *Shakespear*; but there are some Speeches (in one or two Scenes only) the same. . . ."); (5) *Lear,* 1608; (6) *Richard the Second,* 1598, 1608, 1615; (7) *Henry the 4th,* 1599, 1604, 1608; (8) *Second Part of Henry the 4th,* 1600; (9) *Henry the 5th,* 1600, 1608 (Pope comments that there were additions and improvements after these editions.); (10) *Henry the 6th* (He lists what are probably the 1619 "Whole Contention" and the 1600 "First Part" and *The True Tragedie . . . ,* so he may not be counting these as "genuine" plays.); (11) *Richard the 3rd,* 1598, 1602, 1612; (12) *Titus Andronicus,* 1614; (13) *Troilus and Cressida,* 1609 (See his comment on this in the text above.); (14) *Romeo and Juliet,* 1597, 1599; (15) *Hamlet,* 1605, 1611.

52. ". . . where (before) you were abus'd with diuerse stolne, and surreptitious copies, maimed, and deformed by the frauds and stealthes of iniurious imposters, that expos'd them: euen those, are now offer'd to your view cur'd, and perfect of their limbes: and all the rest, absolute in their numbers as he conceiued thē." (Heminge and Condell, "To the great Variety of Readers" [facsimile ed. of First Folio].)

53. Act III, scene ii in modern editions.

54. Pope's printing of *Romeo and Juliet* distinguishes many passages which were not in the quartos and which he finds displeasing. For example, in the first act, he comments on some of the Nurse's lines, "This speech and tautology is not in the first edition"; soon after, a speech by Benvolio has this notation: "In the common edition here follows a ridiculous speech, which is entirely added since the first." And there are other similar footnotes one could cite, including one toward the end of the play in which he asserts, "Some lines are left out here and afterwards, which are unworthy of *Shakespear,* and no hint of them to be found in the old edition."

55. Pope may have had *Othello* in mind, for he notes lines in the opening

scenes of that play which were added after the "first editions" and which might be considered as coming under the heading of mob or plebeian scenes. More relevant is his comment on one of the comic scenes with Speed in *The Two Gentlemen of Verona*: "This whole Scene, like many others in these Plays, (some of which I believe were written by *Shakespear*, and others interpolated by the Players) is compos'd of the lowest and most trifling conceits, to be accounted for only from the gross taste of the age he liv'd in; *Populo ut placerent.*"

56. A search through the *Census of Shakespeare's Plays in Quarto* (Henrietta C. Bartlett and Alfred W. Pollard, New Haven: Yale University Press, 1939) has failed to reveal this text, but to collate and enter manuscript revisions in this way used to be a common practice among readers.

57. Pope restored many lines to the text of *King Lear*. On one occasion he comments, "This Scene [IV, iii], left out in all the common books, is restor'd from the old edition; it being manifestly of *Shakespear*'s writing, and necessary to continue the story of *Cordelia*, whose behaviour here is most beautifully painted" [and it is indeed now a part of the modern text]. In another case, in Act IV of *Richard III*, he notes that a number of lines "have been left out ever since the first editions, but I like them well enough to replace them."

58. Pope was always ready to make a point of what he considered to be unwarranted insertions, noting, for example, at the beginning of Act II of *The Tempest*: "All this . . . seems to have been interpolated, (perhaps by the *Players*) the verses there beginning again; and all that is between in prose, not only being very impertinent stuff, but most improper and ill-plac'd Drollery in the mouths of unhappy shipwreckt people. There is more of the same sort interspers'd in the remaining part of the Scene." Though Pope draws erroneous conclusions from it, he is right in recognizing that a playhouse copy of a play may be subject to all sorts of accretions and excisions. For the same point see the First Folio facsimile, ed. Kökeritz and Prouty (New Haven: Yale University Press, 1954), p. xvii.

59. Pope's solution to the famous crux of *Henry V*, "his nose was as sharp as a pen and a table of green fields," was that "These Words *and a table of green fields* are not to be found in the old editions of 1600 and 1608. This nonsense got into all the following editions by a pleasant mistake of the Stage-editors, who printed from the common piecemeal-written Parts in the Play-house. A table was here directed to be brought in, (it being a scene in a tavern where they drink at parting) and this direction crept into the text from the margin. *Greenfield* was the name of the Property man in that time who furnish'd implements &c. for the actors." (*Works of Shakespear*, III, 422). Theobald, however, questioned this conjecture in the appendix (pp. 137–38) to his *Shakespeare Restored*, pointing out that this type of notation would not have appeared in the prompter's book, nor, at best, in the middle of a scene. He then went on to offer his own famous emendation, "for his nose was as sharp as a Pen, and a'babled of green Fields," which

so carried the day that in his second edition Pope defensively expanded his illustrative note here in the Preface to call attention to the fact that the phrase did
not appear in the quarto editions.

60. For example, at the point in *Henry V* where Pope makes a division for
Act IV, scene xiii, he has this note: "Here in the other editions they begin the
fourth Act, very absurdly, since both the Place and Time evidently continue, and
the words of *Fluellen* immediately follow those of the King just before."

61. In a number of instances Pope restores lines from the quartos or First
Folio in order, he insists, to complete the sense. For example, toward the end of
Act I of *Macbeth,* he comments, "The first of these lines (which in the old edition
is totally different from all the others) and the latter (which is quite omitted in
all the others) entirely restore this very obscure passage to sense, as will appear
upon comparison."

[Compare Pope's ". . . Might be the Be-all and the End-all—*Here* /. . ./
To plague th'inventor:" (I, ix, 5, 10) and the Riverside's ". . . Might be
the be-all and the end-all—here /. . ./ To plague the inventor." (I, vii)
with the Fourth Folio's "Might be the bee all, and the end-all. Here /. . ./
To plague the ingredience of our poyson'd challice. . . ."]

62. Pope also has a note on this type of occurrence. Toward the beginning of
Act V of *Richard III* he has marked such a transposition: "I have placed these
lines here as they stand in the first editions, the rest place 'em three speeches
before. . . . I think 'em more naturally introduced here, when he is retiring to
his tent and considering what he has to do that night."

63. One could cite several instances where Pope notes such "errors" (sometimes
his corrections prevailing, sometimes not): In *Henry VI,* Second Part, he gives a
line to Suffolk which "was falsely put into the Captain's mouth" (Riverside, IV,
i, 50; as in Pope); in *Richard III,* he gives to Brakenbury a whole conversation
with Clarence which the Folio assigned to a Keeper (Riverside [I, iv] follows the
Folio); in *Romeo and Juliet,* he adjusts some lines, between Romeo and Friar Lawrence, where there is confusion in the Folio (Riverside, beg. II, iii; as in Pope);
and in *Julius Caesar* he credits to Casca a speech which had been Brutus'—"In
all the editions this speech is ascrib'd to *Brutus,* than which nothing is more
inconsistent with his mild and philosophical character. But (as I often find speeches
in the later editions put into the wrong mouths, different from the first-publish'd
by the author) I think this liberty not unreasonable" (Riverside, III, i, 105–10;
the speech is retained as coming from Brutus).

64. McKerrow cites among Pope's editorial accomplishments his activity in
regularizing the printing of the text according to whether it is prose or verse.
(Ronald B. McKerrow, *The Treatment of Shakespeare's Text by His Earlier Editors,*

1709–1768, Proceedings of the British Academy, No. 19 [London, 1933],
p. 18.)

65. In reprinting the Preface, Malone annotates this sentence with the suggestion that "Mr. Pope probably recollected the following lines in *The Taming of the
Shrew,* spoken by a Lord, who is giving directions to his servant concerning some
players:

> 'Go, Sirrah, take them to the *buttery,*
> And give them friendly welcome every one.'

But he seems not to have observed that the players here introduced were *strollers:*
and there is no reason to suppose that our author, Heminge, Burbage, Lowin,
etc., who were licensed by K. James, were treated in this manner." (*The Plays &
Poems of William Shakespeare,* ed. Edmund Malone [London, 1790], I, part 1, 94.)

66. "Mr. *Dryden* seems to think that *Pericles* is one of his first Plays; but there
is no judgment to be form'd on that, since there is good Reason to believe that
the greatest Part of the Play was not written by him. . . ." (Rowe, "Some Account
of the Life," p. vii.)

67. In 1727 Theobald had produced at the Drury Lane (publishing it the
next year) "Double Falshood, or the Distressed Lovers," as a Shakespearian work
which had never been printed. Though the point of authorship remains even now
unsettled, there was at the time as later the imputation of forgery to Theobald.

68. The 1664 folio had included seven additional plays (*Pericles Prince of Tyre,
The London Prodigall, The History of Thomas Ld Cromwell, Sir John Oldcastle Lord
Cobham, The Puritan Widow, A Yorkshire Tragedy,* and *The Tragedy of Locrine*). Four
of these had appeared in quarto during Shakespeare's lifetime with his name on
the title page as author; the other three had the initials *W. S.* These seven appeared
in all the subsequent editions until that of Pope, and even then were included in
an accompanying volume (not by Pope) to his second edition, in response either
to demand from the public or demand from the booksellers.

69.   No doubt some mouldy tale,
>   Like *Pericles;* and stale
> As the Shrieues crusts, and nasty as his fish-
>   scraps, out euery dish,
> Throwne forth, and rak't into the common tub,
>   May keepe vp the *Play-club.* . . .
>   ("Ode" to *The Nevv Inne,* 1631, ll. 21–26.)

70. "Hee that will sweare, *Ieronimo,* or *Andronicus* are the best playes, yet,
shall passe unexcepted at, heere, as a man whose Iudgement shewes it is constant,
and hath stood still, these fiue arid twentie, or thirtie Yeeres. Though it be an
Ignorance, it is a vertuous and stay'd ignorance; and next to *truth,* a confirm'd
errour does well. . . ." ("The Induction" to *Bartholomew Fayre,* 1631.)

71. As McKerrow notes, "There seems . . . to have been little justification for Rowe's claim to have consulted all the available editions of Shakespeare in the preparation of his text. It is in fact little more—at least with the exception of *Hamlet*—than a revision of the Fourth Folio." (McKerrow, *The Treatment of Shakespeare's Text,* p. 10.)

72. "I . . . am become, by due gradation of dulness, from a poet a translator, and from a translator, a meer editor." (*Correspondence,* II, 140 [Pope to Caryll, 16 October (1722)].) And there is a comparable complaint to Judith Cowper on 5 November. To such statements Dr. Johnson replied in his Preface: "He understood but half of his undertaking. The duty of a collator is indeed dull, yet, like other tedious tasks, is very necessary; but an emendatory critick would ill discharge his duty, without qualities very different from dulness. In perusing a corrupted piece, he must have before him all possibilities of meaning, with all possibilities of expression. . . . Conjectural criticism demands more than humanity possesses, and he that exercises it with most praise has very frequent need of indulgence. Let us now be told no more of the dull duty of an editor." (Johnson, "Preface," *The Plays of William Shakespeare* (1765), I, sigs. [C8ᵛ]-D.)

73. "I have never indulged my own Conjectures, but kept meerly to such amendments as are authorized by the old Editions in the authors life time. . . ." (*Correspondence,* II, 142 [Pope to Judith Cowper, 5 November (1722)].) To these avowals Lounsbury retorted, "Never has there been exhibited a greater contrast between loftiness of pretension and meagerness of performance. . . . the changes that he made solely on his own authority ran up into the thousands." (T. R. Lounsbury, *The Text of Shakespeare,* [New York: Scribner's, 1906], pp. 85, 86; Lounsbury's figure includes the hundreds of instances in which Pope elicited blank verse lines from passages printed as prose, the greater part of which are still accepted by editors.) For a countering argument, see John A. Hart, "Pope as Scholar-Editor," *Studies in Bibliography,* 23 (1970), 45–59, who defends Pope's achievement as a scholar who collated his texts carefully and systematically even if maintaining his independence of judgment.

74. It would be truer to have said that Shakespeare's alterations are noted occasionally, as in the case of the enlargements in *Henry V,* for Pope was not thorough by today's standards in this matter or in many others, as his goals as an editor were different from those of a modern scholar (see Introduction).

75. Some rejected passages, as Warren notes, were simply omitted. (Warren, p. 127.) In the light of the criticism Pope's practice in this respect has drawn, it is useful to recall McKerrow's statement that "several of the passages which he regarded as interpolations, notably the vision in the fifth act of *Cymbeline,* have been rejected by many other critics, and the total amount of the matter 'degraded,' as he calls it, in his edition, some 1,560 lines, about one and half per cent. of the whole number of lines in the plays, is much less than has been rejected by many more recent writers." (McKerrow, *The Treatment of Shakespeare's Text,* p. 22.)

76. It has been generally acknowledged that Pope's efforts in this sphere were rather meager. (Lounsbury points out that his frequent explanations—often of words less obscure than many he passes over—contain numerous errors in definition and etymology [Lounsbury, *The Text of Shakespeare,* pp. 88–92].) On the other hand, Hart ("Pope as Scholar-Editor") champions Pope's activity: "He defined as many words as he could according to the best authorities of his day; where he failed, the failure may be attributed to the age in which lived" (p. 48).

77. Such starred scenes are rare: Act III, scene v (these are Pope's numberings) of *Othello,* the great scene between Iago and Othello, where Othello's jealousy is aroused; Act IV, scene ii of *Henry VIII,* the last scene with the now divorced and dying Katherine; scenes ii and iii of Act II, and Act III, scene v of *Macbeth,* the preparation for (with Macbeth's famous dagger soliloquy) and the murder of Duncan, and the banquet scene with Banquo's ghost; and Act IV, scene iii of *Julius Caesar,* the argument between Brutus and Cassius. Act III, scene vi of *Romeo and Juliet* and two scenes in *Henry V* are marked, but there I believe the stars refer to notes.

78. "But I wish he [Rymer] would likewise have observ'd some of the Beauties too; as I think it became an Exact and Equal Critique to do." (Rowe, "Some Account of the Life," pp. xxxiv–xxxv.)

79. Pope may be remembering and in a sense responding to Rymer's disparagement: "I have thought our Poetry of the last Age was as rude as our Architecture. . . ." (Thomas Rymer, *The Tragedies of the Last Age Consider'd and Examin'd by the Practice of the Ancients . . .* [London, 1678], p. 142.) (Peter Seary [see n. 14 to Introduction] cites this final paragraph as an example of what he sees as Pope's critical ambivalence about Shakespeare.)

POSTSCRIPT.
By Mr. *POPE*.
to
THE
ODYSSEY
OF
HOMER.

INTRODUCTION

Hang Homer and Virgil! their meaning to seek,
A man must have pok'd in the Latin or Greek;
Those who love our own tongue, we have reason to hope,
Have read them translated by Dryden and Pope.

Matthew Prior, from "Down Hall"

The significance of Pope's Homeric translation is far reaching: for the English-reading world, as for Prior, it meant an elegantly readable version of the *Iliad* and the *Odyssey,* one that soon became a classic.[1] It firmly established the contemporary reputation of its young author and secured for him financial independence at a time when poets had to rely upon patrons or upon other auxiliary sources of income.[2] It marked a long period in Pope's career when his style was put to school to the grand simplicity of Homer's, and though he failed, at least by our standards, to approximate the original in this respect, the experience left its mark. Finally, to the history of eighteenth-century literary theory, it contributed two lively essays, the "Preface" to the *Iliad* and the "Postscript" to the *Odyssey* here printed.

Pope's warning at the opening of the Postscript—that "Whoever reads the Odyssey with an eye to the Iliad, expecting to find it of the same character, or of the same sort of spirit, will be grievously deceived, and err against the first principle of Criticism, which is to consider the nature of the piece, and the intent of its author"—may be equally applied to his two essays in Homeric criticism. In the Preface—eleven years earlier—he had been launching his first great work of translation, what must have seemed to him at the time the culmination and crown of an interest reaching back to childhood.[3] He had been writing too when the controversy between the Ancients and the Moderns still raged, with Homer a crucial figure in the contention. The Preface, then, provided a finely appreciative, broad discussion of Homer, whose characteristic "invention" (seen against Virgil's "judgment" in a traditional, though significant, opposition of Nature and Art) was made the focus for an intensive survey of the epic genre, of the "beauties" and "defects" of the original work, and of the problems of translation.

The Postscript attempts nothing so comprehensive,[4] nor is it so formal in style. Warton quotes Pope's own comment on both pieces: "He used to say it [the Preface] was too pompous and poetical; too much *the great horse,* was his expression; and he preferred his postscript to the *Odyssey*."[5] While this dismisses the Preface too casually, it is true that the Postscript has an interest often overlooked by critics. Like the earlier essay it is organized on a comparison—between the *Odyssey* and the *Iliad*; and, like the previous contrast of Homer and Virgil, the comparison is managed so as to reveal more clearly the distinguishing excellences of each kind of writing rather than to extol either at the expense of the other. Pope realized that too often in the past such pairings had been used to depreciate, and that the *Odyssey* had been disparaged because its merits were not those of its "companion" piece. He takes therefore as a point of departure Longinus's discussion of the two epics, where the *Odyssey* is found to be inferior because it is not so great an example of the sublime, and argues that the criticism is not damning since Longinus is writing on the sublime and not on the nature of the *Odyssey*:

> The Odyssey (as I have before said) ought to be consider'd according to its own nature and design, not with an eye to the Iliad. To censure *Homer* because it is unlike what it was never meant to resemble, is, as if a Gardiner who had purposely cultivated two beautiful trees of contrary natures, as a specimen of his skill in the several kinds, should be blamed for not bringing them into *pairs*; when in root, stem, leaf and flower, each was so entirely different, that one must have been spoil'd in the endeavour to match the other.

If the *Odyssey* is considered on its own terms, and "If *Homer* has fully in these points accomplish'd his own design, and done all that the nature of his Poem demanded or allowed, it still remains perfect in its kind, and as much a master-piece as the Iliad." The comparison of the two epics can now serve to define their distinctive natures and becomes accordingly a comparison of narrative and dramatic, natural and sublime. If the *Odyssey* does not have the sustained "fire and fury" of the *Iliad*, it does not, on the other hand, entirely lack these qualities—and it has its own particular virtues. The "elevated spirit" of the one is matched by the "just moral" of the other. What Longinus saw as a decay of the author's imagination could very well argue a maturing of his judgment. Not only is the *Odyssey* superior in its "Moral," Pope contends; but in the "conduct, turn, and disposition" of its "Fable," it served as a better model for epic writers to follow, as the *Aeneid* and the *Telemachus* attest.

Despite these references to "Moral," "Fable," and "Manners"—Aristotelian categories inherited so strongly through Bossu[6]—such traditional considerations, while explored carefully in the Preface, are only of token interest to Pope here. He may seek the support of Horace, Longinus, and

Aristotle for readers who would recognize the recurrent echoes of Bossu as well as familiar parallels in thought with Mme Dacier, Dryden, Addison, Rapin, and other more contemporary commentators (as the annotations to the text will attempt to indicate); he may announce at the outset that "The Odyssey is the reverse of the Iliad in *Moral, Subject, Manner,* and *Style*" and that its superiority lies in its Moral and Fable (matters of great consequence to the didactic interests of Bossu)—but it is soon apparent that Pope's real aim is to justify the *Odyssey* on poetic grounds, to prove himself that it is, in its own way, as good a *poem* as the *Iliad*:

> And it is certain we shall find in each, the same vivacity and fecundity of invention, the same life and strength of imaging and colouring, the particular descriptions as highly painted, the figures as bold, the metaphors as animated, and the numbers as harmonious and as various.
>
> The Odyssey is a perpetual source of Poetry: the stream is not the less full, for being gentle. . . .

In both his Homeric essays we are kept aware that Pope the critic is Pope the translator, and Pope the translator a practicing poet deeply engaged with problems of contemporary poetics. To make Homer real for Augustan readers he had to cope with what was plainly for them the crux of the epic mode—its levels of discourse.[7] In the *Iliad* it had been a question of Homer's inventive vitality, the sublime of the high style; in the *Odyssey* it was something quite different. In that aspect of Homer's style "where it cannot support a sublimity" and yet "always preserves a dignity, or at least a propriety"—Pope sees one of the greatnesses of the second epic. To describe "low actions" or "little circumstances" without becoming vulgar was a challenge which as translator he found as demanding as anything required in the high style:

> Let it be remember'd, that the same Genius that soar'd the highest, and from whom the greatest models of the *Sublime* are derived, was also he who stoop'd the lowest, and gave to the simple *Narrative* its utmost perfection. Which of these was the harder task to *Homer* himself, I cannot pretend to determine; but to his Translator I can affirm (however unequal all his imitations must be) that of the latter has been much the more difficult.

So the firm concern with poetic values which often distinguishes Pope's criticism from that of his colleagues becomes even more obvious in the Postscript than in the Preface; here in the Postscript it is the essential subject.

Even the exegesis of Longinus, which Austin Warren calls "ingenious but hardly more than quibbling,"[8] soon leads to a provocative discussion of the Longinian view of the *Odyssey* as "Comedy," seen in all its stylistic implications. For, Pope notes, "There is a real beauty in an easy, pure, perspicuous description even of a *low action*." This "natural" style he explores in a discussion of simple and figurative expression, citing Milton's success with archaic language; and he attempts to define its simple dignity by contrasting it with the bombast of the mock heroic. This points to a corollary distinction between low actions and objects, which cannot be raised figuratively without becoming ridiculous, and natural subject matter, which can—as in Virgil's *Georgics*. Although Pope merely touches on this topic of burlesque technique, his few comments are valuable.

Of less interest to the modern reader is the rebuttal to Mme Dacier which concludes the essay. Anne Dacier, a distinguished French scholar and translator of Homer, his supporter against Houdar de La Motte in the Battle of the Ancients and the Moderns, had attacked Pope's preface to the *Iliad*—criticism which he attributes to errors in its translation into French. His rejoinder is illustrative of his basic position in this Homeric phase of the Battle: a characteristic middle ground between the two extremes. He was, of course, an equally staunch defender of Homer—and in the English "quarrel" sided with Temple and Swift for the Ancients— but he could not subscribe to Mme Dacier's idolatry and seems to have enjoyed playing off her exaggerations against La Motte's.[9]

Judiciousness everywhere typifies Pope's activity as a critic. And his Homeric criticism is in the best spirit of neoclassical epic commentary, "a combination of established theory, good sense, and critical perspicacity."[10] Working in a tradition, assimilating from past and current theory,[11] he yet synthesizes his material into critical statements that are very much the expression of his own taste and judgment and concern as reader and poet. For one feels that criticism is never an end in itself for Pope, but a means to the aesthetic experience of an author or a work. In the Preface to the *Iliad* he had written, " 'Tis a great Secret in Writing to know when to be plain, and when poetical and figurative; and it is what *Homer* will teach us if we will but follow modestly in his Footsteps."[12] It is on this concept of "faithfulness" to Homer, on what constitutes it, and on what it taught Pope, that the attention of the reader to the Postscript will inevitably rest.

Notes

1. Dr. Johnson's comment on Pope's Homer was as usual straight to the point: "To a thousand cavils one answer is sufficient; the purpose of a writer is to be read. . . ." (*Lives,* III, 240.)

2.   But (thanks to *Homer*) since I live and thrive,
           Indebted to no Prince or Peer alive. . . .
                (*Imit. Hor.,* Ep. II ii, 68–69; TE IV, 169.)

3. In a letter to Broome (*Correspondence,* I, 297) Pope had noted, "he [Homer] was the first author that made me catch the itch of poetry, when I read him in my childhood. . . ." And that influence is apparent: although Pope destroyed his juvenilia, he told Spence about these youthful imitations—his play composed of speeches from the *Iliad* and his epic, *Alcander, Prince of Rhodes.* (*Anecdotes,* I, 15–17.) Significantly too, one of his first published pieces was his translation of the "Episode of Sarpedon" from the *Iliad.*

4. He already had, for example, at the beginning of the translation an essay, "A General View of the Epic Poem, and of the *Iliad* and *Odyssey.* Extracted from *Bossu.*" (*The Odyssey of Homer* [London, 1725], I, [i]–xxiii.)

5. Joseph Warton, *Essay on the Genius and Writings of Pope,* 4th ed. (London, 1782), I, 116.

6. In 1695 there had appeared in England the single most influential work on the epic, *Monsieur Bossu's Treatise of the Epick Poem, "Done into* English *from the* French, *with a new Original* Preface *upon the same Subject, by* W.J." The weight of Bossu's authority is suggested by Sheffield's encomium upon him:

        Had *Bossu* never writ, the world had still
        Like *Indians* view'd this wondrous piece of Skill;
        As something of Divine the work admired,
        Hoped not to be Instructed, but Inspired;
        Till he, disclosing sacred Mysteries,
        Has shewn where all the mighty Magick lyes,
        Describ'd the Seeds, and in what order sown,
        That have to such a vast proportion grown.
        ("An Essay upon Poetry," Spingarn, II, 295–96.)

So popular was Bossu that even after 1725 there were some thirteen reprintings—published in abbreviated form, with translations of Homer—of the 1719 edition of his treatise; and A. F. B. Clark notes that "this man, who represents that literary *régime* [of the French formalists] at its woodenest, is the most quoted in England of all the French critics (not excepting, I believe, Boileau himself)." (Clark, *Boileau and the French Classical Critics in England (1660–1830)* [Paris: H. Champion, 1925], p. 243.)

7. See, for example, TE VII, lxviii.

8. Warren, p. 117.

9. Audra's feeling too: "Mais n'est-il pas amusant de voir Pope, soufflant le chaud et le froid, morigéner tour à tour La Motte comme Mme Dacier, et

Mme Dacier comme La Motte?" (E. Audra, *L'Influence française dans l'oeuvre de Pope* [Paris: H. Champion, 1931], pp. 244–45.)

10. This description of the criticism of John Dennis is still more applicable to Pope. (H. T. Swedenberg, Jr., *The Theory of the Epic in England, 1650–1800* [Berkeley and Los Angeles: University of California Press, 1944], p. 54.)

11. For a thorough survey of this background see H. T. Swedenberg, Jr., *The Theory of the Epic,* and the "Introduction" to the Twickenham Edition of Pope's translations of Homer (TE VII, xxxv–ccxlix).

12. "Preface" to the *Iliad,* TE VII, 18.

NOTE ON PUBLICATION AND TEXT

The arrangements for the publication of the *Odyssey* were complicated by problems of collaboration and current politics. The first three volumes of the translation appeared in April 1725, six weeks after the edition of Shakespeare and only four months after the subscription announcements. Pope had planned to issue the Proposals late in 1722,[1] but deferred them because of the shadow cast upon him by the Jacobite scandals at that time (the trial for treason of his close friend Bishop Atterbury and the suppression for seditious passages of his edition of Buckingham's *Works*) and later because of the difficulty of securing a publisher and settling financial details with his secret "partners" in the project.[2]

When work on the translation actually got underway is difficult to determine, though the correspondence suggests that Fenton and Broome were active by 1722, with Pope—who was busily engaged in his Shakespeare editing—probably not beginning his translation before May 1723.[3] The undertaking was completed with the publication of the last two volumes in June 1726, volume V concluding with the Postscript, about which Pope had written to Broome on 4 June: "A long postscript relating to critical affairs, which I have taken it into my head to write since we met last, has retarded till now the publication of Homer."[4]

Both the first three volumes and the last two were offered in quarto, small and large folio, and duodecimo.[5] Although the *Odyssey* was never published again in Pope's lifetime, the Postscript was reprinted in the posthumous editions of the translation and in some of the later collections of the *Works* (those by Warton, Johnson, Bowles, and Roscoe), but not included in the editions of the *Works* by Warburton or by Elwin/Courthope; and it is now to be found with the Homeric translations in the Twickenham edition of the poetry. The present text is that of the 1726 quarto:

1726: *The Odyssey of Homer,* Vol. V, quarto, Griffith 170.

Notes

1. *Correspondence,* II, 111.
2. *Early Career,* pp. 250–57.
3. Ibid., p. 250 [*Correspondence,* II, 110 et passim].
4. *Correspondence,* II, 378. He had also written to Broome, on 16 April: "It

is not to be imagined with what sickly reluctance I have at last finished my postscript to Homer." (Ibid., II, 375.)

5. Pope's public subscription had been for quartos, to match the *Iliad* subscription quarto; Lintot set up a rival subscription for his own benefit, offering a cheaper large and small folio, and duodecimos. (*Early Career,* pp. 256–57.)

POSTSCRIPT.
By Mr. *POPE.*

I cannot dismiss this work without a few observations on the true Character and Style of it.[1] Whoever reads the Odyssey with an eye to the Iliad, expecting to find it of the same character, or of the same sort of spirit, will be grievously deceived, and err against the first principle of Criticism, which is to consider the nature of the piece, and the intent of its author.[2] The Odyssey is a moral and political work,[3] instructive to all degrees of men,[4] and filled with images examples and precepts, of civil and domestic life. *Homer* is here a person

> *Qui didicit* patriae *quid debeat,* & *quid* amicis,
> *Quo sit amore* parens, *quo* frater *amandus,* & hospes:
> *Qui quid sit* pulcrum, *quid* turpe, *quid* utile, *quid* non,
> *Plenius* & *melius Chrysippo* & *Crantore dicit.*[5]

The Odyssey is the reverse of the Iliad, in *Moral,*[6] *Subject,*[7] *Manner*[8] and *Style;*[9] to which it has no sort of relation, but as the story happens to follow in order of time, and as some of the same persons are actors in it. Yet from this incidental connexion many have been mis-led to regard it as a continuation or second part,[10] and thence to expect a parity of character inconsistent with its nature.

It is no wonder that the common Reader should fall into this mistake, when so great a Critic as *Longinus* seems not wholly free from it. Although what he has said has been generally understood to import a severer censure of the Odyssey than it really does, if we consider the occasion on which it is introduced, and the circumstances to which it is confined.

"The Odyssey (says he) is an instance, how natural it is to a great Genius, when it begins to grow old and decline, to delight it self in *Narrations* and *Fables.* For, that *Homer* composed the Odyssey after the Iliad, many proofs may be given, &c. From hence in my judgment it proceeds, that as the Iliad was written while his *Spirit* was in its greatest vigor, the whole structure of that work is Dramatick and full of action; whereas the greater part of the Odyssey is employ'd in Narration, which is the taste of *Old Age*: So that in this latter piece we may compare him to the setting Sun, which has still the same greatness but not the same ardor, or force. He speaks not in the same strain; we see no more that *Sublime* of the Iliad which marches on with a constant pace, without ever being stopp'd, or retarded: there appears no more that hurry and that strong tyde of motions and passions, pouring one after another: there is no more the same fury, or the same volubility of diction, so suitable to action, and all along drawing in such innumerable images of nature. But *Homer,* like the Ocean, is always great, even when he ebbs and retires; even when he is lowest and loses himself most in Narrations and incredible Fictions: As instances of this, we cannot forget the descriptions of tempests, the adventures of *Ulysses* with the *Cyclops,* and many others. But tho' all this be *Age,* it is the *Age of Homer*— And it may be said for the credit of these fictions, that they are *beautiful Dreams,* or if you will, the *Dreams of* Jupiter *himself.* I spoke of the Odyssey only to show, that the greatest Poets when their genius wants strength and warmth for the *Pathetic,* for the most part employ themselves in painting the *Manners.* This *Homer* has done, in characterizing the Suitors, and describing their way of life; which is properly a branch of Comedy, whose peculiar business it is to represent the manners of men."[11]

We must first observe, it is the *Sublime* of which *Longinus* is writing: That, and not the nature of *Homer's* Poem, is his subject. After having highly extoll'd the sublimity and fire of the Iliad, he justly observes the Odyssey to have less of those qualities, and to turn more on the side of moral, and reflections on human life. Nor is it his business here to determine, whether the *elevated spirit* of the one, or the *just moral* of the other, be the greater excellence in it self.

Secondly, that fire and fury of which he is speaking, can not well be meant of the general Spirit and Inspiration which is to run through a whole Epic Poem, but of that particular warmth and impetuosity necessary in some parts, to image or represent actions or passions, of haste, tumult, and violence. It is on occasion of citing some such particular passages in *Homer,* that *Longinus* breaks into this reflection; which seems to determine his meaning chiefly to that sense.

Upon the whole, he affirms the Odyssey to have less sublimity and fire than the Iliad, but he does not say it wants the sublime or wants fire. He affirms it to be narrative, but not that the narration is defective. He affirms it to abound in fictions, not that those fictions are ill invented, or ill executed. He affirms it to be nice and particular in painting the manners, but not that those manners are ill painted. If *Homer* has fully in these points accomplish'd his own design, and done all that the nature of his Poem demanded or allowed, it still remains perfect in its kind, and as much a masterpiece as the Iliad.

The Amount of the passage is this; that in his own particular taste, and with respect to the *Sublime, Longinus* preferr'd the Iliad: And because the Odyssey was less active and lofty, he judged it the work of the old age of *Homer.*

If this opinion be true, it will only prove, that *Homer*'s Age might determine him in the choice of his subject, but not that it affected him in the execution of it: And that which would be a very wrong instance to prove the decay of his Imagination, is a very good one to evince the strength of his Judgment. For had he (as Madam *Dacier* observes)[12] compos'd the Odyssey in his youth, and the Iliad in his age, both must in reason have been exactly the same as they now stand. To blame *Homer* for his choice of such a subject, as did not admit the same incidents and the same pomp of style as his former; is to take offence at too much variety, and to imagine, that when a man has written one good thing, he must ever after only copy himself.

The *Battle of* Constantine, and the *School of* Athens, are both pieces of *Raphael*: Shall we censure the School of *Athens* as faulty, because it has not the fury and fire of the other? or shall we say, that *Raphael* was grown grave and old, because he chose to represent the manners of old men and Philosophers? There is all the silence, tranquillity and composure in the one, and all the warmth, hurry and tumult in the other, which the subject of either required: both of them had been imperfect, if they had not been as they are. And let the Painter or Poet be young or old, who designs and performs in this manner, it proves him to have made the piece at a time of life when he was master not only of his art, but of his discretion.[13]

Aristotle makes no such distinction between the two Poems: He

constantly cites them with equal praise, and draws the rules and
examples of Epic writing equally from both.[14] But it is rather to
the Odyssey that *Horace* gives the preference, in the Epistle to *Lollius,*
and in the Art of Poetry. It is remarkable how opposite his opinion
is to that of *Longinus*; and that the particulars he chuses to extoll,
are those very *fictions* and *pictures of the manners* which the other seems
least to approve. Those fables and manners are of the very essence
of the work: But even without that regard, the fables themselves
have both more invention and more instruction, and the manners
more moral and example, than those of the Iliad.[15]

In some points (and those the most essential to the Epic Poem)
the Odyssey is confessed to excel the Iliad; and principally in the
great end of it, the *Moral.*[16] The conduct, turn, and disposition of
the *Fable* is also what the Criticks allow to be the better model for
Epic writers to follow: Accordingly we find much more of the Cast
of this Poem than of the other in the *Æneid,*[17] and (what next to
that is perhaps the greatest example) in the *Telemachus.*[18] In the
Manners, it is no way inferior: *Longinus* is so far from finding any
defect in these, that he rather taxes *Homer* with painting them too
minutely. As to the *Narrations,* although they are more numerous
as the occasions are more frequent, yet they carry no more the marks
of old age, and are neither more prolix nor more circumstantial,
than the conversations and dialogues of the Iliad. Not to mention
the length of those of *Phœnix* in the ninth book,[19] and of *Nestor* in
the eleventh[20] (which may be thought in compliance to their characters) those of *Glaucus* in the sixth,[21] of *Æneas* in the twentieth,[22]
and some others, must be allow'd to exceed any in the whole Odyssey. And that the propriety of style, and the numbers, in the
Narrations of each are equal, will appear to any who compare them.

To form a right judgment, whether the Genius of *Homer* had
suffer'd any decay; we must consider, in both his poems, such parts
as are of a similar nature, and will bear comparison. And it is certain
we shall find in each, the same vivacity and fecundity of invention,
the same life and strength of imaging and colouring, the particular
descriptions as highly painted, the figures as bold, the metaphors
as animated, and the numbers as harmonious and as various.

The Odyssey is a perpetual source of Poetry: The stream is not
the less full, for being gentle;[23] tho' it is true (when we speak only

with regard to the *Sublime*) that a river, foaming and thund'ring in cataracts from rocks and precipices, is what more strikes, amazes and fills the mind, than the same body of water, flowing afterwards thro' peaceful vales and agreeable scenes of pasturage.

The Odyssey (as I have before said) ought to be consider'd according to its own nature and design, not with an eye to the Iliad. To censure *Homer* because it is unlike what it was never meant to resemble, is, as if a Gardiner who had purposely cultivated two beautiful trees of contrary natures, as a specimen of his skill in the several kinds, should be blamed for not bringing them into *pairs*; when in root, stem, leaf, and flower, each was so entirely different, that one must have been spoil'd in the endeavour to match the other.

Longinus, who saw this Poem was *"partly of the nature of Comedy,"* [24] ought not for that very reason to have consider'd it with a view to the Iliad. How little any such resemblance was the intention of *Homer,* may appear from hence, that although the character of *Ulysses* there was already drawn, yet here he purposely turns to another side of it, and shows him not in that full light of glory but in the shade of common life, with a mixture of such qualities as are requisite to all the lowest accidents of it, strugling with misfortunes, and on a level with the meanest of mankind. As for the other persons, none of them are above what we call the higher Comedy: *Calypso,* tho' a Goddess, is a character of intrigue; the *Suitors* are yet more approaching to it; the *Phæacians* are of the same cast; the *Cyclops,* *Melanthius,* and *Irus,* descend even to droll characters: and the scenes that appear throughout, are generally of the comic kind; banquets, revels, sports, loves, and the pursuit of a woman. [25]

From the Nature of the Poem, we shall form an Idea of the *Style.* The diction is to follow the images, and to take its colour from the complexion of the thoughts. Accordingly the Odyssey is not always cloath'd in the majesty of verse proper to Tragedy, but sometimes descends into the plainer Narrative, and sometimes even to that familiar dialogue essential to Comedy. [26] However, where it cannot support a sublimity, it always preserves a dignity, or at least a propriety.

There is a real beauty in an easy, pure, perspicuous description even of a *low action.* [27] There are numerous instances of this both in *Homer* and *Virgil*; and perhaps those natural passages are not the least pleasing of their works. It is often the same in History, where the representations of common, or even domestic things, in clear, plain, and natural words, are frequently found to make the liveliest impression on the reader.

The question is, how far a Poet, in pursuing the description or image of an action, can attach himself to *little circumstances,* without vulgarity or trifling? what particulars are proper, and enliven the image; or what are impertinent, and clog it? In this matter Painting is to be consulted, and the whole regard had to those circumstances which contribute to form a full, and yet not a confused, idea of the thing.[28]

Epithets are of vast service to this effect, and the right use of these is often the only expedient to render the narration poetical.

The great point of judgment is to distinguish when to speak simply, and when figuratively:[29] But whenever the Poet is oblig'd by the nature of his subject to descend to the lower manner of writing, an elevated style would be affected, and therefore ridiculous; and the more he was forc'd upon figures and metaphors to avoid that lowness, the more the image would be broken, and consequen[t]ly obscure.

One may add, that the use of the grand style on little subjects, is not only ludicrous, but a sort of transgression against the rules of proportion and mechanicks: 'Tis using a vast force to lift a *feather.*

I believe, now I am upon this head, it will be found a just observation, that the *low actions of life* cannot be put into a figurative style without being ridiculous, but *things natural* can. Metaphors raise the latter into Dignity, as we see in the *Georgicks;*[30] but throw the former into Ridicule, as in the *Lutrin.*[31] I think this may very well be accounted for: Laughter implies censure; inanimate and ir-rational beings are not objects of censure; therefore these may be elevated as much as you please, and no ridicule follows: but when rational beings are represented above their real character, it becomes ridiculous in Art, because it is vicious in Morality. The *Bees* in *Virgil,*[32] were they rational beings, would be ridiculous by having their actions and manners represented on a level with creatures so superior as men; since it would imply folly or pride, which are the proper objects of Ridicule.

The use of pompous expression for low actions or thoughts is the *true Sublime* of *Don Quixote.* How far unfit it is for Epic Poetry, appears in its being the perfection of the Mock-Epick. It is so far from being the Sublime of *Tragedy*, that it is the cause of all *Bombaste*; when Poets instead of being (as they imagine) constantly lofty, only preserve throughout a painful equality of fustian: That continu'd swell of language (which runs indiscriminately even thro' their lowest characters, and rattles like some mightiness of meaning in the most indifferent subjects) is of a piece with that perpetual elevation of tone which the Players have learned from it; and which is not *speaking*, but *vociferating*.[33]

There is still more reason for a variation of style in *Epic* Poetry than in *Tragic*, to distinguish between that *Language of the Gods* proper to the *Muse* who sings,[34] and is inspir'd; and that of *Men* who are introduced speaking only according to nature. Farther, there ought to be a difference of style observ'd in the speeches of human persons, and those of Deities; and again, in those which may be called set harangues or orations, and those which are only conversation or dialogue. *Homer* has more of the latter than any other Poet: what *Virgil* does by two or three words of narration, *Homer* still performs by speeches: Not only replies, but even rejoynders are frequent in him, a practice almost unknown to *Virgil*.[35] This renders his Poems more animated, but less grave and majestic; and consequently necessitates the frequent use of a lower style. The writers of Tragedy lye under the same necessity, if they would copy nature; whereas that painted and poetical diction which they perpetually use, would be improper even in Orations design'd to move with all the arts of Rhetorick:[36] This is plain from the practice of *Demosthenes* and *Cicero*;[37] and *Virgil* in those of *Drances* and *Turnus*[38] gives an eminent example, how far remov'd the style of them ought to be from such an excess of figures and ornaments: which indeed fits only that *Language of the Gods* we have been speaking of, or that of a *Muse* under inspiration.

To read thro' a whole work in this strain, is like travelling all along on the ridge of a hill; which is not half so agreeable as sometimes gradually to rise, and sometimes gently to descend, as the way leads, and as the end of the journey directs.[39]

Indeed the true reason that so few Poets have imitated *Homer* in these lower parts, has been the extreme difficulty of preserving that mixture of Ease and Dignity essential to them. For it is as hard for an Epic Poem to stoop to the Narrative with success, as for a Prince to descend to be familiar, without diminution to his greatness.

The *sublime* style is more easily counterfeited than the *natural*; something that passes for it, or sounds like it, is common in all false writers:[40] But nature, purity, perspicuity, and simplicity, never walk in the clouds; they are obvious to all capacities; and where they are not evident, they do not exist.

The most plain Narration not only admits of these, and of harmony (which are all the qualities of style) but it requires every one of them to render it pleasing. On the contary, whatever pretends to a share of the Sublime, may pass notwithstanding any defects in the rest, nay sometimes without any of them, and gain the admiration of all ordinary readers.

Homer in his lowest narrations or speeches is ever easy, flowing, copious, clear, and harmonious. He shows not less *invention,* in assembling the humbler, than the greater, thoughts and images; nor less *judgment,* in proportioning the style and the versification to these, than to the other.[41] Let it be remember'd, that the same Genius that soar'd the highest, and from whom the greatest models of the *Sublime* are derived, was also he who stoop'd the lowest, and gave to the simple *Narrative* its utmost perfection. Which of these was the harder task to *Homer* himself, I cannot pretend to determine; but to his Translator I can affirm (however unequal all his imitations must be) that of the latter has been much the more difficult.[42]

Whoever expects here the same pomp of verse, and the same ornaments of diction, as in the Iliad; he will, and he ought to be disappointed. Were the original otherwise, it had been an offence against nature; and were the translation so, it were an offence against *Homer,* which is the same thing.[43]

It must be allow'd that there is a majesty and harmony in the *Greek* language which greatly contribute to elevate and support the narration. But I must also observe that this is an advantage grown upon the language since *Homer*'s time; for things are remov'd from vulgarity by being out of use: And if the words we could find in any present language were equally sonorous or musical in themselves, they would still appear less poetical and uncommon than those of a dead one from this only circumstance, of being in every man's mouth.[44] I may add to this another disadvantage to a Translator, from a different cause: *Homer* seems to have taken upon him the character of an Historian, Antiquary, Divine, and Professor of Arts and Sciences; as well as a Poet.[45] In one or other of these characters he descends into many particularities, which as a Poet only perhaps he would have avoided. All these ought to be preserv'd by a faithful Translator, who in some measure takes the place of *Homer*; and all that can be expected from him is to make them as poetical as the subject will bear. Many arts therefore are requisite to supply these disadvantages, in order to dignify and solemnize these plainer parts, which hardly admit of any poetical ornaments.

Some use has been made to this end, of the style of *Milton*.[46] A just and moderate mixture of old words may have an effect like the working old Abbey stones into a building, which I have sometimes seen to give a kind of venerable air, and yet not destroy the neatness, elegance, and equality requisite to a new work;[47] I mean without rendring it too unfamiliar, or remote from the present purity of writing, or from that ease and smoothness which ought always to accompany Narration or Dialogue. In reading a style judiciously antiquated, one finds a pleasure not unlike that of travelling on an old *Roman* way: but then the road must be as *good,* as the way is *ancient*; the style must be such in which we may evenly proceed, without being put to short stops by sudden abruptnesses, or puzled by frequent turnings and transpositions: No man delights in furrows and stumbling-blocks: And let our love to Antiquity be ever so great, a fine ruin is one thing, and a heap of rubbish another. The imitators of *Milton,* like most other imitators, are not *Copies* but *Caricatura's* of their original; they are a hundred times more obsolete and cramp than he, and equally so in all places: Whereas it should have been observed of *Milton,* that he is not lavish of his exotick words and phrases every where alike, but employs them much more where the subject is marvellous vast and strange, as in the scenes of Heaven, Hell, Chaos, &c. than where it is turn'd to the natural and agreeable, as in the pictures of Paradise, the loves of our first parents, the entertainments of Angels, and the like. In general, this unusual style better serves to awaken our ideas in the descriptions and in the imaging and picturesque parts, than it agrees with the lower sort of narrations, the character of which is simplicity and purity. *Milton* has several of the latter, where we find not an antiquated affected

or uncouth word, for some hundred lines together; as in his fifth
book, the latter part of the eighth, the former of the tenth and
eleventh books, and in the narration of *Michael* in the twelfth. I
wonder indeed that he, who ventur'd (contrary to the practice of all
other Epic Poets) to imitate *Homer*'s Lownesses in the *Narrative,*
should not also have copied his plainness and perspicuity in the
Dramatic parts: Since in his speeches (where clearness above all is
necessary) there is frequently such transposition and forced construction, that the very sense is not to be discover'd without a second or
third reading: And in this certainly he ought to be no example.[48]

To preserve the true character of *Homer*'s style in the present translation, great pains has been taken to be easy and natural. The chief
merit I can pretend to, is, not to have been carried into a more
plausible and figurative manner of writing, which would better have
pleased all readers, but the judicious ones. My errors had been fewer,
had each of those Gentlemen who join'd with me shown as much of
the severity of a friend to me, as I did to them, in a strict animadversion and correction.[49] What assistance I receiv'd from them, was
made known in general to the publick in the original Proposals for
this work, and the particulars are specify'd at the conclusion of it;
to which I must add (to be punctually just) some part of the tenth
and fifteenth books.[50] The Reader will now be too good a judge,
how much the greater part of it, and consequently of its faults, is
chargeable upon me alone. But this I can with integrity affirm, that
I have bestowed as much time and pains upon the whole, as were
consistent with the indispensable duties and cares of life, and with
that wretched state of health which God has been pleased to make
my portion. At the least, it is a pleasure to me to reflect, that I
have introduced into our language this other work of the greatest
and most ancient of Poets, with some dignity; and I hope, with as
little disadvantage as the Iliad. And if, after the unmerited success
of that translation, any one will wonder why I would enterprize the
Odyssey? I think it a sufficient answer to say, that *Homer* himself
did the same, or the world would never have seen it.

I design'd to have ended this Postscript here; but since I am now
taking my leave of *Homer,* and of all controversy relating to him, I

beg leave to be indulg'd if I make use of this last opportunity, to say a very few words about some reflections which the late Madam *Dacier*[51] bestow'd on the first part of my Preface to the Iliad, and which she publish'd at the end of her translation of that Poem*.

To write gravely an answer to them would be too much for the reflections; and to say nothing concerning them, would be too little for the Author. It is owing to the industry of that learned Lady, that our polite neighbours are become acquainted with many of *Homer*'s beauties, which were hidden from them before in *Greek* and in *Eustathius*.[52] She challenges on this account a particular regard from all the admirers of that great Poet, and I hope that I shall be thought, as I mean, to pay some part of this debt to her memory in what I am now writing.[53]

Had these reflections fallen from the pen of an ordinary Critick, I should not have apprehended their effect, and should therefore have been silent concerning them: but since they are Madam *Dacier*'s, I imagine that they must be of weight; and in a case where I think her Reasoning very bad, I respect her Authority.[54]

I have fought under Madam *Dacier*'s banner,[55] and have wag'd war in defence of the divine *Homer* against all the Hereticks of the age. And yet it is Madam *Dacier* who accuses me, and who accuses me of nothing less than betraying our common Cause. She affirms that the most declar'd enemies of this Author have never said any thing against him more injurious or more unjust than I. What must the world think of me, after such a judgment pass'd by so great a Critick? the world, who decides so often, and who examines so seldom; the world, who even in matters of litterature is almost always the slave of Authority? Who will suspect that so much learning should mistake, that so much accuracy should be mis-led, or that so much candour should be byass'd?

All this however has happen'd, and Madam *Dacier*'s Criticisms on my Preface flow from the very same error, from which so many false criticisms of her countrymen upon *Homer* have flow'd, and which she has so justly and so severely reprov'd; I mean the error of depending on injurious and unskilful *translations*.[56]

An indifferent translation may be of some use, and a good one

Seconde Edition, a Paris, 1719.

will be of a great deal. But I think that no translation ought to be
the ground of *Criticism,* because no man ought to be condemn'd
upon another man's explanation of his meaning: Could *Homer* have
had the honour of explaining his, before that august Tribunal where
Monsieur *de la Motte* presides, I make no doubt but he had escap'd
many of those severe animadversions with which some *French* Authors
have loaded him, and from which even Madam *Dacier*'s translation
of the Iliad could not preserve him.

How unhappy was it for me, that the knowledge of our *Island-
tongue* was as necessary to Madam *Dacier* in my case, as the knowledge
of *Greek* was to Monsieur *de la Motte* in that of our great Author; or
to any of those whom she styles *blind Censurers,* and blames for
condemning what they did not understand.

I may say with modesty, that she knew less of my true sense from
that faulty translation of part of my Preface, than those blind censurers might have known of *Homer*'s even from the translation of *la
Valterie,* which preceded her own.[57]

It pleas'd me however to find, that her objections were not level'd
at the general Doctrine, or at any essentials of my Preface, but only
at a few particular expressions. She propos'd little more than (to use
her own phrase) to *combate two or three Similes;*[58] and I hope that to
combate a Simile is no more than to fight with a shadow, since a
Simile is no better than the shadow of an Argument.

She lays much weight where I lay'd but little, and examines with
more scrupulosity than I writ, or than perhaps the matter requires.

These unlucky Similes taken by themselves may perhaps render
my meaning equivocal to an ignorant translator; or there may have
fallen from my pen some expressions, which taken by themselves
likewise, may to the same person have the same effect. But if the
translator had been master of our tongue, the general tenor of my
argument, that which precedes and that which follows the passages
objected to, would have sufficiently determined him as to the precise
meaning of them: And if Madam *Dacier* had taken up her pen a
little more leisurely, or had employ'd it with more temper, she would
not have answered Paraphrases of her own, which even the translation
will not justify, and which say more than once the very contrary to
what I have said in the passages themselves.[59]

If any person has curiosity enough to read the whole paragraphs in my Preface, on some mangled parts of which these reflections are made, he will easily discern that I am as orthodox as Madam *Dacier* her self in those very articles on which she treats me like an Heretick: He will easily see that all the difference between us consists in this, that I offer *opinions,* and she delivers *doctrines*; that my imagination represents *Homer* as the greatest of human Poets, whereas in hers he was exalted above humanity; infallibility and impeccability were two of his attributes. There was therefore no need of defending *Homer* against me, who (if I mistake not) had carry'd my admiration of him as far as it can be carry'd without giving a *real* occasion of writing in his defence.

After answering my harmless Similes, she proceeds to a matter which does not regard so much the honour of *Homer,* as that of the times he liv'd in; and here I must confess she does not wholly mistake my meaning, but I think she mistakes the state of the question. She had said, the Manners of those times were so much the better the less they were like ours: I thought this required a little quali- fication, I confest that in my own opinion the world was mended in some points, such as the custom of putting whole nations to the sword, condemning Kings and their families to perpetual slavery, and a few others. Madam *Dacier* judges otherwise in this;[60] but as to the rest, particularly in preferring the simplicity of the ancient world to the luxury of ours, which is the main point contended for, she owns we agree. This I thought was well, but I am so unfortunate that this too is taken amiss, and call'd adopting or (if you will) stealing *her* sentiment. The truth is she might have said *her words,* for I used them on purpose, being then professedly citing from her:[61] tho' I might have done the same without intending that compliment, for they are also to be found in *Eustathius,* and the sentiment I believe is that of all mankind. I cannot really tell what to say to this whole Remark, only that in the first part of it Madam *Dacier* is displeased that I don't agree with her, and in the last that I do: But this is a temper which every polite man should over-look in a Lady.

To punish my ingratitude, she resolves to expose my blunders, and selects two which I suppose are the most flagrant, out of the many for which she could have chastiz'd me. It happens that the first of these is in part the Translator's, and in part her own, without any share of mine: She quotes the end of a sentence, and he puts in

French what I never wrote in *English*.[62] "*Homer* (I said) open'd a new
and boundless walk for his imagination, and created a world for
himself in the invention of Fable;" which he translates, *Homere crea
pour son usage un monde mouvant, en inventant la fable.*

Madam *Dacier* justly wonders at this nonsense in me; and I, in
the Translator. As to what I meant by *Homer's* invention of Fable, it
is afterwards particularly distinguish'd from that extensive sense in
which she took it, by these words. "If *Homer* was not the first, who
introduced the Deities (as *Herodotus* imagines) into the religion of
Greece, he seems the first who brought them into *a System of Machinery*
for Poetry."

The other blunder she accuses me of is,[63] the mistaking a passage
in *Aristotle,* and she is pleased to send me back to this Philosopher's
treatise of Poetry, and to her Preface on the Odyssey for my better
instruction. Now tho' I am sawcy enough to think that one may
sometimes differ from *Aristotle* without blundering, and tho' I am
sure one may sometimes fall into an error by following him servilely;
yet I own that to quote any Author for what he never said is a
blunder; (but by the way, to correct an Author for what he never
said, is somewhat worse than a blunder.) My words were these. "As
there is a greater variety of Characters in the Iliad than in any other
Poem, so there is of Speeches. Every thing in it has manners, as
Aristotle expresses it; That is, every thing is acted or spoken: very
little passes in narration." She justly says that "Every thing which
is acted or spoken, has not necessarily manners merely because it is
acted or spoken." Agreed: But I would ask the question, whether
any thing can have manners which is neither acted nor spoken? if
not, then the whole Iliad being almost spent in speech and action,
almost every thing in it has Manners: since *Homer* has been prov'd
before in a long paragraph of the Preface, to have excell'd in drawing
Characters and painting Manners, and indeed his whole Poem is one
continued occasion of shewing this bright part of his talent.

To speak fairly, it is impossible she could read even the translation,
and take my sense so wrong as she represents it; but I was first
translated ignorantly, and then read partially. My expression indeed
was not quite exact; it should have been, "Every thing has manners
as *Aristotle* calls them." But such a fault methinks might have been
spared, since if one was to look with that disposition she discovers

towards me, even on her own excellent writings, one might find some mistake which no context can redress; as where she makes *Eustathius* call *Cratisthenes* the *Phliasian, Callisthenes* the *Physician**.[64] What a triumph might some slips of this sort have afforded, to *Homer's*, hers and my enemies, from which she was only screen'd by their happy ignorance? How unlucky had it been, when she insulted Mr. *de la Motte* for omitting a material passage in the † speech of *Helen* to *Hector, Il. 6.* if some champion for the moderns had by chance understood so much *Greek,* as to whisper him, that there was no such passage in *Homer?*[65]

Our concern, zeal, and even jealousy, for our great Author's honour were mutual, our endeavors to advance it were equal, and I have as often trembled for it in her hands, as she could in mine. It was one of the many reasons I had to wish the longer life of this Lady, that I must certainly have regain'd her good opinion, in spite of all mis-representing Translators whatever. I could not have expected it on any other terms than being approved as great, if not as passionate, an admirer of *Homer* as her self. For that was the first condition of her favour and friendship; otherwise not one's Taste alone, but one's Morality had been corrupted, nor would any man's Religion have been unsuspected, who did not implicitly believe in an Author whose doctrine is so comfortable to holy Scripture.[66] However, as different people have different ways of expressing their Belief, some purely by public and general acts of worship, others by a reverend sort of reasoning and enquiry about the grounds of it; 'tis the same in Admiration, some prove it by exclamations, others by respect. I have observed that the loudest huzza's given to a great man in a triumph, proceed not from his friends, but the rabble; and as I have fancy'd it the same with the rabble of Criticks, a desire to be distinguish'd from them has turn'd me to the more moderate, and I hope, more rational method. Tho' I am a Poet, I would not be an Enthusiast; and tho' I am an Englishman, I would not be furiously of a Party. I am far from thinking my self that Genius, upon whom at the end of these remarks Madam *Dacier* congratulates my country: One capable of "correcting *Homer,* and consequently of reforming

*Dacier Remarques sur le 4me livre de l'Odyss.
†De la Corruption du Gout. pag. 467.

mankind, and amending this Constitution."[67] It was not to *Great Britain* this ought to have been apply'd, since our nation has one happiness for which she might have preferr'd it to her own, that as much as we abound in other miserable misguided Sects, we have at least none of the blasphemers of *Homer.*[68] We stedfastly and unanimously believe, both his Poem, and our Constitution, to be the best that ever human wit invented: That the one is not more incapable of amendment than the other; and (old as they both are) we despise any *French* or *English* man whatever, who shall presume to retrench, to innovate, or to make the least alteration in either. Far therefore from the Genius for which Madam *Dacier* mistook me, my whole desire is but to preserve the humble character of a faithful Translator, and a quiet Subject.[69]

Annotations

1. For Pope and his contemporaries, *the* critical authority on the epic was René Le Bossu (*Monsieur Bossu's Treatise of the Epick Poem. . . . "Done into* English *from the* French, *with a new Original* Preface *upon the same Subject, by* W. J." [London, 1695]), Dryden going so far as to comment that "Spenser wanted only to have read the rules of Bossu" ("Dedication of the Aeneis," *Essays,* II, 220; see also "Introduction," n. 6, p. 47). Besides the essay "A general view of the Epic Poem, and of the *Iliad* and *Odyssey.* Extracted from *Bossu*" which introduces Pope's translation of the *Odyssey,* many of the early statements of the Postscript suggest that he was writing with his copy of Bossu close at hand or firmly in mind (and with Mme Anne Lefèvre Dacier's preface to her translation of the *Odyssey* [1716] not much further away!). But Pope's acceptance of prevailing doctrine was never slavish; he remained quite free to burlesque Bossu's formalism (he was the first English writer to do so) in the preface to the *Dunciad* and in the *Peri Bathous's* "Receipt to make an Epic Poem" (originally appearing as *Guardian* No. 78 [10 June 1713]).

2. Inevitably—in the Aristotelian, formalist tradition to which it belongs and in which a critical study is expected to begin by distinguishing and defining—the first book of Bossu's *Treatise* is entitled *Of the Nature of the* Epick Poem; *and of the* Fable. Equally characteristic is the quadrant of "Moral, Subject, Manner, and Style" to which Pope soon refers.

3. Bossu: "The Fable of the *Odysseis* is all for the conduct of a State, and for Policy." (Bossu, p. 192.) Pope's concept of the epic as a work politically relevant to his own age helps give his translation its particularly Augustan character. His version is not to him just a superior presentation of a great classic tale of adventure

but a representation of a heroic vision, rich in humane values, reaching from the Greeks to his own time. As the editors of the Twickenham edition of the translations put it: "Extending the *Iliad* and *Odyssey* beyond poetry and criticism to legislate ordered values to every aspect of his threatened society, Pope made translation a political art." ("Introduction," *Translations of Homer,* TE VII, ccxxi.) *Political* here must be taken in the very broadest sense: when Pope closes the *Odyssey* with the familiar last line of *Absalom and Achitophel* (TE VII, ccxvii–xviii for full discussion), that conclusion does not echo Dryden simply; it reverberates back through Milton to the Bible and on to the most primal contention between order and disorder, between what is destructive, chaotic, and antisocial and what ultimately represents morality, society, civilization.

   4. Bossu:

> This Poem is more useful to the *Vulgar,* than the *Iliad* is, where the Subjects suffer rather by the ill Conduct of their Princes, than through their own fault. . . . it is to be confess'd, that these great Names of *Kings, Hero's, Achilles, Agamemnon,* and *Ulysses,* do no less denote the meanest *Burghers,* than do the *Caesars,* the *Pompeys,* and the *Alexanders* of the Age. The *Commonality* are as subject as the *Grandees,* to lose their Estates, and ruin their Families by Anger and Divisions, by negligence and want of taking care of their business. They stand in as much need of *Homer's* Lessons, as Kings; they are as capable of profiting thereby; and 'tis as well for the *Small* as the *Great,* that the Morality of the *Schools,* that of the *Fable,* and that of the *Chair* deliver those *Truths* we have been just speaking of. (Bossu, p. 26.)

Mme Dacier—no doubt following Bossu—makes much the same observation: ". . . les instructions sont plus marquées & plus frequentes dans l'Odyssée que dans l'Iliade, & ce Poëme est plus moral. Tout est instruit dans l'Odyssée; les peres, les enfants, les maris, les femmes, les Roys, les sujets y trouvent les leçons qui leur sont necessaires pour remplir les principaux devoirs de leur estat." ("Preface," *L'Odyssée d'Homere,* traduite en françois, avec des remarques [Paris, 1716], I, lxxxiii.)

   5. Horace *Ars Poetica* 312–13 (He who has learned what he owes his country and his friends, what love is due a parent, a brother, and a guest . . .); *Epistle* 1. 2. 3–4 (who tells us what is fair, what is foul, what helpful, what not, more plainly and better than Chrysippus or Crantor). (Loeb [1955], pp. 477, 263.)

   6. Bossu:

> The *Odysseis* was not design'd as the *Iliad,* to instruct all the States of *Greece* join'd and confederated in one Body, but for each State in particular. A State is compos'd of two parts; The *Head* which commands is the first, and the *Members* which obey make up the other. There are Instructions requisite for the *Governour,* and some likewise necessary for the *Subjects:* for him to

rule well, and for them to be rul'd by him. . . . But as 'tis necessary that
the Princes in the *Iliad* should be Cholerick and Quarrelssome: So 'tis
necessary in the *Fable* of the *Odysseïs* that the chief Personage should be
Sage, and Prudent." (Bossu, pp. 23, 24.)

7. Bossu: "The better to demonstrate this Length of the *Odysseïs, Aristotle*
adds, *That the Subject of this Poem is a Voyage for Several Years.* . . . This Subject is
indeed a great deal longer than that of the *Iliad*; and it requires a longer time,
and more Actions for all these things, than for the simple Anger of an enrag'd
and pacified person, where every thing was transacted in one and the same place."
(Bossu, pp. 65–66.) "There are *Fables* which naturally contain in them a great
many parts, each of which might make an exact *Fable*: And there are likewise
Actions of the very same nature. The subject Matter of the *Odysseïs* is of this kind
[as compared to a *'Regular simplicity* of the *Fable.* . . . what *Homer* has done with
such success in the Composition of the *Iliad*]." (Bossu, pp. 49, 48.)

8. Bossu: "The Design of the *Odysseïs* is quite different from that of the
Iliad; so likewise is the management of it, as to its *Duration*. The Character of
the Hero is Prudence and Wisdom. And this Moderation gives the Poet liberty
to extend his Action to as long a time as he pleases, and his political Instructions
required. Therefore he did not allow this Action some Weeks as he had that of
the *Iliad*; but he takes up eight years and a half. . . ." (Bossu, p. 108.) Bossu
also contrasts the *Iliad* and the *Odyssey* on the matter of the action (p. 82), the
ordering of events (p. 87), the nature and unity of the intrigue (pp. 93, 102),
the conclusion (p. 104), the characters (p. 120), the invocation (p. 124), the
passions (pp. 140–41), the continuity of the action (p. 149), and the time setting
(p. 156).

9. Bossu: "The *Iliad* consists altogether in Battles, in Anger, and in a continual Commotion without Bounds and measure. The *Odysseis* on the contrary is
full of nothing else but Prudence, Patience, and Wisdom. So that the Learned
observe there is a considerable difference in the Stile and Verses of these two
Poems. There is a great deal of Flegm in the *Odysseis*: But the *Iliad* is all over
one continual Flame." (Bossu, p. 260.)

10. As Pope goes on to indicate, this is an argument advanced by Longinus:
". . . 'Tis certain there are abundance of things in the *Odysses,* which are only
the Sequel of the Misfortunes we read of in the *Ilias*; and which he carry'd into
the *Odysses* as Episodes of the *Trojan* War. Add to this, the Incidents in the *Iliads*
are often lamented by the Heroes of the *Odysses,* as Misfortunes that were known,
and had happen'd a long time before: Wherefore the *Odysses* are properly speaking,
nothing but the Epilogue to the *Iliads*." ("A Treatise of the Sublime," *The Works
of Monsr. Boileau Despreaux* [trans. by Ozell] [London, 1711], II, 29 [sep. pagination for the Treatise].)

11. Scholars are generally agreed that Pope knew Longinus through Boileau—but whether directly from the French or at another remove through English translations has been debated, though TE citations would indicate that there are elements in the French Longinus and not in the English that Pope draws on. Probably it was a matter of using both sources. Pope was familiar enough with John Ozell as a translator to damn him in an early epigram for "murd'ring *Boileau*" (*Minor Poems,* TE VI, 37) and he would certainly have examined a translation as popular as Ozell's three-volume edition of Boileau's *Works* (1711–13). His quotation from Longinus here, though very close, does not quite parallel Ozell's version—to be found in the collected edition—though for convenience's sake that text will be used as a referent, cited as Boileau: "A Treatise of the Sublime," II, 29–31 (sep. pagination for the Treatise).

12. Mme Dacier had devoted the third section of her four-part Preface to just this matter: Longinus's justification of his preference for the *Iliad* by ascribing the *Odyssey* to Homer's failing powers, and her refutation of this commonly held view. Pope's argument follows her closely: she quotes Longinus and then insists that each epic be considered in the light of its own nature:

> L'Iliade, comme Poëme pathetique, doit avoir un caractere different & d'autres couleurs que l'Odyssée, qui est un Poëme moral & il n'y a pas moins de force & de vigueur à avoir conservé à l'Odyssée son veritable caractere, que d'avoir donné à l'Iliade le sien. La veritable marque de l'affoiblissement de l'esprit d'un Poëte, c'est quand il traite mal son sujet; or c'est ce qu'on ne sçauroit reprocher à Homere, le sujet de l'Odyssée n'est pas moins bien traité que celuy de l'Iliade (Dacier, *L'Odyssée,* I, lxvi–lxvii).

She defends the *Odyssey* on its own merits, also drawing on examples from painting (though she is general where Pope is specific), and she argues, plausibly, that no one suggests that Virgil wrote the first part of the *Aeneid,* that based on the *Odyssey,* as an exhausted aftermath to the second part, that patterned on the *Iliad.* Her appreciative defense of the *Odyssey,* made both as reader and translator, provides an interesting preview for several pages of Pope's essay.

13. Mme Dacier:

> On peut rendre cela sensible par un example tiré de la Peinture: Qu'un grand Peintre ait fait deux grands Tableaux; que dans l'un il ait representé tout ce que la colere accompagnée de valeur, peut faire executer à un homme inexorable & injuste, & que dans l'autre il ait imité tout ce que la prudence & la dissimulation peuvent faire attendre d'un homme juste & vaillant, on trouvera dans le premier une vivacité d'action & un esclat qui luy donneront un tres grand relief & qui surprendront l'admiration; & dans ce dernier on trouvera des moeurs, une regularité & une conduite qui se feront admirer des sages. Mais il n'y aura personne qui puisse tirer de l'execution

de ces deux sujets des arguments que ce dernier n'a esté executé que dans la vieillesse du Peintre, & lorsque son esprit commençoit desja à baisser, car rien n'empesche que le dernier n'ait esté fait avant l'autre. (Dacier, *L'Odyssée*, I, lxviii.)

Dryden too had used Raphael—"the greatest of all modern masters"—to illustrate a point of criticism (see "Dedication of the *Aeneis*," *Essays*, II, 199–200) when he wished to point up the superiority of an incident in Virgil over its parallel in a "languishing episode of the *Odysseis*." Raphael's Battle of Constantine is also referred to by Blackmore, in the section on "Machines" in his "Essay upon Epick Poetry." (Sir Richard Blackmore, "An Essay upon Epick Poetry," *Essays upon Several Subjects* [London, 1716].)

14. Mme Dacier: "On ne voit point qu'Aristote dans sa Poëtique ait donné aucune préference marquée à l'un ou à l'autre de ces deux Poëmes. Il a parlé en general de la Poësie. . . ." (Dacier, *L'Odyssée*, I, lxxiii.)

15. Mme Dacier:

Du passage d'Horace, que j'ay rapporté, il me semble qu'on peut inferer que ce grand Critique décide ce qu'Aristote a laissé indécis, & que bien loin de croire que l'Odyssée ait esté faite dans le déclin de l'esprit d'Homere, il luy donne au contraire le préference sur l'Iliade. Cela paroist par le Tableau magnifique qu'il en fait, car il a pris bien plus de plaisir à détailler l'Odyssée que l'Iliade, & d'ailleurs il est tres seur que ce qui enseigne à imiter la vertu, est toujours plus parfait que ce qui enseigne à fuir le vice; car les originaux vicieux sont plus aisez à peindre que ceux qui sont des modelles de vertu & de sagesse. (Dacier, *L'Odyssée*, I, lxxxii.)

In his advice to Lollius—against envy, avarice, debauchery and anger—Horace refers to the *Iliad,* and then, at somewhat greater length, to the *Odyssey*:

Again, of the power of worth and wisdom he has set before us an instructive pattern in Ulysses, that tamer of Troy, who looked with discerning eyes upon the cities and manners of many men, and while for self and comrades he strove for a return across the broad seas, many hardships he endured, but could never be o'erwhelmed in the waves of adversity. You know the Sirens' songs and Circe's cups; if, along with his comrades, he had drunk of these in folly and greed, he would have become the shapeless and witless vassal of a harlot mistress—would have lived as an unclean dog or a sow that loves the mire. We are but ciphers, born to consume earth's fruits, Penelope's good-for-naught suitors, your courtiers of Alcinous, unduly busy in keeping their skins sleek, whose pride it was to sleep till midday and to lull care to rest to the sound of the cithern. (*Epistle* 1. 2. 17–31 [Loeb (1955), pp. 263, 265].)

In *Ars Poetica* (ll. 136ff.) Horace cautions against diffuseness, citing instead the delimited subject of the *Odyssey*—"Sing, Muse for me the man who on Troy's fall / Saw the wide world, its ways and cities all." Next he speaks of "striking and wondrous tales," which he illustrates by episodes from the *Odyssey.* (Loeb [1955], p. 463.)

16. See n. 4. Chapter x of Book I of Bossu's *Treatise* is concerned with the fable of the *Odyssey.* Mme Dacier: ". . . les instructions sont plus marquées & plus frequentes dans l'Odyssée que dans l'Iliade, & ce Poëme est plus moral." (Dacier, *L'Odyssée,* I, lxxxiii.)

17. Cf. Bossu: ". . . *Virgil* had but one Poem to make, and this ought to be more like the *Odysseïs* than the *Iliad,* since the *Roman* State was govern'd by only one Prince." (Bossu, p. 26.) "When he takes an Entire Action, as *Homer* has done for his *Odysseïs,* and *Virgil* for the *Aeneid;* there is nothing to be adjusted, nor any measure to be taken [as in the *Iliad*] to make this Action appear a *Whole,* and not the Part of another Action." (P. 82.) "Therefore *Virgil* has not taken this for the *Matter* of his Poem; but he relates it by such Recitals as *Homer* makes use of in his *Odysseïs.* . . ." (P. 89.) "*Virgil* has divided his Poem as *Homer* did his *Odysseïs.*" (P. 94.) "The Conduct of the *Latin* Poet, in the *Intrigues* he forms, has the same Simplicity. The Tempests are made use of in the first Part of the *Aeneid,* just as in the *Odysseïs.*" (P. 96.) ". . . in the *Odysseïs* and the *Aeneid* the Poets would have been unjust, and the Readers dissatisfied, if such brave Princes and such noble Souls as *Ulysses* and *Æneas* had been suffer'd to sink under any misfortune." (P. 106.) "The *Æneid* is like the *Odysseïs.* The Character of the Hero is Piety and Meekness: and Politicks are likewise essential thereto. Therefore the *Duration* of the Action is continued after the same manner." (P. 109.) ". . . what can be more *Simple* and *Modest* than the *Proposition* of the *Odysseïs* . . . ? We shall find the same *Simplicity* and *Modesty* in the *Proposition* of the *Æneid.*" (P. 121.)

18. Fénelon's *Télémaque* (Paris, 1699).

19. Homer, *Iliad* 9.434–605; in Pope 562–717.

20. Homer, *Iliad* 11.656–803; in Pope 801–934.

21. Homer, *Iliad* 6.145–211; in Pope 179–260.

22. Homer, *Iliad* 20.200–58; in Pope 240–308.

23. Cf. Longinus's commentary on Plato, "whose Stile is very Lofty, tho' it flows without being rapid, and without making a Noise. . . ." (Boileau, p. 37.) Pope had used a comparable image in the Preface: *Homer* like the *Nile* pours out his Riches with a boundless Overflow; *Virgil* like a River in its Banks, with a gentle and constant Stream." ("Preface" to the *Iliad,* TE VII, 12.)

24. In Boileau's translation: "One thing more that oblig'd me to speak of the *Odysses,* was to let you see, that Great Poets and Famous Writers, when their Wit has not Vigour enough for the *Pathetick,* commonly amuse themselves with Painting of Manners. Such is *Homer's* Description of the Life, which *Penelope's* Lovers

led in *Ulysses's* House: For in truth all that Description is a kind of Comedy, wherein the different Characters of Men are Painted." (Boileau, pp. 30–31.)

25. "Comedy, as we have said, is a representation of inferior people. . . ." (Aristotle, *Poetics* 5. 1 [Loeb (1953), p. 19].) Hobbes, in distinguishing poetry in areas of mankind (court, city, and country, with correspondencies in heroic, "scommatique," and pastoral poetry), locates satire and comedy in the scommatique and speaks of "an insincereness, inconstancy, and troublesome humor" of that category. (Thomas Hobbes, "Answer to Davenant's Preface to *Gondibert*," Spingarn, II, 55.)

26. "*Comedy* must likewise yield to *Tragedy,* because it has little of Elevation, and the manner of its Actors Speaking, is too Natural and Familiar." (Bossu, p. 12.)

27. ". . . a *simple* thought in its proper place, is more worth than all the most *exquisite words* and wit out of season." (René Rapin, *Reflections on Aristotle's Treatise of Poesie* [London, 1674], p. 56.)

28. Cf. Dryden: "As in the composition of a picture the painter is to take care that nothing enter into it which is not proper or convenient to the subject, so likewise is the poet to reject all incidents which are foreign to his poem, and are naturally no parts of it; they are wens, and other excrescences, which belong not to the body, but deform it. . . . A painter must reject all trifling ornaments; so must a poet refuse all tedious and unnecessary descriptions." ("A Parallel of Poetry and Painting," *Essays,* II, 139.) Blackmore too has a number of observations in this vein: "An Essay upon Epick Poetry," p. 137; see also pp. 101, 116.

29. This is a matter with which Pope had been concerned in the "Preface" to the *Iliad*: " 'Tis a great Secret in Writing to know when to be plain, and when poetical and figurative. . . ." (TE VII, 18.) Rapin had made a similar point— "There is a particular *Rhetorick* for *Poetry,* which the *Modern* Poets scarce understand at all; this Art consists in discerning very precisely what ought to be said *figuratively,* and what to be spoken *simply*: and in knowing well where ornament is requir'd, and where not. . . . 'Tis onely the talent of great men to know to *speak,* and to be *silent*; to be *florid,* and to be *plain*; to be *lofty,* and to be *low*; to use *figures,* and to speak *simply*. . . ." (Rapin, *Reflections,* pp. 55, 56.)

30. "The greatest *flights* of *Latin Poetry* are in some certain excellent *places* of *Virgil's Georgicks*. . . ." (Ibid., p. 53.)

31. Boileau's mock-heroic poem (Paris: 1674; 1683), in which epic "elevation" is used to mock the pettiness of an ecclesiastical dispute.

32. *Georgics* 4. 67ff.

33. Longinus, in chapter II (Boileau's trans.), discusses the pseudo-tragic style and bombast: "There's certainly nothing more difficult to be avoided in Eloquence than *Bombast*; for as in all Things we naturally seek after something Great, and fear more than any Thing to be accus'd of Driness or Want of Strength, so it

happens, I know not which Way, that the greatest Part of Men fall into this Vice.
. . . However it cannot be deny'd but that *Swelling* in a Discourse is not less
Vicious than Tumours in the Body; it consists of nothing but a false Outside and
a deceitful Appearance, while within 'tis all hollow and empty, and has sometimes
an Effect quite contrary to what is truly Great. . . ." (Boileau, pp. 15–16.) "To
the true Sublime in one Extream, is oppos'd the swelling and fustian Stile; where
weak and trifling Thoughts are set off with all the Ornament that sounding
Words and pompous Periods can bestow, while the slender Sense is effac'd with
too much Colouring and Decoration." (Blackmore, "An Essay upon Epick Poetry,"
p. 154.)

34. Bossu: "At first the *Fables* were employ'd in speaking of the *Divine Nature*
according to the Notion they then had of it. This sublime Subject made the first
Poets to be stil'd *Divines,* and *Poetry the Language of the Gods.* . . . The *Presence of
the Deity,* and the Care such an August Cause ought to take about any Action,
obliges the *Poet* to represent this *Action* as great, important, and manag'd by *Kings*
and *Princes.* It obliges him likewise to think and speak in an elevated way above
the Vulgar, and in a Style that may in some sort keep up the Character of the
Divine Persons he introduces. To this end serves the Poetical and Figurative
Expression, and the Majesty of the *Heroick Verse.*" (Bossu, pp. 3, 5.)

35. This too is a point which Pope had established in the *Iliad* essay ("In
Virgil the Dramatic Part is less in proportion to the Narrative" [TE VII, 8]).
Bossu devotes a chapter (Book III, chapter x) to the "dramatic" narrative, tracing
his emphasis to Aristotle.

36. Cf. Blackmore: "As this often happens on the Theater, when the Tragick
Poet, that wants Judgment and Strength of Imagination, would supply the Defect
of great and elevated Ideas, by turgid and windy Diction, and attempts to terrify
the Audience by the mere Power of raging Words. . . ." (Blackmore, "An Essay
upon Epick Poetry," p. 154.)

37. Longinus: "*Demosthenes*'s Sublime is doubtless most proper for Strong Exaggerations and Violent Passions: On the contrary, Abundance [Cicero's Sublime]
is best, where if I may so express my self, the Orator would shed an Agreeable
Dew on the Minds of his Auditory. A Copious Discourse is certainly most suitable
to common Places, Perorations, Digressions, and generally all Writings, of the
Domonstrative Kind; as also for History, Treatises of Physick, and several other
such like Matters." (Boileau, pp. 36–37.)

38. *Aeneid* 11. 343–75; 11. 378–444.

39. Cf. Davenant: "And surely Poets, whose business should represent the
Worlds true image often to our view, are not less prudent than Painters, who
when they draw Landschaps entertain not the Eye wholly with even Prospect and
a continued Flat, but for variety terminate the sight with lofty Hills, whose
obscure heads are sometimes in the clouds." (Sir William Davenant, "Preface to
Gondibert," Spingarn, II, 3.)

40. Cf. Longinus: "Our Judgment ought to be the same, with respect to Poets and Orators: I mean, we must be very careful that we do not take a certain Appearance, of Dignity, founded upon Great Words jumbl'd together by chance, for Sublime; for if you examine 'em well, you'll find 'em to be nothing but a vain *Flatus* of Words, which deserves rather to be despis'd than admir'd." (Boileau, p. 20.) ". . . we meet with many Poets and Writers, who not being born for the Sublime, have however never been without it; tho' commonly they make use of Mean and Vulgar Ways of Writing: Indeed, they Support themselves by this Placing of Words only, which in some measure, Swells and Heightens their Voices; insomuch, that we do not take Notice of their Meanness." (Boileau, p. 80.)

41. Cf. Boileau: "And never Writer descends sometimes into Particulars so much as he [Homer], nor talks of Little things so often; yet his Phrase is always Noble; and when he makes use of Lower Terms, 'tis with such Art and Industry . . . that he makes 'em Noble and Harmonious:" (Boileau, "Critical Reflections on Some Passages out of Longinus," *Works,* II, 121.)

42. Mme Dacier:

> Je m'estois flattée que la Traduction de l'Odyssée me donneroit moins de peine que celle de l'Iliade, mais j'ay esté bien détrompée à l'essay. Dans l'Iliade j'estois soutenuë par la grandeur des choses & des images; & quoyque je n'aye pû attraper le merveilleux & le sublime des expressions, j'ay conservé la grandeur qui est dans les faits & dans les idées, & cela remplit l'esprit du Lecteur; mais dans l'Odyssée tout est simple, & cependant le Poëte a trouvé dans sa langue des richesses qui l'ont mis en estat de s'expliquer noblement jusques dans les plus petits sujets. (*L'Odysée,* I, lxxxv.)

43. *"Nature* and *Homer* were, he found, the *same"* (*Essay on Criticism,* l. 135 [TE I, 255]).

44. "The Great Masters in Composition know very well that many an elegant Phrase becomes improper for a Poet or an Orator, when it has been debased by common Use. For this Reason the Works of Ancient Authors, which are written in dead Languages, have a great Advantage over those which are written in Languages that are now spoken." (Addison, *Spectator* No. 285 [26 January 1712].)

45. "For out of him, according to our most graue and iudicial *Plutarch,* are all Arts deduced, confirmed, or illustrated." (George Chapman, "Prefaces to the Translation of Homer," Spingarn, I, 67.)

46. *"Milton,* in conformity with the Practice of the Ancient Poets, and with *Aristotle*'s Rule, has infused a great many *Latinisms,* as well as *Græcisms,* and sometimes *Hebraisms,* into the Language of his Poem. . . . The same Reason recommended to him several old Words, which also makes his Poem appear the more venerable, and gives it a greater Air of Antiquity." (Addison, *Spectator* No. 285 [26 January 1712].) Dryden had made a similar observation: "His an-

tiquated words were his choice, not his necessity; for therein he imitated Spenser, as Spenser did Chaucer. And though, perhaps, the love of their masters may have transported both too far, in the frequent use of them, yet, in my opinion, obsolete words may then be laudably revived, when either they are more sounding, or more significant, than those in practice. . . ." (Dryden, "A Discourse concerning the Original and Progress of Satire," *Essays*, II, 29.) ". . . I found in him a true sublimity, lofty thoughts, which were clothed with admirable Grecisms, and ancient words . . . which, with all their rusticity, had somewhat of venerable in them. . . ." (Ibid., p. 109.)

47. ". . . it is doubtful whether Epick Poetry demands that exact and polish'd Diction, which the most careful Writers contend for; there is sometimes a Roughness in the true Sublime, like that in the Surface of some stately Buildings, which makes it appear, if not more Beautiful, yet more Majestick." (Blackmore, "An Essay upon Epick Poety," p. 119.)

48. "If . . . we consider the *Language* of this great Poet, we must allow . . . that it is often too much laboured, and sometimes obscured by old Words, Transpositions, and Foreign Idioms." (Addison, *Spectator* No. 297 [9 February 1712].)

49. Pope to Broome: "I correct daily, and make them seem less corrected, that is, more easy, more fluent, more natural, which, give me leave to say, is the style of Homer, in this work especially. The narrative is perspicuous to the last degree. . . . I will just so far take you down, as to say, you are sometimes too figurative and constrained, not quite easy or clear enough." (*Correspondence*, II, 320 [14 September (1725)].)

50. The history of the collaboration of Pope, Broome, and Fenton is a confused one, complicated by secrecy and half-truths. Apparently the original intention had been to keep the partnership secret until the success of the subscription had been assured, after which Fenton and Broome could step forth to share in the honor. But word leaked out about the project and Pope found it necessary to make some sort of statement, or rather, he got Broome to assert, in a statement at the conclusion of the notes, that "If my performance has merit, either in these, or in any part of the translation (namely in the sixth, eleventh, and eighteenth books) it is but just to attribute it to the judgment and care of Mr. *Pope*, by whose hand every sheet was corrected. His other, and much more able assistant, was Mr. *Fenton*, in the fourth and twentieth books." The real truth is still another matter: correspondence and later acknowledgements have indicated that Broome actually wrote eight books (II, VI, VIII, XI, XII, XVI, XVIII, and XXIII) while Fenton did four (I, IV, XIX, XXII). (*Early Career*, pp. 248–62.)

51. Mme Dacier had died in 1720.

52. Mme Dacier's translation of Homer (the *Iliad* in 1711, the *Odyssey* in 1716) had included prefaces, notes (many of which were taken from the twelfth-

century Byzantine scholar Eustathius, whose *Commentary on the Iliad and Odyssey of Homer* was an important source of critical information) and, with the *Iliad*, a life of Homer. Pope patterned his editions on hers, even to relying heavily on Eustathius for his notes. Although he criticized her for her "thefts" ("Eustathius is transcribed ten times for once that he is quoted" [*Correspondence*, I, 492].), he and his collaborators were guilty of the same sin, borrowing not only from Eustathius, but from Mme Dacier herself. Pope wrote to Broome: "I find upon comparing your notes with Dacier's, many of them much more directly, indeed, entirely copied from her—besides what she takes from Eustathius—than I expected, or than is consistent with the plan I laid down. . . ." (*Correspondence*, II, 363 [20 January 1725/6)].)

53. Cf. Pope's statements to the Duke of Buckingham:

> I cannot think quite so highly of the Lady's learning, tho' I respect it very much. It is great complaisance in that polite nation, to allow her to be a Critic of equal rank with her husband. To instance no further, his remarks on Horace shew more good Sense, Penetration, and a better Taste of his author, and those upon Aristotle's art of poetry more Skill and Science, than any of hers on any author whatever. In truth, they are much more slight, dwell more in generals, and are besides for the most part less her own. . . . Your Grace will believe me, that I did not search to find defects in a Lady; my employment upon the Iliad forc'd me to see them. . . .
>
> (*Correspondence*, I, 492 [1 September 1718].)

The authenticity of this letter, which was first printed in 1737, is called into question by Audra, who thinks that it was fabricated by Pope to make it appear that critical commentary of his preceded hers. In fact, in a preceding letter from Buckingham to Pope—which Audra believes is also spurious—there is an interesting anticipation of what did happen: "I wish, for the sake of the publick which is now so well entertain'd by their quarrel [La Motte's and Mme Dacier's], it may not end at last in their agreeing to blame equally a third man, who is so presumptuous as to censure both, if they should chance to hear of it." (*Correspondence*, I, 485 [August 1718].) (E. Audra, *L'Influence française dans l'oeuvre de Pope* [Paris: H. Champion, 1931], pp. 253–57.)

54. The Twickenham Edition of the translations prints (TE X, 445–56 [Appendix B]) the manuscript text of the surviving portion of the Postscript, which consists of this answer to Mme Dacier. To compare the MS version with the printed text is to see how much Pope characteristically tempered what did appear. The earlier version is more defensive, his response much more a counterattack.

55. Pope is referring to the Battle of the Ancients and Moderns, then focused on Homer, with Mme Dacier and Houdar de La Motte representing the two poles

of opinion. Although Pope was a strong apologist for Homer—answering in his Preface to the *Iliad* many of the charges of the Modernists—his position is usually a moderate one, between the two extremes.

56. Mme Dacier had read Pope's Preface in the French translation by Pérelle.

57. Mme Dacier's translations: *L'Iliade* (3 vols., Paris, 1711; 2d ed., 1719); *L'Odyssée* (3 vols., Paris, 1716). "There had been a very elegant Prose-translation before [in 1709], that by Monsieur de la Valterie, so elegant, that the style of it was evidently the original and model of the famous Télamaque." (*Correspondence*, I, 492.)

58. Mme Dacier had taken exception to what were to her the negative implications of Pope's descriptions of Homer's work as a "wild Paradise" ("Preface," TE VII, 3); as a "copious Nursery which contains the Seeds and first Productions of every kind" (ibid.); and as a "mighty Tree"—"and they who find the justest Faults, have only said, that a few Branches (which run luxuriant thro' a Richness of Nature) might be lopp'd into Form to give it a more regular Appearance" (ibid., p. 17). To her the *Iliad* was the most ordered, symmetrical garden imaginable, its beauties of an achieved and perfected nature, its richness a completely controlled fecundity.

59. As an example of the temper of her argument—she concludes her discussion of this point:

> M. Pope nous auroit rendu un grand service, s'il avait bien voulu nous marquer les branches inutiles qu'il faudroit couper à cet arbre, la symmetrie qu'on devroit donner à ce Jardin brute, pour le rendre plus regulier, & la perfection qui manque aux differentes beautez qu'il dit qu'Homere n'a qu'èbauchées. Il seroit heureux pour nostre siecle & glorieux pour l'Angleterre, d'avoir produit un critique si parfait. ("Reflexions sur la première Partie de la Preface de M. Pope," *L'Iliade*, 2d ed. [Paris, 1719], III, sig. *iiii^r.)

60. She tries to counter by arguing that cruelty and violence are not unknown to later ages either—ages in addition corrupted by ease and luxury; but she is not able to point in modern times to such horrors as Pope cites.

61. She is not actually mentioned by name here; but in any such discussion of Homer's "Censurers and Defenders," her sentiments on this particular matter would have been well known.

62. Dacier, "Reflexions," sig. *[vi]^v.

63. Ibid., sigs. *[vii]^r–[viii]^r.

64. Dacier, *L'Odyssée* (Paris, 1716), I, 385; Eustathius, *Commentarii ad Homeri Odysseam* (Leipzig, 1825), I, 1503:30.

65. This reference is confusing. While Pope alludes to an episode in Book VI, the citation is to a discussion of Helen's speech to Priam in Book III (where

Mme Dacier is indeed critical of La Motte, who "gaste encore le discours"). But although she refers to Helen's blaming the fates (as in her speech to Hector in Book VI), the passage which she then produces as a countering example of "la bonne Morale"—which she accuses La Motte of ignoring when he finds it or changing "en impieté"—is still from that speech of Helen to Priam, where her translation's emphasis on Helen's responsibility ("mais je n'eus ni assez de courage, ni assez de vertu") seems to be her own addition. Later, on p. 493, she does comment on Helen's speech to Hector of Book VI: "Le discours d'Helene à Hector, ce discours plein d'une douceur charmante, n'est pas reconnoissable dans M. de la M."

66. A point which Mme Dacier had pressed in her attack on him: "Après avoir defendu Homere, il faut que je me deffende aussi moymesme, contre une critique qu'il a faite sur un endroit de ma Preface; en parlant des moeurs des heros d'Homere, si semblables à celles des Patriarches. . . ." (Dacier, "Reflexions," sig. *iiii^r.) "Ces moeurs des heros d'Homere ne sont-elles pas tres semblables à celles des Patriarches, & tres dissemblables à celles d'aujourd'huy?" (Ibid., sig. *[v]^r.)

67. "Les fautes que je luy reproche sont si legeres, qu'elles ne doivent pas empescher l'Angleterre d'attendre de ce nouveau poëte les grands advantages qu'on doit esperer d'un reformateur d'Homere. Un homme si habile ne se bornera pas à perfectionner l'art du poëme Epique; ce seroit peu de chose, il perfectionnera l'art de la politique, bien plus estimable & plus important que celuy de l'Epopée. . . ." (Dacier, "Reflexions," sig. *[viii]^r.)

68. Gay was to write to Pope: "All I could hear of you of late hath been by advertisements in news-papers, by which one wou'd think the race of Curls was multiplied; and by the indignation such fellows show against you, that you have more merit than any body alive could have. Homer himself hath not been worse us'd by the French." (*Correspondence*, II, 508 [2 August 1728].)

69. Mme Dacier's political references—including an allusion to Alcibiades ("un homme capable de corriger Homere, sera capable de former des hommes; c'est le jugement qu'en faisoit Alcibiade, car un Grammairien s'estant vanté devant luy, qu'il avoit dans son cabinet, Homere corrigé de sa main, *Eh mon ami*, luy dit-il, *tu es capable de corriger Homere, & tu t'amuses à enseigner des enfants, que ne t'occupes-tu à former des hommes!* Voilà une grande ressource pour un Estat!" [Dacier, "Reflexions," sigs. *[viii]^r–*[viii]^v])—were particularly embarrassing to Pope at this time, when his close friend Atterbury was in the Tower and his edition of Buckingham's *Works* had been suppressed for seditious passages. On 12 February 1722/23 he wrote to Samuel Buckley, in the Foreign Office, through whom he had been sent the volumes containing Mme Dacier's attack:

What indeed most concerns me is her last period, in which she seems both angry & merry (so far I like it very well) but she concludes, that because I sometimes own Homer not to be the Pope, that is not to be infallible; therfore I must think myself wiser, & so correct him. And consequently that I must be qualifyd to Reform all mankind, and be at the Head of the Government. Upon which she cries out,

Voilà une grande Ressource pour l'Etat!

This truly Sir I do not like, & think proper (to you, who are a sort of a Minister, and to all my Friends of the Office) to enter my Protest against such suggestions; especially at this time, when I am told People blame me for having Seen a Book [the Duke of Buckingham's *Works*]. And such a Book (God knows) as I had no more thoughts of Correcting, than of Homer himself. . . . (*Correspondence,* II, 157–58.)

PREFACE.

to

MISCELLANIES

IN

PROSE and *VERSE*.

INTRODUCTION

Dr. Johnson's comment that it was Pope "who prefixed a querulous and apologetical Preface" to the *Miscellanies*[1] is helpful for attribution if perhaps misleading as criticism. Since Swift had delegated to Pope the task of editing the volume,[2] it would seem likely that the latter would prepare the introduction; and though the piece is signed by both and dated May 1727, when Swift was in England, Pope had written to him in Ireland in February, announcing "Our Miscellany is now quite printed."[3] Moreover, the Preface's concern with pirated material particularly reflects Pope's annoyance at Curll's publication of his Cromwell letters the preceding year, and may have been meant, as Dr. Johnson suggests,[4] to prepare the ground—with its references to "ransacked" closets—for Pope's later activities with his correspondence (see *Narrative of the Method*).

Dr. Johnson's strictures (he goes on to write of the "ridiculous and romantick complaint of the robberies committed upon authors by the clandestine seizure and sale of their papers")[5] seem unduly harsh in the light of Pope's quarter-century struggle with Curll to protect his works and his name. A century before the advent of adequate copyright protection, an author's control over his own writings was shockingly tenuous, as Edmund Curll's enterprising career as bookseller and publisher attests.[6] But Curll met his match with Pope, who could be equally energetic and devious in achieving *his* goals. The evils complained of in the Preface are legitimate enough, but they also provided Pope—here and at later times—with a convenient justification for pushing works into print or for accomplishing even more intricate objectives.

Pope's involvement in this particular venture, which includes so few of his own things,[7] does, however, raise the question soon framed by Jonathan Smedley in a contemporary attack, *Gulliveriana: or, A Fourth Volume of Miscellanies*—"How Mr. *Pope* came to condescend to have his Name *tack'd* to this Volume, in which there is not one Line of his writing (except a Share, it may be, of the Preface) is a Riddle, that the Dean and He must unfold. . . . Upon the whole, this plural number, *We*, is ridiculous, P——e having writ so small a Share in these Three Volumes; and as for what A——t and G—— can boast of therein, I own I can hardly find it out. . . ."[8] While it is true that the unauthorized edition of the Cromwell correspondence had made Pope sensitive about his scattered letters and other uncollected pieces, he, also, could be critical of random anthologies, as the close to his letter to Swift of 17 February 1726/7 makes clear:

83

Our Miscellany is now quite printed. I am prodigiously pleas'd with this joint-volume, in which methinks we look like friends, side by side, serious and merry by turns, conversing interchangeably, and walking down hand in hand to posterity; not in the stiff forms of learned Authors, flattering each other, and setting the rest of mankind at nought: but in a free, unimportant, natural, easy manner; diverting others just as we diverted ourselves. The third volume consists of Verses, but I would chuse to print none but such as have some peculiarity, and may be distinguish'd for ours, from other writers. There's no end of making Books, Solomon said, and above all of making Miscellanies, which all men can make. [9]

If the passage as a whole is delightful as an affectionate tribute to his collaborator, the question still remains: Why had he prodded Swift to the task? (Smedley accuses Swift of using Pope as his "Skreen," but the evidence of the letters is that Pope was the moving force.) The answer may be found, in part, in another letter to Swift, written many years later (16 February 1732/3), at the time of Gay's death:

There is nothing of late which I think of more than mortality, and what you mention of collecting the best monuments we can of our friends, their own images in their writings: (for those are the best, when their minds are such as Mr. Gay's was, and as yours is.) I am preparing also for my own; and have nothing so much at heart, as to shew the silly world that men of Wit, or even Poets, may be the most moral of mankind. A few loose things sometimes fall from them, by which censorious fools judge as ill of them, as possibly they can, for their own comfort: and indeed, when such unguarded and trifling *Jeux d'Esprit* have once got abroad, all that prudence or repentance can do, since they cannot be deny'd, is to put 'em fairly upon that foot; and teach the publick (as we have done in the preface to the four volumes of miscellanies) to distinguish betwixt our studies and our idlenesses, our works and our weaknesses. . . . [10]

The concluding phrases are reminiscent of the Preface's "not our Studies, but our Follies; not our Works, but our Idlenesses." And, significantly, when Pope was collecting the second volume of his *Works* in 1735, he wrote, "*Whatever besides I have written, or join'd in writing with Dr.* Swift, *Dr.* Arbuthnot, *or Mr.* Gay *(the only persons with whom I ever wrote in conjunction) are to be found in the four Volumes of Miscellanies by us published: I think them too inconsiderable to be separated and reprinted here. . . .*"[11]

It was one way to clear the field and to do it on his terms, not Curll's; but there were probably even more positive motivations. Just as in 1732 he was preparing his great moral studies, so in 1727 Pope was launching into the brilliant period of the *Dunciad*. However long he had been at work on that poem, Sherburn notes that "The whole trouble with Pope's projects against the Dunces was that they did not 'come off;' they lacked point; and so they lay idle until Swift in his visits of 1726 and 1727 gave the necessary fillip to Pope's ingenuity, and the satirist definitely emerged."[12] It has been suggested,[13] and reasonably, that the *Miscellanies* were part of the strategy that would lead to the *Dunciad*, a preliminary skirmish to rally attention and to draw the fire[14] that would be answered by a full blast to demolish the Dunces once and for all. With the light satiric pieces to scatter shot and the *Peri Bathous* to draw up the battle lines, the fight was on. And now, when the smoke has finally cleared, we can see how in typical fashion Pope once again turned a potential embarrassment into a practical triumph.

Notes

1. Johnson, *Lives*, III, 38.

2. *Correspondence*, II, 420.

3. Ibid., p. 426.

4. Johnson, *Lives*, III, 158.

5. Ibid., p. 144.

6. See Ralph Straus, *The Unspeakable Curll* (London: Chapman and Hall, 1927).

7. In his preface to the 1735 second volume of the *Works*, he acknowledges some of them, but even the complete list is small.

8. Postscript to "Alexanderiana," *Gulliveriana* [by Jonathan Smedley] (London, 1728), pp. 333, 335.

9. *Correspondence*, II, 426.

10. *Correspondence*, III, 347.

11. "The Author to the Reader," *The Works of Mr. Alexander Pope. Volume II* (London, 1735).

12. *Early Career*, p. 305.

13. Peter Quennell, *Alexander Pope: The Education of Genius, 1688–1728* (London: Weidenfeld and Nicolson, 1968), pp. 227–28.

14. As it did; 1728 was a full year for attacks on Pope and Swift. See J. V. Guerinot, *Pamphlet Attacks on Alexander Pope, 1711–1744* (London: Methuen, 1969).

NOTE ON PUBLICATION AND TEXT

With fine understatement Griffith has summarized the bibliographical problems of the *Miscellanies*: "There is confusion, in greater or less degree, from 1728 on."[1] In the case of the Preface it is certainly not less—though Teerink in his Swift bibliography has untangled many of the snarls.[2] After the 1727 publication, by Motte, of the first two volumes of the *Miscellanies in Prose and Verse,* introduced by the Preface, the piece is sometimes present, sometimes lacking, in the later printings of volume one; in some instances (beginning in 1728) it was transferred to the "Last" volume, where it enters into the mix-up between that volume, the third in the series, and the so-called "Third" volume—actually the fourth, though it might be thought of as the third in prose—which followed in 1732. There is further complication: the 1732 duodecimo "Third" volume was so entitled but actually carried (and thus duplicated) the contents of the "Last" volume, and the 1733 edition continued and extended the error by interchanging the title pages of the two volumes; these mistakes and their subsequent correction,[3] as well as the encouragement given to binders to sort the materials and reform the volumes by isolating the prose and poetry,[4] have provided a confounding number of issues.

The Preface then is to be found, at various times, in the First Volume, the Last Volume, and the Third Volume. With all, there is little textual change in the reprintings, except where it was necessary to adapt the opening and closing remarks to cover the transfer of the Preface from Volume I and to extend the remarks to cover more than the three volumes (two of prose, one of poetry) originally projected. Because of the absence of any significant revision and because of Pope's care in seeing into print the first edition (Swift, in Ireland, had delegated to Pope the task of editing the material and seeing it to press),[5] the 1727 printing of the Preface has been followed for the present text, with the substantive variants supplied entirely in textual notes.[6]

Key to the Critical Apparatus

1727 = *Miscellanies in Prose and Verse,* First Vol., octavo, Griffith 184.
1728 = "Last" Vol., octavo, Griffith ‘208a; Teerink/Scouten 25 (3e).
1730a (dated 1731) = First Vol., duodecimo, var. of Griffith 242.
1730b (dated 1731) = "Last" Vol., duodecimo, Griffith 244; Teerink/
Scouten 26 (3).[7]

1732 = "Last" Vol., [second edition?], octavo, var. Griffith 275; var.
          Teerink/Scouten 25 (3f). [Same as 1728.]
1733a (dated 1732) = [mistitled] "Third" Vol., duodecimo, Teerink/
          Scouten 27 (3a).[8]
1733b = "Last" Vol., duodecimo, Teerink/Scouten 27 (3b).[9]
1733c = [mistitled] "Third" Vol., Griffith 286; Teerink/Scouten 27 (3c).
1736 = "Last" Vol., duodecimo, Griffith 440; Teerink/Scouten 28 (3).
1738 = "Last" Vol., duodecimo, Griffith 499.
1742 = *Miscellanies* (in Four Volumes),[10] Vol. I, fourth edition, sm. oc-
          tavo, Griffith 561.

Notes

1. Griffith, p. 444.

2. Dr. H. Teerink, *A Bibliography of the Writings of Jonathan Swift,* 2d. ed.,
ed. by Arthur H. Scouten (Philadelphia: University of Pennsylvania Press, 1963).

3. For a careful study see Teerink/Scouten, pp. 11–21.

4. For example, the 1732 first edition of the "Third" volume has this Booksellers advertisement (the original in reverse italics): "Of the following Volume,
we need only say, that it contains the Remainder of those Miscellaneous Pieces,
which were in some sort promised in the Preface to the former Volumes, or which
have been written since. The *Verses* are paged separately, that they may be added
to that Volume which wholly consisted of Verse, and the Treatise of the *Bathos*
placed in their stead in This."

5. *Correspondence,* II, 420ff.

6. Reviewing the changes in incidentals in these texts in the light of David
Foxon's arguments for Pope's careful revisions and the importance of the 1742
quarto (see n. 6, pp. xiv–xv), I note that the 1742 and 1738 texts are almost
identical as far as incidentals are concerned, and that the changes from the first
edition are toward more capitalization (with the most in the later editions) with
a few shifts in punctuation (not necessarily consistent, as in the practice of reducing punctuation in conjunction with parentheses).

7. Not all copies of 1730b contain the Preface either (e.g., Bodley Vet.
A4f514 and Bodley 12θ1064, Preface; but B.L. 12275.g.4, no Preface); apparently two sets of the Miscellany volumes were issued: (a) with the preface in
volume one and (b) with the preface in the "last" volume.

8. See "Note on the Text"; see also Teerink/Scouten, pp. 11–12.

9. The Griffith volume is all poetry; no doubt its binder followed the suggestion printed in copies of the "Third" volume: "The *Verses* are paged separately,

that they may be added to that Volume which wholly consists of Verse, and the Treatise of the *Bathos* placed in their stead in This."

10. The *Miscellanies* were re-formed after Pope withdrew some of the material for his 1741 *Works in Prose*; this new edition was brought out by Bathurst.

PREFACE.

The Papers that compose the first of these Volumes were printed about sixteen Years ago, to which there are now added two or three small Tracts; and the Verses are transferred into a Volume apart.[1] The second (and perhaps a third)[2] will consist like this, of several small Treatises in Prose, wherein a Friend or two are concerned.[3]

Having both of us been extreamly ill treated by some Booksellers, (especially one *Edmund Curll,*)[4] it was our Opinion that the best Method we could take for justifying ourselves, would be to publish whatever loose Papers in Prose and Verse, we have formerly written; not only such as have already stolen into the World (very much to our Regret, and perhaps very little to our Credit,) but such as in any Probability hereafter may run the same Fate, having been obtained from us by the Importunity, and divulged by the Indiscretion of Friends, although restrain'd by Promises, which few of them are ever known to observe, and often think they make us a Compliment in breaking.

But the Consequences have been still worse: We have been entitled, and have had our Names prefixed at length, to whole Volumes of mean Productions, equally offensive to good Manners and good

Sense, which we never saw or heard of till they appeared in Print.[5]

For a *Forgery,* in setting a false Name to a Writing, which may prejudice another's Fortune, the Law punishes the Offender with the Loss of his *Ears*; but has inflicted no adequate Penalty for such as prejudice another's Reputation, in doing the same Thing in Print; though all and every individual Book so sold under a false Name, are manifestly so many several and multiplied Forgeries.[6]

Indeed we hoped, that the good Nature, or at least the good Judgment of the World, would have cleared us from the Imputation of such Things as had been thus charged upon us, by the Malice of Enemies, the Want of Judgment in Friends, the Unconcern of indifferent Persons, and the confident Assertions of Booksellers.

We are ashamed to find so ill a Taste prevail, as to make it a

necessary Work to do this Justice our selves. It is very possible for

any Author to write below himself; either his Subject not proving
A   so fruitful, or so fitted for him, as he at first imagined; or his Health,
or his Humour, or the present Disposition of his Mind, unqualifying
him at that Juncture: However if he possessed any distinguishing
Marks of Style, or Peculiarity of Thinking, there would remain in
his least successful Writings, some few Tokens, whereby Persons of
Taste might discover him.

But since it hath otherwise fallen out, we think we have sufficiently paid for our Want of Prudence, and determine for the future
to be less communicative: Or rather having done with such Amusements, we are resolved to give up what we cannot fairly disown, to
the Severity of Criticks, the Malice of personal Enemies, and the
Indulgence of Friends.

We are sorry for the Satire interspersed in some of these Pieces,
upon a few People,[7] from whom the highest Provocations have been
received, and who by their Conduct since have shewn that they have
not yet forgiven us the Wrong They did. It is a very unlucky Circumstance, to be obliged to retaliate the Injuries of such Authors,
whose Works are so soon forgotten, that we are in danger already of
appearing the first Aggressors. It is to be lamented, that *Virgil* let
pass a Line, which told Posterity he had two Enemies called *Bavius*
and *Mævius*.[8] The wisest Way is not once to name them, but (as
the Madman advised the Gentleman, who told him he wore a Sword
to kill his Enemies) *to let them alone, and they will die of themselves.*
And according to this Rule we have acted throughout all those
Writings which we design'd for the Press: But in these, the Publication whereof was not owing to our Folly but that of others, the
Omission of the Names was not in our Power. At the worst, we can
only give them that Liberty now for something, which they have so
many Years exercised for nothing, of railing and scribbling against
us. And 'tis some Commendation, that we have not done it all this
while, but avoided publickly to characterise any Person without long
Experience. *Nonum prematur in Annum,* is a good Rule for all Writers,
but chiefly for Writers of Characters; because it may happen to those
who vent Praise or Censure too precipitately, as it did to an eminent
English Poet, who celebrated a young Nobleman for erecting *Dryden's*
Monument, upon a Promise which his Lordship forgot, till it was
done by another.[9]

In regard to two Persons only, we wish our Raillery, though ever so tender, or Resentment, though ever so just, had not been indulged. We speak of Sir *John Vanbrugh,* who was a Man of Wit, and of Honour; and of Mr. *Addison,* whose Name deserves all Respect from every Lover of Learning.[10]

We cannot deny (and perhaps most Writers of our kind have been in the same Circumstances) that in several Parts of our Lives, and according to the Dispositions we were in, we have written some Things which we may wish never to have thought on. Some Sallies of Levity ought to be imputed to Youth, (supposed in Charity, as it was in Truth, to be the Time in which we wrote them;) Others to the Gaiety of our Minds at certain Junctures, common to all A Men. The publishing of these which we cannot quite disown, and without our Consent, is I think, a greater Injury, than that of ascribing to us the most stupid Productions which we can wholly deny.

This has been usually practised in other Countries, after a Man's Decease; which in a great measure accounts for that manifest *Inequality* found in the Works of the best Authors; the Collectors only considering, that so many more Sheets raise the Price of the Book; and the greater Fame a Writer is in Possession of, the more of such Trash he may bear to have tack'd to him. Thus it is apparently the Editor's Interest to insert, what the Author's Judgment had rejected; and Care is always taken to intersperse these Additions in such a manner, that scarce any Book of consequence can be bought, without purchasing something unworthy of the Author along with it.

But in our own Country it is still worse: Those very Booksellers who have supported themselves upon an Author's Fame while he lived, have done their utmost after his Death to lessen it by such Practices: Even a Man's last *Will* is not secure from being exposed in Print; whereby his most particular Regards, and even his dying Tendernesses are laid open.[11] It has been humourously said, that some have fished the very Jakes, for Papers left there by Men of Wit: But it is no Jest to affirm, that the Cabinets of the Sick, and the Closets of the Dead, have been broke open and ransacked, to publish our *private Letters,* and divulge to all Mankind the most secret Sentiments and Intercourses of Friendship. Nay, these Fellows are arriv'd B to that Height of Impudence, as when an Author has publickly disown'd a spurious Piece, they have disputed his own Name with him in printed Advertisements, which has been practis'd to Mr. *Congreve,* and Mr. *Prior.* [12]

A We are therefore compell'd, in respect to Truth, to submit to a very great Hardship; to own such Pieces as in our stricter Judgment we would have suppressed for ever: We are obliged to confess, that this whole Collection, in a manner, consists of what we not only thought unlikely to reach the future, but unworthy even of the *present* Age; not our Studies, but our Follies; not our Works, but our Idlenesses. [13]

Some Comfort however it is, that all of them are Innocent, and most of them, slight as they are, had yet a moral Tendency; either to soften the Virulence of Parties against each other; or to laugh out of Countenance some Vice or Folly of the Time; or to discredit the Impositions of Quacks and false Pretenders to Science; or to humble the Arrogance of the ill-natured and envious: In a word, to lessen the *Vanity,* and promote the *good Humour* of Mankind. [14]

Such as they are, we must in truth confess they are *Ours,* and others should in justice believe they are *All* that are *Ours.* If any thing else has been printed in which we really had any hand, it is either intolerably imperfect, or loaded with spurious Additions; sometimes even with Insertions of Mens Names, which we never meant, and for whom we have an Esteem and Respect. Even those Pieces in which we are least injured, have never before been printed from the true Copies, or with any tolerable Degree of Correctness. We declare, that this Collection contains every Piece, which in the idlest Humour we have written; not only such as came under our
B Review or Correction; but many others, which however unfinished, are not now in our power to suppress. Whatsoever was in our own Possession at the Publishing hereof, or of which no Copy was gone abroad, we have actually destroy'd, to prevent all Possibility of the like Treatment.

These Volumes likewise will contain all the Papers wherein we
C have casually had any Share; particularly those writ in conjunction with our Friends, Dr. *Arbuthnot* and Mr. *Gay*; and lastly, all of this sort composed singly by either of those Hands. The Reader is therefore desired to do the same Justice to these our Friends, as to Us; and to be assured that all the *Things* called our *Miscellanies* (except

the Works of *Alexander Pope*, published by *B. Lintott*, in *Quarto*, and
Folio, in 1717; those of Mr. *Gay*, by *J. Tonson*, in *Quarto*, in 1720;
A and as many of these Miscellanies as have been printed hitherto in
one Volume, *Octavo*) are absolutely spurious, and without our Consent imposed upon the Publick.

Twickenham,   JONATH. SWIFT.
May 27, 1727.   ALEX. POPE.

B P.S. *We could not resist the Opportunity of improving this Collection with
two or three Pieces on parallel Subjects, written by Persons of great Distinction, our particular Friends, for which the Publick ought to thank us,
and with which it was in the Power of none but our selves to have obliged
them.*[15]

Textual Variants

Page 89: A. sixteen] eighteen *1738–42.*
Page 89: B. a] this *1728, 1732*; the fourth *1742.*
Page 89: C. apart.] apart, with the Addition of such others as we since have
            written. *1730a–42.*
Page 89: D. The . . . concerned. *Om 1728, 1732.*
Page 89: E. (and . . . third)] and third *1742.*
Page 89: F. like this, *Om. 1730a–42.*
Page 89: G. wherein] in which *1730a–42.*
Page 89: H. are] is *1730a–42.*
Page 89: I. concerned.] concerned with Us. *1730a–42.*
Page 89: J. or] nor *1733c–42.*
Page 89: K. hoped] hope *1728–38.*
Page 89: L. Justice] Justice to *1730a–42.*
Page 90: A. so *Om. 1733a–42.*
Page 91: A. quite *Om. 1742.*
Page 91: B. Intercourses] Intercourse *1728–42.*
Page 92: A. Judgment] Judgments *1730a–42*
Page 92: B. unfinished] unfurnished *1730a–33b.*
Page 92: C. writ] written *1742.*
Page 93: A. printed . . . *Octavo*)] formerly printed by *Benj. Tooke) 1730a–42;* . . .
            Tooke, 1728, 1732.
Page 93: B. P.S. . . . *Om 1730a–42.*

Annotations

1. The volume was Swift's *Miscellanies in Prose and Verse,* 1711, printed for John Morphew. From it everything was transferred to the first volume of the new *Miscellanies* except the poetry, as noted, and two tracts—"A Meditation upon a Broom-Stick" and "A Famous Prediction of Merlin the British Wizard" (included in volume two). Added were " 'Squire Bickerstaff Detected," "A Proposal for Correcting, Improving, and Ascertaining the English Tongue," "A Letter to a Young Gentleman lately enter'd into Holy Orders," and "Thoughts on Various Subjects"—an expansion of the earlier "Various Thoughts Moral and Diverting." Except for the Preface there is nothing of Pope's in the volume.

2. Originally the plan had been for three volumes, two of prose, one of poetry—and these were published in 1727 and the early spring of 1728. Although the "Last" volume was to have consisted wholly of poetry, Pope in the end substituted the *Peri Bathous* for the intended *Dunciad.* A fourth volume, designated the "Third" and representing the third volume of the prose half-promised in the Preface, appeared in 1732. In time other volumes, containing nothing by Pope, were added and the set came to be considered primarily as a part of Swift's works.

3. Since many of the pieces in the *Miscellanies* were Scriblerian in origin, the inevitable problem of attribution looms. That Arbuthnot and Gay were principally involved is made clear in the closing remarks of the Preface, and when the *Miscellanies* were re-formed in 1742, they were given the new title *Miscellanies in Four Volumes. By Dr. Swift, Dr. Arbuthnot, Mr. Pope, and Mr. Gay. . . .*

4. In 1710 Curll had published Swift's "Meditations upon a Broom-stick and Somewhat Beside . . . ," followed the next year by a volume of his *Miscellanies* which included the *Key to the Tale of a Tub.* Since Swift had not wished his authorship there to be revealed, he was furious—but he got no satisfaction. Several years later, 30 August 1716, he wrote to Pope, ". . . I will grant, that one thorough bookselling Rogue is better qualified to vex an author, than all his contemporary scriblers in Critick or Satire, not only by stolen Copies of what was incorrect or unfit for the publick, but by downright laying other mens dulness at your door. I had a long design upon the ears of that Curl, when I was in credit, but the rogue would never allow me a fair stroke at them, though my penknife was ready and sharp." (*Correspondence,* I, 359).

5. Appropriately enough, the letter (see n. 4) then refers to a rumor of Curll's poisoning—an actuality by which Pope did accomplish his revenge on the bookseller, with whom he had just had his first clash, over the publication of *Court Poems.* Though Swift's and Pope's war with Curll was to be a long-standing one, the 1727 *Miscellanies* were most immediately prompted by Curll's action in 1726 of publishing, in the two volumes of *Miscellanea,* Pope's correspondence with Cromwell and some odd pieces by Swift.

6. Copyright protection for authors was very limited in the eighteenth century (See annotation 2 to *Narrative of the Method*, p. 346. Note also the reference to cutting ears in the Swift letter cited in n. 4). The brutality—potential or actual—in some of the encounters of the time reflects an age which legally did indeed cut off ears, disembowel criminals, and make executions a popular public spectacle. By 1796 one magistrate records, "In the course of the present century, several of the old sanguinary modes of punishment have been either very properly abolished by acts of parliament, or allowed, to the honour of humanity, to fall into disuse:—such as *burning alive, (particularly women) cutting off hands or ears, slitting nostrils, or branding in the hand or face; and the ducking stool*" (*A Treatise on the Police of the Metropolis* [London, 1796], pp. 303–304). The severity of contemporary punishments was also the concern of one of Dr. Johnson's *Rambler* papers (No. 114 [20 April 1751]).

7. While the satires of the first two volumes are broad, general rather than specific in attack, the *Peri Bathous* and some of the accompanying verses of the "Last" Volume point specifically (or suggestively with initials) at targeted individuals. They provoked a pamphlet response: *A Compleat Collection of all the Verses, Essays, Letters, and Advertisements, which have been occasioned by the Publication of Three Volumes of Miscellanies, by Pope and Company* (London, 1728), which included "an Exact LIST of the *Lords, Ladies, Gentlemen* and *others,* who have been abused in those Volumes."

8. Bavius and Mævius—two supposed poetasters, contemporaries of Virgil, who for their attack on the *Georgics* were immortalized by him in a famous line (*Ecologue* 3. 90): "Qui Bavium non odit amet tua carmina, Mævi. . . ."

9. Though Congreve had dedicated his edition of Dryden's dramatic works to the Duke of Newcastle, extolling his generosity in planning a monument to Dryden, nothing was actually provided until the Duke of Buckingham erected a tablet to his name, prompted, it is said, by Pope's reference in his epitaph to Rowe: "Beneath a rude and nameless stone he [Dryden] lies. . . . One grateful woman to thy fame supplies / What a whole thankless land to his denies." (TE VI, 208–209.)

10. The reference to Addison is to the famous Atticus passage, included (in the Last Volume) in "Fragment of a Satire." Though the lines had first been printed in 1722, in the *St. James's Journal,* later reprinted, this is Pope's first acknowledgment of them. Vanbrugh, architect as well as playwright, was lampooned in the same volume, in Swift's "V———'s House" and "The History of V———'s House." While Pope, in the First Epistle of the Second Book of Horace, comments, "How Van wants grace, who never wanted wit!" (l. 289), his remarks to Spence were kindly: "None of our writers have a freer, easier way for comedy than Etherege and Vanbrugh" and "Garth, Vanbrugh, and Congreve were the three most honest-hearted, real good men of the poetical members of the Kit-Cat Club." (*Anecdotes,* I, 206, 50.)

11. So infamous was Curll in this activity that Dr. Arbuthnot was led to remark that a new terror had been added to death. "Did a great man die, Curll immediately announced that his 'Life' was in the press and would speedily be published. This might or might not be true, but the public would be invited to make the proposed publication as complete as possible. In this way it often happened that a few odd biographical scraps from the newspapers would be mingled with any outside contributions that might have been forthcoming, and some sort of 'Life' be made ready before 'the Family' or the dead man's executors, could publish anything at all. And if the available material was not enough for a sixpenny or a shilling pamphlet, what could be better, or easier, than to make the 'Life' the required length by reprinting anything the dead man had happened to write?" (Straus, pp. 23–24.)

Pope's indignation was not merely academic. On 30 June [1727] he had written to Benjamin Motte (the publisher of the *Miscellanies*) about a Curll advertisement that has not been located:

> The advertisement of Curl is a silly piece of Impertinence, not worth notice, & it serves to tell every body what makes for my purpose & reputation, "That those Letters to Mr Cromwell were printed without My Consent or knowledge." The fact of *Cabinets being broke open & dead people's Closets ransackd . . . is nevertheless true,* which this Scoundrel wishes to have applyd to *Cromwells Letters,* only to advance their Sale, tho' it was spoken of other Instances relating to the Dean's as well as mine." (*Correspondence,* II, 438–39.)

One of the other "Instances," as Sherburn suggests, may refer to another event advertised by Curll (in *The Evening Post,* No. 1300, 30 November–3 December 1717): "Letters, Poems, & Amorous, Satyrical, and Gallant, which passed between Sir Andrew Fountain, Dr. Swift, that celebrated Toast Mrs. Anne Long, of Draycot in Wiltshire, the honourable the Lady Mary Chambers, and other Persons of Distinction. Now first published from their respective Originals, found in Mrs. Long's Cabinet since her Decease. Printed for E. Curll over against St. Dunstant's Church in Fleetstreet. . . ."

12. Ralph Straus, in his entertaining history of *The Unspeakable Curll,* gives an account of poor Prior's efforts to counter Curll's business zeal (pp. 25–26). When Prior protested in print to a *second* collection of his poems being brought out by Curll (Curll's first volume was also unsolicited and unauthorized), there was a counter-answer in the paper—"Whereas a nameless Person has taken the Liberty to make use of Mr. Prior's name, and pretended that he had his Order for so doing: This is therefore to assure the Publick, that a Book entitul'd *A Second Collection of Poems* . . . are Genuine, and publish'd from his own correct

Copies: The two last Poems in this Collection being Satyres, Mr. Prior has never yet publicly own'd them. . . ." As Straus comments, "It was no reply to poor Mr. Prior, but it served its purpose well enough." (P. 26.) Whatever the incident referred to here with Congreve (On 6 May, probably of 1727, Congreve had written to Pope and complained: "P.S. By the inclosed you will see I am like to be impress'd, and enroll'd in the list of Mr. Curll's Authors; but I thank God I shall have your company. I believe it is high time you should think of administring another *Emetick*" [*Correspondence*, II, 434]), he was shortly to be further victimized by Curll, in a fulfillment of Pope's direst predictions: after Congreve's death in 1729 (with the bulk of his fortune left to the young Duchess of Marlborough in a will that was an open invitation to Curll), the latter issued *the Memoirs of the Life, Writings, and Amours of William Congreve,* rumored to be so scandalous that its publication became a matter of great concern to the playwright's friends.

13. Even so, as editor of the collection, Pope used the discretionary powers given him by Swift ("I am mustring as I told you all the little things in verse that I think may be Safely printed, but I give you despotick Power to tear as many as you please" [*The Correspondence of Jonathan Swift,* ed. by Harold Williams (Oxford: Clarendon Press, 1963), III, 172; see 193 also]), for the latter writes to Motte in December of 1727: "As to the poeticall Volumes of miscellanys I believe five parts in six at least are mine. Our two friends [Pope and Gay] you know have printed their works already, and we could expect nothing but slight loose papers. There is all the Poetry I ever writ worth printing. Mr Pope rejected some, I sent him, for I desired him [to] be severe as possible; and I will take his judgment." (Ibid., p. 258.)

14. From the beginning, Pope was consistently concerned with his "image": that he appear (and *be*) a certain kind of writer and, equally important, a certain kind of man. One can trace through his introductions, his letters, as well as the works themselves, this self-conscious projection of an ideal. Over the years it evolved from the gentlemanly but gifted amateur to the committed moral satirist, but always it is a speaker of good sense and equability.

15. For instance, Vol. I included " 'Squire Bickerstaff Detected," with the prefacing note, *"This Piece being on the same Subject, and very rare, we have thought fit to add it, tho' not written by the same Hand."* (In Faulkner's 1735 edition of Swift's *Works,* the heading was revised to attribute the piece to *"that famous Poet* Nicholas Row, *Esq. . . ."*) Jonathan Smedley, in his satiric *Gulliveriana* (London, 1728), had commented: "The *Postscript* to this Preface, is the most trifling thing that was ever read: The *Doctor* can't tell whether his *Friends of Distinction* writ two or three Pieces; but I can tell that they writ three, or four, or five Pieces, and that they are all so dull in their Kind, that I shall not disgrace his *Friends,* by guessing at their Names, tho' I think it is no Offence to say, that the Author of

the *Dullest,* died not long since." (P. 335.) The attribution of the poetry in particular is difficult: of the seventy-five pieces of the Last Volume, thirty-seven are thought by Harold Williams to be Swift's and twenty-four are included in the Pope canon by Griffith. The authorship of the rest, mostly trifles, remains problematical.

MEMOIRS
Of *P. P.*
Clerk of THIS PARISH.

INTRODUCTION

Any account of the *Memoirs of P. P.* is inevitably bound up with the history of the Scriblerus Club, that association of Augustan wits which produced this essay along with so many other satirical pieces in censure of pomposity and false learning. Composed primarily of Pope, Swift, Gay, Dr. Arbuthnot, Parnell, and Robert Harley, earl of Oxford, the Club had grown out of a two-fold concept: Swift's efforts to form a brilliant Tory group (in opposition to Addison's "little Senate" at Button's) into an "academy" which would encourage young writers and serve to refine and fix the language; and Pope's plan for a monthly journal, *The Works of the Unlearned*, which, as a parody of a well-known and recently defunct monthly abstract, *The History of the Works of the Learned*, would satirize absurdities in learning and criticism.[1] What emerged was something different from both, yet appropriate to each—a small social group of kindred spirits whose collaboration, at three stages over a fifteen-year period (1714, when the Club was formally organized with scheduled dinner meetings; 1716–18; and 1726–29, the occasion of Swift's visits to England and the publication of *The Dunciad*), resulted in an outline for a broad satire of human folly, organized around a hero-pedant, who was to function as the author of such satires as they would themselves write or to whom they could ascribe the works of contemporaries whom they wished to ridicule. Although the *Memoirs of Martinus Scriblerus*, the fictitious biography of their hero which was to provide a base for all the peripheral pieces, was not put into final shape and published until much later—in the 1741 *Prose Works*—the discussions of the group inspired the many "Scriblerian" items which eventually preceded the central work into print, and certainly gave impetus to such Scriblerus-related masterpieces as *Gulliver's Travels*, *The Dunciad*, and *The Beggar's Opera*.

If the *Memoirs of P. P.* is not one of the more serious or significant efforts of the Scriblerians—in this instance, Pope and Gay[2]—it is, nevertheless, characteristic of their spirit and method. Like so many of the Augustan satires, it is an attack both specific and general. In particular it is a parody, or travesty, on the best-known memoirs of the day, Bishop Burnet's *History of My Own Time*; more generally it belongs—in a humble vein—to the great tradition of *MacFlecknoe*, in which self-satisfied mediocrity is presented in its own terms and allowed to damn itself out of hand. The pompous, complacent P. P.—with his toad's eye view of a puddle world—is fit game, a victim of his own pretensions and a deadly example of what the memoir writer may easily become.

Gilbert Burnet, bishop of Salisbury, was especially vulnerable to the satirists. With his Broad Church views in religion and politics, his *History,* published posthumously by his son in 1724, was offensive to them and generally evoked a storm of protest because of its obvious Whig bias. Even Burnet's nineteenth-century editor, while extolling the Bishop's virtues, manages to describe him damningly; "although busy and intrusive, [he was] at least as honest as most partisans."[3] Swift—a historian himself, of a very different color (especially in his interpretation of Queen Anne's reign)—did not bother even with such faint praise, but in his notes to his own copy of the *History*[4] relentlessly underlined its author's egocentricity, his moralizing, his—to Swift—specious argument, and, above all, the limitations of his style.[5] These matters are the loci too of Pope and Gay's satire, though they focus more on the memoirist aspect of Burnet's memoir-history than on the political. With the burlesque technique of deflation, P. P's petty world becomes an ironic microcosm of the Bishop's aggrandized scene. High or low, self-importance makes a telling target, but one more visible when reduced to P. P.'s absurdities. His posturings—whether within the Church as one of its least significant functionaries, or without in his pedestrian trades and in the political fantasies of his little cabal—ridicule Burnet's equally self-conscious career as churchman, self-acclaimed counselor to the great (a role more advertised than actual according to his enemies), and amateur scientist.

While the satiric thrusts, then, are essentially broad, the annotations to the text will show that they are barbed with references to particulars of Burnet's life, references that to the contemporary reader would open all sorts of associations. Even the most oblique allusion to barrenness, for example, could recall Burnet's notorious arguments for divorce, a youthful indiscretion (on a particularly sensitive issue for Charles II) that the Jacobite press was to put to damaging use against him. In the same way, a casual mention of 30 January—the anniversary of King Charles's martyrdom—would suggest several widely published sermons for that occasion, where the Bishop had vigorously preached royalist sentiments that proved embarrassing when he later presented himself as instrumental in bringing William and Mary to the throne. It might well be because of this past to be lived down, that the satirists provided him, eminent Broad Churchman and Whig that he had become, with a High Church, Jacobite-Tory counterpart in P. P.—whose proclivities might also stand as sorry testimony to the Bishop's well-known pastoral zeal in shaping and regulating the clergy, politically as well as theologically.[6]

Basic to the satire is parody of the style that so enraged Swift. But where Swift was nettled by awkwardnesses and inelegancies, the "jumping periods" of the history, Pope and Gay have fastened onto the pervasive unctuousness of tone as it reverberates in the introductory and concluding comments. P. P.'s pronouncements at the outset of his account are pompous in the best tradition of the Burnet who wrote, "I look on the perfecting of this work, and the carrying it through the remaining part of my life, as the greatest service I can do to God and to the world . . .";[7] caught too are his sentiments in conclusion: "I pray God it may be read with the same candour and sincerity with which I have written it, and with such a degree of attention as may help those who read it to form just reflections, and sound principles of religion and virtue, of duty to our princes, and of love to our country, with a sincere and incorruptible zeal to preserve our religion, and to maintain our liberty and property."[8] When the Bishop demurs, "I have on design avoided all laboured periods or artificial strains, and have writ in as clear and plain a style as was possible, choosing rather a copious enlargement than a dark conciseness,"[9] he may not be a very astute self-critic but he has hit at the heart of the narrative technique that he shares with P. P.—"copious enlargement." However sleazy the fabric that P. P. spins out of the mean threads of his life, it is made in the spirit of the master ("I was in court a great part of the years 1662, 1663, and 1664; and was as inquisitive as I could possibly be . . .").[10] Like Swift's spider each narrator is at the center of his self-generated web.

In their scorn, the Scriblerians were not alone. Almost all of Burnet's publications (with their controversial stands on nonconformity, nonresistance and resistance, toleration, exclusion . . .) had provoked heated rebuttal,[11] and he had figured as the Buzzard in Dryden's *Hind and the Panther* ("The Third Part," ll. 1120–94). That personal "character"— perhaps a last minute addition inspired by Burnet's pamphlet "Reasons against the Repealing the Acts of Parliament concerning the Test"[12]—also points up his characteristic impudence, vanity, and ingratitude. Two decades later, when the Club was getting underway in 1714, the Bishop was still very much in the critical eye as he plunged into the polemical squabbles of the last years of Queen Anne's reign with a series of new militant prefaces and introductions.[13] Undoubtedly the Club members would have been alert to the memoirs on which he was busily engaged and which were probably available to some of them or to their friends in manuscript form; and his death, in 1715, would have focused their interest. To keep the issue in their minds, there were other considerations. Around 1715, the Bishop's youngest son, Thomas, a staunch Whig of Addison's coterie, was attacking Pope in his periodical *The Grumbler* and was playing his part in the events that attended the launching of Pope's translation of the *Iliad*. He tried to promote Tickell's rival edition and after that fiasco, composed with George Duckett two satiric pamphlets, both entitled *Homerides*. Their activity rankled the poet sufficiently for him to have included them in the *Dunciad*,[14] so at the time one can assume he was sensitive to Burnets of any age or persuasion. In fact, Pope may well have been, if not the actual author, certainly the instigator of a pamphlet called *Homer in a Nut-Shell: or, the Iliad of* Homer *in Immortal Doggrel. By* Nickydemus Ninnyhammer, *F. G.* (London, 1715),[15] which, in burlesque of Tickell's dedication of his *Iliad* to the recently deceased Lord Halifax, carried its dedication to "the late *Pious* B——p of S———m," "he being a Man of such an exorbitant Muttonfist, and withal of so uncommon an Head-piece, I take upon me for once to strike out of the Road of *Common Sense,* and inscribe this Epic Poem to his *Ghost.*"[16]

Because the productions of the Scriblerians were as collective as their closely shared attitudes and antagonisms,[17] matters of attribution are some-times—though not in this instance—difficult, and problems of dating are often insoluble. Here Pope himself confuses the situation, perhaps not undeliberately, by asserting that "these memoirs were written at the seat of the Lord Harcourt in Oxfordshire, before that excellent person (bishop Burnet's) death, and many years before the appearance of that history, of which they are pretended to be an abuse."[18] The only time that he and Gay were together at Stanton Harcourt for any length was in the summer of 1718—when there was, appropriately, a Scriblerian reunion: yet Bishop Burnet had, of course, died in 1715. Whatever the exact truth, it is very probable that the *Memoirs of P. P.,* like other Scriblerian papers, was con-ceived in the early days of the Club, while Burnet was still involved in writing, and may well have been actually pulled together some years later, at a time when there was a renewal of Scriblerian activity, as there was in 1716–18. In any event, more years were to pass before the *Memoirs* finally appeared in print. Then, with so many other Scriblerian pieces, it was included in that great "catch-all," the Pope-Swift *Miscellanies.*

Notes

1. See *Spectator* No. 457 (14 August 1712) for Pope's proposal for this bur-lesque. For a detailed account of the Scriblerus Club see Chap III of the *Early Career* and the Preface to Charles Kerby-Miller's edition of the *Memoirs . . . of Martinus Scriblerus* (New Haven: Yale University Press, 1950).

2. In "The Booksellers to the Reader," from *The Works in Prose,* Vol. II (London, 1741), Pope had noted, "We have also obtain'd the *Memoirs* of Scriblerus, being the beginning of a considerable Work undertaken so long ago as in 1713 by several great Hands. As much of it as is here publish'd, and all the *Tracts* in

the same Name, were written by our Author and Dr. *Arbuthnot*, except the *Essay on the Origine of Sciences*, in which Dr. *Parnelle* had some hand, as Mr. *Gay* in the *Memoirs of a Parish-Clerk*."

3. *Bishop Burnet's History of His Own Time* (Oxford: Clarendon Press, 1823), I, xv.

4. Swift's notes, reproduced in the edition cited above (n. 3), were taken from speaker Onslowe's copy, where, in turn, they had been copied from Swift's copy, which had come into the possession of the Marquis of Landsdowne.

5. Swift's "Cursory Remarks" (characterized by the editor as "shrewd, caustic, and apposite, but not written with the requisite decorum; indeed, three of them are worded in so light a way, that even modesty forbad their admission" [*Burnet's History*, I, x]) are typically sharp. Beginning with the Preface, where he responded to the Bishop's promise to retouch and polish his work, with the comment, "Rarely polished; I never read so ill a style" (I, 7), Swift continues in the same vein throughout: "Stupid moralist" (I, 446), "Style of a gamester" (II, 436), "Vain fop" (III, 200), "Strange inconsistent stuff" (I, 267), "Nonsense" (I, 171, 494). . . .

6. As Burnet's biographer, H. C. Foxcroft, comments,

Burnet's later prefaces . . . rank with the curiosities of literature. They are in fact semi-political manifestoes; in which religious exhortation and political appeals jostle one another with truly amusing vehemence. In this instance [a new preface to his *Pastoral Care*], the complaints of clerical ignorance, which excited High Church spleen, seem to have been well founded; and were in any case strictly appropriate to the theme. The defence of the good Low Churchman might even pass muster; did not Burnet dilate on the politics of that exemplary individual. His thankful acceptance (without any equivocal reservation) of the Revolution and the Hanoverian settlement; his dread of the Pretender—whose love of Tyranny and Popery will have grown with his sufferings on their behalf—seem topics hardly relevant to the *Pastoral Care*. Nor can we trace any valid connection between clerical avocations and the terms of the impending Peace. (*A Life of Gilbert Burnet* [Cambridge: Cambridge University Press, 1907], pp. 457–58.)

7. Burnet, *History*, I, 6.

8. Ibid., VI, 168.

9. Ibid., I, 7.

10. Ibid., I, 345.

11. Temperamentally as well as ideologically the Bishop was a stormy petrel; in arguing his similarity to William Penn, the DNB describes him succinctly as unquestioningly self-confident and controversially eager.

12. *The Works of John Dryden* (Berkeley and Los Angeles: University of California Press, 1969), III, 449–54.

13. His preface to the third edition of his *Pastoral Care* provoked George Sewell's *Antidotum Sarisburiense* (February 1713); in return his 1713 preface to the revised *Homilies* of 1690 was followed by a second Sewell *Letter.* In September 1713 another vehement introduction, this time to the final volume of his *History of the Reformation* and fanatical in its Popish fears, inspired a satire by Parnell and a wicked parody by Swift as "Gregory Misosarum." (Foxcroft, *Life of Burnet,* pp. 457–64.)

14. In the 1728 *Dunciad,* III, 173–80:

"Behold yon Pair, in strict embraces join'd;
How like their manners, and how like their mind!
Fam'd for good-nature, B** and for truth;
D** for pious passion to the youth.
Equal in wit, and equally polite,
Shall this a Pasquin, that a Grumbler write;
Like are their merits, like rewards they share,
That shines a Consul, this Commissioner."

(TE, V, 168.)

Pope had also added a footnote epigram for the *Dunciad Variorum*:

Burnet *and* Duckit, *friends in spite,*
   Came hissing forth in Verse;
Both were so forward, each wou'd write,
   So dull, each hung an A——
Thus Amphisboena (*I have read*)
   At either end assails:
None knows which leads, or which is led,
   For both Heads are but Tails.

(TE V, 169n.)

In the 1742 *New Dunciad* the epigram is removed and the lines naming the two are deleted from the text.

15. For attribution see *Early Career,* p. 141.

16. The attack which follows dwells on familiar faults: "*His consummate* Pretensions *to all kinds of Business, his* awaking Sonorousness in his *extempore* Rhapsodies, *his active Zeal for the* Interest of old Glorious, *and the* Dexterity *he had in* the Art of Conveyancing, *are Subjects easy to be enlarged upon, but* 'tis much easier to let 'em alone."

17. On this issue, for example, we also have Dr. Arbuthnot's *Notes and Memorandums of the Six Days, preceeding the Death of a late Right Reverend,* printed in 1715. Here, Burnet feverishly contemplates his death and his literary remains

("Call for my Man: Order him to bring the *Folio* in Manuscript, of my *own Life* and *Times*. Consider what a great Name I shall leave behind me"), while he and his son squabble: "Tom [Burnet]. . . . I know one way that may make my *Legacy* doubled in a short Time—. . . . Why, a *certain* Book written by a *certain* grave Man about *Certain Times*, which I hope *certainly* to publish, and get a round sum for the Copy." (*The Miscellaneous Works of the Late Dr. Arbuthnot* [Glasgow, 1751], I, 233, 243.)

18. "Testimonies of Authors," *The Dunciad Variorum* (TE V, 34). Pope was replying to an attack attributed to James Moore Smythe: "The Memoirs of a Parish Clerk was a very dull and unjust abuse of a person who wrote in defence of our Religion and Constitution, and who has been dead many years." The letter from which it was taken, signed "Philo-Ditto," had appeared in the *Daily Journal* for 3 April 1728 (No. 2254); earlier, in the London *Evening-Post* of 19 March 1728 (No. 44), one "Philalethes" had addressed himself *"To the Author of the* Daily Journal": "Having in yours of March 18, inform'd the Publick of a flagrant Piece of Plagiary in the last Volume of *Pope* and *Swift*'s Miscellanies; I desire you will add a much more considerable one in wrong of the same Ingenious Gentlemen. I see no Reason why you should suppress the Name of Mr. *James Moore Smythe,* to whom this Injury has been done . . . But I must further acquaint you, Sir, that the whole Piece, entituled, *Memoirs of a Parish Clerk,* in the Second Volume of that Collection, has to my Knowledge above two years ago been own'd by Mr. *Smith* in several Companies." In the *Dunciad* "Testimonies" cited above, Pope had also commented satirically on Moore Smythe's purported authorship of the *Memoirs.*

NOTE ON PUBLICATION AND TEXT

However much earlier it was actually composed (see Introduction), the *Memoirs of P. P.* was not published until 1727, in the second volume of the Swift-Pope *Miscellanies*. It is present in all the later reprintings of that volume, in 1730, 1733, and 1736; and it was included in the 1741 edition of Pope's prose works, in the reorganized *Miscellanies in Four Volumes* of 1742, and in the posthumously published Warburton edition of his works in 1751. In these various printings, changes in the text are few and minor and, for the most part, are to be found in the later editions, when Pope was revising and reassembling his works. The copytext is that of the first edition (1727), but incorporates the poet's later revisions in the accidentals of the edition in which they first appeared. Textual notes supply all the other substantive variants.

Key to the Critical Apparatus

1727 = *Miscellanies in Prose and Verse*, Second Vol., octavo, Griffith 185.

1730 (dated 1731) = Second Vol., duodecimo, Griffith 243.

1733 = Second Vol., second edition, duodecimo, Griffith 285.

1736 = Second Vol., duodecimo, Griffith 436, 437.

1741 = *Works in Prose*, Vol. II, folio, Griffith 529; l. p. folio, Griffith 530; quarto, Griffith, 531.

1742 = *Miscellanies* (in Four Volumes), Second Vol., sm. octavo, Griffith 562.

1751 = *Works*, ed. Warburton, Vol. VI, octavo, Griffith 648.

MEMOIRS
Of *P. P.*
Clerk of THIS PARISH.

Advertisement.   [On facing page, original
in reverse italics.]

The Original of the following extraordinary Treatise consisted of
two large Volumes in Folio;[1] which might justly be entituled,
The Importance of a Man to Himself:[2] But, as it can be of very little
to any body besides, I have contented my self to give only this short
Abstract of it, as a taste of the *true Spirit* of *Memoir-Writers.*[3]

In the Name of the Lord. *Amen.* I, *P.P.* by the Grace of God,
Clerk of this Parish, writeth this History.[4]

Ever since I arrived at the Age of Discretion I had a Call to take
upon me the Function of a Parish-Clerk;[5] and to that end, it seemed
unto me meet and profitable to associate myself with the Parish-
Clerks of this Land; such I mean, as were right worthy in their
Calling, Men of a clear and sweet Voice, and of becoming Gravity.[6]

Now it came to pass, that I was born in the Year of our Lord
Anno Domini 1655, the Year, wherein our worthy Benefactor, Esquire
Bret,[7] did add one Bell to the Ring of this Parish. So that, it hath
been wittily said, that "one and the same Day did give to this our
Church two rare Gifts, its *great Bell* and its *Clerk.*"

Even when I was at School, my Mistress did ever extol me above
the rest of the Youth, in that I had a laudible Voice. And it was
furthermore observed, that I took a kindly Affection unto that black
Letter[8] in which our Bibles are Printed. Yea, often did I exercise my
self in singing godly Ballads,[9] such as the *Lady and Death,* the
Children in the Wood, and *Chevy-Chace*; and not, like other Children,
in lewd and trivial Ditties. Moreover, while I was a Boy, I always
adventured to lead the Psalm next after Master William *Harris* my
Predecessor; who (it must be confessed to the glory of God) was a
most excellent Parish-Clerk in that his Day.[10]

Yet be it acknowledged, that at the Age of sixteen, I became a
Company-keeper,[11] being led into idle Conversation by my extraor-
dinary Love to *Ringing*;[12] insomuch, that in a short Time I was
A   acquainted with every Set of Bells in the whole Country. Neither
B   could I be prevail'd upon to absent my self from *Wakes*;[13] being
called thereunto by the Harmony of the Steeple. While I was in
C   these Societies, I gave my self up to unspiritual Pastimes, such as
Wrestling, Dancing and *Cudgel-playing*; so that I often returned to my
Father's House with a broken Pate: I had my Head broken at *Milton*
by *Thomas Wyat,* as we play'd a bout or two for an Hat that was
edged with Silver-Galloom.[14] But in the Year following, I broke the
D   Head of *Henry Stubbs,* and obtained an Hat not inferior to the former:
At *Yelverton* I encountred *George Cummins* Weaver, and behold my
Head was broken a second Time! At the Wake of *Waybrook,* I engaged
William Symkins Tanner, when lo, thus was my Head broken a third
Time! and much Blood trickled therefrom. But I administred to my
comfort, saying within my self, "What Man is there, howsoever
E   dextrous in any Craft, who is for aye on his guard?" A Week after,
I had a *base-born Child* laid unto me; for in the days of my Youth I
was look'd upon as a follower of Venereal Fantasies: Thus was I led
into Sin by the comeliness of *Susanna Smith,* who first tempted me,
and then put me to Shame;[15] for indeed, she was a Maiden of a
seducing Eye and pleasant Feature. I humbled my self before the
Justice, I acknowledged my Crime to our Curate, and to do away
mine Offences, and make her some Atonement, was joined to her
in holy Wedlock on the Sabbath-Day following.

How often do those things which seem unto us Misfortunes,
redound to our Advantage! For the Minister (who had long looked
on *Susanna* as the most lovely of his Parishioners)[16] liked so well of
my demeanour, that he recommended me to the Honour of being
his *Clerk,* which was then become vacant by the decease of good
Master *William Harris.*

*Here ends the first Chapter; after which follow fifty or sixty Pages of his
Amours in general, and that particular one with* Susanna *his present Wife;
but I proceed to Chapter the 9th.*

No sooner was I elected into mine Office, but I layed aside the
powder'd Gallantries of my Youth, and became a new Man. I considered my self as in some wise of Ecclesiastical Dignity, since by
wearing a Band, which is no small part of the Ornament of our

Clergy,[17] I might not unworthily be deemed as it were a *Shred* of the *Linen Vestment* of *Aaron.*[18]

Thou mayst conceive, O Reader, with what concern I perceived the Eyes of the Congregation fixed upon me,[19] when I first took my Place at the Feet of the Priest. When I raised the Psalm, how did my Voice quaver for fear! And when I arrayed the Shoulders of the Minister with the Surplice, how did my Joints tremble under me! I said within my self, "Remember, *Paul,* thou standest before Men of high Worship, the wise Mr. Justice *Freeman,* the grave Mr. Justice *Tonson,* the good Lady *Jones,* and the two virtuous Gentlewomen her Daughters, nay, the great Sir *Thomas Truby,*[20] Knight and Baronet, and my young Master the Esquire, who shall one Day be Lord of this Manor:" Notwithstanding which, it was my good hap to acquit my self to the good liking of the whole Congregation; but the Lord forbid I should glory therein.

The next Chapter contains an Account how he discharg'd the several Duties of his Office; in particular, he insists on the following.

I was determined to reform the manifold Corruptions and Abuses which had crept into the Church.[21]

First, I was especially severe in whipping forth Dogs from the Temple, all excepting the Lap-dog of the good Widow *Howard,*[22] a sober Dog which yelped not, nor was there Offence in his Mouth.

Secondly, I did even proceed to moroseness, though sore against my Heart, unto Poor Babes; in tearing from them the half-eaten Apples, which they privily munched at Church. But verily it pitied me, for I remembered the Days of my Youth.

Thirdly, With the sweat of my own Hands I did make plain and smooth the Dogs-ears throughout our great Bible.

Fourthly, The Pews and Benches which were formerly swept but once in three years, I caused every *Saturday* to be swept with a Beesom[23] and trimmed.

Fifthly and Lastly, I caused the Surplice to be neatly darned, washed, and laid in fresh Lavender, (yea, and sometimes to be sprinkled with Rose-Water) and I had great Laud and Praise from all the neighbouring Clergy, forasmuch as no Parish kept the Minister in cleaner Linen.

Notwithstanding these his publick Cares, in the eleventh Chapter he informs us he did not neglect his usual Occupations as a Handy-craftsman.

Shoes, *saith he,* did I make, (and, if intreated, mend) with good

Approbation. Faces also did I shave; and I clipped the Hair. Chirurgery also I practised, in the Worming of Dogs; but to Bleed adventured I not, except the Poor.[24] Upon this my twofold Profes-

A sion, there passed among Men a merry Tale delectable enough to be

B rehearsed: How that being overtaken with Liquor[25] one *Saturday*-Evening, I shaved the Priest with *Spanish* Blacking[26] for Shoes, in-

C stead of a Wash-ball,[27] and with Lamp-Black powdered his Perriwig. But these were Sayings of Men, delighting in their own Conceits more than in the Truth. For it is well known that great was my

D,E Care and Skill in these my Crafts: Yea, I once had the Honour of trimming Sir *Thomas* himself, without fetching Blood. Furthermore, I was sought unto to geld the Lady *Frances* her Spaniel, which was wont to go astray. He was called *Toby*, that is to say, *Tobias*.[28] And thirdly, I was entrusted with a gorgeous pair of Shoes of the said Lady, to set an Heelpiece thereon; and I received such Praise therefore, that it was said all over the Parish I should be recommended unto the *King* to mend Shoes for his Majesty:[29] Whom God preserve, Amen.

The rest of this Chapter I purposely omit, for it must be own'd that when he speaks as a Shoemaker he is very absurd.[30] *He talks of* Moses's *pulling off his* Shoes, *of tanning the* Hides *of the* Bulls of Basan, *of*

F *Simon* the Tanner, &c. *and takes up to four or five Pages to prove, that when the* Apostles *were Instructed to Travel* without Shoes, *the Precept did not extend to their* Successors.

G *The next Chapter relates, how he* discover'd a Thief with a Bible and Key, *and experimented* Verses of the Psalms that had cured Agues.[31]

I pass over many others which inform us of Parish Affairs only; such as of the Succession of Curates; a List *of the* weekly Texts; *what* Psalms

H *he chose on* proper Occasions; *and what* Children *were* Born *and* Buried:[32] *The Last of which Articles he concludes thus,*

That the Shame of Women may not endure, I speak not of *Bastards*; neither will I name the *Mothers,* altho' thereby I might delight many grave Women of the Parish: Even her who hath done Penance in the Sheet[33] will I not mention, forasmuch as the Church hath been Witness of her Disgrace. Let the Father, who hath made due Composition with the Churchwardens to conceal his Infirmity, rest in Peace; my Pen shall not bewray him, for I also have sinned.[34]

The next Chapter contains what he calls a great Revolution in the Church;[35] *part of which I transcribe.*

Now was the long expected Time arrived, when the Psalms of King *David* should be hymned unto the same Tunes to which he played them upon his Harp; so was I informed by my Singing-Master, a Man right cunning in *Psalmody*. Now was our over-abundant *Quaver* and *Trilling* done away, and in lieu thereof was instituted the *Sol-fa,* in such guise as is sung in his Majesty's Chappel. We had *London* Singing-Masters sent into every Parish, like unto *Excisemen*; and I also was ordained to adjoin my self unto them, though an unworthly Disciple, in order to instruct my fellow Parishioners in this new manner of Worship.[36] What tho' they accused me of humming through the Nostril, as a Sacbut?[37] Yet would I not forgoe that Harmony, it having been agreed by the worthy Parish-Clerks of *London,* still to preserve the same. I tutored the young Men and Maidens[38] to tune their Voices as it were a Psaltery, and the Church on the Sunday was filled with these new Hallelujahs.

Then follow full seventy Chapters containing an exact detail of the Law-Suits of the Parson *and his* Parishioners, *concerning* Tythes,[39] *and near a Hundred Pages left blank, with an earnest desire that the* History might be compleated by any of his Successors, in whose time these Suits should be ended.

A *The next Chapter contains an Account of the* Briefs[40] *read in the Church, and the* Sums *collected upon each.* For the Reparation of nine Churches,
B,C collected at nine several times, 2*s.* and 7*d.* ¾. For fifty Families ruin'd by Fire, 1*s.* ½. For an Inundation, a King *Charles*'s Groat[41] given by Lady *Frances,* &c.

In the next, he laments the disuse of Wedding-Sermons, *and celebrates the Benefits arising from those at* Funerals, *concluding with these Words.* Ah! Let not the Relations of the Deceas'd grudge the small Expence of an Hatband, a pair of Gloves, and ten Shillings, for the satisfaction they are sure to receive from a pious Divine, that their Father, Brother, or bosom Wife, are certainly in Heaven.[42]

In another, he draws a Panegyrik on one Mrs. Margaret Wilkins, *but after great Encomiums concludes, that,* notwithstanding all, she was an unprofitable Vessel, being a barren Woman,[43] and never once having furnished God's Church with a Christening.

We find in another Chapter, how he was much stagger'd in his belief, and disturb'd in his Conscience by an Oxford Scholar, *who had prov'd to him by* Logick, *that* Animals might have rational,[44] nay, immortal Souls; *but how he was again comforted with the Reflection,* that if so, they might be allowed Christian Burial, and greatly augment the Fees of the Parish.

In the two following Chapters he is overpower'd with Vanity. We are told, how he was constantly admitted to all the Feasts and Banquets of the Church-Officers,[45] *and the* Speeches *he there made for the good of the* Parish. *How he gave* hints *to young* Clergy-men *to Preach;*[46] *but above all, how he gave a* Text *for the* 30th *of* January, *which occasion'd a most excellent Sermon,*[47] *the Merits of which he takes entirely to himself. He gives an account of a Conference he had with the Vicar concerning the use of Texts. Let a Preacher (saith he) consider the Assembly before whom he Preacheth, and unto them adapt his Text.*[48] *Micah the 3d and 11th affordeth good matter for Courtiers and Courtserving-men. The Heads of the Land judge for reward; and the People thereof judge for Hire; and the Prophets thereof divine for money: Yet will they lean upon the Lord, and say, Is not the Lord among us?* Were the first Minister to appoint a Preacher before the House of Commons, would not he be wise to make choice of these Words? *Give, and it shall be given unto ye.* Or before the Lords, *Giving no Offence, that the Ministry be not blamed,* 2 Cor. vi. 3. Or praising the warm Zeal of an Administration, *Who maketh his Ministers a flaming fire,* Psalm 104.4. We omit many other of his Texts, as too tedious.

From *this period, the Style of the Book rises extreamly.*[49] *Before the next Chapter was pasted the Effigies*[50] *of Dr.* Sacheverel, *and I found the opposite Page all on a foam with* Politicks.[51]

We are all now (says he) arrived at that celebrated Year, in which the *Church of England* was tried in the Person of Dr. *Sacheverel.*[52] I had ever the Interest of our High-Church at Heart, neither would A I at any season mingle my self in the Societies of Fanaticks, whom I from my Infancy abhorred, more than the *Heathen* or *Gentile.*[53] It was in these Days I bethought my self, that much Profit might accrue unto our Parish, and even unto the Nation, could there be assembled together a number of chosen Men of the right Spirit, who might argue, refine, and define, upon high and great Matters.[54] Unto this purpose, I did institute a weekly Assembly of divers worthy Men at the *Rose and Crown Ale-House,* over whom my self (tho' unworthy) did preside. Yea, I did read unto them the *Post-Boy* of Mr. *Roper,* and the written Letter of Mr. *Dyer,*[55] upon which we communed afterwards among our selves. Our Society was composed of the following Persons: *Robert Jenkins,* Farrier; *Amos Turner,* Collar-maker; *George Pilcocks,* late Excise-man; *Thomas White,* Wheel-wright; and my self.[56] First, of the first, *Robert Jenkins.*

He was a Man of bright Parts and shrewd Conceit, for he never shooed an Horse of a Whig or a Fanatic, but he lamed him sorely.[57]

Amos Turner, a worthy Person, righly esteemed among us for his Sufferings, in that he had been honoured in the Stocks for wearing an Oaken Bough.[58]

George Pilcocks, a Sufferer also, of zealous and laudable freedom of Speech, insomuch that his Occupation had been taken from him.

Thomas White, of good repute likewisse, for that his Uncle, by the Mother's side, had, formerly, been Servitor[59] at *Maudlin*-College, where the glorious *Sacheverel* was Educated.

Now were the Eyes of all the Parish upon these our Weekly Councils. In a short space, the Minister came among us; he spake concerning us and our Councils to a multitude of other Ministers at the Visitation, and they spake thereof unto the Ministers at *London,* so that even the *Bishops* heard and marvelled thereat. Moreover, Sir *Thomas,* Member of Parliament, spake of the same to other Members of Parliament; who spake thereof unto the Peers of the Realm. Lo! thus did our Counsels enter into the Hearts of our Generals and our Law-givers; and from henceforth, even as we devised, thus did they.[60]

A   *After this, the whole Book is turn'd on a sudden, from his own Life,[61] to a* History *of all the* publick transactions *of* Europe, *compil'd from the* News-Papers *of those Times. I could not comprehend the meaning of this,*

B   *till I perceived at last (to my no small Astonishment) that all the measures of the four last Years of the* Queen,[62] *together with the* Peace *at* Utrecht, *which have been usually attributed to the* E—— *of* O——, D—— *of* O——, *Lords* H—— *and* B——, *and other great Men;[63] do here most plainly appear, to have been wholly owing to* Robert Jenkins, Amos Turner, George Pilcocks, Thomas White, *but above all* P. P.

  The Reader may be sure I was very inquisitive after this extraordinary Writer, whose Work I have here abstracted. I took a Journey into the Country

C   *on purpose: but could not find the least trace of him: till by accident I met an old Clergyman, who said he cou'd not be positive, but thought it might*

D,E   *be one* Paul Philips, *who had been Dead about twelve years. And upon*

F   *enquiry, all he cou'd learn of that person from the neighbourhood, was,*

That he had been taken notice of for swallowing Loaches,[64] *and remember'd by some people by a* black and white Cur with one Ear, *that constantly follow'd him.*

In the Churchyard, I read his Epitaph, *said to be written by himself.*

> O Reader, if thou canst read,
> Look down upon this Stone;
> Do all we can, Death is a Man,
> That never spareth none.[65]

Textual Variants

Page 110: A. whole *Om. 1742.*

Page 110: B. upon] with *1727–36.*

Page 110: C. my self up] up my self *1727.*

Page 110: D. *Henry*] *Harry 1727–36.*

Page 110: E. Craft] Knowledge or Craft *1727–36.*

Page 111: A. *Tonson*] *Tomson 1727–36;* Thomson *1742.*

Page 111: B. own *Om. 1742.*

Page 112: A. Men] pleasant Men *1727–36.*

Page 112: B. with] in *1742.*

Page 112: C. Perriwig] perruke *1742.*

Page 112: D. Care and *Om. 1742.*

Page 112: E. these] all these *1727–36.*

Page 112: F. &c. *Add. 1741–51.*

Page 112: G. *Chapter Om. 1742.*

Page 112: H. *and Add. 1741–51.*

Page 113: A. *Chapter Om. 1742.*

Page 113: B. and *Add. 1733–51.*

Page 113: C. ¾.] ¼. *1727–30.*

Page 114: A. season] seasons *1727–36.*

Page 115: A. *whole Om. 1742.*

Page 115: B. *last*] *the last 1727.*

Page 115: C. *purpose; . . . might be*] *purpose. The Neighbourhood there thought it must be 1727–36.*

Page 115: D. *about*] *above 1736.*

Page 115: E. And . . . him.] *I could learn no more from my Enquiry, but that such a one had liv'd and dy'd there: And there was nothing they knew remarkable of him, only this circumstance which all agree in, "That he had*

a black and white Cur with one Ear, that constantly follow'd him."
1727–36.

Page 115: F. he] we *1742.*

Annotations

1. Burnet's *History* was also first published in two large folio volumes. Though volume two did not appear until 1734, ten years after the first, it was clearly indicated in the first volume that a second would follow.

2. Arbuthnot had concluded one part of his *Notes and Memorandums of the Six Days, preceeding the Death of a late Right Reverend* . . . with the Bishop's raving, "Resolve to minute every Thing I can remember of myself 'till I depart this Life." (*Miscellaneous Works* [Glasgow, 1751], I, 245.)

3. See Lord Hervey's introduction to his *Memoirs of the Reign of George the Second*: "As to the disagreeable egotisms with which almost all memoir-writers so tiresomely abound, I shall endeavour to steer as clear of them as I can. . . . I leave those ecclesiastical heroes of their own romances—De Retz and Burnet—to aim at that useless imaginary glory of being thought to influence every considerable event they relate. . . ." (London: John Murray, 1848, I, 3.)

4. Perhaps more justifiably but as unctuously, Burnet had dedicated his efforts: "I look on the perfecting of this work, and the carrying it on through the remaining part of my life, as the greatest service I can do to God and to the world. . . . And now, O my God, the God of my life, and of all my mercies, I offer this work to thee, to whose honour it is chiefly intended; that thereby I may awaken the world to just reflection on their own errors and follies . . . ," to which Swift retorted, "This I take to be nonsense." (*Bishop Burnet's History of His Own Time* [Oxford: Clarendon Press, 1823], I, 6, 7, 7n.)

5. Especially in the eighteenth century there was considerable argument over whether the office of the parish clerk was a temporal or spiritual position; but in general the term was applied, as here, to one whose duty was to take part in the singing and to make arrangements, under the direction of the resident clergyman, for the due performance of any of the services. The prestige of the clergy had sunk to a marked low at this time (witness John Eachard's popular satire of 1670, *The Grounds and Occasions of the Contempt of the Clergy and Religion enquired into*), depreciating all the more the small honor attaching to the lower incumbencies: "However mean and inconsiderable the Office of Parish-Clerks has been esteemed, in Places remote and distant from *London* . . ." ("An Essay concerning the Office and Duties of Parish-Clerks," *Collectanea Ecclesiastica* [London, 1752], p. 399).

6. As Bishop Burnet made clear in his introductory remarks, he too had come early to his avocation and to his much-vaunted association with important personages: "I had while I was very young a greater knowledge of affairs than is

usual at that age. . . . I fell into great acquaintance and friendships with several persons, who either were or had been ministers of state. . . ." (Burnet, I, 3, 4.) As for his vocation, Dryden characterized him (as the Buzzard in the *Hind and the Panther,* Part III, l. 1147) as "A Theologue more by need, than genial bent"; though the Bishop himself asserted "I have always had a true zeal for the church of England" (VI, 172), his son, in his "Life of the Author," informs us that his father had first "applied himself to the law, much to the regret of his father, who had always designed him for a clergyman" (VI, 236). To his detractors, his interests had always remained too political and secular.

7. Perhaps a glancing allusion to Col. Henry Brett (d. 1724), a well-known member of Addison's circle? Col. Brett, characterized by Sherburn as "a representative courtier and man about town" (*Early Career,* p. 116), had married the notorious countess of Macclesfield, putative mother of Richard Savage, and with her fortune bought a country estate, Sandywell Park, which he rebuilt. More broadly, the reference is suggestive of Burnet's obtrusive vanity in linking personal history with national affairs: e.g., "Upon the king's death the Scots proclaimed his son king, and sent over sir George Wincam, that married my great aunt . . ." (Burnet, *History,* I, 88). As Swift commented, "Was that the reason he was sent?" (Ibid., I, 88n.)

8. Although black letter was most in vogue in the sixteenth century, it was used until the end of the seventeenth (the Authorized Bible of 1611 was in that character) and even persisted into the eighteenth century in law books, proclamations, licenses, etc.

9. Ballad singing was a popular rural pastime, as Gay suggests in his "Shepherd's Week" when Bowzybeus entertains the folk: "Then sad he sung *The Children in the Wood*" and "To louder Strains he rais'd his Voice, to tell / What woeful Wars in *Chevy-Chace* befell. . . ." These two popular ballads ("The Children in the Wood" is somtimes designated a "vulgar ballad" or broadside) were also the subject of Addison's famous *Spectator* papers Nos. 70 (21 May 1711), 74 (25 May 1711), and 85 (7 June 1711)—the first formal notice of the type in the eighteenth century and a major event in the history of ballad criticism. "The Lady and Death" is a variant of "Death and the Lady," one of a series of moral ballads deriving from the *Dance of Death,* with a modern counterpart in Schubert's "Der Tod und das Mädchen." "Death and the Lady" was especially popular in the eighteenth century and apparently a favorite of Goldsmith, for he refers to it on several occasions. (Anne G. Gilchrist, " 'Death and the Lady' in English Balladry," *Journal of the English Folk Dance and Song Society,* 4 [1941], 37–48.)

10. This might be a squib at a candidate (Mr. Harris) for whom Burnet had unsuccessfully campaigned in the General Election of 1705. As Miss H. C. Foxcroft notes in her life of Burnet (Cambridge: Cambridge University Press, 1907), "Burnet's method of canvassing is not likely to have been discreet; and in fine,

to use his own words, 'I failed in my attempt, and it raised a most violent storm against me from the Tories. . . .' " (P. 417.)

11. "A frequenter of company, esp. in bad sense, a reveller" (OED).

12. No doubt change ringing, a peculiarly English art of bell ringing which developed during the seventeenth century and which consists of intricate variations in the order in which a set of bells may be rung.

13. John Ashton (*Social Life in the Reign of Queen Anne,* London: Chatto and Windus, 1882) notes that such rough village sports as cudgel-playing—and football, wrestling, boxing, running—were kept alive by country "wakes," a term used in rural England for annual parish festivals. In cudgel-playing a hat seems to have been the traditional prize, awarded to whichever contestant drew first blood from his opponent's head.

14. Galloom, or galoon, a kind of narrow, closewoven ribbon or braid used as trimming.

15. One of the basic satiric devices of this piece being ironic incongruity (pomposity of language and unctuousness of tone set against the actual trivialities narrated), there may be intended irony in P. P.'s seduction by Susanna, a primal Eve "who first tempted me," whereas the biblical Susanna (to be called to mind by the biblical cadences of the passage?) was the traditional model of the beautiful but God-fearing woman basely accused of seduction by her hypocritical elders.

16. In his satiric sketch of Burnet as the Buzzard in the *Hind and the Panther,* Dryden touches upon (Part III, ll. 1145–46) his contemporary notoriety for improper behavior toward (i.e., undue influence on) ladies under his spiritual guidance. (*Works of John Dryden* [Berkeley and Los Angeles: University of California Press, 1969], III, 451–52.) See also n. 38.

17. Vestments had become a controversial issue: the Royal Commission on Ecclesiastical Reform (1689) had reviewed the use of the surplice (Foxcroft, *Life of Burnet,* p. 277) and Burnet, in his *Four Discourses delivered to the Clergy of the Diocess of Sarum* (London, 1694), noted, "Some except to our habit, as a Ceremony taken from the Service of the Jewish Temple: and this, tho it is now esteem'd the least considerable of all the exceptions made against us, yet was that which first began those unhappy disputes that have since increased so fatally upon us."

18. Aaron, the prototype of the High Priest, had been chosen by God to be Israel's first High Priest, and with Moses was instructed at length (Exodus 28) about the holy vestments proper to his office. Ironically, it was also Aaron who had directed the Israelites in constructing the Golden Calf—a not inappropriate thread in the fabric of P. P.'s "Shred" of vestment.

19. It was Burnet's tendency too to see himself as the focus of attention. More characteristic than the disclaimer is the inherent egotism of such a statement in the *History* as, "I must now mix in somewhat with relation to my self, though that may seem too inconsiderable to be put into a series of matters of such importance." (Burnet, *History,* II, 437.)

20. It is hard to tell whether these names had contemporary significance or not: certainly the *Tonson* catches the eye (Jacob Tonson, Pope's first publisher), although in the earlier versions it was *Tomson,* a name as generic as *Freeman* or *Jones.* There are possible contemporary references (Mr. Ralph Freeman; "Mr Freeman"—the duke of Marlborough; Sir William Jones; Richard Jones, first earl of Ranelagh) but the allusions don't quite fit nor does any pattern of satire emerge. The name *Truby,* on the other hand, might well have had current associations because of Truby's Coffee House, which catered primarily to the clergy. (G. M. Trevelyan, *Illustrated English Social History* [London: Longmans, Green, 1957], III, 22, 30.)

21. P. P.'s self-important attack on the "corruptions" of the church, with its wrenched biblical echoes, is further example of the burlesque technique of the satire, here playing on one of Burnet's favorite topics. In fact, in his preface to the *History,* he inveighed, ". . . indeed the peevishness, the ill nature, and the ambition of many clergymen, has sharpened my spirits perhaps too much against them: so I warn my reader to take all that I say on these heads with some grains of allowance . . ." (Burnet, *History,* I, 6). Swift noted laconically, "I will take his warning" (ibid., I, 6 n.). In his concluding chapter, Burnet harangued lengthily on behavior and duties of the gentry, nobility, royalty, clergy, bishops. . . . Much earlier, in *A Discourse of the Pastoral Care* (1692), he had argued that "Scandalous persons ought, and might be more frequently presented than they are, and both Private and Publick Admonitions might be more used than they are" (p. 95).

22. A playful reference to Henrietta Howard, later countess of Suffolk? A sort of "grass widow," Mrs. Howard, one of the maids-of-honor of the princess of Wales, became the mistress of the prince; on his succession to the throne as George II, she formally separated from her husband. She was a long-time friend of Pope (and Gay) and, from 1724, a neighbor at Marble Hill at Twickenham. Norman Ault argues that her dog Fop is the subject of a poem "Bounce to Fop: An Heroic Epistle, from a Dog at Twickenham to a Dog at Court" which he attributes to Pope, dating it originally from 1726 or 1727, with a fuller rewriting years later. (*New Light on Pope* [London: Methuen, 1949], pp. 342–48.) Possibly it is Fop that is alluded to here, or, just possibly, it is Mrs. Howard's lover, the Prince.

23. An obsolete form of *besom,* a broom, usually made from a bunch of twigs bound around a handle.

24. It is typical of the satiric technique of inflation/deflation that P. P.'s activity in "surgery" is linked to the worming of dogs. Although technically the treatment for worming was medicinal rather than surgical (see, for example, *An Account of the Breeding of Worms in Human Bodies* by Nicholas Andry, trans. from the French [London, 1701]), the undertaking reminds one that it was not until the end of the century that British surgery was raised from the technical trade of

the barber-surgeon to the science of the specialist—largely through the efforts of the Scots-born Hunter brothers. Bloodletting, however, continued a popular practice until far into the next century. It is interesting to note Member-of-the-Royal-Society Burnet's own concern for the study of anatomy. In a treatise "Thoughts on Education," published long after his death (London, 1761) but ascribed to him as written in about 1668, there is the advice: "I should begin with anatomy, as one easy and useful piece of knowledge, not troubling the youth to get by heart the names of veins, arteries, nerves and muscles, but to make him understand the use, function, situation, figure, and dependance of the chieff parts of the body; and this will be neither a tedious nor ane unpleasant work; especially if wee be where wee may see dissections." (P. 67.)

25. When in 1692 there appeared puritanical royal proclamations against drunkenness and "Sabbath-breach," these were charged to Burnet as chief contriver. (Foxcroft, *Life of Burnet*, p. 314.)

26. The OED cites Ure *Dict. Arts* 341 (1839): "When this cork [*sc.* the white cork of France] is burned in close vessels it forms a pigment called Spanish black."

27. A ball of soap used for washing and for shaving.

28. While *Toby* is indeed the familiar form of *Tobias,* it did have vulgar contemporary reference—to the buttocks and genitals.

29. Burnet's appetite for royal favor and intimacy was well known; whether exhorting Charles to better behavior, encouraging William of Orange in his English aspirations, basking in the confidence of Queen Mary, or rushing to be the first to throw himself on his knees to the new Queen Anne, he could not resist in his *History* calling attention to his place at court.

30. The folly of P. P.'s interpreting scripture by artisan concerns may be equated with the Bbishop's practice of arguing politics on biblical precedent (as in his preface to *Four Discourses delivered to the Clergy of the Diocess of Sarum* [London, 1694], where he justifies taking arms against the government by Old Testament example.)

31. The death, in 1692, of Robert Boyle, the father of modern chemistry, was the occasion of a celebrated sermon by the Bishop, an amateur experimental scientist himself. The eulogy stressed the interrelationship of science and religion, which may be what is parodied here. Certainly in his advice to priests in *A Discourse of the Pastoral Care* (London, 1692) Burnet had admonished, "The Study and Practice of *Physick,* especially that which is safe and simple, puts the Clergy in a capacity of doing great Acts of Charity, and of rendring both their Persons and Labours very acceptable to their People; it will procure their being soon sent for by them in Sickness, and it will give them great advantages in speaking to them, of their Spiritual Concerns, when they are so careful of their Persons, but in this nothing that is *sordid* must mix" (p. 91).

32. To a contemporary reader, the reference to children born and buried and,

then, to bastardy might well suggest the controversy over the legitimacy of the "Old Pretender" and Burnet's part in the affair, with his very suspicious account in his *History* of the birth of the Prince of Wales. Yoked to the complaints about the lack of proper witnesses to the event were all sorts of rumors, detailed by the Bishop: of miscarriages, of babies introduced into the royal bed in warming pans, of later infant substitutions. Such was Burnet's further interest that shortly after the confinement, in the summer of 1688, he published, anonymously, a paper on the safeguards provided by Roman law for presumptive heirs in cases of posthumous birth.

33. The OED cites this usage of *sheet*: "In phr. referring to performing penance in a sheet (orig. for fornication)." *The Daily Courant* for 11 December 1733 has this account: "On Sunday last a Woman did Penance in the Parish Church of St. Bride's, by standing in a White Sheet, with a Wand in her Hand, on a Stool in the middle Isle, during the Time of Divine Service, for Adultery and Fornication, and having a Bastard Child; and behaved the whole Time with seeming Penitence for her Crimes, by shedding Tears plentifully, and afterwards received a proper Admonition for the same."

34. No such consideration deterred the Bishop, who stalwartly took his sovereigns to task for their profligate behavior (e.g., his letter to Charles II: ". . . I resolved to write a very plain letter to the king: I set before him his past life, and the effects it had on the nation, with the judgments of God that lay on him, which was but a small part of the punishment that he might look for: I pressed him upon that earnestly to change the whole course of his life. . . ."). (Burnet, *History*, II, 287.)

35. P. P.'s "great" Revolution must inevitably suggest the Glorious Revolution of 1688, in which Burnet played so self-important a role ("The prince [of Orange] desired me to go along with him [on the expedition to England] as his chaplain, to which I very readily agreed: for, being fully satisfied on my conscience that the undertaking was lawful and just, and having had a considerable hand in advising the whole progress of it. . . ." [Burnet, *History*, III, 288]). It might more directly refer to the subsequent Commission on Ecclesiastical Reform (meeting from 3 October to 18 November 1689), in which Burnet actively participated too. As usual P. P. reduces everything to the lowest common denominator of his own petty interests.

36. In many cases the parish clerk was the chief musical functionary of the church, who taught the choir and, during the service, gave out the metrical psalm or anthem and served as precentor, sounding the notes of the psalm tune. The Restoration had seen a reinstallation of choral services after their curtailment by the Puritans, but with changes, for King Charles advocated a livelier style of sacred music. Dr. Burney reports, "It was honest John Playford who new strung the harp of David, and published, in 1671, the first edition of his 'Psalms and

Hymns in solemn Musick, in foure Parts on the common Tunes to Psalms in Metre used in Parish-churches. . . .' The several editions of this work published in various forms, at a small price, rendered its sale very general, and psalm-singing in parts, a favourite amusement in almost every village in the kingdom" (*A General History of Music* . . . [London, 1789], III, 464). While Sternhold and Hopkins had compiled the chief metrical psalter, Tate and Brady's version, which appeared in 1696, soon became equally important.

37. The nasal singing of the extreme Protestants had become almost traditional in satire; and Burnet's Scotch-Presbyterian connections and sympathies as well as his Broad Church positions were never forgotten by his detractors.

38. Maidens with lovely voices was a sore topic. As Miss Foxcroft reports: After his second wife's death, the Bishop's household was run by a Scotch couple named Tofts, with a daughter Katherine—"beautiful, fascinating, and dowered with a magnificent voice. It is possible that the kindly employer had extended to the wayward genius a rather ill-judged patronage; and when, somewhere about 1700 she left the Palace (under circumstances which do not seem to have reflected credit on the discipline of the establishment she quitted) to become the most brilliant of contemporary English opera-singers the Tory Jacobite gutterpress found a theme for scandalous variations" (Foxcroft, *Life of Burnet,* p. 379).

39. Tithes: dues legally payable to the established church. "The immemorial system went on, with its steady crop of litigation, without much complaint till the early years of the 19th century" (*Dict. of English Church History,* p. 611). Burnet had discussed tithes in his *History of the Rights of Princes in the disposing of ecclesiastical benefices and Church lands* (1682) and he returns to the subject in *Four Discourses Delivered to the Clergy of the Diocess of Sarum* (1694): "And therefore not to enter upon the discussion of any antecedent right to *Tythes,* it is certain that Publick Laws may appropriate such proportion of Soil, or of its growth, to such uses as they think fitting: And when that is once done, private persons must bear that, even when they do not approve of the use" (p. 109).

40. The OED defines *brief* as "a letter patent issued by the sovereign as Head of the Church, licensing a collection in the churches throughout England for a specific object of charity" and cites a reference from Pepys' *Diary* for 30 June 1661: "To church where we observed the trade of briefs is come now up to so constant a course every Sunday, that we resolve to give no more to them."

41. A groat—a coin equal to four pence which ceased to be issued for circulation in 1662—became, according to the OED, "the type of a very small sum."

42. In a contemporary ballad entitled *The Parish Clerk,* there is this stanza:

> But, greedy as Death, until his last breath
> This method he ne'er fail'd to use;

> When interr'd a corpse lay, Amen he'd scarce say,
> Before he cry'd, Who pays the dues?
> (From a collection "Fowler, Salisbury *Scraps*":
> B. L. 1347.m8. 37.)

Miss Foxcroft reports, "In the spring of 1695 died two of Burnet's early friends; the Duke of Hamilton and Lord Halifax. He had ceased to respect either; while it is said that Halifax declined Burnet's last ministrations; lest the Divine (using him, as he had used Rochester, to 'point' a pious 'moral') should 'triumph over him after his death.' " (Foxcroft, *Life of Burnet*, p. 333.) The Bishop had effected the deathbed conversion of the profligate earl of Rochester, which he chronicled in *Some Passages of the Life and Death of the right honourable John Earl of Rochester* (1680).

43. See *Dr. Gilbert Burnet's Resolution of two important Cases of Conscience: Is a Woman's Barrenness a just Ground for a Divorce, or for Polygamy? Is Polygamy in any Case lawful under the Gospel?* (1671). Not published by the author (who lived to regret a youthful and ill-considered display of Civil Law), the piece, which answered both questions in the affirmative, was prompted by the interest of Lauderdale and Moray in the question of divorce for King Charles, who was without legitimate offspring after nine years of marriage.

44. Perhaps a jibe at the recognition of the seventeenth-century Broad Church as "Rationalistic" or "Latitudinarian." Burnet, in 1675, had answered "A Rational Compendious Way to Convince without Dispute all persons whatsoever Dissenting from the true Religion" with his "A Rational Method For proving the Truth of the Christian Religion, As it is Professed in the Church of England"; in it he—like P. P. in this instance—turns his opponent's opening arguments to his own purpose: "Hitherto I have waited on *J. K.* in the survey of these Truths about which we are agreed, and I hope, upon a review of what we have both performed, he will not deny but I have strengthened his Position with the accession of many more, and better arguments than any he brought" (p. 31).

45. The position of the parish clerk was lower than that of the rector or vicar but higher than that of the sexton; these three constituted the salaried officials of the parish church.

46. The final section of Burnet's favorite work of his own, *A Discourse of the Pastoral Care* (London, 1692), was devoted to "Preaching."

47. The anniversary of the martyrdom of Charles I—30 January—was the occasion of several sermons by the Bishop. Their effusive Royalism caused them to be maliciously reprinted in later years by the Jacobite press.

48. In his essay on preaching (see n. 46) Burnet had just so counselled his young clergymen, admonishing them that "great regard is to be had to the Nature of the Auditory, that so the Point explained may be in some measure proportioned

to them" (p. 109). P. P.'s literal application of these words of wisdom points up the dangers of truistic advice. And some of Burnet's own texts bear mention too: for his first sermon before Queen Anne (15 March 1702), Isaiah 49.23: "And Kings shall be thy nursing Fathers, and their Queens thy nursing Mothers."

49. Burnet's style—whether in its exuberance or in its revised insipidity—was a prime target of his critics; and he himself acknowledged, "When a Man writes his own Thoughts, the heat of his Fancy, and the quickness of his Mind, carry him so much after the Notions themselves, that for the most part he is too warm to judg of the aptness of Words, and the justness of Figures; so that he either neglects these too much or overdoes them." (Burnet's "Preface" to his trans. of More's *Utopia* [London, 1684], sig. A3 and [A3]ᵛ.)

50. As the OED explains, the archaic form *effigies*—likeness, image, portrait . . .—is now superseded by *effigy*, except "as humourously pedantic."

51. P. P.'s political involvements and pretensions parody the Bishop's tendency to consider history in theological terms and to bring political emphasis to pastoral matters. In 1712 he had written a new preface to the third edition of his *Discourse of the Pastoral Care* (London, 1713). Here he discussed the distinctions between High and Low Churchmen, with the political implications of their positions: "This is a short Account of the *Low* Churchmens Notions, with Relation to Matters of Religion among us: As to our temporal Concerns, they think all that Obedience and Submission that is settled by our Laws, to the Persons of our Princes, ought to be paid them for Conscience sake: But if a misguided Prince shall take on him to dissolve our Constitution, and to subject the Laws to his Pleasure, they think that if God offers a Remedy, it is to be received with all Thankfulness. For these Reasons they rejoyced in the Revolution, and continue Faithful and True to the Settlement then made; and to the subsequent Settlements" ([A6ᵛ–A7]; the original in reverse italics). "Every Look in the *Low* Church-man towards a Popish Pretender, is to him both Perjury and Treason" ([A7]ᵛ).

52. On 5 November 1709 Dr. Henry Sacheverell had preached an inflammatory sermon, *The Perils of False Brethren,* which reiterated his usual attacks against Whigs, dissenters, latitudinarians, Low Churchmen, the Hanoverian succession, and the principles of the Glorious Revolution. His subsequent impeachment and trial in 1710 aroused a storm of High Church-Tory agitation and helped bring about the fall of the Whig ministry. Despite this, many of the leading Tories apparently disliked him. (See Swift, *Journal to Stella,* ed. Harold Williams [Oxford: Clarendon Press, 1948], I, 342: "And Sacheverell will be the next bishop? He would be glad of an addition of two hundred pounds a year to what he has; and that is more than they will give him, for aught I see. He hates the new ministry mortally, and they hate him, and pretend to despise him too. They will not allow him to have been the occasion of the late change; at least some of them will not: but my lord keeper owned it to me t'other day." Later he

recounts [II, 469] meeting Sacheverell, for whose brother he helped secure a post: "I will let Sacheverell know this, that he may take his measures accordingly; but he shall be none of my acquaintance.") Burnet was very much involved in the Sacheverell fracas: he was personally insulted in the sermon (where Sacheverell had wickedly cited Burnet's own early—and now very embarrassing—arguments for nonresistance) and, after impeachment proceedings began, an inflamed mob gutted a meeting house close by the bishop's London residence and threatened his own house, before which "one, with a spade, cleft the skull of another, who would not shout as they did" (Burnet, *History,* V, 430).

53. Applied to Nonconformists, *Fanatick,* like *Enthusiast,* was a term of opprobrium in a period which was generally hostile to dissenters. *Gentile,* a now obsolete synonym for heathen or pagan.

54. In the life of his father appended to the *History,* Thomas Burnet reported on the Bishop's life in Clerkenwell (where he lived for his last six years) and his gathering there with a "most select and intimate acquaintance"—distinguished members of the right wing of the Whig party. As Burnet's later biographer, Miss Foxcroft, comments, "Such exclusive intercourse however with the members of a single party cannot have tended to enlarge the political views of the Bishop." (Foxcroft, *Life of Burnet,* p. 441.)

55. *The Post Boy* and Dyer's *News Letter* were two early periodicals, both in existence before the succession of Queen Anne. Handwritten newsletters, such as John Dyer's, were common in the late seventeenth century, with a fairly wide circulation among the country squires. So popular were they, in fact, that the other well-known newsletter, Dawk's, was printed in script letters to simulate the manuscript form. Abel Roper's *Post Boy* became one of the most important of the periodicals and the leading Tory organ.

56. Again there is the question of names and how far one can push satiric possibilities. Since three are very common surnames, it is not difficult to locate candidates for them (and even for Pilcocks if one accepts the audial equivalency of *Sherlock*), but, as in earlier instances, no convincing pattern emerges.

57. While it seems unlikely that this is an ironic allusion to Sir Lionel Jenkins, secretary of state under Charles II, his "character" by Burnet (a typical device of the *History*) may well illustrate the characteristic style that is being parodied in these portraits:

> He was a man of exemplary life, and considerably learned: but he was dull and slow: he was suspected of leaning to popery, though very unjustly: but he was set on every punctilio of the church of England to superstition, and was a great assertor of the divine right of monarchy, and was for carrying the prerogative high: he neither spoke nor writ well: but being so eminent for the most courtly qualifications, other matters were the more easily dispensed with. (Burnet, *History,* II, 245.)

58. Since in his flight from Cromwell's soldiers the future Charles II had been sheltered by an oak tree (later celebrated as the Royal Oak), oak sprays became a Jacobite symbol.

59. *Servitor* is an ambiguous designation. Commonly meaning a manservant (chiefly one who waited table), in certain Oxford colleges it referred to a class of undergraduate members who received their lodging and most of their board free and were excused lecture fees. The OED further notes, "Originally the servitors acted as servants to the fellows, and although the requirement of menial services from them gradually fell into disuse, they continued to be regarded as socially the inferiors of the Commoners." Burnet was all too prone to press family connections, even when they were irrelevant (see n. 7; or "Waristoun was my own uncle: [but I will not be more tender in giving his character, for all that nearness in blood:]" [Burnet, *History*, I, 48]).

60. One of the central complaints against Burnet's *History* was that he had so aggrandized his role in the events he was narrating. As he himself announced in the preface, "And now for above thirty years I have lived in such intimacy with all who have had the chief conduct of affairs, and have been so much trusted, and on so many important occasions employed by them, that I have been able to penetrate far into the true secrets of counsels and designs." (Burnet, *History*, I, 4.)

61. The *History* was originally written with the biographical and historical strands interwoven, with the "life" the narrative thread; it was in 1702–03 that the work was revised to place the events of the author's life in a supplementary section, later reworked for publication by his son. In part the revision was prompted by the appearance of a tract, subtitled "With . . . the Discovery of a certain Secret History not yet published," which "leaked" certain of Burnet's strictures against the clergy, which he consequently modified. (H. C. Foxcroft, *A Supplement to Burnet's History of My Own Time* [Oxford: Clarendon Press, 1902], pp. xii–xv.)

62. Although Burnet had originally planned his *History* to cover the fifty years from May 1660, the impending peace led him to extend his work to July 1713: "I am now come to the end of the war and of this parliament both at once: it was fit they should bear some proportion to one another; for as this was the worst parliament I ever saw, so no assembly, but one composed as this was, could have sat quiet under such a peace. But I am now arrived at my full period, and so shall close this work. I had a noble prospect before me, in the course of many years, of bringing it to a glorious conclusion; now the scene is so fatally altered, that I can scarce restrain myself from giving vent to a just indignation in severe complaints. . . . (Burnet, *History*, VI, 168.) It was against such attacks and in defense of Queen Anne and the ministry, that Swift had written his own *History of the Four Last Years of the Queen* (". . . the chief cause of my writing was, not to

let such a Queen and Ministry be under such a load of infamy, or posterity be so
ill informed . . ." [*The Correspondence of Jonathan Swift,* ed. Harold Williams
(Oxford: Clarendon Press, 1963), V, 63]). Though not published until 1758, it
was written in 1712–13 and was very much in Swift's thoughts during the
probable periods of composition of the P. P. *Memoirs* (see *ibid.,* II, 36, 46).

63. The Treaty of Utrecht, which ended the War of the Spanish Succession,
was finally signed in April 1713, after a long period of interrupted peace negotiations marked by contention between Whigs and Tories. The general election of
1710 had brought to power a Tory ministry (involving the earl of Oxford, the
duke of Ormonde, and Lords Harcourt and Bolingbroke) which was committed
to making the peace.

64. A small European freshwater fish prized for food. All too appropriately it
had a colloquial meaning at the time of simpleton or fool.

65. P. P.'s rather anticlimactic epitaph stands in marked contrast to Bishop
Burnet's formidably long Latin one (Nichols, *Literary Anecdotes of the 18th Century*
[1812], I, 283–84). Dr. Arbuthnot had provided some lines too (in Latin *and*
English) for his bishop (see *Introduction,* n. 17) including "Many have had *purer
Doctrine* / No one Stronger Sides and Lungs"; and Swift was reported to have
chalked the following epitaph on a tombstone in the close of Burnet's see:

> Here Sarum lies, who was as wise
> And learn'd as Tom Aquinas;
> Lawn sleeves he wore, yet was no more
> A Christian than Socinus.
> Oaths pro and con he swallowed down,
> Loved gold like any layman;
> He preached and prayed, and yet betrayed
> God's holy church and mammon.
> If such a soul to heaven stole
> And passed the devil's clutches,
> I do presume there may be room
> For Marlbro' and his Duchess.
>   (Hist. MSS Comp. Rep. VI 468.)

Stradling *versus* Stiles.

INTRODUCTION

S hakespeare put it more bluntly—"The first thing we do, let's kill all
the lawyers"—and Dickens more memorably in the great chapters on
Chancery in *Bleak House*. But the Scriblerians were deadly too in their
attacks on legal practices and procedures. Swift (especially), Pope,[1] Gay,
Arbuthnot (whose John Bull series was initiated with the pamphlet *Law
is a Bottomless Pit*)—all individually satirized law and lawyers. Collectively,
they collaborated on Chapter XV of the *Memoirs*: *"Of the Strange and never
to be parallel'd Process at Law upon the Marriage of Scriblerus, and the
Pleadings of the Advocates."* It was this episode which no doubt prompted
Stradling versus Stiles, for Chapter XVI of the *Memoirs* announces:

> But we must not here neglect to mention, that during the whole Course
> of this Process, his continual attendance on the Courts in his own Cause,
> and his invincible Curiosity for all that past in the Causes of others, gave
> him a wonderful insight into this Branch of Learning, which must be
> confess'd to have been so improved by the Moderns, as beyond all compar-
> ison to exceed the Ancients. From the day his first Bill was filed, he began
> to collect *Reports*; and before his Suit was ended, he had time abundantly
> sufficient to compile a very considerable Volume. His Anger at his ill success
> caus'd him to destroy the greatest part of these *Reports*; and only to preserve
> such, as discover'd most of the Chicanery and Futility of the practice. These
> we have some hopes to recover, if they were only mislaid at his Removal;
> if not, the world will be enough instructed to lament the loss, by the only
> one now publick, viz. The *Case of* Stradling *and* Stiles, *in an Action concerning
> certain* black *and* white Horses.[2]

This separate little Scriblerian burlesque, a parody of a lawsuit with its
absurd argument propounded in the equally absurd (if all too real) jargon
of the courts, was, Pope told Spence, written by him "with the help of a
lawyer,"[3] Spence commenting "and by what he added, it seemed to be the
late Master of the Rolls, Fortescue."[4] Certainly by 1716, when he was
probably at work on the piece (not published, however, until 1727, in the
second volume of the *Miscellanies*), Pope had become good friends with the
legal adviser of the Scriblerus Club, William Fortescue, who the year
before had been called to the bar. It remained a lifelong friendship, with
Fortescue's help here in technical matters typical of the interest and generosity acknowledged later in the First Satire of the Second Book of Horace:

> I come to Council learned in the Law.
> You'll give me, like a Friend both sage and free,
> Advice; and (as you use) without a Fee.[5]

Despite Pope's esteem for his adviser and friend, the law was still fair game, even if this satire was somewhat peripheral to the main thrust—if not the spirit—of the Scriblerian project with its Martinus-centered attack on the follies of the "learned" rather than on broader, institutionalized absurdities. In fact, the nature of the satire in this piece makes an interesting link with *Gulliver's Travels*—the reference suggested in Chapter XVI again of the *Memoirs,* where, in the passage following the one cited above, is to be found: "We cannot wonder that he contracted a violent Aversion to the *Law,* as is evident from a whole Chapter of his Travels."[6] Complicated as is the relationship between the projected travels of Martinus and those of Gulliver,[7] the allusion is clearly to the fifth chapter of Part IV, Swift's longest attack on law and lawyers as Gulliver explains the English legal system to his Houyhnhnm Master. The section begins, "I said there was a Society of Men among us, bred up from their Youth in the Art of proving by Words multiplied for the Purpose, that *White* is *Black,* and *Black* is *White,* according as they are paid."[8] Gulliver illustrates the point by the example of a man's futile attempt to defend his right to his own property, a cow. Swift then goes on to cite the techniques of lawyers to dwell on irrelevant circumstances, always consulting precedents, appropriate or not, with as many adjournments as possible to forestall decisions. And he observes, toward the end of the section, ". . . this Society hath a peculiar Cant and Jargon of their own, that no other Mortal can understand, and wherein all their Laws are written, which they may take special Care to multiply; whereby they have wholly confounded the very Essence of Truth and Falshood, of Right and Wrong; so that it will take Thirty Years to decide whether the Field, left me by my Ancestors for six Generations, belong to me, or to a Stranger three Hundred Miles off."[9]

Stradling versus Stiles is indeed a case in point. It is, however, a lighthearted example of such legal quibbling, a reductio ad absurdum with none of the virulence that marks Swift's account. But there are all the irrelevancies, all the gratuitous citations, all the hedgings, and the final splendid inconclusiveness that Swift describes. Given the difficulty of pinpointing dates for Scriblerus papers, it is not profitable to speculate here on who might have been influencing whom; rather, once again, we see the two satirist-friends proceeding "side by side . . . and walking hand in hand to posterity. . . ."[10]

Notes

1. A glance, in *A Concordance to the Poems of Alexander Pope* (ed. Bedford and Dilligan [Detroit, Michigan: Gale Research Co., 1974]), at such entries as *Bar, Bench, Judges, Lawyer, Lawyer's, Lawyers* . . . will suggest the range and spirit of Pope's views (e.g., "Plundered by Thieves, or Lawyers which is worse" or "And [all the Plagues in one] the bawling Bar").

2. *Memoirs,* p. 164.

3. *Anecdotes,* I, 57.

4. Ibid.

5. TE IV, 5.

6. *Memoirs,* p. 164.

7. This matter is reviewed at length by Professor Kerby-Miller in his edition of the *Memoirs,* pp. 315–20.

8. *Gulliver's Travels,* ed. Herbert Davis (Oxford: Basil Blackwell, 1965), p. 248.

9. Ibid., p. 250.

10. *Correspondence,* II, 426.

NOTE ON PUBLICATION AND TEXT

In one of the 1742 printings of the *Memoirs* (Griffith 566) there appears a concluding advertisement of "Pieces *of* Scriblerus *(written in his Youth)* *already published,*" which lists "The *Report* of a *Case* in an *Action at Law* concerning certain *Pyed,* or *Black* and *White* Horses." This is *Stradling versus Stiles,* first published in the Pope-Swift *Miscellanies,* although originally composed much earlier.

According to Professor Kerby-Miller, this legal spoof was probably drafted in 1716[1] about the time Pope was working on the Double Mistress episodes which prompted it.[2] The piece was not published until 1727, when it was included in the second volume of the *Miscellanies,* to be reprinted in the editions of 1730, 1733, 1736, and 1742. While it was not included (perhaps, Kerby-Miller thinks, because of copyright difficulties)[3] in the 1741 *Prose Works* with the *Memoirs* and most of the other previously published Scriblerian tracts, Warburton added it to the collection in his 1751 edition of the *Works.*

Since there are no significant substantive changes after the first edition beyond an early substitution of *Inspection* for *Injunction* in the last lines of the text, a change from a more appropriate legal term which suggests a printer's error, the first edition has been used as a copytext with the few, minor variants recorded in notes. (The only other changes that occur involve unimportant punctuation, capitalization, italicization, and spelling.) To complete the history of the text, the 1751 edition has been included in the collation.

Playing on ironic authenticity, the original texts used—along with the jargonish legal French—occasional black letter. Black letter (or "Gothic" letter) was devised by the inventors of printing for sacred works—in imitation of the formal hand of German monastic scribes. Appearing first in England with Caxton and used extensively by all the early presses, black letter persisted in English printing to a late date, being used for bibles, law books, royal proclamations, and acts of Parliament. For ease in reading, small capitals have been substituted for black letter in this text, a practice followed too in the annotations.

Key to the Critical Apparatus

1727 = *Miscellanies in Prose and Verse,* Second Vol., octavo, Griffith 185.
1730 (dated 1731) = Second Vol. duodecimo, Griffith 243.
1733 = Second Vol., second edition, duodecimo, Griffith 285.

1736 = Second Vol., duodecimo, Griffith 436, 437.
1742 = *Miscellanies* (in Four Volumes), Second Vol., sm. octavo, Griffith 562.
1751 = *Works,* ed. Warburton, Vol. VI, octavo, Griffith 648.

Notes

1. *Memoirs,* p. 46.

2. Having discovered what is apparently part of the first draft of the Double Mistress on the back of some of Pope's *Iliad* manuscript sheets, Professor Sherburn surmised that the fragment got into Pope's pile of scrap paper early in the autumn of 1717. (*Memoirs,* Appendix IV, p. 364.)

3. Ibid., p. 65n.

Stradling *versus* Stiles.

Le Report del Case[1] argue en le commen Banke[2] devant touts les Justices de mesme le Banke en le quart. An. du raygne de Roy *Jacques* entre *Matthew Stradling* Plaint. et *Peter Styles* Def.[3] en un Action propter certos Equos coloratos *Anglice* PYED-HORSES port per le dit *Matthew* vers le dit *Peter.*

Le recitel del Case. SIR John Swale, OF Swale-Hall IN Swale-Dale, FAST BY THE RIVER Swale, KT.[4] MADE HIS LAST-WILL AND TESTAMENT: IN WHICH, AMONG OTHER BEQUESTS WAS THIS, *viz.* Out of the kind Love and Respect that I bear unto my much honoured and good Friend Mr.

A *Matthew Stradling,* Gent. I do bequeath unto the said Mr. Matthew Stradling, *Gent. all my black and white Horses.* THE TESTATOR HAD SIX BLACK HORSES, SIX WHITE HORSES, AND SIX PYED HORSES.

THE DEBATE THEREFORE WAS, WHETHER OR NO THE SAID

Le Point. Matthew Stradling SHOULD HAVE THE SAID PYED HORSES BY VIR-TUE OF THE SAID BEQUEST.

Pour le Pl. Atkins APPRENTICE[5] POUR LE Pl. MOI SEMBLE QUE LE Pl. RE-COVERA.

AND FIRST OF ALL IT SEEMETH EXPEDIENT TO CONSIDER, WHAT IS THE nature of Horses, AND ALSO WHAT IS THE nature of Colours;

B AND SO THE ARGUMENT WILL CONSEQUENTIALLY DIVIDE ITSELF
C INTO A TWOFOLD WAY, THAT IS TO SAY, THE Formal Part, AND
D the Substantial Part. Horses ARE THE Substantial Part OR THING
E BEQUEATHED: Black and White THE Formal AND DESCRIPTIVE PART.

Horse IN A PHYSICAL SENSE DOTH IMPORT a certain Quadrupede or four-footed Animal, which by the apt and regular disposition of certain proper and convenient Parts, is adapted, fitted and consti-tuted for the use and need of Man. YEA, SO NECESSARY AND CON-DUCIVE WAS THIS ANIMAL CONCEIVED TO BE TO THE BEHOOF OF THE COMMON-WEAL, THAT SUNDRY AND DIVERS ACTS OF PAR-LIAMENT HAVE FROM TIME TO TIME BEEN MADE in favour of Horses.

1st Edw. VI. MAKES THE TRANSPORTING OF Horses OUT OF THE KINGDOM, NO LESS A PENALTY THAN THE FORFEITURE OF 40 l.[6]

2d & 3d Edw. VI. TAKES FROM Horsestealers THE BENEFIT OF THEIR CLERGY.[7]

And the Statutes of the 27th and 32d of Hen. VIII. CONDESCEND SO FAR AS TO TAKE CARE OF THEIR VERY Breed:[8] THESE OUR WISE ANCESTORS PRUDENTLY FORESEEING, THAT THEY COULD NOT BETTER TAKE CARE OF THEIR OWN POSTERITY, THAN BY ALSO TAKING CARE OF THAT OF THEIR Horses.

AND OF SO GREAT ESTEEM ARE Horses IN THE EYE OF THE COMMON-LAW, THAT WHEN A Knight of the Bath COMMITTETH A ANY GREAT OR ENORMOUS CRIME, HIS PUNISHMENT IS TO HAVE HIS Spurs chopt off with a Cleaver,[9] BEING, AS MASTER Bracton B WELL OBSERVETH, unworthy to ride on an Horse.[10]

Littleton, Sect. 315.[11] saith, IF TENANTS IN COMMON MAKE A LEASE RESERVING FOR RENT a Horse, THEY SHALL HAVE BUT ONE ASSIZE, BECAUSE, saith the Book, THE LAW WILL NOT SUFFER a Horse to be severed. ANOTHER ARGUMENT OF WHAT HIGH ESTIMATION THE LAW MAKETH OF AN HORSE.

BUT AS THE GREAT DIFFERENCE SEEMETH NOT TO BE SO MUCH TOUCHING THE SUBSTANTIAL PART, Horses, LET US PROCEED TO THE FORMAL OR DESCRITIVE PART, viz. WHAT HORSES THEY ARE THAT COME WITHIN THIS BEQUEST.

COLOURS ARE COMMONLY of various Kinds and different Sorts; OF WHICH White AND Black ARE THE TWO EXTREAMS, AND CONSEQUENTLY comprehend within them all other Colours whatsoever.

BY A BEQUEST THEREFORE of black and white Horses, grey or C pyed Horses may well pass; FOR WHEN TWO EXTREAMS, OR REMOTEST ENDS OF ANY THING ARE DEVISED, THE LAW BY COMMON INTENDMENT[12] WILL INTEND whatsoever is contained between them to be devised too.

BUT THE PRESENT CASE IS STILL STRONGER, COMING NOT ONLY WITHIN THE INTENDMENT, BUT ALSO THE VERY LETTER OF THE WORDS.

BY THE WORD Black, ALL THE HORSES THAT ARE black are devised; BY THE WORD White, ARE DEVISED THOSE THAT are

white; AND BY THE SAME WORD, WITH THE CONJUNCTION COP-
ULATIVE, And, BETWEEN THEM, the Horses that are black and
white, THAT IS TO SAY, pyed, are devised also.

WHATEVER IS black and white IS pyed, AND WHATEVER is pyed
IS black and white; *ergo,* Black and White IS Pyed, AND *vice versa,*
Pyed IS Black and White.

IF THEREFORE Black and White Horses ARE DEVISED, Pyed
Horses shall pass by such devise, but Black and White Horses are
devised, *ergo* the Pl. shall have the Pyed Horses.

Pour le   A   Catlyne SERJAUNT,[13] MOY SEMBLE AL CONTRARY, THE PLAIN-
Defend.   TIFF SHALL not have the Pyed Horses by Intendment; FOR IF BY
THE DEVISE OF Black and White Horses, NOT ONLY BLACK AND
WHITE HORSES, BUT HORSES OF ANY COLOUR BETWEEN THESE
TWO EXTREAMS MAY PASS, then not only Pyed and Grey Horses,
but also Red or Bay Horses would pass likewise, which would be
absurd and against Reason. AND THIS IS ANOTHER STRONG AR-
GUMENT IN LAW, *nihil quod est contra rationem est licitum,*[14] for Reason
is the Life of the Law, NAY, THE Common Law is nothing but
Reason; WHICH IS TO BE UNDERSTOOD OF artificial Perfection and
Reason GOTTEN BY LONG STUDY, AND not of Man's natural Reason,
FOR *nemo nascitur Artifex,* AND Legal Reason *est summa ratio;*[15] AND
THEREFORE IF ALL THE REASON THAT IS DISPERSED INTO SO MANY
DIFFERENT HEADS, WERE UNITED INTO ONE, HE COULD NOT
MAKE SUCH A LAW AS THE LAW OF England; BECAUSE BY MANY
B   SUCCESSIONS OF AGES IT HATH BEEN FIXED AND REFIXED BY
GRAVE AND LEARNED MEN; SO THAT THE OLD RULE MAY BE
VERIFIED IN IT, *Neminem oportet esse legibus sapientiorem.*[16]

AS THEREFORE Pyed Horses DO NOT COME WITHIN THE IN-
TENDMENT OF THE BEQUEST, SO NEITHER DO THEY WITHIN THE
LETTER OF THE WORDS.

A Pyed Horse IS NOT A White Horse, NEITHER IS A Pyed a Black
Horse; HOW THEN CAN Pyed Horses COME UNDER THE WORDS OF
Black and White Horses?

BESIDES, WHERE CUSTOM HATH ADAPTED A CERTAIN DETER-
MINATE NAME TO ANY ONE THING, IN ALL DEVISES,[17] FEOF-
MENTS,[18] AND GRANTS, that certain Name shall be made use of,
and no uncertain circumlocutory Descriptions shall be allowed; FOR

Certainty is the Father of Right and the Mother of Justice.

A   Le reste del Argument jeo ne pouvois oyer, car jeo fui disturb en mon place.

B   Le Court fuit longement en doubt de cest Matter; et apres grand deliberation eu,

   Judgment fuit donne pour Le Pl. nisi causa.

Motion in Arrest of Judgment,[19] that the Pyed Horses were
C Mares; and thereupon an Injunction was prayed.

   Et sur ceo le Court advisare vult.[20]

Textual Variants

Title: A/SPECIMEN/OF/SCRIBLERUS'S REPORTS. *Add. 1742–51.*
Page 136: A. Mr. *Om. 1742.*
Page 136: B. CONSEQUENTIALLY] CONSEQUENTLY *1736–51.*
Page 136: C. INTO] IN *1736–51.*
Page 136: D. the *Om. 1736–51.*
Page 136: E. AND] OR *1742–51.*
Page 137: A. OR] AND *1733–51.*
Page 137: B. an] a *1733–51.*
Page 137: C. FOR] SO *1733.*
Page 138: A. AL] AT *1736;* AL' *1751.*
Page 138: B. HATH] HAS *1736, 1751.*
Page 139: A. disturb] distrub *1727–36.*
Page 139: B. CEST] C'EST *1751.*
Page 139: C. Injunction] Inspection *1731–36, 1751.*

Annotations

1. "The report of the case argued in the Court of Common Pleas before all the Justices of that same Bench in the fourth year of the reign of King James between Matthew Stradling, Plaintiff, and Peter Styles, Defendant, in an action over certain colored horses—in English "pied-horses"—brought by the said Matthew against the said Peter."

Although Latin was the language of formal court records (usually printed in black letter) up until 1731, the use of French for instruction, pleading, and casual records carried down from the Middle Ages into the eighteenth century—despite the interim of the Commonwealth, when only English was allowed. In his *Discourse on the Study of Laws,* Roger North (1653–1734), lawyer and historian, argued: "For really the Law is scarce expressible properly in English, and, when it is done, it must be *Françoise,* or very uncouth." "A man may be a wrangler, but never a lawyer, without a knowledge of the authentic books of law in their genuine language [French]." "Some may think that because the law French is no better than the old Norman corrupted, and now a deformed hotch-potch of the English and Latin mixed together, it is not fit for a polite spark to foul himself with; but this nicety is so desperate a mistake, that laywer and law French are coincident; one will not stand without the other." (London: C. Baldwyn, 1824, pp. 13, 14, 11–12.) That law French became more and more Anglicized until it degenerated into a slang can be seen from the passage translated above. What sounds like a parody is actually typical: cf. this description of a case from Andrew Vidian's *The Exact Pleader* (London, 1684):

> C. vers W. & Sa. Feme. Cas port' pur ceo que Feme def' puis Marriage affirme al Plaintiff que elle fuit single woman & sollicit' le plt' a marrier luy. Et que le plt' ad marry luy, per que it fuit trouble en sa ment ad dam' Et adjudge per tout le Court que accon' ne gist pur ceo que le offence del' Cheat fuit per le marriage fait Felony & ferra punie per indictment. (P. 13.)

2. "The COMMON PLEAS, termed otherwise *Common Bench,* is one of the King's Courts. . . . It hath Jurisdiction in all Causes concerning Lands and Inheritances. . . ." (Giles Jacob, *A Law Grammar . . .* [In the Savoy, 1749], p. 100.)

3. Whether the names are significant is conjectural. As the OED notes, John——a——Stiles and John——a——Nokes are usually coupled as fictitious names for parties in law suits. Beyond this, as with the case, there is a nice ambiguity: What is a stile but a straddling device; and, yet, just as Matthew's position straddles the color issue, so does "stile" have an appropriately counter legal meaning: "Authorized form [in Scots Law] for drawing up a deed or instrument" or "In generalized sense: Legal technicality of language or construction" (OED).

4. In J. S. Fletcher's *Picturesque History of Yorkshire* (3 vols., London: Dent, 1899–), there is an account of a Sir Soloman Swale of Swale Hall, Swalesdale, "famous as a litigant." His suits in Chancery in the first decades of the eighteenth century—over which he wasted the family fortune—might have been known to Fortescue, then a law student.

5. "In like Manner you may be deemed a Lawyer in some competent Degree, when, as a Learner, You shall become acquainted with the Principles, Causes and Elements of the Law. It will not be convenient, by Severe Study, or at the Expence of the best of your Time, to pry into Nice Points of Law; such like Matters may be left to your Judges and Counsel, who in *England* are called *Serjeants at Law,* and others well Skilled in it, whom in Common Speech We call *Apprentices* of the

Law . . ." (Sir John Fortescue, *De Laudibus Legum Angliae* [in the Savoy, 1737], pp. 14–15). "Apprentices" originally were trained in the Inns of Court and the Inns of Chancery; but by the eighteenth century the Inns had lost their collegiate character and became, rather, professional bodies with the privilege of admitting their members to practice in the courts. Students learned by a private course of reading or by being articled to a practicing attorney. See also n. 13.

6. Anno. 1. Edw. 6. cap. 5.

7. Anno. 2. Edw. 6. cap. 33.

8. Anno. 27. Hen. 8. cap. 6; Anno. 32. Hen. 8. cap. 13.

9. "At the Chapel Door, the King's Master Cook, with a White Apron, and Chopping-knife in his Hand, having a little Table before him, covered with a Linnen-Cloth, as they passed by, said thus unto them.

Gentlemen, You know what a great Oath you have taken, which is to defend the Gospel, succour the Widows and Fatherless, right the Wronged, &c. which, if you perform, and keep, it will be to your great Honour; but if you break it, I must hack off your Spurs from your Heels, as unworthy of this Dignity, which will be a great Dishonour to you, which God forbid."

(*An Historical Account of the* Honourable *Order of the Bath* [London, 1725], pp. 22–23.)

10. Henry de Bracton (Bratton or Bretton) (d. 1268) wrote the first comprehensive treatise on the law in England, "De Legibus et Consuetudinibus Angliae." Although I do not find in Braction the actual observation to which Pope refers, Bracton does record (in discussing the crime of rape and its punishment), "If he should be a knight, his horse for his disgrace shall be stripped of the skin of his upperlip, and his tail cut off close to his rump. . . ." (Ed. and trans., Twiss [London: Longman, 1880], II, 485.)

11. Thomas Littleton (1402–1481), judge and legal author, whose "Tenures" (with Coke's comments) was long the principal authority on English real property law. As Roger North, in the Augustan period, described his work: "A student begins with books that are institutionary, and of them, in the first place, LITTLETON, the text of which is accounted law, and no other book hath that authority" (North, *Discourse on the Study of the Laws,* p. 10). Actually it is Sect. 314 (Lib. III, Cap. IV) which is referred to here.

12. "INTENDMENT, in our Law, signifies the Understanding, Intention and true Meaning of a Thing; which supplies what is not fully expressed or apparent." (Jacob, *A Law Grammar,* p. 130.)

13. See also n. 5. In a history going back to the Middle Ages, the serjeants, whether at the bench or at the bar, were leaders of the legal profession, the order from which judges were appointed. During this period they had a monopoly of

practice in the Court of Common Pleas, though their power and prestige were beginning to wane.

14. Or, as Giles Jacob put it ("Of Maxims and General Rules"): *"Quod est inconveniens, & contra Rationem non est permissum in Lege*: Whatever is inconvenient, and contrary to Reason, is not permitted in the Law." (*A Law Grammar,* p. 54.) Earlier in this work, in section II, "Of Grounds and Principles," Jacob lists first "The *Law of Reason . . .* it is termed the first Rule, that all Things must be ruled by." (P. 4.)

15. ". . . for no one is born ingenious, and Legal Reason is the highest reason. . . ."

16. ". . . no one should be wiser than the laws."

17. Devise: "Is properly where a Man gives away any Lands or Tenements by Will in Writing." (Giles Jacob, *A New Law Dictionary* [In the Savoy, 1729].)

18. Feoffment: "Is a Gift or Grant of any Manors, Messuages, Lands, or Tenements, to another in *Fee,* or to him and his Heirs for ever, by the Delivery of Seisen and Possession of the Thing given or granted. . . ." (Ibid.)

19. "To move in *Arrest of Judgment,* is to shew Cause why Judgment should be staid, notwithstanding Verdict given. . . ." One of the reasons listed as cause for this action is "where Persons are misnamed" or "the Declaration doth not lay in the Thing with Certainty. . . ." (Ibid.)

20. "The rest of the argument I could not hear because I was disturbed at my seat.

The Court was long in doubt about resolving the matter; and after a long deliberation was had

Judgment was given for the plaintive *nisi causa* [except for cause].

[There was a] motion "in Arrest of Judgment" that the pied horses were mares; therefore an injunction was requested.

And on this the Court wished to deliberate."

THOUGHTS
ON
Various Subjects.

INTRODUCTION

In an age self-conscious about wit and elegance in its conversation and correspondence, the practice of keeping (and perusing) commonplace-book collections of aphorisms, sententiae, or bon mots is not surprising. However ironic Swift is being in his "Complete Collection of Genteel and Ingenious Conversation" and its author Simon Wagstaff's account of gathering these "Flowers of Wit, Fancy, Humour, and Politeness":

> I always kept a large Table-Book in my Pocket; and as soon as I left the Company, I immediately entred the choicest Expressions that passed during the Visit. . . . If my favourable and gentle Readers could possibly conceive the perpetual Watchings, the numberless Toyls, the frequent Risings in the Night, to set down several ingenious Sentences, that I suddenly, or accidentally recollected; and which, without my utmost Vigilance, had been irrecoverably lost for ever: If they would consider, with what incredible Diligence, I daily, and nightly attended, at those Houses where Persons of both Sexes, and of the most distinguished Merit used to meet, and display their Talents: With what Attention I listened to all their Discourses, the better to retain them in my Memory; and then, at proper Seasons withdrew unobserved, to enter them in my Table-Book, while the Company little suspected what a notable Work I had then in Embrio. . . .[1]

at the same time he must have been doing much the same thing for himself—though not necessarily in the same way![2] For there exists a pocket notebook of his in which he set down proverbs and sayings,[3] and over the years he published a series of "serious" *Thoughts on Various Subjects*.[4]

Swift's inspiration and model for these "Thoughts" was no doubt La Rochefoucauld, "my Favorite because I found my whole character in him."[5] Although Pope never produced the "Set of Maximes in opposition to all Rochefoucaults Principles"[6] about which he wrote to Swift in 1725, he had apparently made another proposal which did materialize:

> When Dr. Swift and I were in the country for some time together, I happened one day to be saying that 'if a man was to take notice of the reflections that came into his mind on a sudden, as he was walking in the fields or sauntering in his study, there might be several of them perhaps as good as his most deliberate thoughts.' On this hint we both agreed to write down all the volunteer reflections that should thus come into our heads all

the time we stayed there. We did so, and this was what afterwards furnished out the maxims published in our *Miscellanies*. Those at the end of one volume are mine, and those in the other Dr. Swift's.[7]

Here, then, Pope's *Thoughts on Various Subjects* from Vol. II of the *Miscellanies* (Swift's, an expansion of his earlier collection in the 1711 *Miscellanies in Prose and Verse*, appearing in Vol. I). But Pope's account to Spence is not a very satisfactory accounting. The "some time" that he and Swift were in the country together would have been the several days of July 1714 at Letcombe (more likely, given, as we shall see, the style of the Thoughts) or the spring and summer of 1726. Or, there is Herbert Davis's contention in his "Conversation of the Augustans" that what we read here are the bon mots from actual Scriblerian conversations ("even if in their printed form they have been carefully cut and polished"),[8] without, generally, the impersonal and aphoristic quality of Swift's earlier series. Neither argument for spontaneity, though, recognizes that a good number of these "volunteer reflections" can be found in Pope's correspondence (see annotations), going back as early as the first recorded letter in 1704. Just as the Swift/Wagstaff conversational gems have been traced to contemporary books of proverbs rather than to spot recordings, "hot as he heard them,"[9] so Pope's maxims must be considered studied observations, more "literary" and well remembered[10] than sudden insights, hot as he thought them or uttered them in unrestrained Scriblerian company—as Davis would have it.

The identified aphorisms come largely from Pope's early, very self-conscious letters—in fact, his mannered exchanges with Wycherley read like the dialogue of a Restoration comedy. For the twenty or so *bon* phrases that he collected in the *Thoughts,* there are just as many that might have been:

As a Man in love with a Mistress, desires no Conversation but hers, so a Man in love with himself, (as most Men are) may be best pleased with his own.[11]

. . . if a Man be a Coxcomb, Solitude is his best School; and if he be a Fool, it is his best Sanctuary.[12]

. . . the great dealers in Wit, like those in Trade, take least Pains to set off their Goods; while the Haberdashers of small Wit, spare for no Decorations or Ornaments.[13]

Conceit is to Nature what *Paint* is to Beauty; it is not only needless, but impairs what it wou'd improve[14]

A mutual commerce makes Poetry flourish; but then Poets like Merchants, shou'd repay with something of their own what they take from others; not like Pyrates, make prize of all they meet.[15]

It is the unfortunate consequence of a compliment, that a man, for hearing a good deal more than his due said of him by another, must afterwards say a great deal less than his due of himself.[16]

And on and on. Since he writes in these terms, it is not surprising to find him mentioning maxims on several occasions ("It is certainly the truest maxim in nature that no people are to be so little feared, or so easy to be satisfied with the common course of our actions and addresses, as those of the highest pitch of understanding")[17] and he counsels Wycherley, whose works he was editing for publication, "it is . . . my sincere Opinion, that the greater Part would make a much better Figure, as *Single Maxims* and *Reflections* in Prose, after the manner of your favourite *Rochefoucaut,* than in Verse"[18] (and later he will echo one or two of Wycherley's subsequent "Maxims and Moral Reflections").

If La Rochefoucauld was not the favorite for Pope that he was for Swift and Wycherley ("As L'Esprit, Rochefoucauld, and that sort of people prove that all virtues are disguised vices, I would engage to prove all vices to be disguised virtues. Neither, indeed, is true, but this would be a more agreeable subject, and would overturn their whole scheme"),[19] still Pope's *Thoughts* have some flavor of the master: compare Pope's "I never knew any man in my life, who cou'd not bear anothers misfortunes perfectly like a Christian" with La Rochefoucauld's "We all have enough strength to bear the misfortunes of others"—with perhaps Pope having the edge here.

Later, when Pope revised his Thoughts, adding eleven and dropping thirteen and part of another, he moved in the direction that his correspondence had also taken. As he wrote to Swift in 1729, "it is many years ago since I wrote as a Wit. How many occurrencies or informations must one omit, if one determin'd to say nothing that one could not say prettily? . . . it was not unentertaining to my self to observe, how and by what degrees I ceas'd to be a witty writer; as either my experience grew on one hand, or my affection to my correspondents on the other."[20] Half of the passages he omitted are those that can be traced to the belletristic youthful letters, as those he added echo the political and social concerns of the correspondence of the thirties, that less "imitative" period. But even earlier, in the original series, the bulk of the observations that found their way into the *Miscellanies* were more moral and political than the predominantly urbane and literary ones which adorn the correspondence of that time. As such, Pope's Thoughts—early and late—are not unlike Swift's. What essentially distingishes the two collections is that Pope's are stylistically more cadenced, more antithetically balanced: the writer of couplets has a different ear from the prose master, with his pithy punchlines. Together, the two series stand both as models of Augustan "conversational style" and as testimonials, in however inverted a way, of the impact such conversation is thought to have exerted on the prose and poetry of the age.[21]

Notes

1. *A Proposal for Correcting the English Tongue, Polite Conversation, Etc.*, ed. Davis and Landa (Oxford: Basil Blackwell, 1964), pp. 100, 121–22. Although Swift did not publish the piece until 1738, the editors argue that it was begun not later than 1704.

2. Mackie L. Jarrell, in "Proverbs in Swift's *Polite Conversation*," *The Huntington Library Quarterly*, 20 (1956), pp. 15–38, argues that actually Swift's "smart turns" were gathered not from drawing rooms but from his reading in contemporary collections of proverbs.

3. Ibid., p. 15.

4. Dated 1706, these first appeared in the *Miscellanies in Prose and Verse*, 1711, and were extended to almost twice their original length for inclusion in the 1727 Pope-Swift *Miscellanies*, with a further collection published by Dodsley in 1745 and reprinted in the Hawkesworth London edition of 1755.

5. *Correspondence*, II, 343.

6. Ibid., II, 333.

7. *Anecdotes*, I, 60.

8. Herbert Davis, "The Conversation of the Augustans" in *The Seventeenth Century*, ed. R. F. Jones et al. (Stanford: Stanford University Press, 1965), p. 184.

9. See Mackie L. Jarrell, "Proverbs in Swift's *Polite Conversation*" (and n. 2).

10. Pope's verbal memory is, of course, remarkable; the letters echo and re-echo with favorite phrases.

11. *Correspondence*, I, 11.

12. Ibid.

13. Ibid., I, 16.

14. Ibid., I, 19.

15. Ibid., I, 20.

16. Ibid., I, 193.

17. Ibid., I, 204; see also I, 198; I, 243; II, 201; II, 315.

18. Ibid., I, 86.

19. *Anecdotes*, I, 219.

20. *Correspondence*, III, 79.

21. James Sutherland, *A Preface to Eighteenth Century Poetry* (Oxford: Clarendon Press, 1958), pp. 65–66.

NOTE ON PUBLICATION AND TEXT

Pope and Swift both gathered "thoughts on various subjects" which "afterwards furnished out the maxims published in our *Miscellanies.* Those at the end of one volume are mine, and those in the other Dr. Swift's" (so Pope reported to Spence).[1] Swift's series, an amplification of those aphorisms published in his 1711 miscellany, are to be found in the first volume of the joint 1727 *Miscellanies in Prose and Verse,* and Pope's in the second.[2] The latter's were reprinted in the 1730 (dated 1731), 1733, and 1736 editions of that volume without real change. Pope then revised the collection considerably, adding and deleting, to use it as the concluding section of the *Letters* of 1737, but those sheets were subsequently cancelled and saved for the 1741 *Works in Prose.* It was that text that was printed, with negligible changes, in *The Second Volume* of the reformed *Miscellanies* of 1742; interestingly enough, when Elwin/Courthope included the piece, as their final selection, they used the earlier text.

Because this work illustrates so graphically Pope's evolving prose style and shifting concerns, the present text reproduces both the original selections (with those passages later deleted set off by brackets) and the 1741 additions, using the numbering system that Pope adopted then and following the other, minor revisions of that text (where there is less capitalization and italicization),[3] with substantive variants noted. (Retention of all the 1727 maxims, many of which reiterate the author's early epistolary witticisms [as the annotations reveal], allows one also to trace more easily the youthful Pope's tendency to echo himself.)

Key to the Critical Apparatus

1727 = *Miscellanies in Prose and Verse,* Second Vol., octavo, Griffith 185.
1730 (dated 1731) = Second Vol., duodecimo, Griffith 243.
1733 = Second Vol., second edition, duodecimo, Griffith 285.
1736 = Second Vol., duodecimo, Griffith 436, 437.
1741 = *Works . . . in Prose,* Vol. II, folio, Griffith 529; l.p. folio, Griffith 530; quarto, Griffith 531.
1742 = *Miscellanies* (in Four Volumes), Second Vol., sm. octavo, Griffith 562.

Notes

1. *Anecdotes,* I, 60.
2. Despite Pope's clear identification, John Hayward, in his edition of Swift's

prose works (London: The Cresset Press, 1949), announces that "In Swift's own annotated copy of the *Miscellanies,* 1727 . . . Swift has marked in volume II those "Thoughts" which he claimed as his" (p. 12). Herbert Davis correctly questions this assumption, especially since those passages so marked include the two designated *T. K.* and *D. A.*; Davis, on the other hand, is willing to attribute the authorship broadly, seeing all the maxims as "the choicest fruits of the conversation of the Scriblerians." ("The Conversation of the Augustans" in *The Seventeenth Century,* ed. R. F. Jones et al. [Stanford: Stanford University Press, 1965], p. 185.)

3. This is consistent with some of David Foxon's observations on Pope's revisions, argued in his unpublished Lyell lectures (see n. 6, pp. xiv–xv).

THOUGHTS
ON
Various Subjects.

I.

Party is the madness of Many, for the gain of a Few. [1]

II.

There never was any Party, Faction, Sect, or Cabal whatsoever, in which the most ignorant were not the most violent: For a Bee is not a busier animal than a Blockhead. However, such instruments are necessary to Politicians; and perhaps it may be with States as with Clocks, which must have some dead weight hanging at them, to help and regulate the motion of the finer and more useful parts. [2]

III.

To endeavour to work upon the Vulgar with fine Sense, is like attempting to hew Blocks with a Razor.

IV.

Fine Sense and exalted Sense are not half so useful as common Sense: [3] There are forty Men of Wit for one man of Sense: And he that will carry nothing about him but Gold, will be every day at a loss for want of readier change.

V.

Learning is like Mercury, one of the most powerful and excellent things in the world in skilful hands; in unskilful, the most mischievous. [4]

VI.

The nicest Constitutions of Government are often like the finest pieces of Clockwork: which depending on so many Motions, are therefore more subject to be out of order.

VII.

Every man has just as much Vanity as he wants Understanding.

VIII.

Modesty, if it were to be recommended for nothing else, this were enough, that the pretending to little leaves a man at ease, whereas Boasting requires a perpetual labour to appear what he is not. If we have Sense, Modesty best proves it to others; if we have none, it best hides our want of it. For as Blushing will sometimes make a Whore pass for a virtuous Woman, so Modesty may make a Fool seem a man of Sense.[5]

IX.

It is not so much the being exempt from Faults, as the having overcome them, that is an advantage to us: it being with the follies of the mind as with the weeds of a field, which if destroy'd and consum'd upon the place of their birth, enrich and improve it more, than if none had ever sprung there.[6]

X.

To pardon those Absurdities in our selves, which we cannot suffer in others, is neither better nor worse than to be more willing to be fools our selves, than to have others so.

XI.

A Man shou'd never be asham'd to own he has been in the wrong, which is but saying, in other words, that he is wiser to day than he was yesterday.

A   [The best way to prove the clearness of our Mind, is by shewing its Faults; as when a Stream discovers the Dirt at the bottom, it convinces us of the transparency and purity of the Water.][7]

XII.

Our Passions are like Convulsion-Fits, which tho' they make us stronger for the time, leave us the weaker ever after.[8]

XIII.

To be angry, is to revenge the fault of others upon our selves.

XIV.

A brave man thinks no one his Superior who does him an injury, for he has it then in his power to make himself superior to the other, by forgiving it.[9]

XV.

To relieve the Oppress'd is the most glorious Act a Man is capable of; it is in some measure doing the business of God and Providence.[10]

A   [I as little fear that God will damn a Man that has Charity, as I hope that the Priests can save one who has not.]

XVI.

Superstition is the Spleen of the Soul.

XVII.

Atheists put on a false courage and alacrity in the midst of their Darkness and apprehensions; like Children, who when they go in the dark, will sing for fear.

XVIII.

An Atheist is but a mad ridiculous derider of Piety, but a Hypocrite makes a sober jest of God and Religion. He finds it easier to be upon his knees, than to rise to do a good Action; like an impudent Debtor, who goes every day and talks familiarly to his Creditor, without ever paying what he owes.

XIX.

What Tully says of War,[11] may be apply'd to disputing, it should be always so manag'd as to remember that the only end of it is Peace: But generally true Disputants are like true Sportsmen, their whole delight is in the pursuit; and a Disputant no more cares for the Truth, than the Sportsman for the Hare.

XX.

The Scripture in time of Disputes is like an open Town in time of War, which serves indifferently the occasions of both Parties; each makes use of it for the present turn, and then resigns it to the next comer to do the same.

XXI.

Such as are still observing upon others, are like those who are always abroad at other mens houses, reforming every thing there, B   while their own runs to ruin.

XXII.

When Men grow virtuous in their old Age, they only make a Sacrifice to God of the Devil's leavings.

A   [Some old Men by continually praising the time of their Youth, would almost perswade us that there were no Fools in those days; but unluckily they are left themselves for Examples.][12]

XXIII.

When we are young, we are slavishly employ'd in procuring some-thing whereby we may live comfortably when we grow old; and
B   when we are old, we perceive it is too late to live as we propos'd.

C   [The World is a thing we must of necessity either laugh at, or be angry at; if we laugh at it, they say we are proud; if we are angry at it, they say we are ill-natur'd.][13]

XXIV.

People are scandaliz'd if one laughs at what they call a serious thing. Suppose I were to have my head cut off to morrow, and all the world were talking of it to day, yet why might not I laugh to think, what a bustle is here about my head?

XXV.

The greatest advantage I know of being thought a Wit by the world, is that it gives one the greater freedom of playing the Fool.

XXVI.

We ought in humanity no more to despise a man for the misfor-tunes of the Mind, than for those of the Body, when they are such as he cannot help. Were this thoroughly consider'd, we should no more laugh at one for having his brains crack'd, than for having his head broke.

XXVII.

A Man of Wit is not incapable of Business, but above it. A sprightly generous Horse is able to carry a Pack-saddle as well as an Ass, but he is too good to be put to the drudgery.[14]

XXVIII.

Whereever I find a great deal of Gratitude in a poor man, I take it for granted, there wou'd be as much Generosity if he were a rich man.

XXIX.

Flowers of Rhetoric in Sermons and serious discourses,[15] are like the blue and red Flowers in Corn, pleasing to those who come only for amusement, but prejudicial to him who would reap the profit from it.

A

XXX.

When two people compliment each other with the choice of any thing, each of them generally gets that which he likes least.

XXXI.

He who tells a lye, is not sensible how great a task he undertakes, for he must be forc'd to invent twenty more to maintain that one.[16]

XXXII.

Giving advice is many times only the privilege of saying a foolish thing one's self, under pretence of hindring another from doing one.

XXXIII.

'Tis with followers at Court, as with followers on the Road, who first bespatter those that go before, and then tread on their heels.

XXXIV.

False Happiness is like false Money, it passes for a time as well as the true, and serves some ordinary occasions: but when it is brought to the touch, we find the lightness and allay, and feel the loss.

XXXV.

Dastardly Men are like sorry Horses, who have but just spirit and mettle enough to be mischievous.

XXVI.

Some people will never learn any thing, for this reason, because they understand every thing too soon.

XXXVII.

A Person who is too nice an observer of the business of the crowd, like one who is too curious in observing the labour of the Bees, will often be stung for his curiosity.

XXXVIII.

A Man of Business may talk of Philosophy, a Man who has none may practice it.

XXXIX.

There are some Solitary wretches who seem to have left the rest of mankind only as Eve left Adam, to meet the Devil in private.

XL.

The Vanity of human life is like a River, constantly passing away, and yet constantly coming on.[17]

XLI.

I seldom see a noble Building, or any great piece of Magnificence and pomp, but I think, how little is all this to satisfy the ambition, or to fill the Idea, of an immortal Soul?[18]

XLII.

'Tis a certain truth, that a man is never so easy or so little impos'd upon, as among people of the best sense: It costs far more trouble to be admitted or continu'd in ill company than in good; as the former have less understanding to be employ'd, so they have more vanity to be pleas'd; and to keep a fool constantly in good humour with himself and with others, is no very easy task.

XLIII.

The difference between what is commonly call'd ordinary company and good company, is only hearing the same things said in a little room, or in a large Salon, at small tables, or at great Tables, before two candles or twenty Sconces.

A   [Two Women seldom grow intimate but at the expence of a third Person; they make Friendships as Kings of old made Leagues, who sacrific'd some poor Animal betwixt them, and commenc'd strict Allies: So the Ladies, after they have pull'd some Character to pieces, are from thenceforth inviolable Friends.][19]

XLIV.

It is with narrow-soul'd people as with narrow-neck'd bottles: The less they have in them, the more noise they make in pouring it out.[20]

XLV.

Many men have been capable of doing a wise thing, more a cunning thing, but very few a generous thing.[21]

XLVI.

Since 'tis reasonable to doubt most things, we should most of all doubt that Reason of ours which wou'd demonstrate all things.

XLVII.

To buy Books, as some do who make no use of them, only because they were publish'd by an eminent Printer, is much as if a man should buy Cloaths that did not fit him, only because they were made by some famous Taylor.

XLVIII.

'Tis as offensive to speak Wit in a fool's company, as it would be ill manners to whisper in it; he is displeas'd at both for the same reason, because he is ignorant of what is said.

A   [A good-natur'd Man has the whole World to be happy out of: Whatever Good befals his Species, a well-deserving Person promoted, a modest Man advanced, an indigent one relieved, all this he looks upon but as a remoter Blessing of Providence on himself; which then seems to make him amends for the narrowness of his own Fortune, when it does the same thing he would have done had it been in his power. For what a luxurious Man in Poverty wou'd want for Horses and Footmen, a goodnatur'd Man wants for his Friend or the Poor.][22]

XLIX.

False Criticks rail at false Wits, as Quacks and Impostors are still cautioning us to beware of Counterfeits, and decry others cheats only to make more way for their own.[23]

L.

Old Men, for the most part, are like old Chronicles, that give you dull but true accounts of times past, and are worth knowing only on that score.

LI.

There should be, methinks, as little merit in loving a Woman for her Beauty, as in loving a Man for his Prosperity; both being equally subject to change.

A   [Wit in Conversation is only a readiness of Thought and a facility of Expression, or (in the Midwives Phrase) a quick Conception and an easy Delivery.][24]

LII.

B   We should manage our Thoughts in composing any work, as Shepherds do their Flowers in making a Garland, first select the choicest, and then dispose them in the most proper places, where
C   they give a lustre to each other. [Like the Feathers in *Indian* Crowns, which are so manag'd that every one reflects a part of its Colour and Gloss on the next.][25]

LIII.

As handsome Children are more a dishonour to a deform'd Father than ugly ones, because unlike himself; so good thoughts, own'd by a Plagiary, bring him more shame than his own ill ones. When a poor thief appears in rich garments, we immediately know they are none of his own.

D   [If he who does an Injury be his own Judge in his own Cause, and does Wrong without Reason, by being the first Agressor; then surely it is no wonder the Injur'd should think the same way, and right himself by Revenge; that is, be both Judge and Party too, since the other was so who first wrong'd him.]

LIV.

Human Brutes, like other beasts, find snares and poison in the
A provisions of life, and are allur'd by their Appetites to their destruction.

LV.

The most positive men are the most credulous; since they most
believe themselves, and advise most with their falsest Flatterer and
worst enemy, their own Self-love.

LVI.

Get your Enemies to read your works, in order to mend them,
for your friend is so much your second-self, that he will judge too
like you. [26]

LVII.

Women use Lovers as they do Cards; they play with 'em a while,
and when they have got all they can by 'em, throw 'em away; call
for new ones, and then perhaps lose by the new ones all they got by
the old ones.

LVIII.

Honour in a Woman's mouth, like the oath in the mouth of a
B Gamester, is ever still most us'd as their truth is most question'd.

C [Your true Jilt uses Men like Chess-Men, she never dwells so long
on any single Man as to over-look another who may prove more
advantagious; nor gives one another's place, till she has seen 'tis for
her Interest; but if one is more useful to her than others, brings
him in over the Heads of all those others.]

LIX.

Women, as they are like riddles in being unintelligible, so generally resemble them in this, that they please us no longer when
once we know them. [27]

LX.

A Man who admires a fine Woman, has yet no more reason to
wish himself her husband, than one who admir'd the Hesperian
Fruit wou'd have had to wish himself the Dragon that kept it.

LXI.

He who marries a wife because he can't always live chastly, is
A much like a man who finding a few humours in his body, resolves
to wear a perpetual blister.

LXII.

Marry'd people, for being so closely united, are but the apter to
part; as knots, the harder they are pull'd, break the sooner.

LXIII.

A Family is but too often a Commonwealth of Malignants: What
we call the Charities and Ties of affinity, prove but so many separate
and clashing interests: the son wishes the death of the father; the
younger brother that of the elder; the elder repines at the sisters
portions: When any of them marry, there are new divisions, and
new animosities. It is but natural and reasonable to expect all this,
and yet we fancy no comfort but in a Family.[28]

LXIV.

Authors in France seldom speak ill of each other, but when they
have a personal pique; Authors in England seldom speak well of
each other, but when they have a personal friendship.

LXV.

There is nothing wanting to make all rational and disinterested
people in the world of one Religion, but that they should talk
together every day.[29]

LXVI.

Men are grateful, in the same degree that they are resentful.[30]

LXVII.

The longer we live, the more we shall be convinc'd, that it is
reasonable to love God, and despise Man, as far as we know either.

B   [It is impossible that an Ill-natured Man can have a Publick-
spirit. For how should he love ten thousand Men, who never loved
one? *T.K.*][31]

LXVIII.

That character in conversation which commonly passes for Agreeable, is made up of civility and falshood.

LXIX.

A short and certain way to obtain the character of a reasonable and wise man, is, whenever any one tells you his opinion, to comply with it.

LXX.

What is generally accepted as Virtue in women, is very different from what is thought so in men: A very good woman would make but a paltry man.

LXXI.

Some people are commended for a giddy kind of Good humour, which is as much a virtue as Drunkenness.

LXXII.

Those people only will constantly trouble you with doing little offices for them, who least deserve you should do them any.

A   [Whoever has flatter'd his Friend successfully, must at once think himself a Knave, and his Friend a Fool.]

B   [We may see the small value God has for Riches, by the People he gives them to. D.A.][32]

C   [Who are next to Knaves? Those that converse with 'em.]

LXXIII.

We are sometimes apt to wonder, to see those people proud who have done the meanest things, whereas a consciousness of having
D done poor things, and a shame of hearing of it, often make the composition we call Pride.

LXXIV.

An Excuse is worse and more terrible than a Lye: For an excuse is a *Lye guarded*.[33]

LXXV.

Praise is like Ambergrise: a little whiff of it, and by snatches, is very agreeable; but when a man holds a whole lump of it to your nose, it is a stink, and strikes you down.[34]

LXXVI.

The general cry is against Ingratitude, but sure the complaint is misplac'd, it shou'd be against Vanity. None but direct villains are capable of wilful Ingratitude; but almost every body is capable of thinking he hath done more than another deserves, while the other thinks he hath receiv'd less than he deserves.

LXXVII.

I never knew any man in my life, who cou'd not bear anothers misfortunes perfectly like a Christian.[35]

LXXVIII.

A   Several Explanations of Casuists, to multiply the Catalogue of Sins may be called *Amendments* to the *Ten Commandments*.

LXXIX.

'Tis observable that the Ladies frequent Tragedies more than Comedies: The reason may be, that in Tragedy their sex is deify'd and ador'd, in Comedy expos'd and ridicul'd.

LXXX.

The Character of covetousness is what a man generally acquires more through some niggardliness, or ill grace, in little and incon-
B   siderable things, than expences of any consequence. A very few pounds a year would ease that man of the scandal of Avarice.

LXXXI.

Some men's Wit is like a dark lanthorn, which serves their own turn, and guides them their own way: but is never known (according to the Scripture Phrase) either to shine forth before Men, or to glorify
C   their Father in heaven.

LXXXII.

It often happens that those are the best people, whose characters have been most injur'd by slanderers: As we usually find that to be the sweetest fruit which the birds have been pecking at.

LXXXIII.

The people all running to the Capital city, is like a confluence of all the animal spirits to the heart, a symptom that the constitution is in danger.

A
LXXXIV.

The wonder we often express at our neighbours keeping dull company, wou'd lessen, if we reflected, that most people seek companions less to be talk'd to, than to talk.

B
LXXXV.

Amusement is the happiness of those that cannot think.

C
LXXXVI.

Never stay dinner for a Clergyman who is to make a morning visit e'er he comes; for he will think it is his duty to dine with any greater man that asks him.

D
LXXXVII.

A contented man is like a good tennis player, who never fatigues and confounds himself with running eternally after the ball, but stays till it comes to him.

E
LXXXVIII.

Two things are equally unaccountable to reason, and not the object of reasoning; the Wisdom of God, and the Madness of Man.[36]

F
LXXXIX.

Many men, prejudic'd early in disfavour of mankind by bad maxims, never aim at making friendships; and while they only think of avoiding the Evil, miss of the Good that would meet them. They begin the world knaves, for prevention, while others only end so, after disappointment.

G
XC.

No woman ever hates a man for having been in love with her; but many a woman hates a man for being a friend to her.

XCI.

The eye of a Critick is often like a Microscope, made so very fine and nice, that it discovers the atoms, grains, and minutest particles, without ever comprehending the whole, comparing the parts, or seeing all at once the harmony.[37]

XCII.

A King may be a Tool, a thing of straw; but if he serves to frighten our enemies, and secure our property, it's well enough: A scarecrow is a thing of straw, but it protects the Corn.

XCIII.

The greatest things and the most praise-worthy, that can be done for the publick good, are not what require great parts, but great honesty: Therefore for a King to make an amiable character, he needs only to be a man of common honesty, well advised.[38]

XCIV.

Notwithstanding the common complaint of the knavery of men in power, I have known no great Minister or man of parts in business, so wicked as their Inferiors; their sense and knowledge preserves them from a hundred common rogueries, and when they become bad, it is generally more from the necessity of their situation, than from a natural bent to evil.[39]

XCV.

Whatever may be said against a Premiere or Sole Minister, the evil of such an one, in an Absolute Government, may not be great: For it is possible that almost any Minister may be a better man than a King born and bred.[40]

XCVI.

A man coming to the water-side, is surrounded by all the crew: every one is officious, every one making applications, every one offering his services; the whole bustle of the place seems to be only for him. The same man going from the water-side, no noise made about him, no creature takes notice of him, all let him pass with utter neglect! The picture of a Minister when he comes into power, and when he goes out.

FINIS.

Textual Variants

Title: THOUGHTS/ON/*Various Subjects*. *1727–36*.
Page 152: A. The . . . Water. *Om. 1741–42*.
Page 153: A. I . . . not. *Om. 1741–42*.
Page 153: B. runs] run *1742*.
Page 154: A. Some . . . Examples. *Om. 1741–42*.
Page 154: B. is *Om. 1733–36*.
Page 154: C. The . . . ill-natur'd. *Om. 1741–42*.
Page 155: A. from it. *Om. 1742*.
Page 156: A. Two . . . Friends. *Om. 1741–42*.
Page 157: A. A . . . Poor. *Om. 1741–42*.
Page 158: A. Wit . . . Delivery. *Om. 1741–42*.
Page 158: B. any work] a Poem *1727–36*.
Page 158: C. Like . . . next. *Om. 1741–42*.
Page 158: D. If . . . him. *Om. 1741–42*.
Page 159: A. Appetites] Appetite *1727–36*.
Page 159: B. Gamester] cheating Gamester *1727–36*.
Page 159: C. Your . . . others. *Om. 1741–42*.
Page 160: A. a man] one *1727–36*.
Page 160: B. It . . . . *T.K. Om. 1741–42*.
Page 161: A. Whoever . . . Fool. *Om. 1741–42*.
Page 161: B. We . . . D. A. *Om. 1741–42*.
Page 161: C. Who . . . 'em. *Om. 1741–42*.
Page 161: D. of it] it *1727–36*; of them *1742*.
Page 162: A. to . . . Sins] by multiplying Sins, *1727–36*.
Page 162: B. than] than in *1727–36, 1742*.
Page 162: C. Father] Father who is *1727–36*.
Page 163: A. LXXXIV. *Add. 1741–42*.
Page 163: B. LXXXV. *Add. 1741–42*.
Page 163: C. LXXXVI. *Add. 1741–42*.
Page 163: D. LXXXVII. *Add. 1741–42*.
Page 163: E. LXXXVIII. *Add. 1741–42*.
Page 163: F. LXXXIX. *Add. 1741–42*.
Page 163: G. XC. *Add. 1741–42*.
Page 164: A. XCI. *Add. 1741–42*.
Page 164: B. XCIII. *Add. 1741–42*.
Page 164: C. XCIV. *Add. 1741–42*.
Page 164: D. Minister or man]. Ministers or men *1742*.
Page 164: E. XCV. *Add. 1741–42*.

Annotations

1. Cf. ". . . party-spirit, which at best is but the madness of many for the gain of a few." (*Correspondence*, I, 247.) This letter was written to Edward Blount on 27 August 1714; it might argue that the Thoughts are, as by Pope's account, essentially the product of his visit with Swift at Letcombe in July (see "Introduction," p. 146).

2. The simile of the clock weight was one that Pope worked over in Wycherley's poem "A Panegyrick on Dulness" ("So Clocks to Lead their nimble Motions owe"); see *Correspondence*, I, 32.

3. Cf. "We talk much of fine sense, refin'd sense, and exalted sense; but for use and happiness give me a little common sense." (*Correspondence*, I, 306.)

4. Believed at the time to be a primal substance found in all metals, mercury also had a popular figurative meaning as an emblem of volatility of temperament, as Pope was to use it in the *Essay on Man*: " 'Tis thus the Mercury of Man is fix'd" (TE III i, 76). Or, in a letter to Martha Blount, writing about "Duke" Disney, "The Duke is too Sedate for me, nothwithstanding he has so much Mercury in him" (*Correspondence*, I, 315). The general idea of the Thought, of course, has been immortalized in "A little learning is a dangerous thing. . . ."

5. In the "Collection of Maxims and Moral Reflections" that Pope persuaded Wycherley to make out of some of his poetic sentiments, there is a comparable observation: "Modesty is the Embellishment of the Body, as of the Mind; and the best Atonement for the Deficiency of Beauty in Women, or Wit in Men." (*The Posthumous Works of William Wycherley Esq; in Prose and Verse* [London, 1728], p. 17.)

6. Cf. ". . . I believe 'tis with the Errors of the Mind as with the Weeds of a Field, which if they are consum'd upon the place, enrich & improve it more, than if none had ever grown there." (*Correspondence*, I, 139.)

7. Cf. "The cleanness and purity of one's mind is never better prov'd, than in discovering its own faults at first view: as when a Stream shows the dirt at its bottom, it shows also the transparency of the water." (*Correspondence*, I, 274.)

8. A metaphor which Pope uses in the *Epistle to a Lady*:

> In this one Passion man can strength enjoy,
> As Fits give vigour, just when they destroy.
>   (TE III ii, 34.)

9. Cf. "Whoever is really brave, has always this comfort when he is oppressed, that he knows himself to be superior to those who injure him. For the greatest power on earth can no sooner do him that injury, but the brave man can make himself greater by forgiving it." (*Correspondence*, I, 335.)

10. Cf. "To relieve the injured (if you will pardon a poetical expression in

prose) is no less than to take the work of God himself off his hands, and an easing Providence of its care: 'Tis the noblest act that human nature is capable of. . . ." (*Correspondence*, I, 119.)

11. Cicero, *De Officiis* I. ll. 35–36: "Quare suscepienda quidem bella sunt ob eam causam, ut sine iniuria in pace vivatur . . ." ("The only excuse, therefore, for going to war is that we may live in peace unharmed . . ." [Loeb (1961), p. 37]). Cicero (Marcus Tullius) was an old favorite: as Pope told Spence, " 'When I came from the last of them [his early schools], all the acquisition I had made was to be able to construe a little of Tully's *Offices*' " (*Anecdotes*, I, 10).

12. This is in the spirit of La Rochefoucauld's "Old people are fond of giving good advice to console themselves for being no longer able to give bad examples" (London: Humphrey Milford, 1939, #93).

13. Cf. " 'Tis very hard, this World is a Thing which every unfortunate Thinking Creature must necessarily either laugh at, or be angry at: And if we laugh at it, People will say we are Proud, if we are angry at it they'l say we are ill-humor'd." (*Correspondence*, I, 315.)

14. Or, as Wycherley put it, "The best Wits make the worst Men of Business, as Beasts of Pleasure are least fit for Burthens." (*The Posthumous Works of William Wycherley*, p. 15.)

15. In justifying his attribution of *The Dignity, Use, and Abuse of Glass-Bottles* to Pope, Norman Ault cites several instances of verbal echoes, one of them this phrase, which he compares with "the most beautiful Flowers of their Pulpit-Rhetorick" from the 1715 "sermon." (*The Prose Works of Alexander Pope, Vol. I* [Oxford: Basil Blackwell, 1936], p. lxxxii.)

16. In a similar vein: "For indeed 'tis the constant character of all fools that they are never contented with saying or doing one foolish thing; they will always commit another to maintain or defend it." (*Correspondence*, I, 93.)

17. The image is one that a youthful Pope had used in an early poem, "The River":

> Thy stream, like his [time's], is never past,
> And yet is ever on the way.

(TE VI, 14.)

18. Cf. "Buildings, Gardens, Writings, Pleasures, Works, of whatever stuff Man can raise! none of them (God knows) capable of advantaging a Creature that is mortal, or of satisfying a Soul that is Immortal!" (*Correspondence*, II, 45.)

19. Cf. " 'Tis a common practice now for ladies to contract friendships as the great folks in ancient times entered into leagues. They sacrificed a poor animal betwixt 'em, and commenced inviolable allies, *ipso facto*; so now they pull some harmless little creature into pieces, and worry his character together very com-

fortably. . . ." (*Correspondence*, I, 170–71.) See also, *A Letter to a Noble Lord*, p. 446.

20. Again (see n. 15) Ault uses a verbal parallel to confirm Pope's authorship of *The Dignity, Use, and Abuse of Glass-Bottles*, citing this Thought and a comparable statement from the Sermon: "But narrow-soul'd Men, like narrow-neck'd Bottles, hold much but give little, nay, and that little too with much Difficulty and murmurings; . . . the less they bestow, the more Noise they make about it." (*The Prose Works of Alexander Pope*, I, lxxix.)

21. There is perhaps an echo of this in the *Epistle to a Lady*:

> She speaks, behaves, and acts just as she ought;
> But never, never, reach'd one genr'ous Thought.
> (TE III ii, 64.)

22. Cf. "Only what a luxurious Man wants for horses and foot-men a good-natur'd Man wants for his friends, or the indigent." (*Correspondence*, I, 169.)

23. Cf. " 'Tis indeed the common Method of all Counterfits in Wit, as well as in Physic, to begin with warning us of others' cheats, in order to make the more way for their owne." (*Correspondence*, I, 139.)

24. Cf. "True Wit I believe, may be defin'd a Justness of Thought, and a Facility of Expression; or (in the Midwives phrase) a perfect Conception, with an easy Delivery." (*Correspondence*, I, 2.) This is just one of a series of *bon* phrases that Pope prepared for his first letter, as a boy of sixteen, to the distinguished Wycherley.

25. Cf. "According to a Simile Mr. *Dryden* us'd in conversation, of Feathers in the Crowns of the wild *Indians*, which they not only chuse for the beauty of their Colours, but place them in such a manner as to reflect a Lustre on each other." (*Correspondence*, I, 34.)

26. In a similar verbal vein: ". . . you have show'd me most of my Faults, to which as you are the more an implacable Enemy, by so much the more are you a Kind Friend to Me." (*Correspondence*, I, 68.)

27. Something of this idea Pope was to use in the *Epistle to a Lady*:

> Woman and Fool are two hard things to hit,
> For true No-meaning puzzles more than Wit.
> (TE III ii, 59.)

28. Cf. "A family nowadays is a little Commonwealth of malignants, where each has a paltry, separate interest from the other. The son wishes the death of the father, the younger brother of the elder, the elder grudges the portion of the sisters; and when any of them marry, then rise new interests and new divisions *in saecula saeculorum*." (*Correspondence*, I, 475.)

29. Cf. "And after all, I verily believe your Lordship and I are both of the same religion, if we were thoroughly understood by one another; and that all

honest and reasonable christians would be so, if they did but talk enough together every day; and had nothing to do together, but to serve God and live in peace with their neighbour." (*Correspondence,* I, 454.)

30. Cf. La Rochefoucauld's ". . . but there is scarcely anyone who has anything but ingratitude for great acts of generosity." (London: Humphrey Milford, 1939, #229.)

31. Cf. "I am certain that whoever wants these, can never have a *Publick-Spirit*; for (as a friend of mine says) how is it possible for that man to love twenty thousand people, who never loved one? (*Correspondence,* I, 357n [textual variant]; see also II, 333.) I have not identified "T.K." beyond Pope's reference to "a friend of mine."

32. Herbert Davis identifies "D. A." as Dr. Arbuthnot ("The Conversation of the Augustans" in *The Seventeenth Century,* ed. R. F. Jones *et al.* [Stanford: Stanford University Press, 1965]).

33. Cf. ". . . if I were not more asham'd to tell a Lye, or to make an Excuse, which is worse than a Lye (for being built upon some probable Circumstance, it makes use of a degree of Truth to falsify with: It is a Lye *Guarded*)." (*Correspondence,* II, 319.)

34. Cf. "For Praise is like Ambergrize; a little unexpected Whiff of it . . . is the most agreeable thing in the world; but when a whole lump of it is thrust to your nose, it is a Stink, and strikes you down." (*Correspondence,* II, 349.) Pope was later to use the image in the *Epistle to Bathurst,* this time talking about wealth:

> In heaps, like Ambergrise, a stink it lies,
> But well-dispers'd, is Incense to the Skies.
> (TE III ii, 111.)

35. Cf. La Rochefoucauld, Maxim #19: "We all have enough strength to bear the misfortunes of others." (London: Humphrey Milford, 1939.)

36. While this makes a good aphorism, Pope's position on the limits of reason is more complex: there are his famous lines in the *Essay on Man* (I, 113–22 [TE III i, 29–30]) but then there is his statement to Spence: "At present we can only reason of the divine justice from what we know of justice in man. When we are in other scenes we may have truer and nobler ideas of it, but while we are in this life we can only speak from the volume that is laid open before us" (*Anecdotes,* I, 135).

37. This is a recurrent theme with Pope:

> The critic Eye, that microscope of Wit,
> Sees hairs and pores, examines bit by bit:
> How parts relate to parts, or they to whole,
> The body's harmony, the beaming soul,

> Are things which Kuster, Burman, Wasse shall see,
> When Man's whole frame is obvious to a *Flea.*

(*Dunciad*, IV, 233–38; note also the *Essay on Man*, I, 193ff., *Epistle to Dr. Arbuthnot*, 169–70, and *Essay on Criticism*, 243ff.)

38. So central to Pope's political thinking is honesty that, in his index to the *Correspondence*, Sherburn lists a section "The great lack of honest men" (V, 185); typical of Pope's comments is this in a letter to Allen, 8 February 1741/2:

> I content myself as You do, with honest wishes, for honest men to govern us, without asking for any Party, or Denomination, beside. That is all the Distinction I know: and tho they call Kings the Fountains of Honour, I think them only the Bestowers of Titles; which they are generally most profuse of, to wh——s and kn——s. (Ibid., IV, 386–87.)

39. In a different but related vein Pope had written: ". . . in some times [it is] fitter that Knaves should govern, to stand charged with the Infamy of them [mischiefs] to Posterity." (*Correspondence*, IV, 249.)

40. There are a number of anecdotes that illustrate Pope's notorious "disesteem of Kings" (to use Dr. Johnson's phrase); Spence records his assertion: "Kings now (except the King of Sardinia) [are] the worst things upon earth. They are turned mere tradesmen: *cauponantes bellum, non belligerantes.*" (*Anecdotes*, I, 246.)

ΠΕΡΙ ΒΑΘΟΥΣ:

OR,

Martinus Scriblerus

HIS

TREATISE

OF THE

ART of SINKING

IN

POETRY.

INTRODUCTION

Nothing is more characteristic of the Augustan world of letters than that even in the domain of literary criticism one of the best productions of the period should be a mock *Ars,* or handbook of poetics. Like *MacFlecknoe, A Modest Proposal, The Beggar's Opera,* and *The Rape of the Lock, Peri Bathous: or, The Art of Sinking in Poetry* is a brilliant example of the technique by which indirections find directions out. Pope had already demonstrated the effectiveness of burlesque criticism in his *Guardian* paper on pastorals and in the *Receipt to Make an Epic Poem.*[1] Here, in a work of broader scope, he deployed the method at its fullest. The result is a critical commentary as telling as any of the more "serious" efforts of the time.[2]

With its collection of initialed bathetic dunces, *Peri Bathous* was probably conceived by Pope as a prelude to the more devastating *Dunciad,* which appeared two months later—a clever provocation of enemies whom he could then answer in that forthcoming volume.[3] But the work may also be read as a Scriblerian attack, one of the series of pieces projected to satirize pretentious learning. Like his colleagues, Pope felt a strong distaste for fools, along with a sense, inherited from the Humanists, of moral obligation to do battle against the mediocre and irrational. In this, the *Peri Bathous* can be seen as a direct descendant of Dryden's *MacFlecknoe* (or even the *Praise of Folly*), where likewise the aberrant and second-rate had been taken extravagantly at its own worth and rendered damningly superlative. Flecknoe, "Thro' all the realms of *Nonsense* absolute," had proved to be, as Dryden predicted, the sire of a long line, while the conditions that Dryden decried—not only in *MacFlecknoe* but in his prologues and epilogues—had not appreciably improved in thirty-five years. The hack and the pedant still flourished. And it was still up to the guardians of reason and morality to cope with them.

So, at any rate, the members of the Scriblerus Club, pooling their wry responses to such matters in the winters of 1713–1714 (when most of the seeds of the later productions were sown), seem to have felt. The Club, as Professor Sherburn has commented, though far from originating a satirical bent in Pope, "helped to fix in him habits of satirical thought and expression."[4] For a period of roughly two years and at a formative age, he was in a position to exchange ideas at close range with some of the foremost wits in England, and to collaborate in a program which, had it ever been completed, was "to have ridiculed all the false tastes in learning, under the character of a man of capacity enough that had dipped in every art

and science, but injudiciously in each."⁵ The composite character of the
Club hero, Martinus Scriblerus, gave rein to the individual talents of the
group, so that from their collective thinking in that rather narrowly academic enterprise grew a variety of major and minor works—most to be
published long after the short period of the Club's formal meetings. *Gulliver's Travels* (1726), *Peri Bathous* (1728),⁶ the *Dunciad* (1728), and the
Memoirs of Martinus Scriblerus (1741)—the focal work—were the most important, but there were also such jeux d'esprit as *The Origine of Sciences,
Stradling versus Stiles, Memoirs of P. P., Annus Mirabilis,* and *Virgilius Restauratus.* Even works so different as Pope's *Key to the Lock* and Gay's *Three
Hours after Marriage* and *The Beggar's Opera* owe something to the Scriblerian method.

Peri Bathous, however, became and remains more than just a preliminary
drawing of fire in anticipation of the *Dunciad*; indeed the real value of the
Bathos is better appreciated by modern readers than by Pope's contemporaries, who inevitably were concerned with its personalities.⁷ We are not
interested, except historically, in the exact identification of "W. H." or in
the number of times Blackmore's poetry is allowed to damn him; much
more significant are the entertaining insights into the forms of bad writing,
applicable in any age.

To the student of literary theory, moreover, *Peri Bathous* brings further
elaboration of matters opened up in the Postscript to the *Odyssey,* published
two years before. Pope's preoccupation there with style, particularly the
distinction between the natural and the sublime, is transparently related
to his satiric inversion in *Peri Bathous* of Longinus's *Peri Hupsous.* Though
his references to Longinus and Longinian concerns—sublimity, enthusiasm, natural genius—extend far beyond this period, it is here, under the
somewhat ambiguous cover of satire, that we come closest perhaps to his
real attitudes. *Peri Bathous* also touches upon other traditional topics such
as the Battle of the Ancients and Moderns, the place of rules, the moral
function of poetry, the state of the theater. Finally, in Pope's own words
to Spence: "*The Profound,* though written in so ludicrous a way, may well
be worth reading seriously as an art of rhetoric."⁸

Informing the whole—and perhaps this is most important of all—is
the judgment of an accomplished craftsman and astute critic, who in the
more subtle shadings of the satire is setting his poetic sensibility, representative of the best of the neoclassic mode, against the extravagances
inherent in a cult of enthusiasm and passion, identified, on the whole,
with Longinus because of advocates like John Dennis⁹ and Leonard Welsted
(whose translation of Longinus was prefaced by a critical essay that epit-
omized everything that Pope despised in contemporary modernist theory:

an indiscriminant adulation of current writers—like Ambrose Philips; a glorification of untutored taste; a devaluation of classical precepts and models).[10] But the question of Pope's attitude toward Longinus and his theory of the sublime (or at least what the period understood this to be)[11] is, of course, complex. Certainly the title and structure of the *Peri Bathous* must be taken as parody, the play on the word *profound,* lifted from one of Longinus's statements, leading Pope to his inversion.[12] Whether Longinus's sentiments are parodied is another matter. The most recent previous editor of the *Peri Bathous* thinks not: "Pope's handling of the Longinian principles seems not to be animated by ridicule. In Pope's work there is paid to Longinus the lip service of the period."[13]

That Longinus was one of the accepted authorities of the age goes without question: the first half of the eighteenth century saw nine printings of the Greek text as well as a number of English editions and translations of Boileau's French version.[14] In the catalogue of critics in the *Essay on Criticism,* Pope ackowledges him at length:

> Thee, bold *Longinus!* all the Nine inspire,
> And bless *their Critick* with a *Poet's Fire,*
> An ardent *Judge,* who Zealous in his Trust,
> With *Warmth* gives Sentence, yet is always *Just;*
> Whose *own Example* strengthens all his Laws;
> And *Is himself* that great *Sublime* he draws.
> (TE I, 316.)

It is true too that the Longinian emphasis on natural genius and on the emotive character of art can be traced in Pope's commentaries on Shakespeare and Homer, especially in the Preface to the *Iliad,*[15] where he announces:

> It is to the Strength of this amazing Invention we are to attribute that unequal'd Fire and Rapture, which is so forceful in *Homer,* that no Man of a true Poetical Spirit is Master of himself while he reads him. . . . Exact Disposition, just Thought, correct Elocution, polish'd Numbers, may have been found in a thousand; but this Poetical *Fire,* this *Vivida vis animi,* in a very few. Even in Works where all those are imperfect or neglected, this can over-power Criticism, and make us admire even while we disapprove.
> (TE VII, 4.)

This is strong language from a man who stated, also in the *Essay on Criticism,* that "Fools *Admire,* but Men of Sense *Approve.*" Is the apparent contradiction a real inconsistency, as Austin Warren would have it, "based on Pope's genuine enjoyment of two different types of art without a full consciousness of their difference"?[16] Or is it Pope's natural taste—always flexible—recognizing poetic genius basically outside his own artistic canon?

Actually, Pope no more denigrates the true sublime than he would the true heroic which is the basis of the mock heroic; it is the absurdities, the inflations, the misjudgments to which the sublime is particularly susceptible that constitute the bathetic—at a polar distance from the true high style and yet only a misstep away (as Longinus himself had acknowledged when, in passing, he touched upon the bombastic, puerile, and "empty" styles).[17] The danger is the lure of the heights, as seductive in art as in nature: "In *fearless Youth* we tempt the Heights of Art," Pope recognized early, in the *Essay on Criticism* and in some of his own juvenile heroics. It is a temptation of which he learned to be suspicious.[18]

Pope makes the point best himself, in a passage closing Chapter IV of the *Bathos*:

> The Sublime of Nature is the Sky, the Sun, Moon, Stars, &c. The Profund of Nature is Gold, Pearls, precious Stones, and the Treasures of the Deep, which are inestimable as unknown. But all that lies between these, as Corn, Flower, Fruits, Animals, and Things for the meer use of Man, are of mean price, and so common as not to be greatly esteem'd by the curious. It being certain that any thing, of which we know the true Use, cannot be invaluable: Which affords a solution, why common Sense hath either been totally despis'd, or held in small repute, by the greatest modern Critics and Authors.

What is being satirized here is the attitude which values excessively what is remote and unknown. The despising of the close, familiar, and useful (as the Laputans in *Gulliver's Travels* despised Lord Munodi and his accomplishments) turns paradoxically on the word "invaluable," ambiguously capable of meaning both priceless and worthless; the useful is indeed not "without value": it has *real* value. And it is common sense that discovers such value—usually grounded in appropriateness—without being dazzled by the exotic or extravagant. Or to move from nature to art (for which it is, after all, to Pope "the *Source,* and *End,* and *Test*"), true judgment regards suitability to the occasion, not an absolute worth inherent in certain conditions or styles. So it is that Pope devotes much consideration to Homer's sublimity in the Preface to the *Iliad* (a sublimity which he relates to a high style, even though Longinus essentially—and in Boileau's interpretation, emphatically—did not), while it is the nonsublime, natural style that is the concern of his Postscript to the *Odyssey,* which he recognizes to be a stylistically very different epic.

Pope's attitude in the *Peri Bathous* is then fundamentally conservative and "classical." It champions the Ancients against the "every way industrious Moderns" who excel them "both in the Weight of their writings, and in the Velocity of their judgments" (Chap. I). It distrusts—like Dryden and Swift—the values of the modern "Majority," whose "true design is Profit or Gain" (Chaps. I and II). It situates, ironically, the poetic afflatus among secretions and evacuations—a placing that could conceivably be a counterthrust to Longinus's stress on natural genius ("Poetry is a natural or morbid Secretion from the Brain" [Chap. III]) and (like Swift on the Aeolists) a parody of his later tribute to *in*spiration. And it returns again and again to the celebration of that common sense (judgment allied to wit) which the bathetic poets scorned and feared: "I will venture to lay it down, as the first Maxim and Corner-Stone of this our Art; that whoever would excel therein, must studiously avoid, detest, and turn his head from all the ideas, ways, and workings of that pestilent Foe to Wit, and Destroyer of fine Figures, which is known by the Name of *Common Sense*" (Chap. V).

Although "fine Figures" refers to the imagery used by denizens of the deep (those literary flying fishes, porpoises, etc.) in Chapter VI, it cannot but contain a sardonic glance at Longinus's recommendation of figures and of elaborated diction[19] to support a style whose very ornateness made it vulnerable to easy and usually unhappy imitation. How easy is acknowledged by Pope's inclusion among the "profound" examples of a number of lines from his own juvenilia—ambitious, exuberant excesses whose badness lies precisely in their being ornaments that have nothing to adorn. To quote again from Professor Sherburn, "The examples [of bad writing cited in *Peri Bathous*] are not unjustly cited, and they must have served as warning guides to poets. They show the true bent of Pope's genius, exemplified in his works after the *Dunciad*; it was a bent toward the rational plainness of common sense and away from the strained floridity of his baroque predecessors."[20]

What Pope learned and shares with his readers in the catalogue of bathetic excerpts (those "warning guides") from Chapters V, VII, VIII, IX, X, XI, and XII, does indeed constitute the "art of rhetoric" of which he spoke to Spence. While there could scarcely be a more convincing argument for the neoclassical virtues of decorum, restraint, correctness, and sense than these testimonials to debased taste, a closer examination gives vivid insight as well into how tropes and images "work": where does the proper "locus" of a figure lie? how far can—or cannot—an image be extended? how do figures interrelate? what does precision in expression really mean? what is the "logic" of poetry? and so forth. Some of the examples are simply and joyously inflated and inflationary bombast masquerading as eloquence—especially those from Blackmore, Pope's favorite, peerless source; had Pope commissioned them, they could not have served him better. Other examples—often the anonymous ones that are probably Pope's own creations, either from his youth or for the occasion—reveal an imagery gone berserk:

> *Behold a scene of misery and woe!*
> *Here Argus soon might weep himself quite blind,*
> *Ev'n though he had Briareus' hundred hands*
> *To wipe those hundred eyes——*

For students of Pope's own poetic, occasional judgments reflect a sensibility we may no longer share: to an age brought up on the metaphysicals, for instance, the passage from Cleveland on the bee (Chap. VIII) seems less offensive than it obviously did to Pope; we may accept an extravagance that he found diffuse or over-nice. But these discrepancies are rare indeed; for the most part, the horrors in Pope's museum are horrors still.

The four chapters that follow upon this ironic handbook, making up its appendix, are not so closely related to the rest, largely because they lie outside the Longinian framework. But they partake of the same satiric perspective and they, too, have their literary commentary to make. Chapter XIII is a mad, expediter's scheme of rhetorical assembly lines. Chapter XIV, *"How to make Dedications, Panegyrics or Satires, and of the Colours of Honourable and Dishonourable,"* is a manual, not without its modern applications, on how to win friends and influence patrons. Chapter XV, *"A Receipt to make an Epic Poem,"* is a Scriblerian parody, already printed in the *Guardian,* of Bossu's famous treatise on the epic. And Chapter XVI is an attack on the stage, no doubt prompted by Pope's experiences with the production of *Three Hours after Marriage.*

Most of what Pope argues for and against in the *Peri Bathous* is familiar to readers of his conventional critical writings—from the early *Essay on Criticism* through the Homeric essays and his Shakespearean commentary. What makes the *Peri Bathous* unique is the witty intelligence at play, both in the initial transfiguration of the Longinian "Profound" and in everything that follows from it. Where more appropriate to exploit fascinating ambiguities of language than in a rhetoric itself structured on a verbal inversion? "Is there not an Art of Diving as well as of Flying? And will any sober practitioner affirm, that a diving Engine is not of singular use in making him long-winded . . . ?" Again: "The Physician, by the study and inspection of urine and ordure, approves himself in the science; and in the like sort should our author accustom and exercise his imagination upon the dregs of nature." Long live Sh[adwell]!

For all the spirited extravagances of the Treatise, the realities that lie beneath the irony remain doctrinal to our time as well as Pope's:

> Let us look round among the Admirers of Poetry, we shall find those who have a taste of the Sublime to be very few; but the Profund strikes universally, and is adapted to every capacity.

> . . . obscurity bestows a cast of the wonderful, and throws an oracular dignity upon a piece which hath no meaning. [How apt for much writing about hermeneutics and self-destructing artifacts today!]

> And since the great Art of all Poetry is to mix Truth with Fiction, in order to join the *Credible* with the *Surprizing*; our author shall produce the Credible, by painting nature in her lowest simplicity; and the Surprizing, by contradicting common opinion.

> An Universal Genius rises not in an age; but when he rises, armies rise in him! he pours forth five or six Epic Poems with greater facility, than five or six pages can be produced by an elaborate and servile copyer after Nature or the Ancients.

> For Choice and distinction are not only a curb to the spirit, and limit the descriptive faculty, but also lessen the book; which is frequently the worst consequence of all to our author.

> *Periphrase* is another great aid to *Prolixity*; being a diffus'd circumlocutionary manner of expressing a known idea, which should be so mysteriously couch'd, as to give the reader the pleasure of guessing what it is that the author can possibly mean? and a strange surprize when he finds it.

> It must always be remember'd that Darkness is an essential quality of the Profund, or, if there chance to be a glimmering, it must be as Milton expresses it, *"No light, but rather darkness visible."*

And much remains pure fun:

> It is with the Bathos as with small Beer, which is indeed vapid and insipid, if left at large and let abroad; but being by our Rules confin'd and well stopt, nothing grows so frothy, pert, and bouncing.

> [Anticlimax is] A Surprize resembling that of a curious person in a cabinet of Antique Statues, who beholds on the pedestal the names of Homer, or Cato; but looking up, finds Homer without a head, and nothing to be seen of Cato but his privy member.

> For the first [Cumbrous imagery] is the proper engine to depress what is

high, so is the second [Buskin, or *Stately*] to raise what is base and low to a ridiculous Visibility. When both of these can be done at once, then is the Bathos in perfection; as when a man is set with his head downward, and his breech upright, his degradation is compleat: One end of him is higher than ever, only that end is the *wrong one*.

Therefore when we sit down to write, let us bring some great author to our mind, and ask our selves this question; How would Sir Richard have said this? Do I express myself as simply as Ambrose Philips? or flow my numbers with the quiet thoughtlessness of Mr. Welsted?[21]

According to Professor Sherburn, *Peri Bathous* appeared in a French translation as early as 1740, "and thus may have had an international influence on the art of the eighteenth century."[22] It is a happy thought.

Notes

1. *Guardian* No. 40 (27 April 1713) was Pope's ironic rebuttal of Thomas Tickell's praise of Ambrose Philips' pastorals; the *Receipt* was originally published also in the *Guardian*, 10 June 1713, and reprinted as Chap. XV of the *Peri Bathous*.

2. It has been suggested that Pope might have been spurred to organize his "high flights of Poetry" by the news in 1726 of John Oldmixon's projected *Essay on Criticism* (1728), itself in anticipation of Oldmixon's translation of Abbé Bouhours' *La Manière de bien penser*, which it imitated (as Bouhours had imitated Longinus) in providing examples of right and wrong "thinking." But Oldmixon's *Essay* is a dull affair, largely a conventional collection of "beautiful Descriptions, Similes, Allusions, &c. . . . ." (as Charles Gildon entitled his own offering in *The Complete Art of Poetry*, 1718). Pope's pointed examples in a lively ironic context were unique.

3. In the preface to the 1728 editions of the *Dunciad* appears this complaint, "that every week for these two Months past, the town has been persecuted with . . . Pamphlets, Advertisements, Letters, and weekly Essays, not only against the Wit and Writings, but against the Character and Person of Mr. *Pope*." (TE V, 202.)

4. *Early Career*, p. 82.

5. *Anecdotes*, I, 56.

6. Individual authorship of works published under the collective pseudonym *Martinus Scriblerus* is difficult to assign. *Peri Bathous* has been generally ascribed to Pope; although his own statements of responsibility are contradictory, there is his admission to Swift: "The third Volume of the Miscellanies is coming out post now, in which I have inserted the Treatise περὶ βαθοῦς I have entirely Methodized

and in a manner written, it all, the Dr [Arbuthnot] grew quite indolent in it, for something newer, I know not what." (*Correspondence*, II, 468.) See also Mrs. Steeves' résumé of the matter in her edition of *Peri Bathous* (New York: King's Crown Press, 1952; reprinted, Atheneum Press, 1968), pp. xxiiiff.

7. This has also been true of the *Dunciad*: "It was not long before the public began to feel the need of some sort of key to the dunces. The Earl of Oxford wrote on May 27 to say that many of his friends had been asking for one, and three weeks later Pope was able to tell him that the curiosity of George II had been sufficiently aroused for him to make a similar demand." (TE V, xxiii.)

8. *Anecdotes*, I, 57.

9. Dennis's critical position was so well known that there was no question as to who was being satirized as Sir Tremendous [Longinus] in Gay's farcical *Three Hours after Marriage*.

10. Leonard Welsted, "A Dissertation concerning the Perfection of the *English* Language, the state of Poetry, &c.," *Epistles, Odes, &c.* (London, 1724).

11. As A. F. B. Clark's study, *Boileau and the French Classical Critics in England,* has revealed, most Englishmen (including, probably, Pope) knew Longinus through Boileau's very free translation (from which the term *sublime* as a translation of *hupsos* came into vogue) and through the critical commentaries of the preface to that translation.

12. Longinus had asked whether there was an art of sublimity or profundity (ὕφους τις ἢ βάθους); it was Pope who first gave to *bathos* its now current sense of "ludicrous descent from the elevated to the commonplace." (OED)

13. Edna Leake Steeves, "Introduction," *The Art of Sinking in Poetry* (New York: King's Crown Press, 1952), p. liv.

14. Samuel H. Monk, *The Sublime: A Study of Critical Theories in XVIII–Century England* (New York, 1935), pp. 21–22.

15. In fact, Warton described the Preface as "a declamatory piece of criticism in the way of Longinus." (Joseph Warton, *An Essay on the Genius and Writings of Pope* [London, 1806], II, 400.)

16. Warren, p. 12.

17. See annotation 4 to the text.

18. Others were not so perceptive, as the *Peri Bathous* and *The Dunciad* record memorably (e.g., "The Senior's judgment all the crowd admire, / Who but to sink the deeper, rose the higher" [TE V, 309, ll. 288–89]).

19. Longinus's statement here is rather ambiguous: "figures bring support to the sublime, and on their part derive support in turn from it to a wonderful degree. Where and how, I will explain. The cunning use of figures is particularly subject to suspicion, and produces an impression of ambush, plot, fallacy. . . . Wherefore a figure is at its best when the very fact that it is a figure escapes attention. Accordingly, sublimity and passion form an antidote and a wonderful

help against the mistrust which attends upon the use of figures. The art which craftily employs them lies hid and escapes all future suspicion, when once it has been associated with beauty and sublimity" (*Longinus on the Sublime,* ed. W. Rhys Roberts, 2d ed. [Cambridge: Cambridge University Press, 1907], pp. 95, 97 [Chap. XVII]); i.e., "we don't see the figure if there is passion"—but how do we know there is passion except *through* the figure?

20. *Early Career,* p. 82.

21. These passages are to be found in Chapters II, XII, V, VI, VIII, VIII, XI, IV, XI, XII, and IX.

22. *Early Career,* p. 82.

NOTE ON PUBLICATION AND TEXT

Although Pope had originally meant the *Dunciad* for the "last" volume (the third in order of publication) of the Pope-Swift *Miscellanies,* he decided instead to issue it separately, substituting for it the provocative *Peri Bathous.* As he wrote to Swift, "The third Volume of the Miscellanies is coming out post now [7 March 1727/28], in which I have inserted the Treatise περὶ βαϑοῦς I have entirely Methodized and in a manner written, it all, the Dr grew quite indolent in it, for something newer, I know not what. It will be a very Instructive piece."[1]

Published, then, in octavo early in 1728, it was reissued later in the year and reprinted in 1732. In 1730 the *Miscellanies* were published in 12mo., dated 1731. When early in 1733 (some volumes were dated 1732) these three volumes were reprinted and a fourth ("the Third Volume") added, confusion began over the so-called "Last" volume and the new "Third," these volumes being originally mistitled and later (including a 1736 reprinting) the error corrected either with the insertion of a new title page or a reprinting.[2] A duodecimo "Last" volume was also issued in 1738. When the *Miscellanies* were reordered in 1742 in small octavo, to match Pope's other works in that format, the *Peri Bathous* was moved to the Second Volume with Pope's other prose works. And in 1741 the Treatise had appeared in Volume II of his *Works . . . in Prose,* where it accompanied the *Memoirs* and other Scriblerian tracts,[3] with which it was reprinted by Warburton in Volume VI of his 1751 edition of Pope's works.

Because of Pope's late decision to include the *Peri Bathous* in the *Miscellanies,* the first printing in 1728 was a rushed affair and Pope expanded and corrected the text for the 1730 duodecimo edition, among other things moving his footnotes to the bottom of the page. (The table of contents for some reason always appeared at the end.) Even more revisions—with some further categories of bad writing and examples—were made in the 1741 *Works . . . in Prose,* an edition which also reduces considerably the extensive capitalizations and italics of the earlier printings. These changes were incorporated in the 1742 *Miscellanies,* which has its own corrections and changes, minor but significant, which argue for its being used as a base text. Since it, though, is less consistent in its practice of capitalizing and italicizing, the 1741 text is followed in those particulars, and, for the numberings of Chap. XI, Warburton's edition, where the sequence is a little less confusing. All substantive variants are recorded in textual notes (reproducing the accidentals of the edition in which the variant first appears), with the 1751 edition included in the collation to complete the history of the text.

Key to the Critical Apparatus

1728 (dated 1727) = *Miscellanies in Prose and Verse,* "Last" Vol., octavo, Griffith 196; Teerink/Scouten 25 (3a).

[1728 = "Last" Vol., octavo, Griffith 208a; Teerink/Scouten 25 (3e).]

1730 (dated 1731) = "Last" Vol., duodecimo, Griffith 244; Teerink/ Scouten 26.

1732 = "Last" Vol., octavo, Griffith 275; Teerink/Scouten 25 (3f).

1733a (dated 1732) = [mistitled] "Third" Vol., duodecimo, Teerink/ Scouten 27 (3a).

1733b = "Last" Vol., duodecimo, Teerink/Scouten 27 (3b).

1733c = [mistitled] "Third" Vol., duodecimo, Griffith 286; Teerink/ Scouten 27 (3c).

1736 = "Last" Vol., duodecimo, Griffith 440; Teerink/Scouten 28 (3).

1738 = "Last" Vol., duodecimo, Griffith 499; Teerink/Scouten 30 (1).

1741 = *Works . . . in Prose,* Vol. II, folio, Griffith 529; l. p. folio, Griffith 530; quarto, Griffith 531.

1742 = *Miscellanies* (in Four Volumes), Second Vol., sm. octavo, Griffith 562.

1751 = *Works,* ed. Warburton, Vol. VI, octavo, Griffith 648.

Notes

1. *Correspondence,* II, 468.

2. For a review of these bibliographical confusions see the Teerink/Scouten *Bibliography of the Writings of Jonathan Swift* (Philadelphia: University of Pennsylvania Press, 1963), pp. 11–20. In her edition of the *Peri Bathous,* Edna Leake Steeves, in conjunction with R. H. Griffith, has included a bibliographic study of the 1727 [1728] "Last Volume" (*The Art of Sinking in Poetry* [New York: King's Crown Press, 1952], pp. 195–207).

3. The history of this printing is interesting. Earlier, sheets had been prepared of the *Peri Bathous,* the *Key to the Lock,* and *Virgilius Restauratus* to be used in the *Works* of 1735, following the *Dunciad* (and made-up, thick-paper copies in that form are to be found at Harvard and Oxford [see Maynard Mack, "Two Variant Copies of Pope's *Works . . . Volume II*: Further Light on Some Problems of Authorship, Bibliography, and Text" (*Library,* 12 [1957], 48–53)]). After these Scriblerian pieces were withheld, though, because Pope did not own the copyright,

he saved them for a separate expanded publication, *Tracts of Martinus Scriblerus: And other Miscellaneous Pieces,* when, in 1737, he was projecting simultaneous and matching editions of his letters and "tracts"—a plan that again failed apparently because of publication rights (David Foxon reviews the whole account in his unpublished collection of Lyell Lectures, *Pope and the Early Eighteenth-Century Book Trade* [1975], pp. 142–43, 151–65). Finally the tracts, both those of 1735 and 1737, were published in the 1741 *Works,* some copies of which carry the originally prepared 1737 title page to introduce the Scriblerian pieces.

MARTINUS SCRIBLERUS,
ΠΕΡΙ ΒΑΘΟΥΣ:
OR,
Of the Art of SINKING in
POETRY.

CHAP. I.

A It hath been long (my[1] dear Countrymen) the subject of my concern and surprize, that whereas numberless Poets, Critics, and Orators have compiled and digested the Art of ancient Poesy, there hath not arisen among us one person so publick-spirited, as to perform the like for the Modern.[2] Altho' it is universally known, that our every way industrious Moderns, both in the Weight of their writings, and in the Velocity of their judgments, do so infinitely excel the said Ancients.[3]

Nevertheless, too true it is, that while a plain and direct road is paved to their ὕψος, or Sublime; no track has been yet chalk'd out, to arive at our βάθος, or Profund.[4] The Latins, as they came between the Greeks and Us, make use of the word *Altitudo,* which implies equally height and depth. Wherefore considering with no small grief, how many promising Genius's of this age are wandering (as I may say) in the dark without a guide, I have undertaken this arduous but necessary task, to lead them as it were by the hand, and step by step, the gentle down-hill way to the Bathos; the bottom, the end, the central point, the *non plus ultra,* of true Modern Poesy!

B When I consider (my dear Countrymen) how extensive, fertile and populous are our Lowlands of Parnassus, the flourishing state of our Trade, and the plenty of our Manufacture; there are two reflections which administer great occasion of surprize: the one, that all dignities and honours should be bestowed upon the exceeding few meager inhabitants of the Top of the mountain;[5] the other, that our own nation should have arriv'd to that pitch of greatness it now possesses, without any regular System of Laws.[6] As to the first, it is with great pleasure I have observ'd of late the gradual decay of Delicacy and Refinement among mankind, who are become too reasonable to require that we should labour with infinite pains to come up to the taste of these Mountaineers, when they without any, may condescend to ours. But as we have now an unquestionable Majority on our side, I doubt not but we shall shortly be able to level the Highlanders, and procure a farther vent for our own product, which is already so much relish'd, encourag'd, and rewarded, by the Nobility and Gentry of Great Britain.[7]

Therefore to supply our former defect, I purpose to collect the scatter'd Rules of our Art into regular Institutes, from the example and practice of the deep Genius's of our nation; imitating herein my predecessors the Master of Alexander, and the Secretary of the renown'd Zenobia.[8] And in this my undertaking I am the more animated, as I expect more success than has attended even those great Critics; since their Laws (tho' they might be good) have ever been slackly executed, and their Precepts (however strict) obey'd only by fits, and by a very small number.

At the same time I intend to do justice upon our neighbours, inhabitants of the upper Parnassus; who taking advantage of the rising ground, are perpetually throwing down rubbish, dirt and stones upon us, never suffering us to live in peace. These men, while they enjoy the chrystal stream of Helicon, envy us our common water, which (thank our stars) tho' it is somewhat muddy, flows in much greater abundance. Nor is this the greatest injustice that we have to complain of; for tho' it is evident that we never made the least attempt or inrode into Their territories, but lived contented in our native fens; they have often not only committed Petty Larcenys upon our borders, but driven the country, and carried off at once whole Cart-loads of our manufacture; to reclaim some of which stolen goods is part of the design of this Treatise.

For we shall see in the course of this work, that our greatest Adversaries have sometimes descended towards us;[9] and doubtless might now and then have arrived at the Bathos itself, had it not been for that mistaken opinion they all entertained, that the Rules

of the Ancients were equally necessary to the Moderns; than which
there cannot be a more grievous Error, as will be amply proved in
the following discourse.

A   And indeed when any of these have gone so far, as by the light
of their own Genius to attempt *new* Models, it is wonderful to
observe, how nearly they have approach'd us in those particular
B   pieces; tho' in their others they differ'd *toto cælo* from us.

CHAP. II.

*That the Bathos, or Profund, is the natural Taste of Man, and in par-
ticular, of the present* Age.

The Taste of the Bathos is implanted by Nature itself in the soul of
man;[10] till, perverted by custom or example, he is taught, or rather
compell'd, to relish the Sublime. Accordingly, we see the unpreju-
diced minds of Children delight only in such productions, and in
such images, as our true modern writers set before them. I have
observ'd how fast the general Taste is returning to this first Simplicity and Innocence: and if the intent of all Poetry be to divert
and instruct, certainly that kind which diverts and instructs the
greatest number is to be preferr'd. Let us look round among the
Admirers of Poetry, we shall find those who have a taste of the
Sublime to be very few; but the Profund strikes universally, and is
adapted to every capacity. 'Tis a fruitless undertaking to write for
men of a nice and foppish Gusto,[11] whom after all it is almost
impossible to please; and 'tis still more chimerical to write for Posterity, of whose Taste we cannot make any judgment, and whose
Applause we can never enjoy. It must be confess'd our wiser authors
have a present end,

Et prodesse volunt & delectare Poetæ.[12]

Their true design is Profit or Gain; in order to acquire which, 'tis
necessary to procure applause by administring pleasure to the reader:
From whence it follows demonstrably, that their productions must
be suited to the *present* Taste. And I cannot but congratulate our
age on this peculiar felicity, that tho' we have made indeed great
progress in all other branches of Luxury, we are not yet debauch'd
with any high Relish in Poetry, but are in this one Taste less nice

than our ancestors.[13] If an Art is to be estimated by its success, I appeal to experience whether there have not been, in proportion to their number, as many starving good Poets, as bad ones?

Nevertheless, in making Gain the principal end of our Art, far be it from me to exclude any great Genius's of *Rank* or *Fortune* from diverting themselves this way. They ought to be praised no less than those Princes, who pass their vacant hours in some ingenious mechanical or manual Art. And to such as these, it would be ingratitude not to own, that our Art has been often infinitely indebted.[14]

CHAP. III.

The Necessity of the Bathos, Physically consider'd.

Farthermore, it were great cruelty and injustice, if all such Authors as cannot write in the other way, were prohibited from writing at all. Against this I draw an argument from what seems to me an undoubted physical Maxim, That Poetry is a natural or morbid Secretion from the Brain.[15] As I would not suddenly stop a cold in the head, or dry up my neighbour's Issue, I would as little hinder him from necessary writing. It may be affirmed with great truth, that there is hardly any human creature past childhood, but at one time or other has had some Poetical Evacuation, and no question, was much the better for it in his health; so true is the saying, *Nascimur Poetæ.* Therefore is the Desire of Writing properly term'd *Pruritus,* the "Titillation of the Generative Faculty of the Brain," and the Person is said to conceive; now such as conceive must bring forth.[16] I have known a man thoughtful, melancholy and raving for divers days, who forthwith grew wonderfully easy, lightsome and cheerful, upon a discharge of the peccant humour, in exceeding purulent Metre.[17] Nor can I question, but abundance of untimely deaths are occasion'd for want of this laudable vent of unruly passions: yea, perhaps, in poor wretches, (which is very lamentable) for meer want of pen, ink, and paper! From hence it follows, that a suppression of the very worst Poetry is of dangerous consequence to the State: We find by experience, that the same humours which vent themselves in summer in Ballads and Sonnets, are condens'd by the winter's cold into Pamphlets and Speeches for and against the Ministry: Nay I know not, but many times a piece of Poetry may be the most innocent composition of a Minister himself.

It is therefore manifest that *Mediocrity* ought to be allow'd, yea indulged, to the good Subjects of England.[18] Nor can I conceive how the world has swallowed the contrary as a Maxim, upon the single authority of that* Horace?[19] Why should the golden Mean, and quintessence of all Virtues, be deem'd so offensive in this Art? Or Coolness or Mediocrity be so amiable a quality in a Man, and so detestable in a Poet?

However, far be it from me to compare these Writers with those great Spirits, who are born with a *Vivacité de pesanteur,* or (as an English Author calls it) an "Alacrity of sinking;"[20] and who by strength of Nature alone can excel.[21] All I mean is to evince the Necessity of Rules to these lesser Genius's, as well as the Usefulness of them to the greater.

A

CHAP. IV.

That there is an Art of the Bathos, or Profund.

We come now to prove, that there is an Art of Sinking in Poetry.[22] Is there not an Architecture of Vaults and Cellars,[23] as well as of lofty Domes and Pyramids? Is there not as much skill and labour in making Dikes,[24] as in raising Mounts? Is there not an Art of Diving as well as of Flying? And will any sober practitioner affirm, that a diving Engine is not of singular use in making him long-winded, assisting his descent, and furnishing him with more in-genious means of keeping under water?

B

C,D

If we search the Authors of Antiquity, we shall find as few to have been distinguish'd in the true Profund, as in the true Sublime. And the very same thing (as it appears from Longinus) had been imagin'd of that, as now of this: namely, that it was entirely the Gift of Nature.[25] I grant that to excel in the Bathos a Genius is requisite; yet the Rules of Art must be allow'd so far useful, as to add weight, or as I may say, hang on lead,[26] to facilitate and enforce

E   *   *Mediocribus esse poetis*
Non dii, non homines, etc.   Hor.

our descent, to guide us to the most advantageous declivities, and habituate our imagination to a depth of thinking. Many there are that can fall, but few can arrive at the felicity of falling gracefully; much more for a man who is amongst the lowest of the creation, at the very bottom of the Atmosphere,[27] to descend beneath himself, is not so easy a task unless he calls in Art to his assistance. It is with the Bathos as with small Beer, which is indeed vapid and insipid, if left at large and let abroad; but being by our Rules confin'd and well stopt, nothing grows so frothy, pert, and bouncing.[28]

A   The Sublime of Nature is the Sky, the Sun, Moon, Stars, etc. The Profund of Nature is Gold, Pearls, precious Stones, and the Treasures of the Deep, which are inestimable as unknown. But all that lies between these, as Corn, Flower, Fruits, Animals, and Things for the meer use of Man, are of mean price, and so common as not to be greatly esteem'd by the curious.[29] It being certain that any thing, of which we know the true Use, cannot be invaluable: Which affords a solution, why common Sense[30] hath either been totally despis'd, or held in small repute, by the greatest modern Critics and Authors.

CHAP. V.

Of the true Genius for the Profund, and by what it is constituted.

And I will venture to lay it down, as the first Maxim and Corner-Stone of this our Art; that whoever would excel therein, must studiously avoid, detest, and turn his head from all the ideas, ways, and workings of that pestilent Foe to Wit, and Destroyer of fine Figures,[31] which is known by the Name of *Common Sense*. His business must be to contact the true *Gout de travers*;[32] and to acquire a most happy, uncommon, unaccountable Way of Thinking.[33]

B   He is to consider himself as a grotesque painter,[34] whose works would be spoil'd by an imitation of nature, or uniformity of design. He is to mingle bits of the most various, or discordant kinds, landscape, history, portraits, animals, and connect them with a great deal of flourishing, by head or tail, as it shall please his imagination, and contribute to his principal end, which is to glare by strong oppositions of colours, and surprize by contrariety of images.

> *Serpentes avibus geminentur, tigribus agni.* Hor.[35]

His design ought to be like a labyrinth, out of which no body
A can get clear but himself. And since the great Art of all Poetry is
B to mix Truth with Fiction,[36] in order to join the *Credible* with the
Surprizing; our author shall produce the Credible, by painting nature
in her lowest simplicity; and the Surprizing, by contradicting common opinion. In the very Manners he will affect the *Marvellous*; he
will draw Achilles with the patience of Job;[37] a Prince talking like
a Jack-pudding;[38] a Maid of honour selling bargains;[39] a footman
speaking like a philosopher; and a fine gentleman like a scholar.[40]
Whoever is conversant in modern Plays, may make a most noble
collection of this kind, and at the same time, form a complete body
of *modern Ethics and Morality.*[41]

Nothing seem'd more plain to our great authors, than that the
world had long been weary of *natural things.* How much the contrary
C are form'd to please, is evident from the universal applause daily
given to the admirable entertainments of Harlequins and Magicians
on our stage.[42] When an audience behold a coach turn'd into a
wheelbarrow, a conjurer into an old woman, or a man's head where
his heels should be; how are they struck with transport and delight?[43] Which can only be imputed to this cause, that each object
is chang'd into that which hath been suggested to them by their
own low ideas before.

He ought therefore to render himself master of this happy and
anti-natural way of thinking to such a degree, as to be able, on the
appearance of any object, to furnish his imagination with ideas
infinitely *below* it. And his eyes should be like unto the wrong end
of a perspective glass, by which all the objects of nature are lessen'd.[44]

For Example; when a true genius looks upon the Sky, he immediately catches the idea of a piece of blue lutestring,[45] or a child's
mantle.

> c *The skies, whose spreading volumes scarce have room,*
> *Spun thin, and wove in nature's finest loom,*[46]

D   c Prince Arthur, p. 41, 42.[47]

> *The new-born world in their soft lap embrac'd,*
> *And all around their starry mantle cast.*

A   If he looks upon a Tempest, he shall have an image of a tumbled bed, and describe a succeeding calm in this manner;

> d *The Ocean, joy'd to see the tempest fled,*
> *New lays his waves, and smooths his ruffled bed.*

The Triumphs and acclamations of the Angels at the Creation of the Universe, present to his imagination "the Rejoycings of the Lord B Mayor's Day;" and he beholds those glorious beings celebrating their Creator, by huzzaing, making illuminations, and flinging squibs, crackers and sky-rockets.

> e *Glorious Illuminations, made on high*
> *By all the stars and planets of the sky,*
> *In just degrees, and shining order plac'd,*
> *Spectators charm'd, and the blest dwelling grac'd.*
> *Thro' all th' enlighten'd air swift fireworks flew,*
> *Which with repeated shouts glad Cherubs threw.*
> *Comets ascended with their sweeping train,*
> *Then fell in starry showers and glittering rain.*
> *In air ten thousand meteors blazing hung,*
> *Which from th' eternal battlements were flung.*

If a man who is violently fond of *Wit,* will sacrifice to that passion his friend or his God,[49] would it not be a shame, if he who is smit with the love of the *Bathos* should not sacrifice to it all other transitory regards? You shall hear a zealous Protestant Deacon[50] invoke C a Saint, and modestly beseech her to do more for us than Providence.

> f *Look down, bless'd saint, with pity then look down,*
> *Shed on this land thy kinder influence,*

d P. 14.
  N.B. In order to do Justice to these great Poets, our Citations are taken from the best, the last, and most correct Editions of their Works. That which we use of Prince Arthur, is in *Duodecimo,* 1714. The fourth Edition revised.[48]
D   e *ibid.,* p. 50.
  f A. Philips on the Death of Queen Mary.

> *And guide us through the mists of providence,*
> *In which we stray.*——[51]

Neither will he, if a goodly Simile come in his way, scruple to affirm himself an eye-witness of things never yet beheld by man, or never in existence; as thus,

> [g] *Thus have I seen in Araby the bless'd,*
> *A Phœnix couch'd upon her fun'ral nest.*[52]

But to convince you that nothing is so great which a marvellous genius, prompted by this laudable zeal, is not able to lessen; hear how the most sublime of all Beings is represented in the following images,[53]

First he is a PAINTER.

> [h] *Sometimes the Lord of Nature in the air,*
> *Spreads forth his clouds, his sable canvas, where*
> *His pencil, dipp'd in heavenly colour bright,*
> *Paints his fair rain-bow, charming to the sight.*[54]

Now he is a CHYMIST.

> [i] *Th' Almighty Chymist does his work prepare,*
> *Pours down his waters on the thirsty plain,*
> *Digests his lightning, and distils his rain.*[55]

Now he is a WRESTLER.

> [k] *Me in his griping arms th' Eternal took,*
> *And with such mighty force my body shook,*
> *That the strong grasp my members sorely bruis'd,*
> *Broke all my bones, and all my sinews loos'd.*

Now a RECRUITING OFFICER.

> [l] *For clouds, the sun-beams levy fresh supplies,*
> *And raise recruits of vapours, which arise*
> *Drawn from the seas, to muster in the skies.*[56]

[g] Anon.
A [h] Blackm. opt. edit. Duod. 1716. p. 172.
[i] Blackm. Ps. civ. p. 263.
[k] Page 75.
[l] P. 170.

Now a peaceable GUARANTEE.
^m *In leagues of peace the neighbours did agree,*
   *And to maintain them, God was Guarantee.*⁵⁷

Then he is an ATTORNEY.
ⁿ *Job, as a vile offender, God indites,*
   And terrible decrees against me writes.
      God will not be my advocate,
   *My cause to manage or debate.*⁵⁸

In the following Lines he is a GOLDBEATER.
^o *Who the rich metal beats, and then, with care,*
   Unfolds the golden leaves, to gild the fields of air.

Then a FULLER.
^p ——*th' exhaling reeks that secret rise,*
   Born on rebounding sun-beams thro' the skies,
   Are thicken'd, wrought, and whiten'd, 'till they
         grow
   A heav'nly fleece——

A MERCER, or PACKER.
^q *Didst thou one end of air's wide curtain hold,*
   And help the Bales of Æther to unfold;
   *Say, which cærulean pile was by thy hand unroll'd?*⁶⁰

A BUTLER.
^r *He measures all the drops with wondrous skill,*
   Which the black clouds, his floating Bottles, fill.

And a BAKER.
^s *God in the wilderness his table spread,*
   *And in his airy Ovens bak'd their bread.*⁶¹

^m P. 70.
ⁿ P. 61.
^o P. 181.
^p P. 18 [error for 180].⁵⁹
^q P. 174.
^r P. 131 [misprinted 132 in 1742].
^s Black. Song of Moses, p. 218.

CHAP. VI.

Of the several Kinds of Genius's in the Profund, and the Marks, and Characters of each.

I doubt not but the reader, by this Cloud of examples, begins to be convinc'd of the truth of our assertion, that the Bathos is an *Art*; and that the Genius of no mortal whatever, following the mere ideas of Nature, and unassisted with an habitual, nay laborious peculiarity of thinking, could arrive at images so wonderfully low and unaccountable. The great author, from whose treasury we have drawn all these instances (the Father of the Bathos, and indeed the Homer of it)[62] has like that immortal Greek, confin'd his labours to the greater Poetry, and thereby left room for others to acquire a due share of praise in inferior kinds. Many painters who could never hit a nose or an eye, have with felicity copied a small-pox, or been admirable at a toad or a red herring. And seldom are we without genius's for *Still-life,*[63] which they can work up and stiffen with incredible accuracy.

An Universal Genius rises not in an age; but when he rises, armies rise in him! he pours forth five or six Epic Poems with greater facility, than five or six pages can be produced by an elaborate and servile copyer after Nature or the Ancients.[64] It is affirm'd by Quintilian, that the same genius which made Germanicus so great a General, would with equal application have made him an excellent Heroic Poet.[65] In like manner, reasoning from the affinity there appears between Arts and Sciences, I doubt not but an active catcher of butterflies, a careful and fanciful pattern-drawer, an industrious collector of shells, a laborious and tuneful bagpiper, or a diligent breeder of tame rabbits, might severally excel in their respective parts of the Bathos.[66]

I shall range these confin'd and less copious Genius's under proper classes, and (the better to give their pictures to the reader) under the names of *Animals* of some sort or other;[67] whereby he will be enabled, at the first sight of such as shall daily come forth, to know to what Kind to refer, and with what Authors to compare them.[68]

1. The *Flying Fishes:* These are writers who now and then rise upon their fins, and fly out of the Profund; but their wings are soon dry, and they drop down to the bottom. G.S.[69] A.H.[70] C.G.[71]

2. The *Swallows*[72] are authors that are eternally skimming and fluttering up and down, but all their agility is employ'd to *catch flies.* L.T.[73] W.P.[74] Lord. H.[75]

3. The *Ostridges* are such, whose heaviness rarely permits them to raise themselves from the ground; their wings are of no use to lift them up, and their motion is between flying and walking; but then they *run very fast.* D.F.[76] L.E.[77] The Hon. E.H.[78]

4. The *Parrots* are they that repeat *another's* words, in such a hoarse odd voice, as makes them seem their *own.* W.B.[79] W.S.[80] C.C.[81] The Reverend D.D.[82]

5. The *Didappers*[83] are authors that keep themselves long out of sight, under water, and come up now and then where you least expected them.[84] L.W.[85] G.D. Esq;[86] The Hon. Sir W.Y.[87]

6. The *Porpoises* are unweildy and big; they put all their numbers into a great turmoil and tempest, but whenever they appear in plain light, (which is seldom) they are only shapeless and ugly monsters. I.D.[88] C.G.[89] I.O.[90]

7. The *Frogs* are such as can neither walk nor fly, but can *leap* and *bound* to admiration: They live generally in the bottom of a ditch, and make a great noise whenever they thrust their heads above water. E.W.[91] I.M. Esq;[92] T.D. Gent.[93]

8. The *Eels* are obscure authors, that wrap themselves up in their own mud, but are mighty nimble and pert.[94] L.W.[95] L.T.[96] P.M.[97] General C.[98]

9. The *Tortoises* are slow and chill, and, like pastoral writers, delight much in gardens: they have for the most part a fine embroider'd Shell, and underneath it, a heavy lump. A.P.[99] W.B.[100] L.E.[101] The Right Hon. E. of S.[102]

These are the chief *Characteristicks* of the *Bathos,* and in each of these kinds we have the comfort to be bless'd with sundry and manifold choice Spirits in this our Island.

CHAP. VII.

Of the Profund, when it consists in the Thought.[103]

We have already laid down the Principles upon which our author is to proceed, and the manner of forming his Thought by familiarizing his mind to the lowest objects; to which it may be added, that

Vulgar Conversation will greatly contribute. There is no question but the Garret or the Printer's boy may often be discern'd in the compositions made in such scenes and company; and much of Mr. Curl himself has been insensibly infused into the works of his learned writers. [104]

The Physician, by the study and inspection of urine and ordure, approves himself in the science; and in like sort should our author accustom and exercise his imagination upon the dregs of nature. [105]

This will render his thoughts truly and fundamentally low, and carry him many fathoms beyond Mediocrity. For, certain it is, (tho' some lukewarm heads imagine they may be safe by temporizing

A between the extremes) that where there is not a Triticalness[106] or Mediocrity in the Thought, it can never be sunk into the genuine and perfect Bathos, by the most elaborate low Expression: It can, at most, be only carefully obscured, or metaphorically debased. But 'tis the Thought alone that strikes, and gives the whole that spirit, which we admire and stare at. For instance, in that ingenious piece on a lady's drinking the Bath-waters.

> [t] *She drinks! She drinks! Behold the matchless dame!*
> *To her 'tis water, but to us 'tis flame:*
> *Thus fire is water, water fire by turns,*
> *And the same stream at once both cools and burns.*

What can be more easy and unaffected than the Diction of these verses? 'Tis the Turn of Thought alone, and the Variety of Imagination, that charm and surprize us. And when the same lady goes into the Bath, the Thought (as in justness it ought) goes still deeper.

> [u] *Venus beheld her, 'midst her crowd of slaves,*
> *And thought herself just risen from the waves.*

How much out of the way of common sense is this reflection of Venus, not knowing herself from the lady?

Of the same nature is that noble mistake of a frighted stag in
B,C a full chace, who (saith the Poet,)

[t] Anon. [107]
[u] Idem.

Hears his own feet, and thinks they sound like more;
And fears the hind-feet will o'ertake the fore. [108]

So astonishing as these are, they yield to the following, which is Profundity itself,

    [x] *None but Himself can be his Parallel.* [109]

Unless it may seem borrowed from the Thought of that Master of a Show in Smithfield, [110] who writ in large letters, over the picture of his elephant,

    This is the greatest Elephant in the world, except Himself. [111]

However our next instance is certainly an original: Speaking of a beautiful infant,

So fair thou art, that if great Cupid be
A child, as Poets say, sure thou art he.
Fair Venus would mistake thee for her own,
Did not thy eyes proclaim thee not her son.
There all the lightnings of thy Mother's shine,
And with a fatal brightness kill in thine. [112a]

First he is Cupid, then he is not Cupid; first Venus would mistake him, then she would not mistake him; next his Eyes are his Mother's, and lastly they are not his Mother's, but his own.

Another author describing a Poet that shines forth amidst a circle of Critics,

Thus Phœbus thro' the Zodiac takes his way,
And amid Monsters rises into day. [112b]

What a peculiarity is here of invention? The Author's pencil, like the wand of Circe, turns all into monsters at a stroke. A great Genius takes things in the lump, without stopping at minute con-
A siderations: In vain might the ram, the bull, the goat, the crab, the scorpion, the fishes, all stand in his way, as mere natural animals: much more might it be pleaded that a pair of scales, an old man, and two innocent children, were no monsters: There were only the

B   [x] Theobald, Double Falshood.

Centaur and the Maid that could be esteem'd out of nature. But
what of that? with a boldness peculiar to these daring genius's,
what he found not monsters, he made so.

CHAP. VIII.

*Of the Profund, consisting in the Circumstances, and of Amplification and
Periphrase in general.*[113]

What in a great measure distinguishes other writers from ours, is
their chusing and separating such circumstances in a description as
A enoble or elevate the subject.

The circumstances which are most natural are *obvious,* therefore
not *astonishing* or peculiar. But those that are far-fetch'd or unexpected, or hardly compatible, will surprise prodigiously. These
therefore we must principally hunt out; but above all, preserve a
laudable *Prolixity*; presenting the whole, and every side at once, of
the image to view. For Choice and distinction are not only a curb
to the spirit, and limit the descriptive faculty, but also lessen the
book; which is frequently of the worst consequence of all to our
author.[114]

B,C   Job says in short, "He washed his feet in butter,"[115] a circumstance some Poets would have soften'd, or past over: now hear how
this butter is spread out by the great Genius.

> [y] *With teats distended with their milky store,*
> *Such num'rous lowing herds, before my door,*
> *Their painful burden to unload did meet,*
> *That we with butter might have wash'd our feet.*

How cautious and particular! "He had (says our author) so many
herds which herds thriv'd so well, and thriving so well gave so much
milk, and that milk produc'd so much butter, that if he did not,
he might have wash'd his feet in it."

The ensuing description of Hell is no less remarkable in the
circumstances.

[y] Blackm. Job, p. 133.

> ^z *In flaming heaps the raging ocean rolls,*
> *Whose livid waves involve despairing souls;*
> *The liquid burnings dreadful colours shew,*
> *Some* deeply red *and others* faintly blue.

A   Could the most minute Dutch-painter have been more exact?[116]
How inimitably circumstantial is this also of a war-horse![117]

> ^a *His eye-balls burn, he wounds the smoaking plain,*
> *And* knots *of* scarlet ribbond *deck his mane.*

Of certain Cudgel-players.

> ^b *They brandish high in air their threatning staves,*
> *Their Hands a* woven guard *of* ozier *saves,*
> *In which they fix their* hazle weapon's end.

Who would not think the Poet had past his whole life at Wakes
B   in such laudable diversions? since he teaches us how to hold, nay
how to make a Cudgel![118]

Periphrase is another great aid to *Prolixity*; being a diffus'd circumlocutory manner of expressing a known idea, which should be
so mysteriously couch'd, as to give the reader the pleasure of guessing
C   what it is that the author can possibly mean? and a strange surprize
when he finds it.

The Poet I last mentioned is incomparable in this figure.

> ^c *A waving sea of heads was round me spread,*
> *And still fresh streams the gazing deluge fed.*

Here is a waving sea of heads, which by a fresh stream of heads,
grows to be a gazing deluge of heads. You come at last to find, it
means a *great crowd.*

How pretty and how genteel is the following?

> ^d *Nature's Confectioner——*
> *Whose suckets are moist alchimy:*

^z Pr. Arth. p. 89.
^a Anon.
^b Pr. Arth. p. 197.
^c Job, p. 78.
^d Cleveland.

> *The still of his refining mold*
> *Minting the garden into gold.*[119]

What is this but a Bee gathering honey?

> [e] *Little Syren of the stage,*
> *Empty warbler, breathing lyre,*
> *Wanton gale of fond desire,*
> *Tuneful mischief, vocal spell.*———[120]

Who would think, this was only a poor gentlewoman that sung finely?

We may define *Amplification* to be making the most of a Thought; it is the Spinning-wheel of the Bathos, which draws out and spreads [A] it into the finest thread. There are Amplifiers who can extend half a dozen thin thoughts over a whole Folio; but for which, the tale of many a vast Romance, and the substance of many a fair volume, might be reduced into the size of a primmer.

In the book of Job, are these words, "Hast thou commanded the morning, and caused the day spring to know his place?"[121] How is this extended by the most celebrated Amplifier of our age?

> [f] *Canst thou set forth th' etherial* mines *on high,*
> *Which the refulgent* ore *of light supply?*
> *Is the celestial* furnace *to thee known,*
> *In which I* melt *the golden metal down?*
> *Treasures, from whence I deal out light as fast,*
> *As all my stars and lavish suns can waste.*[122]

The same author hath amplified a passage in the civ[th] Psalm; "He looks on the earth, and it trembles. He touches the hills, and they smoke."[123]

> [g] *The hills forget they're fix'd, and in their fright,*
> *Cast off their weight, and ease themselves for flight:*
> *The woods, with terror wing'd, out-fly the wind,*
> *And leave the heavy, panting hills behind.*[124]

---

[e] A Philips to Cuzzona.
[B] [f] Job, p. 108.
[g] P. 267.

A   You here see the hills not only trembling, but shaking off the woods from their backs, to run the faster: After this you are presented with a foot-race of mountains and woods, where the woods distance the mountains, that, like corpulent pursy fellows come puffing and panting a vast way behind them.

CHAP. IX.

Of Imitation, and the Manner of Imitating.[125]

That the true authors of the Profund are to imitate diligently the examples in their *own way,* is not to be question'd, and that divers have by this means attain'd to a depth whereunto their own weight
B could never have carried them, is evident by sundry instances. Who
,D sees not that De Foe was the poetical son[126] of Withers,[127] Tate of
G Ogilby,[128], E. Ward of John Taylor,[129] and Eusden of Blackmore?[130] Therefore when we sit down to write, let us bring some great author to our mind, and ask ourselves this question; How would Sir Richard
H have said this? Do I express my self as simply as Ambrose Philips? Or flow my numbers with the quiet thoughtlessness of Mr.
I Welsted?[131]

But it may seem somewhat strange to assert, that our Proficient should also read the works of those famous Poets who have excelled in the *Sublime:* Yet is not this a paradox? As Virgil is said to have read Ennius, out of his dunghill to draw gold, so may our author read Shakespear, Milton, and Dryden for the contrary end, to bury their gold in his own dunghil[l]. A true Genius, when he finds any thing lofty or shining in them, will have the skill to bring it down, take off the gloss, or quite discharge the colour, by some ingenious Circumstance or Periphase, some addition or diminution, or by some of those Figures, the use of which we shall shew in our next chapter.

The book of Job is acknowledged to be infinitely sublime, and
J yet has not the father of the Bathos reduced it in every page? Is there a passage in all Virgil more painted up and labour'd than the description of Ætna in the third Æneid?

> ——*Horrificis juxta tonat Ætna ruinis,*
> *Interdumque atram prorumpit ad æthera nubem,*
> *Turbine fumantem piceo, & candente favilla,*

Attollitque globos flammarum, & fidera lambit.
Interdum scopulos avulsaque viscera montis
Erigit eructans, liquefactaque saxa sub auras
Cum gemitu glomerat, fundoque exæstuat imo. [132]

A   (I beg pardon of the gentle English reader, and such of our writers as understand not Latin.) Lo! how this is taken down by our British Poet, by the single happy thought of throwing the mountain into a *fit* of the *cholic.*

      [h] *Ætna, and all the burning mountains, find*
      Their kindled stores with inbred storms of wind
      Blown up to rage; and, roaring out, *complain,*
      As torn with inward gripes, *and tort'ring pain:*
      Lab'ring, they cast their dreadful vomit *round,*
      And with their melted bowels *spread the ground.*

   Horace, in search of the Sublime, struck his head against the Stars[i];[133] but Empedocles, to fathom the Profund, threw himself into
B   Ætna.[134] And who would not imagine our excellent Modern had also been there, from this description?

   Imitation is of two sorts; the first is when we force to our own purposes the Thoughts of others; the second consists in copying the Imperfections, or Blemishes of celebrated authors.[135] I have seen a
C   Play professedly writ in the style of Shakespear; wherein the resemblance lay in one single line,

      And so good morrow t'ye, good master Lieutenant. [136]

And sundry poems in imitation of Milton, where with the utmost exactness, and not so much as one exception, nevertheless was constantly *nathless,* embroider'd was *broider'd,* hermits were *eremites,* disdain'd was *'sdeign'd,* shady *umbrageous,* enterprize *emprize,* pagan *paynim,* pinions *pennons,* sweet *dulcet,* orchards *orchats,* bridge-work *pontifical;* nay, her was *hir,* and their was *thir* thro' the whole poem.[137] And in very deed, there is no other way by which the true modern poet could read, to any purpose, the works of such men as Milton and Shakespear.

   [h] Pr. Arth., p. 75.
   [i] Sublimi feriam sidera vertice.

It may be expected, that like other Critics, I should next speak of the *Passions:* But as the main end and principal effect of the Bathos is to produce *Tranquillity of Mind,* (and sure it is a better design to promote *sleep* than madness) we have little to say on this subject. [138] Nor will the short bounds of this discourse allow us to treat at large of the *Emollients* and *Opiats* of Poesy, of the Cool, and the manner of producing it, or of the methods us'd by our authors in managing the Passions. I shall but transiently remark, that nothing contributes so much to the *Cool,* [139] as the use of *Wit* in expressing passion: The true genius rarely fails of points, conceits, and proper *similes* on such occasions: This we may term the *Pathetic epigrammatical,* in which even puns are made use of with good success. [140] Hereby our best authors have avoided throwing themselves or their readers into any indecent Transports.

A   But as it is sometimes needful to excite the *passions* of our antag-
B   onist in the polemick way, the true students in the low [141] have constantly taken their methods from low life, where they observ'd, that to move Anger, use is made of scolding and railing; to move Love, of bawdry; to beget Favour and Friendship, of gross flattery;
C   and to produce Fear, of calumniating an adversary with crimes obnoxious to the State. As for Shame, it is a silly passion, of which as our authors are incapable themselves, so they would not produce it in others.

CHAP. X.

D   *Of* Tropes *and* Figures: *And first of the variegating, confounding, and reversing Figures.*

But we proceed to the *Figures.* [142] We cannot too earnestly recommend to our authors the study of the *Abuse of Speech.* They ought to lay it down as a principle, to say nothing in the usual way, but (if possible) in the direct contrary. Therefore the Figures must be so turn'd, as to manifest that intricate and wonderful Cast of Head
E   which distinguishes all writers of this kind; or (as I may say) to refer exactly the Mold in which they were formed, in all its inequalities, cavities, obliquities, odd crannies, and distortions.

It would be endless, nay impossible to enumerate all such Figures;

but we shall content ourselves to range the principal, which most
powerfully contribute to the Bathos,[143] under three Classes.

A   I. The Variegating, Confounding, or Reversing Tropes and Fig-
       ures.
      II. The Magnifying, and
     III. The Diminishing.

We cannot avoid giving to these the Greek or Roman Names:
But in tenderness to our countrymen and fellow writers, many of
whom, however exquisite, are wholly ignorant of those languages,
we have also explained them in our mother tongue.

B   Of the first sort, nothing so much conduces to the Bathos,[144] as
the

CATACHRESIS.

A Master of this will say,

> Mow the Beard,
> Shave the Grass,
> Pin the Plank,
> Nail my Sleeve.

C From whence results the same kind of pleasure to the mind, as to
the eye when we behold Harlequin trimming himself with a hatchet,
hewing down a tree with a rasor, making his tea in a cauldron, and
brewing his ale in a tea-pot, to the incredible satisfaction of the
British spectator. Another source of the Bathos is,

The METONYMY,

the inversion of Causes for Effects, of Inventors for Inventions, &c.[145]

> *Lac'd in her* [k]*Cosins new appear'd the bride,*
> *A* [l]*Bubble-boy and* [m]*Tompion at her side,*
> *And with an air divine her* [n]*Colmar ply'd:*

[k] Stays.
[l] Tweezer-case.
[m] Watch.
[n] Fan.

Then oh! she cries, what slaves I round me see?
Here a bright Redcoat, there a smart °Toupee.[146]

The SYNECHDOCHE,

which consists, in the use of a part for the whole. You may call a young woman sometimes Pretty-*face* and Pigs-*eyes,* and sometimes Snotty-*nose* and Draggle-*tail.*[147] Or of Accidents for Persons; as a Lawyer is called Split-cause, a Taylor Prick-louse, &c. Or of things belonging to a man, for the man himself; as a *Sword*-man, a *Gown*-man, a *T——m-T——d*-man;[148] a White-*Staff,*[149] a Turn-*key,* &c.

The APOSIOPESIS,[150]

An excellent figure for the Ignorant, as "What shall I say?" when one has nothing to say: or "I can no more," when one really can no more. Expressions which the gentle reader is so good as never to take in earnest.

The METAPHOR.

The first rule is to draw it from the *lowest things,* which is a certain way to sink the highest; as when you speak of the Thunder of Heaven, say,

[1] *The* Lords above *are* angry *and* talk big.[151]

Or if you would describe a rich man refunding his treasures, express it thus,

[m] *Tho' he (as said) may Riches* gorge, *the Spoil*
Painful in massy Vomit shall recoil,
Soon shall he perish with a swift decay,
Like his own Ordure, cast with scorn away.[152]

Secondly, that whenever you start a Metaphor, you must be sure to *run it down,* and pursue it as far as it can go. If you get the scent of a State negotiation, follow it in this manner.

° A sort of Perriwig: All words in use at this present writing.
[1] Lee Alex.
[m] Black. Job. p. 91, 93.

> [n] *The stones and all the elements with thee*
> *Shall* ratify *a strict* confederacy;
> *Wild beasts their savage temper shall forget,*
> *And for a firm* alliance *with thee* treat;
> *The finny tyrant*[153] *of the spacious seas*
> *Shall send a* scaly embassy *for peace*:
> *His* plighted faith *the Crocodile shall keep,*
> *And seeing thee, for joy sincerely weep.*

Or if you represent the Creator denouncing war against the wicked, be sure not to omit one circumstance usual in proclaiming and levying war.

> [o] Envoys *and* Agents, *who by my command*
> *Reside in Palestina's land,*
> *To whom* commissions *I have given,*
> *To manage there the* interests *of heaven.*
> *Ye* holy heralds *who* proclaim
> *Or war or peace, in mine your master's name,—*
> *Ye* pioneers *of heaven, prepare a* road,
> *Make it plain, direct and broad;———*
> *For I* in person *will my people* head;
> *———For the divine deliverer*
> *Will* on his march *in majesty appear,*
> *And needs the aid of no* confed'rate pow'r.[154]

[A] We come next to the Confounding, under which we rank

[B]   1. The MIXTURE OF FIGURES,

which raises so many images, as to give you no image at all. But its principal beauty is when it gives an idea just *opposite* to what it seem'd meant to describe. Thus an ingenious artist painting the Spring, talks of a *Snow of Blossoms,* and thereby raises an unexpected picture of Winter. Of this sort is the following:

> [p] *The gaping clouds pour lakes of sulphur down,*
> *Whose livid flashes sickning sunbeams drown.*

[n] Job, p. 22.
[o] Blackm. Isa. c[hap]. xl.
[C] [p] Pr. Arthur, p. 73.

What a noble Confusion? clouds, lakes, brimstone, flames, sun-
beams, gaping, pouring, sickning, drowning! all in two lines.

2. The JARGON. [155]

> q *Thy head shall rise, tho' buried in the dust,*
> *And 'midst the clouds his*[156] *glittering turrets thrust.*

Quære, What are the glittering turrets of a man's head?

> r *Upon the shore, as frequent as the sand,* [157]
> *To meet the Prince, the glad Dimetians stand.*

Quære, Where these Dimetians stood? and of what size they were?

A Add also to the *Jargon* such as the following.

> s *Destruction's empire shall no longer last,*
> *And Desolation lye for ever waste.* [158]

B

> t *Here Niobe, sad mother, makes her moan,*
> *And seems converted to a stone in stone.* [159]

C But for Variegation, nothing is more useful than

D   ## 3. The PARANOMASIA, or PUN,

where a Word, like the tongue of a jack-daw, speaks twice as much
by being split: As this of Mr. Dennis,

> *Bullets that wound, like Parthians, as they* fly: [w160]

or this excellent one of Mr. Welsted,

> x *—Behold the Virgin lye*
> *Naked, and only* cover'd *by the* Sky. [161]

To which thou may'st add,

q Job, p. 107.
r Pr. Arthur, p. 157.
s Job, p. 89.
t T. Cook, Poems.
w Poems 1693, pag. 13.
x Welsted, Poems, Acon & Lavin.

To see her beauties no man needs to stoop,
She has the whole Horizon for her hoop. [162]

4. The ANTITHESIS, or SEE-SAW,

whereby Contraries and Oppositions are balanced in such a way, as
to cause a reader to remain suspended between them, to his exceeding delight and recreation. Such are these, on a lady who made
herself appear out of size, by hiding a young princess under her
cloaths.

[y] *While the kind nymph changing her faultless shape*
Becomes unhandsome, handsomely *to scape.* [163]

On the Maids of Honour in mourning:

[z] *Sadly they charm, and dismally they please.* [164]
——*His eyes so bright*
[a] *Let in the object and let out the light.* [165]
[b] *The Gods look pale to see us look so red.* [166]
——*The ᶜFairies and their Queen*
In mantles blue came tripping o'er the green. [167]
[d] *All nature felt a reverential shock,*
The sea stood still to see the mountains rock.

CHAP. XI.

The Figures continued: Of the Magnifying and Diminishing Figures.

A Genuine Writer of the Profund will take care never to *magnify*
any object without *clouding* it at the same time: His Thought will
appear in a true mist, and very unlike what is in nature. It must
always be remember'd that Darkness is an essential quality of the

[y] Waller.
[z] Steel on Queen Mary.
[a] Quarles.
[b] Lee, Alex.
[c] Phil. Past.
[d] Blackm. Job, p. 176.

Profund, or if there chance to be a glimmering, it must be as Milton expresses it,

> No *light, but rather darkness visible.*[168]

The chief Figure of this sort is,

A

> 1. The HYPERBOLE, or Impossible.

For instance, of a Lion;

> [e] *He roar'd so loud, and look'd so wond'rous grim,*
> *His very shadow durst not follow him.*[169]

Of a Lady at Dinner.

> *The silver whiteness that adorns thy neck,*
> *Sullies the plate, and makes the napkin black*

Of the same.

> ——*Th'[f] obscureness of her birth*
> *Cannot eclipse the lustre of her eyes,*
> *Which make her all one light.*[170]

Of a Bull-baiting.

> [g] *Up to the stars the sprawling mastives fly,*
> *And add new monsters to the frighted sky.*[171]

Of a Scene of Misery.

> [h] *Behold a scene of misery and woe!*
> *Here Argus soon might weep himself quite blind,*
> *Ev'n tho' he had Briareus' hundred hands*
> *To wipe those hundred eyes*——

B

And that modest request of two absent lovers:

> *Ye Gods! annihilate but Space and Time,*
> *And make two lovers happy.*

C
[e] Vet. Aut.
[f] Theob. Double Falshood.
[g] Blackm.
[h] Anon.

A   2. The PERIPHRASIS, which the Moderns call the *Circumbendibus,* whereof we have given examples in the ninth chapter, and shall again in the twelfth.

To the same class of the *Magnifying* may be referr'd the following, which are so excellently modern, that we have yet no name for them. In describing a country prospect,

> [i] *I'd call them mountains, but can't call them so,*
> *For fear to wrong them with a name too low;*
> *While the fair vales beneath so humbly lie,*
> *That even humble seems a term too high.*

B   III. The third Class remains, of the *Diminishing* Figures: And 1. the ANTICLIMAX, where the second line drops quite short of the first, than which nothing creates greater surprize.

On the extent of the British Arms.

> [k] *Under the Tropicks is our language spoke,*
> *And Part of Flanders hath receiv'd our Yoke.* [172]

On a Warrior.

> [l] *And thou Dalhoussy the great God of War,*
> *Lieutenant Colonel to the Earl of Mar.* [173]

On the Valour of the English.

C
D
> [m] *Nor* Art *nor* Nature *has the force*
> *To stop its steddy course,*
> *Nor* Alps *nor* Pyrenæns *keep it out,*
> ——*Nor fortify'd Redoubt.* [174]

At other times this figure operates in a larger extent; and when the gentle reader is in expectation of some great image, he either E finds it surprizingly imperfect, or is presented with something low, or quite ridiculous: A surprize resembling that of a curious person in a cabinet of Antique Statues, [175] who beholds on the pedestal the

[i] Anon.

[k] Wall.

[l] Anon.

[m] Denn. on Namur.

names of Homer, or Cato; but looking up finds Homer without a
head, and nothing to be seen of Cato but his privy member.[176] Such
A are these lines of a Leviathan at sea,

> [n] *His motion works, and beats the oozy mud,*
> *And with its slime incorporates the flood,*
> *'Till all th' encumber'd, thick, fermenting stream*
> B Does *like* one Pot of boiling Ointment seem.
> *Where'er he swims, he leaves along the lake*
> *Such frothy furrows, such a foamy track,*
> *That all the waters of the deep appear*
> Hoary——*with age, or* grey *with sudden fear.*[177]

But perhaps even these are excelled by the ensuing.

> [o] *Now the resisted flames and firey store,*
> *By winds assaulted, in wide forges roar,* }
> *And raging seas flow down of melted Ore.* }
> *Sometimes they hear long* Iron Bars remov'd,
> *And* to *and* fro *huge* Heaps of Cynders shov'd.[178]

C   2. The VULGAR,

D is also a Species of the *Diminishing:* By this a spear flying into the
air is compared to a boy whistling as he goes on an errand.

> [p] *The mighty* Stuffa *threw a massy spear,*
> *Which, with its* Errand *pleas'd, sung thro' the air.*[179]

A Man raging with grief to a Mastiff Dog.

> [q] *I cannot stifle this*[180] *gigantic woe,*
> *Nor on my raging grief a* muzzle *throw.*

And Clouds big with water to a woman in great necessity:

> Distended *with the* Waters *in 'em pent,*
> *The clouds* hang deep *in air, but* hang unrent.[181]

[n] Blackm. Job, p. 197.
[o] Pr. Arthur. p. 157.
[p] Pr. Arthur.
[q] Job, p. 41.

3. The INFANTINE.

This is when a Poet grows so very simple, as to think and talk like a child. I shall take my examples from the greatest Master in this way: Hear how he fondles, like a meer stammerer.

> [r] Little Charm *of placid mien,*
> Miniature *of beauty's queen,*
> *Hither, British muse* of mine,
> *Hither, all ye* Græcian Nine,
> *With the lovely Graces* Three,
> *And your* pretty Nurseling *see.*
>
> *When the meadows next are seen,*
> *Sweet enamel, white and green.*
> *When again the* lambkins *play,*
> Pretty Sportlings *full of* May.
>
> *Then the neck so white and round,*
> (Little Neck *with brilliants bound.*)
> *And thy* Gentleness *of mind,*
> (Gentle *from a* gentle *kind*) &c.
> Happy *thrice, and* thrice agen,
> Happiest *he of* happy *men,* &c.[182]

[A]   and the rest of those excellent Lullabies of his composition. How prettily he asks the sheep to teach him to bleat?

> [s] *Teach me to grieve with bleating moan, my sheep.*[183]

Hear how a babe would reason on his nurse's death:

> [t] *That ever she* could *die! Oh most* unkind!
> *To die, and leave poor* Colinet *behind?*
> *And yet,——Why blame I her?*——[184]

[B]   With[185] no less simplicity does he suppose that shepherdesses tear their hair and beat their breasts, at their own deaths:

[r] Amb. Philips on Miss C[uzonna].
[s] Philips's Pastorals.
[t] Ibid.

^v *Ye brighter maids, faint emblems of my fair,*
With looks cast down, and with dishevel'd hair,
In bitter anguish beat your breasts, and moan,
Her death untimely, as it were your own. [186]

A

4. The INANINITY, or NOTHINGNESS.

B Of this the same author furnishes us with most beautiful instances: where you easily perceive the Nothingness of every second
Verse.

^y *Ah silly I, more silly than my sheep,*
(Which on the flow'ry plain I once did keep.) [187]

^z *To the grave Senate she could counsel give,*
(Which with astonishment they did receive.) [188]

^a *He whom loud cannon could not terrify,*
Falls, (from the grandeur of his Majesty.) [189]

C

^b *Happy, merry as a king,*
Sipping dew——you sip, and sing. [190]

The Noise *returning with returning* Light,

What did it?

D

^c *Dispers'd the* Silence, *and dispell'd the* Night.

^d *The glories of proud* London *to survey,*
The Sun himself shall rise——by break of day. [191]

E

5. The EXPLETIVE.

admirably exemplified in the Epithets of many authors.

^v Ibid.
^x Ibid.
^y Ibid.
^z Phil. on Q. Mary.
^a Ibid.
^b T. Cook, on a Grashopper.
^c Anon.
^d Autor Vet.

Th' umbrageous shadow, and the verdant green,
The running current, and odorous fragrance,
Chear my lone solitude with joyous gladness. [192]

A   Or in pretty drawling words like these,

ᵉ *All men his tomb, all men his sons adore,*
And his son's sons, till there shall be no more. [193]
The rising sun our grief did see,
The setting sun did see the same,
While wretched we remembred thee,
ᶠ*O Sion, Sion, lonely name.* [194]

6. The MACROLOGY and PLEONASM [195]

are as generally coupled, as a lean rabbit with a fat one; nor is it a wonder, the superfluity of words and vacuity of sense, being just the same thing. I am pleased to see one of our greatest adversaries [196] employ this figure.

ᵍ *The growth of meadows, and the pride of fields.*
The food of armies and support of wars.
Refuse of swords, and gleanings of a fight.
Lessen his numbers, and contract his host.
Where'er his friends retire, or foes succeed,
Cover'd with tempests, and in oceans drown'd. [197]

Of all which the Perfection is

The TAUTOLOGY.

Break thro' the billows, and——divide the main. [198]
ʰ *In smoother numbers, and——in softer verse.* [199]
ⁱ *Divide—and part—the sever'd World—in two.* [200]

With ten thousand others, equally musical, and plentifully flowing thro' most of our celebrated modern Poems.

ᵉ T. Cook, Poems.
ᶠ Ibid.
ᵍ Camp.
ʰ Tons. Misc. 12° vol. 4. p. 291. 4th Edit.
ⁱ Ibid. vol. 6. p. 121.

CHAP. XII.

Of Expression, *and the several Sorts of* Style *of the present Age.*[201]

The *Expression* is adequate, when it is proportionably low to the Profundity of the Thought. It must not be always *Grammatical,* lest A it appear pedantic and ungentlemanly; nor too clear, for fear it become vulgar; for obscurity bestows a cast of the wonderful, and throws an oracular dignity upon a piece which hath no meaning.

For example, sometimes use the wrong Number; *The Sword and Pestilence at once devours,* instead of *devour.* [k] Sometimes the wrong Case; *And who more fit to sooth the God than thee?* instead of *thou.* And rather than say, *Thetis saw Achilles weep,* she *heard* him weep.[202]

We must be exceeding careful in two things; first, in the *Choice* of *low Words:* secondly, in the *sober* and *orderly* way of *ranging* them. Many of our Poets are naturally bless'd with this talent, insomuch that they are in the circumstance of that honest Citizen, who had made *Prose* all his life without knowing it.[203] Let verses run in this manner, just to be a vehicle to the words. (I take them from my last cited author, who, tho' otherwise by no means of our rank, seem'd once in his life to have a mind to be simple.)[204]

[l] *If not, a prize I will myself decree,*
From him, or him, or else perhaps from thee.

[m] *— —full of Days was he;*
Two ages past, he liv'd the third to see.

[n] *The king of forty kings, and honour'd more*
By mighty Jove than e'er was king before.

[o] *That I may know, if thou my pray'r deny,*
The most despis'd of all the Gods am I.

[p] *Then let my mother once be rul'd by me,*
Tho' much more wise than I pretend to be.

[k] Ti. Hom. Il. I.
[l] Ti. Hom. Il. I. p. 11.
[m] Idem. p. 17.
[n] Id. p. 19.
[o] P. 34.
[p] P. 38.

Or these, of the same hand,[205]

> q *I leave the arts of poetry and verse*
> *To them that practise them with more success.*
> *Of greater truths I now prepare to tell,*
> *And so at once, dear friend and muse, farewel.*[206]

A   Sometimes a single *Word* will vulgarize a poetical idea; as where a Ship set on fire owes all the *Spirit* of the *Bathos* to one choice word that ends the line.

> r *And his scorch'd ribs the hot Contagion* fry'd.

And in that description of a World in ruins,

> s *Should the whole frame of nature round him break,*
> *He unconcern'd would hear the mighty* Crack.[207]

So also in these,

> t *Beasts tame and savage to the river's brink*
> *Come, from the fields and wild abodes*—to drink.[208]

Frequently two or three words will do it effectually,

> v *He from the clouds does the* sweet liquor squeeze,
> *That chears the* Forest and the Garden *trees.*[209]

It is also useful to employ *Technical Terms,* which estrange your style from the great and general Ideas of nature: and the higher your subject is, the lower should you search into mechanicks for your expression.[210] If you describe the garment of an angel, say that his x *Linnen* was *finely spun,* and *bleach'd on the happy Plains.* y Call an

---

q Tons. Misc. 12° vol. 4. p. 292, fourth Edit.
r Pr. Arthur, p. 151.
s Tons. Misc. vol. 6, p. 119.
t Job, 263 [error for 262].
v Id. Job, 264.
x Prince Arthur, p. 19.
B   y Ibid. p. 339.

army of angels, *Angelic Cuirassiers,* and, if you have occasion to mention a number of misfortunes, style them

> [z] *Fresh* Troops *of Pains, and* regimented *Woes.*[211]

STYLE is divided by the Rhetoricians into the Proper and the Figured.[212] Of the Figur'd we have already treated, and the Proper is what our authors have nothing to do with. Of Styles we shall mention only the Principal which owe to the moderns either their chief Improvement, or entire Invention.

A

1. The FLORID Style,

B than which none is more proper to the Bathos, as flowers which are the *Lowest* of vegetables, are most *Gaudy,* and do many times grow in great plenty at the bottom of *Ponds* and *Ditches.*[213]

A fine writer in this kind presents you with the following Posie:

> [a] *The groves appear all drest with wreaths of flowers,*
> *And from their leaves drop aromatic showers,*
> *Whose fragrant heads in mystic twines above,*
> *Exchang'd their sweets, and mix'd with thousand kisses,*
> *As if the willing branches strove*
> *To beautify and shade the grove,*[214]

C which indeed most branches do. But this is still excell'd by our Laureat,

> [b] *Branches in branches twin'd compose the grove,*
> *And shoot and spread, and blossom into love.*
> *The trembling palms their mutual vows repeat,*
> *And bending poplars bending poplars meet.*
> *The distant platanes seem to press more nigh,*
> *And to the sighing alders, alders sigh.*[215]

Hear also our Homer.

[z] Job, p. 86.
[a] Behn's Poems, p. 2.
[b] Guardian, 12° 127.

His Robe of State *is form'd of light refin'd,*
An endless Train *of lustre* spreads behind.
His throne's of bright compacted Glory *made,*
With Pearls *celestial, and with Gems* inlaid:
Whence Floods *of joy, and* Seas *of splendor flow,*
On all th' angelic gazing throng below.[216]

2. The PERT Style:[217]

This does in as peculiar a manner become the low in wit, as a pert air does the low in stature. Mr. *Thomas Brown,* the author of the *London Spy,* and all the *Spies* and *Trips* in general, are herein to be diligently studied: In Verse Mr. *Cibber's Prologues.*[218]

But the beauty and energy of it is never so conspicuous, as when it is employ'd in *Modernizing* and *Adapting* to the *Taste of the Times* the works of the *Antients.* This we rightly phrase *Doing* them into English,[219] and *Making* them English; two expressions of great Propriety, the one denoting our *Neglect* of the *Manner how,* the other the *Force* and *Compulsion* with which it is brought about. It is by virtue of this Style that Tacitus talks like a Coffee-House Politician,[220] Josephus like the British Gazetteer,[221] Tully is as short and smart as Seneca or Mr. Asgill,[222] Marcus Aurelius is excellent at Snip-snap,[223] and honest Thomas à Kempis as Prim and Polite as any preacher at court.[224]

3. The ALAMODE[225] Style:

which is fine by being *new,* and has this happiness attending it, that it is as durable and extensive as the poem itself. Take some examples of it, in the description of the Sun in a Mourning coach upon the death of Queen Mary.

See Phœbus *now, as once for* Phaeton,[226]
Has mask'd his face; and put deep Mourning on;
Dark clouds his fable Chariot *do surround,*
And the dull Steeds stalk o'er *the* melancholy round.

Blackm. Ps. 104.
Amb. Philips.

Of Prince Arthur's Soldiers drinking.

> ᵉ *While rich* Burgundian *wine, and bright* Champaign,
> *Chase from their minds the terrors of the main.*²²⁷

(whence we also learn, that *Burgundy* and *Champaign* make a man on shore despise a storm at sea.)

Of the Almighty encamping his Regiments.

> ᶠ —*He sunk a vast capacious deep,*
> *Where he his* liquid Regiments *does keep,*
> *Thither the waves* file off, *and make their way,*
> *To form the* mighty body *of the sea;*
> *Where they* encamp, *and in their* station stand,
> Entrench'd *in* Works *of* Rock, *and* Lines *of* Sand.²²⁸

Of two Armies on the Point of engaging.

> ᵍ *Yon' armies are the* Cards *which both must play;*
> *At least come off a* Saver *if you may:*
> Throw boldly *at the* Sum *the* Gods *have* set;
> *These on your side will all their fortunes* bet.²²⁹

ᴀ All perfectly agreeable to the present Customs and best Fashions of our Metropolis.

But the principal branch of the *Alamode* is the PRURIENT, a Style greatly advanced and honoured of late by the practice of persons of the *first Quality*; and, by the encouragement of the *Ladies,* not unsuccessfully introduced even into the Drawing-room.²³⁰ Indeed its incredible Progress and Conquests may be compared to those of the great *Sesostris,*²³¹ and are every where known by the *same Marks,* the images of the genital parts of men or women.²³² It consists wholly of metaphors drawn from two most fruitful sources or springs, the very Bathos of the human body, that is to say * * * and * * * *Hiatus Magnus lachrymabilis.*²³³* * * * * * * * * * * * * * * * *
* * * * * * * * * * * * * * * * *

And *selling of Bargains,*²³⁴ and *double Entendre,* and Κιββέρισμος and Ὀλδφιέλδισμος,²³⁵ all derived from the said sources.

ᵉ Pr. Arthur, p. 16.
ᶠ Blackm. Ps. 104. p. 261.
ᵍ Lee, Sophon.

A   4. The FINICAL Style,

which consists of the most curious, affected, mincing metaphors,
B and partakes of the *alamode*: as the following,

C   Of a Brook dry'd by the Sun.

  h Won *by the summer's* importuning *ray,*
    Th' eloping *stream did from her channel stray,*[236] }
    And with enticing *sun-beams* stole away.

                    Of an easy Death.

  i *When watchful death shall on his harvest look,*
    And see thee ripe with age, invite *the hook;*
    He'll gently *cut thy* bending *Stalk, and thee*
    Lay kindly *in the* Grave, *his* Granary.

                    Of Trees in a Storm.

D k *Oaks whose extended arms the winds defy,*
    The tempest sees *their strength,* and sighs, and passes by.[237]

                    Of Water simmering over the Fire.

  l *The sparkling flames raise water to a* Smile,
    Yet the pleas'd *liquor* pines, *and lessens all the while.*[238]

    5. LASTLY, I shall place the CUMBROUS, which moves heavily
under a load of metaphors, and draws after it a long train of words.
And the BUSKIN,[239] or *Stately,* frequently and with great felicity
mix'd with the former. For as the first is the proper engine to depress
what is high, so is the second to raise what is base and low to a
ridiculous Visibility. When both these can be done at once, then is
the Bathos in perfection; as when a man is set with his head downward, and his breeach upright, his degradation is compleat: One
E end of him is higher than ever, only that end is the *wrong one.* Will

  h Blackm. Job, p. 26.
  i Ibid. p. 23.
  k Denn.
  l Anon. Tons. Misc. Part 6. p. 234 [misprinted 224 in 1741–
52].

not every true lover of the Profund be delighted to behold the most
A vulgar and low actions of life exalted in the following manner?[240]

Who knocks at the Door?

For whom thus rudely pleads my loud-tongu'd gate,
That he may enter?——

See who is there?

[m] *Advance the fringed curtains of thy eyes,*
And tell me who comes yonder.——[241]

Shut the Door.

The wooden guardian of our privacy
Quick on its axle turn.——

Bring my Cloaths.

Bring me what Nature, taylor to the Bear,
To Man *himself deny'd: She gave me Cold,*
But would not give me Cloaths.——

Light the Fire.

Bring forth some remnant of Promethean *theft,*
Quick to expand th' inclement air congeal'd
By Boreas' *rude breath.*——

Snuff the Candle.

Yon' Luminary amputation needs,
Thus shall you save its half-extinguish'd life.

Open the Letter.

[n] *Wax! render up thy trust.*——[242]

Uncork the Bottle, and chip the Bread.

Apply thine engine to the spungy door,
Set Bacchus *from his glassy prison free,*
And strip white Ceres *of her nut-brown coat.*

[m] Temp.
B [n] Theob. Double Falshood.

A   CHAP. XIII.[243]

A Project for the Advancement of the Bathos.[244]

Thus have I (my dear Countrymen) with incredible pains and diligence, discovered the hidden sources of the *Bathos,* or, as I may say,
broke open the Abysses of this *Great Deep.* And having now esta-
B blish'd good and wholesome Laws, what remains but that all true
moderns[245] with their utmost might do proceed to put the same in
execution? In order whereto, I think I shall in the second place
highly deserve of my Country, by proposing such a *Scheme,* as may
facilitate this great end.[246]

As our Number is confessedly far superior to that of the enemy,
there seems nothing wanting but Unanimity among ourselves. It is
therefore humbly offer'd, that all and every individual of the Bathos
do enter into a firm association, and incorporate into One regular
Body, whereof every member, even the meanest, will some way
contribute to the support of the whole;[247] in like manner, as the
weakest reeds, when joined in one bundle, become infrangible. To
which end, our Art ought to be put upon the same foot with other
Arts of this age. The vast improvement of modern manufactures
ariseth from their being divided into several branches, and parcel'd
out to several trades: For instance, in Clock-making, one artist
makes the balance, another the spring, another the crown-wheels,
a fourth the case, and the principal workman puts all together: To
this oeconomy we owe the perfection of our modern watches, and
doubtless we also might that of our modern Poetry and Rhetoric,
were the several parts branched out in the like manner.

Nothing is more evident than that divers persons, no other way
remarkable, have each a strong disposition to the formation of some
particular Trope or Figure. Aristotle saith, that "the *Hyperbole* is an
C ornament fit for young Men of Quality;"[248] accordingly we find in
those Gentlemen a wonderful propensity toward it, which is marvellously improved by Travelling. Soldiers also and Seamen are very
happy in the same Figure. The *Periphrasis* or *Circumlocution* is the
peculiar talent of Country Farmers; the *Proverb* and *Apologue* of old
Men at their clubs; the *Ellipsis* or Speech by half words, of Ministers

A and Politicians, the *Aposiopesis*[249] of Courtiers, the *Litotes* or Diminution, of Ladies, Whisperers and Backbiters; and the *Anadiplosis*[250] of common Cryers and Hawkers, who by redoubling the same words, persuade people to buy their oysters, green hastings,[251] or new ballads. *Epithets* may be found in great plenty at Billinsgate,[252] *Sarcasm* and *Irony* learned upon the Water,[253] and the *Epiphonema* or *Exclamation* frequently from the Beargarden,[254] and as frequently from the *Hear him* of the House of Commons.

Now each man applying his whole time and genius upon his particular Figure, would doubtless attain to perfection; and when each became incorporated and sworn into the Society, (as hath been proposed) a Poet or Orator would have no more to do but to send to the particular Traders in each Kind, to the *Metaphorist* for his *Allegories,* to the *Simile-maker* for his *Comparisons,* to the *Ironist* for his *Sarcasms,* to the *Apothegmatist* for his *Sentences,* &c. whereby a Dedication or Speech would be compos'd in a moment, the superior artist having nothing to do but to put together all the Materials.

I therefore propose that there be contrived with all convenient dispatch, at the publick expence, a *Rhetorical Chest of Drawers,*[255] consisting of three Stories, the highest for the *Deliberative,* the middle for the *Demonstrative,* and the lowest for the *Judicial.* These shall be divided into *Loci* or *Places,* being repositories for Matter and Argument in the several kinds of oration or writing; and every Drawer shall again be sub-divided into Cells, resembling those of Cabinets for Rarities. The apartment for *Peace* or *War,* and that of the *Liberty of the Press,* may in a very few days be fill'd with several arguments perfectly new; and the *Vituperative Partition* will as easily be replenished with a most choice collection, entirely of the growth and manufacture of the present age. Every composer will soon be taught the use of this Cabinet, and how to manage all the Registers B of it, which will be drawn out much in the manner of those in an Organ.[256]

The Keys of it must be kept in honest hands, by some *Reverend Prelate,* or *Valiant Officer,* of unquestion'd Loyalty and Affection to every present Establishment in Church and State; which will sufficiently guard against any mischief which might otherwise be apprehended from it.[257]

And being lodg'd in such hands, it may be at discretion *let out*
by the *Day,* to several great Orators in both Houses; from whence
A it is to be hop'd much *Profit* and *Gain* will also accrue to our Society.

CHAP. XIV.[258]

How to make Dedications, Panegyrics, *or* Satires, *and of the* Colours
of Honourable and Dishonourable.

Now of what necessity the foregoing Project may prove, will appear
from this single consideration, that nothing is of equal consequence
to the success of our Works, as *Speed* and *Dispatch.* Great pity it is,
that solid brains are not like other solid bodies, constantly endow'd
with a velocity in sinking, proportion'd to their heaviness: For it is
with the Flowers of the Bathos as with those of Nature, which if
B the careful gardener brings not hastily to market in the Morning,
must unprofitably perish and wither before Night. And of all our
Productions none is so short-liv'd as the *Dedication* and *Panegyric,*
which are often but the *Praise of a Day,* and become by the next,
utterly useless, improper, indecent, and false.[259] This is the more to
C,D be lamented, inasmuch as these two are the sorts whereon in a
E,F manner depends that *Profit* (which must still be remember'd to be
the main end) of our *Writers* and *Speakers.*

We shall therefore employ this chapter in shewing the quickest
method of composing them; after which we will teach a *short Way
to Epic Poetry.* And these being confessedly the works of most Importance and Difficulty, it is presum'd we may leave the rest to each
author's own learning or practice.

First of *Panegyric:* Every man is *honourable,* who is so by Law,
Custom, or Title. The *Publick* are better judges of what is honourable, than private Men. The Virtues of great Men, like those of
Plants, are inherent in them whether they are exerted or not; and
the more strongly inherent, the less they are exerted; as a Man is
the more rich, the less he spends. All great Ministers, without either
private or oeconomical Virtue, are *virtuous* by their *Posts;*[260] liberal
G and generous upon the *Publick Money,* provident upon *Publick Supplies,*

just by paying *Publick Interest,* couragious and magnanimous by the
A *Fleets* and *Armies,* magnificent upon the *Publick Expence,* and prudent
by *Publick Success.* They have by their Office, a right to a share of
the *Publick Stock* of Virtues; besides they are by *Prescription immemorial*
invested in all the celebrated virtues of their *Predecessors* in the same
stations, especially those of their own Ancestors.

As to what are commonly call'd the *Colours* of *Honourable* and
Dishonourable, they are various in different Countries: In this they
are *Blue, Green,* and *Red.* [261]

But forasmuch as the duty we owe to the Publick doth often
require that we should put some things in a strong light, and throw
a shade over others, I shall explain the method of turning a vicious
Man into a Hero.

The first and chief rule is the *Golden Rule* of *Transformation,* which
consists in converting Vices into their bordering Virtues. A Man
who is a Spendthrift, and will not pay a just Debt, may have his
Injustice *transform'd* into Liberality; Cowardice may be metamor-
phos'd into Prudence; Intemperance into good Nature and good
Fellowship; Corruption into Patriotism; and Lewdness into Tenderness and Facility. [262]

The second is the *Rule of Contraries:* It is certain, the less a Man
is endu'd with any Virtue, the more need he has to have it plentifully
bestow'd, especially those good qualities of which the world generally believes he hath none at all: For who will thank a Man for
giving him that which he *has?*

The Reverse of these Precepts will serve for *Satire,* wherein we
are ever to remark, that whoso loseth his place, or becomes out of
B favour with the Government, hath forfeited his share in *publick Praise*
and *Honour.* Therefore the truly-publick-spirited writer ought in duty
C to strip him whom the government hath stripped; which is the real
poetical Justice of this age. For a full collection of Topicks and Epithets
to be used in the Praise and Dispraise of Ministerial and Unmin-
isterial Persons, I refer to our *Rhetorical Cabinet;* concluding with an
earnest exhortation to all my brethren, to observe the Precepts here
laid down, the neglect of which hath cost some of them their *Ears*
in a *Pillory.* [263]

CHAP. XV.

A Receipt to make an Epic Poem.[264]

An Epic Poem, the Critics agree, is the greatest work human nature
is capable of. They have already laid down many mechanical rules
for compositions of this sort, but at the same time they cut off
almost all undertakers from the possibility of ever performing them;
for the first qualification they unanimously require in a Poet, is a
Genius.[265] I shall here endeavour (for the benefit of my Countrymen)
to make it manifest, that Epic Poems may be made *without a Genius,*
nay without Learning or much Reading. This must necessarily be
of great use to all those who confess they never *read,* and of whom
A   the world is convinc'd they never *learn.*[266] Moliere observes of making
a dinner, that any man can do it with *Money,* and if a profess'd Cook
cannot do it without, he has his Art for nothing;[267] The same may
be said of making a Poem, 'tis easily brought about by him that
has a *Genius,* but the skill lies in doing it without one. In pursuance
of this end, I shall present the reader with a plain and certain
Recipe,[268] by which any author in the Bathos may be qualified for
this grand performance.[269]

For the FABLE.[270]

Take out of any old Poem, History-book, Romance, or Legend,
(for instance, *Geoffry of Monmouth,* or *Don Belianis of Greece*) those
parts of story which afford most scope for *long Descriptions:*[271] Put
these pieces together, and throw all the adventures you fancy into
B   *one Tale.* Then take a Hero, whom you may chuse by the sound of
his name, and put him into the midst of these adventures:[272] There
let him *work* for twelve books; at the end of which you may take
him out, ready prepared to *conquer* or to *marry*; it being necessary
that the conclusion of an Epic Poem be *fortunate.*

To make an EPISODE.

Take any remaining adventure of your former collection, in which
you could no way involve your Hero: or any unfortunate accident
that was too good to be thrown away; and it will be of use, applied
to any other person, who may be lost and *evaporate* in the course of
the work, without the least damage to the composition.[273]

For the MORAL and ALLEGORY.

These you may extract out of the Fable afterwards, at your leisure:[274] Be sure you *strain* them sufficiently.

For the MANNERS.[275]

For those of the Hero, take all the best qualities you can find in
the most celebrated Heroes of antiquity; if they will not be reduced
A to a *Consistency*, lay them *all on a heap* upon him. But be sure they
are qualities which your *Patron* would be thought to have; and to
prevent any mistake which the world may be subject to, select from
the alphabet those capital letters that compose his name, and set
them at the head of a Dedication before your Poem. However, do
not absolutely observe the exact quantity of these Virtues, it not
being determin'd whether or no it be necessary for the Hero of a
Poem to be an *honest Man?*[276] For the *Under-Characters,* gather them
from Homer and Virgil, and change the names as occasion serves.

For the MACHINES.

Take of *Deities,* male and female, as many as you can use: Separate
them into two equal parts, and keep Jupiter in the middle; Let Juno
put him in a ferment, and Venus mollify him. Remember on all
occasions to make use of volatile Mercury. If you have need of *Devils,*
draw them out of Milton's Paradise, and extract your *Spirits* from
B Tasso. The use of these Machines is evident; since no Epic Poem can
possibly subsist without them,[277] the wisest way is to reserve them
for your greatest necessities: When you cannot extricate your Hero
by any human means, or yourself by your own wit, seek relief from
Heaven, and the Gods will do your business very readily. This is
according to the direct Prescription of Horace in his Art of Poetry,

> *Nec Deus intersit, nisi dignus vindice* Nodus
> *Inciderit.——*[278]

That is to say, *A Poet should never call upon the Gods for their Assistance,
but when he is in great Perplexity.*

For the DESCRIPTIONS.

For a *Tempest.* Take Eurus, Zephyr, Auster, and Boreas, and cast them together in one verse: add to these of Rain, Lightning and Thunder (the loudest you can) *quantum sufficit:* mix your Clouds and Billows well together 'till they foam, and thicken your Description here and there with a Quick-sand. Brew your Tempest well in your head, before you set it a blowing.[279]

For a *Battle.* Pick a large quantity of Images and Descriptions from Homer's Iliads, with a spice or two of Virgil, and if there remain any overplus, you may lay them by for a *Skirmish.* Season it well with *Similes,* and it will make an excellent Battle.

For a *Burning Town.* If such a Description be necessary, (because it is certain there is one in Virgil) old Troy is ready burnt to your hands. But if you fear that would be thought borrow'd, a Chapter or two of Burnet's Theory of the *Conflagration,* well circumstanced and done into verse, will be a good *Succedaneum.*[280]

As for *Similes* and *Metaphors,* they may be found all over the Creation; the most ignorant may *gather* them, but the difficulty is in *applying* them. For this advise with your *Bookseller.*

CHAP. XVI.
A Project for the Advancement of the Stage.

It may be thought that we should not omit the *Drama,* which makes so great and so lucrative a part of Poetry. But this Province is so well taken care of, by the present *Managers*[281] of the Theatre, that it is perfectly needless to suggest to them any other Methods than they have already practised for the advancement of the Bathos.

Here therefore, in the Name of all our Brethren, let me return our sincere and humble Thanks to the most August Mr. Barton Booth,[282] the most Serene Mr. Robert Wilks,[283] and the most Un-daunted Mr. Colly Cibber;[284] of whom let it be known, *when the People of this Age shall be Ancestors,* and to all *the Succession of our Successors,* that to this present Day they continue to *Out-do* even their *own Out-doings:*[285] And when the inevitable Hand of sweeping Time shall have brush'd off all the Works of *To-day,* may this Testimony of a *Co-temporary Critic* to their Fame, be extended as far as *To-morrow.*

Yet, if to so wise an Administration it be possible any thing can be added, it is that more ample and comprehensive Scheme which
A   Mr. Dennis and Mr. Gildon, (the two greatest Critics and Reformers then living) made publick in the year 1720, in a Project sign'd with their Names, and dated the 2ᵈ of February. I cannot better conclude than by presenting the Reader with the Substance of it.[286]

1. It is proposed, That the two *Theatres* be incorporated into one Company;[287] that the *Royal Academy of Musick* be added to them as an *Orchestra*;[288] and that Mr. Figg with his Prize-fighters,[289] and Violante with the Rope-dancers, be admitted in Partnership.[290]

2. That a spacious Building be erected at the Public expence, capable of containing at least *ten thousand* Spectators,[291] which is become absolutely necessary by the great addition of Children and Nurses to the Audience, since the new Entertainments.[292] That there be a Stage as large as the Athenian, which was near ninety thousand geometrical paces square, and separate divisions for the two Houses of Parliament, my Lords the Judges, the honourable the Directors of the Academy, and the Court of Aldermen, who shall all have their Places frank.[293]

3. If *Westminster-Hall*[294] be not allotted to this service, (which by reason of its proximity to the two Chambers of Parliament above-mentioned, seems not altogether improper;) it is left to the wisdom of the Nation whether *Somerset-House*[295] may not be demolished, and a Theatre built upon that Scite, which lies convenient to receive Spectators from the County of *Surrey,* who may be wafted thither by water-carriage, esteemed by all Projectors the cheapest whatsoever. To this may be added, that the river *Thames* may in the readiest manner convey those eminent Personages from Courts beyond the seas, who may be drawn either by Curiosity to behold some of our most celebrated Pieces, or by Affection to see their Countrymen, the Harlequins and Eunuchs; of which convenient notice may be given, for two or three months before, in the public Prints.[296]

4. That the *Theatre* abovesaid be environ'd with a fair Quadrangle of Buildings, fitted for the accommodation of decayed *Critics* and *Poets*; out of whom *Six* of the most aged (their age to be computed from the year wherein their first work was published) shall be elected

to manage the affairs of the Society, provided nevertheless that the
Laureat for the time being, may be always one. The Head or President over all, (to prevent disputes, but too frequent among the
A learned) shall be the most ancient *Poet* and *Critic* to be found in the
whole Island.[297]

5. The *Male-Players* are to be lodg'd in the garrets of the said
Quadrangle, and to attend the persons of the Poets dwelling under
them, by brushing their apparel, drawing on their shoes, and the
like. The *Actresses* are to make their beds, and wash their linnen.

6. A large room shall be set apart for a *Library,* to consist of all
the modern Dramatick Poems, and all the Criticisms extant. In the
midst of this room shall be a round table for the *Council of Six* to
sit and deliberate on the Merits of *Plays.*[298] The *Majority* shall determine the Dispute; and it it should happen that *three* and *three*
should be of each side, the President shall have a *casting Voice,* unless
where the Contention may run so high as to require a decision by
Single Combat.

7. It may be convenient to place the *Council of Six* in some conspicuous situation in the Theatre, where after the manner usually
practised by composers in musick, they may give *Signs* (before settled
and agreed upon) of Dislike or Approbation. In consequence of these
Signs the whole audience shall be required to *clap* or *hiss,* that the
Town may learn certainly when and how far they ought to be
pleas'd?[299]

8. It is submitted whether it would not be proper to distinguish
the *Council of Six* by some particular Habit or Gown of an honourable
B shape and colour, to which may be added a square Cap and a white
Wand.[300]

9. That to prevent unmarried Actresses making away with their
Infants,[301] a competent provision be allowed for the nurture of them,
who shall for that reason be deemed the *Children of the Society*; and
that they may be educated according to the Genius of their parents,
the said Actresses shall declare upon Oath (as far as their memory
will allow) the true names and qualities of their serveral fathers. A
private Gentleman's Son shall at the publick expence be brought up
a Page to attend the *Council of Six:* A more ample provision shall be
made for the son of a *Poet*; and a greater still for the son of a *Critic.*

10. If it be discovered that any Actress is got with Child, during
the Interludes of any Play wherein she hath a Part, it shall be

reckoned a neglect of her Business, and she shall *forefeit* accordingly. If any Actor for the future shall commit Murder, except upon the stage, he shall be left to the laws of the land; the like is to be understood of *Robbery* and *Theft.* In all other cases, particularly in those for *Debt,* it is propos'd that this, like the other Courts of *Whitehall* and *St. James's,*[302] may be held a *Place of Privilege.* And whereas it has been found, that an obligation to satisfy paultry Creditors has been a Discouragement to Men of Letters,[303] if any Person of Quality or others shall send for any *Poet* or *Critic* of this Society to any remote quarter of the town, the said Poet or Critic shall freely pass and repass without being liable to an *Arrest.*

11. The forementioned Scheme in its several regulations may be supported by Profits arising from every Third-night throughout the year.[304] And as it would be hard to suppose that so many persons could live without any food, (tho' from the former course of their lives, a *very little* will be deemed sufficient) the masters of calculation will, we believe, agree, that out of those Profits, the said persons might be subsisted in a sober and decent manner. We will venture to affirm farther, that not only the proper magazines of Thunder and Lightning,[305] but *Paint, Diet-drinks, Spitting-pots,* and all other *Necessaries* of *Life,* may in like manner fairly be provided for.

12. If some of the Articles may at first view seem liable to Objections, particularly those that give so vast a power to the *Council of Six* (which is indeed larger than any entrusted to the great Officers of state) this may be obviated, by swearing those *Six* Persons of his Majesty's Privy Council,[306] and obliging them to pass every thing of moment *previously* at that most honourable Board.[307]

CONTENTS

TO THE

Art of SINKING in POETRY.

Textual Variants

Title: ΠΕΡΙ ΒΑΘΟΥΣ: / OR, / *Martinus Scriblerus*/ HIS / TREATISE / OF
THE / ART of SINKING / IN / POETRY. *1728–38*; Written in the Year
1727. Add. 1741, 1751.

Page 186: A. *Footnote reference* [†] *inserted here, with accompanying footnote:* † *Martinus
Scriblerus,* tho' of *German* Extraction, was born in *England. Vid.* his
Life and *Memoirs,* which will speedily be publish'd. *1728–38.*

Page 186: B. how . . . are] the extent, fertility, and populousness of *1728–41,
1751.*

Page 187: A. these] those *1728–38.*

Page 187: B. that *Add. 1741–51.*

Page 188: A. attempt] attempt upon *1728–38.*

Page 188: B. in] in all *1728–38.*

Page 189: A. ones.] ones? *1728–41.* [Since such question-mark changes do not
actually affect meaning, they will not be cited as variants after
this.]

Page 189: B. who . . . grew] but . . . grow *1728–38.*

Page 189: C. for] by *1728–38.*

Page 190: A. offensive] offensive only *1728–38.*

Page 190: B. making . . . raising] making of . . . raising of *1728–38.*

Page 190: C. descent,] sight, *1728–41, 1751.*

Page 190: D. more] other *1728–41, 1751.*

Page 190: E. *Warburton identified such annotations with a "P."*

Page 191: A. Flower] Flowers *1728–38.*

Page 191: B. head or tail] Heads or Tails *1728–41, 1751.*

Page 192: A. get] get you *1728–38.*

Page 192: B. with] and *1728–38.*

Page 192: C. are] is *1728–38.*

Page 192: D. *Notes transferred from margin to bottom of page and identifying letters added 1730–51.*

Page 193: A. an] the *1728–38.*

Page 193: B. their] the *1728–41, 1751.*

Page 193: C. to . . . Providence.] only to change the Course of Providence and Destiny, for the sake of three or four weighty Lines. *1728–38.*

Page 193: D. *ibid. Add. 1742.* [Footnote variants, which are usually negligible, will not be indicated after this unless significant.]

Page 194: A. Blackm.] *Blackm. Job. 1728.*

Page 197: A. L.T] *L.T. 1728.*

Page 197: B. Lord H.] Lord *R. 1728–38.*

Page 197: C. as] that *1728–38.*

Page 197: D. W.S.] *W.H. 1728–41, 1751.*

Page 197: E. G.D.] ——*D. 1728–38.*

Page 197: F. Thought] Thoughts *1728–38.*

Page 198: A. not *Add. 1741–51.*

Page 198: B. a *Add. 1741–51.*

Page 198: C. who . . . Poet,)] of which the Poet, *1728–38.*

Page 199: A. goat, the crab] Goat, the Lion, the Crab *1728–41, 1751.*

Page 199: B. Falshood] *Distress 1728.*

Page 200: A. enoble] illustrate *1728–38.*

Page 200: B. Job] When *Job 1728–41, 1751.*

Page 200: C. a . . . butter] (a . . . over) hear how it *1728–38;* (a . . . over) now . . . butter *1741.*

Page 201: A. Dutch-painter] Dutch-painters *1741, 1751.*

Page 201: B. since he . . . , nay how] He even . . . , and *1728–38.*

Page 201: C. strange *Add. 1741–51.*

Page 202: A. into] in *1728–41, 1751.*

Page 202: B. 108] 180 *1728–38.*

Page 203: A. the] their *1728–38.*

Page 203: B. never] not *1728–38.*

Page 203: C. De Foe] *DeF—— 1728–38.*

Page 203: D. Tate] *T——te 1728–38.*

Page 203: E. Ward] *W——rd 1728–38.*

Page 203: F. Eusden] *E——n 1728–41, 1751.*

Page 203: G. Blackmore] *Bl——k——re 1728–38.*

Page 203: H. Ambrose Philips] *A. Ph—— 1728–38;* Amb. Philips *1741.*

Page 203: I. Welsted] *W——st——d 1728–38.*

Page 203: J. the] our *1728–38.*

Page 204: A. Lo!] But lo! *1728–38.*

Page 204: B. would not] but would *1728–41, 1751.*

Page 204: C. resemblance] greatest Resemblance *1728–38.*

Page 205: A. as] for as much as *1728–38.*

Page 205: B. low] law *1741, 1751.*

Page 205: C. of] by *1728–38.*

Page 205: D. *confounding] confusing 1728–38.*

Page 205: E. kind] Genius *1728–38.*

Page 206: A. Confounding] Confusing *1728–38.*

Page 206: B. *Sentence introduced by I in 1751;* Bathos] *Abuse* of Speech *1728.*

Page 206: C. as] as doth *1728–38.*

Page 207: A. *Then] And 1728–38.*

Page 207: B. Or *Add. 1742.*

Page 207: C. Secondly,] The Second, *1728–41, 1751.*

Page 207: D. at . . . writing.] in this present Year 1727. *1728–41, 1751.*

Page 208: A. We . . . which] Under the Article of the *Confusing, 1728–38;* Under . . . *Confounding, 1741–51.*

Page 208: B. *Numbers 1–4 add. 1741–51; only sections 3 and 4 numbered, as 1 and 2 1730–38.*

Page 208: C. p. 73.] p. 37. *1741–51.*

Page 209: A. Add . . . following. *Add. 1741–51.*

Page 209: B. *Here . . . stone.* [plus footnote] *Add 1730–51.*

Page 209: C. Variegation,] Variegation and Confusion of Objects, *1728–38.*

Page 209: D. *Section 3 add. 1730–51.*

Page 211: A. *Number add. 1751.*

Page 211: B. those] his *1742* [Printer's change?]

Page 211: C. Falshood.] *Distress. 1728*

Page 212: A. *Number 2 add. 1741, 1751; as number 3 1742.*

Page 212: B. And 1.] And first, *1728–41; om. 1742.*

Page 212: C. *Nor . . . out,] Nor Death, nor Hell it self can keep them out, 1728.*

Page 212: D. *steddy] noisy 1730.*

Page 212: E. low,] very low, *1728–38*.

Page 213: A. of] on *1728–38*.

Page 213: B. *like* one] one vast *1728–38*.

Page 213: C. *Numbers 2–4 add 1741–51; numbers 5, 6 add. 1751*.

Page 213: D. into] in *1728–38*.

Page 214: A. and] With *1728–38*.

Page 214: B. *At this point there was a passage now omitted:* His Shepherd reasons as much like an Innocent, in Love:

> *I love in secret all a beauteous Maid,*   *Ibid.*
> *And have my Love in secret all repay'd:*
> *This coming* Night *she does* reserve *for me.*

The Love of this Maiden to him appears by her allowing him the Reserve of one Night from her other Lovers; which you see he takes extreamly kindly. *1728–38*.

Page 215: A. Inaninity] Inanity *1728–38, 1751*.

Page 215: B. where . . . Verse. *Add. 1742*.

Page 215: C. *Happy . . . sing. Add. 1730–51*.

Page 215: D. *Following this quotation in 1741, 1751:* You easily perceive the Nothingness of every second Verse. [See p. 215: B]

Page 215: E. *Numbers 5, 6, add. 1751*.

Page 216: A. Or . . . name. *Add. .1730–51*.

Page 217: A. become] becomes *1741, 1751*.

Page 218: A. vulgarize] familiarize *1728–38*.

Page 218: B. p. 339.] p. 239. *1728*.

Page 219: A. Style *Add. 1741–51*.

Page 219: B. most] the most *1728–41*.

Page 219: C. which . . . do.] (Which . . . do) *1728–41, 1751*.

Page 220: A. Pearls] Pearl *1728–41, 1751*.

Page 220: B. Queen] Q. *1728–38*.

Page 221: A. of] of this *1728–38*.

Page 222: A. Style *Add. 1741–51*.

Page 222: B. partakes . . . following,] partakes of the last mentioned. *1728–38*; partakers of the *alamode: 1751*.

Page 222: C. Of] As this, of *1728–41, 1751*.

Page 222: D. *whose] with 1728–38*.

Page 222: E. higher than] as high as *1728–41, 1751*.

Page 223: A. the following] this *1728–38*.

Page 223: B. Falshood.] *Distress. 1728*.

Page 224: A. *This section (Chaps. XIII–XVI) was headed APPENDIX 1728–38*.

Page 224: B. good] the good *1728–38*.

Page 224: C. ornament] Ornament of Speech *1728–38*.

Page 225: A. *Litotes*] *Littole 1728.*

Page 225: B. in] of *1728–38.*

Page 226: A. and] or *1728–38.*

Page 226: B. market] the market *1728–38.*

Page 226: C. these two] they *1728–38.*

Page 226: D. sorts] very two sorts *1728–38.*

Page 226: E. *Profit*] *Gain* or *Profit, 1728–38.*

Page 226: F. (which . . . main end)] which . . . whole end *1728–38;* which . . . main end *1741, 1751.*

Page 226: G. *Publick*] *Parliamentary 1728–38.*

Page 227: A. *Expence,*] *Expences, 1728–41, 1751.*

Page 227: B. in] of *1728–38.*

Page 227: C. hath] has *1728–38.*

Page 228: A. Moliere] What Moliere *1728–38.*

Page 228: B. by] for *1728–41, 1751.*

Page 229: A. them] 'em *1728–38.*

Page 229: B. since] for since *1728–38.*

Page 230: A. Thunder] of Thunder *1728–38.*

Page 230: B. Burnet's] the *1728–41, 1751.*

Page 230: C. difficulty] Danger *1728–38.*

Page 230: D. not] not wholly *1728–41, 1751.*

Page 230: E. Barton Booth] *B——t—— B——th 1728–38.*

Page 230: F. Robert Wilks] *W——ll——m W——lks 1728–38.*

Page 230: G. Colly Cibber] *C——ll——y C——bb——r 1728–38.*

Page 231: A. Dennis] *D——nn——s 1728–38.*

Page 232: A. most ancient] *oldest 1728–38.*

Page 232: B. may] might *1728–38.*

Page 233: A. for] by *1728–38.*

Page 233: B. deem'd *Add. 1741–51.*

Page 233: C. *Followed, in 1728–38, by: Vale & Fruere. / MAR. SCRIB.*

Page 233: D. Art . . . POETRY.] BATHOS. *1728–38.*

Page 233: E. *Chapter Numbers (and "Introduction") add. 1742–51.*

Page 234: A. *Genius*] *Genius's 1728–38.*

Page 234: B. *confounding, confusing, 1728–38.*

Annotations

N.B. In these annotations, general references to Longinus are made from W. Rhys Roberts' translation (*Longinus on the Sublime*, 2d ed. [Cambridge: Cambridge University Press, 1907]), cited as "Roberts"; those bearing more closely on Pope's text are located in the Boileau translation, which he probably used ("A Treatise of the Sublime," *The Works of Monsr Boileau Despreaux* [trans. Ozell], vol. II [sep. pagination for the Treatise] [London, 1711]), cited as "Boileau." The copious notes of Edna Leake Steeves' edition of the *Peri Bathous* (*The Art of Sinking in Poetry* [New York: King's Crown Press, 1952; reprinted, Atheneum Press, 1968]) have been consulted and some (identified, if not otherwise, by "E. L. S." in brackets) are, with grateful acknowledgment, incorporated into this commentary.

1. The early editions carried a footnote (see textual variant), dropped after the 1741 printing of the *Memoirs,* when it was no longer appropriate.

2. While John Oldmixon in *An Essay on Criticism* (1728) had avowedly not attempted to "enter into the philosophical Part of Criticism," he had, in the manner of Abbé Bouhours (and in anticipation of his translation of Bouhours' *La Manière de bien penser,* which appeared later that year), provided "Examples of every Kind of right Thinking." Oldmixon's modern editor, R. J. Madden, thinks that Pope, alerted in 1726 to the forthcoming volumes, might have been spurred to organize his own treatise and its illustrative excerpts, the presentation of which, Madden feels, does bring to mind the *Essay*. Earlier, in 1718, Charles Gildon had published *The Complete Art of Poetry* in six parts, the sixth being "A Collection of the most beautiful Descriptions, Similes, Allusions, &c. from *Spenser,* and our best *English* Poets . . ."; even earlier, of course, were Roscommon's and Buckingham's rhymed Artes as well as Pope's own *Essay on Criticism*. None of these provided the kind of "modern" rhetoric, however ironically presented here, that Pope had in mind.

3. In his Homeric criticism Pope had taken his stand in the contemporary Quarrel of the Ancients and Moderns. There, as here and in the *Essay on Criticism,* we see him staunchly on the side of the classicists (although his positions are usually moderate and mediating). In the topography of Parnassus that follows and in this sense of the *weighty* moderns, Pope echoes Swift's metaphors in the *Battle of the Books,* an important document in the Quarrel.

4. Longinus's query, at the beginning of Section II, as to whether there is such a thing as an art of the sublime (ὕφος) or lofty (βάθος) has given rise to much semantic and textual confusion. Most translators treat the two words as synonymous, using "sublime" to cover both, while Pope, on the other hand, exploits the opposite meaning possible in *Bathos*: the profound, or deep; to complicate matters, some scholars have argued that Longinus's βάθος is a misprint for πάθος, pathos or passion. Longinus, in defining the sublime, distinguishes it from the tumid, puerile, and a kind of empty passion, all three pitfalls for those seeking to attain it. He hints at the paradox that Pope seizes on: ". . . all who aim at elevation are so anxious to escape the reproach of being weak and dry that they are carried, as by some strange law of nature, into the opposite extreme.

. . . While tumidity desires to transcend the limits of the sublime, the defect which is termed puerility is the direct antithesis of elevation, for it is utterly low and mean and in real truth the most ignoble vice of style" (Roberts, pp. 47, 49). Here again one is reminded of Swift, who in the Conclusion to *A Tale of a Tub* (Oxford: Basil Blackwell, 1965) speaks of *"Profound Writers"*—with whom it is, as with wells, that *"wondrous Deep"* is often mistaken for *"wondrous Dark."* (P. 133.) Pope focuses in this paragraph on the ambiguities of both terms. Note, too, Swift's comment in his Preface to the *Tale*: "However, being extreamly sollicitous, that every accomplished Person who has got into the Taste of Wit . . . should descend to the very *bottom* of all the *Sublime* throughout this Treatise . . ." (p. 26).

5. Cf. "This Quarrel [Ancients and Moderns] first began . . . about a small Spot of Ground, *lying* and *being* upon one of the two Tops of the Hill *Parnassus*; the highest and largest of which, had it seems, been time out of Mind, in quiet Possession of certain Tenants, call'd the *Antients*; And the other was held by the *Moderns*." (Swift, *Battle of the Books,* in *A Tale of a Tub {with Other Early Works},* p. 142). The Moderns challenge the Ancients either to relinquish their heights to them (for they feel their "Prospects" are being blocked) or to allow them to level the high point.

6. Pope here as elsewhere takes a commonsensical view of "Laws" and rules. Derivable from the practice of great predecessors, especially the ancients, they are in general to be respected, but must always allow for exceptions (a *"Grace* beyond the Reach of Art") and must never become a straitjacket as in modern theories of the epic (see Chapter XV).

7. The commercial language of this paragraph (Trade, Manufacture, vent, product) reflects a typical Scriblerian distrust of the burgeoning mob-majority, whose mercenary values and general levelling instincts were felt to be infecting those who by birth and education should have been the promoters of taste and culture. It is a conclusion familiar to readers of *Absalom and Achitophel, the Beggar's Opera,* and *Tale of a Tub.* More specifically the spirit of the whole section may echo ironically Leonard Welsted's defensive "State of the Union" argument: ". . . our Trade, our Peace, our Liberty, the Complexion of our Language and of our Government, and the Disposition and Spirit of the *Britons,* admirably turn'd by Nature for succeeding in Poetry, all would conspire to make this Nation the Rival of the most renown'd among the Ancients for Works of Wit and Genius . . ." ("A Dissertation concerning the Perfection of the *English* Language . . . ," *Epistles, Odes, &c.* [London, 1724], p. xv). Or it could recall Sir Richard Blackmore, about whom Dr. Johnson was to comment: "Here is again discovered the inhabitant of Cheapside, whose head cannot keep his poetry unmingled with trade." (Johnson, *Lives,* II, 241).

8. Aristotle and Longinus; Boileau's preface to his translation of Longinus had included an account of his service to the queen.

9. Among the quotations, Pope did include some from Waller and Dryden (and young Pope). Their lapses, however, can only contrast with the wealth of citations from a "natural" like Blackmore.

10. Spingarn traces the history of the term "taste" from classical times, when it was used in its original physical sense, through the French critics, especially Saint-Evremond, for whom it meant a natural instinct, independent of reason and authority (*je ne sais quoi*). (Spingarn, I, xci–cv.) By the time of *The Essay on Criticism*, taste, "good" taste, was to be equated with good sense, as the natural response of the educated and cultivated, schooled in the practice of the ancients. On the other hand, a "Modernist" critic like Leonard Welsted still argued for spontaneous taste, untrammeled by education ("True Conceptions of Poetry can no more be communicated to one born without Taste than adequate Ideas of Colours can be given to one born without Sight . . ." [Welsted, "A Dissertation," p. xx]).

11. "Individual or particular liking, relish, or fondness" (OED, citing this passage).

12. Horace *Ars Poetica* 333; the line actually reads, "Aut prodesse volunt aut delectare poetae . . .": "Poets aim either to benefit, or to amuse. . . ." (Loeb [1955], p. 479.) Pope exploits the double meaning of "profit" as a translation of "prodesse" (do good, benefit, profit).

13. The Renaissance concept of the decay of the world ("We're scarse our Fathers shadowes cast at noone") carries the corollary, espoused by advocates of the Ancients in the "Quarrel," of a similar diminution of talent and sensibility in the arts, despite the "progress" shown in science and in "all other branches of Luxury." For this last phrase, cf. Leonard Welsted, ". . . assemble in one View the different Refinements of Architecture, Painting, Sculpture, Music, and many others [other than poetry], and what do any or all of them promote, except the Luxury and the Ornaments of Life?" (Welsted, "A Dissertation," p. xliii.) The modernism of Pope's speaker is particularly evident in this relegation of poety to a Luxury.

14. For "Genius's of *Rank* or *Fortune*," Pope might have had Blackmore in mind, given his own modest disclaimer:

> . . . *Poetry has been so far from being my* Business *and* Profession, *that it has imploy'd but a small part of my Time; and then, but as my* Recreation, *and the Entertainment of my idle hours. If this Attempt succeeds so far, as to excite some other Person that has a noble Genius, Leisure, and Application, to Honour his Country with a just Epick Poem, I shall think the Vacancies and Intervals that for about two years past, I have had from the Business of my Profession, which notwithstanding was then greater than at any time before, have been very well imploy'd.* ("The Preface," *Prince Arthur* [London, 1695])

For "Princes"———? The reference could no doubt include Peter the Great, who was well known for his interest in technical and mechanical arts, having in 1698 spent six weeks in England, studying shipbuilding at Deptford (and shocking his hosts by his uncouth social behavior); Gilbert Burnet in his *History of His Own Time* (Edinburgh, 1753, IV, 322) speaks of him as "mechanically turned." Whether George I or George II had any such bent I have not discovered; certainly they were notorious for their lack of concern for any of the arts except music.

15. While Longinus, in Section II, presents the argument that the Sublime is natural to man, later (in Sec. XIII of Roberts, Sec. XI of Boileau), talking about Plato and imitation, he says "Similarly from the great natures of men of old there are borne in upon the souls of those who emulate them (as from sacred caves) what we may describe as *effluences.* . . ." Pope's elaboration and inversion of effluence and *in*spiration (familiar from Plato onwards) is reminiscent of Swift's discussion, in *A Tale of a Tub,* of "wind," where similarly afflatus and flatulence are confounded.

16. Just as there is a deliberate confusion in this section between the figurative and the literal/physical (the poetic itch [*Pruritus*], conceptions, and bringing forth), so the familiar idea of poets not being made but born (*Nascimur Poetae*) gets caught up in the different, but related, idea of the naturalness of the activity of giving birth to poetry.

17. As Steeves observes (p. 99), "It is difficult to resist a surmise that this passage, which parodies currently popular medical phraseology, may have been suggested or even sketched by Dr. Arbuthnot, since it is so definitely within his province. Arbuthnot's posthumous works contain a piece entitled 'An Essay upon an Apothecary' which ridicules the pseudoscientific lingo of the trade (*Miscellaneous Works,* 1751, II, 110–14)."

18. This argument is again suggestive of Swift, whose *Argument against Abolishing Christianity in England* defends blasphemy on similar grounds: "if they cannot be allowed a *God* to revile or renounce; they will speak *Evil of Dignities,* abuse the Government, and reflect upon the Ministry."

19. *Ars Poetica* 372–73: "But that poets be of a middling rank, neither men nor gods [nor booksellers ever brooked]." (Loeb [1955], p. 481.) Pope felt strongly about this: "Middling poets are no poets at all" (*Anecdotes,* I, 177). "In Pope's copy of Sir William Soame's translation of Boileau's *Art of Poetry* . . . Pope wrote in the margin next to the paraphrase of this passage [Horace's], 'That there is no medium in Poetry' " (ibid., 178n).

20. Pope's "English Author" is probably Shakespeare: "You may know by my size that I have a kind of alacrity in sinking" (Falstaff, *The Merry Wives of Windsor,* III, v, 11–13). The earl of Dorset had, however, appropriated the phrase in a way more pertinent to this context in "To a Person of Honour, upon his Incomparable, Incomprehensible Poem" [Edward Howard and his *The British Princes*] (London, 1718), describing Howard's verse:

> In this way of writing without thinking,
> Thou hast a strange alacrity of sinking.

21. Perhaps recalling Flecknoe's advice to his son: "Trust Nature, do not labor to be dull. . . ."

22. Cf. Longinus, Section II.

23. An architecture in which Pope may have interested himself as in the 1720s he worked on his famous grotto.

24. I.e. ditches.

25. This is a popular oversimplification of Longinian doctrine, either Pope's own or his modernist spokesman's. Longinus's actual view is balanced: "nature is the original and vital underlying principle in all cases, but system can define limits . . . and can also contribute the safest rules for use and practice" (Roberts, p. 45).

26. A figure Pope had originally contributed to some lines by Wycherley on Dulness (London, 1728) and was to use again in the *Dunciad.*

27. Man, that is, has many orders above him in the Great Chain of Being to which he belongs, and resides at the lowest point of the vaporous envelope of air surrounding the earth.

28. Cf. *Dunciad,* III, 169–72 (TE V, 328):

> "Flow Welsted, flow! like thine inspirer, Beer,
> Tho' stale, not ripe; tho' thin, yet never clear;
> So sweetly mawkish, and so smoothly dull;
> Heady, not strong, and foaming tho' not full."

29. The vanity of man's pursuit of precious stones and metals had become conventional. Less cited, scorn for the familiar and useful is central to Swift's satire in Book III of *Gulliver's Travels.*

30. Pope appears to use "common Sense" here in its familiar meaning, but as a literary term its meanings could be controversial. On the one hand, it was the rallying cry of the French rationalistic school of criticism (with Rymer its English proponent); on the other, as Austin Warren notes, "sense," with its variant phrases, "good sense," "men of sense," "superior sense," occurs eighteen times in the *Essay on Criticism* without implying censure of the classics or the "received critics" (Warren, p. 36). Pope attempted to bridge the critical gap by affirming that since nature and reason were best exemplified in the ancients, their practice was more trustworthy as a guide for poets and critics than idiosyncratic individual judgment.

31. Cf. Longinus: ". . . they [Figures], if handled in the proper manner, will contribute . . . in no mean degree to sublimity" (Roberts, p. 91). See a reference to this point in the "Introduction," p. 177, and the covering note, no. 19, pp. 181–82.

32. I.e. spirit of wrong-headedness. ". . .'Ah, what a *gout de travers* rules the understanding of the illiterate!' The exclamation is from Phoebe Clinket, the lady dramatist in *Three Hours after Marriage,* when the actors object that her play will not please an audience" [E. L. S., p. 101.]

33. In section IV (Boileau), Longinus had commented, "All this Affectation, as Mean and Puerile as 'tis, comes from one only Cause, and that is the Seeking too much after Novelty in Thoughts. . . ." (P. 19.)

34. The OED traces the term *grotesque* through early modern French to the Italian *grottesca,* defined by Florio as "a kinde of rugged unpolished painters worke, anticke worke" (with possible etymological relation to grottos and paintings appropriate to them). Early on, the word took the meaning "A kind of decorative painting or sculpture, consisting of representations of portions of human and animal forms, fantastically combined and interwoven with foliage and flowers" and a little later came to be applied to any design "characterized by comic distortion or exaggeration." As Dryden describes it, in *A Parallel of Poetry and Painting,* "There is yet a lower kind of poetry and painting, which is out of nature; for a farce is that in poetry, which *grotesque* is in a picture" (*Essays,* II, 132).

35. *Ars Poetica* 13: "['Painters and poets,' you say, 'have always had an equal right in hazarding anything.' We know it: this license we poets claim and in our turn we grant the like; but not so far that savage should mate with tame, or] serpents couple with birds, lambs with tigers." (Loeb [1955], p. 451.)

36. Cf. *Ars Poetica* 151–52. While Horace speaks of blending facts and fiction, it is in the context of inventing a consistent story.

37. Cf. Horace *Ars Poetica* 120–22: "If haply, when you write, you bring back to the stage the honouring of Achilles, let him be impatient, passionate, ruthless, fierce. . . ." (Loeb [1955], p. 461.)

38. "A buffoon, clown, or merry-andrew, *esp.* one attending on a mountebank." (OED.)

39. "An allusion in Swift's *Strephon and Chloe* all but completely glosses the phrase:

> No maid at court is less ashamed,
> Howe'er for selling bargains famed,
> Than she to name the parts behind.

Scott, in a note on Dryden's Prologue to Beaumont and Fletcher's *The Prophetess,* explains it as 'the seller naming his or her hinder parts in answer to the question "What?" which the buyer was artfully led to ask.' Both Dryden and Dorset refer to the practice as part of the badinage of the theater." [E. L. S., pp. 102–03.]

40. A letter to the *Daily Journal* of 23 April 1728, included in *A Compleat Collection of All the Verses, Essays, Letters and Advertisements, which have been occasioned by the Publication of Three Volumes of Miscellanies, by Pope and Company* (London,

1728), accuses Pope of treacherously attacking his friend Congreve by reference here to Jeremy and Valentine from *Love for Love,* but it is a very dubious identification. The description of Martinus Scriblerus in the *Memoirs* as an eccentric, unkempt, and unwordly figure makes clear the contemporary stereotype of the scholar as the direct opposite of a gentleman, also stereotyped in the *Memoirs* in the young nobleman at Court of Chapter XI.

41. While Pope's enmity toward the theater and actors has been exaggerated, the experience of *Three Hours after Marriage* (1717) had done little to make him sanguine about the contemporary stage, his general attitude being reflected in the last chapter of the *Peri Bathous.*

42. The great popularity of pantomimes is often cited as an example of the debased taste of the period. Developed as a form by John Rich of the Lincoln's Inn Fields Theatre and, on their success, also produced by Colley Cibber at the Drury Lane, these fantastical entertainments are satirized in the *Dunciad* (TE V, 176ff. and 331ff.). They are associated also with the attacks on *Three Hours after Marriage,* for three months after that production, there was staged at the Drury Lane a piece called *The Shipwreck; or Perseus and Andromeda* (with a "Crocodile Monster" suggestive of the earlier play) while, some two weeks later, the rival theater came out with *The Jealous Doctor; or the Intriguing Dame,* with John Rich, as "Lun," playing Harlequin. (George Sherburn, "The fortunes and misfortunes of *Three hours after marriage,*" *Modern Philology,* 24 [1926], 108).

43. Steeves has located several of these references in contemporary pantomimes: the conjuror into an old woman, in Theobald's *Harlequin Sorcerer* (1725); a man's head where his heels should be, probably in *Harlequin, Dr. Faustus* (1723); and men and women—if not coaches—turned into wheelbarrows by Harlequin's wand, in Rich's pantomimes, according to accounts in Davies' *Memoirs of the Life of Garrick.* (Pp. 104–05.)

44. An effect with which many had grown familiar by Pope's time, when "the telescope was a common spectacle in public parks, and became one of the holiday sports of the populace" (Marjorie Nicolson, "The 'New Astronomy' and the English Literary Imagination," *Studies in Philology* 22 [1935], 428–62).

45. Lutestring or lustring: "A kind of glossy silk fabric; a dress or ribbon of this material" and the OED cites a passage from Pope's letters as illustration: "Think of flouncing the petticoat so very deep, that it looks like an entire coat of lutestring!"

46. This line had also caught the critical attention of Aaron Hill, notes Guy Laprevotte ("Notes sur le *Peri Bathous* . . . [*Revue des langues vivantes,* 39 (1973), 325–45]), who argues that Hill served Pope not only as "victim" in the *Peri Bathous* but also as source for some of his observations there. Laprevotte points out that in his preface to the *The Creation* Hill had attacked Blackmore ("In this tremendous Exercise of his Divinity, to compare him to a *Weaver,* and his Expansion

of the Skies, to the low Mechanism of a *Loom,* is injudiciously to *diminish* an Idea, he pretends to *heighten* and *illustrate*") and Addison in ways that are echoed by Pope. (See also n. 196.)

47. An epic poem in ten books by Sir Richard Blackmore (1655?–1729), physician in ordinary to William III and Anne, and voluminous author. Although he had also offended Pope personally, he deserves his star billing in the *Bathos* on literary "merit" alone.

48. This carefully pedantic establishment of texts suggests, along with a letter from Arbuthnot to Swift on 26 June 1714 ("Pope has been collecting high flights of poetry, which are very good, they are to be solemn nonsense" [*The Correspondence of Jonathan Swift,* ed. Harold Williams (Oxford: Clarendon Press, 1965), II, 43], that work on the *Peri Bathous* was underway early in Scriblerian history. Though the piece was not pulled together until just before its printing in 1728 (see [Pope's] *Correspondence,* II, 468), the bathetic excerpts came largely from this much earlier period.

49. This could be a thrust at Blackmore in retaliation for his railing against Pope's impiety in his "adaptation" of the First Psalm (a sore point since the adaptation was off-color and never meant for publication). If so, referring to the man who had written an attack against the Wits in *A Satyr against Wit* (1700) as one "violently fond of *Wit*" would be doubly ironic.

50. According to M. G. Segar (*The Poems of Ambrose Philips* [Oxford: Basil Blackwell, 1937]), Philips was ordained deacon while still at Cambridge. As one of Addison's "little Senate," Philips (1674–1749) had early earned Pope's rancor for (as Pope believed) abusing him and his *Iliad* undertaking in the coffeehouses and detaining subscriptions paid in to Philips by members of the Hanover Club, of which he was Secretary.

51. "Lament for Queen Mary" was Philips' first poem, which appeared in the spring of 1694/5 and later that year was collected in a volume of elegies presented to the royal family by Cambridge University. Pope's quotation omits three lines which in the original followed the first line cited, and he changes *these* Mists to *the* Mists.

52. In his citation for *Peri Bathous* (first printed in the "Last" volume of the *Miscellanies* [item 196]), Griffith attributes all the pieces signed "Anon." (as in Pope's footnote here) to Pope as quotations from his juvenile epic, *Alcander, Prince of Rhodes.* Steeves records (p. 108) a comment by Swift (in the *Public Spirit of the Whigs,* 1714) relevant to this passage: " 'I have known a poet, who was never out of England, introduce a fact by way of simile, which could probably nowhere happen nearer than in the plains of Lybia; and begin with, "So have I seen." ' "

53. These diminishing metaphors recall, suggests Guy Laprevotte (see n. 46), a similar complaint by Aaron Hill, who in #54 of *The Plain Dealer* attacked the "Hymn to the Creator" for the false sublime in much the same terms.

While it cannot be proved that Pope read *The Plain Dealer* before composing the *Peri Bathous*, Laprevotte sees a strong case that Pope was indeed inspired by Hill in his attacks on Blackmore.

54. The passages (see nn. 55–61) that follow are taken, as Pope indicates, from the second, 1716, edition of Blackmore's *Paraphrase on the Book of Job*, a volume that includes paraphrases of the songs of Moses, of some of the Psalms, and of some chapters of *Isaiah,* from which Pope draws also. There are some textual changes (usually to make sense from the cuttings), though only substantive variants will be noted: Clouds] cloud; Colour bright] Colours made; and Pope drops two lines following the third cited here.

55. Work] Works; Lightning] Light'nings; the order of the second and third lines has been reversed.

56. For Clouds, the Sun-Beams] Where for Clouds they.

57. In] To; the] their.

58. God will not be] He'll be no more; manage, or] manage in; Steeves has properly located the last two lines of this passage in Blackmore's paraphrase of *Isaiah,* p. 298.

59. Modern editions have noted an error in pagination (no doubt a printer's omission), correcting the original 18 to 180.

60. Of Air's] of the; Say] Tell; Hand] Hands.

61. God] He; their] the.

62. Sir Richard Blackmore. Longinus had, of course, celebrated the accomplishments of Homer, "whose Thoughts were all Sublime" (Boileau, p. 25). Like Flecknoe's, Blackmore's was a crowning achievement. In Pope's own words (in a footnote glossing the line in the *Dunciad,* "who sings so loudly, and who sings so long"):

> A just character of Sir *Richard Blackmore,* Kt. . . . whose indefatiguable Muse produced no less than six Epic poems: *Prince* and *King Arthur,* 20 Books [sic]; *Eliza,* 10; *Alfred,* 12; *The Redeemer,* 6: besides *Job* in folio, the whole *Book of Psalms, the Creation,* 7 Books, *Nature of Man,* 3 Books, and many more. 'Tis in this sense he is stiled afterwards, the *Everlasting Blackmore.* (TE V, 131n.)

The note then continues with a reference to a statement of Charles Gildon, which Pope might have had in mind here: "As for Mr. *Lamode*'s putting the modern *Authors* on a Foot with *Homer,* I am very confident, that the *admirable* Author of *the Creation,* has too much *Judgment,* and too much *Modesty,* to have any such Thought himself. Let it suffice, that the Author of the *Arthurs,* has the Glory of excelling *Lucretius,* it is a Palm gain'd only by him. . . ." (Charles Gildon, *The Complete Art of Poetry* [London, 1718], I, 108.)

63. The relatively low contemporary estimate (encouraged in England by

Reynolds) of still life, as a notably "lesser" genre, can be understood given the critical attitudes of the time. Dryden, for example, in the *Parallel of Poetry and Painting* argues that "both these arts . . . are not only true imitations of Nature, but of the best Nature, of that which is wrought up to a nobler pitch. . . . They are imitations of the passions, which always move, and therefore consequently please; for without motion there can be no delight, which cannot be considered but as an active passion." (*Essays,* II, 137.)

64. Note Blackmore's creative torrent; see n. 62.

65. *The Institutio Oratoria of Quintilian* (Loeb [1922], IV, 53). The argument actually runs that Germanicus's skill in war would particularly qualify him to write of war, given his already established interest in poetry (10. 1. 91).

66. A typical attitude of the age. Spence records that "Sir Isaac Newton, though he scarce ever spoke ill of any man, could scarce avoid it towards your virtuoso collectors and antiquarians. Speaking of Lord Pembroke once, he said, 'Let him have but a stone doll and he's satisfied. I can't imagine those gentlemen but as enemies to classical studies; all their pursuits are below nature.' " (*Anecdotes,* I, 350.) Cf. the *Tatler,* No. 216, 26 August 1710: "it is, methinks, the Mark of a little Genius to be wholly conversant among Insects, Reptiles, Animalcules, and these trifling Rarities, that furnish out the Apartment of a Virtuoso."

67. As Steeves has noted (p. 110), these are untraditional animals, though appropriate, as she suggests, because as inhabitants of air and water they are particularly capable of rising and sinking. One wonders if Pope was inspired in this classification by Dryden's very suggestive metaphor in *An Essay of Dramatic Poesy,* " 'these swallows which we see before us on the Thames are the just resemblance of his wit: you may observe how near the water they stoop, how many proffers they make to dip, and yet how seldom they touch it; and when they do, 'tis but the surface: they skim over it but to catch a gnat, and then mount into the air and leave it' " (*Essays,* I, 32). Since this whole section of the *Essay* is on bad writing and since just preceding this passage there is the statement, " 'he is a very Leveller in poetry: he creeps along with ten little words in every line,' " which Pope echoes in the *Essay on Criticism,* one suspects that these were well-read pages.

68. Austin Warren asserts that "It was probably for this chapter and these allegedly random initials that the treatise was written" (Warren, p. 165). Certainly this was a popular contemporary view: in a pamphlet published in April 1730, *One Epistle to Mr. A. Pope, Occasion'd by Two Epistles Lately Published,* Leonard Welsted and James Moore Smythe announced that "Mr. Dean Swift never saw the *Profund,* till made publick, and Dr. Arbuthnot, who originally sketch'd the Design of it, desired that the Initial Letters of Names of the Gentlemen abused might not be inserted, that they might be *A* or *B,* or *Do* or *Ro,* or any thing of that Nature, which would make this Satire a general one upon any dull Writers

in any Age: This was refused by Pope. . . . Some Replies which were made to
the *Profund*, occasioned the Publication of the *Dunciad*, which was first of all
begun with a general Malice to all Mankind, and now appears under an Excuse
of Provocations, which he had received, after he himself had struck the first Blow
in the above-mentioned Miscellanies" (p. vii). Although Pope protested to Aaron
Hill, "those Letters were set at Random to occasion what they did occasion, the
Suspicion of bad and jealous Writers" (*Correspondence*, III, 165), their lending
themselves so well to identification and to individuals who figure in the *Dunciad*
argues against this demurrer. Pope's audience, at any rate, was quick to conjecture
names for initials (see, for example, *A Compleat Collection. . . . To which is added
an Exact List of the Lords, Ladies, Gentlemen and others, who have been abused in those
Volumes* [the *Miscellanies*] [London, 1728] and *Characters of the Times* [London,
1728]). For a history of the ascriptions, see Steeves, who argues that "there seems
to be neither remarkable appropriateness nor special consistency in the classifications" (p. 111).

69. Variously assigned to George Stepney, George Sewell, or Dr. George
Stanhope. The best candidate seems to be George Sewell (d. 1726): after an
unsuccessful career as a physician, he became a booksellers' hack and controver-
sialist; most pertinently, he added an unsolicited seventh volume of poems to
Pope's edition of Shakespeare's plays (1725). In *Fragment of a Satire* (later incorporated into the *Epistle to Dr. Arbuthnot*), published also in the "Last" volume of
the *Miscellanies* (1728), Pope had written of "sanguine Sew——," later changed
to "Slashing Bentley."

70. Though applicable to Anthony Hammond, this was generally assumed—
especially by the paranoid "victim" himself—to be Aaron Hill (1683–1750),
whose checkered career as a speculator and dull author (with a reputation for self-
importance and pomposity) invited his inclusion here and in the *Dunciad* as one
of the divers who can also succeed in mounting among the swans (as the flying
fishes occasionally rise out of the Profound). The long history of his relations with
Pope is marked by recriminations and reconciliations; in Professor Sutherland's
words (TE V, 445), "Pope had to pay dearly for his enmity, but still more for his
friendship"—as he was subjected to long, tedious letters and manuscript tragedies
to be read and criticized. In "Notes sur le *Peri Bathous* . . ." (see nn. 46 and 53),
Guy Laprevotte also considers the Pope-Hill relationship, arguing that Hill, if a
mediocre poet, was often an astute critic whose attacks on Blackmore might have
directed Pope's attention to certain bathetic examples. He traces much of Pope's
enmity to Hill's stalwart defense of his friend Dennis at a time when Pope was
smarting from Dennis's strictures on his translation of Homer.

71. This same set of initials appears under the Porpoises. In both instances
they are taken to be Charles Gildon (1665–1724), who had a long career of
attacking Pope: he disparaged the *Pastorals*, attacked the *Rape of the Lock* in a

pamphlet called *The New Rehearsal* (1714), collaborated with Dennis on a particularly scurrilous pamphlet *A True Character of Mr. Pope and his Writings* (1716), and tried to discredit Pope and his family in the *Memoirs of the Life of William Wycherley* (1718). The real cause of his enmity is not known, though Professor Sherburn places him and his "venal quill" in the hireling class of Pope's detractors.

72. In the first edition the list of Swallows had read "L [no period] T. WP. Lord R." Such was the speculation over these initials (see n. 68) that readers were quick to notice the absence of periods. One writer, to the *London Evening Post* of 26 March 1728 (a letter included in the *Compleat Collection*), proposed that the absence of periods between letters would indicate first and last names while periods would separate different surnames (e.g., E. W. would mean Eusden and Welsted rather than Edward Ward). It seems more likely that the omission of the periods was a typographical error, perhaps prompted by the form of "Lord R."

73. For *Shakespeare Restored* (1726), his self-announcing response to Pope's edition of Shakespeare, Lewis Theobald (1688–1744)—whom Pope also blamed for *A Compleat Key to . . . The What D'Ye Call It* (1715) and the suppression of whose life of Buckingham had been laid to Pope—was enthroned in the *Dunciad*. Here he is "lowered" by two listings (under the eels as well as swallows) and three quotations. Pope's aesthetic quarrel with him is summarized in the reference (in *Fragment of a Satire,* published in the same volume as the *Peri Bathous*) to such as "piddling T——s," "a Word-Catcher, that lives on syllables."

74. Steeves has reviewed three possibilities—William Pattison, William Philips, and William Pulteney—and further search has not turned up any more likely candidates. Although William Pulteney may have been in Pope's mind in the *Dunciad* (Book IV, ll. 517ff.), the allusion there is political rather than poetical. William Pattison (1706–1727)—rather than William Philips, a minor dramatist—seems the best prospect since he was one of Curll's minions (rumored to have been starved to death by him) and associated with such recognized bathetic types as Eusden and Concanen.

75. In editions of 1741 and after, there is this change to "Lord H.," where the reference is clearly to Lord Hervey, one of the most famous/infamous antagonists of Pope's later years (for an account of their relationship, see *Letter to a Noble Lord*). The identity of the original "Lord R." is less obvious: though contemporary sources suggest the earls of Rochester and Roscommon, neither seems particularly appropriate for a niche here. While Pope considered the Restoration Wits "holiday writers"—"gentlemen that diverted themselves now and then with poetry, rather than as poets" (*Anecdotes*, I, 201–02)—that is a judgment many leagues from the Bathos. Swift has uncomplimentary things to say about Charles Robartes, second earl of Radnor (*Journal to Stella,* ed. Harold Williams [Oxford: Clarendon Press, 1974], II, 452), who has been cited too as a possible source for Cotta's son in the *Epistle to Bathurst* (TE III ii, 108–09n), but there is nothing to suggest that he was a writer.

76. Daniel Defoe (1661?–1731), whose family name was originally Foe; after the author changed it, it was usually spelled De Foe. Although Pope had told Spence, "De Foe wrote a vast many things, and none bad, though none excellent. There's something good in all he has writ" (*Anecdotes,* I, 213), he probably felt he must include in the *Bathos* (see Chap. IX too) and in the *Dunciad* a figure so notorious at the time as a political hireling, author of "catch-penny" lives of criminals, and, in general, a prolific and indiscriminant writer for the masses.

77. As the poetical son of Blackmore (see Chap. IX and the *Dunciad,* I, l. 104), Laurence Eusden (1688–1730) too was a "natural" for the *Bathos,* one who, though a miserable poet, had in 1718 been named Poet Laureate. Even the author of the rebutting *Characters of the Times* was hard put to justify him: "A Man of insuperable Modesty, since certainly it was not his Ambition, that led him to seek this illustrious Post, but his Affection to the Perquisite of Sack" (Eusden was notorious for his drinking!).

78. Edward Howard (fl. 1669); "High-born Howard" of the *Dunciad*—also known as "foolish Ned"—was a well-established butt of the Restoration Wits (see n. 20) for his bad poetry and bad plays.

79. The Rev. William Broome (1689–1745)—who also appears under the Tortoises—was one of Pope's assistants in translating the *Odyssey.* The collaboration was not a happy one for either and the whole episode reflects badly on Pope. (See *Early Career,* pp. 248–62, and TE VII, xliv.) In the rancor that persisted for some years afterward, Pope included a passage from Broome, without any identification, in Chapter VII of the *Bathos* (for, parrot-like, if he was not a bad imitator, he was inadequate on his own) and commented in the *Dunciad* (a reference later dropped):

> Hibernian Politicks, O Swift, thy doom,
> And Pope's translating three whole years with Broome.
>
> (TE V, 190–91.)

80. In their documentation of the *Peri Bathous,* the EC editors just ignore this set of initials, and one is tempted to follow suit. For no likely candidate for "W. H.," the earlier listing, has surfaced; the list of the "abused" in *A Compleat Collection* includes a Mr. Hodges, but there is no further identification for him. Perhaps significantly, with the 1742 printing there is a change in the text to "W. S."; this, though, is scarcely better. Steeves has suggested William Shippen, but this is surely wrong, for Pope admired "downright Shippen." Perhaps it is William Sherwin, to whom Hervey addressed verses (see *A Most Proper Reply to the Nobleman's Epistle to a Doctor of Divinity*). The whole matter is puzzling: if the original "W. H." was a printer's error, one wonders why it would not have been corrected much earlier, especially given the furor over the initials.

81. Though his exaltation was not, of course, to come until the 1743 *Dun-*

ciad, Colley Cibber (1671–1757) (as a parrot here, and as the "Most Undaunted Mr. Colly Cibber," in Chap. XVI, "A Prospect for the Advancement of the Stage") pays for his contemporary reputation as a popular writer, actor, and producer, pandering to the current taste. As such Pope had lightly satirized him in *Three Hours after Marriage,* which he then, in turn, lampooned in a revival of the *Rehearsal* a few weeks later.

82. Steeves follows the EC identification: the Rev. Dean of Armagh, Richard Daniel (1681–1739). Besides being an enemy of Swift's, he had imitated (parroted?) Pope's "Messiah" in verses appearing in Lintot's 1712 *Miscellany.*

83. "A small diving water-fowl"—"applied ludicrously to people" (OED, citing this passage).

84. The first printings of these initials (L. W.——D. Esq;) immediately invited speculation whether two names were meant or just one: Leonard *Welsted* or Welsted, and, say, Duckett. One of the letter writers represented in *A Compleat Collection* argued for the single name, largely, one feels, so that he could then attack Pope with the familiar and vicious A. P.——E. Since in 1741, the letter "G" was substituted for the dash, one can, sooner or later, look for two names.

85. Leonard Welsted (1688–1747), heralded in the later *Bathos* (in Chap. IX: "flow my Numbers with the quiet thoughtlessness of Mr. Welsted?") and in the *Dunciad* (see n. 28), might well have earned his bathetic immortality simply with his own poetry and criticism. His "Dissertation concerning the Perfection of the *English* Language, the State of Poetry, &c.," which prefaced his translation of Longinus (1728), presents so exactly what Pope is burlesquing in the opening chapters of the *Peri Bathous* that one wonders if he worked with Welsted's essay (in which he was gratuitously snubbed) at hand. In addition Welsted, as an old Buttonian, had made a career of attacking Pope: in *Palaemon to Caelia, at Bath* (1717); in *One Epistle to Mr. A. Pope* (in collaboration with James Moore Smythe) (1730); in *Of Dulness and Scandal* (1731); and in *Of True Fame* (1732).

86. Steeves argues for George Bubb Dodington or, more likely, George Duckett (1684–1732). Dodington's role as a dubious patron better qualifies him for the *Dunciad* and the *Epistle to Dr. Arbuthnot,* where he has obviously contributed something to the character of Bufo, while Duckett's career as a pamphleteer/ journalist and almost professional antagonist to Pope makes his inclusion here appropriate. He and Thomas Burnet are so closely linked as fellow Buttonians and joint collaborators against Pope that the early omission of his first initial may be a swipe at this half-identity. Together they wrote *Homerides: or a Letter to Mr. Pope* (1715), attacking Pope's translatiaon of the *Iliad; Homerides, or Homer's First Book Moderniz'd* (1716), a further attack on him as translator and Catholic; and some papers in *Pasquin* (February and May 1723) at the time of Atterbury's trial and the problems over Buckingham's *Works.* Duckett was accused of writing, with

Dennis, *Pope Alexander's Supremacy* (1729), a post-*Dunciad* pamphlet, but Guerinot questions the attribution.

87. According to Steeves, Warburton expanded this to "Sir W. Young" (as it appears in EC), so there is no question of the identification, though, like the author of *Characters of the Times*, one wonders why this essentially political figure (however worthy as a type of fatuous orator and Whig henchman) was singled out here and at this time (he does figure in some of Pope's later poems). But perhaps the *Characters of the Times* provides its own answer: "I own, I have formerly seen a little Piece of his, or generally attributed to him, written on the Occasion of a Centinel's weeping on the Stage at some Incident in one of Mr. *Philip*'s Tragedies" (pp. 10–11). Sir William Yonge or Young (d. 1755) did have verses printed in the *Gentleman's Magazine* and Dodsley's *Collection of Poems* (1782) and he had been involved in reworking Broome's *A Jovial Crew* as a ballet-opera for Cibber's Drury Lane Theatre (in 1730/1) with Concanen and Roome, two of Pope's dunces.

88. The position of John Dennis, "Sir Tremendous [Longinus]" (1657–1734), in this bathetic catalogue among the corpulent porpoises was a fate guaranteed him by what seemed to Pope the uncritical emotionalism of his literary theory and by a history of bitter feuding between the two. Dennis published an outraged response (*Reflections . . . upon . . . an Essay on Criticism*, 1711) to an unflattering reference in the *Essay*; Pope retorted with *Narrative of Dr. Robert Norris* (1713)—or earlier if the *Critical Specimen* is his—and the fight was on. Following the *Reflections*, Dennis contributed four more scathing pamphlets: *A True Character of Mr. Pope* (1716), *Remarks upon Pope's Homer* (1717), *Remarks on the Rape of the Lock* (1728), and *Remarks upon Several Passages in the Preliminaries to the Dunciad* (1729). Pope also attributed *Pope Alexander's Supremacy* to him and Duckett, but it is not clear that either was involved. Guy Laprevotte ("Notes sur le *Peri Bathous*," p. 326) interestingly conjectures that Pope not only ridicules Dennis by designating him a porpoise but, even more ironically, borrows from him the idea of the identification, for in Dennis's adaptation of the *Merry Wives of Windsor* (*The Comical Gallant or the Amours of Sir John Falstaffe*), allusion is made to Falstaff as a Porpus—an association Pope might well have enjoyed.

89. See n. 71.

90. Traditionally assigned to John Oldmixon (1673–1742), whose qualifications are indeed impressive, though one might argue too for John Ozell (d. 1743). Both men were Curll hirelings, Oldmixon essentially a vehemently Whig historian and dramatist and Ozell a translator. Pope would have known Oldmixon's translation of Boileau (1711), but their first encounter seems to have involved the publication—in Oldmixon's miscellany of 1714—of a poem of Pope's retitled for the occasion "Receipt to make a Cuckold," a small piece of ribaldry that added little to his reputation, especially when Oldmixon went out of his way to call attention to the poem. Two years later Oldmixon was responsible for Curll's

possessing the poems that he published, without authorization, as *Court Poems*—insinuating embarrassingly that they might be by Pope, whose resulting war with Curll was further fueled in 1716 by Oldmixon's abusive *The Catholic Poet*. Oldmixon's own *Essay on Criticism* (1728) was a serious work but included, in passing, a number of swipes at Pope, some of them repeated in *The Arts of Logick and Rhetorick,* which appeared several months later and commented on the *Peri Bathous.*

Ozell had annoyed Pope too. His edition of *Le Lutrin* (1708) contained an insult to Wycherley, which Pope had answered in an epigram, "The Translator." In 1715, moreover, Ozell published the *Works* of Voiture "to which is prefixed the Author's Life and a Character of his Writings by Mr. Pope"—a pirated reprint, according to Sherburn, of Pope's "Epistle to a Lady with the Works of Voiture." So whether or not he belongs in the *Bathos,* he has an assured spot in the *Dunciad* (TE V, 91, 290, in the company of Cibber and first Johnson and then "Tibbald") with a nice, "defending" summary of his career in the "Errata" to the 1729 edition.

91. Edward (Ned) Ward (1667–1731), for whom there is no record of controversy with Pope before the *Bathos* and the *Dunciad,* was probably included in both because of his wide reputation as a "popular" writer, catering to the taste of the town with his *London Spy* and other such fare. In *Durgen* (1728) and *Apollo's Maggot in his Cups* (1729) (which included a "Postscript" or "Falsehoods by Alexander Pope against Edward Ward"), he replied—the second a vicious, personal attack.

92. James Moore (1702–34), who added to himself the name Smythe on coming into an inheritance in 1729, was, according to the *Characters of the Times,* "a very bright promising young Gentleman ["Esq"!]," who died young. In his comedy, *The Rival Modes* (1727), he used some unacknowledged verses of Pope (though Pope had withdrawn permission) so that when Pope later published them himself he was accused of plagiarism. *The Compleat Collection* includes an exchange of letters (from the *Daily Journal* and the *London Evening Post*) on this matter, the second letter being such an ironic attack that it may be Pope-inspired: it "defends" the abused Smythe and his play and in support of his skill attributes to him the *Memoirs of P. P.* (q. v.)! Pope included Smythe in the *Dunciad,* to which he responded by collaborating with Welsted on *One Epistle to Mr. A. Pope* (1730). But Pope had the last word, writing his literary epitaph in the *Epistle to Dr. Arbuthnot:* "Arthur [Moore], whose giddy Son neglects the Laws, / Imputes to me and my damn'd works the cause. . . ." (TE IV, 97.)

93. Thomas (Tom) D'Urfey or Durfey (1653–1723)—writer of poems, songs, and plays—seems to be introduced here, as in the *Dunciad,* "not because Pope felt spiteful towards him, but because every one was prepared to treat Durfey as a joke" (TE V, xlv). Like Ned Ward, with whom he is linked in the *Dunciad,* Durfey had enjoyed a long career in Augustan "popular" culture (delighting the squires, as the youthful Pope writes jocularly to Cromwell [*Correspondence,* I, 81]).

94. Guy Laprevotte ("Notes sur le *Peri Bathous*," p. 325) has pointed out the similarity between Pope's phrase and a line from Dorset's "To Mr. Edward Howard, on His Incomparable, Incomprehensible Poem, called the British Princes" ("So the dull eel moves nimbler in the mud, / Than all the swift-finn'd racers of the flood"), a poem which Pope very obviously had in mind—see n. 20.

95. See n. 85.

96. See n. 73.

97. Peter Motteux (1660–1718), French immigrant dramatist and translator. As the *Bathos*'s fish/fowl go, Motteux seems innocuous, though he is included in the *Dunciad* probably for the same reason he appears here: a reputation for long-windedness ("Talkers, I've learned to bear; *Motteux* I knew. . ." [*Fourth Satire of Dr. John Donne*, l. 50; TE IV, 29]). Given the definition of the eels, it might not be an inappropriate category for a tedious figure and a prolific, second-rate writer.

98. "General C." is supposed by the author of *Characters of the Times* to be General Christopher Codrington (1668–1710). But this is unlikely, since he had retired to the Barbados while Pope was still a boy. General William Cadogan, on the other hand, first earl Cadogan (1675–1726), Marlborough's quartermaster general in the War of the Spanish Succession, was "a favourite *bête noir* of Pope's" (TE III ii, 187n), earning Pope's lasting hostility because of a ruthless witticism directed at Atterbury when the latter was in the Tower (*Anecdotes*, I, 101–02). Though Cadogan's achievements were diplomatic and military rather than literary, the DNB quotes a reference to "early days in Dublin, 'when you was really a poet,' " which may suggest contemporary awareness of poetic pretensions.

99. See n. 50. This category was perhaps created intentionally for Philips, whose pastorals, published at the same time as Pope's, had been accorded disproportionate praise by the *Guardian*—in consequence of which, Pope's ironic *Guardian* paper No. 40 (27 April 1713). Like Blackmore, Philips was a "natural" for the *Bathos*, his writings furnishing Pope with twelve illustrations, making him second only to the Master.

100. See n. 79.

101. See n. 77.

102. As Steeves notes, this is probably Charles Douglas, earl of Selkirk (1663–1739), who appears also in *Epilogue to the Satires, Epistle to Bathurst,* and *Epistle to Cobham,* and in a manuscript version of the *Dunciad*. We do not know what writings of his Pope refers to, but his general reputation is clear from Lord Hervey's quip: "Let Nauseous Selkirk shake his empty head / Through six courts more, when six have wish'd him dead" (TE III ii, 23n).

103. Longinus, sections VIII, IX, X: "First and most important is the power of forming great conceptions" (Roberts, p. 57). ". . . the truly eloquent must be free from low and ignoble thoughts" (p. 61).

104. Pope's continuing war with Curll was sustained both by personal pub-

lishing confrontations (e.g., see *Narrative of the Method*), and by his contempt for Curll's role in promoting hack writing in his "Literary" (Curll's own term!) and in pirating and misusing the works of decent authors. This is the only mention of him in the *Peri Bathous*; he will appear in a major role in the *Dunciad*.

105. The reference to Physician brings to mind Blackmore (one of Curll's "learned writers") whose medical experience colored his theories of imagination (*Essays upon Several Subjects* [London, 1716], I, 153), and whose essay "Of the Sublimity of the Thoughts" Pope may, in part, be parodying here (ibid., pp. 94–97); there is also the general reminder of the *Tale of a Tub*.

106. Citing Pope's phrase (mistakenly attributed to the *Memoirs*), the OED defines only the adjectival form ("of a trite or commonplace character"), giving as first illustration Swift's "A Tritical Essay upon the Faculties of the Mind" (*Miscellanies in Prose and Verse* [London, 1711]).

107. "Spence informed Warton that 'some of the anonymous verses . . . of the *Art of Sinking in Poetry* [Chapter vii] were such as our poet remembered from his own ALCANDER' " (*Anecdotes*, I, 19n). The lines are reminiscent of Crashaw, about whom Warton noted, ". . . .from the dregs of Crashaw, of Carew, of Herbert, and others, (for it is well known he was a great reader of all these poets,) [the young] Pope has very judiciously collected gold." (*On the Genius and Writings of Pope* [London, 1806], I, 85.) In his youthful letters to Cromwell, Pope quoted Crashaw (*Correspondence*, I, 103) and later commented: "nothing regular or just can be expected from him." (*Correspondence*, I, 109–11.)

108. "Scott notes: 'Dr. Ridley is said to have told Mr. Steevens, Mr. Spence informed him that these lines originally stood in Pope's *Windsor Forest*. Mr. Spence, on the other hand, affirmed to Dr. Warton, that they were quoted from his unpublished epic, called Alcander. Amid this contradictory evidence, we may be excused believing that Pope had written them "for the nonce" to fill the place which they occupy in this treatise' (Swift's *Works*, ed. Sir Walter Scott, 2nd ed., 1824, XIII, 44 note)." [E. L. S., pp. 138–39.]

109. Steeves records that the line, from Lewis Theobald's *Double Falshood* (1727), was parodied by other amused satirists (p. 139). In the first edition of *Peri Bathous* the play, from which Pope quotes twice more, is mistitled the *Double Distress*. Theobald responded in a letter to *Mist's Weekly Journal*, 27 April 1728 (reprinted in *A Compleat Collection*), not only dismissing the error bitterly ("But 'tis meer *Wordcatching* [a reference to Pope's criticism of him in those terms in *Fragment of a Satire*], and beneath a great Genius to be *exact* in any Thing") but trying to justify his lines by comparing them to Shakespeare's or alleging, in this case, that it is Shakespeare's own ("the Line is in *Shakespeare's* old Copy").

110. Site of Batholomew Fair.

111. A reference Pope also makes in a letter to the duchess of Hamilton in October 1717 (*Correspondence*, I, 437).

112. A letter from Fenton to Broome (7 April [1728]; *Correspondence*, II, 487–88) reports on the inclusion of these two passages from Broome: "He has challenged you to a public defence, and if you do not think it worth your while to take up the gauntlet, the sullen silence of Ajax will be the most manly revenge." Sherburn notes that the first passage is from "On the birthday of a Gentleman [Mr. Robert Trefusis] when three Years Old." The second passage (with l. 2 actually "And rises amid monsters . . .") is from Broome's "Epistle to my Friend Mr. Elijah Fenton," 1726. About this Pope wrote to Broome (2 May 1730; *Correspondence*, III, 107): "Indeed, when I saw that passage in the book, I never suspected it to be yours, but imagined I had remembered it in Cowley, mistaking the one for the other." As Sherburn comments, ". . . he may be sincere here, but is probably disingenuous" (ibid., 107n).

113. Longinus: Roberts, Chaps. X, XI, XII; Boileau, Chap. VIII, "Of the Sublimity which is drawn from Circumstances," Chap. IX, "Of Amplification," Chap. X, "What Amplification is."

114. Longinus: " 'Twou'd be an infallible Secret for us to reach the *Sublime*, if we knew how to make a right Choice of the most considerable, and by connecting them well together, form 'em into one Body: For this Choice on one Hand, and the Connection of select Circumstances together on the other, are as a Powerful Charm upon the Mind. . . . all the grand Circumstances distinguish'd *a propos*, and collected with Judgment, are the Chief Beauty. . . ." (Boileau, pp. 31–32). Cf. Blackmore: "Anything is therefore admirable, because it is surprizing, and therefore surprizing because extraordinary and unexpected. All unusual Occurrences, especially the Excursions and Transgressions of Nature in her Operations, move the Imagination with great Force. . . . Our Wonder is likewise mov'd by common Objects represented in uncommon Circumstances. . . ." (*Essays upon Several Subjects*, I, 36, 35.)

115. Job 29.6—"When I washed my steps with butter, and the rocks poured me out rivers of oil. . . ."

116. Cf. *Spectator*, No. 83 (5 June 1711): "His [Dutch artist's] Figures were wonderfully laboured; if he drew the Portraiture of a Man, he did not omit a single Hair in his Face; if the Figure of a Ship, there was not a Rope among the Tackle that escaped him."

117. "The war horse with the burning eyes and hoofs that wound the earth had appeared in one of the most popular paraphrases of *Job*, by George Sandys. This read:

> Him cans't thou as a grasshopper affright,
> Who from his nostrils throws a dreadful light,
> Exults in his own courage, proudly bounds,
> With trampling hoofs the sounding centre wounds,

> Breaks through the order'd ranks with eyes that burn!
> Nor from the battle-axe or sword will turn.
> (*Poetical Works,* ed. Richard Hooper, 1872, pp. 71–72.)

The 'burning eyes' and 'wounding hoofs' were not in Sandys' source, but later paraphrases of *Job* borrowed these gratuitous additions. It is impossible to believe that the scarlet ribbons are anything but an addition of Pope's. . . ." [E. L. S., pp. 141–42]

118. Wake: Not (here) a funeral vigil, but the local annual festival of an English parish. *Spectator* No. 161 (4 September 1711) has a letter on the sporting contests at a Country Wake, beginning with cudgel-players, "who were breaking one another's Heads in order to make some Impression on their Mistresses Hearts."

119. The opening lines of "Fuscara, or the Bee Errant." In the original, the first line reads, "Nature's confectioner, the bee," and the next three lines are enclosed in parentheses. According to John M. Berdan, *The Poems of John Cleveland* (New York: Grafton Press, 1903), "It is quoted as the best example of wit in the 1677 preface, and it is the first poem in that edition. Many modern writers cite it as an example of the lack of restraint of the period." (P. 201.) Pope had a low opinion of Cleveland. (*Anecdotes,* I, 188.)

120. "To Signora Cuzzoni," 25 May 1724. Pope has dropped the second line ("Charmer of an idle age") and then, after line 4, the next four lines. Signora Francesca Cuzzoni was a much heralded operatic diva, whose position was challenged in 1736 by the arrival of Faustina Bordoni, the rivalry between the two causing quite a stir.

121. Job 38.12—"Hast thou commanded the morning since thy days. . . .?"

122. Pope omits a couplet after the fourth line; suns] Sun.

123. Psalm 104.32—"He looketh on the earth and it trembleth: he toucheth the hills, and they smoke."

124. Pope has omitted a couplet (about rocks) following line 2.

125. Longinus: Roberts, Chaps. XIII and XIV; Boileau, Chap. XI, "Of Imitation," and Chap. XII, "Of the Manner of Imitation."

126. Literary genealogies had become traditional: cf. *Dunciad* (TE V, 276), "She saw, with joy, the line immortal run, / Each sire imprest and glaring in his son. . . ." Sutherland notes that "The introduction of such men [Blackmore, etc.], and of Taylor, the water poet, Withers, Quarles, Ogilby, Tate, and others, was intended by Pope to put his scribblers in a historical setting of dullness. Every one was agreed about Ogilby and Tate; the assumption was that every one would see that Eusden and Welsted, Oldmixon and Cooke were of the same dull order, differing only in the scarcely relevant fact that they were still alive" (TE V, xlv).

127. Defoe (see n. 76) and George Wither or Withers (1588–1667) are linked

as fellow-pamphleteers. As a poet, Wither himself acknowledged that his reputation had "withered" (DNB); certainly by Pope's day he was well established as a feeble writer.

128. It was as a translator that Nahum Tate (1652–1715) [also adapter of Shakespeare], Poet Laureate, "a cold writer, of no *invention* but sometimes translated tolerably when befriended by Mr. *Dryden*" (TE V, 72n), was joined with John Ogilby (1600–76), whose translations of Homer, Virgil, and Aesop were scorned, though the eight-year-old Pope had been thrilled by his Homer ("It was that great edition with pictures" [*Anecdotes*, I, 14]).

129. Ned Ward (see n. 91) could be seen in a line descending from John Taylor (1580–1653), the "water poet," since both were recognizably popular writers catering to vulgar taste. To quote the DNB: "Although Taylor complacently styled himself the 'king's water poet' and the 'queen's waterman,' he can at best be only regarded as a literary bargee."

130. Or, as the *Dunciad* put it, "And Eusden eke out Blackmore's endless line . . ." (TE V, 72 and 276).

131. Cf. Longinus: "How wou'd *Homer* have said such a thing? What wou'd *Plato, Demosthenes,* or even *Thucydides* . . . have done . . . ?" (Boileau, p. 39.) See notes on Chap. VI for commentary on Philips and Welsted, though the particular reference here to Philips is probably to the style of his children's poems, which earned him the name of "Namby-Pamby." (see n. 182.)

132. *Aeneid* 3. 571–77. Dryden's translation may be compared with Blackmore's adaptation, which Pope next cites.

> The Port capacious, and secure from Wind,
> Is to the foot of thundring *Etna* joyn'd.
> By turns a pitchy Cloud she rowls on high;
> By turns hot Embers from her entrails fly;
> And flakes of mounting Flames, that lick the Skie.
> Oft from her Bowels massy Rocks are thrown,
> And shiver'd by the force come piece-meal down.
> Oft liquid Lakes of burning Sulphur flow,
> Fed from the fiery springs that boil below.

133. *Odes* I. I. 36: ["But if you rank me among Lyric bards,] I shall touch the stars with my exalted head" (Loeb [1952], p. 5).

134. See Horace, *Ars Poetica* 464–65: "deus immortalis haberi / dum cupit Empedocles, ardentem frigidus Aetnam / insiluit."

135. Cf. Longinus: "Thus by presenting those Great Men we propose to Imitate, to our Imagination, they stand us instead of a Torch to light us, and raise our Souls almost as high as the Idea we have conceiv'd of those Illustrious Genius's . . ." (Boileau, p. 39).

136. Identified by Warton as a line from Nicholas Rowe's *Lady Jane Grey* (V, i, 36): "And so good morning, good Master Lieutenant." As Pope had observed parenthetically to Spence (speaking about *Jane Shore*, which Rowe said was written in imitation of Shakespeare's style), "(It was mighty simple in Rowe to write a play now, professedly in Shakespeare's style, that is, professedly in the style of a bad age.)" (*Anecdotes*, I, 183.)

137. According to Warton, "He alluded particularly to Philip's 'Cyder,' of which he often expressed a strong disapprobation, and particularly on account of those antiquated words." (EC X, 372n.) Spence, on the other hand, records, "Though his [Milton's] formed style may fit the higher parts of his own poem, it does very ill for others who write on natural and pastoral subjects. Philips, in his *Cyder*, has succeeded extremely well in his imitation of it, but was quite wrong in endeavouring to imitate it on such a subject." (*Anecdotes*, I, 197.) In his Postscript to the *Odyssey* (see above, p. 59), Pope had complained, "The imitators of *Milton*, like most other imitators, are not *Copies* but *Caricatura's* of their original; they are a hundred times more obsolete and cramp than he. . . ."

138. Cf. Longinus: "I would affirm with confidence that there is no tone so lofty as that of genuine passion, in its right place, when it bursts out in a wild gust of mad enthusiasm and as it were fills the speaker's words with frenzy" (Roberts, p. 59).

139. Longinus: Boileau's Chap. III, "Of the Cold Stile," and Chap. IV, "Of the Origin of the Cold Stile."

140. Speaking of the three vices opposite to the Sublime (the bombastic, puerile, and emptily pathetic), Longinus comments on those who "by confining themselves too much to the Figurative Stile . . . at last sink into a ridiculous Affectation" and he goes on, in the next chapter, to cite examples of bathetic puns (Boileau, pp. 16, 18).

141. Dubiously emended to *law* in 1741, 1751 and subsequent editions.

142. Longinus too had turned at the close of his treatise (Chap. XIII, Boileau; Chap. XV, Roberts) to the discussion of images and figures.

143. Cf. Longinus; "But 'twou'd be a Work of too much Breath, not to say Infinite; if we shou'd here treat of all the *Figures* that may be admitted into Discourse, Wherefore we shall content our selves with running over some of the Principal ones; we mean those that contribute most to the *Sublime* . . ." (Boileau, pp. 45–46).

144. Pope's original phrase here, "nothing so much conduces to the *Abuse* of *Speech*, as the Catachresis" (corrected in an "Errata" leaf in the first edition [E. L. S., p. 148]), defines the term: i.e., "Improper use of words; application of a term to a thing it does not properly denote; abuse or perversion of a trope or metaphor" (OED).

145. James Bramston's lines (from the *Art of Politicks*, 1729, cited by the OED) reflect on the situation:

Think we that modern Words eternal are?
Toupet, and *Tompion, Cosins,* and *Colmar*
Hereafter will be called by some plain Man
A *Wig,* a *Watch,* a *Pair of Stays,* a *Fan.*

The equations are, for the most part, obvious: Tompion, for example, was a celebrated watchmaker of Queen Anne's day, and Cosins a famous corsetier (see also TE IV, 85, 85n and Lady Mary's "The Basset Table"). The OED knows no origin for Colmar as a fan beyond the place-name in Alsace; for *bubble-boy* it cites Pope's line and his footnote identification, suggesting that the term may come from *bubble* and *beau,* i.e., beau-befooler.

146. According to Warton these lines come from Pope's own youthful poems.

147. Cf. Longinus: "The expression of Herodotus to the effect that beautiful women are 'eye-smarts' is not much better [than other examples of frigidity]" (Roberts, p. 53).

148. Tom-Turdman, a "night man"—one who, by night, empties cesspools, etc.

149. White staves were carried by important court officers, the Lord Treasurer, etc.

150. "A rhetorical artifice, in which the speaker comes to a sudden halt, as if unable or unwilling to proceed"—and the OED cites this passage as example. According to Steeves, "I can no more" had become a trite phrase in the dramatic literature of the day. (P. 149.)

151. From "The Rival Queens, or the Death of Alexander the Great" (I, i), the best known of Nathaniel Lee's tragedies. Lee (1653?–1692), who as bombastic playwright furnished two other quotations to *Peri Bathous,* had spent some time in Bedlam:

In Durance, Exile, Bedlam, or the Mint
Like *Lee* or *Budgell,* I will Rhyme and Print.
(TE IV, 15.)

152. The first two lines come from p. 93, the second two from p. 91; shall recoil] will revoil; Soon shall he] The'Unrighteous.

153. tyrant] Tyrants.

154. After his l. 6, Pope omits 24 lines; after l. 7, one line; after l. 8, three lines; after l. 9, 13 lines; and after l. 11, 31 lines (Blackmore, *A Paraphrase on the Book of Job . . .* , pp. 289–92). For I] for he; his] my; And needs] He needs.

155. "Any mixture of heterogeneous elements"; "Unintelligible or meaningless talk or writing; nonsense, gibberish" (OED).

156. His] its.

157. Upon the shore] Along the Coast; the sand] its Sand.

158. Pope has omitted a line between these two verses.

159. The lines, from Thomas Cooke's epistle to the earl of Pembroke, read:

> Then, *Niobe,* thy hapless Offsprings fall;
> The Forest waves the Branches on the Wall;
> Thick fly the Darts, the Mother makes her Moan,
> And seems converted to a Stone in Stone. . . .
> (*Tales, Epistles, Odes, Fables, &c.* [London, 1729], p. 48.)

Poet, pamphleteer, translator, one of Curll's authors and associate of Moore Smythe, Concanen, and Theobald—Cooke (1703–56) earned his inclusion first in the *Dunciad* and later in the 1730 reprinting of the *Bathos* for his dubious taste (judging A. Philips superior to Pope in the *Battle of the Poets* [1725]), for his own bathetic verse, and for his attacks on Pope after the *Peri Bathous* and the *Dunciad*: an anonymous letter to the *Daily Journal* of 23 April 1728, reprinted in the *Compleat Collection,* in which he commented, from three passages of the Treatise, on "the *extraordinary Gratitude, Modesty,* and *Learning* of that Gentleman" (p. 35); a rewritten *Battle of the Poets* (1729); "The Episode of Thersites" (denigrating Pope as translator) (1729). And then, in 1732, a further attack: "A Letter in Prose to Mr. Alexander Pope, occasioned by his Epistle in Verse to the Earl of Burlington."

160. The conflated lines, from "Upon our Victory at Sea," read:

> Bullets, amain, unseen by mortal Eye,
> Fly in whole Legions thro' the darkened Sky,
> And kill and wound, like *Parthians,* as they fly.
> (*Miscellanies in Verse and Prose* [London, 1693], p. 13.)

161. Pope has modified Welsted's lines (in *Epistles, Odes, &c.,* 1724):

> Now, *Acon,* the coy Nymph is wholly thine:
> Nor will her Fame permit her to decline
> His suit, who saw her, with familiar Eyes,
> Asleep, and only cover'd with the Skies:
>   (P. 14.)

162. Since Pope does not identify the passage (and I have been unable to trace it), it may well be his own "addition."

163. From Waller's "To my Lady Morton on New-years-day, 1650. at the Louvre in Paris" (London, 1711), p. 170. While] Where. That Pope's attacks in the *Peri Bathous* are essentially critical, not vindicative, is demonstrated by his inclusion of lines here and in Chapter XI from a poet whom he greatly admired, citing him among a list of writers who "might serve as authorities for poetical language" (*Anecdotes,* I, 171).

164. The line, from Steele's *The Procession. A Poem on Her Majesties Funeral* (By a Gentleman of the Army) (London, 1695), was omitted when Steele reprinted the poem, this time under his name, in his *Poetical Miscellanies,* 1714 [1713], a

collection which included some of Pope's early translations. Despite extensive revisions, the poem provoked a lampoon, "Upon Mr. Steele's Incomparable Elegy on the Death of Queen Mary. Publish'd Eighteen Years after it was Written—" (Rae Blanshard, ed., *The Occasional Verse of Richard Steele* [Oxford: Clarendon Press, 1952], p. 74). Since this was the period of Pope's *Guardian* paper No. 40 and Swift's "The First Ode of the Second Book of Horace Paraphras'd: And Address'd to Richard St——le, Esq," Pope was no doubt attuned to matters involving Steele, though, as Sherburn argues (*Early Career,* p. 154), there is no history of real rancour between them.

165. The lines, from Quarles' *Divine Fancies* (Book I, XLII: "On the Body of Man" [London, 1722, p. 18]) read:

> His Eyes like Christal *Windows* clear and bright
> Let in the *Object,* and let out the Sight.

Popular with less sophisticated readers because of the quaint illustrations to his poems, Quarles is included here, as in the *Dunciad* and the Horatian imitations, as a dull writer:

> But Kings in Wit may want discerning spirit.
> The Hero William, and the Martyr Charles,
> One Knighted Blackmore, and one pension'd Quarles . . . .
> (TE IV, 227.)

166. The line is from Lee's *Sophonisba* (London, 1676, Act I, p. 3) rather than the *Death of Alexander.* The Gods look] And then look'd.

167. From Philips' *Sixth Pastoral* (ll. 107–08; and] with.

168. Cf. Longinus: "For as in all things, we are most taken with what Shines and Strikes most . . . : Which Image Striking his Imagination, hinders his examining the Strength of the Proofs more narrowly; Dazling him with the great Lustre, with which it Covers and Surrounds a Discourse." (Boileau, p. 45.)

169. Pope's "Vetus Autor" has not been identified, nor has his source for the next quotation.

170. *Double Falshood,* I, iii.

171. Steeves notes that the passage is not from the edition of *Prince Arthur* that Pope elsewhere cites, but from the first edition (1695), p. 232:

> Rais'd to the Clouds, the sprawling Mastives fly,
> And add new Monsters to th'affrighted Sky.

She notes too that the verses are quoted in Edward Bysshe's *Art of English Poetry* (5th ed., 1714), whence Pope may have remembered them. (P. 154.)

172. Edmund Waller, "Upon the Death of the Lord Protector in the Year 1658" (London, 1711), p. 219. Tropics] Tropick.

173. Although Griffith assigns the lines to *Alcander,* Steeves argues that they

may be from an authentic Scots poem since the compliment is in "the overwhelming Scotch fashion of the time." (Pp. 155–56.)

174. It was EC that noted that these lines are actually from Dennis's ode on the Battle of Aghrim, "A Pindaric Ode on the King, written Aug 2, 1691" (from *Miscellanies in Verse and Prose* [London, 1693], p. 3). After the first edition of the *Peri Bathous,* Pope changed the lines to conform to the original, later substituting *steddy* for *noisy* (see textual variants).

175. The OED illustrates its definition ("A room devoted to the arrangement or display of works of art and objects of vertu") from this reference.

176. The contemporary zeal for collecting antiquities is satirized in the *Memoirs* and *Three Hours after Marriage.* Bufo, too, it will be recalled (*Epistle to Dr. Arbuthnot,* l. 236), owns "a true *Pindar* . . . without a head."

177. like one Pot] one vast Pot; no ellipsis in original.

178. Pp. 156–57.

179. As Steeves notes, the lines are from *King Arthur* (London, 1697, p. 103), not *Prince Arthur.* (P. 157.) The mighty] Then mighty; a massy] his massy.

180. this] such.

181. Steeves locates the lines in the first edition (1700) of Blackmore's *Job,* but Pope's version comes from the 1716 edition that he was using (p. 122); The clouds] Their Wombs; hang] float.

182. The first passage is from "To Miss Georgiana Youngest Daughter to Lord Carteret" (1725). After line 2, Pope omits ten lines; ye] the; pretty] promis'd. The rest of the quotation consists of scattered couplets from "To the Honourable Miss Carteret" (1725); Then the necks] And the neck; no parentheses. After his pastorals, Philips' five poems to children are his best known (most notorious) work, earning him the nickname of Namby-Pamby and provoking numerous parodies (see M. G. Segar, *The Poems of Ambrose Philips* [Oxford: Basil Blackwell, 1937], pp. 181–82).

183. Philips, the *Fourth Pastoral,* l. 55.

184. Ibid., ll. 49–51; die] go; poor] thy; no ellipsis. The two lines preceding were ridiculed by Pope in the *Guardian* paper. (See n. 99.)

185. See textual variant (Page 214:B) for a passage omitted *1741–51.* Those lines (ll. 45–47 from Philips' *Sixth Pastoral*) were probably dropped by Pope because he had unfairly distorted the author's meaning.

186. Philips, the *Fourth Pastoral,* ll. 63–66; breast] Breasts; death] Hour.

187. Philips, the *Second Pastoral,* ll. 61–62; the flowery plain] thy flow'ry Banks; no parentheses in original. Not surprisingly Pope had included these lines in his satiric *Guardian* No. 40 of 27 April 1713.

188. Philips, "Lament for Queen Mary," ll. 36–37; no parentheses. (See n. 51.)

189. Ibid. The original (ll. 50–53) reads,

He whom the Terrours of a bloody Fight

. . . .

Nor the loud Cannon's Roar can terrifie,
Falls from the Grandeur of his Majesty.

190. This 1730 addition is from Cooke's translation of Anacreon, "To the Grasshopper" (*Tales, Epistles, Odes, Fables, &c.*, p. 191).

191. "The second verse of this couplet may be found in a one-act farce of 1731 by 'Scriblerus Tertius' (a pseudonym frequently used by Cooke) called *The Battle of the Poets; or, The Contention for the Laurel.* The line is spoken by Sir Fopling Fribble who represents Cibber. The inference seems to be that the line is from one of Cibber's plays, but a search . . . failed to unearth it. Since the farce postdates *Peri Bathous* the author may have picked up the line from Pope's treatise." [E. L. S., p. 159.]

192. Warton thought this passage "glanced at Thomson," but if Pope had intended such a "glance" it seems likely he would have produced a better imitation. Everything suggests it was created for the occasion.

193. From "Tyrtaeus, on Martial Virtue" (Cooke, *Tales, Epistles, Odes, Fables, &c.*, p. 189); there] they.

194. From Cooke too, his "Psalm the 137th paraphrased" (ibid., p. 160); grief] Griefs; sun did see] Sun beheld; While] When.

195. "Prolixity of speech" and "redundancy of expression," with the OED in the first case citing this passage as illustration.

196. As Steeves notes (p. 160), the compliment to Addison suggested here is undercut by the number of illustrations that follow. Pope later mentioned to Spence, "Tautology, a frequent fault of Addison: more such faults in his *Campaign* than any one would easily imagine" (*Anecdotes*, I, 76). For a history of the complex relations between Addison and Pope, especially at the time Pope was collecting his "flights," see *Early Career,* Chapter V; Spence's *Anecdotes*, I, 60–80; and, especially, Norman Ault, *New Light on Pope* (London: Methuen, 1949), Chap. VI.

197. Addison's *Campaign,* ll. 199, 202, 192 (in parentheses in original), 268, 168, 190.

198. Pope's footnote reference to Tonson's *Miscellany* (which has been moved to locate properly the next two lines) was originally printed here by mistake; actually this line (which never appeared in any of Tonson's miscellanies) is, as Steeves notes (p. 161), from a poem of Tickell's entitled *The Royal Progress.* In *Spectator* No. 620 (15 November 1714), it is glowingly introduced as "the Work of a Master." Break] Breaks; divide] divides; no ellipsis.

199. See n. 198. Correctly located by the citation, this line is from Addison's "Account of the Greatest English Poets," about which Pope later commented to Spence, "That was not published till after his death [obviously wrong—a lapse

in memory?], and I dare say he would not have suffered it to be printed had he been living, for he himself used to speak of it as a poor thing" (*Anecdotes*, I, 73, 74n). and . . . in] and a.

200. As printed in "Horace, Ode III. Book III," the lines read:

> [*Europe* from *Afric* shall] divide
> And part the sever'd World in two:

The poem, as Steeves reports, was first published anonymously in *Spectator* No. 615 (3 November 1714) and then included by Tickell in his edition of Addison's works (1721). Whether Pope knew it to be Addison's is conjectural, though Steeves has collected some evidence that others did (pp. 162–63).

201. Longinus had concluded his discussion with a consideration of "Disposition of Words" (Boileau, Chap. XXXII) and "Mean Expressions" (Chap. XXXIV).

202. From Thomas Tickell's *The First Book of Homer's Iliad* (London, 1715), ll. 80, 178, 407. This rival translation, perhaps prompted by Addison and certainly promoted by the Buttonians, was a sore issue for Pope, though, according to Sherburn, in later years Tickell was a friend to both Pope and Swift (*Early Career*, pp. 127ff.).

203. M. Jourdain in Molière's *Le Bourgeois gentilhomme*.

204. Pope's identifications ascribe the five following passages to Tickell; but his reference to the next two, which are by Addison, as from "the same hand" makes clear his belief that Addison was the actual translator of Tickell's translation (see also *Anecdotes*, I, 70). He was not alone in this belief. Warton held it, as did Addison's friend Steele and many contemporaries. The truth appears to be that Addison corrected Tickell's work (see Ault, *New Light on Pope*, pp. 105–06; and *Early Career*, p. 131).

205. See n. 204.

206. From Addison's "An Account of the Greatest English Poets"; I now] I'll now.

207. From "Horace, Ode III. Book. III"; Pope has omitted a line between the two cited.

208. Pope's page reference to this passage from Psalm 104 is incorrect.

209. That] Which; Forest] Forests.

210. In his "Proposal for Correcting, Improving, and Ascertaining the English Tongue" (Oxford: Basil Blackwell, 1964), Swift had complained of all the "cant words" and "new Terms" that were debasing the language. Terms related to "Mechanic" may be either technical or base and lowly, as appropriate here.

211. Fresh Troops of Pains] Fierce Troops of Pain.

212. As Steeves points out, Pope's discussion of style here takes hints from

Parnell's *Essay on the different Styles of Poetry* (1713), where he allegorically describes good and bad practices. (P. 165.)

213. One is reminded that the "excessively ornate" is indeed etymologically "flowery."

214. From Aphra Behn's "The Golden Age," *Poems Upon Several Occasions* (London, 1684), p. 2; appear] appear'd; drop] dropt. Pope elsewhere cites her as "Authoress of several obscene Plays, &c." (TE IV, 219n).

215. From Laurence Eusden (appointed Laureate in 1718), "The Court of Venus from Claudian . . ." in *Guardian* No. 127 of 6 August 1713; alders, alders] Alder, Alders.

216. P. 260; with Gems] blest Gems.

217. Cf. *Spectator* No. 616 (Friday, 5 November 1714), "Our little Burlesque Authors, who are the Delight of ordinary Readers, generally abound in these pert Phrases, which have in them more Vivacity than Wit."

218. Cf. Swift ("A Proposal for Correcting the English Tongue," p. 12): "Thus furnished, they [young men from the Universities] come up to Town; reckon all their Errors for Accomplishments, borrow the newest Set of Phrases; and if they take a Pen into their Hands, all the odd Words they have picked up in a Coffee-House, or a Gaming Ordinary, are produced as Flowers of Style; and the Orthography refined to the utmost. To this we owe those monstrous Productions, which under the Names of *Trips, Spies, Amusements,* and other conceited Appelations, have over-run us for some Years past." Edward Ward (1667–1731), not Thomas Brown (1663–1704), was the author of the *London Spy.* According to the DNB, in a deathbed letter, Brown protested "against being responsible for 'lampoons, trips, London Spies,' in which he had no hand." But as the DNB also notes, "his knowledge of London was certainly 'extensive and peculiar,' " and the sizable posthumous collection of his works included such essays as "Amusements Serious and Comical," "A Pocket-Book of Common Places," and "A Walk round London and Westminster." Cibber's verse is memorably described in the *Dunciad*: "Nonsense precipitate, like running Lead" (TE V, 278).

219. Common title page locutions in Pope's time.

220. Thomas Gordon (d. 1750), one of Walpole's gazetteers, had dedicated his very recently published *Tacitus* (1728) to him. He appears as Silenus in the *Dunciad* (TE V, 390) because his reward for his journalistic services was to be made a Commissioner for Wine Licences.

221. Pope commented to Spence, "L'Estrange's excellent fable style is abominable in his translation of Josephus" (*Anecdotes*, I, 204). Roger L'Estrange (1616–1704), Tory journalist and pamphleteer, supplemented his meager income with hack translations, having also translated Tully's (Cicero's) *Offices* and Seneca's *Morals*—which Pope may have in mind in his next statement. *The British Gazeteer* (or *Weekly Journal*) of George Read (often called *Read's* to distinguish it from *Mist's Weekly Journal*) was a Whig newspaper published from 1715 to 1761.

222. As Steeves points out, John Asgill (1659–1738) wrote in a style "characterized by an anonymous satirist of the time as a series of contradictions, pert remarks, abrupt questions, common similes, low comparisons and inappropriate jests" (p. 167). (She mentions too that Pope may be alluding here to Dr. Cockman's translation of Cicero's *Offices,* which had six editions between 1706 and 1723.)

223. Snip-snap = "smart repartee" (OED). Pope, speaking of L'Estrange's *Josephus* (see n. 221) adds (*Anecdotes,* I, 204) "and 'tis the same with his imitator Collier [Jeremy Collier (1650–1726)] as to his lighter pieces and his translation of Marcus Antoninus" (*The Emperor M. Aurelius Antoninus His Conversation with Himself,* 1701).

224. John Stanhope (1660–1728), Dean of Canterbury, had translated Kempis's *Imitatio Christi* (1698), "modernizing" his texts and following, as the DNB phrases it, a "paraphrastic system."

225. I.e. fashionable or voguish.

226. Pp. 83–84; see nn. 188 and 51.

227. Chase] Chas'd.

228. He sunk] Th' Almighty sunk; does keep] might keep; station] Stations.

229. The first two lines are from Act IV (London, 1676, p. 45); Yon] You. The final two come from Act II (p. 20), where the original read:

> Throw boldly at the sum which the Gods set,
> A hundred thousand lives at once are met,
> That on your side, with all their fortunes bet.

230. Pope may be glancing at Lady Mary, whose somewhat scandalous "Roxana: or the Drawing Room" had been published in 1716 by Curll, attributed to a "lady of quality."

231. The Greek name of a legendary king of Egypt, who, according to Greek tradition, conquered the whole of Asia and introduced the worship of Serapis, a god of fertility.

232. Cf. Swift: "What I mean, is that highly celebrated Talent among the *Modern* Wits, of deducing Similitudes, Allusions, and Applications, very Surprizing, Agreeable, and Apposite, from the *Pudenda* of either Sex, together with *their proper Uses*" (*Tale of a Tub* [Oxford: Basil Blackwell, 1965], p. 92).

233. Ostensibly, "deplorable large gap"—a traditional scribal notation here used comically to account for the omitted names; but also, more literally, "large, tear-shaped (or even weeping) cleft."

234. See note 39.

235. "Cibberism and Oldfieldism." As Steeves comments, these references to Colley Cibber and Anne Oldfield (1683–1730) reflect upon "the ribaldry and

equivocality of the comedy roles in which Cibber and Mrs. Oldfield won applause"
(p. 168).

236. stream] Flood; her] its.

237. Identified by EC as from John Dennis's verses on the sea fight at La
Hogue ("Upon our Victory at Sea," *Miscellanies in Verse and Prose* [London, 1693],
p. 16). The original first line reads, speaking of oaks: "Their huge extended Arms
the Winds defy. . . ." (See also n. 160.)

238. From "The Celebrated Beauties," p. 234 (incorrectly paged in later editions). The sparkling] So sparkling.

239. I.e., the tragic vein.

240. Only two of the passages that follow are identified; given the nature of
these examples, one might hazard the guess that they were composed for the
occasion.

241. As Steeves notes (p. 169) Pope may be quoting from Shakespeare's *Tempest* (I, ii, 409–10) or from the Dryden-Davenant version, which is closer to the
Peri Bathous lines:

> Advance the fringed curtains of thine eyes
> And say what thou seest yonder.
> (III, v, 1–2 [London, 1670, p. 44].)

or may just be quoting from memory.

242. Act II, scene ii.

243. In the first edition, the four chapters that follow were listed under
Appendix, and the parody of Longinus concludes with Chapter XII. Steeves argues
plausibly (pp. 181–84) that the treatise originally finished there and that Pope
added the remaining chapters to flesh out the piece for inclusion in the "Last"
Volume of *Miscellanies* in place of the *Dunciad.* Chapter XV, "The Receipt to make
an Epic Poem"—published in 1713 as a *Guardian* paper—he had on hand and
the other chapters might well have evolved from related Scriblerian interests,
especially Arbuthnot's and Swift's concern with "projects" like those outlined in
Chapter XIII.

244. As Steeves points out, there are actually two projects here: an Academy
of letters and a "Rhetorical Chest." The very word *projects* (and *projectors*) would
have had particular meaning for the readers of *Gulliver's Travels,* recently published.
To Guy Laprevotte the whole title recalls Bacon's "Advancement of Learning,"
and he goes on too to consider the chapter's satire as modeled on scientific societies,
particularly the Royal Society and Sprat's history of it. Laprevotte also sees in the
title a possible allusion to "The Advancement and Reformation of Modern Poetry"
of John Dennis, one of the most vociferous supporters of the Moderns, who had
also defended them in his "Reflections . . . upon . . . An Essay upon Criticism."
(Laprevotte, "Notes sur le *Peri Bathous,*" pp. 339–45.)

245. As Laprevotte reminds us, this returns to the satire advanced at the outset of the *Peri Bathous* against the "Moderns." Here their confusion between scientific and literary "progress" is as absurd as the "Affinity . . . between Arts and Sciences" heralded in Chap. VI. (Ibid., pp. 341–43.)

246. Like the speaker's unctuous civic protestations in *A Modest Proposal*.

247. This concept Laprevotte ("Notes sur le *Peri Bathous*," pp. 339–40) traces to Bacon and Sprat and the organization of scientific societies at the time.

248. *Rhetoric* 3. 11. 16: "There is something youthful about hyperboles; for they show vehemence." (Loeb [1959], p. 417.)

249. See n. 150.

250. "The beginning of a sentence, line, or clause with the concluding, or any prominent, word of the one preceding" (OED).

251. "An early-ripening fruit or vegetable" (OED, citing this phrase as reference).

252. London's oldest city market, primarily a fish market, so that the name became synonymous with the coarse scolding of fish wives.

253. From Thames watermen, "whose licentious ribaldry was known as 'River Wit' " (John Ashton, *Social Life in the Reign of Queen Anne* [London: Chatto and Windus, 1882], II, 144).

254. Beargardens, originally sites of bearbaiting, later became arenas for fighting matches (see *Spectator* No. 436 [21 July 1712]: "a Place of no small Renown for the Gallantry of the lower Order of Britons, namely, to the Bear-Garden at *Hockley in the Hole*; Where . . . there was to be a Tryal of Skill to be exhibited between Two Masters of the Noble Science of Defence. . . ."

255. Laprevotte suggests that the word "repositories" was meant to bring to mind the famous "repository" "dans lequel la Société Royale conservait ses spécimens; d'ailleurs, il est précisé que chaque tiroir de la commode sera subdivisé en cosiers semblables à ceux dans lequels on mettait 'les raretés' " ("Notes sur le *Peri Bathous*," p. 341). In any case, this schema is derived from Aristotle's *Rhetoric* (". . . there are necessarily three kinds of rhetorical speeches, deliberative, forensic, and epideictic" [1. 3.3 (Loeb [1959], p. 33)]), where the discussion touches upon the further subdivisions or classifications cited here (e.g., Peace or War, Liberty of the Press). It has been noted that Hobbes's translation of Aristotle provides specifically Pope's terms: deliberative, demonstrative, and judicial [E. L. S., pp. 185–86].

256. One is inevitably reminded of Lagado's frames "for improving speculative Knowledge by practical and mechanical Operations." Certainly Swift's influence seems very pervasive in this chapter.

257. Cf. Blackmore's suggestion for theater censors: "It might, perhaps be desirable, that a few Persons of Importance, Men of Learning, Gravity, and good Taste, might be commission'd by Authority, as a Check upon the Actors, to

censure and suppress any Dramatic Entertainments that shall offend against Religion, Sobriety of Manners, or the Publick Peace . . ." (*Essays upon Several Subjects,* I, 229). Or— ". . . .generally Men of a plain Understanding and good Sense, but of great Industry and Capacity for Business, are in all Governments advanc'd to Posts of Trust and great Employments in the State, while meer Wits are regarded as Men of the lowest Merit, and accordingly are promoted to the meaner and less profitable Places, being look'd on, by reason of their Inapplication and volatile Temper, as unfit for a higher Station. (Ibid., p. 216—this observation precedes an attack on *A Tale of a Tub* and that "impious Buffoon," its author!)

258. According to Warton, "It will be difficult to find more knowledge of life, more wit, more satire, more good sense, in any passage of equal length than is comprized in this fourteenth chapter" (Pope's *Works* [London, 1797], VI, 264.)

259. Cf. Swift: "There is a Problem in an ancient Author, why Dedications, and other Bundles of Flattery run all upon stale musty Topicks . . ." (Preface to *A Tale of a Tub,* p. 30).

260. Possibly Pope anticipates here his later campaign against the Court and its "great Minister," Walpole.

261. The reference to the colors of the Orders of the Garter, the Bath, and the Thistle, is heightened by the topical implication: as the two last had been revised by Walpole in 1727, they were particularly "objects of ridicule to the Opposition" (EC X, 399n).

262. Aristotle's "golden mean" between the vices of excess and defect is here transformed into the "Golden Rule" of semantic "Transformation."

263. Defoe, to his sorrow, had learned that anyone writing against the government ran the risk of imprisonment and the pillory—if not worse. Even the slippery Curll in his war against the King's Bench on other issues ended up in the pillory though not, as has been asserted, with the loss of his ears (Straus, p. 98).

264. This chapter is Pope's *Guardian* paper No. 78 of Wednesday, 10 June 1713, revised for its new context. It is highly unlikely that Pope, as Warton thought, intended a "severe animadversion . . . on Bossu," whose *Traité du poème épique* (1675) he had recommended in his Preface to the *Iliad* and an abstract of which he had prefixed to his translation of the *Odyssey.* More probably, as Loyd Douglas argues (" 'A severe animadversion on Bossu,' " *PMLA,* 62 [1947], 690–706), Pope's scorn is aimed at those guilty of mechanical applications of Bossu's principles, e.g. particularly Blackmore. We may usefully note in this connection that the English translation of Bossu which Pope probably used is dedicated to the author of *Prince Arthur, "wherein you have in a great measure confin'd your self to the Rules and Precepts which* Aristotle *and* Horace *and even our* Bossu, *have prescrib'd to the* Epick Poem."

265. Cf. Bossu: "all *Arts* depend upon a great many other things [beyond the

Light of Nature], such as the *Choice* and *Genius* of those, who first invented them, or of those who have labour'd at them with an Universal Applause" (Bossu, p. 1).

266. Douglas (see n. 264) cites Blackmore's avowal in his preface to *King Arthur,* "I had read but little Poetry throughout my whole Life . . ." [London, 1697, p. v].

267. In *L'Avare,* III, i.

268. Steeves points out the device of the "Recipe" was a familiar one, Pope himself having used it earlier in "Epigram upon Two or Three" (or "A Receipt to make a Cuckold"), 1713. (P. 188.)

269. It is significant that this is precisely what Bossu did *not* intend for his Treatise: "Having no Design by this Treatise to make *Poets* . . . but only to furnish my self with some sort of Foundation in the Design then I have of explaining the *Aeneid* of Virgil . . ." (Bossu, p. 2).

270. Pope follows Bossu's divisions: fable, epic action, narration, manners, machines, and expression.

271. Cf. Blackmore (from his preface to *King Arthur* [London, 1697], the original in reverse italics): "And that the Reader may better observe whence the Action of this takes its Rise, I will tell in short *King Arthur's* Story, as tis related by *Geofry* of Monmouth. That there was . . . a King of *Britain* nam'd *Arthur.* . . . And tho' the above-cited *Geofry* of Monmouth is indeed a Fabulous Author, yet his Authority, especially considering that there was such a War-like Prince as *Arthur,* is a sufficient Foundation for an *Epick Poem*" (pp. xi–xii). "And several friends to *Prince Arthur* did very early convince me, that in several Instances the Descriptions, Digressions, and Similes, were lyable to the same Objection [of being too long]" (p. iv).

272. Cf. Bossu: "We may disguise the *Fiction,* render the Action more singular, and make it a *Rational Fable* by the Names of Men invented at Pleasure" (Bossu, p. 16). "But the better to carry on this Disguise, search must be made in *History* for the Names of some Persons to whom this feign'd Action might either *Probably* or *Really* have happen'd . . ." (ibid., p. 17).

273. Cf. Bossu: "But can an Author put nothing into his Poem, but what is purely the Matter of it? Or has he not the Liberty of inserting . . . some pieces of rich and gay Stuff, that have nothing to do with the Ground-work? . . . they [dictates of right reason, practices of good poets, rules of the best masters] do not approve of the Recital of an Incident that has not one of these two Conditions, *viz.* Such a one as is neither the Matter of the Epopéa, nor necessary to illustrate any part of the *Action.*" (Bossu, p. 55.) An *Episode,* according to *Artistotle,* should not be taken from something else and added to the Action . . ." (ibid., p. 64).

274. This is a complete inversion of Bossu's theory that the epic narration is invented to illustrate the moral: "The first thing we are to begin with for Composing a *Fable,* is to chuse the Instruction, and the point of Morality, which is to

serve as its Foundation, according to the Design and End we propose to our selves" (Bossu, p. 15).

275. Although Warton (Pope's *Works* [London, 1797], VI, 270–71n) foot-notes this as "A stroke of ridicule on Bossu," reviewing then the traditional critical discussion of whether manners should be poetically or morally good, Douglas (" 'A severe animadversion on Bossu,' " p. 700) acknowledges the dispute but does not see it as a relevant attack on Bossu, only one of the many critics who had dealt with the question. He argues too that the opening statements about the hero are more illustrative of Blackmore's practice than Bossu's theory.

276. Cf. Bossu: Book IV ("Concerning the Manners of the Epick Poem"), chap. v: "Whether the Hero of the Poem ought to be an Honest Man, or no?" And Bossu answers no, distinguishing between a "Hero in Morality" and one "in Poetry" (well behaved vs. well defined).

277. Cf. Bossu: "We may in short affirm, that *Machines* are to be made use of all over, since *Homer* and *Virgil* do nothing without them" (Bossu, p. 225).

278. Ll. 191–92: "And let no god intervene, unless a knot come worthy of such a deliverer . . ." (Loeb [1955], p. 467). Bossu cites the same passage in his discussion of the use of Machines (Book V, chap. IV, p. 226).

279. Douglas argues, "The section on the descriptions is likewise clearly not a take-off on Le Bossu's discussion of the subject, but an *a posteriori* prescription based on the sort of thing which permeates all Blackmore's epics," and he cites some of Blackmore's "stormy concoctions"—with several references of quicksands. (" 'A severe animadversion on Bossu,' " p. 701.)

280. Warton: "An undeserved sarcasm on a work full of strong imagery, Burnet's theory" (Pope's *Works* [1797], VI, 273). Thomas Burnet's *Telluris Theora Sacra* (1681, 1689), translated as *The Theory of the Earth* (1684, 1690), devoted Book III to "the Burning of the World," the author commenting, "If one should now go about to represent *the World on Fire,* with all the confusions that necessarily must be, in Nature and in Mankind, upon that occasion, it would seem to most Men a Romantick Scene (Chap. 12; London, 1697, p. 72).

281. The three contemporary actor-managers of the Drury Lane Theatre: Barton Booth, Robert Wilks, and Colley Cibber. Hogarth has a print, "A Just View of the British Stage" (1724), depicting the three plotting various pantomimes.

282. Barton Booth (1681–1733), whose fame and fortune reached its height with his impersonation of Addison's Cato, had a career advanced by aristocratic patronage, his admission to the management of the Drury Lane having been effected through Queen Anne's influence.

283. Robert Wilks (1665?–1732) was characterized by Cibber as the "most diligent, laborious, and useful actor that had been on the stage for fifty years" (DNB). His name was long associated with the management of the Haymarket Theatre and then the Drury Lane during its most prosperous period.

284. See n. 81. Cibber might have been a successful dramatist, a popular comedian, and a judicious manager; but Pope still had a low opinion (intensified by his experience with *Three Hours after Marriage*) of everything and everyone to do with the stage.

285. "The notorious phrase 'Out-do even their own Outdoings' is quoted from the Preface to Cibber's *Provoked Husband,* first performed at Drury Lane on Jan. 10, 1728, and published—where the Preface first appeared—on Jan. 31, 1728. Mrs. Oldfield had played the leading feminine role, and Cibber relates how she 'outdid her usual excellence.' Apparently Cibber's phrase vastly tickled the wits, for it was parodied time and time again and was quoted in numerous burlesques written upon the new laureate. An obscene interpretation was immediately given the phrase as applied to Mrs. Oldfield. Cibber later made excuses for it in his *Apology,* and though not an especially sensitive person, he seems to have felt the prick of the many gibes at his unlucky words." [E. L. S., p. 190.]

286. Steeves reviews (pp. 190–91) the history of speculation on this elusive "Project." Advertised at the time as *A New Project for the Regulation of the Stage,* the pamphlet is listed in bibliographies, though no modern commentator has seen a copy of it. Following Dennis's disclaimers, critics reject it as a work of his, Hooker (Dennis's editor) arguing that it is actually a satire *on* Dennis and Gildon; "and the fact that Pope happily summarizes it . . . suggests that he was privy to the secret of its authorship" (Dennis, *Works,* II, ix). The specificity of the date of publication might also have reminded readers of a pertinent series of exchanges at that same time between Dennis and Steele over Steele's new paper, *the Theatre,* Dennis having addressed four letters to "Sir John Edgar [Steele], Called by Himself Sole Monarch of the Stage in Drury Lane; and his Three Deputy Governors." And Gildon's name was identified (whether correctly or not) with *A Comparison between the Two Stages* [Drury Lane and Lincoln's Inn Fields], 1702—a reference that makes a nice transitional link with the paragraph that follows.

287. The two major theaters of the time were the Drury Lane and the Lincoln's Inn Fields; the very idea of merging the two competitive companies would no doubt have been titillating to contemporary readers.

288. *The Royal Academy of Music* had been established in 1719 precisely to separate opera from the legitimate stage so that the music could develop properly (and Pope was invited to prepare a seal with suitable motto for the organization, though he did not do so). (E. L. Avery, *The London Stage 1660–1800,* Part II [Carbondale, Illinois: Southern Illinois University Press, 1960], p. lxxiv.) In less than a decade, troubled by financial problems and internal squabbles, the opera company closed with the 1727–28 season.

289. James Figg (d. 1734), pugilist celebrated in Hogarth's prints and a humorous poem by John Byrom, established an amphitheatre or academy of arms, whose entertainments were so popular that doors were opened three hours before performances. (DNB.)

290. Cf. *Spectator* No. 258 (26 December 1711): "In short, Sir, I would have something *done* as well as *said* on the stage. . . . I would fain ask any of the present Mismanagers why should not Rope-dancers, Vaulters, Tumblers, Ladder-walkers, and Posture-makers appear again on our Stage?" ("Signor and Signora Violante, Turks, were rope-dancers whose performances were much in demand with the theatrical audiences of the day. Peg Woffington was a pupil of the Signora's" [E. L. S., p. 191].)

291. To be compared, for example, with the 1400 seating capacity of the Lincoln's Inn Fields theater (Avery, *The London Stage 1660–1800*, p. xxxiv).

292. Avery reports that *Mist's Weekly Journal* (for 14 January 1727) "stressed the rage for the 'irrational class' of entertainments (operas, rope-dancing, Italian farces, and pantomimes)" (ibid., pp. clxxv–xxvi).

293. The implied link between theater and government is reminiscent of Addison's admonition (*Spectator* No. 446 [1 August 1712]): "If the *English* Stage were under the same Regulations the *Athenian* was formerly, it would have the same Effect that had, in recommending the Religion, the Government and Publick Worship of its Country." Dennis had made a similar observation in *The Stage Defended* (*Works*, II, 319). In fact the period was full of arguments for the public regulation of the stage (ibid., I, 510).

294. For centuries the seat of the chief law court of England (scene of the trials of More, Guy Fawkes, Charles I), Westminister Hall was part of Westminster Palace, where Parliament met until in 1834 fire destroyed the building except for the Hall and Chapel.

295. By the early eighteenth century, Somerset House had become a residence for the poorer nobility, "and after this its garden became a spot of popular resort. James Stuart, the Old Pretender, was supposed to have been secreted there in 1725, though the suspicion was probably mere legend. An expense for many years before its demolition in 1775, probably the point of Pope's proposal is directed at its uselessness and the impracticality of keeping it in repair" [E. L. S., p. 192].

296. "Would it be foolish to imagine that the reference to the convenience of the proposed theater to the Thames waterside, so that 'Eminent Personages from Courts beyond the Seas' could come up the Thames to see the Italian singers and French comedians [the "Eunucks" and Harlequins], might possibly suggest the still general fear of a Jacobite naval-military coup? The Old Pretender was then living in Rome. Cf. Arbuthnot's 'The Devil to Pay at St. James's' (*Misc. Works*, I, 213): '. . . it would be a great Security to the Protestant Interest to have a Clause added to some Act of Parliament, obliging all foreign Singers, Dancers, and Tumblers, to objure the Devil, the Pope, and the Pretender, before they appear in Publick.' " [E. L. S., p. 192.)

297. Two somewhat later references suggest that his description could well fit Dennis, who, in *Harlequin-Horace*, is apostrophized as "eldest of the scribbling

Throng" (London, 1731, p. 49) while in "Essays, Letters, and Occasional Pieces Relating to the Late War of the Dunces" (in *A Collection of Pieces in Verse and Prose, Which have been publish'd on Occasion of the Dunciad* [London, 1732], he is referred to as "the worthy President of our Society [of Dunces]," and hailed as prime candidate for the Laureate (pp. 29–30).

298. In the "Epistle Dedicatory" to his *Stage Defended* (1726), Dennis had proposed that the Government set up a board of judges to review plays and award prizes to the best comedy and tragedy submitted each year. (*Works,* II, 303.) See n. 257 for Blackmore's advice on theater censorship and censors.

299. As it was, there were claques and party factions that disrupted performances and greatly influenced the success or failure of productions (Avery, *The London Stage 1660–1800,* pp. clix, clxiii).

300. See n. 149.

301. With Jeremy Collier's attack on the stage calling attention to the "immorality" of theaters, the profession of acting did not rank high socially or legally, actors in court often being treated no better than vagabonds or vagrants. (Avery, *The London Stage 1660–1800,* pp. cxxi, cxxin.)

302. Whitehall, the palace of the sovereigns of England since Henry VIII, had burned in 1698 (it was never rebuilt though Pope in *Windsor Forest* [l. 380] heralds the projected restoration), and St. James became the official London royal residence.

303. Cf. Hogarth's "The Distressed Poet."

304. Theater finances were already complicated by the system of benefit performances (in fact, from a third to a half of the performances from March through June were usually set aside for actors and other employees [Avery, *The London Stage 1660–1800,* p. xcvi]). From the record of receipts at Lincoln's Inn Fields between 1726 and 1728, we learn that on the night of 24 October 1728, for example, £76 10s was collected, with orders valued at an additional £9 17s (ibid., p. lix).

305. Since Pope uses "magazine" (storehouse for explosives) in a figurative sense in the *Iliad,* in Jove's "cloudy magazine of storms" (XII, 332), he may really be punning here with "Thunder and Lightning" referring to "cloth, app. of glaring colors, worn in 18c" (OED).

306. The old function of the Privy Council as a sovereign's chief consultative body became superseded as the advisors to the crown tended more and more to belong to one party and the Council became, as it is today, a body used merely to ratify decisions already taken.

307. The early editions had concluded with "Vale & Fruere ["Farewell and flourish"]. / *MAR. SCRIB."*—Martinus's customary valediction.

AN
ESSAY
Of the Learned
MARTINUS SCRIBLERUS,
Concerning the ORIGINE of
SCIENCES.

Written to the most Learned Dr.——
F.R.S. *from the* Deserts *of* NUBIA.

INTRODUCTION

Although not one of the better known Scriblerian pieces, *An Essay of the Learned Martinus Scriblerus, Concerning the Origine of Sciences* provides an entertaining example of the satire by the Club on abuses of learning. Presented as a discourse by their pedant-hero, directed to "the most Learned Dr. ——F.R.S." (Dr. John Woodward, prime target of several Scriblerian attacks), the *Essay,* as Pope explained to Spence, "was to ridicule such as build general assertions upon two or three loose quotations from the ancients."[1] With this satiric perspective and with the engaging argument "that all learning was derived from the monkeys in Ethiopia,"[2] the little treatise has good fun with both the theory and its contemporary implications.

Listed first in the catalogue (to be found at the end of the 1742 printing of the *Memoirs*) of "Pieces *of* Scriblerus (*written in his Youth) already published*," *The Origine of Sciences* was indeed probably an early effort, although it was not published until 1732, in the Pope-Swift *Miscellanies.* Spence records uncertainly that Pope attributed the piece to himself and Arbuthnot ("I think he added"[3]) and/or "Parnell?";[4] Pope is more explicit in the preface to his 1741 *Works . . . in Prose,* where he reprinted the *Essay* along with the first publication of the *Memoirs* and other Scriblerian papers, asserting, ". . . all the *Tracts* in the same name, were written by our Author and Dr. *Arbuthnot,* except the *Essay on the Origine of Sciences,* in which Dr. *Parnelle* had some hand. . . ."[5] Certainly Arbuthnot's involvement would be expected, since the essay burlesques the kind of scientific moonshine for which he had already challenged Dr. Woodward, who was the very model of the virtuoso described by the Scriblerians in their characterization of Martinus: "a man of capacity enough that had dipped in every art and science, but injudiciously in each."[6]

John Woodward, professor of Physick at Gresham College, member of the Royal Society, fellow of the College of Physicians, scientist, antiquarian, collector . . . , was unquestionably a man of many parts, a volatile mixture of strengths and weaknesses, talents and liabilities, insights and blind spots. As his most recent historian concludes, "Our hero was not a great man but he was a man of near-greatness, a flawed genius who left his mark upon his own time and indeed for a long time afterward, but who slipped (like his shield [satirized in the *Memoirs*]) gradually and finally into oblivion."[7] Irascible and eccentric, he tangled with most of the leading scientists of his day—Newton, Dr. Hans Sloane, Dr. Richard Mead—and inevitably attracted the notice of Arbuthnot, his colleague in the Royal Society, and hence of the other Scriblerians, who saw in him all that they found wrong in the new science, all that was actually hindering, they believed, achievement in learning.

And what a delicious butt they had in Dr. Woodward. If his interests and enthusiasms were boundless, equally expansive (and unbridled) were his theories and conclusions, which all too often in their absurdity discredited his valid observations and experimentation. By the turn of the century he had gained fame and notoriety with *An Essay Toward a Natural History of the Earth,* offering a new theory of the Deluge,[8] over which he and Dr. Arbuthnot first crossed swords. As a physician he studied the nature and function of the bile, concluding that vomits were the sovereign remedy for all diseases, a notion which not surprisingly was seized upon in the *Memoirs.* More central to that work, though (and featured in its second chapter), was the topical controversy over Dr. Woodward's shield, a small embossed iron shield, for which extravagant claims were made by its proud owner and his supporters. In the same capacity, as collector and antiquarian, Woodward was satirized as Dr. Fossile in *Three Hours After Marriage.*

In *The Origine of Sciences* it is less Dr. Woodward's subject matter than, as Pope suggests, his methodology which is being burlesqued, although the germ of the essay might well have come from a discourse on the learning of the Egyptians which Woodward prepared, one can assume, in the nineties, although it was not published until almost fifty years after his death, in 1777. Written to attack the growing belief toward the end of the seventeenth century in the primacy of Egyptian culture[9] and to rebut arguments (in 1685, 1699) by Dr. John Spencer, master of Corpus Christi College, Cambridge, that the Hebrews had derived much of their religion from the Nile, the treatise gets underway with the loftily casual remark that its author looked forward to the time when he would have the leisure to "set forth the first appearances of science in the world, and trace her through all ages and climates."[10] This does seem an irresistible hint for the *Origine*; and since at the time Dr. Arbuthnot was publishing *An Examination of Dr. Woodward's Account of the Deluge* (1697), it appears possible that the doctor, alert to Woodwardian activity, got wind of the manuscript or heard rumors of the projected *magnum opus.*

Seventeen years later, in 1714, about the time the *Memoirs* were being planned and the *Origine* drafted, Woodward was again attracting a good deal of attention. In addition to a new version of his theory of the Flood and the publication of a dissertation by Henry Dodwell on his shield, he had come forth in 1713 with an account of some Roman remains uncovered in London. The latter seems particularly pertinent here in its techniques of argument. Woodward describes with great precision, for example, a portion of the city wall which had been exposed, but when he starts conjecturing from his evidence, we begin to see the source of some of the *Origine*'s splendidly bald assertions. From the ruin of a wall, Dr. Woodward is willing to infer the failure of a civilization:

> And yet so vast a Bulk and Strength had not been able to secure it from being beat down in former Ages, and near levell'd with the Ground. This rightly reflected upon, will alone be sufficient to give us an Idea of the Difference betwixt those Times, and ours: betwixt that State of Things, and the present.

Or, again, after considering the Druids, he concludes:

> This is the main of what Antiquity hath transmitted down to us of the Theology and Philosophy of the Druids: and, by this, 'twill not be hard to frame a Judgment of their Science, as to the *Stars,* the *World, Nature,* and *the Power of the Gods*; of which we have not the Particulars.[11]

These mental operations compare favorably with Martinus's "reflections" on the pygmies:

> I cannot but persuade my self, from those Accounts in Homer, Aristotle and others, of their history, wars, and revolutions, and from the very Air in which those authors speak of them as of things known, that they were then a part of the study of the Learned. And tho' all we directly hear is of their Military atchievements, in the brave defence of their country from the annual invasions of a powerful enemy, yet I cannot doubt but that they excell'd as much in the arts of peaceful government, tho' there remains no traces of their civil institutions.

Delightful in the same off-handed manner are Scriblerus's explanations of the fabulous rapes of mythology, which he attributes to satyrs:

> I am sensible it may be objected, that they [the victims] are said to have been compress'd in the shape of different animals; but to this we answer, that women under such apprehensions hardly know what shape they have to deal with.

In such vein, the *Origine*—whether unencumbered by supportive evidence (as in the history of spread of hair over the bodies of the "Sylvans") or airily documented by classical references or contemporary citations (to works like Tyson's *Orang-Outang . . . or, the Anatomy of a Pygmie,* which reflects the current interest in the monkey kind exploited by the essay)[12]—

draws to a characteristic Woodwardian close: "This account, which is entirely my own, I am proud to imagine has traced knowledge from a fountain correspondent to several opinions of the Ancients, tho' hitherto undiscover'd both by them and the more ingenious moderns." It is in the rollicking finale—"And now what shall I say to mankind in the thought of this great discovery?"—that the modern reader, no doubt like his Augustan counterpart, finds the chief wit of the Essay, as the author exhorts the world to recapture the noble inheritance which he has just evolved from the pygmies and satyrs of classical lore, through the simian Aesop and Socrates, down to our own "elder brothers by a day in the creation"—monkeys, apes, and baboons. "Might not the talents of each kind of these be adapted to the improvement of the several sciences? The man-tegers to instruct heroes, states-men, and scholars? baboons to teach ceremony and address to Courtiers? monkeys, the art of pleasing in conversation, and agreeable affectations, to ladies and their lovers? apes of less learning, to form comedians and dancing masters: and marmosets, court pages and young English travellers." —and all of it enhanced by the implication that England, however, is too obsessed with politics to be interested in a revival of learning, even of this kind, whereas France is capable of no other.

Notes

1. *Anecdotes,* I, 57.
2. Ibid.
3. Ibid.
4. Ibid., I, 58.
5. *The Works of Mr. Alexander Pope, in Prose. Vol. II.* (London, 1741), p. vi.
6. *Anecdotes,* I, 56.
7. Joseph M. Levine, *Dr. Woodward's Shield* (Berkeley and Los Angeles: University of California Press, 1977), pp. 3–4.
8. Geology and paleontology were developing interests of the late seventeenth century. In 1681 Thomas Burnet had stirred considerable controversy with his *Sacred Theory of the Earth,* a theologically oriented account of the primeval earth transformed by the Flood. He ignored the contemporary speculation about fossils and earth strata which was the basis of Woodward's 1695 *Essay,* which argued, in opposition, a great dissolution and resettling of matter after the "universal deluge." Woodward's thesis left many unanswered questions and it was these that Arbuthnot raised as he challenged the philosophical method of the *Essay.*
9. See annotation 3 to the text.

10. *Of the Wisdom of the Antient Egyptians, &c.* (London, 1777), p. 7.

11. *An Account of some Roman Urns . . . with Brief Reflections upon the Antient and Present State of London* (London, 1713), pp. 11, 19.

12. In the *Memoirs* too there are references to mantegars and fabulous apes.

NOTE ON PUBLICATION AND TEXT

The sporadic activity of a group working—sometimes cooperatively, sometimes independently—over a span of almost three decades makes the dating and assigning of authorship for the Scriblerian pieces very difficult—as difficult as sorting out the bibliographic muddle of the various editions of the *Miscellanies* in which many of these works appeared. But internal and external evidence suggests that *The Origine of Sciences* was essentially composed, by Pope, Dr. Arbuthnot, and Parnell, in 1714, the year of the Club's formal existence.[1]

The *Origine* was not published, however, until 1732, when Pope included it in the fourth volume ("The Third Volume"—so called because the actual third had been published as "The Last") of the *Miscellanies*, where it was reprinted, in his lifetime, in the subsequent octavo (?), duodecimo, and small octavo editions: an unlocated second octavo edition in 1732 (possibly a ghost),[2] 1732–33 duodecimos, a 1736 duodecimo, and a 1742 small octavo. The history of the duodecimos is complicated by the publishers' confusion over the "Last" volume and the "Third," those volumes being originally mistitled and the error later corrected either with the insertion of a new title page or a reprinting.[3] When the piece appeared in the small octavo *Miscellanies* of 1742, brought out to match Pope's other works in that format, it was moved, in a general reshuffling of contents, to the Second Volume.

In 1741 the essay had been included in Vol. II of Pope's *Works . . . in Prose,* where it accompanied the *Memoirs* and other Scriblerian tracts. Surprisingly enough it was not reprinted in the 1751 *Works,* Warburton, who reproduced all the other Scriblerian items from 1741, having substituted *Stradling versus Stiles.*

For the 1741 *Works* Pope made some textual revisions, adding a few more when he reordered the *Miscellanies* in 1742 (writing to Bathurst, "I wish you would resolve upon printing in the manner I mentioned your Miscellanies, for I am now perfectly at leisure, which I shall not be a month longer. I am sure it will turn out much to their advantage; and, as for mine, I have no terms to make with you, but only to serve you in the little improvements that I shall make").[4] The present text, then, follows this last edition, though maintaining the 1741 text's more consistent practice of reducing the extensive capitalization and italics of the earlier editions.[5] Substantive variants are recorded in the textual notes. (And the original footnotes are now identified by letters of the alphabet rather than by the asterisks and other symbols used then.)

Key to the Critical Apparatus

1732 = *Miscellanies in Prose and Verse,* "Third" Vol., octavo, Griffith 276; Teerink/Scouten 25 (4a).

[1733 (dated 1732) = 1733a (with correct title page): *Miscellanies,* "Third" Vol., duodecimo, Teerink/Scouten 27 (4b)].

1733a = *Miscellanies,* [mistitled] "Last" Vol., duodecimo, Teerink/Scouten 27 (4a).

1733b = *Miscellanies,* "Third" Vol., duodecimo, Teerink/Scouten 27 (4c).

1736 = *Miscellanies,* "Third" Vol., duodecimo, Griffith 438; Teerink/Scouten 29 (4b).

1741 = *Works . . . in Prose,* Vol. II, folio, Griffith 529; l. p. folio, Griffith 530; and quarto, Griffith 531.

1742 = *Miscellanies* (in Four Volumes), Second Vol., sm. octavo, Griffith 562.

Notes

1. See Introduction, p. 279, and Kerby-Miller, *Memoirs,* p. 41.

2. Cited by Griffith (278) as listed in the Hoe Catalogue; Teerink/Scouten does not mention it.

3. For the history of this see Teerink/Scouten, pp. 11–21.

4. *Correspondence,* IV, 353.

5. As with the *Peri Bathous,* this is consistent with David Foxon's observations on Pope's revisions, argued in his unpublished Lyell lectures (see n. 6, pp. xiv–xv).

AN
ESSAY
Of the Learned
MARTINUS SCRIBLERUS,
Concerning the ORIGINE of
SCIENCES.

Written to the most Learned Dr.—— F.R.S.[1]
from the Deserts *of* NUBIA.[2]

A mong all the enquiries which have been pursu'd by the curious and inquisitive, there is none more worthy the search of a learned head, than the Source from whence we derive those Arts and Sciences which raise us so far above the vulgar, the Countries in which they rose, and the channels by which they have been

A,B convey'd.[3] As those who first brought them amongst us attain'd them by travelling into the remotest parts of the earth, I may boast of some advantages by the same means; since I write this from the Deserts of Æthiopia, from those plains of sand which have buried the pride of invading armies, with my foot perhaps at this instant ten fathom over the grave of Cambyses;[4] a solitude to which neither Pythagoras nor Appollonius ever penetrated.[5]

C   It is universally agreed, that Arts and sciences were deriv'd to us from the Ægyptians and Indians; but from whom they first receiv'd

D them, is yet a secret. The highest period of time to which the learned

E attempt to trace them, is the beginning of the Assyrian Monarchy, when their inventors were worship'd as Gods.[6] It is therefore necessary to go backward into times even more remote, and to gain some knowledge of their history, from whatever dark and broken hints may any way be found in ancient authors concerning them.

    Nor Troy nor Thebes were the first of Empires; we have mention, tho' not histories, of an earlier warlike people call'd the Pygmaeans.[7]

F I cannot but persuade my self, from those Accounts in [a]Homer,[8]

[a] Il. 3. Hom.

A   Aristotle[9] and others, of their history, wars, and revolutions, and
from the very Air in which those authors speak of them as of things
known, that they were then a part of the study of the Learned. And
tho' all we directly hear is of their Military atchievements, in the
brave defence of their country from the annual invasions of a powerful
enemy, yet I cannot doubt but that they excell'd as much in the arts
of peaceful government, tho' there remain no traces of their civil
institutions. Empires as great have been swallow'd up in the wreck
B   of Time, and such sudden periods have been put to them as occasion
a total ignorance of their story. And if I should conjecture that the
like happen'd to this nation, from a general extirpation of the people
by those flocks of monstrous birds, wherewith Antiquity agrees they
were continually infested; it ought not to seem more incredible,
than that one of the Baleares was wasted by rabbits,[10] [b]Smynthe by
mice,[11] and of late [c]Bermudas almost depopulated by rats.[12] Nothing
is more natural to imagine, than that the few survivers of that
empire retired into the depths of their Deserts, where they liv'd
undisturb'd, till they were found out by Osyris in his travels to
instruct mankind.

He met, says [d]Diodorus, in Æthiopia, a sort of "little Satyrs,
who were hairy one half of their body, and whose leader Pan accompanied him in his expedition for the civilizing of mankind."[13] Now
of this great personage Pan, we have a very particular description
in the ancient writers;[14] who unanimously agree to represent him
shaggy-bearded, hairy all over, half a man and half a beast, and
C   walking erect with a staff, (the posture in which his race do to this
day appear among us). And since the chief thing to which he apply'd
himself was the civilizing of mankind, it should seem that the first
D,E   principles of science must be receiv'd from that nation, to which
the Gods were by [e]Homer said to resort twelve days every year, for
the conversation of its wise and just inhabitants.[15]

If from Ægypt we proceed to take a view of India, we shall find
that their knowledge also deriv'd itself from the same source. To

[b] Eustathius in Hom. Il. 1.

[c] Speede, in Bermudas.

[d] L. 1. ch. 18. Diod.

[e] Il. 1st.

that country did these noble creatures accompany Bacchus in his expedition, under the conduct of Silenus, who is also describ'd to us with the very same marks and qualifications. "Mankind is ignorant, saith 'Diodorus, whence Silenus deriv'd his birth, through his great antiquity; but he had a tail on his loins, as likewise had all his Progeny, in sign of their descent."[16] Here then they settled a colony, which to this day subsists with the same tails. From this time they seem to have communicated themselves only to those men, who retir'd from the converse of their own species to a more uninterrupted life of contemplation. I am much inclin'd to believe, that in the midst of those solitudes they instituted the so much celebrated order of Gymnosophists.[17] For whoever observes the scene and manner of their life, will easily find them to have imitated with all exactness imaginable, the manners and customs of their masters and instructors. They are said to dwell in the thickest woods, to go naked, to suffer their bodies to be over-run with hair, and their nails to grow to a prodigious length.[18] gPlutarch says, "they eat what they could get in the fields, their drink was water, and their bed made of leaves or moss."[19] And hHerodotus tells us, that they esteem'd it a great exploit to kill very many Ants or creeping things.[20]

Hence we see that the two nations which contend for the origine of learning, are the same that have ever most abounded with this ingenious race. Tho' they have contested which was first blest with the rise of science, yet have they conspir'd in being grateful to their common masters. Ægypt is well known to have worshipp'd them of old in their own images; and India may be credibly suppos'd to have done the same, from that adoration which they paid in latter
A times to the Tooth of one of these hairy Philosophers; in just gratitude as it should seem, to the Mouth from which they receiv'd their knowledge.[21]

Pass we now over into Greece, where we find Orpheus returning out of Ægypt, with the same intent as Osyris and Bacchus made their expeditions.[22] From this period it was, that Greece first heard

---

f L. 3. ch. 69. Diod.
B g Plutarch in his Orat. on Alexander's Fortune.
   h Herod. L. 1.

the name of Satyrs, or own'd them for *Semi-dei*. And hence it is
surely reasonable to conclude, that he brought some of this wonderful
species along with him, who also had a leader of the line of Pan, of
the same name, and expressly call'd King by 'Theocritus.[23] If thus
much be allow'd, we easily account for two of the strangest reports
A   in all antiquity. One is that of the beasts following the musick of
Orpheus, which has been interpreted of his taming savage tempers,
B   but will thus have a literal application: The other, which we most
C,D insist upon, is the fabulous story of the Gods compressing women
in woods under bestial appearances, which will be solved by the
love these sages are known to bear to the females of our kind. I am
sensible it may be objected, that they are said to have been com-
press'd in the shape of different animals; but to this we answer, that
women under such apprehensions hardly know what shape they have
to deal with.

From what has been last said, 'tis highly credible that to this
ancient and generous race the world is indebted, if not for the Heroes, at least for the acutest Wits of antiquity. One of the most
remarkable instances, is that great mimick genius ʲÆsop, for whose
extraction from these *Sylvestres Homines* we may gather an argument
from Planudes, who says, that Æsop signifies the same thing as
Æthiop, the original nation of our people. For a second argument
we may offer the description of his person, which was short, deform'd, and almost savage; insomuch that he might have liv'd in
the woods, had not the benevolence of his temper made him rather
adapt himself to our manners, and come to court in wearing apparel.[24] The third proof is his acute and satyrical wit; and lastly, his
great knowledge in the nature of beasts, together with the natural
pleasure he took to speak of them upon all occasions.

The next instance I shall produce is ᵏSocrates. First, it was a
tradition that he was of an uncommon birth from the rest of men;
secondly, he had a countenance confessing the line he sprung from,
being bald, flat-nos'd, with prominent eyes, and a downward look:[25]
thirdly he turn'd certain fables of Æsop into verse,[26] probably out

ⁱ Παν Ἄναξ, Theo. Id. 1st.
ʲ Vit. Æsop. initio.
ᵏ Vid. Plato and Xenophon.

of his respect to beasts in general, and love to his family in particular.

In process of time, the women, with whom these Sylvans would
have lovingly cohabited, were either taught by mankind, or induc'd
by an abhorrence of their shapes, to shun their embraces; so that
our sages were necessitated to mix with beasts. This by degrees
occasion'd the hair of their posterity to grow higher than their
middles, it arose in one generation to their arms, in the second it
invaded their necks, in the third it gain'd the ascendant of their
heads, till the degenerate appearance in which the species is now
immers'd became compleated. Tho' we must here observe, that there
were a few who fell not under the common calamity; there being
some unprejudic'd women in every age, by virtue of whom a total
A   extinction of the original race was prevented. It is remarkable also,
that even where they were mix'd, the defection from their nature
B   was not so intire, but there still appear'd marvellous qualities among
them, as was manifest in those who follow'd Alexander in India.[27]
How did they attend his army and survey his order! How did they
cast themselves into the same forms for march or for combat! What
an imitation was there of all his discipline! the ancient true remains
of a warlike disposition, and of that constitution which they enjoy'd
C   while they were yet a monarchy.

To proceed to Italy: At the first appearance of these wild philosophers, there were some of the least mix'd who vouchsafed to converse with mankind; which is evident from the name of [1]Fauns, a
fando, or speaking.[28] Such was he who coming out of the woods in
hatred to tyranny, encourag'd the Roman army to proceed against
the Hetruscans who would have restor'd Tarquin.[29] But here, as in
all the western parts of the world, there was a great and memorable
Æra in which they began to be silent. This we may place something
near the time of Aristotle, when the number, vanity, and folly of
human philosophers encreas'd, by which men's heads became too
D   much puzzled to receive the simpler wisdom of these ancient Sylvans;
the questions of that academy[30] were too numerous to be consistent
with their ease to answer; and too intricate, extravagant, idle, or
pernicious, to be any other than a derision and scorn unto them.

[1] Livy.

From this period, if ever we hear of their giving answers, it is only when caught, bound, and constrain'd, in like manner as was that ancient Grecian prophet, Proteus.[31]

Accordingly we read in [m]Sylla's time, of such a philosopher taken near Dyrrachium, who wou'd not be persuaded to give them a lecture by all they cou'd say to him, and only shew'd his power in sounds, by neighing like a horse.[32]

But a more successful attempt was made in Augustus's reign by the inquisitive genius of the great Virgil; whom, together with Varus,[33] the commentators suppose to have been the true persons who are related in the 6th Bucolick to have caught a philosopher, and doubtless a genuine one, of the race of the old Silenus. To prevail upon him to be communicative (of the importance of which Virgil was well aware) they not only ty'd him fast, but allur'd him likewise
A by a courteous present of a comely maiden call'd Ægle, which made him sing both merrily and instructively. In this song we have their doctrine of the Creation, the same in all probability as was taught so many ages before in the great Pygmean empire,[34] and several hieroglyphical fables under which they couched or embellish'd their morals.[35] For which reason I look upon this Bucolick as an inestimable treasure of the most ancient science.

In the reign of Constantine, we hear of another, taken in a net, and brought to Alexandria, round whom the people flock'd to hear his wisdom; but as Ammianus Marcellinus reporteth, he proved a dumb philosopher, and only instructed by action.[36]

The last we shall speak of who seemeth to be of the true race, is said by St. Jerome to have met St. [n]Antony in a desert, who enquiring the way of him, he shewed his understanding, and courtesy by pointing, but wou'd not answer, for he was a dumb philosopher also.[37]

These are all the notices which I am at present able to gather, of
B the appearance of so great and learned a people on your side of the world. But if we return to their ancient native seats, Africa and India, we shall there find even in modern times, the traces of their original conduct and valour.

[m] Plutarch in Vit. Syllae.
[n] Vit. St. Ant.

In Africa (as we read among the indefatigable Mr. Purchas's collections) a body of them, whose leader was inflamed'd with love for a woman, by martial powers and stratagem won a fort from the Portuguese.[38]

But I must leave all others at present to celebrate the praise of two of their unparallell'd Monarchs in India. The one was Perimal the magnificent, a Prince most learned and communicative, to whom in Malabar their excess of zeal dedicated a temple,[39] rais'd on seven hundred pillars, not inferior in °Maffaeus's opinion to those of Agrippa in the Pantheon.[40] The other, Hanimant the marvellous, his relation and successor, whose knowledge was so great, as made his followers doubt if even that wise species cou'd arrive at such perfection; and therefore they rather imagin'd him and his race a sort of Gods form'd into apes.[41] His was the Tooth which the Portuguese took in Bisnagar 1559, for which the Indians offer'd, according to ᴾLinschotten, the immense sum of seven hundred thousand ducats.[42] Nor let me quit this head without mentioning with all due respect Oran Outang the great, the last of this line; whose unhappy chance it was to fall into the hands of Europeans. Oran Outang, whose value was not known to us, for he was a mute philosopher: Oran Outang, by whose dissection the learned Dr. Tyson has added a confirmation to this system, from the resemblance between the Homo Sylvestris and our humane body, in those organs by which the rational soul is exerted.[43]

We must now descend to consider this people as sunk into the *bruta Natura,* by their continual commerce with beasts. Yet even at this time, what experiments do they not afford us, of relieving some from the spleen, and others from imposthumes,[44] by occasioning laughter at proper seasons? With what readiness do they enter into the imitation of whatever is remarkable in humane life? and what surprizing relations have LeComte and others given, of their appetites, actions, conceptions, affections, varieties of imaginations, and abilities capable of pursuing them?[45] If under their present low circumstances of birth and breeding, and in so short a term of life as is now allotted them, they so far exceed all beasts, and equal many

° Maff. l. 1.
ᴾ Linschot. ch. 44.

men; what prodigies may we not conceive of those, who were *nati melioribus annis,* those primitive, Longaeval and Antideluvian man-

A tegers,[46] who first taught science to the world?

This account, which is entirely my own, I am proud to imagine has traced knowledge from a fountain correspondent to several opinions of the Ancients, tho' hitherto undiscover'd both by them and

B the more ingenious moderns. And now what shall I say to mankind in the thought of this great discovery? What, but that they should abate of their Pride, and consider that the authors of our knowledge are among beasts. That these, who were our elder brothers by a day

C in the creation, whose kingdom (like that in the scheme of Plato) was govern'd by philosophers, who flourish'd with learning in

D Æthiopia and India, are now undistinguish'd, and known only by the same appellation as the man-tyger, and the monkey!

As to speech, I make no question, that there are remains of the first and less corrupted race in their native deserts, who yet have the power of it. But the vulgar reason given by the Spaniards, "that they will not speak for fear of being set to work,"[47] is alone a sufficient one, considering how exceedingly all other learned persons affect their ease. A second is, that these observant creatures having been eye-witnesses of the cruelty with which that nation treated their brother Indians, find it necessary not to show themselves to be men, that they may be protected not only from work, but from cruelty also. Thirdly, they cou'd at best take no delight to converse with the Spaniards, whose grave and sullen temper is so averse to that natural and open chearfulness, which is generally observ'd to accompany all true knowledge.[48]

E But now were it possible that any way cou'd be found to draw forth their latent qualities, I cannot but think it would be highly serviceable to the learned world, both in respect of recovering past knowledge, and promoting the future. Might there not be found

F certain gentle and artful methods, whereby to endear us to them? Is there no Nation in the world, whose natural turn is adapted to engage their society, and win them by a sweet similitude of manners? Is there no nation, where the men might allure them by a distinguishing civility, and in a manner fascinate them by assimilated motions? no nation, where the women with easy freedoms, and the gentlest treatment, might oblige the loving creatures to sensible returns of humanity? The love I bear my native country prompts me to wish this nation might be Great Britain, but alas! in our present wretched, divided condition, how can we hope, that foreigners of so great prudence will freely declare their sentiments in the midst of violent parties,⁴⁹ and at so vast a distance from their friends, relations, and country? The affection I bear our neighbour-state, wou'd incline me to wish it were Holland⁵⁰—*Sed laevâ in parte mamillae Nil salit Arcadico.*⁵¹ 'Tis from France then we must expect this restoration of learning, whose late Monarch took the sciences under his protection, and rais'd them to so great a height.⁵² May we not hope their Emissaries will some time or other have instructions, not only to invite learned men into their country. but learned beasts, the true ancient man-tegers (I mean) of Æthiopia and India? Might not the talents of each kind of these be adapted to the improvement of the several sciences? The man-tegers to instruct heroes,

A states-men and scholars? baboons to teach ceremony and address to Courtiers? monkeys, the art of pleasing in conversation, and agree-

B,C able affectations to ladies and their lovers? apes of less learning, to

D form comedians and dancing masters: and marmosets, court pages and young English travellers. But the distinguishing each kind, and

E allotting the proper business to each, I leave to the inquisitive and penetrating Genius of the Jesuits in their respective Missions.⁵³

F   *Vale & Fruere.*

Textual Variants

Page 286: A. those] they *1732–36.*

Page 286: B. attain'd . . . earth,] travell'd into the remotest Parts of the Earth to attain them, *1732–36.*

Page 286: C. were deriv'd to us from] took their Rise among *1732–36.*

Page 286: D. to] from *1741.*

Page 286: E. is] is from *1732–36.*

Page 286: F. in] of *1732–36.*

Page 287: A. of . . . Learned.] that their History Wars and Revolutions were then a part of the Study of the Learned, from the very Air in which those Authors speak of them, as of things universally known. *1732–36.*

Page 287: B. sudden] certain *1736.*

Page 287: C. do . . . appear] are . . . shown *1732–36.*

Page 287: D. that nation] this People *1732–36*; this nation *1741*.

Page 287: E. which] whom *1732–36*.

Page 288: A. in . . . seem,] as it should seem, in just Gratitude *1732–41*.

Page 288: B. his] *his first 1732–36*.

Page 289: A. One . . . beasts] One, that the Tradition of *Beasts 1732–36*.

Page 289: B. but *Add. 1741–42*.

Page 289: C. is . . . kind.] is, that the Love which these Sages bear to the Females of our Kind affords a Solution of all those Fables of the *Gods compressing Women* in Woods under *bestial appearances*. *1732–36*.

Page 289: D. story] one *1741*.

Page 290: A. It] And it *1732–41*.

Page 290: B. so intire, but] intire; *1732–41*.

Page 290: C. yet *Add. 1741–42*.

Page 290: D. simpler *Add. 1742*.

Page 291: A. a courteous] making him a *1732–41*.

Page 291: B. on] in *1732–41*.

Page 293: A. science] Sciences *1732–41*.

Page 293: B. more ingenious *Add. 1742*.

Page 293: C. (like . . .) was] was like the scheme of *Plato 1732–36*.

Page 293: D. undistinguish'd] undistinguish'd from *1732–41*.

Page 293: E. found] found out *1732–41*.

Page 293: F. and *Add. 1741–42*.

Page 294: A. ceremony . . . Courtiers?] the Courtiers, Ceremony and Address? *1732–36*.

Page 294: B. apes] The apes *1732–36*.

Page 294: C. to form *Add. 1742*.

Page 294: D. :and] :the *1732–36*.

Page 294: E. the . . . each,] them to their proper Business, *1732–41*.

Page 294: F. *Following this was the signature "M.S." in 1732–36*.

Annotations

1. Dr. John Woodward (see "Introduction," pp. 279–80).

2. A place of satiric and exotic interest for Scriblerus, who announced (in an advertisement appearing with the *Memoirs* in *The Works of Alexander Pope*, Vol. III. Part II [London, 1742]), among some projected additional volumes of *Memoirs*, ". . . .the THIRD BOOK never before publish'd, Containing his Journey thro' the Desarts of *Nubia* to the Court of *Ætheopia*. . . ."

3. The Battle of the Ancients and Moderns had focused attention on such

investigations and investigators. Cf. Sir William Temple, "On Ancient and Modern Learning" (1690):

> There is nothing more agreed than, That all the Learning of the *Greeks* was deduced Originally from *Egypt* or *Pheonicia*; but, Whether theirs might not have flourished to that Degree it did by the Commerce of the *Ethiopians, Chaldaeans, Arabians*, and *Indians* is not so evident, though I am very apt to believe it; and to most of these Regions some of the *Grecians* travelled in Search of those Golden Mines of Learning and Knowledge. Not to mention the Voyages of *Orpheus, Musaeus, Lycurgus, Thales, Solon, Democritus, Herodotus, Plato*, and that vain Sophist, *Apollonius*, who was but an Ape to the Ancient Philosophers, I shall only trace those of *Pythagoras*, who seems of all others to have gone the farthest upon this Design, and to have brought home the greatest Treasures. (Spingarn, III, 38.)

4. The major achievement of the Persian king Cambyses II was his conquest of Egypt in 525 B.C.; while he planned an expedition against Ethiopia too, he managed only the annexation of the northern part. According to Herodotus, he actually died in Syria, returning from Egypt to put down an uprising in Persia.

5. See n. 3.

6. See n. 3. Temple emphasizes the Indian influence too (with a discourse on the Indian "Brachmans"). He concludes in summary, "They [Science and Arts] are generally agreed to have held their course from *East* to *West*, to have begun in *Chaldaea* and *Ægypt*. . . ." (Spingarn, III, 50.) A treatise by Woodward (see "Introduction"), *Dr. Woodward's Discourse on the Wisdom of the Egyptians*, challenged this generally held view of Egyptian learning, arguing the primacy of the Mosaic tradition: ". . . the arts and learning of Judaea were, in truth, very considerable a long time before ever Thales, Pythagoras, or any of the most early of the Greek sages had ever visited Egypt." (P. 100.)

7. The fable of pygmies and their wars with cranes is to be found in numerous classical writers (besides Homer and Aristotle, among others Ovid [*Fast.* 6. 176; *Met.* 6. 90] and Juvenal [13. 167], and illustrated in classical art. In "A Philological Essay concerning the Pygmies of the Ancients" (*Orang-Outang, sive Homo Sylvestris* . . . [London, 1699]), Dr. Edward Tyson had reviewed the "scientific" references to them in antiquity (in Aristotle, Pliny, Strabo, Ctesias . . .) in his attempt to prove that the pygmies and satyrs of classical lore were actually apes and monkeys; his work was an important source for the Scriblerians.

8.   To Warmer Seas the Cranes embody'd fly,
       With Noise, and Order, thro' the mid-way Sky;
       To Pygmy-Nations Wounds and Death they bring,
       And all the War descends upon the Wing.
                                        (TE VII, 188 [ll. 7–10].)

9. ". . . these birds [cranes] migrate from the steppes of Scythia to the marshlands south of Egypt where the Nile has its source. And it is here . . . that they are said to fight with the pygmies; and the story is not fabulous, but there is in reality a race of dwarfish men. . . ." (*Historia Animalium* [vol. IV of *The Works of Aristotle* (Oxford, Clarendon Press, 1910)], 8. 12. 597ᵃ.)

10. In the time of *Octavius Augustus,* the *Baleares* dispatched an Embassy to the Senate, begging Succours against the Rabbets, which having multiplied to an excessive Number, destroy'd the Corn, Plants and Trees, and would not suffer them to live in quiet in these Islands: Thus *Pliny* and *Strabo* adds, that they begged to have other Lands to Inhabit, because these Animals had driven them out of their Houses. ([Colin Campbell] *The Ancient and Modern History of the Balearick Islands* [London, 1716], p. 95.)

11. As in Mme Dacier's note (derived from the twelfth-century Greek scholar Eustathius), from Ozell's English translation of her *Iliad,* 1712 (Pope made extensive use of these notes [TE VII, xl]):

Smyntha was the Name of a Temple, which *Apollo* had at *Tenedos* and *Chrysa,* where a Statue of that God was ador'd, which had a Mouse at his Feet. The Reason whereof was this, according to *Callinous,* an ancient Elegiac Poet; a Colony from *Crete,* going to *Troas,* receiv'd an Oracle from *Apollo,* ordering them to settle in the Place, where the Children of the Earth shou'd attack them; and one Night an infinite Number of Rats and Mice gnaw'd to pieces all their Bucklers, and other Leathern Utensils; and this they took for an Accomplishment of the Oracle. (P. 7.)

12. In his time, the Lord sent upon the Countrey a very grievous scourge and punishment, threatning the utter ruine and desolation of it. . . . a wonderful annoyance by silly Rats: These Rats coming at the first out of a Ship, few in number, increased in the Space of two year, or lesse, so exceedingly, that they filled not only those places where they first landed: But swimming from place to place, spread themselves into all parts of the Countrey.

Speed continues with a lengthy account of this infestation. (John Speed, "The Description of the Sommer Islands," *A Prospect of the Most Famous Parts of the World* [London, 1662], p. 41.)

13. This is a composite of several passages from Diodorus: "Of Osiris they say that, being of a beneficent turn of mind, and eager for glory, he gathered together a great army, with the intention of visiting all the inhabited earth and teaching the race of men how to cultivate the vine and sow wheat and barley; for he supposed that if he made men give up their savagery and adopt a gentle manner of life he would receive immortal honours because of the magnitude of his bene-

factions." "He also took Pan along on his campaign, who is held in special honour by the Egyptians. . . ." "While he was in Ethiopia, their account continues, the Satyr people were brought to him, who, they say, have hair upon their loins." (Loeb [1960], I, 55, 57, 59 [bk. 1. 17, 18].)

14. For example, *Lucian* (*Dialogues of the Gods* 2[22]): ". . . you [Pan] with your horns and ugly snout and shaggy beard and a goat's cloven hooves and a tail over your behind." (Loeb [1961], VII, 245.)

15.   The Sire of Gods, and all th'Etherial Train
        On the warm Limits of the farthest Main,
        Now mix with Mortals, nor disdain to grace
        The Feasts of *Æthiopia*'s blameless Race:
        Twelve Days the Pow'rs indulge the Genial Rite,
        Returning with the twelfth revolving Light.
                      (TE VII, 114–15 [ll. 554–59].)

In his note on this passage from the *Iliad,* Pope refers to Diodorus's observation that the Ethiopians were the "Inventors of Pomps, Sacrifices, solemn Meetings and other Honours paid to the Gods." (TE VII, 114n.)

16. Again, this is a conflation of several passages from Diodorus: "Then he [Dionysus] made a campaign into India . . . (4.3)." "They also add that he was accompanied on his campaigns by a personal attendant and caretaker, Seilenus, who was his adviser and instructor in the most excellent pursuits and contributed greatly to the high achievements and fame of Dionysus (4. 4)." "And companions of his on the campaign [against Cronus], they say, were also the most nobly born of the Nysaeans, those, namely, who bear the name Seileni. For the first man of all, they say, to be king of Nysa was Seilenus, but his ancestry was unknown to all men because of its antiquity. This man had a tail at the lower part of his back and his descendants also regularly carried this distinguishing mark because of their participation in his nature (3. 72)." (Loeb [1961], II, 347, 351, 321–23.)

17. The name given by the Greeks to a sect of Indian ascetic philosophers, who went about naked.

18. In his *Geography,* Strabo reports: "Speaking of the philosophers, Megasthenes says that those who inhabit the mountains hymn the praises of Dionysus and point out as evidences [of his former presence there] the wild grape vine . . . ." "As for the Garmanes, he says that the most honourable of them are named Hylobii [Forest dwellers, sometimes called Gymno-sophists] and that they live in forests, subsisting on leaves and wild fruits, clothed with the bark of trees. . . ." (Loeb [1961], VII, 97, 103 [bk. 15. 1. 58, 60].)

19. Even there it is said that there are certain holy men, a law unto themselves, who follow a rigid gymnosophy and give all their time to God; they are more frugal than Diogenes since they have no need of a wallet. For they

do not store up food, since they have it ever fresh and green from the earth; the flowing rivers give them drink and they have fallen leaves and grassy earth to be upon. (Plutarch, "On the Fortune or the Virtue of Alexander," 1. 332 [Loeb *Moralia* (1962), IV, 413–15].)

20. Pope appears confused in his references here. Book 1 of Herodotus (140) does have an account of those who "kill all alike, ants and snakes, creeping and flying things, and take much pride therein," but these are the Magians, a Median tribe of magicians. In Book 3 (102) Herodotus writes of Indian ants, a strange breed indeed of sandy desert ants, "bigger than foxes," who mine gold as they burrow in the sand. (Loeb Herodotus (1921), I, 179–81; II, 129–31.)

21. Tyson (see n. 7), in another appendix to his *Orang-Outang*, "A Philological Essay concerning the Satyrs of the Ancients," had argued, "*Pan* was a Name of this sort of *Monkey* . . . 'tis certain that this *Animal* was worshipped in *India* as a *Deity*, as a Dog was by the *Ægyptians* . . ." (p. 54), citing also the passage in Diodorus (1. 18) about Pan's veneration by the Egyptians, referred to earlier (see n. 13). He then continues:

> The Superstition of worshipping this *Animal* obtained not only amongst the Ancients, but there are Instances likewise of a later date, and what *Johannes Linschoten* relates, is very remarkable. "How that in the year 1554, the *Portuguese* having taken the Island of *Ceylon*, they proposed to rob a Temple on the top of *Adam's Pike*; but they found nothing there, but a little Cabinet adorned with Gold and Jewels, in which was kept the *Tooth* of an *Ape*, which they took away, to the great grief of the Kings of that Place; who sent Ambassadors to the *Portuguese*, and offered them Seventy thousand Ducats for the *Tooth*; which the *Portuguese* were willing enough to take, but were disswaded from it by their Bishop *Gaspar*, who told them, that it was a Crime, thus to encourage the Idolatry of the *Indians*; whereupon he burnt the *Tooth*, and flung the Ashes into the River.

22. "And after he [Orpheus] had devoted his entire time to his education and had learned whatever the myths had to say about the gods, he journeyed to Egypt, where he further increased his knowledge. . . ." (Diodorus 4. 25 [Loeb (1961), II, 425].)

23. "Come, mighty King, come, *Pan*, and take my Pipe. . . ." ("Idyllium 1," *The Idylliums of Theocritus*, made English by Mr. Creech [London, 1713], p. 6.)

24. "Æsop (according to *Planudes, Camerarius* and Others) was by birth . . . of a mean Condition, and in his person deformed, to the highest degree: Flat-Nos'd, Hunch-Back'd, Blobber-Lipp'd; a Long Mishapen Head; his Body Crooked all over, Big-Belly'd, Baker-Legg'd, and his Complexion so swarthy, that he took

his very Name from't; for *Æsop* is the same with *Æthiop*." ("The Life of Æsop," *Fables* [London, 1694], p. 1.)

25. In Xenophon's *Symposium,* Socrates humorously defends his appearance (bulbous eyes, short, upturned nose, thick lips) on the grounds of beauty linked to utility, concluding, "And, lastly, I must excel you in *Beauty* for this Reason: the *Naiades,* notwithstanding they are Sea-Goddesses, are said to have brought forth the Sileni; And sure, I am much more like them, than you can pretend to be." (*The Banquet of Xenophon,* trans. James Welwood [London, 1710], p. 140.)

26. Plato, in the "Phaedo," has Socrates report his making metrical versions of Aesop's fables while in prison. (Loeb [1960], pp. 211–13.)

27. According to Arrian (*Anabasis Alexandri* [The Campaigns of Alexander], 5. 1–2.3 [Loeb (1958), II, 3–7]), the city of Nysa, supposed to have been founded by Dionysus and Seilenus (see n. 16), provided Alexander with three hundred cavalrymen and was reportedly the scene of Bacchanalian revels by the Macedonians. Although he does not identify these descendants of Seilenus as animal-like, the tradition of Bacchus and monkey warriors persists through to modern times, as in Bishop Heber's account (*Narrative of a Journey through the Upper Provinces of India* [London: John Murray, 1828]) of a festival in Allahabad with a figure of Hunimân, the famous monkey general, "as naked and almost as hairy as the animal whom he represented . . . with a long tail tied round his waist, a mask to represent the head of a baboon, and two great painted clubs in his hands. His army followed, a number of men with similar tails and masks. . . . I was never so forcibly struck with the identity of Rama and Bacchus. Here were before me Bacchus, his brother Amphelus, the Satyrs (smeared with wine lees) and the great Pan commanding them" (I, 337–38).

28. Pope's footnote must be misplaced, the Livy reference more logically going with the account which follows (see n. 29). *Fando* is the gerund of the defective verb *for,* meaning *to speak* or *to say,* in a poetical sense. Livy uses the form as a participial adjective in 10. 41. 3, but there it has more the sense of *right* or *proper* (that it may be spoken).

29. "To the story of this fight common report adds a prodigy: that in the silence of the following night a loud voice was heard coming out of the Arsian forest, which was believed to be the voice of Silvanus, and that this was what he said: 'The Tuscans have lost one more man in the battle-line; the Romans are conquerors in the war.' At all events the Romans left the field like victors, and the Etruscans like an army that has been defeated." (Loeb Livy [1961], I, 239, [2. 7. 2–4].)

30. The school founded by Plato (c. 385 B.C.).

31. See *Odyssey* 4. 521ff. (TE IX, 145ff.).

32. "Here, they say, a satyr was caught asleep, such an one as sculptors and painters represent, and brought to Sulla, where he was asked through many

interpreters who he was. And when at last he uttered nothing intelligible, but with difficulty emitted a hoarse cry that was something between the neighing of a horse and the bleating of a goat, Sulla was horrified, and ordered him out of his sight." (Loeb Plutarch: "Sulla" [27], *Lives,* IV, 409–11.)

33. The sixth eclogue, "The Song of Silenus," is dedicated to a Varus, whose identity is still conjectural.

34. Actually the Vergilian account is a summary of that given by Lucretius in *The Nature of Things.*

35. The fables Silenus touches upon include those of Prometheus, Hylas, Pasiphaë, Atalanta, Scylla, Philomela.

36. A search through Ammianus Marcellinus's history has not turned up this anecdote. But Tyson, remarking on St. Jerome (see n. 37) comments, "And tho St. *Jerome,* to confirm this Relation, adds, That in *Constantine*'s time one of these Monsters was seen alive at *Alexandria* in *Ægypt,* and after it's Death, it's Carcass was embalmed and sent to *Antioch* for the Emperor to see it. . . ." ([from Tyson, *Orang-Outang*] "A Philological Essay Concerning the Satyrs of the Ancients," p. 53.) He cites further Philostorgius's account of the story, in which the creature was sent to Constantius by the King of India.

37. In the history of St. Paul, sometimes attributed to Jerome but now to Palladius, St. Anthony is described as encountering in the desert a centaur ("And the creature returned him an answer in a barbarous language with words of impurity, and his mouth was full of fear; so the old man went on his journey seeking out the way"); he then meets another animal, who identifies himself as a "satyr." (*Stories of the Holy Fathers,* trans. Sir Ernest Budge [London: Oxford University Press, 1934], pp. 262–63.) In the "Life of St. Anthony" by St. Athanasius, the hermit encounters a demon "from its head to its side it was like a man, and its legs and feet were those of an ass," which at the mention of Christ flees and "bursts assunder." (Ibid., pp. 60–61.) Tyson in *Orang-Outang* also alludes to the story ("A Philological Essay Concerning the Satyrs of the Ancients," pp. 52–53), challenging this view of satyrs as demons.

38. A search through Purchas has not located this reference, though there is an account of "troopes" of baboons and monkeys in Africa: "The Baboones goe three or foure thousand in a Herd, marching in ranke, some of the greater being Leaders the smaller following . . ." ([London, 1625], II, 1575).

39. In Purchas's *Pilgrimes,* the letters of Nicolas Pimenta record: "There is a Temple of *Perimal,* in which is worshipped an ape called *Hanimant,* whom they report to haue beene a God, and for I know not what offence, with many other thousands of Gods (in like wise metamorphosed) to haue transformed into an Ape, and to haue ruled over all those Apes in that place." ([London, 1625], II, 1745.) Later in the account there is reference to the "Feast of Perimal's Marriage," with the notation "The *Feast of Kowes* was solemnized a month before, and all

wayes filled with them: for they hold *Perimal* to haue been the sonne of a Kow."
(Ibid., II, 1750.)

40. Ioannes Petrus Maffeius, *Historiarum Indicarum* (Florentiae, 1588), p. 25
(Bk. I, Chap. XXV in the 1655 French trans.).

41. This ape god (Hanniman, Hanuman, Hanumat, Harman, etc.), appearing
often in the accounts of European travelers (A. and J. Churchill, *Collection of
Voyages and Travels* [London, 1704], III, 838–39, 862–63), is also referred to in
the *Memoirs,* where, in the "Double Mistress" episode, Martin encounters in the
raree show a manteger, "true descendant of the celebrated Hanniman the Magnificent." (*Memoirs,* p. 144.)

42. See n. 21. (*The Voyage of John Huyghen van Linschoten,* Hakluyt Society
[London, 1855] I, 292–94.)

43. "From what is generally received, *viz.* That the *Brain* is reputed the more
immediate Seat of the *Soul* it self; one would be apt to think, that since there is
so great a disparity between the *Soul* of a *Man,* and a *Brute,* the *Organ* likewise
in which 'tis placed should be very different too. Yet by comparing the *Brain* of
our *Pygmie* with that of a *Man*; and, with the greatest exactness, observing each
Part in both; it was very surprising to me to find so great a resemblance of the
one to the other, that nothing could be more. (Tyson, *Orang-Outang,* p. 54.)
Tyson's conclusion is that while his "Pygmie" more resembled human beings than
apes and monkeys, yet it was no man but "a sort of *Animal* between both. . . ."
(P. 91.)

44. Or impostume(s): an abscess or (used physically or temperamentally) a
swelling.

45. "What is to be seen in the Isle of *Borneo,* is yet more remarkable, and
surpasseth all that ever the History of Animals hath hitherto related to be most
admirable . . . a sort of Beast, called the *Savageman*; whose Shape, Stature, Countenance, Arms, Legs, and other Members of the Body, are so like ours, that
excepting the Voice only, one should have much ado not to reckon them equally
Men with certain Barbarians in *Africa,* who do not much differ from Beasts." Le
Compte continues with a description of this "Savage Man," following it with
lengthy comment on a species of ape he himself had seen in the Straits of Molucca.
(Louis Le Compte, *Memoirs and Observations . . . made in a late Journey Through the
Empire of China* [London, 1697], pp. 510–12.)

46. Charles Kerby-Miller, in footnoting a reference to a mantegar in the *Memoirs* (Chap. XIV, p. 143; see n. 41), quotes a mid-eighteenth-century description
of such a "Man-Tiger" kept in the yard of the Tower of London: ". . . a curious
Animal, somewhat of the Baboon Kind, but of astonishing Strength, and very
mischievous if affronted." (P. 301.)

47. Again the Scriblerians have their Tyson close at hand, for he cites examples
of apes being put to work, with the observation, "A great many Instances of this

Nature might be given that are very surprising. And in another place [Acosta, quoted by Garcilosso de la Vega] tells us, That the Natives think that they can speak, but will not, for fear of being made to work" ([from Tyson, *Orang-Outang*] "A Philological Essay Concerning the Pygmies of the Ancients," p. 37.)

48. The *Memoirs* open: "In the Reign of Queen Anne . . . thou may'st possibly, gentle Reader, have seen a certain Venerable Person, who frequented the Out-side of the Palace of St. James's; and who, by the Gravity of his Deportment and Habit, was generally taken for a decay'd Gentleman of Spain." (*Memoirs*, p. 91.) As Kerby-Miller notes, this was a common characterization of Spaniards. In Chapter IV of the *Memoirs*, Cornelius holds a long disquisition on national temperament and diet.

49. At the time the *Essay* was being composed, England was going through the political turmoil of the last days of Queen Anne, with the Tory ministry divided and the Whigs belligerently in the wings.

50. Though England and Holland had been allies in the recently terminated War of the Spanish Succession, the relationship had never been easy, and Arbuthnot, in his John Bull pamphlets, had satirized the Dutch in Nicholas Frog—and the French in Lewis Baboon!

51. This is part of a passage from Juvenal's satire, "Learning and Letters Unprofitable":

> culpa docentes
> scilicet arguitur, quod laevae parte mamillae
> nil salit Arcadico iuveni, cuius mihi sexta
> quaque die miserum dirus caput Hannibal implet. . . .

"It is the teacher's fault, of course, that the Arcadian youth feels no flutter in his left breast when he dins his 'dire Hannibal' into my unfortunate head on every sixth day of the week. . . ." (Loeb [1957], pp. 150–51 [7. 158–61].)

52. Unlike the Royal Society, The Académie Royale des Sciences, organized 1665–66, under the aegis of Louis XIV (d. 1715), was an institution of the State, its professional scientists appointed and supported by the government. Since the Scriblerians were sympathetic with the French government's support of the Académie française, this may be another jibe at the offical lack of interest in intellectual concerns in England.

53. The Jesuits (always suspect, from the days of the Popish Plot and earlier) were of course famous, or infamous, for their missionary zeal and their successes around the globe, where Catholic influence—political and economic as well as theological—was an issue with British explorers and traders. Even within the Catholic church, the Jesuits' methods were ultimately challenged and restricted.

TO THE
READER.
from
THE
Posthumous WORKS
OF
William Wycherley, Esq;
In PROSE and VERSE.
VOL. II.

INTRODUCTION

In the tempestuous history of Pope and his correspondence,[1] round two (following upon Curll's initiative in publishing in 1726 the letters of Cromwell) involved his 1729 edition of *The Posthumous Works of William Wycherley, Esq; in Prose and Verse. Vol. II.* The "sequel" was prompted by the appearance the year before of Wycherley's *Posthumous Works* edited by Lewis Theobald. Pope, still smarting from *Shakespeare Restored,* Theobald's commentary on his editing of Shakespeare, saw a further opportunity to discredit the man whom he had newly enthroned as King of the Dunces, by publishing his own so-to-speak "Wycherley Restored." As a young man, Pope had worked with Wycherley on preparing some of the aged playwright's poems for publication, an undertaking finally abandoned—and Pope had letters from Wycherley that traced their "collaboration" and made clear Wycherley's poetic limitations. But on the dramatist's deathbed marriage (an event along with its consequent litigation as sordid as anything he ever satirized on the stage)[2] and with Theobald as co-executor of the heavily mortgaged estate, his widow's new husband (and former lover)— who was also Wycherley's cousin and the agent behind the coerced marriage—had decided to have the poems published after all. It was a collection that Pope considered dubious in every sense: its authenticity was questionable since it contained poems that had apparently been silently "improved upon" by Theobald as well as some of those he had himself corrected or which were printed only partially corrected, and some poems that he knew were simply spurious;[3] moreover, the quality of the whole was such as to reflect badly on Wycherley's reputation. Pope's volume, then, would be a defense of Wycherley (and of himself as youthful adviser—and friend to the famous) as well as an indictment of Theobald as unscrupulous and irresponsible editor; it could present texts at least more genuine and also make available the correspondence between Wycherley and himself that, while adding luster to his own early career, would justify his publication and document the assertions made in Wycherley's behalf in his preface to the volume, here printed. Though the edition was supressed, probably because of copyright problems, the unused sheets of the correspondence were to turn up again, in Pope's next—and this time highly successful—venture with his letters.[4]

Notes

1. See Introduction to *Narrative of the Method,* pp. 319–22.
2. Howard P. Vincent has an account of the episode in "The Death of Wil-

liam Wycherley," *Harvard Studies and Notes in Philology and Literature*, 15 (1933), 219–42.

3. For a discussion of both volumes, see Vinton A. Dearing, "Pope, Theobald, and Wycherley's *Posthumous Works*," *PMLA*, 68 (1953), 223–36.

4. See *Narrative of the Method* and the introduction to the prefaces of the 1735 and 1737 editions of the letters. While it has usually been thought that the Wycherley sheets had been held for future use, J. McLaverty argues that at that time (1729), a complete volume of letters was printed (without design for immediate publication) as a safeguard against Curll, with those letters (including the Wycherley ones, reprinted from the original type) incorporated in the 1735 publication. ("The first printing and publication of Pope's letters," *Library*, 2 [1980], 264–80.)

NOTE ON PUBLICATION AND TEXT

G iven Pope's deviousness in the publication of his letters, it is not to be expected that he would acknowledge any role in producing *The Posthumous Works of William Wycherley, Esq; in Prose and Verse. Vol. II,* let alone claim its prefatory "To the Reader." Nor does Griffith, who recognized Pope's editorship of the volume, include the preface in his listings. Yet one must agree with Vinton A. Dearing that "Consideration of the volume as a unit makes it clear Pope wrote the preface. . . ."[1]

Except for being reprinted in the Sherburn *Correspondence,* in the collection entitled "Pope's Own Prefaces to His Letters, 1729–42," the piece has not appeared since the original publication, itself a rarity. What happened to that volume is not clear: certainly it did not sell, for Pope was to acquire the sheets containing the letters—some six hundred of them— for the early editions of his 1735 *Letters;*[2] probably it was suppressed because of copyright infringement since one of the central poems, the "Epistle to Mr. Dryden," was reprinted from an earlier miscellany by Lintot, whom Pope had just been satirizing in the *Dunciad.*[3]

The present printing of the preface, then, reproduces that of the 1729 edition, which it follows in all respects, except for the italic type in which the original was printed:

1729: *The Posthumous Works of William Wycherley, Esq; In Prose and Verse.* Vol. II. Consisting of Letters and Poems Publish'd from Original Manuscripts. London: Printed for J. Roberts in Warwick-lane, octavo, Griffith 223. "To the Reader": A2ʳ–A3ᵛ.

Notes

1. Vinton A. Dearing, "Pope, Theobald, and Wycherley's *Posthumous Works,*" *PMLA,* 68 (1953), 223.

2. For a more recent discussion of the Wycherley publication and Pope's *Letters* see J. McLaverty's "The first printing and publication of Pope's letters" (*Library,* 2 [1980], 264–80), referred to in n. 4 to the Introduction, p. 308.

3. Dearing, "Pope, Theobald, and Wycherley's *Posthumous Works,*" pp. 235– 36.

TO THE
READER.

Having heard that there were, in the *Harley Library,*[1] some Papers
of the late Mr. *Wycherley,* beside what are published in the
First Part of his *Posthumous Works;*[2] and particularly several *Letters,*
which we doubted not would be highly acceptable to the Curious:
We made it our Business to apply to the Possessor of them, the
Right Honourable the *Earl* of *Oxford.* His Lordship has been pleas'd,
in the most Generous Manner, to comply with our Request,[3] and
to sacrifice a Private Curiosity to the Gratification of the Publick.
Tho' we doubt not, one Cause to which we are to attribute this
Favour, is the known Benevolence of that Noble Lord to Learned
Men, which extends not only to their *Persons,* but to their *Memories.*

It is always some Question, Whether *Posthumous Works* are Genuine?[4] These Poems in particular will be suspected, from the manifest *Disparity* between them, and the *Folio* printed by Mr. *Wycherley*
himself in his Life-time;[5] nay, between some and others of these
very Verses. We therefore judg'd the ensuing *Letters* of the more
Consequence, as they happen to be a Proof (and indeed the *only one,*
to all such who have not been favour'd with a Sight of the *Manuscripts*) that some of the said Poems are Genuine, and let us into the
History of their Correction, 'till now a Secret.

They will further enable the Reader to distinguish, which of the
Pieces were touch'd upon, with the Author's own Consent and Con-
currence, by his Friend;[6] and which may have been finger'd after his
Death, by others,[7] without any Warrant but their own Arrogance,
or Motive but their own Lucre. The Fact is, that tho' none of them
had the last Hand, many were once in a better Condition than they
now appear; as may be seen by the *Epistle to* Mr. *Dryden* and a few
others, by great Chance preserv'd in the State Mr. *Pope* left them.[8]

It will be ask'd, Why for so long a Time, as from the Beginning
of this Design (which appears by the Letters to have been in 1705,)
'till the Death of Mr. *Wycherley* which happen'd in 1715, no farther
Progress was made in correcting either these, or the vast Number
of other Verses he left behind? We here see the Reasons were many:

The known Inability of Mr. *Wycherley* in *Versification*,[9] added to the Decay of his *Memory*;[10] the *Impossibility* which his Friend at last found of rendring them perfect *Pieces of Poetry*,[11] even tho' he should have entirely new-written them; the Conviction by several Instances, that the more he should bring them to approach to it, the less he should obtain the *End propos'd* of having them pass for Mr. *Wycherley*'s; and lastly, his sincere Opinion that they would make a worse Figure as Verses unequal and undigested, without Ornament Method or Musick, than as single *Maxims* or *Apothegmes* of good Sense in Prose.[12] Never was more friendly Advice, or a truer Judgment given. It was also a Task which the Author (notwithstanding his unhappy Defects of *Ear* and *Memory*) might *himself* perform, and upon which it appears he had actually begun, by the *three hundred and odd Maxims* found among his Papers, which only of that whole Book (as we are inform'd) were sent to the Press in Mr. *Wycherley*'s own Hand.

It is no unpleasing Reflection to us, that (after more than twenty Years, in which this Transaction has been a Secret) we can thus far consult the Fame of Two Eminent Writers, remarkable for so long a Friendship at so great an Inequality of Years,[13] for it appears to have commenc'd when the one was above *Seventy,* the other not *Seventeen*:[14] And that in this we publish an *Example,* (very rarely to be found among any Authors, and never but among the Best,) of so much Temper, Sense of his own Deficiencies, and Deference to the Judgment of a Friend, in the One; and of so much Sincerity, Candor and Zeal for the Reputation of a Friend, in the Other.

There cannot certainly be a greater Injury to a dead or living Author, than to publish such Works, the unfinish'd Parts of which will be ascrib'd to the one, the more finish'd to the other, and yet answerable to the Intent or Character of neither. It was therefore thought, that to represent the True State of this Case, would be doing the best Justice to the Memory of Mr. *Wycherley.*

A few Passages and Parts of the Letters are omitted, for Reasons which will be obvious to any who compare them.[15]

To which End, the *Originals,* in the Authors own Hand-writing, (together with some other material Papers) may, upon Application, be view'd in the HARLEY-LIBRARY, by any Gentleman, or other Person, of such a Character as to be admitted.[16]

Annotations

1. Robert Harley (1661–1724), first earl of Oxford, and his son Edward (1689–1741), second earl of Oxford, were both good friends to Pope. The first earl, Queen Anne's Lord Treasurer, was "patron" of the Scriblerus Club and founder of a magnificent library, which was to figure importantly in Pope's epistolary schemes. Wishing to disassociate himself from the publication of his letters—and at the same time control it—Pope used the Harleian Library, by then inherited by the second earl, as a depository for the papers he was busy collecting from his correspondents. There transcripts were made of letters that could be "released" ambiguously for the publications that did ensue over the years (this Wycherley volume, the collections of 1735–37, and, less directly, the Pope-Swift correspondence of 1741). Around 15 September 1729, Pope had written to Edward Harley: "The mention of your Library (which I should Envy any man, but One who both makes a good use of it himself, & suffers others to do so) brings back into my mind a Request I have had at heart, for half a year & more; That you would suffer some Original papers & Letters, both of my own and some of my Friends, to lye in your Library at London. There seems already an occasion for it, from a publication of certain Posthumous pieces of Mr Wycherley; very unfair & derogatory to His memory, as well as injurious to me; who had the sole supervisal of 'em committed to me, at his Earnest desire in his Life time: And Something will be necessary to be done, to Clear both his & my reputation, which the Letters under hand will abundantly do: for which particular reason I would desire to have them lodged in our Lordships hands." (*Correspondence*, III, 54.) For background, see too George Sherburn, "Pope's Letters and the Harleian Library," *English Literary History*, 7 (1940), 177–87.

2. *The Posthumous Works* of William Wycherley *Esq; in Prose and Verse.* Faithfully publish'd from *His* Original Manuscripts, by Mr. *Theobald*. London: Printed for A. Bettesworth, J. Osborn, W. Mears, W. and J. Innys, J. Peele, T. Woodward; and F. Clay. 1728. Theobald's volume had promised another (*"What is here offered, being but one Moiety of Mr. Wycherley's Manuscripts, the Remainder of which, according to the Reception of these, will in a short time follow"* ["To the Reader," p. iv]), which Pope's "Vol. II" could ironically represent.

3. Pope had written to Oxford, 16 October 1729, "I am extreamly obliged to you for your kind permission to Quote your Library, and to mention it in what manner I pleas'd: I consulted Mr Lewis upon the Turn of the Preface to those papers relating to Mr. Wycherley and have exceeded perhaps my Commission in one point, (tho we both judged it the Right way) for I have made the Publishers say, that Your *Lordship permitted them a Copy* of some of the papers from the Library, where the Originals remain as Testimonies to the Truth. It is indeed no more than a justice due to the Dead, and to the Living author; one of which (I have

the happiness to know) You are Concernd for; and the other had too much Merit to have his Laurels blasted fourteen years after his death by an unlicencd & presumptuous Mercenary." (*Correspondence*, III, 58–59.)

4. The author of the preface to Theobald's volume had these closing comments: "*As* Plain Dealing *is in all Cases best, the most captious Critic must allow it to be a sufficient Character of these Miscellanies, that they are the Genuine Remains of the Author of the* Plain Dealer." (P. iv.)

5. *Miscellany Poems*: As Satyrs, Epistles, Love-Verses, Songs, Sonnets, &c. by W. Wycherley, *Esq.* London: Printed for *C. Brome, J. Taylor,* and *B. Tooke*; at the *Gun* at the West-End of St. *Paul*'s, the *Ship* in St. *Paul*'s Church-Yard, and at the *Middle-Temple* Gate, *Fleet-street.* MDCCIV.

6. For example, Wycherley to Pope, 5 February 1705/6: "Now, Sir, to make you another Excuse for my boldness in inviting you to Town, I design'd to leave with you some more of my Papers, (since these return so much better out of your Hands than they went from mine) . . ." (*Correspondence*, I, 13); 22 March 1705/6: "I must lay a pennance upon you which is to desire you to look over that Damnd Miscellany of Madrigals of mine [the folio volume of *Miscellany Poems* (1704)] to pick out (if possible) some that may be so alterd that they may yet apeare in print again I hope with better Success than they hether to have done" (ibid., I, 15); 22 November 1707: "Now, as for my owning your assistance to me, in overlooking my unmusical Numbers, and harsher Sense, and correcting them both, with your Genius, or Judgment; I must tell you I always own it, (in spite of your unpoetick Modesty) who would do with your Friendship as your Charity; conceal your Bounty to magnify the Obligation; and even whilst you lay on your Friend the Favour, acquit him of the Debt: But that shall not serve your turn; I will always own, 'tis my infallible Pope has, or would redeem me from a poetical Damning, the second time; and save my Rhimes from being condemn'd to the Criticks Flames to all Eternity" (ibid., I, 33); see also pp. 30, 50, 70, 80, 82–83, 84–85. Pope, in reply, wrote questioning what he should do, reporting what he was doing, and advising what should be done. (Ibid., I, 15–16, 31–32, 33–34, 83–84, 86.)

7. Pope's volume includes a reprint of Theobald's table of contents, annotated to designate works as spurious, as those revised by that editor, and as those incorrectly or imperfectly reproduced.

8. The "Epistle to Mr. Dryden"—the inclusion of which may have led to the suppression of the volume since the copyright belonged to Lintot—provided Pope with a good argument, as he could compare his revision, authorized by Wycherley ("I have receiv'd your kind Letter, with my Paper to Mr. *Dryden* corrected. I own you have made more of it by making it less . . ." [*Correspondence*, I, 13]), with the longer version printed by Theobald. Dearing, in his "Pope, Theobald, and Wycherley's *Posthumous Works*," has studied the two texts, and he

concludes: "It is probably safe to assume that Wycherley was responsible for few, if any, of the subtle variations, and to generalize that where Pope's version is better the revision is his, where Theobald's is better the revision is Theobald's. Wycherley could not have approved Theobald's revisions, of course, but there is no evidence that he did not welcome Pope's. Once again, we shall never know how Theobald came to print from the unrevised original." (Dearing, *PMLA*, 68 [1953], 234.) In a note (to his letter to Wycherley of 20 November 1707), Pope draws attention to what had happened to his reworking of "A Panegyrick on Dulness"—a revision that he had sketched in some detail in the letter—where Theobald had only partially reproduced the changes. (*Correspondence*, I, 32n.)

9. Pope had had his problems trying to embellish Wycherley's "stale, antiquated, poetical Puss"; as he explains, "I have done all that I thought could be of advantage to them [some particular verses]: Some I have contracted, as we do Sun-beams, to improve their Energy and Force; some I have taken quite away, as we take Branches from a Tree, to add to the Fruit; others I have entirely new express'd, and turned more into Poetry. . . . You have commission'd me to paint your Shop, and I have done my best to brush you up like your Neighbours." (*Correspondence*, I, 16.)

10. Wycherley to Pope, 27 April 1710: "You give me an Account in your Letter, of the trouble you have undergone for me, in Compareing my Papers, you took down with you, with that old printed Volume, and with one another, of that Bundle, you have in your Hands: amongst which, (You say,) you find numerous repetitions of the same thoughts, and Subjects, all which, I must confess my want of memory has prevented me from imagining; as well as commiting them. . . ." (*Correspondence*, I, 84–85.) Pope had observed to Spence,

> Wycherley used to read himself asleep o'nights, either in Montaigne, Rochefoucault, Seneca, or Gratian, for those were his favourite authors. He would read one or other of them in the evening and the next morning perhaps write a copy of verses on some subject similar to what he had been reading. [He would] have all their thoughts, only expressed in a different turn, and that without knowing that he was obliged to them for any one thought in the whole poem. I have experienced this in him several times (for I visited him for a whole winter, almost every evening and morning) and look upon it as one of the strangest phenomenons that I ever observed in the human mind. (*Anecdotes*, I, 37.)

11. Pope had finally written to Wycherley, in the last letter of the collection, "Be certain I shall most carefully observe your Request, not to cross over, or deface the Copy of your Papers for the future, and only to mark in the Margin the Repetitions; But as this can serve no further than to get rid of those Repetitions, and no way rectify the *Method*, nor *connect* the *Matter*, nor improve the

Poetry in *Expression* or *Numbers,* without further blotting, adding, and altering; so it really is my opinion, and desire, that you should take your Papers out of my hands into your own. . . . Do not be so unjust, as to imagine from hence that I would decline any part of this Task: On the contrary you know, I have been at the pains of transcribing some Pieces, at once to comply with your desire of not defacing the Copy, and yet to lose no Time in proceeding upon the Correction. I will go on the same way if you please; tho' truly it is (as I have often told you) my sincere Opinion, that the greater Part would make a much better Figure, as *Single Maxims* and *Reflections* in Prose, after the manner of your favourite Rochefoucaut, than in Verse. And this, when nothing more is done but marking the Repetitions in the Margin, will be an easy Task for your self to do, notwithstanding the bad Memory you complain of." (*Correspondence,* I, 86–87.)

12. See n. 11. This was a point that Pope had made to Wycherley on more than one occasion. On 29 November 1707, he had written: "To *methodize* in your Case, is full as necessary as to *strike out*: otherwise you had better destroy the whole Frame, and reduce them into *single Thoughts* in *Prose,* like Rochfoucault, as I have more than once hinted to you." (*Correspondence,* I, 34.)

13. Pope's candid criticism apparently caused an estrangement, at least for a while, between them, but as Sherburn comments, "except for a temporary coolness in 1710 the friendship lasted until Wycherley's death." (*Correspondence,* I, 1 [section note].) Spence records, "We [Pope and Wycherley] were pretty well together to the last, only his memory was so totally bad that he did not remember a kindness done to him, even from minute to minute. He was peevish too, latterly, so that sometimes we were out a little and sometimes in. He never did any unjust thing to me in his whole life, and I went to see him on his death-bed." (*Anecdotes,* I, 41.)

14. In one of his early, and very self-conscious, letters to his famous correspondent, the young Pope had postured:

But I separate from all the rest that Paragraph or two, in which you make me so warm an Offer of your Friendship. Were I possess'd of That, it would put an End to all those Speeches with which you now make me blush; and change them to wholesome Advices and free Sentiments, which might make me wiser and happier. I know 'tis the general Opinion, that Friendship is best contracted betwixt Persons of equal Age: but I have so much Interest to be of another Mind, that you must pardon me if I cannot forbear telling you a few Notions of mine, in opposition to that Opinion. . . . Now, as a young Man who is less acquainted with the Ways of the World, has in all probability less of Interest; and an old Man who may be weary of himself, less of Self-love; so the Friendship between them is the more likely to be true, and unmix'd with too much Self-regard. One may add to this, that such a Friendship is of greater Use and Advantage to both; for the old Man will grow more gay and agreeable to please the young one; and the young Man more discreet and prudent by the help of the old one; so it may prove a Cure of those epidemical Diseases of Age and Youth, Sourness and Madness." (*Correspondence*, I, 8.)

15. As Pope had written to Edward Harley, "to ask your leave to deposite certain Memorandums of me, & the best part of me, (my Friendships & Correspondence with my Betters) in your Library. I foresaw some dirty Trick in relation to my Friend Wycherley's papers which they were publishing; & nothing can at once do justice so well to Him & to Me, who was by him employd in them, as the divulging some parts of his & my Letters (with proper Guard & Caution to reserve what should not be publishd of private Letters pour raisons (as the French express it) d'Honneteté.") (*Correspondence*, III, 55.) And he excised such passages as Wycherley's account of a drunken accident (ibid., I, 58) and his bawdy commentary on a coach trip with four women (ibid., I, 14). While omissions and other manipulations of his text by Pope incensed his Victorian editors Elwin and Courthope, who questioned the validity of the whole correspondence, modern commentators like Sherburn conclude that "the unscrupulous editing of Pope does not notably alter the truth concerning his friendship with the great dramatist. . . ." (*Correspondence*, I, 1n.; see also Dearing, "Pope, Theobald, and Wycherley's *Posthumous Works*," pp. 228–29.)

16. Pope reclaimed the papers in 1735, for he wrote to Oxford that year, "I recollect that your Lordship has still in your custody the Brouillons of verses, & some Letters of Wycherley, I think in a red leather Cover with your arms upon it. I beg also that I may have it" (*Correspondence*, III, 469), and apparently never returned them to the Library; but Harleian transcripts of twelve of the letters were discovered at Longleat and these, with Pope's printings, are the basis of modern editions of the thirty-six letters of the correspondence (twenty-six of which Pope printed in the *Posthumous Works*).

A

NARRATIVE

OF THE

METHOD

BY WHICH THE

PRIVATE LETTERS of Mr. POPE
Have been procur'd and publish'd by
EDMUND CURLL, Bookseller.

NB. *The Original Papers, in* Curl's *own
Hand, may be seen at* T. Cooper's.

INTRODUCTION

Pope's publication of his letters is a subject that has teased investigators since the time of Dr. Johnson, who remarked laconically that this was a passage in Pope's life "which seems to deserve some enquiry."[1] That challenge was taken up hotly in the mid-nineteenth century, when Charles Wentworth Dilke's acquisition of the manuscript letters of Pope to Caryll revealed the liberties Pope had taken in "editing" his correspondence.[2] To Dilke, and more particularly Pope's editor Elwin, the poet seemed guilty of tampering, and the latter devoted the greater part of his introduction to the *Works* to an account of the printing of the letters, seeing the complex of intrigue as further evidence of the turpitude of a man whose morals he was constantly calling into question.[3] Recent judgment has been more objective; without attempting to whitewash Pope, modern commentators like Griffith[4] and, most recently of course, Sherburn[5] and Winn[6] have reviewed the facts with an awareness of the unique problems of the Augustan author and with insight into Pope's personal motives.

The events of this story make a remarkable tale of dealings and double-dealings, often verging on the melodramatic. Yet such ingenuities were, in a sense, inevitable given Pope's taste for subterfuge and given the situation of the time. According to contemporary convention, letters were private communications and it was a breach of taste to publish one's own. Although eventually Pope's action did much to establish letter writing as a literary mode—for he looked upon his letters as significant "works," as testimonies "of my own love for good men"[7]—he was still sensitive about his reputation. He would publish the letters,[8] in the way that he wanted them published, but he was determined to seem innocent of involvement.[9] The appearances of his various correspondence were accordingly marked by complex transactions. And no transaction is more tangled or more exciting (or brought down more censure on his head from the Victorians) than that which engineered the 1735 publication of his letters—the publication with which *A Narrative of the Method*, here printed, is concerned.

The anonymously published *Narrative* is Pope's version of his maneuvers with his old enemy Edmund Curll,[10] which culminated in Curll's publishing of *Mr. Pope's Literary Correspondence for Thirty Years; from 1704 to 1734*. When taken with rebutting statements and documents to be found in Curll's second volume of the letters[11] (traced in the annotations to the text), the *Narrative* provides a connected "history"[12] of the affair, the two accounts together reproducing in all their contradiction and confusion the various letters and advertisements which were a part of the intrigue. Conveniently, too, for the interested reader, the *Narrative* recapitulates some earlier history, for it opens with a review of Pope's previous experiences with his letters—the unauthorized printing of his correspondence with Henry Cromwell and his printed but suppressed volume, including letters, of the works of Wycherley[13]—and Curll's role in both those publications. With that as background, the reader is then brought to more immediate events, and Pope's elaborate scheme begins to unfold.[14]

In October 1733, Curll had received from an alleged acquaintance of Pope,[15] an unknown P. T. (later ruefully identified by Curll as "Trickster Pope"), some biographical information about the poet—linking his family elegantly, if erroneously, with a noble Irish one—with the offer of more such memoirs. The letter made a plausible response to advertisements Curll had published earlier that year inviting information for a projected life of the celebrated author, soliciting encouraged no doubt by a letter which Curll had received in March from an unidentified E. P., who sent him some unflattering anecdotes about Pope's early schooling.[16] Curll was as ready to exploit popular interest with an abusive biography, as Pope, one may assume, was willing to feed him facts, comfortably false, which he might be duped into printing. Then followed another communication from P. T., this time tendering a large collection of letters by Pope, the letters to be delivered to Curll as soon as he published an advertisement, provided by P. T., of the forthcoming volume. Although this was enticing—especially since this latest note implied animosity between P. T. and Pope—Curll was too wary to act merely upon the promise of letters; he did not comply and the matter was dropped until March 1735, when, as he himself reports, he came upon the advertisement again by chance, while "regulating some Papers in my Scritoire."[17]

Whatever may have prompted Curll's renewed interest at that time, he used the paper in an overture of conciliation, sending it to Pope along with the suggestion of a new edition of the Cromwell letters. Pope, ostensibly suspicious of a trick, responded with a public advertisement denying all knowledge of P. T. or any collection of his letters and spurning Curll's advances. There things might have rested except that P. T. popped up again, with a letter to Curll announcing that he had seen Pope's message and was eager to release the letters, which in the interim he had printed but which he now wished Curll to publish. The day after Pope's advertisement Curll replied in turn, advertising that the correspondence would appear, that

> No longer now like Suppliants we come,
> E. C. makes War, and A. P. is the Drum——[18]

for he had made an appointment with P. T. to see one of the books in sheets. That appointment was never kept. P. T. withdrew on the grounds that Pope might have learned of the rendezvous, though as Curll shrewdly commented, "how Mr *Pope* was to know of this Meeting is the Cream of the Jest."[19]

Curll was obviously suspicious by this point, but after further negotiations with P. T. there materialized a new figure of mystery, R. S.—"a short, squat Man. . . . He had on a Clergyman's Gown, and his neck was surrounded with a large, Lawn Barrister's Band"[20]—who brought to Curll, on the night of 7 May, a "Book in sheets, almost finished,"[21] and some dozen original letters. Matters then began to move swiftly, although there were still numerous communications between Curll and P. T. and R. S.—now further revealed in these notes as R. Smythe—about money and about the earlier correspondence between them, which P. T. wished returned. Both he and R. S. exhorted Curll to advertise the forthcoming publication; but until he had books in hand, Curll was cautious. By 12 May he had received fifty copies—lacking title pages and prefaces— which he soon sold, and at one-thirty that afternoon five bundles, amounting to 190 more books, were delivered to his house. The venture must have seemed a success: the advertisement had appeared that morning, and the *Letters* were finally on the market.

But the plot had not yet run its full course. One half hour after the delivery of the five bales of books, the whole lot was impounded by messengers from the House of Lords, and Curll was summoned to appear before that body the next day on the charge of breach of privilege. For the advertisement, released just a few hours earlier, had indicated that the correspondence included letters *from* lords as well as to them, and no such publication was allowed without the consent of the peers involved. Lord Ilay (a neighbor of Pope), who had brought the charges, complained that in the copy he had purchased from Curll there was a letter containing abuse against the earl of Burlington.[22] But when the books were examined, that letter was not to be found, nor were there any letters from the lords included in the text. As no infringements on rights had occurred, the charges were dropped and the letters were returned, to be made available to a public now even more eager for them.

In the course of the proceedings, messages had passed furiously between R. S., writing in behalf of P. T., and P. T. himself, and Curll: Curll was warned to reveal nothing of the transactions with P. T.; he was instructed to assume full responsibility for the printing and publishing of the edition; and he was informed, very casually, that the "Rogue" of a printer had sent incomplete copies of the last books. When Curll ignored these injunctions—by denying any knowledge of the source of the books, which his wife had received, and then by circulating among some of the lords the latest letter of instruction from P. T.—the communications became hostile. Before long Curll was denouncing P. T. as a "Will o' the Wisp" and threatening to publish their correspondence, while P. T. and R. S. were disputing Curll's title to the Pope letters and were threatening in turn to publish his letters to them. And there was Pope himself, as the outraged victim of all three, advertising "that if either of the said Persons [P. T. or R. S.] will discover the whole of this Affair, he shall receive a Reward of *Twenty Guineas*; or if he can prove he hath acted by *Direction of any other,* and of *what Person,* he shall receive double that Sum."[23]

Neither the shadowy P. T. or his more substantial agent attempted to collect the reward; it was left for Curll, in a prefatory *"To Mr Pope"*[24]— included along with the threatened "Initial Correspondence" in the second volume of his edition of the letters—to bill Pope for forty guineas. For Curll had learned from Gilliver, the publisher of Pope's volume of Wycherley papers, that Pope himself had bought up the sheets of that volume, sheets that were again used in the books brought to Curll. "*P. T.* is Trickster *Pope, R. S.* is Silly Rascal," Curll raged, but with his infamous reputation, he raged in vain. P. T. and R. S. disappeared behind the anonymous *A Narrative of the Method by which the Private Letters of Mr. Pope have been procur'd and publish'd by Edmund Curll, Bookseller,* which Cooper, Pope's current publisher, brought out in June.

The game was over—at least for the present. The letters were out, with Curll the popular villain, and Pope could look forward, as the postscript to the *Narrative* suggests, to publishing his "own" edition within the next few years. And the letters themselves, whether issued by P. T., Curll,[25] or, later, Pope himself, continued to sell, for as Griffith comments, "If Pope is not the greatest among English poets, he is the greatest advertiser and publisher among them."[26] Should this seem to damn with faint praise, one may recall Griffith's preceding observations on Pope and his age: "A dependable patron was gone, a sustaining public was not yet come. With such a recalcitrant condition Pope wrestled; from it he wrestled success. He resorted at times to subterfuges we think undignified, but he lost no contemporary prestige by them; we pronounce them base; he thought them fire by which to whip the devil."[27]

Notes

1. Johnson, *Lives,* III, 155.

2. Dilke, *The Papers of a Critic* (London: John Murray, 1875), I, 93ff. A detailed account of the publication of the letters begins on p. 287.

3. EC I, xxvi–cxlvii.

4. Griffith, I part ii, xlvii.

5. *Correspondence,* I, "Introduction."

6. James Anderson Winn, *A Window in the Bosom* (Hamden, Connecticut: Archon Books, 1977), particularly Chapter I. And in the recent "The first printing and publication of Pope's letters" (*Library,* 2 [1980], 264–80), J. McLaverty reviews sympathetically Pope's maneuvers as a plan to discredit Curll before the House of Lords at a time when Parliament was considering the Booksellers' Bill, where, Pope hoped, "the Legislature will be pleas'd not to *extend* the *Privileges,* without at the same Time *restraining the License, of Booksellers.*"

7. *Correspondence,* II, 419.

8. As Swift commented (*Correspondence,* III, 92): "I find you to have been a writer of Letters almost from your infancy, and by your own confession had Schemes even then of Epistolary fame."

9. Dr. Johnson understood both Pope and the problem when he made his analysis of what subsequently took place: "It seems that Pope, being desirous of printing his letters, and not knowing how to do, without imputation of vanity, what in this country has been done very rarely, contrived an appearance of compulsion: that when he could complain that his letters were surreptitiously published, he might decently and defensively publish them himself." (*Lives,* III, 157.)

10. For the history of that long relationship see Ralph Straus, *The Unspeakable Curll* (London: Chapman and Hall, 1927).

11. *Mr. Pope's Literary Correspondence. Volume the Second.* London: Printed for E. Curll. . . . M.DCC.XXXV. This volume includes a number of interesting prefatory pieces, among them a reprint of the *Narrative*—with rebutting notes— and "The Initial Correspondence," Curll's version of what had happened.

12. For as James Winn comments, "it is prose fiction, not documentary" (*A Window in the Bosom,* p. 41). See also n. 14.

13. For an account of this volume see V. A. Dearing's "Pope, Theobald, and Wycherley's *Posthumous Works,*" *PMLA,* 68 (1953), 223–36 and Pope's preface to the volume, pp. 305–16, above.

14. In an appendix, Winn (*A Window in the Bosom*) provides "one possible timetable" of these events, reviewing in detail the two accounts with all their inherent murkiness. As he acknowledges, "no one will ever know what happened beyond a few basic facts" (p. 36).

15. "I was well acquainted with his Father, and with the first part of his own Life, tho' since he hath treated me as a Stranger." (Curll, "Initial Correspondence," p. 8.)

16. The letter—which Curll reproduced in his "Initial Correspondence" (pp. 6–7)—was one guaranteed to attract his attention, for it offered "proof of that *natural spleen* which constitutes his [Pope's] *Temperament,* and from which he

has never deviated in the whole course of his Life"—the proof being a brief account of the poet's career in his "last School": "Mr *Alexander Pope* before he had been four Months at this School (or was able to construe *Tully's Offices*) employed his Muse in satirizing his Master. It was a Libel of at least one hundred Verses, which a Fellow-Student having given informatin of, was found in his pocket, and the young Satirist was soundly whipp'd, and kept a Prisoner to his Room seven days; whereupon his Father fetch'd him away, and I have been told, he never went to School more." According to Sherburn (*Correspondence,* III, 359n), "The information as to the poet's schooling is so completely wrong that one assumes that it is fabricated by Pope in a wilful desire to mislead Curll."

17. Curll, "Initial Correspondence," p. 12.

18. Appendix II to Curll's "Initial Correspondence," p. 29.

19. Curll, "Initial Correspondence," p. 13.

20. Ibid., p. 14.

21. Ibid.

22. Straus, pp. 166–68; EC VI, Appendix II, pp. 432–35.

23. *Narrative,* p. 334.

24. "*To Mr* Pope," *Mr. Pope's Literary Correspondence* (London, 1735), II, xiii–xiv.

25. Newspaper reading at the time must have been considerably enlivened by the advertisements—simultaneous and vociferous—of the rival publications. In the *Daily Post-Boy* of 28 May 1735, for example, readers are admonished in one column, "We hope it is sufficient to Prefer this Edition, to say it is NOT printed for *Edmund Curl,* and it is entirely free from his Notes and Impertinences"; while in the next column Curll counters with

> Edmund Curll's *Follies and Impertinence*
> *Will prove a Match for* Pope's *Satiric Sense*

and warns them (*Daily Post-Boy,* 29 May 1735) to "Beware of Pyrated Editions, Defective and without Cutts."

26. Griffith, I part ii, xlvii.

27. Ibid.

NOTE ON PUBLICATION AND TEXT

Although *A Narrative of the Method by which the Private Letters of Mr. Pope have been procur'd and publish'd by Edmund Curll, Bookseller* was an anonymous publication, Pope's responsibility for it seems as apparent as his participation in the events which it records.[1] Except for Curll's statements, it is the only account of how Pope's letters came to be published, prior to the prefaces to the 1737 editions of the letters. Even then, Pope's preface to the authorized Quarto (still written in the anonymity of the third person) does not attempt to supplant it, but, rather, echoes it suggestively in details.

The present text is taken from the original edition, published by T. Cooper in June of 1735, with the slightly different caption title used as a heading. The *Narrative* was subsequently reprinted in each of the duodecimo editions of the *Letters of Mr. Pope, and Several Eminent Persons, from the Year 1705 to 1735. Vol. I*; it was also reprinted by Curll, as the "True Narrative . . . ," in his second volume of *Mr. Pope's Literary Correspondence*. Sherburn reproduces it in the *Correspondence* (III, 458–67).

1735: *A Narrative of the Method by which the Private Letters of Mr. Pope have been procur'd and publish'd by Edmund Curll, Bookseller.* N.B. *The Original Papers, in* Curl's *own Hand, may be seen at* T. Cooper's. London: Printed for T. Cooper in Pater-noster Row, duodecimo, Griffith 382.
{1735: *Letters,* Vol. I, duodecimo, Griffith 384.
1735: *Letters,* Vol. I, duodecimo, Griffith 396.
1735: *Letters,* Vol. I, duodecimo, Griffith 397.
1735: *Letters,* Vol. I, duodecimo, Griffith 400.
1735: *Letters,* Vol. I, duodecimo, Griffith 408.
1735: *Mr. Pope's Literary Correspondence,* Vol. the Second, octavo, Griffith 386.[2]}

Notes

1. Most commentators attribute the piece to Pope. Griffith states: "That Pope was the author appears probable" (Griffith, 304) and Winn concurs, though Sherburn merely designates it as "Pope-inspired" (*Correspondence,* I, xiv).

2. Curll's printing of the *Narrative,* with rebutting notes, is modified by the transfer of some of the material: the Thomas-Cromwell letters, to the "Preface"

to volume one of the *Correspondence*; and one of the advertisements and two of the early P. T. letters, to the "Initial Correspondence" (in volume two)—Curll's own narrative of the affair, supported by such papers as he had in his possession. The "Initial Correspondence" and the *Narrative* together provide a complete account, such as it is, of the publication of the letters, reproducing all the documents which were a part of the intrigue.

A

NARRATIVE

OF THE

METHOD *by which Mr. Pope's Private Letters were procured and published by* EDMUND CURL, *Bookseller.*

It has been judg'd, that to clear an Affair which seem'd at first sight a little mysterious, and which, tho' it concern'd only one Gentleman,[1] is of such a Consequence, as justly to alarm every Person in the Nation, would not only be acceptable as a *Curiosity,* but useful as a *Warning,* and perhaps flagrant enough as an *Example,* to induce the LEGISLATURE to prevent for the future, an Enormity so prejudicial to every private Subject, and so destructive of Society it self.[2]

This will be made so plain by the ensuing Papers, that 'twill scarce be needful to attend them with any Reflections, more than what every Reader may make.

In the Year 1727, *Edmund Curl,* Bookseller, published a Collection of several private Letters of Mr. *Pope* to *Henry Cromwell,* Esq;[3] which he obtain'd in this Manner.

Mr. *Cromwell*[4] was acquainted with one Mrs. *Thomas,*[5] to whom he had the Indiscretion to lend these Letters, and who falling into Misfortunes, seven Years after, sold them to Mr. *Curll,* without the Consent either of Mr. *Pope* or Mr. *Cromwell,*[6] as appears from the following Letters.

To HENRY CROMWELL, *Esq;*

June 27, 1727.

After so long a Silence, as the many and great Oppressions I have sigh'd under has occasion'd, one is at a Loss how to begin a Letter to so kind a Friend as your self. But as it was always my Resolution, if I must sink to do it as decently (that is as silently) as I could: So when I found my self plung'd into unforeseen, and unavoidable Ruin, I retreated from the World, and in a manner buried my self in a dismal Place, where I knew none, nor none knew me. In this dull unthinking Way, I have protracted a lingering Death (for Life it cannot be called) ever since you saw me, sequestered from Company, deprived of my Books, and nothing left to converse with but the Letters of my dead, or absent Friends, amongst which latter I always placed yours, and Mr. *Pope*'s in the first Rank. I lent some of them indeed to an ingenious Person, who was so delighted with the Specimen, that he importun'd me for a Sight of the rest, which having obtain'd, he conveyed them to the Press, I must not say altogether with my Consent, nor wholly without it. I thought them too good to be lost in Oblivion, and had no Cause to apprehend the disobliging of any. The Publick, *viz.* All Persons of Taste and Judgment, would be pleased with so agreeable an Amusement; Mr. *Cromwell* could not be angry, since it was but Justice to his Merit, to publish the solemn and private Professions of Love, Gratitude and Veneration, made to him by so celebrated an Author; and surely Mr. *Pope* ought not to resent the Publication, since the early Pregnancy of his Genius was no dishonour to his Character. And yet had either of you been ask'd, common Modesty would have oblig'd you to refuse what you would not have been displeas'd with if done without your Knowledge; and besides, to end all Dispute, you had been pleased to make me a free Gift of them to do what I pleased with them: And every one knows that a Person to whom a Letter is address'd, has the same Right to dispose of it, as he has of Goods purchased with his Money.[7] I doubt not but your Generosity and Honour will do me the Right of owning by a Line that I came honestly by them. I flatter my self in a few Months I shall again be visible to the World, and whenever thro' good Providence that Turn shall happen, I shall joyfully acquaint you with it, there being none more truly your obliged Servant than, Sir,

Your faithful and
most humble Servant,
E. THOMAS.

P.S. A Letter, Sir, directed to Mrs. *Thomas,* to be left at my House, will be safely transmitted to her by

E. CURL.

To Mr. Pope.

Epsom, July 6. 1727.

When these Letters were first printed, I wonder'd how *Curl* could come by them, and could not but laugh at the pompous Title; since whatever you wrote to me was Humour and familiar Raillery. As soon as I came from *Epsom,* I heard you had been to see me, and I writ you a short Letter from *Will's,* that I long'd to see you. Mr. *D——s*[8] about that time charg'd me with giving them to a Mistress, which I positively denied; not in the least, at that time, thinking of it: But some time after finding in the News-Papers, Letters from Lady *Packington,* Lady *Chudleigh,* and Mr. *Norris,*[9] to the same *Sapho,*[10] or *E. T.* I began to fear that I was guilty. I have never seen these Letters of *Curl's,* nor would go to his Shop about them; I have not seen this *Sapho,* alias *E. T.* these seven Years;—— her writing, *That I gave her them to do what she would with them,* was straining the Point too far: I thought not of it; nor do I think she did then: But severe Necessity, which catches hold of a Twig, has produced all this; which has lain hid, and forgot by me, so many Years. *Curl* sent me a Letter last Week, desiring a positive Answer about this Matter, but finding I would give him none, he went to *E. T.* and writ a Postscript, in her long romantick Letter, to direct my Answer to his House, but they not expecting an Answer, sent a young Man to me, whose Name it seems is *Pattisson,*[11] I told him I should not write any thing, but I believed it might be so as she writ in her Letter. I am extreamly concern'd that my former Indis-cretion, in putting them into the Hands of this *Pretieuse,*[12] should have given you so much Disturbance; for the last thing I should do would be to disoblige you; for whom I have ever preserved the greatest Esteem, and shall ever be, Sir,

Your faithful Friend,
and most humble Servant,
HENRY CROMWELL.

To Mr. POPE.

August 1. 1727.

Tho' I writ my long Narrative from *Epsom* till I was tired, yet was I not satisfied; lest any Doubt should rest upon your Mind. I could not make Protestations of my Innocence of a grievous Crime;

but I was impatient till I came to Town, that I might send you those Letters, as a clear Evidence, that I was a perfect Stranger to all their Proceedings. Should I have protested against it, after the Printing, it might have been taken for an Attempt to decry his Purchase; and as the little Exception you have taken, has serv'd him to play his Game upon us for these two Years; a new Incident from me might enable him to play it on for two more:[13]——The great Value she expresses for all you write, and her Passion for having them, I believe was what prevailed upon me to let her keep them. By the Interval of twelve Years at least, from her Possession to the Time of printing them, 'tis manifest that I had not the least Ground to apprehend such a Design: But as People in great Straits, bring forth their Hoards of old Gold, and most valuable Jewels, so *Sapho* had recourse to her hid Treasure of Letters, and plaid off, not only yours to me, but all those to her self (as the Ladies last Stake) into the Press.——As for me, I hope, when you shall cooly consider the many thousand Instances of our being deluded by Females, since that great Original of *Adam* by *Eve,* you will have a more favourable Thought of the undesigning Error of,

Your faithful Friend,
and humble Servant,
HENRY CROMWELL.

This Treatment being extreamly disagreeable to Mr. *Pope,* he was advised to recal any Letters which might happen to be preserved by any of his Friends, particularly those written to Persons deceas'd, which would be most subject to such an Accident. Many of these were return'd him.[14]

Some of his Friends advised him to print a Collection himself, to prevent a worse; but this he would by no means agree to.[15] However, as some of the Letters served to revive several past Scenes of Friendship, and others to clear the Truth of *Facts* in which he had been misrepresented by the common Scribblers, he was induced to preserve a few of his own Letters, as well as of his Friends. These, as I have been told, he inserted in TWO BOOKS, some Originals, others Copies, with a few Notes and Extracts here and there added. In the same Books he caused to be copied some small Pieces in Verse and

Prose, either of his own, or his Correspondents; which, tho' not finish'd enough for the Publick, were such as the Partiality of any Friend would be sorry to be depriv'd of.

To this Purpose, an Amanuensis or two were employ'd by Mr. *Pope,* when the Books were in the Country, and by the Earl of *Oxford,* when they were in Town.[16]

It happen'd soon after, that the *Posthumous Works* of Mr. *Wycherly* were publish'd, in such a Manner, as could no way increase the Reputation of that Gentleman, who had been Mr. *Pope*'s first Correspondent and Friend;[17] And several of these Letters so fully shew'd the State of that Case, that it was thought but a Justice to Mr. *Wycherly*'s Memory to print a few, to discredit that Imposition. These were accordingly transcrib'd for the Press from the *Manuscript Books* above-mention'd.[18]

They were no sooner printed, but *Edmund Curl* look'd on these too as his Property; for a Copy is extant, which he corrected in order to another Impression, interlin'd, and added marginal Notes to, in his own Hand.[19]

He then advertis'd anew the Letters to Mr. *Cromwell,* with *Additions,* and promis'd Incouragement to all Persons who should send him more.[20]

This is a Practice frequent with Booksellers, to swell an Author's Works, in which they have some Property, with any Trash that can be got from any Hand; or where they have no such Works, to procure some. *Curl* has in the same manner since advertiz'd the *Letters* of Mr. *Prior,* and Mr. *Addison.*[21] A Practice highly deserving some Check from the Legislature; since every such Advertisement, is really a *Watch-word* to every *Scoundrel*[22] in the Nation, and to every *Domestick* of a Family, to get a Penny, by producing any Scrap of a Man's Writing, (of what Nature soever) or by picking his Master's Pocket of Letters and Papers.

A most flagrant Instance of this kind was the Advertisement of an intended Book, call'd *Gulliveriana Secunda*; where it was promis'd "that *any Thing,* which *any Body* should send as Mr. *Pope*'s or Dr. *Swift*'s, should be printed and inserted *as Theirs.*"

By these honest means, Mr. *Curl* went on encreasing his Collection,[23] and finding (as will be seen hereafter by No. 5) a further

Prospect of doing so, he retarded his Edition of Mr. *Cromwell's* Letters till the Twenty-Second of March 1734–35, and then sent Mr. *Pope* the following Letter, the first he ever receiv'd from him.[24]

No. I.

SIR,

To convince you of my readiness to oblige you, the *Inclosed* is a Demonstration. You have, as he says, disoblig'd a Gentleman, the initial Letters of whose Name are P. T. I have some other Papers in the same Hand relating to your *Family,* which I will show if you desire a Sight of them. Your letters to Mr. *Cromwell* are out of Print, and I intend to Print them very beautifully in an *Octavo Volume.* I have more to say than is proper to write, and if you'll give me a Meeting, I will wait on you with Pleasure, and close all Differences betwixt you and yours

E. CURL.

Rose-Street 22 March 1735.
P.S. I expect the Civility of an Answer or Message.

The *Inclos'd* were two Scraps of Paper, suppos'd to be P. T's (a feigned Hand) the first containing this Advertisement.

No. II.

Letters of *Alexander Pope* Esq; and several eminent Hands. From the Year 1705. to 1727. Containing a Critical, Philological, and Historical Correspondence between him and *Henry Cromwell* Esq; *William Wycherly* Esq; *Wiliam Walsh* Esq; *William Congreve* Esq; Sir *William Trumbull*; Sir *Richard Steele*; E. O———, Mr. *Addison*; M. *Craggs*; Mr. *Gay*; Dean *Swift,* &c. with several Letters to Ladies; to the Number of two Hundred. *N. B.* The Originals will be shewn at *Ed. Curl's* when the Book is Published.

The other Paper was a Scrap of some Letter in the same Hand, which exprest "a Dissatisfaction at *Curl* for not having printed his Advertisement"———What more cannot be seen, for the rest is cut off close to the Writing.

Mr. *Pope's* Friends imagin'd that the whole Design of E. *Curl* was to get him but to look on the Edition of *Cromwel's* Letters, and so to print it as *revis'd* by Mr. *Pope*,[25] in the same manner as he sent an *obscene Book* to a *Reverend Bishop*, and then Advertis'd it as *corrected* and *revis'd* by him.[26] Or if there was any such Proposal from *P. T. Curl* would not fail to embrace it, perhaps pay for the Copy with the very Mony he might draw from Mr. *P*—— to suppress it, and say *P. T.* had kept another Copy. He therefore answer'd the only way he thought it safe to correspond with him, by a publick Advertisement in the *Daily Post-Boy.*[27]

No. III.

Whereas *A. P.* hath received a Letter from *E. C.* Bookseller, pretending that a Person, the Initials of whose Name are *P. T.* hath offered the said *E. C.* to print a large Collection of Mr. *P*'s Letters, to which *E. C.* requires an Answer, *A. P.* having never had, nor intending to have, any private Correspondence with the said *E. C.* gives it him in this Manner. That he knows no such Person as *P. T.* that he believes he hath no such Collection, and that he thinks the whole a Forgery, and shall not trouble himself at all about it.

Ed. Curl return'd an impertinent Answer[28] in the same Paper the next Day, denying that he *endeavour'd to correspond with Mr. P.* and affirming that he wrote by *Direction,* but declaring that he would *instantly print the said Collection.* In a few Days more he publish'd the *Advertisement of the Book* as above, with this Addition, "*E. C.* as before in the like Case, will be faithful"[29] He now talk'd of it every where, said "That *P. T.* was a LORD,[30] or a PERSON OF CONSEQUENCE, who printed the Book at a *great Expence,* and sought no Profit, but *Revenge* on Mr. *Pope, who had offended him:*" particularly, "That some of the Letters would be such as both *Church* and *State would take Notice of;* but that *P. T.* would by no means be known in it, that he never would once be *seen* by him, but treated in a very *secret Manner.*" He told some Persons that sifted him in this Affair, "that he had convers'd only with his Agent, a Clergyman of the Name of *Smith,*[31] who came, as he said, from *Southwark.*" With this Person it was that *Curl* transacted the Affair, who before all the Letters of the Book were delivered to *Curl,* insisted on the Letters of *P. T.* being return'd him, to secure him from all possibility of a Discovery, as appears from No. 12.

Mr. *Pope,* on hearing of this *Smith,* and finding when the Book came out, that several of the *Letters* could only have come from the *Manuscript*-Book before-mention'd, publish'd this Advertisement.[32]

Whereas a Person who signs himself *P. T.* and another who writes himself *R. Smith* and passes for a Clergyman, have Transacted for some time past with *Edm. Curl,* and have in combination printed the *Private Letters* of Mr. *Pope* and his Correspondents [some of which could only be procured from his own Library, or that of a Noble Lord, and which have given a Pretence to the publishing others as his which are not so, as well as Interpolating those which are;] This is to advertise, that if either of the said Persons will discover the Whole of this Affair, he shall receive a Reward of *Twenty Guineas*; or if he can prove he hath acted by* *Direction of any other,* and of *what Person,* he shall receive double that Sum.

Whether this Advertisement, or the future Quarrel of *Curl* and *Smith* about Profits produced what follow'd we cannot say, but in a few Days the ensuing Papers, being the whole[34] Correspondence of *P. T.* and *Edm. Curl* were sent to the Publisher *T. Cooper,*[35] which we shall here lay before the Reader.

They begin as high as[36]

No. IV.

October the 11*th,* 1733.

Mr. CURL,

Understanding you propose to write the *Life* of *Mr. Pope,*[37] this is only to inform you, I can send you diverse Memoirs which may be serviceable, if your Design be really to do him neither Injustice, nor shew him Favour. I was well acquainted with his Father, and with the first part of his own Life, tho' since he has treated me as a Stranger. It is certain some late Pamphlets are not fair in respect to his Father, who was of the younger Branch of a Family in good

* *For* Curl *had said in his advertisement, that he wrote to Mr. P. By* Direction, *and another of his drawing up of Mr.* Pope's Life *began thus,* By Direction.———[33]

Repute in *Ireland,* and related to the Lords *Downe,* formerly of the same Name. He was (as he hath told me himself, and he was [very different from his Son] a modest and plain honest Man) a Posthumous Son, and left little provided for, his elder Brother having what small Estate there was, who afterwards Study'd and dy'd at *Oxford.* He was put to a Merchant in *Flanders,* and acquir'd a moderate Fortune by Merchandize, which he quitted at the Revolution in very good Circumstances, and retir'd to *Windsor* Forrest, where he purchas'd a small Estate, and took great Delight in Husbandry and Gardens. His Mother was one of seventeen Children of *W. Turnor* Esq; formerly of *Burfit Hall* in the ——Riding of *Yorkshire.* Two of her Brothers were kill'd in the Civil Wars. This is a true Account of Mr. *Pope*'s Family and Parentage.[38] Of his Manners I cannot give so good an one, yet as I would not wrong any Man, both ought to be True; and if such be your Design, I may serve you in it, not entering into any Thing in any wise Libellous. You may please to direct an Answer in the *Daily Advertiser* this Day-sennight in these Terms ——*E. C. hath received a Letter, and will comply with P. T.*

Yours.

On the backside of this Letter is endors'd in *Curl's* Hand,
Notice was accordingly given, as Desir'd, in the Daily Advertiser, *upon which was sent the following Letter.*[39]

No. V.

Nov. 15 1733.

SIR,

I troubled you with a Line some time since, concerning your Design of the *Life* of Mr. *Pope,* to which I desir'd your Answer in the *Daily Advertiser* of *Thursday* the 10th[40] Instant *October.* I do not intend my self any other Profit in it, than that of doing Justice to, and on, that Person, upon whom, Sir, you have conferr'd some Care as well as Pains in the Course of your Life; and I intend him the like for his Conduct towards me. *A propos* to his Life, there have lately fall'n into my Hands a large Collection of his *Letters,* from the former Part of his Days to the Year 1727. which being more considerable than any yet seen, and opening very many Scenes new to the World, will alone make a Perfect and the most authentick *Life* and *Memoirs* of him that could be. To shew you my Sincerity and determinate Resolution of assisting you herein, I will give you an Advertisement, which you may publish forthwith if you please, and on your so doing the Letters shall be sent you. They will make a Four or Five Sheet[41] Book, yet I expect no more than what will barely pay a Transcriber, that the Originals may be preserved in mine or your Hands to vouch the Truth of them. I am of Opinion these alone will contain his whole History (if you add to them what you formerly printed of those to *Henry Cromwell,* Esq; [*Here a part of the Letter is cut off, and the following Words indors'd by Curl*——But you must put out an Advertisement for——] otherwise I shall not be justify'd to some People who have *Influence,* and on whom I have some *Dependance*; unless it seem to the Publick Eye as no entire Act of mine; but I may be justify'd and excus'd, if, after they see such a Collection is made by you, I acknowledge I sent some Letters to contribute thereto. They who know what hath pass'd betwixt Mr. *Pope* and me formerly, may otherwise think it dishonourable I should set such a thing a-foot. Therefore print the Advertisement I sent you, and you shall instantly hear from or see me. Adieu, *T. P. Here a Postscript is cut off.*

There appears no other Letter from *P. T.* till one of *April* the *4th,* which must be in 1735, as it relates plainly to Mr. *Pope's* Advertisement in Answer to *Curl's* Letter to him of *March* 22*d.* which see above No. 3.

No. VI.

April 4.

I see an Advertisement in the Daily Advertisements, which I take to relate to Me. I did not expect you of all Men would have betray'd me to Squire *Pope*; but you and he both shall soon be convinc'd it was no *Forgery.* For since you would not comply with my Proposal to advertise, I have printed them at my own Expence, being advis'd that I could safely do so. I wou'd still give you the Preference, if you'll pay the Paper and Print, and allow me handsomely for the Copy. But I shall not trust you to meet and converse upon it [after the Suspicion I have of your Dealings with Master *P.*] unless I see my Advertisement of the Book printed first, within these Four or

Five days. If you are afraid of Mr. *P.* and dare not set your Name to it, as I propos'd at first, I do not insist thereupon, so I be but conceal'd. By this I shall determine, and if you will not, another will. It makes a Five Shilling Book. I am

Your servant,
P. T.

No. VII.

On a Scrap of Paper torn from a Letter, the Direction crost out,
SIR,
   I should not deal thus Cautiously or in the Dark with you, but that 'tis plain from your own Advertisement, that you have been Treating with Mr. *Pope.*

No. VIII.

On another Piece cut off,
   I still give you, Sir, the Preference. If you will give me 3*l.* a Score for 650 [each Book containing 380 Pages 8*vo.*] and pay down 75*l.* of the same, the whole Impression shall be yours, and there are Letters enough remaining (if you require) to make another 30 Sheets 8*vo.* a Five Shillings Book. You need only Answer thus in the *Daily Post* or *Advertiser* in four Days——[42] [*E. C.* will meet *P. T.* at the *Rose Tavern* by the Play-House at Seven in the Evening *April* 22d] and one will come, and show you the Sheets.

Mr. CURL'S ANSWERS.
No. IX.

29th April 1735.

SIR,
I have not ever met with any thing more inconsistent than the several Proposals of your Letters. The First bearing Date *Oct.* 11*th* 1733. gives some Particulars of Mr. *Pope's Life,* which I shall shortly make a publick Use of, in his Life now going to the Press.
   The Second of your Letters of *Nov.* 15*th* 1733, informs me That if I would publish an Advertisement of a Collection of Mr. *Pope's*

Letters in your Custody, the Originals should be forthwith sent me, and for which you would expect no more than what would pay for a Transcript of 'em.

In your Third Letter of the Fourth Instant, you groundlesly imagine I have attempted to betray you to Mr. *Pope*; say you have printed these Letters your self, and now want to be handsomely allow'd for the Copy, *viz.* 3*l.* a Score, which is 2*l.* more than they cost Printing; appoint a Meeting at the *Rose* on the 22*d.* Instant, where I was to see the Sheets, dealing thus, as you truly call it, in the Dark.

April 21, You put off this Meeting, fearing a Surprize from Mr. *Pope.* How should he know of this Appointment, unless you gave him Notice? I fear no such Besettings either of him or his Agents. That the paying of seventy-five Pounds would bring you to Town in a Fortnight, would I be so silly as to declare it. By your last Letter, of last Night, a Gentleman is to be at my Door, at Eight this Evening, who has full Commission from you.

You want seventy-five Pounds for a Person you would serve; That Sum I can easily pay, if I think the Purchase would be of any Service to me. But in one Word, Sir, I am engaged all this Evening, and shall not give my self any further Trouble about such jealous, groundless, and dark Negociations. An HONOURABLE and OPEN DEALING is what I have been always used to, and if you will come into such a Method, I will meet you any-where, or shall be glad to see you at my own House, otherwise apply to whom you please.

Yours,
E. C.

For P. T. *or the Gentleman who comes from him at Eight this Evening.*
This appears to be the first Time *Curl* had any personal Conference with *R. Smith* the Clergyman.

No. X.
To the Reverend Mr. ***

SIR,

I am ready to discharge the Expence of Paper, Print, and Copy-Money, and make the Copy my own, if we agree. But if I am to be your Agent, then I insist to be solely so, and will punctually pay every Week for what I sell to you.——

No. XI.
Answer to P. T.'s *of 3d of* May.

SIR,

You shall, as all I have ever had any Dealings with have, find a JUST and HONOURABLE Treatment from me. But consider, Sir, as the Publick, by your Means entirely, have been led into an Initial Correspondence betwixt *E. C.* and *P. T.* and betwixt *A. P.* and *E. C.* the Secret is still as recondite as that of the Free-Masons. *P. T.* are not, I dare say, the true Initials of your Name; or if they were, Mr. *Pope* has publickly declar'd, *That he knows no such Person as* P. T. how then can any thing you have communicated to me, discover you, or expose you to his Resentment?

I have had Letters from another Correspondent, who subscribes himself *E. P.*[43] which I shall print as Vouchers, in Mr. *Pope's* Life, as well as those from *P. T.* which, as I take it, were all sent me for that Purpose, or why were they sent at all?

Your Friend was with me on *Wednesday* last, but I had not your last till this Morning, *Saturday* 3d of *May.* I am, Sir, *Yours,*

E. C.

P. S. What you say appears by my Advertisement in relation to Mr. *Pope,* I faithfully told your Friend the Clergyman. I wrote to Mr. *Pope,* to acquaint him that I was going to print a new Edition of his Letters to Mr. *Cromwell,* and offer'd him the Revisal of the Sheets, hoping likewise, that it was now time to close all former Resentments, which, ON HONOURABLE TERMS, I was ready to do. I told him likewise I had a large Collection of others of his Letters, which, *from your two Years Silence on that Head, I thought was neither unjust nor dishonourable.*

No. XII.

———I cannot send the *Letters now, because I have them not all by me, but either this Evening or To-morrow, you shall not fail of them, for some of them are in a Scrutore of mine out of Town, and I have sent a Messenger for them, who will return about Three or

* P. T.'s *Letters to* Curl.

Four this Afternoon. Be not uneasy, I NEVER BREAK MY WORD, and as HONOURABLE and JUST Treatment shall be shewn by me, I shall expect the same Return.

The Estimate and Letters you shall have together, but I desire the Bearer may bring me fifty more Books. Pray come to Night, if you can.

I am faithfully yours,
E. CURL.

For the Reverend Mr Smith
(*half an Hour past Ten.*)

Curl was now so elated with his Success, the Books in his Hands, and, as he thought, the Men too, that he raised the Style of his Advertisement, which he publish'd on the 12th of *May,* in these Words, in the *Daily Post-Boy.*[44]

No. XIII.

This Day are published, and most beautifully printed, Price five Shillings, Mr. Pope's *Literary Correspondence for* thirty *Years; from* 1704 *to* 1734. *Being a Collection of Letters, regularly digested, written by him to the Right Honourable the late Earl of* Hallifax, *Earl of* Burlington, *Secretary* Craggs, *Sir* William Trumbull, *Honourable* J. C. *General****, Honourable* Robert Digby, *Esq; Honourable* Edward Blount, *Esq; Mr.* Addison,, *Mr.* Congreve, *Mr.* Wycherly, *Mr.* Walsh, *Mr.* Steele, *Mr.* Gay, *Mr.* Jarvas, *Dr.* Arbuthnot, *Dean* Berkeley, *Dean* Parnelle, *&c. Also Letters from Mr.* Pope *to Mrs.* Arabella Fermor, *and many other Ladies.* With the respective Answers of each Correspondent. *Printed for* E. Curl *in* Rose-street, Covent-Garden, *and sold by all Booksellers. N. B. The* Original Manuscripts (*of which Affidavit is made*) *may be seen at Mr.* Curl's *House by all who desire it.*

And immediately after he writes thus to *Smith*.

No. XIV.

12th *May,* 1735.

SIR,

Your Letter written at Two Afternoon on *Saturday,* I did not receive till past Ten at Night. The *Title* will be done to Day, and

according to your Promise, I fully depend on the Books and MSS. To-morrow. I hope you have seen the *Post-Boy*, and *approve the* Manner *of the Advertisement.* I shall think every Hour a long Period of Time till I have more Books, and see you, being, Sir,
(*For the Reverend Mr. Smith.*) *Sincerely yours,*
E. CURL.

But the Tables now began to turn. It happened that the Booksellers Bill (*for so it was properly called, tho' entitled,* An Act for the better Encouragement of Learning) *came on this Day in the House of Lords:*[46] *Some of their Lordships having seen an Advertisement of so* strange a Nature, *thought it very unfitting such a Bill should pass, without a* Clause *to prevent such an enormous* License *for the future. And the Earl of* I— —y[47] *having read it to the House, observed further, that as it pretended to publish several Letters to* Lords, *with the* respective Answers of each Correspondent, *it was a* Breach of Privilege,[48] and *contrary to a standing Order of the House. Whereupon it was order'd that the Gentleman Usher of the Black Rod do forthwith seize the Impression of the said Book, and that the said* E. Curl, *with* J. Wilford, *for whom the* Daily Post-Boy *is printed, do attend the House To-morrow. And it was also order'd that the* Bill for the better Encouragement of Learning, *be read a second time on this Day Sevennight.* BY THIS INCIDENT THE BOOKSELLERS BILL WAS THROWN OUT.[49]

May 13, 1735.

The Order made Yesterday upon Complaint of an Advertisement in the Post-Boy, *of the Publication of a Book entitled Mr.* Pope's Literary Correspondence for thirty Years past, *being read, Mr.* Wilford *the Publisher, and Mr.* E. Curl, *were severally called in and examined, and being withdrawn,*

Order'd, That the Matter of the said Complaint be refer'd to a Committee to meet To-morrow, and that E. Curl *do attend the said Committee. And that the Black Rod do attend with some of the said Books.*

May 14. *P. T.* writes to *Curl,* on the unexpected Incident of the Lords, to instruct him in his Answers to their Examination, and with the utmost Care to conceal himself, to this effect.

* *By this it appears, it was of* Curl's *own drawing up, which he deny'd to the Lords.*[45]

No. XV.

That he congratulates him on his Victory over the Lords, *the* Pope, *and the* Devil; *that the* Lords *could not touch a Hair of his Head, if he continued to behave boldly; that it would have a better Air*[50] *in him to own the* Printing *as well as the* Publishing, *since he was no more punishable for one than for the other; that he should answer nothing more to their Interrogatories, than that he receiv'd the Letters from* different Hands; *that some of them he* bought, *others were* given him, *and that some of the* Originals he had, *and the rest he should shortly have.* P. T. tells him further, *That he shall soon take off the* Mask *he complains of; that he is not a* MAN OF QUALITY (*as he imagined*) *but* one conversant with such, and was concern'd particularly with a noble Friend of Mr. Pope's, in preparing for the Press the Letters to Mr. Wycherly; *that he caused a Number over and above to be printed, having from that time conceived the Thought of publishing a Volume of* P's Letters, *which he went on with, and order'd, as nearly as possible,* to resemble That Impression. *But this was only* in ordine ad, *to another more material Volume, of his Correspondence with Bishop* Atterbury, *and the late Lord* Oxford *and* Bolingbroke. *And he confesses he made some* Alterations *in* these Letters, *with a* View to those, *which Mr.* Curl *shall certainly have, if he behaves as he directs, and every way conceals* P. T.

We have not this original Letter, but we hope Mr. *Curl* will print it;[51] if not, it can only be for this Reason, That as it preceded their Quarrel but one Day,[52] it proves the Letters to Bishop *Atterbury*, Lord *Bollingbroke*, &c. cannot be in *Curl*'s Hands, tho' he has pretended to advertise them.[53]

The next day *Curl* answers him thus.

No. XVI.

Thursday 9 *Manè,* 15th *May,* 1735.
Dear Sir,

I am just again going to the Lords to finish *Pope*. I desire you to send me the Sheets to perfect the first fifty Books, and likewise the remaining three hundred Books, and pray be at the *Standard* Tavern this Evening, and I will pay you twenty pounds more. My Defence is right, I only told the Lords, I did not know from whence the

Books came, and that my Wife receiv'd them. This was strict Truth, and prevented all further Enquiry. The *Lords declar'd* they had been made *Pope's Tool.* I put my self upon this single Point, and insisted, as there was not any Peer's Letter in the Book, I had not been guilty of any Breach of Privilege.——*Lord* Delawar *will be in the Chair by Ten this Morning,* and the House will be up before Three.——I depend that the Books and the Imperfections will be sent, and believe of *P. T.* what I hope he believes of me.

For the Reverend Mr. Smith.

The Book was this Day produc'd, and it appearing that, contrary to the Advertisement,[54] there were no Letters of Lords contain'd in it, and consequently not falling under the Order of the House, the Books were re-deliver'd.

At the same time *Curl* produc'd, and shew'd to several of the Lords the *foregoing Letter* of *P. T.*[55] which seems extraordinary, unless they had begun to quarrel about *Profits* before that Day. But after it, it is evident from the next Letter, that they had an Information of his Willingness to betray them, and so get the whole Impression to himself.[56]

No. XVII.

To the Reverend Mr. Smith.

Rose Street past Three
Friday 16 *May* 1735.

SIR,

1. I am falsly accus'd, 2. I value not any man's Change of Temper; I will never change MY VERACITY for Falshood, in owning a Fact of which I am Innocent. 3. I did not own the Books came from *across the Water,* nor ever *nam'd you,* all I said was, that the Books came *by Water.* 4. When the Books were seiz'd I sent my Son to convey a Letter to you, and as you told me every body knew you in *Southwark,* I bid him make a *strict Enquiry,* as I am sure you wou'd have done in such an Exigency. 5. Sir I HAVE ACTED JUSTLY in this Affair, and that is what I shall always think wisely. 6. I will be kept no longer in the Dark: *P. T.* is *Will o' the Wisp;* all the Books I have had are Imperfect; the First 50 had no Titles nor Prefaces, the last 5 Bundles seiz'd by the Lords contain'd but 38 in each Bundle,

which amounts to 190, and 50, is in all but 240 Books. 7. As to the Loss of a Future Copy, I despise it, nor will I be concern'd with any more such dark suspicious Dealers. But now Sir I'll tell you what I will do; when I have the Books perfected which I have already receiv'd, and the rest of the Impression I will pay you for them. But what do you call this Usage? First take a Note for a Month and then want it to be chang'd for one of Sir *Richard Hoare's*——My Note is as good, for any Sum I give it, as the BANK, and shall be as punctually paid. I always say, *Gold is better than Paper,* and 20 *l.* I will pay, if the Books are perfected to morrow Morning, and the rest sent, or to Night is the same thing to me. But if this dark converse goes on, I will Instantly *reprint the whole Book,* and as a Supplement to it, *all the Letters* P. T. *ever sent me,* of which I have *exact copies*; together with *all your Originals,* and give them in upon Oath to my Lord Chancellor. You talk of *Trust*; *P. T.* has not repos'd any in me, for he has my Mony and Notes for imperfect Books. Let me see, Sir, either *P. T.* or your self, or you'll find the *Scots* Proverb verify'd

> *Nemo me impune lacessit.*
> *Your abus'd humble Servant,*
> E. CURL.

P. S. LORD—— I attend this Day. LORD DELAWAR I SUP WITH TO NIGHT. Where *Pope* has one Lord, I have twenty.[57]

Mr. *Curl,* just after, in the *London Post* or *Daily Advertiser,* printed this Advertisement[58]

No. XVIII.

—Mr. *Pope's* Litterary Correspondence &c. with a Supplement, of the *Initial Correspondence* of *P. T.   E. P.   R. S. &c.*

To which in two Days more his Correspondents return'd the following[59]

No. XIX.

To manifest to the World the Insolence of *E. Curl,* we hereby declare that neither *P. T.* much less *R. S.* his Agent, ever did give, or could pretend to give any Title whatever in Mr. *Pope's* Letters to the said *E. Curl,* and he is hereby challeng'd to produce any Pretence to the Copy whatsoever. ———We help'd the said *E. Curl* to the Letters, and join'd with him, on Condition he should pay a certain Sum for the Books *as he sold them*; accordingly the said *E. Curl* receiv'd 250 Books which he sold (Perfect and Imperfect) at 5 *shill.* each, and for all which he never paid more than 10 Guineas, and gave *Notes* for the rest which prov'd *not Negotionable.* Besides which, *P. T.* was perswaded by *R. S.* at the Instigation of *E. Curl,* to pay the Expence of the whole Impression, *viz* 75 *l.* no part whereof was repaid by the said *Curl.* Therefore every Bookseller will be indemnify'd every way from any possible Prosecution or Molestation of the said *E. Curl,* and whereas the said *E. Curl* threatens to publish our Correspondence, and as much as in him lies, to *betray his Benefactors,* we shall also publish *his Letters to us,* which will open a Scene of Baseness and Foul Dealing that will sufficiently show to Mankind his Character and Conduct.[60]

May 23d. 1735. P. T. R. S.

The Effect of this Quarrel has been the putting into our Hands all the Correspondence above; which having given the Reader, to make what Reflections he pleases on, we have nothing to add but our hearty Wishes, (in which we doubt not every honest Man will concur,) that the next *Sessions,* when the BOOKSELLERS BILL shall be again brought in, the Legislature will be pleas'd not to *extend* the *Privileges,* without at the same Time *restraining the Licence, of Booksellers.*[61] Since in a Case so *notorious* as the printing a Gentleman's PRIVATE LETTERS, most Eminent,[62] both *Printers* and *Booksellers,* conspired to assist the Pyracy[63] both in printing and in vending the same.

P. S.

We are Inform'd, that notwithstanding the Pretences of Edmund Curl,[64] *the Original Letters of Mr.* Pope *with the Post-Marks upon them, remain still in the Books from whence they were copy'd, and that so many Omissions and Interpolations have been made in this Publication as to render it Impossible for Mr. P. to own them in the Condition they appear.*[65]

FINIS.

Annotations

1. "Mr *Pope* is the Son of a Trader, and so is Mr *Curll*——*par nobile.*" [Curll.] [This and subsequent notes marked *Curll* are the rejoinders he appended to his reprinting of the *Narrative* to be found in the second volume of his first 1735 edition of the letters (Griffith 386).]

2. Protective legislation was limited in the eighteenth century. In Pope's time the author's legal rights had been more clearly established than ever before with the Act of Queen Anne in 1710 ("An Act for the Encouragement of Learning by Vesting the Copies of Printed Books in the Authors, or Purchasers of such Copies, during the Times therein mentioned"), but its provisions had expired by 1731 and the confused distinction between authorship and ownership of literary pieces still made publishing a risky business. In 1721 a provision made it a breach of privilege to publish a lord's work without his consent; other individuals were not equally protected.

The Booksellers' Bill—An Act for the better Encouragement of Learning— being considered by Parliament at the time of the *Narrative,* was concerned with protecting booksellers' interests, but Pope apparently hoped that his current experience with Curll, brought as it was to the attention of the House of Lords, might lead to a "*Clause* to prevent such an enormous *License* for the future." It was not, though, until 1741, again in a confrontation with Curll, that Pope was to be successful in establishing an author's copyright in personal letters. (See Pat Rogers, "The Case of Pope *v.* Curll," *Library,* 27 [1972], 326–31.)

3. *Miscellanea*: Griffith 177. Dated 1727, the work was published in 1726.

4. Henry Cromwell, critic and man about town, an early friend of Pope, and one of the coffeehouse group with whom he associated when first he went up to London. Their friendship and correspondence, most active between 1709 and 1711, cooled as hostility developed between Pope and Cromwell's great friend John Dennis.

5. Elizabeth Thomas, poetaster and celebrity hunter, who under the name of "Corinna" contributed her share to Curll's long and dubious list of publications. She was to tangle again with Pope when, in retaliation for a rather brutal attack in the *Dunciad,* she and Curll brought out the ineffectual *Codrus: or, the Dunciad Dissected.*

6. "These Letters were a free Gift; so that there was not any Occasion to ask the Consent of either of those Parties. Mr *Curll* purchased them as justly as Mr *Lintot* did the Copy of Mr *Pope's Homer,* &c." [Curll.] This contention by Curll was refuted in a court case in 1741 over his publication of the Pope-Swift correspondence. At that time it was ruled that before transmission a letter was the absolute property of the author, that the receiver acquired only a special or qualified property, perhaps to the paper but not to the contents of the letter, and that

this gave him no right of publication. (Pope *vs.* Curll, 2 Atk[yns's Reports, Chancery, Br.] 342.)

7. See n. 6.

8. Evidently John Dennis, the critic and adversary of Pope, who was a close friend of Cromwell; in fact it was Cromwell who first introduced Pope to him.

9. Cf. Sherburn, *Correspondence,* II, 439n: "On a fly-leaf of the Bodleian MSS. Rawlinson Letters 90 is written 'Original Letters under the Hands of Mr John Dryden, Charles Dryden, ——Norris, —— Pope, Lady Chudleigh, Mrs Thomas, Dr. Ed: Young.' Rawlinson was an antiquary who published through Curll, from whom he must have got those Cromwell letters, now in Bodley." In the second volume of *Pylades and Corinna* ("Memoirs of the Lives, Amours, and Writings of Richard Gwinnett and Mrs. Eliz. Thomas"), published in 1732, there is a collection of letters between Mrs. Thomas and Norris [John Norris (1657–1711), author of philosophical essays and poems], Lady Chudleigh [Lady Mary Chudleigh (1656–1710), poetical writer], Lady Packington [Lady Hester Packington (d. 1715), of Westwood, Wor.], and others.

10. Though Cromwell refers to Mrs. Thomas as "Sapho," she was more generally known as "Corinna"—especially in her capacity as one of Curll's little band of hacks. The name was conferred upon her (by her own request according to the DNB) by Dryden, who is also reported to have commented, "I would have called you Sapho, but that I hear you are handsomer."

11. William Pattison, another of the number of needy authors in the employ of Curll. Shortly after this reference, on 11 July 1727, he died of smallpox—though Pope is supposed to have accused Curll of starving him to death (EC VI, 133n). His posthumously printed works were subscribed to by Pope and included a poem addressed to him.

12. Précieuse.

13. Curll was always ready to exploit any publicity for his publications. As it was, not long after this letter, in November, he was advertising a "new" edition of the correspondence (see n. 20).

14. Pope, for instance, had written Caryll (5 December 1726): ". . . .I will begin by entreating of you to consult my fame, such as it is, and to help me to put out of Curl's power [the Cromwell letters had come out that summer] any trifling remains of mine. If therefore you have preserved any verses or letters, I beg you to send them to me (as I will desire every man to do whom I know to be my friend)." (*Correspondence,* II, 419.) The entreaties were not in vain, for as he reported to Swift on one occasion, "I lately receiv'd from the widow of one dead correspondent, and from the father of another, several of my own letters of about fifteen or twenty years old. . . ." (*Correspondence,* III, 79; 28 November 1729.)

15. "This is a notorious Falshood, for it will be proved that the Books sold

by *R. S.* to Mr *Curll,* were printed at Mr *Pope's* Expence." [Curll.] Pope's public attitude on this matter, however, was unwavering. The very day that saw the publication of his letters by Curll—the result, of course, of his own careful engineering—found him writing to Caryll,

> But what makes me sick of writing is the shameless industry of such fellows
> as Curle, and the idle ostentation, or weak partiality of many of my cor-
> respondents, who have shewn about my letters (which I never writ but in
> haste, and generally against the grain, in mere civility), for almost all
> letters, are impertinent farther than *si bene valeas, bene est, ego valeo* to such
> a degree that a volume of 200, or more are printed by that rascal: But he
> could never have injured me this way, had not my friends furnished him
> with the occasion by keeping such wretched papers as they ought to have
> burned. (*Correspondence,* III, 455.)

Five years later, when he was again embroiled in epistolary publication, this time with seeing into print his and Swift's correspondence, he was equally con-cerned that there be no "Imputation" of his involvement. (*Correspondence,* IV, 286.) Yet one can appreciate Pope's dilemma, bound as he was by the conventions of the day which proscribed normal publication of his letters: he would have them published—but not until they had been properly prepared for the public, many of them being the extravagances of his youth.

16. For Pope to appear innocent, it was necessary for the letters to be out of his hands; therefore, the library of his good friend Edward Harley, earl of Oxford, which served both as a depository for his papers and as a source for transcriptions, was an important factor in his plans. See George Sherburn, "Pope's Letters and the Harleian Library," *English Literary History,* 7 (1940), 177–87.

17. In his youthful friendship with Wycherley, Pope had undertaken to assist the then elderly poet in preparing some poems for publication, a project which they later deemed wise to abandon. In spite of this decision, a posthumous volume was brought out in 1728 by his widow's next husband and Lewis Theobald, who had already incurred Pope's enmity by criticism of his edition of Shakespeare. See V. A. Dearing, "Pope, Theobald, and Wycherley's *Posthumous Works,*" *PMLA* 68 (1953), 223–36.

18. Pope's countering volume, which he entitled *The Posthumous Works. . . . Vol. II* (Griffith 223), was suppressed—perhaps because of copyright problems; but he acquired the sheets and saved them for his [P. T.'s] 1735 edition of the letters. Even from the Wycherley volume, Pope chose to remain nominally dis-engaged. Its preface (q.v.: pp. 305ff.) cites Lord Oxford as the party responsible for freeing the papers from his library.

19. "This is another Falshood, Mr *Curll* only gave a Copy of this Pamphlet to *R. S.* to shew *P. T.* that he had reprinted those Letters which came out in

1728, and corrected the *Errata* therein." [Curll.] It will be noticed that Curll's reply, though labelling Pope's charge a "falshood," fails to answer it.

20. "Falshood the *Third*. Mr *Curll* defies any Man living to produce any such Advertisement." [Curll.] In 1727 (*St. James's Evening Post*, 9/11 November) and again in 1729 (*St. James's Evening Post*, 25/27 February), Curll had advertised "This Day was publish'd a New Edition of Mr. Pope's Familiar Letters to Henry Cromwell, Esq." When he was advertising the *Literary Correspondence* (in May 1735) he called attention to the "Letters to Mr. Cromwell" as also available at his house—with no mention this time, though, of a new edition.

21. In the *Daily Post-Boy* for 19 May 1735, following an advertisement of Pope's letters, Curll listed among "Books now in the Press" the Letters of Mr. Prior and Mr. Addison.

22. "None can be more a *Scoundrel* than the Writer of this Narrative, as many Falshoods detected in it will prove." [Curll.] Curll's self-righteous indignation might provoke more sympathy if his reputation were not so unsavory on this very score. As Swift, another of his victims, commented (from "On the Death of Dr. Swift"):

> He'll treat me as he does my betters,
> Publish my will, my life, my letters:
> Revive the libels born to die,
> Which Pope must bear, as well as I.

For an engaging account of Curll's ingenuities in this area, see Straus, pp. 23ff.

23. "Stupid Impertinence! what has Mr *Curll* to do with Dean *Smedley*'s Book called *Gulliveriana*? or with the Conduct of any Other Person? nor was Mr *Curll* any ways concern'd in printing *Gulliveriana*." [Curll.] The reference is to a collection published in 1728 for Jonathan Smedley by J. Roberts: *Gulliveriana: or, A Fourth Volume of Miscellanies. Being A Sequel of the Three Volumes, published by Pope and Swift. To which is added, Alexanderiana; or, A Comparison between the Ecclesiastical and Poetical Pope. And many Things, in Verse and Prose, relating to the latter. With an ample Preface; and a Critique on the Third Volume of Miscellanies lately publish'd by those two facetious Writers*. Curll is of course sidestepping the issue of disclaiming any connection with *Gulliveriana*, since the charge concerns a sequel to it or an advertisement of such a sequel. [I have not come across the advertisement.]

24. "A greater Favour than Mr *Pope* deserved at his Hands." [Curll.]

25. "Doubtless that was Mr *Curll*'s Intent, or he need not have acquainted Mr *Pope* with his Design of printing a new Edition." [Curll.]

26. Falshood the *Fourth*. One hundred Guineas will be paid to this Narrative-Writer if he can produce any such Advertisement of Mr *Curll*'s. This is founded on a merry Story, and the Fact as follows, *viz*. Mr *Henry Hoare*,

eldest Son of Sir *Richard Hoare*, came to Mr *Curll* and told him, that Dr *Robinson*, then Bishop of *London*, heard he was concern'd in printing an Edition of the Earl of *Rochester*'s Poems. Mr *Curll* told Mr *Hoare*, that he was, among other Booksellers and Printers, (*viz.* Mr *Darby* in *Batholomew-Close*, Mr *Bettesworth*, in *Pater-noster-row*, Mr *Rivington*, in *St. Paul's Church-yard*, Mr *Pemberton*, in *Fleet-street*, &c.) concerned in an Edition of that Nobleman's Works. But likewise told Mr *Hoare*, that he would get a Book interleav'd for my Lord Bishop, and whatever his Lordship saw amiss, if he would be pleased to strike out any Lines, or Poems therein, such Leaves should be re-printed, and render'd conformable to his Lordship's Opinion. Away goes Mr *Hoare*, overjoy'd with this Message from Mr *Curll*, with a tender of his Duty to the Bishop, and opens his Credentials; upon hearing which the Bishop smil'd, and made the following Reply to Mr *Hoare*. Sir, I am told that Mr *Curll* is a shrewd Man, and should I revise the Book you have brought me, he would publish it as approv'd by me. This no doubt Mr *Curll* might justly have done, for whatever is not condemn'd is approv'd; a Standing-Maxim This, in Civil, Canon, and Common Law. [Curll.]

Again it is to be noted that in denying the fact Curll admits the intent; in fact, Straus, who reproduces this account, comments on Curll's fondness for bishops and cites also his vain attempts to persuade the Bishop of Peterborough to consent to the republication of some of his youthful indiscretions. Curll's Rochester publications illustrate, too, another of his techniques, mentioned earlier (see n. 22). He had advertised, in the *Post-Boy* of 14 March 1708, the appearance of a new edition of the works of Rochester and Roscommon "with some Memoirs"; there were no books but subsequently there were numerous public appeals for material: "Those Gentlemen that have any Papers by them of the Earl of Rochester's, or Roscommon's, if they please to send 'em as soon as possible, they shall have so many of the Books neatly bound as is proportional to what they communicate, or any other gratification of the undertaker E. Curll." (Straus, p. 23.)

27. The advertisement, in slightly different form ("Whereas E. C. Bookseller, has written to Mr. P——. . . ."), appeared in the *Daily Post-Boy* on 3 April [Griffith mistakenly lists it as 4 April], the same day it appeared in the *Grub-Street Journal*. It was also published in the *Daily Journal*, on the 4th.

28. "It was universally allow'd to be a very pertinent one." [Curll.] Curll's reply did not appear in the *Daily Post-Boy* of 4 April ("the same Paper the next Day"); it might have been printed in the 5 April issue, but I have not seen a copy of that to check. However, Curll included the document in his "Initial Correspondence" (see n. 34), where it runs as follows:

Whereas *A. P.* Poet, has certified in the *Daily Post-Boy*, that he shall not trouble himself at all about the Publication of a large Collection of the said Mr *P*——'s Letters which *P. T.* hath offered *E. C.* to print. This is to certify, that Mr *C.* never had, nor intended ever to have, any private Correspondence with *A. P.* but was directed to give him Notice of these Letters. Now to put all *Forgeries,* even *Popish ones,* to flight; this is to give Notice, that any Person, (or, *A. P.* himself) may see the ORIGINALS, in Mr *P*——'s own Hand, when printed. *Initials* are a *Joke*; Names at length are *real.*

> *No longer now like Suppliants we come,*
> E. C. *makes War, and* A. P. *is the drum.*

(Curll, Appendix II to "Initial Correspondence," pp. 28–29.)

29. The advertisement appeared at the end of a long listing by Curll in the *Daily Post-Boy* of 8 April 1735.

30. "This is false: *E. P.* is a Nobleman, *P. T.* is a Scrub." [Curll.] According to Curll, on 27 March 1733—some six months before his first communication from P. T.—he had received from an unidentified "E. P." some anecdotes about Pope's early schooling. Since these accounts, whatever their source, were not very complimentary to the poet, being "a Proof of that *natural spleen* which constitutes his *Temperament,*" Curll was happy to include the letter in his prefatory "Anecdotes of the Life and Family of *Alexander Pope,* Esq." to be found, with the P. T. papers, in the second volume of his 1735 printing of the letters. And he had advertised (*Daily Journal,* 30 March 1733) *The Life of Mr. Pope,* where "Nothing shall be wanting but his (universally desired) Death" [with a notation following about the anecdotes that he had received the few days before].

31. "Smith" (Curll's Smythe) was supposedly enacted by a painter named James Worsdale. Dr. Johnson, who reported the alleged role, characterized him as one "employed in clandestine negotiations, but whose veracity was very doubtful." (*Lives,* III, 158.)

32. Curll reprinted the advertisement (which had appeared in the *Daily Post-Boy* for 20 May 1735) in the Appendix to his "Initial Correspondence" (see n. 34) along with his reply (taken from the *Daily Post-Boy* of 21 May): "Whereas it is promised in Mr. *Pope's* Name (in the *Daily Post-Boy*) that *Twenty Guineas* shall be paid to a Person who signs himself *P. T.* to discover *R. S.* or *Forty Guineas* shall be paid to *R. S.* if he will discover *P. T.* or any body else who was in the Confederacy of publishing Mr. *Pope's* Letters. This is to give Notice, that another Person who writes himself *E. P.* was likewise concerned with *Edm. Curll* in the said Important Confederacy, who have all jointly and severally agreed to oblige Mr. *Pope,* if he will make it worth their while, and let *E. Curll* print his Works for the future. . . ." (Appendix to "Initial Correspondence," pp. 29–30.) Once the "Plot" was "discovered"—to use Curll's own words—and he was writing up his account of it, he concluded his "*To Mr. Pope*" (in volume two of the *Literary*

Correspondence) with a bill, one item of which was forty-two pounds, "To discover the *Publishers* of Mr. *Pope's Letters*"—his last word on the famous forty guineas.

33. "N. B. *This was true,* E. Curll." [Curll.]

34. "False. It is not *Half*; see the *Initial Correspondence* hereto subjoined." [Curll.] In the second volume of his 1735 edition of the letters, Curll not only reprinted the "Narrative" [see n. 1] but he reproduced those letters and documents in his possession, with his own explanatory narrative, as "The *Initial Correspondence:* or, Anecdotes on the Life and Family of Mr Pope." This material supplements the *Narrative,* providing the reader with a connected account and with the complete series of letters and advertisements.

35. Although the *Narrative* was the first Pope volume to bear Cooper's imprint, he had brought out the "Booksellers" edition of the letters, and from this time became, along with Dodsley, one of Pope's preferred publishers. (Griffith, p. 304.)

36. In his reprinting of the *Narrative* Curll omits the next two letters, for he includes those in his "Initial Correspondence" [see n. 34], where they, as the first communications to him from P. T., introduce his version of what subsequently happened.

37. See n. 30. Curll was famous—or infamous—for his biographies, which Arbuthnot described as adding "a new terror to death." (Quoted in *Early Career,* p. 162.) For example, Curll's advertisement of "The Last Will and Testament" of Matthew Tindale, in the *Daily Journal* of 31 August 1733, listed twenty other "Lives and Last Wills" currently available.

> 38. The *Oxford* Antiquary informs us, that, *Thomas Pope,* the young Earl of *Downe,* died in St. *Mary*'s Parish in *Oxford,* 28 *Dec.* 1660, aged 38 Years leaving behind him one only Daughter named *Elizabeth,* who was first married to *Henry-Francis Lee* of *Dichley* in *Oxfordshire,* and afterwards to *Robert* Earl of *Lindsey.* The Earldom of *Downe,* went to *Thomas Pope,* Esq; his Uncle, who, likewise, having no Male-Issue, the Estate went away among *Three* Daughters; the *Second* of whom was married to Sir *Francis North,* afterwards Lord *North* of *Guilford.* Both these Earls of *Downe* were buried at *Wroxton,* near *Banbury,* in *Oxfordshire* with their Ancestors. (See *Wood*'s *Athen. Oxon.* Vol. II, pag. 543, Edit. ult.) [Curll: "Initial Correspondence," p. 9n.]

Although in a footnote to the "Epistle to Dr. Arbuthnot," Pope reported that his father was "of a gentleman's family in Oxfordshire, the head of which was the Earl of Downe," Sherburn has found nothing to indicate that Pope's family, the Andover Popes, were related to the Oxfordshire Popes; as he comments, "This account contains certain strikingly authentic facts—the posthumous birth would not be remembered outside the family—and certain equally striking bits of fiction:

William Pope shared alike with his brother in the family fortune, and so far as is known he neither studied nor died at Oxford." (*Early Career*, pp. 30–31.) The information about the poet's mother seems to be accurate.

39. My own investigations support Sherburn's statement that "search discovers no such advertisement." (*Correspondence*, I, xiii.)

40. Obviously a misprint for 18 October, seven days ("sen-night") from 11 October.

41. Corrected in reprintings to Four and Five *Shilling* Book.

42. The notice appeared in the *Daily Post-Boy*, 17 April 1735, as a postscript in Curll's advertisement—"E. C. hereby gives Notice, that he will be ready to receive the Papers relating to A. P. on the 22d instant, at Seven in the Evening, at the Place appointed."

43. See n. 30.

44. Where it did appear.

45. "This is *False*. Mr *Curll* told the Lords he copied the Advertisement, and returned the Original. This *R. S.* knows to be *True*." [Curll.] See n. 54.

46. The Act of Queen Anne [see n. 2], which had expired by this time, had, for a limited period, established copyright for the protection of authors, though it also served to cover booksellers. The booksellers, however, were really interested in perpetual copyright—and were constantly trying to get such a measure through Parliament. On the grounds that their rights were being infringed by imported publications, they had drawn up another petition in 1735, which passed Commons on 1 May and was then brought to the House of Lords. Here it was shelved when the second reading was indefinitely postponed.

47. Archibald Campbell, earl of Ilay (Islay) and later third duke of Argyle, was a neighbor of Pope at Whitton Park.

48. See n. 2.

49. "This is likewise a flagrant FALSHOOD." [Curll.] Though Pope may have had private information from his friends in the Lords, there is nothing to suggest that the failure of the bill was determined by this episode. Later bills, in 1737 and 1774, met the same fate; the only perpetual copyright remaining in the century was that held by the Universities, whose rights were confirmed by an act of Parliament in 1775.

50. "Mr. *Curll* was resolved not to put on that *Air of Lying P. T.* advised, but told the Lords *strict Truth*; which occasioned the Breach (not Quarrel) between them" [Curll.]

51. "Which he has done, in the *Initial Correspondence*, with several others." [Curll.]

52. "Mr *Curll* knows of no Quarrel, but much Roguery." [Curll.]

53. "Bishop *Atterbury*'s Letters, &c. are in Mr *Curll*'s Hands, which he is ready to produce." [Curll.] Pope's correspondence with Atterbury, a tender matter

because of the background of treason, became an issue in the publication of the later volumes of Curll's *Literary Correspondence* (see *Correspondence,* III, 473ff.).

54. *"False.* The Advertisement did not say there were any Peers Letters in the Book." [Curll.] Curll's testimony to the lords was that he had merely copied the advertisement sent him, and that by correspondents (in the advertisement's "respective Answers of each Correspondent") he had meant only such persons as had answered the letters. (From *Journals* of the House of Lords, extracted in EC VI, 433–34.) Whether Curll copied the advertisement, as he claimed, or copied it with significant alterations, or manufactured it himself (his statement of what *he* had meant by "respective Answers" points to one of the two latter), he undoubtedly appreciated the selling advantages of the implication that there were letters from noblemen.

55. *"False* again. Mr. Curll shewd the Letter at *Large,* not the *Extract* herein recited." [Curll.] This quibble is typical of many of Curll's rejoinders: while appearing to deny charges—and deny them vigorously—he often merely sidesteps the issue.

56. "This is false, *R. S.* having before contracted with Mr *Curll* for 600 books, and given him a Receipt for 300, but deliver'd only 240, and those all imperfect." [Curll.]

57. "This *P. S.* as Cooper printed it, contradicts itself. Mr *Curll* called at Lord *Delawar*'s House, and found him and Lord *Cowper* gone to *Holland.* And that Evening Mr *Curll* had the Honour to spend with Lord *Haversham.* As to Lords, Mr *Curll* might have double his Number." [Curll.] In Curll's own reprinting of the *Narrative,* the postscript reads, "Lord 0——, and Lord *Delaware,* I attend this Day. I'll Sup with you to Night. Where *Pope* has *one* Lord, I have twenty."

58. It appeared in the *Daily Post-Boy* on Thursday, 22 May 1735. On 17 May and 19 May R. S. had written to Curll (see Curll, "Initial Correspondence," pp. 25–27), first querulously about his behavior and then ingratiatingly, promising to "bring the Remainder of the Impression Thursday Evening." Curll retorted, on 22 May, with two manifestoes—"To the Most Noble and Right Honourable the PEERS of *Great-Britain*" and "To the Booksellers"—in which he crowed over his "triumph" before the Lords and announced a new edition of the letters: "Now, my Lords, to Matter of Fact, I shall this Week publish a new Edition of Mr *Pope's Literary Correspondence,* &c. wherein the Letters to Mr *Jarvas,* Mr *Digby,* Mr *Blount,* and Dr *Arnuthnot* (which were wanting in all the Copies seized by your Lordships' Order) shall be by me delivered *gratis.* And as I am resolved to detect, if possible, the Contrivers of this gross Imposition upon your Lordships. [*sic*] I will, by way of Supplement, print all the Letters I have received from *E. P. P. T.* and *R. S.* with some other Correspondence which, as Mr *Bays* says, shall both *Elevate* and *Surprize* the Public." (Appendix to "Initial Corre-

spondence," p. 31.) Griffith cites 23 May (error for 24 May) for the publication of the *Literary Correspondence,* referring to an advertisement in the *Daily Journal* No. 4480. The advertisement in that issue, however, is for the *Letters of Mr. Pope and several Eminent Hands,* not the Curll edition; in the same issue appeared P. T. and R. S.'s declaration "To manifest to the World . . ." (see n. 59).

59. Printed in the *Daily Journal,* 24 May 1735 (No. 4480).

60. To this Mr *Curll* replied, in the *Daily Post-Boy* of *May* 27, *viz.* Gentlemen, The Scurility of your Advertisement I despise; *Falshood* under your own Hands I shall here prove upon you; and as to your *Scandal* in affirming that *my Notes proved not Negotiable,* I will take proper Measures. It is declared, that neither *P. T.* much less *R. S.* his Agent, ever did give, or could pretend to give, any Title whatever, in Mr *Pope's* Letters to Mr *Curll,* and he is challenged to produce any Pretence to the Copy whatsoever. *P. T.* in his first Letter to Mr *Curll,* writes thus; To shew you my Sincerity and determinate Resolution, these Letters shall be sent you, they will make a four or five Shilling Book, yet *I expect no more than what will barely pay a Transcriber,* that the Originals may be preserved in your Hands to vouch the Truth of them. *Your's,* P. T. *P. S. I would have you add to them what you formerly printed of those to Mr* Cromwell. In a Letter from *R. S.* to Mr *Curll,* he thus writes. Sir, my Cousin (*P. T.*) desires you will get 600 of the Titles printed with all Expedition; and assures you, that no Man whatsoever shall vend a Book but yourself, for you shall have the whole Impression to be sure. *I shall leave it to your Generosity to consider me for the Copy.* I am, your Friend and Servant, *R. S.* On *Monday* the 12th Instant, Mr *Curll,* published these Letters, tho' he had but 50 Books, and those wanting Titles and Prefaces: But the same Day at Noon *R. S.* sent for Mr *Curll* to the *Standard* Tavern in *Leicester-Fields,* where Mr *Curll* paid him 30 *l.* (in Cash 10 *l.* by a negotiable Note, payable in a Month, 15 *l.* and a conditional Note for 5 *l.*) for which *R. S.* gave a Receipt to Mr *Curll* in full for 300 Books, delivering then by two Porters, five Bundles of 38 Books in each, making 190, which he said came by Water, and they sent to Mr *Curll's* House, and his Wife received them in his Absence. Mr *Curll* having had in all but 240 Books, tho' a Receipt given for 300, and the last 190 all delivered imperfect. I therefore desire to know, if this does not open a scene of Baseness and foul Dealing, that sufficiently shew to Mankind the Character and Conduct of *P. T.* and *R. S.?* I shall say no more till I publish the whole of their Transactions upon Oath. *E. Curll.* [Curll.]

61. It is J. McLaverty's argument that Pope designed the whole scheme against Curll with this in mind: that the episode would illustrate pointedly the unscrupulousness of some booksellers and the vulnerability of authors. ("The first printing and publication of Pope's letters," *Library,* 2 [1980], 264–80.)

62. "Mr *Pope* is no more a Gentleman than Mr *Curll,* nor more eminent as a Poet, than he as a Bookseller." [Curll.]

63. "T. *Cooper's* Edition [The Booksellers of London edition] is the pirated one, and which all honest Booksellers, and the Public, have agreed to discourage." [Curll.]

64. "Mr *Curll* never pretended to have any more Letters of Mr *Pope's* than he produced to the Lords in Committee." [Curll.]

65. "Mr *Pope* well knows that these Letters now *appear* as he directed them to be printed; which will hereafter be made more fully *appear.*" [Curll.]

TO THE
READER.
from
LETTERS
OF
Mr. *POPE,*
AND
Several Eminent Persons.

PREFACE.
to
LETTERS
OF
Mr. *ALEXANDER POPE,*
And Several of his FRIENDS.

THE
Booksellers to the Reader.
from
THE
WORKS
OF
ALEXANDER POPE, Esq;
VOL. V.

INTRODUCTION

After having had his letters to Cromwell published without his leave and after the failure of his Wycherley volume with its letters, Pope settled down to plot with a vengeance the destiny of his correspondence. To have it published properly and to see it accepted as a legitimate part of his *Works* was his goal, but contemporary convention about the privacy of personal papers made it an end toward which he could not work directly. That did not deter him. Once again by indirections (chronicled in the *Narrative of the Method*) he found direction out, and 1735–37 saw the triumph of his immediate schemes: letters appeared "surreptitiously" and notoriously—their publication *and* publicity to be capped by the "authorized" editions that he had made sure were called for.

Except for the earliest, "morning" books,[1] the 1735 *Letters* were preceded by an introductory "To the Reader," which even the disgruntled Curll—pawn in all these maneuvers—reprinted in some of his countering volumes. For the "official" quartos and folios of 1737, Pope prepared another introduction, self-justifying to a further degree, and both prefaces—with an additional explanatory "The Booksellers to the Reader" from the octavo editions of that year—were reproduced in the later reprintings of the letters as part of the collected *Works*. Pope had indeed achieved his purpose: a large collection of his letters was out and was certainly being read in all its numerous editions, and he, vindicated by the prefaces and the *Narrative of the Method,* could bask in the reflecting glory.

But the publication of the letters is more than a fascinating chapter in what Griffith has called the "risky business" of eighteenth-century publishing, and more than a colorful footnote to Pope's talent for subterfuge; it is what Griffith, again, relates to a "dynamic moment," an "initiating impulse."[2] For, historically, it meant a convention broken, a changed popular attitude toward letter-writing and letter-reading; after Pope the way is paved for a Walpole or Gray. Equally important, as Pope helped to elevate correspondence to an art, he also helped to define and emphasize that art. Although the longer 1737 Preface only begins to touch upon the subject, it does suggest how Pope saw himself as an epistolary writer, which in turn says much about how Pope saw himself as a man—an interrelationship characteristic of and necessary to his artistic vision.[3]

Notes

1. According to Sherburn the first edition of the *Letters* appeared in at least four variant issues (*Correspondence,* I, xix), the first of which (Griffith 374) was

the batch of fifty books, lacking title pages and prefaces, which was delivered to Curll on the morning of 12 May and soon sold. (See *Narrative of the Method,* p. 343.) See also Note on Publication and Text for "To the Reader" (1735), n. 1, p. 362.

2. Griffith, I part ii, xl.

3. For further discussion of this point, see "Shadow and Substance: A Discussion of Pope's Correspondence," *The Familiar Letter in the Eighteenth Century* (Lawrence: University of Kansas Press, 1966), pp. 34–48.

NOTE ON PUBLICATION AND TEXT
[TO THE READER (1735)]

The first edition of the *Letters* appeared, according to Sherburn, in at least four variant issues, all but the earliest including the prefatory "To the Reader," here printed.[1] In the third of these issues a new, second paragraph was introduced that was retained in the subsequent octavo and duodecimo reprints of these so-called "surreptitious" editions[2] (except where the *Narrative of the Method* was substituted as an introduction, as in Griffith 396, 397, and 400). While the "official" quartos and folios of 1737 printed a new preface, the Roberts octavo of that year (published later but actually prepared and printed earlier) and the subsequent small octavo *Works of Alexander Pope,* Vol. V. . . . The Second Edition—a revised conflation of Roberts and the authorized editions—saw both prefaces used together (accompanied by the brief "Booksellers to the Reader"), the earlier one being labelled "Preface of the Publisher of the Surreptitious Edition, 1735" and being printed without the added paragraph. The pair appear also in the 1739 *Works* and the 1742 *Works,* Vol. IV. Part I.

Since the later changes in the text, beyond the new second paragraph, are negligible, involving only minor variations in punctuation, capitalization, and spelling,[3] the first printing, except for the italic typeface of the original, has been followed for the present text, with the added paragraph (dropped later because the Wycherley references had been incorporated into the 1737 Preface) reproduced in a textual note. All of the pertinent editions containing "To the Reader" are cited below, by their Sherburn listings, to complete the history of the publication.

Key to the Critical Apparatus

1735a2 = *Letters of Mr. Pope, and Several Eminent Persons.* In the Years 1705, &c to 1717. London: Printed for J. Roberts . . . , octavo, Griffith 375.

[1735a3 = *Letters of Mr. Pope, and Several Eminent Persons,* From the Year 1705, to 1711. Vol. I. London: Printed and sold by the Booksellers of London and Westminster, octavo, Griffith 378.

1735a4 = *Letters* . . . , octavo, Griffith 380.

1735c = *Letters* . . . , octavo, Griffith 381.

1735d = *Letters* . . . , octavo, Griffith 383.

1735e = *Letters of Mr. Pope, and Several Eminent Persons,* From the Year 1705 to 1735. Vol. I. London: Printed for T. Cooper, and sold by the Booksellers of London and Westminster, duodecimo, Griffith 384.

1735n = *Letters of Mr. Pope, and Several Eminent Persons.* From the Year 1705, to 1735. N.B. This Edition contains more Letters, and more correctly printed, than any other extant. Printed for J. Smith; and sold by the Booksellers of London and Westminster, duodecimo, Griffith 408.

1737a = *The Works of Alexander Pope, Esq;* Vol. V. Consisting of letters, Wherein to those of the Author's own Edition, are added all that are genuine from the former Impressions, with some never before printed. London; Printed for J. Roberts in Warwick-lane, sm. octavo, Griffith 461.

1737e = *The Works of Alexander Pope, Esq;* Vol. 5 . . . The Second Edition, Corrected. London: Printed for T. Cooper . . . , sm. octavo, Griffith 472.

1739a = *The Works* . . . , Vol. V. . . . London: Printed for T. Cooper . . . , sm. octavo, Griffith 511.

1739b = *The Works* . . . , Vol. V. . . . London: Printed for T. Cooper . . . , sm. octavo, Griffith 512.

1742Lb = *The Works* . . . , Vol. IV. Part I. Containing an Authentic Edition of his Letters. London: Printed for T. Cooper . . . , sm. octavo, Griffith 568.}

Notes

1. Sherburn, *Correspondence,* I, xix. J. McLaverty argues plausibly that the preface used first in the "Afternoon edition" (Griffith 375) came from an unpublished collection of letters Pope had printed in 1729, at the time of the Wycherley volume, as a safeguard against Curll ("The first printing and publication of Pope's letters," *Library,* 2 [1980], 264–80).

2. Curll's genuinely surreptitious publication, *Mr. Pope's Literary Correspondence for Thirty Years,* also reprinted the preface; see Griffith 376 and 385.

3. There is one minor verbal change, probably accidental: in the added paragraph, *those* is altered to *these* in 1735a4, 35e, and 35n.

TO THE
READER.
[1735]

We presume we want no Apology to the Reader for this Publication, but some may be thought needful to Mr. *Pope:* However he cannot think our Offence so great as Theirs, who first separately published what we have here but collected in a better Form and Order.[1] As for the Letters we have procur'd to be added,[2] they serve but to compleat, explain, and sometimes set in a true light, those others, which it was not in the Writer's or Our power
A   to recall.[3]

This Collection hath been owing to several Cabinets;[4] some drawn from thence by Accidents, and others (even of those to Ladies) voluntarily given. It is to one of that Sex we are beholden for the whole Correspondence with *H. C.* Esq; which Letters being lent her by that Gentleman, she took the liberty to print;[5] as appears by the following, which we shall give at length, both as it is something Curious, and as it may serve for an Apology for our selves.

[Following were inserted the three letters, of E. Thomas to Henry Cromwell of 27 June 1727 and Cromwell's to Pope of 6 June 1727 and 1 August 1727 (*Correspondence,* II, 437–38; 439–41), which Pope also printed in the *Narrative of the Method,* pp. 327–30.]

Now, should our Apology for this Publication be as ill receiv'd, as the Lady's seems to have been by the Gentlemen concerned;[6] we shall at least have *Her Comfort* of being Thank'd by the rest of the world. Nor has Mr. *P.* himself any great cause to think it much Offence to his Modesty, or Reflexion on his Judgment; when we take care to inform the publick, that there are few Letters of his in this Collection which were not written under Twenty years of age:[7] On the other hand, we doubt not the Reader will be much more surpriz'd to find, at that early period, so much Variety of Style, Affecting Sentiment, and Justness of Criticism, in pieces which must have been writ in haste, very few perhaps ever re-view'd, and none intended for the Eye of the Publick.[8]

Textual Variants

Page 363: A. *In the third issue of the first edition, a new (second) paragraph was added:* "The Letters to Mr. *Wycherley* were procured some Years since, on account of a surreptitious Edition of his Posthumous Works: As those Letters shewed the true state of that Case, the Publication of them was doing the best Justice to the Memory of Mr. *Wycherley.*" *The following paragraph then opened,* "The rest of this Collection. . . ." *Add.* *1735a3, a4, c, d, e, n.*

Annotations

1. The reference is, of course, to Curll's surreptitious publication of Pope's letters to Cromwell in the *Miscellanea* of 1726 but also —as the paragraph Pope added to the preface was to indicate—to Pope's own, if unacknowledged, publication of his Wycherley correspondence in the 1729 *Posthumous Works of William Wycherley. Vol. II* (see above). There Pope had printed twenty-six letters; in the 1735 collection he omitted two and added two others, one fabricated from the two letters to Caryll. Such manipulations outraged Pope's Victorian editors; modern scholars find the matter of textual rather than moral concern. As Sherburn observes, in discussing a Cromwell letter: "In his 1735 editions Pope was desirous of discrediting Curll's earlier (1726) texts. This letter [of 27 April 1708], for which no original exists, would discredit the letter written only two days earlier (of which Curll had the autograph), which Pope never reprinted and from which he took one bit for insertion in his letter of 18 Mar. 1708. One can only surmise the origin of this present letter." (*Correspondence,* I, 48n.)

2. Besides the Wycherley and Cromwell correspondence, the volume contains his letters to and from Walsh, "Letters to Several Ladies," correspondence with Sir William Trumbull, Steele, Addison, and other miscellaneous acquaintances, and a collection of letters to Gay.

3. See "The the Reader" from *The Posthumous Works of William Wycherley. Vol. II,* above.

4. Ransacked cabinets, notable scritoires—such is the furniture of epistolary drama; for the whole extravagant tale see the *Narrative of the Method.*

5. As the letters reproduced in the preface made clear, Curll had acquired the Cromwell letters from the latter's discarded mistress, Elizabeth Thomas, who had become one of his hack writers. This episode only served to intensify Pope's anxiety about his correspondence, and the following years found him busily soliciting friends for the return of his letters.

6. In importuning Caryll for letters, Pope had argued, "For the letters, I am obliged to the care you have taken, in the endorsement and order you mention:

however, I beg once more to see them. You cannot conceive the pain which Cromwell's partiality to those things (which only could occasion their coming into the public) has given me." (*Correspondence*, II, 423.)

7. In general Pope liked to exploit the precocity of his talent; but when the wit of his early letters became an outmoded style, he was quick, as Sherburn notes, to attribute these "follies" to his youthfulness. (*Correspondence*, I, 1 [head note].)

8. Though Swift's tease may have been excessive—"I find you have been a writer of Letters almost from your infancy, and by your own confession had Schemes even then of Epistolary fame" (*Correspondence*, III, 92)—Pope was certainly never as artless about his writing as this statement suggests. As early as 1712 he was trying to recall his letters for one literary "design" or another, and once he was engaged in seeing them into print, he edited them as carefully as any other of his *Works*.

NOTE ON PUBLICATION AND TEXT
[PREFACE (1737)]

Once Pope had achieved the publication of his letters in the "surreptitious" texts of 1735 (both Curll's and his own), it was only a
question of time before the "authentic" editions followed. [1] And follow they
did, in 1737—handsome official quartos and folios, worthy to stand with
the collected *Works* of 1717 and 1735. Promoted by Pope's newfound friend
Ralph Allen, [2] this authorized subscription edition supplanted the octavo
edition he had originally planned, though unacknowledged octavos were
also printed. As Sherburn traces the bibliographic history: "The text of
the official edition was frequently 'improved' from a small octavo edition,
evidently prepared, most of it, before the official edition, but published
as volumes v and vi of Pope's *Works,* with the imprint of J. Roberts, a
month after the official edition was out." [3] All three—the authorized quartos and folios and the unacknowledged octavos—carried a new preface,
here printed.

Since the text of this preface differs somewhat between the large paper
editions and the octavos, the question of authority becomes difficult. Sherburn, who reproduces the quarto's preface, argues that "The differences
in text are many but are almost always merely rhetorical. The text printed
represents Pope's considered revision of the Preface—probably! The matter
is confused by a passage in 'The Booksellers to the Reader'[4] prefixed to
1737a [the Roberts octavo], where the 'Booksellers' say, 'We have prefix'd
the *Author's Preface*; and to make it known to be such, have put it into
the *First Person* (as it stood originally in his Specimen) instead of the *Third*
(as he since alter'd it) lest future times shou'd be led to mistake it for
some other Editor's.' Quite possibly, of course, Pope here speaks for the
'Booksellers.' "[5]

Although Pope very probably does speak for the "Booksellers," the
quarto third-person rendering of the preface (in later editions entitled
"Preface: Prefixed to the First Genuine Edition in 4°. 1737") is printed
here too as carrying the unmistakable authority of the "official" edition,
the substantive variants (all from the 1737a octavo) being indicated in the
textual notes. (Pope's footnotes are here identified alphabetically rather
than numerically, as in the original.) The list of editions collated—cited
by their Sherburn numbers—provides a history of the publication.

Key to the Critical Apparatus

1737a = *The Works of Alexander Pope, Esq*; Vol. V. Consisting of letters,
Wherein to those of the Author's own Edition, are added all
that are genuine from the former Impressions, with some never
before printed. London: Printed for J. Roberts in Warwick-lane,
sm. octavo, Griffith 461.

1737b1 = *Letters of Mr. Alexander Pope, and Several of his Friends.* London:
Printed by J. Wright for J. Knapton . . . L. Gilliver . . .
J. Brindley . . . and R. Dodsley, quarto, Griffith 454.

1737b2 = *Letters . . . ,* folio, Griffith 456.

1737e = *The Works* . . . Vol. V. The Second Edition, Corrected. London:
Printed for T. Cooper, sm. octavo, Griffith 472.

1739a = *The Works* . . . Vol. V. London: Printed for T. Cooper in Pater-
noster-Row, sm. octavo, Griffith 511.

1739b = *The Works* . . . Vol. V. . . . , sm. octavo, Griffith 512.

1742Lb = *The Works of Alexander Pope, Esq*; Vol. IV. Part I. Containing
an Authentic Edition of his Letters. London: Printed for
T. Cooper in Pater-noster-Row, sm. octavo, Griffith 568.

Notes

1. In July 1735 Pope had announced in *The London Gazette* (No. 7419: 12–
15 July 1735): *"Whereas several Booksellers have printed several surreptitious and incorrect Editions of* Letters *as mine, some of which are not so, and others interpolated; and
whereas there are Daily Advertisements of* Second *and* Third *Volumes of more such*
Letters, *particularly my Correspondence with the late* Bishop of Rochester; *I think my
self under a Necessity to publish such of the said Letters as are genuine, with the Addition
of some others of a Nature less insignificant; especially those which pass'd between the said*
Bishop *and my self, or were any way relating to him: Which shall be printed with all
convenient Speed."*

2. It was Pope's recently published letters that had attracted the interest and
support of the wealthy Ralph Allen of Bath; see *Correspondence,* IV, 19, 23.

3. Ibid., I, xv; see Note on Publication and Text of "The Booksellers to the
Reader" (1737).

4. See p. 381.

5. *Correspondence,* I, xxxvin.

PREFACE. [1737]

A   If what is here offer'd the Reader should happen in any degree to
please him, the thanks are not due to the Author, but partly to
B,C   his Friends, and partly to his Enemies: It was wholly owing to the
D,E   Affection of the former, that so many Letters of which he never kept
F   copies were preserv'd, and to the Malice of the latter that they were
produc'd in this manner.

He had been very disagreeably us'd, in the publication of some
G,H   Letters written in his youth, which fell into the hands of a Woman
I,J   who printed them without his, or his correspondent's consent, in
1727.[1] This treatment, and the apprehension of more of the same
K,L,M kind, put him upon recalling as many as he could from those who
N,O   he imagin'd had kept any.[2] He was sorry to find the number so
great, but immediately lessen'd it by burning three parts in four of
P   them:[3] The rest he spar'd, not in any preference of their Stile or
writing, but merely as they preserv'd the memory of some Friend-
Q   ships which will ever be dear to him,[4] or set in a true light some
Matters of fact, from which the Scriblers of the times had taken
R,S,T occasion to asperse either his Friends or himself. He therefore lay'd
U   by the originals, together with those of his Correspondents, and
caus'd a Copy to be taken to deposite in the Library of a noble
Friend;[5] that in case either of the revival of slanders, or the publi-
V   cation of surreptitious letters, during his life or after, a proper use
might be made of them.

The next year, the Posthumous works of Mr. *Wycherley* were
printed, in a way disreputable enough to his memory: It was thought
a justice due to him, to shew the world his better judgment; and
that it was his last resolution to have suppress'd those Poems. As
W   some of the letters which had pass'd between him and our Author
clear'd that point, they were publish'd in 1729, with a few marginal
X   notes added by a friend.[6]

Y   If in these letters, and in those which were printed without his
consent,[7] there appear too much of a juvenile ambition of Wit, or
Z,AA affectation of Gayety, he may reasonably hope it will be consider'd
BB,CC *to whom,* and at *what age,* he was guilty of it, as well as how soon

it was over.[8] The rest, every judge of writing will see, were by no
means Efforts of the Genius but Emanations of the Heart: and this
alone may induce any candid reader to believe their publication an
act of necessity, rather than of vanity.

A,B   It is notorious, how many volumes have been publish'd under the
title of his Correspondence,[9] with promises still of more, and open
and repeated offers of encouragement to all persons who should send
C   any letters of his for the press.[10] It is as notorious what methods
were taken to procure them, even from the Publisher's own accounts
D   in his prefaces, viz. by transacting with people in necessities,[a] or of
abandon'd[b] characters, or such as dealt without names in the[c] dark.
Upon a quarrel with one of these last, he betray'd himself so far as
E   to appeal to the publick in Narratives and Advertisements:[13] like
F,G   that Irish Highway-man a few years before, who preferr'd a Bill
H   against his Companion, for not sharing equally in the mony, rings
and watches, they had traded for in Partnership upon *Hounslow-
heath.*

J,K   Several have been printed in his name which he never writ, and
address'd to persons to whom they never were written;[d] counterfeited
„M   as from Bishop *Atterbury* to him, which neither that Bishop nor he
ever saw;[e] and advertiz'd even after that period when it was made
Felony to correspond with him.

Ɔ,P   I know not how it has been this Author's fate, whom both his
R,S *Situation* and his *Temper* have all his life excluded from rivalling any
man, in any pretension, (except that of pleasing by Poetry) to have
T   been as much aspers'd and written at, as any First Minister of his
U   time: Pamphlets and Newspapers have been full of him,[16] nor was
it *there only* that a private man, who never troubled either the world
or common conversation with his opinions of Religion or Govern-

V   [a] See the Preface to Vol. I. of a Book called Mr. Pope's Literary
Correspondence.[11]

   [b] Postscript to the Preface to Vol. 4.[12]

   [c] Narrative and Anecdotes before Vol. 2.

W   [d] In Vol. 3. Letters from Mr. Pope to Mrs. Blount, &c.[14]

   [e] Vol. 2 of the same, 8° pag. 20.[15] and at the end of the Edition
of his Letters in 12° by the Booksellers of London and Westminster;
and of the last Edition in 12° printed by T. Cooper, 1725 {1735}.

ment has been represented as a dangerous member of Society, a
A bigotted Papist, and an enemy to the Establishment. The unwar-
rantable publication of his Letters hath at least done him this service,
to show he has constantly enjoy'd the friendship of worthy men;[17]
B,C and that if a Catalogue were to be taken of his friends and his
D,E enemies, he needs not to blush at either. Many of them having been
written on the most trying occurrences, and all in the openness of
F,G friendship, are a proof what were his real Sentiments, as they flow'd
warm from the heart, and fresh from the occasion; without the least
H thought that ever the world should be witness to them.[18] Had he
I,J sate down with a design to draw his own Picture,[19] he could not
have done it so truly; for whoever sits for it, (whether to himself or
K,L another) will inevitably find the features more compos'd, than his
M appear in these letters. But if an Author's hand, like a Painter's, be
more distinguishable in a slight sketch than in a finish'd picture,
this very carelessness will make them the better known from such
Counterfeits, as have been, and may be imputed to him, either thro'
a mercenary, or a malicious design.

N,O   We hope it is needless to say, he is not accountable for several
P passages in the surreptitious editions of those letters, which are such
as no man of common sense would have publish'd himself. The
Q,R errors of the press were almost innumerable, and could not but be
S extreamly multiply'd in so many repeated editions; by the Avarice
T and Negligence of pyratical Printers, to not one of whom he ever
gave the least Title, or any other encouragement than that of not
prosecuting them.

U,V   For the *Chasms* in the correspondence, we had not the means to
W,X supply them, the Author having destroy'd too many letters to pre-
Y,Z serve any Series. Nor would he go about to amend them, except by
AA the omission of some passages, improper, or at least impertinent,[20]
to be divulg'd to the publick: or of such entire letters, as were either
not his, or not approv'd of by him.

BB   He has been very sparing of those of his Friends, and thought it
a respect shewn to their memory, to suppress in particular such as
were most in his favour. As it is not to *Vanity* but to *Friendship* that
CC,DD,EE he intends this Monument, he would save his Enemies the mortifi-
cation of showing any farther how well their Betters have thought
FF,GG of him; and at the same time secure from their censure his living

A Friends, who (he promises them) shall never be put to the blush,
B this way at least, for their partiality to him.

C   But however this Collection may be receiv'd, we cannot but lament the *Cause* and the *Necessity* of such a publication, and heartily
wish no honest man may be reduc'd to the same. To state the case
fairly in the present situation.[21] A Bookseller advertises his intention
to publish your Letters: He openly promises encouragement, or even
pecuniary rewards, to those who will help him to any; and ingages
to insert whatever they shall send: Any scandal is sure of a reception,
and any enemy who sends it skreen'd from a discovery. Any domestick or servant, who can snatch a letter from your pocket or cabinet,
is encouraged to that vile practise. If the quantity falls short of a
volume, any thing else shall be join'd with it (more especially scandal) which the collector can think for his interest, all recommended
under your Name: You have not only Theft to fear, but Forgery. Any
Bookseller, tho' conscious in what manner they were obtain'd, not
caring what may be the consequences to your Fame or Quiet, will
sell and disperse them in town and country. The better your Reputation is, the more your Name will cause them to be demanded,
and consequently the more you will be injur'd. The injury is of such
a nature, as the Law (which does not punish for *Intentions*) cannot
prevent; and when done, may punish, but not redress. You are
therfore reduc'd, either to enter into a personal treaty with such a
man, (which tho' the readiest, is the meanest of all methods) or to
take such other measures to suppress them, as are contrary to your
Inclination, or to publish them, as are contrary to your Modesty.
Otherwise your Fame and your Property suffer alike; you are at once
expos'd and plunder'd. As an *Author,* you are depriv'd of that Power
which above all others constitutes a good one, the power of rejecting,
and the right of judging for your self, what pieces it may be most
useful, entertaining, or reputable to publish, at the time and in the
manner you think best. As a *Man,* you are depriv'd of the right
D even over your own Sentiments, of the privilege of every humane
creature to divulge or conceal them; of the advantage of your second
thoughts; and of all the benefit of your Prudence, your Candour, or
your Modesty. As a *Member of Society,* you are yet more injur'd; your
private conduct, your domestick concerns, your family secrets, your
passions, your tendernesses, your weaknesses, are expos'd to the

Misconstruction or Resentment of some, to the Censure or Impertinence of the whole world. The printing private letters in such a
manner, is the worst sort of *betraying Conversation,* as it has evidently
the most extensive, and the most lasting ill consequences. It is the
highest offence against *Society,* as it renders the most dear and intimate intercourse of friend with friend, and the most necessary
commerce of man with man, unsafe, and to be dreaded. To open
Letters is esteem'd the greatest breach of honour; even to look into
them already open'd or accidentally dropt, is held an ungenerous, if
not an immoral act. What then can be thought of the procuring
A them merely by Fraud, and the printing them merely for Lucre? We
B cannot but conclude every honest man will wish, that if the Laws
have as yet provided no adequate remedy, one at least may be found,
to prevent so great and growing an evil.

Textual Variants

Page 368: A. are not . . . Author] will not be . . . me *1737a.*
Page 368: B. his] my *1737a.*
Page 368: C. his] my *1737a.*
Page 368: D. Affection] Partiality *1737a.*
Page 368: E. he] I *1737a.*
Page 368: F. were] are *1737a.*
Page 368: G. Letters] I had *1737a.*
Page 368: H. his] my *1737a.*
Page 368: I. his] mine *1737a.*
Page 368: J. his] my *1737a.*
Page 368: K. him] me *1737a.*
Page 368: L. as many as he] what letters I *1737a.*
Page 368: M. who *Om. 1737a.*
Page 368: N. he] I *1737a.*
Page 368: O. he] I *1737a.*
Page 368: P. he] I *1737a.*
Page 368: Q. him] me *1737a.*
Page 368: R. his] my *1737a.*
Page 368: S. himself] my self *1737a.*
Page 368: T. he] I *1737a.*
Page 368: U. his] my *1737a.*
Page 368: V. his] my *1737a.*
Page 368: W. him and our Author] us *1737a.*

Page 368: X. added. . . . *Om. 1737a.*

Page 368: Y. his] my *1737a.*

Page 368: Z. he] I *1737a.*

Page 368: AA. may reasonably *Om. 1737a.*

Page 368: BB. he] I *1737a.*

Page 368: CC. as . . . over.] and how soon the folly was over? *1737a.*

Page 369: A. his] my *1737a.*

Page 369: B. open and *Om. 1737a.*

Page 369: C. letters of his] of my Letters *1737a.*

Page 369: D. necessities] necessity *1737a.*

Page 369: E. *After "Advertisements" there was a footnote* (4): Ibid. *1737a.*

Page 369: F. like] just like *1737a.*

Page 369: G. a few years before, *Om. 1737a.*

Page 369: H. , rings *Om. 1737a.*

Page 369: I. his] my *1737a.*

Page 369: J. he] I *1737a.*

Page 369: K. and *Om. 1737a.*

Page 369: L. him] me *1737a.*

Page 369: M. he] I *1737a.*

Page 369: N. this Author's] my *1737a.*

Page 369: O. whom] when *1737a.*

Page 369: P. his] my *1737a.*

Page 369: Q. his] my *1737a.*

Page 369: R. his] my *1737a.*

Page 369: S. excluded] excluded me *1737a.*

Page 369: T. his] my *1737a.*

Page 369: U. him] me *1737a.*

Page 369: V. of . . . . *Om. 1737a.*

Page 369: W. , &c. *Om. 1737a.*

Page 370: A. The . . . he has] I hope a better opinion will be entertain'd of me, by those who read these letters. They may show, that I have *1737a.*

Page 370: B. his] my *1737a.*

Page 370: C. his] my *1737a.*

Page 370: D. he needs] I need *1737a.*

Page 370: E. of them *Om. 1737a.*

Page 370: F. are a proof] will prove *1737a.*

Page 370: G. his] my *1737a.*

Page 370: H. he] I *1737a.*

Page 370: I. his] my *1737a.*

Page 370: J. he] I *1737a.*

Page 370: K. the] his *1737a.*

Page 370: L. his] mine *1737a.*

Page 370: M. But] And *1737a.*

Page 370: N. We] I *1737a.*

Page 370: O. he is] I am *1737a.*

Page 370: P. those] my *1737a.*

Page 370: Q. press] press too *1737a.*

Page 370: R. almost *Om. 1737a.*

Page 370: S. in . . . editions] in . . . Impressions *1737a and transferred to follow*
        "Printers," *1737a.*

Page 370: T. he] I *1737a.*

Page 370: U. in] of *1737a.*

Page 370: V. we had not] I have neither the desire nor *1737a.*

Page 370: W. the Author *Om. 1737a.*

Page 370: X. many] many of the *1737a.*

Page 370: Y. he] I *1737a.*

Page 370: Z. amend them,] alter or amend any thing *1737a.*

Page 370: AA. some. . . . .] here and there a passage wholly impertinent to the
        publick, or of a thought or two which I disapprov'd on a review.
        1737a.

Page 370: BB. He. . . .] I have been sparing in the letters of my Correspondents;
        and particularly shown respect to their memory in suppressing
        such as are most in my favour. *1737a.*

Page 370: CC. he intends] I intend *1737a.*

Page 370: DD. he] I *1737a.*

Page 370: EE. save his] spare my *1737a.*

Page 370: FF. him] me *1737a.*

Page 370: GG. his] my *1737a.*

Page 371: A. he promises] I promise *1737a.*

Page 371: B. him] me *1737a.*

Page 371: C. receiv'd, we] receiv'd, or whatever credit may be deriv'd to me
        from that part of it which is not my own, I *1737a.*

Page 371: D. humane] human *1737a, 1737e–42Lb.*

Page 372: A. We] I *1737a.*

Page 372: B. wish] wish with me *1737a.*

Annotations

1. These were the Cromwell letters, published by Curll, who got them from
Cromwell's discarded mistress, Elizabeth Thomas, by then one of his stable of
writers. See *Narrative of the Method.*

2. See, for example, letters to Caryll (*Correspondence,* II, 419, 423, 449; III,

14, 31), to Hugh Bethel (II, 501), to Fortescue (III, 478), to Spence (III, 498), to Broome (III, 510). . . .

3. That Pope actually destroyed many, or any, of his letters seems doubtful, but certainly he was to publish only a very small part of his correspondence; in fact such letters account for only slightly more than ten percent of those in the Sherburn *Correspondence*. It is possible, of course, that he here refers (equivocally) to brief notes.

4. While the concern for friendship—a persistent refrain in this apologia— may here be rhetoric, Pope's letters do stand as a monument to his enduring (and endearing) relationships with those close to him. As Maynard Mack has put it, "His tone may vary in the letters with the subject or the addressee, but their real substance is almost always the substance of a love letter, if that term may still be used today without sexual or romantic implications. . . . The 'business' of the letters tends to be subsidiary to the sense of being in affectionate communication with someone very dear." (Review of *Correspondence, Philological Quarterly*, 36 [1957], 394.)

5. The library of Edward Harley, second earl of Oxford, to whom Pope had written circa 15 September 1729: "The mention of your Library (which I should Envy any man, but One who both makes a good use of it himself, & suffers others to do so) brings back into my mind a Request I have had at heart, for half a year & more; That you would suffer some Original papers & Letters, both of my own and some of my Friends, to lye in your Library at London. There seems already to be an occasion of it, from a publication of certain Posthumous pieces of Mr. Wycherley. . . ." (*Correspondence*, III, 54.) Oxford's gracious response ("I received the favor of your letters both and designed troubling you before the last came, you may be assured I shall think my library very much Honoured by the deposite you propose, and if you please to have those papers put in a box and left with my porter he has orders to put the Box into the library, and what ever mention you make of that Library I shall be pleased with" [ibid., III, 56]) gave Pope unrestricted use of a convenient screen behind which to manipulate the various publications of his letters.

6. See "To the Reader" from the *Posthumous Works of William Wycherley. Vol. II*. The "marginal" notes appeared as footnotes.

7. In the Cooper edition of 1737, there is appended to the section "Letters to Several Ladies" this note: "Most of these the Author has left out of his own Edition. They were printed without his Consent, and no doubt are the same upon which the censure is past in the Preface. 'That they have too much of a juvenile, ambition of Wit, and affectation of Gayety.' And it is pleaded in Excuse, 'that they were written very young, and the folly was soon over.' "

8. The young Pope, self-consciously exchanging compliments and bon mots with such mannered correspondents as Wycherley, affected a pretentious, witty

style, which he later, just as self-consciously, abandoned, as he notes to Swift: (28 November 1729) "I lately receiv'd from the widow of one dead correspondent, and the father of another, several of my own letters of about fifteen or twenty years old; and it was not unentertaining to my self to observe, how and by what degrees I ceas'd to be a witty writer; as either my experience grew on the one hand, or my affection to my correspondents on the other." (*Correspondence*, III, 79.)

   9. These were the Curll publications: *Mr. Pope's Literary Correspondence*, in five volumes. Pope's 1737 octavos printed "A Catalogue of the *Surreptitious* and *Incorrect* Editions of Mr. Pope's Letters," which comprised all the Curll volumes and the other 1735 editions.

   10. In an introductory "To the Subscribers" in Vol. III, Curll had advertised: "Mr *Pope's* Project to usher his Letters into the World by my Means, was the Foundation of this Scheme of *A Literary Correspondence*; which has been so well received, that it shall be continued while People of Taste approve of it: And that will be as long as People of Taste, who have valuable Performances in this Kind in their Power, contribute their Stores to the Emolument of Mankind. Not but that I am always ready and willing to purchase any Genuine Pieces from such Possessors as expect a *Premium*."

   11. The reference is to Elizabeth Thomas, whose letter to Cromwell, reproduced in the 1735 Preface and in the *Narrative of the Method,* lamented how she had "plung'd into unforeseen, and unavoidable ruin. . . ." ("Preface," *Mr Pope's Literary Correspondence* (London: Printed for E. Curll, 1735), I, [A2ᵛ].

   12. Sherburn heralds (*Correspondence*, I, xxxviiin) as "a document in abuse" this postscript to the Preface (of Curll's fourth volume [1736]) to which Pope refers in this footnote:

> Pray, with my *Respects* to Mr. POPE, tell him I am sorry that *Ill health, Ill Humour, Ill Weather, and the Want of a Coach,* should all conspire to prevent his paying that Visit to LUCRETIA [identified by Curll as "A noted Cast-off-Punk, of his pious *Saint-John*. Mrs. *Griffith,* alias *Butler,* alias *Lucretia Lindo,* who has several Letters of Mr. *Pope's* not worth Printing"], which she lately expected from Him; and tho' she will not by any Means admit of the Term *Affectionate,* he may subscribe Himself her *humble Servant*. The Lady is eloped from her last Lodging, but *He* may hear of his *Deary* at the *Old Place*. She hopes the Picture will please, now the Painter has re-touched it.

> 'Tis strange! that still our Bard the *Truth* will shun,
> For *Wrong* is *Wrong,* where-ever it be done.
>   *Adv.* from *Hor.*

13. Like those collected in *A Narrative of the Method.*

14. The reference is to four letters of Voiture printed as from Pope to Martha Blount by Curll, who—as Sherburn points out—"well knew that they came from the translation of Voiture's letters that he himself was just then publishing." (*Correspondence*, I, xxi.)

15. Sherburn comments that the letter cited in the footnote as from page 20 (third series) of Curll's third volume was "pretty certainly not by Pope, although it expressed ideas later found in the *Essay on Man.*" The other two letters he designates as "to him from Atterbury, which Pope later disowned." (*Correspondence*, I, xxxviii, xx.)

16. For the nature and range of these, see J. V. Guerinot, *Pamphlet Attacks on Alexander Pope, 1711–1744* (London: Methuen, 1969).

17. Pope's relationships played a central role in his life, one that he commemorates repeatedly in his personal remarks. Forced by health, religion, and politics to live outside the main currents of Augustan life, retired to the seclusion of Twickenham, for many years in the company of an aging mother, he was inevitably dependent upon his friends—often those similarly alienated from normal domestic, social, or political involvements: Swift, Gay, Atterbury, Bolingbroke. Because these friends were so dispersed, in Ireland, on the Continent, and throughout England, letters had to carry most of the burden of their long association.

18. Cf. Dr. Johnson's view: "Pope may be said to write always with his reputation in his head; Swift perhaps like a man who remembered that he was writing to Pope; but Arbuthnot like one who lets thoughts drop from his pen as they rise to his mind." (*Lives*, III, 160.)

19. One must remember Pope's interest and practice in portraiture ("I have thrown away three Dr. *Swift*'s, each of which was once my Vanity, two Lady *Bridgwaters*, a Dutchess of *Montague*, besides half a dozen Earls, and one Knight of the Garter. I have crucify'd *Christ* over-again in effigie, and made a *Madona* as old as her mother St. *Anne.*" (*Correspondence*, I, 187]).

20. As Sherburn has described Pope's editorial activity,

> The improved offical texts illustrate Pope's principles of revision. Trivialities concerning daily life or finances are omitted; so also are small indecorous remarks, either slightly salacious or profane. Personal names also are frequently excised. Perhaps the most common changes are purely stylistic: the letters are made more concise, the sentences more straightforward, the diction more elegant. There is little change in the sense of any letter except such as is due to omissions. . . . In moral and literary quality the revised official texts were to Pope the more satisfactory—were 'a more perfect image of himself'. In making an edition that he called 'authentic', he omitted many letters found in the earlier editions and added between sixty and seventy new letters. (*Correspondence*, I, xv.)

Pope himself wrote to Hugh Bethel—"For all it can do is to shew, I disapprove many things I formerly thought & wrote, by my omitting them in this Edition." (Ibid., IV, 39.)

21. Curll's career as a publisher stands as all too real testimony to the validity of Pope's complaints. For an engaging account of what an Augustan author had to contend with, see Ralph Straus's *The Unspeakable Curll* (1927).

NOTE ON PUBLICATION AND TEXT
[THE BOOKSELLERS TO
THE READER (1737)]

In reviewing the history of the 1737 publication of the letters, Sherburn notes that a "minute study of the editions involved shows that Pope's intention would have been satisfied by a small octavo edition; but he was persuaded to project a subscription edition in folio and quarto."[1] When the "official" edition appeared, it was indeed followed a month later by a small octavo edition (*The Works of Alexander Pope, Esq;*, Vol. V), under the imprint of J. Roberts, which apparently had been prepared and printed before the authorized volumes. This edition carried the 1735 preface, retitled "Preface of the Publisher of the Surreptitious Edition, 1735," as well as the new official preface—but now rendered in the first person. To explain this change ("lest future times shou'd be led to mistake it for some other Editor's")[2] and to continue the account of Pope's contest with Curll, a brief "The Booksellers to the Reader," generally acknowledged as Pope's,[3] was added along with "A Catalogue of the *Surreptitious* and *Incorrect* Editions of Mr. Pope's *Letters*" and a table of contents marked to indicate unauthorized letters (i.e., not included in the official edition) and new inclusions.

As the later editions of the letters—the subsequent 1737 and 1739 octavos and the 1742 *Works,* Vol. IV. Part I—were essentially based on the Roberts edition, they also carry the Booksellers' preface, with some modifications, since there Pope reprinted the "Preface Prefixed to the First Genuine Edition in 4°. 1737" in its third-person form. The present text follows the Roberts printing with the later changes incorporated in textual notes. (For the collation, Sherburn's listings have been used.)

Key to the Critical Apparatus

1737a = *The Works of Alexander Pope, Esq;* Vol. V. Consisting of letters, Wherein to those of the Author's own Edition, are added all that are genuine from the former Impressions, with some never before printed. London: Printed for J. Roberts in Warwick-lane, sm. octavo, Griffith 461.

1737e = *The Works . . .* Vol. V. The Second Edition, Corrected. London: Printed for T. Cooper, sm. octavo, Griffith 472.

1739a = *The Works* . . . Vol. V. London: Printed for T. Cooper in Pater-
noster-Row, sm. octavo, Griffith 511.

1739b = *The Works* . . . Vol. V. . . . , sm. octavo, Griffith 512.

1742Lb = *The Works of Alexander Pope, Esq*; Vol. IV. Part I. Containing
an Authentic Edition of his Letters. London: Printed for
T. Cooper in Pater-noster-Row, sm. octavo, Griffith 568.

Notes

1. *Correspondence,* I, xiv; see also Vinton A. Dearing, "The 1737 Editions of
Alexander Pope's Letters," *Essays Critical and Historical Dedicated to Lily B. Campbell* (Berkeley and Los Angeles: University of California Press, 1950), pp. 185–
97.

2. But as Elwin/Courthope interpreted it, "Pope was anxious to conceal that
while he was urging false pleas to compel his friends to subscribe for his expur-
gated quarto, he had printed a full edition of the letters which he kept ready to
be thrown on the market at any convenient opening, and rather than be at the
cost of reprinting the preface to the octavo, he invented a futile pretext to account
for its departure from the later version in the quarto." (EC VI, xliv.)

3. See Maynard Mack, review of *Correspondence, Philological Quarterly,* 36
(1957), 391–92.

THE
Booksellers to the Reader.
[1737]

M^r. *Pope* having been obliged to publish an authentic Edition of his *Letters,* in order to reject many which were not his, and to show his disapprobation of the publishing of others, written in his youth, and printed without his knowledge; has seem'd willing to deprive the publick of what Writings of this sort he could.[1] Nevertheless the same Persons who began the Injury having since
A continued it toward him, not only *publickly advertizing* they wou'd
B pyrate his Edition, and *replace* all the Letters he rejected, but such an Impression being actually prepared for the Press and the first
C Sheets of it published;[2] we have taken the liberty to prevent them, in a more correct and reputable manner.[3] We have done the Writer
D,E the justice to insert only genuine Letters, and to distinguish those which were printed without his consent from those of his own Edi-
F tion, by an Asterisk * in the Index prefix'd to the former: Those which have a double Asterisk ** are in no Impression except this:[4] but were in such hands, as to be in imminent danger of being printed. We have prefix'd the *Author's Preface*; and to make it known to be such, have put it into the *First Person* (as it stood originally in his Specimen)[5] instead of the *Third* (as he since alter'd it) lest future times shou'd be led to mistake it for some other Editor's.[6] We have also given a *Catalogue* of the many *Surreptitious Editions* of his Letters; in every one of which are several he disapprov'd, or were falsely imputed to him.[7]

Textual Variants

Page 381: A. not only . . . *replace*] by pyrating his Edition, and *replacing* 1737e–42Lb.
Page 381: B. , but . . . published. *Om.* 1737e–42Lb.
Page 381: C. liberty to prevent them,] Liberty in this to add those Letters, but 1737e–42Lb.
Page 381: D. to insert . . . and *Om.* 1737e–42Lb.

Page 381: E. those . . . consent] them *1737e–42Lb*.

Page 381: F. prefix'd. . . . Editor's.]: And we can safely say, there is not one but is genuine. *1737e–42Lb*.

Annotations

1. See Preface to the 1737 *Letters*.

2. A cursory examination of newspapers for November 1736 (when Curll's *New Letters of Mr Alexander Pope* [Griffith 429; Sherburn 1736c] was published and the Roberts edition was being printed) and May–June 1737 (when the official volumes and the Roberts octavo appeared) has not turned up any such advertisement. But in a prefatory "To My Subscribers *encore*," dated 5 November 1736, Curll had written [the original printed in reverse italics]:

> Having, as you All know, honestly Purchased the *First* Volume of Mr. *Pope's Literary Correspondence* of his Agent the Reverend Mr. *Smith*; Published and paid my Respects to my *Benefactor* in the *Second*; Dispatched *Brocade* and *Tim Lancet* in the *Third*; and, Got rid of the *Shifters* in the *Fourth*; I now come to give you a just Account of the Contents of this *Fifth* Volume.
>
> Beside, what is here presented to You, I have Several other very valuable Originals in my Custody, which, with these, were Transmitted to me from *Ireland*. And this Volume will be closed with whatever *additional Letters* Mr. *Pope* shall think fit to insert in his *Works* in *Prose,* now printing in *Quarto,* Price a Guinea; but the Controversy between *Me* and Mr. *Pope* will never be ended till the Eyes of one of Us are *closed* (I mean by *Death,* not by Dr. *Taylor*) if *Mine* are open longest, to the last Volume of *Literary Correspondence* shall be prefixed A faithful Account of Mr. *Pope's* Life and Writings, with a true Copy of his Last Will and Testament, if he makes one.

The British Library's copy of this fifth volume of the *Literary Correspondence* (which carries also the "New Letters" title page of the 1736 pamphlet, Sherburn noting that Curll's 1737 Volume V was in part a second edition, the first part a reissue of the 1736 volume) does include an "Advertisement," dated 8 June 1737, which comments, "Besides these [list of omissions and changes], many considerable Paragraphs are omitted in the Letters which remain; others, are *interpolated,* and upon the whole, this *Guinea Edition* is so far from being an *Authentic one,* that it is only a *Select Collection* of Mr. *Pope's* Letters, more *old Letters* being *omitted,* than there *New ones* added." Actually, there was a pirated edition (Griffith 470), but by James Watson rather than Curll, and of the Roberts octavo, not the official quarto. (See Maynard Mack, review of *Correspondence, Philological Quarterly,* 36 [1957], 391.)

3. Dearing ("The 1737 Editions of Pope's Letters," *Essays Critical and Historical Dedicated to Lily B. Campbell* [Berkeley and Los Angeles: University of California Press, 1950], p. 196) argues plausibly that the omissions of the official volume were due to Pope's desire to produce a single volume of manageable size to match the quartos and folios of his poetical *Works* and his translations of Homer, and that "it seems equally likely that Pope was influenced in his selection and revision by the tastes and standards of the restricted audience to which the price of the official edition would confine it."

4. The Roberts edition's Table of Contents lists forty letters identified by a single asterisk and eleven by a double. In the later editions, where the "new" category no longer pertained, only a single asterisk was used, to distinguish letters not included in the official edition.

5. See Note on Publication and Text, p. 379.

6. In the subsequent editions, though, Pope reverted back to the Preface as found in the quarto edition.

7. This "catalogue" includes Curll's edition of the Cromwell letters, his four (later five) volumes of *Mr. Pope's Literary Correspondence* and the 1735 editions of the *Letters*.

To the READER.

from
LETTERS
BETWEEN
Dr. *SWIFT,* Mr. *POPE,* &c.

THE
BOOKSELLERS
TO THE
READER.
from
THE
WORKS
OF
Mr. *ALEXANDER POPE,*
In PROSE.
VOL. II.

INTRODUCTION

The publication of the Pope-Swift correspondence brings to a close, with an appropriate bang, the history of the letters, a final chapter worthy of the earlier ones in its machinations and bibliographic confusion. Just as Pope's association with Swift was one of his most valued relationships, personal as well as literary, so their correspondence—which was to be its memorial[1]—became a culminating venture. And though the means by which Pope again achieved publication without appearing to be involved show him at his worst, the objective—that memorable exchange lasting nearly thirty years—often reflects the best of a man who could indeed claim to be known by his friendships.

Both the "authorized" London edition of the correspondence, *The Works of Mr. Alexander Pope, in Prose. Vol. II,* and the rare reissuing of the "clandestine" volume of 1740, *Letters Between Dr. Swift, Mr. Pope, &c. From the Year 1714 to 1736. Publish'd from a Copy Transmitted from Dublin,* carried individual prefaces, "The Booksellers to the Reader" and "To the Reader," behind which Pope characteristically disavowed any connection with the publications. As the "Booksellers to the Reader" argues, the responsibility for the appearance of the letters belongs to Swift in Ireland, with Pope merely contributing a few additional letters "a little to clear up the History of their Publication. . . ." Those letters of his which would have revealed his determined efforts to collect, edit, and print this correspondence were, of course, suppressed. But from letters which passed between Pope and Lord Orrery and Mrs. Whiteway (Swift's cousin), now available in the Sherburn correspondence, and from the bibliographic studies of Sherburn, Mack, Dearing, and Elias,[2] one can begin to piece together the real story.

Once Pope's correspondence began to appear in print in 1735, he started importuning Swift to return his letters, his interest in their recovery heightened no doubt by Lord Orrery's reports of the Dean's failing health. The communications among the three in 1736–37, when Orrery was in Ireland and could serve as Pope's "agent" in his negotiations, is full of reference to these letters and their possible "Ill use"[3]—a danger apparently realized (perhaps with Pope's own help) when late in 1736 Curll published two letters to Swift, one from Pope and one from Bolingbroke, advertised as "from the Original Manuscripts, transmitted from Ireland."[4] Pope could now renew his pressures on a Swift not so much unwilling as unwell (in May 1737 he writes to Pope, "It is true, I owe you some letters, but it has pleased God, that I have not been in a condition to pay you."),[5] with the result that Orrery did collect a packet of letters, which he delivered to Pope later in the summer.

Even at this time there was talk of a "Chasm of Letters" (from 1717–22) lost, stolen, or "not return'd by Those with whom he entrusted his Papers on some certain occasions."[6] A year later, Swift asserted:

> "I can faithfully assure you, that every letter you have favour'd me with these twenty years and more, are sealed up in bundles, and delivered to Mrs. W[hiteway], a very worthy, rational, and judicious Cousin of mine, and the only relation whose visit I can suffer: All these Letters she is directed to send safely to you upon my decease."[7]

—but then added in a final postscript: "I shewed my Cousin the above letter, and she assures me 'that a great Collection of your/my letters to me,/you are put up and sealed, and in some very safe hand.' " Given this bewildering revelation and the earlier suspicions voiced by Orrery about Swift's friends and servants, there were reasons for Pope's concern that not all his letters were safely back to him. There were no grounds, however, for his unscrupulously using "these grounds to deceive the public into thinking in 1741 that his letters had not been returned to him, but had been printed first in Ireland."[8]

Events had played into his hands. In 1740 Pope learned, first indirectly, then directly, from Mrs. Whiteway that she had some further letters of the Dean to relay to him. In September he wrote Orrery (there is another, even longer "justifying" narrative letter on 30 December), bringing him up-to-date on these and subsequent developments as well as reviewing all that had transpired before—but significantly omitting to mention the letters that he had already received from Swift:

> Mrs. Whiteway then acquainted Mr Nugent [a mutual acquaintance, who had married Pope's old friend Mrs. Knight], that the Letters were found, and that she would transmit them to me. He came away without them; but wrote at my request, & proposed some methods of conveying them safely. . . . In the mean time Mrs. W. was pleas'd to write to me confirming Mr N.'s account, but chusing to send them by another hand. I answered her with all respect, accepted her offer with all acknowledgment and remained in full expectation of the Favour.
>
> Her letter bore date the 3d of June last, and was followed the next month by one from Mr Faukener the Bookseller, which in short acquaints me,
>
> "That a Collection of Letters betwixt the Dean & me, had been sent to the Dean by some unknown persons (from London he supposes, tho they

call themselves in their letter, His Countrymen, & speak of his Merits to Ireland) And that the Dean having read, & thinking them genuine, has given them to him to be printed."

I am sure I need make no Reflections on this whole Proceeding from the beginning to the end; they will be abundantly suggested to a Man of your Candor & Honour. We shall both join in One, which is to lament the Dean's Condition, & not to irritate, but pity him.[9]

Pope pretended dismay and outrage as he forged his insinuations that Mrs. Whiteway and her son-in-law Deane Swift exploited Swift's condition and were ultimately responsible for Faulkner's undertaking—which he maneuvered to delay until his own long-planned but unacknowledged London edition of the correspondence had appeared. This publication he tried also to impute to Mrs. Whiteway: (writing to Orrery, 3 December 1740) "I entirely agree with you, that we can not hinder their publication, either on this side or your side of the water, longer than while we hold up a Negotiation with the Lady. They will infallibly be published here as soon as Falkner has printed his, or as soon as he has desisted from it."[10] But despite his efforts to cover his tracks, to protect himself from any "Imputation"[11] of involvement by scattering the blame where he could, subsequent scholarship has made it clear that in May or June Pope had surreptitiously sent Swift, through the agency of an old friend Samuel Gerrard, a secret printing of those letters he had retrieved from Ireland in 1737—the so-called "clandestine volume"—with an anonymous covering letter: "You may be assured there is *no other Copy* of this Book in any Hands but your own: So that, while you live, it will be in the Power of no other, but yourself, to bestow it on the Publick."[12] When Swift—who doubtlessly took these protestations as well as the furtiveness with a large grain of salt—edited the collection and gave it to Faulkner to publish, Pope was all set to protest the authenticity of the text, which he apparently allowed Cooper to publish as the rare *Letters Between Dr. Swift, Mr. Pope, &c. From the Year 1714 to 1736. Publish'd from a Copy Transmitted from Dublin,*[13] and which he made the basis of his other, major London editions, even reissuing the sheets of the clandestine volume for the 1742 Cooper octavo *The Works of Alexander Pope, Esq; Vol. VII.*

Shameless as Pope's actions were, he had accomplished his goal; as he wrote to Allen, 17 April 1741, ". . . Two of my great Cares are over, one agreable, the other disagreable, as the Cares of this Life generally run mingled: my Grotto is finished, & my Letters are printed. . . ."[14] The two "subterranean" achievements are not so incompatible—certainly not for Pope, whose transforming hand could be devious as well as deft.

Notes

1. *Correspondence,* IV, 59.

2. Sherburn, *Correspondence,* I, xv–xviii et passim; Maynard Mack, "The First Printing of the Letters of Swift and Pope," *The Library,* 19 (1939), 465–85; V. A. Dearing, "New Light on the First Printing of the Letters of Swift and Pope," *The Library,* 24 (1943), 74–86; A. C. Elias, Jr., "The Pope-Swift *Letters* (1740–41): Notes on the First State of the First Impression," *Papers of the Bibliographical Society of America,* 69 (1975), 323–43.

3. *Correspondence,* IV, 8, 42, 50, 52, 58, 60, 63.

4. *The London Evening Post,* No. 1402, 9–11 November 1736. Curll had printed these letters in a volume entitled *New Letters of Mr. Alexander Pope,* and included them in Vol. V of *Mr. Pope's Literary Correspondence.*

5. *Correspondence,* IV, 71.

6. Ibid., IV, 73.

7. Ibid., IV, 115–16.

8. Ibid., IV, 130n.

9. Ibid., IV, 263–64.

10. Ibid., IV, 301.

11. Ibid., IV, 286.

12. Ibid., IV, 243.

13. See Note on Publication and Text, p. 391.

14. *Correspondence,* IV, 340.

NOTE ON PUBLICATION AND TEXT
[TO THE READER (1741)]

The "as yet unidentified" earliest printing of the Pope-Swift correspondence cited by Griffith[1] was originally traced by Maynard Mack to a rare volume, under the imprint of T. Cooper, 1741: *Letters Between Dr. Swift, Mr. Pope, &c. From the Year 1714 to 1736. Publish'd from a Copy Transmitted from Dublin.*[2] The relationship of this text to the "clandestine" volume has long remained conjectural, with Sherburn referring to "modified copies of this printing as issued later,"[3] and Teerink and Scouten distinguishing three different states of the edition.[4] The recent discovery of another, fourth copy of the edition leads A. C. Elias, Jr. to argue that "the known copies of the Cooper edition fall into two neat categories— those belonging to the trade edition, with its later title page (Penn and Yale [Mack's copy]), and those belonging to the earlier period . . . when Pope needed copies for private use."[5]

It is this "trade" edition, the third state, which was eventually published by Cooper and which bears the preface, "To the Reader," here printed. Different from the prefatory "Booksellers to the Reader" of the later London editions of the letters, but like it in spirit, the piece, as Mack noted, "contains some curious echoes of the anonymous letter sent to Swift with the printed sheets of this correspondence.[6] There can be no doubt that Pope is the author of both."[7]

"To the Reader" appears only in the Cooper volume *Letters Between Dr. Swift, Mr. Pope, &c.*, from which the present text (originally printed in italic) is taken:

1741: *Letters Between Dr.* Swift, *Mr.* Pope, *&c. From the Year 1714 to 1736. Publish'd from a Copy Transmitted from* Dublin. London: Printed for T. Cooper, octavo, Teerink/Scouten 60.

Notes

1. Griffith, p. 423.
2. Maynard Mack, "The First Printing of the Letters of Swift and Pope," *The Library*, 19 (1939), 465–85. See also V. A. Dearing, "New Light on the First Printing of the Letters of Pope and Swift," *The Library*, 24 (1943), 74–86.
3. *Correspondence*, I, xxiv.
4. Teerink/Scouten, pp. 139–41.

5. A. C. Elias, Jr., "The Pope-Swift *Letters* (1740–41): Notes on the First State of the First Impression," *Papers of the Bibliographical Society of America,* 69 (1975), 333.

6. [Pope] to Swift, ? May 1740 (*Correspondence,* IV, 242–43).

7. Mack, "The First Printing of the Letters of Swift and Pope," p. 467n.

To the READER. [1741]

W e could not but embrace an Opportunity that was offer'd
some Time since, of preserving the following Letters to Posterity. But it was resolved not to publish them, without first sending
a Copy to Dr. *Swift* himself, and leaving him absolute Master
whether it should be done during his Life, or not?[1] The Dean was
pleas'd to approve, declare it genuine, and gave it with his own
Hands to be printed.[2] We are well inform'd it is making its Appearance in *Ireland*; after which we presume, there can be no Scruple
in our doing the same in *England*.[3] Nor should it be thought any
Wrong (as it cannot be any *Discredit*) to his *Correspondent,* unless he
intended to print it himself:[4] And in that Case, Dr. *Swift* has a Prior
Right, as three Parts in four of the Collection are his.[5] This Publication therefore being perfectly agreeable to the Dean's Inclination,
it ought not to be look'd upon as Pyratical, but will surely deserve
the Thanks of the Publick.

Annotations

1. Maynard Mack has noted the similarity between this statement and the
anonymous letter which accompanied the clandestine volume:

> Sir,—The true Honour which all the honest and grateful Part of this Nation
> must bear you, as the most publick spirited of Patriots, the best of private
> Men, and the greatest polite Genius of this Age, made it impossible to
> resist the Temptation, which has fallen in our Way, of preserving from all
> Accidents a Copy of the *inclosed Papers,* which at once give so amiable a
> Picture of your own excellent Mind, and so strong a Testimony of the Love
> and Respect of those who nearest know, and best can judge of it.
>
> As there is Reason to fear they would be lost to Posterity after your
> Death, if either of your Two great Friends should be possessed of them,
> (*as we are informed you have directed*) they are here collected and submitted
> to your own mature Consideration. Envy itself can find Nothing in them
> that either You, or They, need be ashamed of. But you, Sir, are the Person
> *most* concerned, and ought to be made the *only* Judge in this Case. You may
> be assured there is *no other Copy* [as Sherburn notes (*Correspondence,* IV, 243n),
> this is an improbable statement] of this Book in any Hands but your own:
> So that, while you live, it will be in the Power of no other, but yourself,

to bestow it on the Publick. In so doing You shall oblige all Mankind in general, and *benefit any deserving Friend* in particular. But if during your Life, you suppress is, yet after your Death it is not fit that either You should be robbed of so much of your Fame, or We of so much of your Example;— We are,/Worthy Sir,/your sincere Admirers, Obliged *Country-Men,* and/ Faithful, Affectionate Servants. (*Correspondence,* IV, 242–43.)

2. The history of Faulkner's printing of the letters and Pope's ambiguous efforts to stop publication can be traced through his correspondence with and through the earl of Orrery in the fall and winter of 1740 and the spring of 1741 (*Correspondence,* IV, 262 et passim). In characteristic vein he also wrote to Robert Nugent, 14 August 1740:

. . . last week I received an account from Faukener the Dublin Bookseller, "That the Dean himself has given him a Collection of Letters; of his own & mine & others, to be printed; & he civilly asks my Consent: assuring me the D. declares them genuine, & that Mr Swift, Mrs Whiteway's Son in law, will correct the press, out of his great respect to the Dean & myself." He says, they were collected by some unknown persons, & the Copy sent with a Letter, importing that "it was criminal to suppress such an amiable picture of the Dean, & his private Character appearing in those letters, & that if he would not publish them in his life time, others would after his death."

I think I can make no Reflections upon this strange Incident, but what are truly melancholy, & humble the Pride of human Nature. That the great-est of Genius's tho Prudence may have been the Companion of Wit (which is very rare) for their whole Lives past, may have nothing left them at last but their Vanity. No Decay of Body is half so miserable! I shall write, & do, all I can upon this vexatious Incident, but I despair of stopping what is already no doubt in many hands. (*Correspondence,* IV, 256.)

3. The suggestion of English publication rises early in the intrigue: the earl of Orrery to Pope, 6 October 1740—"If they are printed in England they will soon be published there. . . ." (*Correspondence,* IV, 276.) And Pope wrote to Orrery 27 December: "If ever such an Impression appears in England, I know what to do, & shall do Mr Falkener's Edition no small service, by applying to the Laws in force here to suppress or destroy this." (Ibid., IV, 311–12.)

4. An imputation which Pope consistently and vehemently disavowed; see, for example, his letter to Orrery 25 October 1740 (*Correspondence,* IV, 286), or, just before the appearance of the correspondence, his last letter to Swift (Ibid., IV, 337).

5. Pope had complained to Swift in his last letter to the Dean: "My Part of them [the letters] is far too mean. . . ." (*Correspondence,* IV, 337.)

NOTE ON PUBLICATION AND TEXT
[THE BOOKSELLERS TO THE READER (1741)]

While Pope was manipulating into print the various editions of his correspondence with Swift, he had written to the earl of Orrery: "My Intention is, if I see the printed book come out, either here or in Ireland, to cause any bookseller to add to it a few of the *Dean's* Letters which verify the narrative you see, (And (if you have no Objection) one or two of your own of a former date here cited) and *not to say a word in my own person,* but leave those additional Letters to show the Course of the affair. Unless by their trumpeting the Falsity about, you should judge it necessary to print at the End of the book this very Narrative."[1] It developed that Pope chose to maintain the pose of aloofness, and did not publish his account nor acknowledge the brief preface which introduces *The Works of Alexander Pope, in Prose. Vol. II,* which appeared in London in April 1741 (two months before Faulkner's Dublin edition), in quarto and folio. According to Sherburn the quarto impression preceded the folios, though all three were published simultaneously.[2] Curll then reprinted the quarto as *Dean Swift's Literary Correspondence, for Twenty-four Years; from 1714 to 1738.* In 1742 Pope issued an octavo edition, printed by Cooper, *The Works of Alexander Pope, Esq; Vol. VII,* which Maynard Mack discovered was, in large part, a reissue of the sheets used in the "clandestine volume" (the "clandestine volume" itself was published by Cooper in a rare edition—*Letters Between Dr. Swift, Mr. Pope &c. . . .*—with its own preface [q.v.]).[3] There was another Cooper octavo with the Booksellers' preface that year, *The Works of Alexander Pope, Esq; Vol. IV. Part III,* though Sherburn contends that Pope probably did not read proof or make revision in this printing.[4]

The present text of "The Booksellers to the Reader" follows the 1741 quarto with the substantive changes in the 1742 octavo noted as textual variants.[5] To complete the history of the publication all the editions collated are cited by their Sherburn listings. The piece was also reprinted in the Elwin-Courthope edition of the *Works,* VI, xlv.

[In some copies of the *Works in Prose* the Scriblerian pieces that make up the second half of the volume are introduced by a separate title page (*Tracts of Martinus Scriblerus: And other Miscellaneous Pieces*), directions to the binder, and another "Booksellers to the Reader"—all originally pre-

pared in 1737 for the simultaneous and matching editions of his letters
and "tracts" that Pope was projecting at that time, a plan that failed
apparently because of publication rights.[6] This earlier and shorter "Booksellers to the Reader," which anticipates the preface here printed, runs as
follows (the original in italics):

> There having been formerly published together with the *Dunciad*, Part
> of the *Works* in *Prose* of Mr. *Pope*, &c. and now an Authentic Edition of his
> *Letters*, and those of his Friends, in Folio and Quarto; the Proprietors of the
> following Pieces which have hitherto lain dispers'd in divers irregular Vol-
> umes, thought it would be agreeable to the Purchasers of the large Edition,
> to collect the same in the like Form.
>
> The Treatise of the *Art of Sinking*, and *Virgilius Restauratus*, were written
> between our Author and Dr. *Arbuthnot*; Dr. *Parnelle* had a hand in that of
> the Origine of Sciences; Mr. *Gay* in the Memoirs of a Parish-Clark, and
> two of the Guardians. The Tracts in the name of *Scriblerus* are manifestly
> related to the *Dunciad*, as the Guardians, &c. are to the *Letters*; and may
> therefore be properly bound either at the End of the Dunciad, or with the
> Letters, which shall be most convenient to the Purchaser, as his Books are
> already bound, or not.]

Key to the Critical Apparatus

1741La1 = *The Works of Mr. Alexander Pope, in Prose.* Vol. II. London:
Printed for J. and P. Knapton, C. Bathurst, and R. Dodsley,
quarto, Griffith 531.

1741La2 = *The Works of . . . Pope, in Prose.* Vol. II. . . . folio, Griffith
529, 530.

1742La = *The Works of Alexander Pope, Esq;* Vol. VII. Containing the
Third and Last Part of Letters, Between him and Dr Swift.
London: Printed for T. Cooper, small octavo, Griffith 560.

[1742Ld1 = *The Works of Alexander Pope, Esq.* Vol. IV. Part III. Containing the Third Part of Letters. London: Printed for
R. Dodsley, and Sold by T. Cooper, small octavo, Griffith
570.

1742Ld2 = *The Works of Alexander Pope, Esq.* Vol. IV. Part III. . . . small
octavo, Griffith 571.

1742Le = *The Works of Alexander Pope*, Esq. Vol. IV. Part III. Containing
the third Part of Letters. London: Printed for R. Dodsley, and
Sold by T. Cooper, small octavo, Griffith 572.]

Notes

1. *Correspondence,* IV, 313.
2. Ibid., I, xxiv.
3. See "Introduction," p. 389.
4. *Correspondence,* I, xxv.
5. While this piece is much too short for significant evidence of textual changes in accidentals, one might note that there are only two variations: one comma added ("being an Authentic Edition of his Letters, with those of his Friends") and one deleted ("and not only continued without his Consent but after his absolute Refusal"), neither change crucial.
6. See Maynard Mack, "Two Variant Copies of Pope's *Works* . . . *Volume II:* Further Light on Some Problems of Authorship, Bibliography, and Text," *Library,* 12 (1957), 48–53. David Foxon also reviews the matter in his unpublished collection of Lyell Lectures, *Pope and the Early Eighteenth-Century Book Trade* (1975).

THE
BOOKSELLERS
TO THE
READER.
[1741]

A,B   There having been formerly publish'd, in Folio and Quarto, one Volume of the Works in *Prose* of Mr. *Pope,* being an Authentic Edition of his *Letters* with those of his *Friends,*[1] we thought it would

C   be agreeable to the Purchasers of that Edition to have likewise the *Letters* between him and Dr. *Swift*: These we have copied from an Impression sent from *Dublin,* and said to be printed by the Dean's Direction.[2]

     As it was begun without our Author's Knowledge, and not only continued without his Consent, but after his absolute Refusal, he would not be prevail'd upon to revise those Letters;[3] but gave us a few more of the Dean's, a little to clear up the History of their Publication; which the Reader may see in one View, if he only

D   observes the Passages marked with Comma's in Letters,[4] 75,[5] 77,[6] 81,[7] 84,[8] 86,[9] 87,[10] 88,[11] of this Book.

E   We also obtain'd the *Memoirs* of SCRIBLERUS, being the beginning of a considerable Work undertaken so long ago as in 1713 by several great Hands.[12] As much of it as is here publish'd, and all the *Tracts* in the same Name, were written by our Author and Dr. *Arbuthnot,* except the *Essay on the Origine of Sciences,* in which Dr. *Parnelle* had some hand, as Mr. *Gay* in the *Memoirs of a Parish-Clerk.*[13] The rest were Mr. *Pope's.* And the Reader may be assured he has now a complete Edition, not only of all this Author has written singly, but of whatsoever he wrote in Conjunction with any of his *Friends.*[14]

Textual Variants

Page 398: A. publish'd,] publish'd among the Works of Mr. *Pope, 1742La.*
Page 398: B. in . . . being *Om. 1742La.*
Page 398: C. of that Edition *Om. 1742La.*

Page 398: D. *Numbers appear as follows* 74, 76, 80, 83, 85, 86, 87, 88 *1742La.*
Page 398: E. *Last paragraph om.* *1742La.*

Annotations

1. The "official" folio and quarto editions of 1737: *The Letters of Mr. Alexander Pope, and Several of his Friends.* London: Printed by J. Wright for J. Knapton . . . L. Gilliver . . . J. Brindley and R. Dodsley.

2. From the "clandestine volume" of 1740, secretly printed by Pope and furtively relayed to Swift in May or June of that year, Faulkner reprinted the first Dublin edition, sheets of which were sent to Pope, who protested vigorously and rushed his own London edition through first.

3. Pope had written to the earl of Orrery (27 December 1740): "I can only repeat to Mr Faukener what I told him before, that I utterly dis-approve the Printing it [the Dublin edition of the letters]; tho I agree with your Lordship, it is now as impossible to be supprest as it was at first unworthy to be printed. . . . To what purpose does Mr Falkener offer me to alter or correct any thing? when at the same time he assures me there is Another Edition somewhere over which he hath no Influence? In a word therefore, I will have nothing to do in it; I will neither *Revise, alter, omit,* nor *touch,* a single line of it." (*Correspondence,* IV, 311.) For a full rendering of Pope's protestations and machinations, see the run of letters between him, Orrery, Mrs. Whiteway, and Faulkner from September 1740 through March 1741 (*Correspondence,* IV, 262–338).

4. There is one additional letter so marked, no. 89, the last of the letters and unlisted in the table of contents. The passage in "Comma's" reads as follows:

(Letter LXXXIX: *The Earl of Orrery to Mr. Pope.* Oct. 4, 1738) "Mrs. W—— did assure me she had not one of them [the letters], and seem'd to be under great uneasiness that you shou'd imagine they were left with her. She likewise told me she had stopt the Dean's letter which gave you that information; but believ'd he would write such another; and therefore desir'd me to assure you from her, that she was totally ignorant where they were." [I am ready to testify it; and think it ought to be known,] "That the Dean says they are deliver'd into a safe hand, and Mrs.* W—— declares she has them not. The Consequence of their being hereafter publish'd may give uneasiness to some of your Friends, and of course to you: so I would do all in my power to make you entirely easy in that point." [* (footnote originally printed in reverse italics) "This *Lady* since gave Mr. *Pope* the Strongest Assurances that she had used her utmost Endeavours to prevent the Publication; nay, went so far as to *secrete* the Book, till it was commanded from her, and delivered to the *Dublin* printer: Whereupon her Son in law, D. *Swift,* Esq; insisted upon writing a Preface, to justify Mr. *P.*

from having any Knowledge of it, and to lay it upon the corrupt Practices of the Printers in *London*; but this he would not agree to, as not knowing the Truth of the Fact."]

5. From Swift, 3 September 1735: "You need not fear any consequence in the commerce that both so long passed between us; although I never destroy'd one of your letters. But my Executors are men of honour and virtue, who have strict orders in my will to burn every letter left behind me."

6. From Swift, 21 October 1735: "You need not apprehend any Curll's medling with your letters to me; I will not destroy them, but have ordered my Executors to do that office."

7. From Swift, 22 April 1736:

As to what you say of your Letters, since you have many years of life more than I, my resolution is to direct my Executors to send you all your letters, well sealed and pacqueted, along with some legacies mentioned in my will, and leave them entirely to your disposal: Those things are all tied up, endors'd and locked in a cabinet, and I have not one servant who can properly be said to write or read: No mortal shall copy them, but you shall surely have them when I am no more.

8. To Swift, 30 December 1736: [While the commas are missing here, probably through error, it is easy to locate the relevant passage.]

But I have much reason to fear, those [letters] which you have too partially kept in your hands will get out in some very disagreeable shape, in case of our mortality: and the more reason to fear it, since this last month Curl has obtain'd from Ireland two letters, (one of Lord Bolingbroke and one of mine, to you which we wrote in the year 1723,) and he has printed them, to the best of my memory, rightly, except one passage concerning Dawley which must have been since inserted, since my Lord had not that place at that time. Your answer to that letter he has not got; it has never been out of my custody; for whatever is lent is lost, (Wit as well as Mony) to these needy poetical Readers.

9. From Swift, 31 May 1737:

All the letters I can find of yours, I have fastened in a folio cover, and the rest in bundles endors'd; But, by reading their dates, I find a chasm of six years, of which I can find no copies; and yet I keep them with all possible care: But, I have been forced, on three or four occasions to send all my papers to some friends, yet those papers were all sent sealed in bundles, to some faithful friends; however, what I have, are not much above sixty.

10. From Swift, 23 July 1737: ["he (Lord Orrery) will take with him"] "all the letters I preserved of yours, which are not above twenty-five. I find there is a

great chasm of some years, but the dates are more early than my two last journeys to England, which makes me imagine, that in one of these journeys I carry'd over another Cargo."

11. From Swift, 8 August 1738: "I can faithfully assure you, that every letter you have favour'd me with, these twenty years and more, are sealed up in bundles, and delivered to Mrs. W——, a very worthy, rational, and judicious Cousin of mine, and the only relation whose visits I can suffer: All these Letters she is directed to send safely to you upon my decease."

12. Sherburn notes: "Swift spent the summer of 1713 in Ireland, and very likely only after his return to England another design—possibly also Pope's originally—appealed to the group: that of writing burlesque memoirs of a many-sided pedant, whose name was early determined as Martinus Scriblerus." (*Early Career*, p. 76.) Pope had told Spence, "The design of the *Memoirs of Scriblerus* was to have included all the false tastes in learning, under the character of a man of capacity enough that had dipped in every art and science, but injudiciously in each. It was begun by a club of some of the greatest wits of the age: Lord Bolingbroke, Lord Oxford, the Bishop of Rochester, Mr. Pope, Congreve, Arbuthnot, Swift, and others." (*Anecdotes*, I, 56.)

13. In a chapter "The Authorship, Composition, and Publication of the *Memoirs*," Kerby-Miller reviews the difficult matter of attribution during the various periods of Scriblerus activity (*Memoirs*, pp. 57–67). While the works were ultimately a product of several hands and even more heads, the Pope-Arbuthnot-Gay collaboration seems to have been central.

14. Not included from the previously published Scriblerian satires were *Annus Mirabilis*, *Stradling versus Stiles*, and the notes and prolegomena to the *Dunciad*, the first two omitted, suggests Kerby Miller, because of copyright difficulties. (*Memoirs*, p. 65n.)

A Master Key to Popery

or

*A True and Perfect Key
to Pope's Epistle to
the Earl of Burlington*

INTRODUCTION

For the George Sherburn *Festschrift* John Butt printed, for the first time, a prose pamphlet he discovered in the Chatsworth library,[1] *A Master Key to Popery*, which he established as being Pope's ironic response to the barrage of attacks that greeted his *Epistle to Burlington*.[2] The dunces, aroused by the *Peri Bathous*, the 1728 *Dunciad*, and the *Dunciad Variorum*, had found an ideal issue for revenge in the identification of Timon in the poem—a man of wealth but little taste—with the duke of Chandos, an unpopular millionaire with a pretentious country seat, who, rumor had it, having befriended the poet, was then ruthlessly turned on by his beneficiary. As Dr. Johnson later summarized the situation (in his own turn fostering, with his misrepresentations, the myth of the vicious satirist), "A violent outcry was therefore raised against the ingratitude and treachery of Pope, who was said to have been indebted to the patronage of Chandos for a present of a thousand pounds, and who gained the opportunity of insulting him by the kindness of his invitation."[3]

The unwarranted charges (for the details of the portrait do not particularly well fit either Chandos or his mansion "Cannons," nor, in any case, was he Pope's close friend or patron) came fast and furious—"And if I have not lost my Senses, the Town has lost 'em, by what I heard so late, as but two Days ago, of the Uproar on this Head."[4] Three days after the poem was published on 13 December 1731, Pope had been moved to write (later ascribing the original unsigned letter to William Cleland)[5] two letters, printed as one in the *Daily Post-Boy* for 22 December and reprinted in divided form in the *Daily Journal* the next day, in which he rebutted the accusations ("Why, in God's Name, must a *Portrait* apparently collected from twenty different Men, be applied to one only?").[6] The accusations, however, prevailed, Guerinot noting that "Seven pamphlets in the next few months rejoiced in Pope's ingratitude."[7]

That the slanders were not limited to Grub-Street lampoons but reflected gossip in high places too is perhaps the reason that Pope was so disturbed and defensive; in the open letter to Burlington that he prefixed to the third edition of the *Epistle*, he comments, "This way of Satire is dangerous, as long as Slander rais'd by Fools of lowest Rank, can find any countenance from those of a Higher."[8] And it is a matter of record that on 21 December Lord Hervey had written to his great friend Stephen Fox:

Everybody concurs in their opinion of Pope's last performance, and condemns it as dull and impertinent. I cannot but imagine, by the 18 lines in the last page but one, that he designed ridiculing Lord Burlington as much as he does the Duke of Chandois. It is astonishing to me that he is not afraid this prophecy will be verified, which was told him a year or two ago,

> "In black and white whilst satire you pursue,
> Take heed the answer is not black and blue."[9]

It is also a matter of record that the *Master Key* carries the first mention of "Lord Fanny"—in all probability Lord Hervey here as elsewhere in Pope's satires. Indeed, one of F. W. Bateson's arguments for attributing the pamphlet (which he reprints in Appendix C of the Twickenham edition of the *Epistles*) to Pope is that it includes not only Pope's established enemies but a new group, familiar now from later works—Lord Hervey, Bubb Dodington, Sir Gilbert Heathcote. . . .[10] It demonstrates, then, in a signal way, the shift taking place in Pope's satiric career as he begins to move from the miry ground of the attacks on the dunces to the more elite battlefields of the Horatian poems of the 30s.

As for this particular skirmish, time has vindicated the poet, unearthing documents that disprove allegations like Johnson's and support Pope's own defense (though the question of identification still persists).[11] It has also brought to light *A Master Key*, the oblique version of that defense. For in this ironic parody Pope has, by taking at face value his critics' absurd interpretations, exposed their intrinsic foolishness. As he wryly argues, in one of the partially "straight" assertions of the satire:

> But what seems very unaccountable is, that A Man of any *Genius* (which one wou'd think has its foundation in *Com̃on Sense*) shou'd be the *Greatest Fool* in his age, & constantly choose for the Objects of his Satire, the Best Friends he has? All the Noblemen whom we shall prove him to abuse in this Epistle are such, whose Esteem and Distinction he seem'd most to Court, & to possess; or whose Power and Influence cou'd best protect or credit him: Nay all the Criticks who have been most provok'd at it, are such, as either had been his Friends or call'd themselves so, or had made some pretence to his Acquaintance or Correspondence.

The passage is significant beyond its basic insight into the ridiculousness of the critical storm, in that it underlines Pope's dismay at attack from that segment of society which never before had he had to consider hostile: "The Honour & Veracity of such I will not doubt: especially of so honourable Persons as Lord Fanny, Mᶜ Dorimant, the Lady De-la-Wit, the Countess of Methusalem, & others." With these new antagonists he no doubt felt the need to be more circumspect, more self-protective; and this may well be the central reason why *A Master Key*, like the *Letter to a Noble Lord*, was never published—though as Bateson acknowledges, it "reads as though it had been written for publication."[12]

There are other explanations that could be advanced. Scholars have determined that the piece was probably composed in late January or February 1732;[13] perhaps by the time it was finished, and the attacks were beginning to subside, Pope was ready to let the matter die rather than add fresh fuel to an embarrassing fire, preferring to rest his case on the dignified letter he had prepared for the third edition of the *Epistle*. In another context, writing to Oxford on 22 January about the postponement of the *Epistle to Bathurst* because of its compliment to Chandos (later transferred to the *Epistle to Cobham*), he had explained, "But to print it, now, would be interpreted by Malice (& I find it is Malice I am to expect from the World, not Thanks, for my writings) as if I had done it in atonement, or thro' some apprehension, or sensibility of having meant that Duke an abuse: which I'm sure was far from my Thought,"[14] a danger that could equally apply to the *Master Key* and its even more lavish encomiums. But what in 1732 might not have been tactical or prudent, several hundred years later reminds us that the satire that must provoke does at the same time promote pleasure for the general reader, who even now responds to its sense and wit.

Notes

1. The unsigned MS., in the hand of Lady Burlington, who occasionally served as Pope's copyist in the early 30s, may well be the pamphlet referred to by Pope in a letter to the Earl: "I have a favor to beg of my Lady B. . . . to give me the Copy of my Pamphlet which she writ out, & to keep my original among her papers of greater value. . . ." (*Correspondence*, III, 272.)

2. John Butt, " 'A Master Key to Popery,' " *Pope and His Contemporaries*, ed. Clifford and Landa (Oxford: Clarendon Press, 1949), pp. 41–57.

3. *Lives*, III, 152. Dr. Johnson's charges, developed in two additional paragraphs, have been refuted by Sherburn (see n. 11). The whole matter is also reviewed by F. W. Bateson in Appendix B of the Twickenham Edition of the *Epistle to Several Persons* (TE III ii, 170–74).

4. Pope to Hill, 22 December 1731 (*Correspondence*, III, 260).

5. Pope reprinted the letter with his correspondence: in the 1735 texts with the heading "To J. Gay, Esq." and in the octavos of 1737–43 headed "Mr. Cleland to Mr. Gay." It is included by Sherburn in the *Correspondence* (III, 254–57).

6. Ibid., p. 256.

7. Guerinot, p. xxiv. He lists the following relevant works: Leonard Welsted, *Of Dulness and Scandal. Occasion'd by the Characters of Lord Timon.* (3 January 1732); [Matthew Concanen] *A Miscellaney on Taste. By Mr. Pope, &c. Viz. I. Of Taste in Architecture. An Epistle to the Earl of Burlington. With Notes Variorum, and a Compleat Key.* (15 January 1732); [John Cowper?] *Of Good Nature. An Epistle Humbly Inscrib'd to His G{ra}ce the D{u}ke of C{hando}s.* (22 January 1732); *Malice Defeated. A Pastoral Essay. Occasioned By Mr. Pope's Character of Lord Timon, In his Epistle to the Earl of Burlington, and Mr. Welsted's Answer.* (1 February 1732); *On P{op}e and W{elste}d. Occasion'd by their late Writings.* (8 February 1732); *Mr. Taste, the Poetical Fop* (retitled, *The Man of Taste. A Comedy.*) (5 April 1732); [Thomas Cooke] "A Letter in Prose to Mr. Alexander Pope, occasioned by the Epistle in Verse to the Earl of Burlington," *The Comedian,* Numb. II (May 1732).

8. To the earl of Burlington [January 1731/2], *Correspondence,* III, 266.

9. Earl of Ilchester, *Lord Hervey and His Friends 1726–38* (London: John Murray, 1950), pp. 124–25.

10. TE III ii, 175.

11. If George Sherburn (" 'Timon's Villa' and Cannons," *The Huntington Library Bulletin,* 8 [1935], pp. 131–52) and F. W. Bateson (TE III ii, Appendix B) finally acquitted Pope of the Chandos charges, the matter of identification of "Timon" and his villa is far from resolved. Cases have been made for Walpole and his estate (by Kathleen Mahaffey ["Timon's Villa: Walpole's Houghton," *Texas Studies in Literature and Language,* 9 (1967), 193–222] and Maynard Mack [*The Garden and the City* (London: Oxford University Press, 1969), Appendix F]), for Walpole but Blenheim (by Morris R. Brownell [*Alexander Pope & the Arts of Georgian England* (Oxford: Clarendon Press, 1978), Appendix C]), and for Chatsworth, among other possibilities (by Pat Rogers ["Timon's Villa Again," *British Journal for Eighteenth-Century Studies,* II (1979), 63–65]). Most recently, James R. Aubrey, in an article significantly entitled "Timon's Villa: Pope's Composite Picture" (*Studies in Philology,* 80 [1983], 325–48), reviews the situation and argues just that—that Pope's satire is broadly, rather than specifically, directed, with Timon's villa a "synthesis of offensive objects."

12. TE III ii, xxxii.

13. Ibid., pp. 175–76.

14. *Correspondence,* III, 267.

NOTE ON PUBLICATION AND TEXT

The pamphlet *A Master Key to Popery: or, A True and Perfect Key to Pope's Epistle to the Earl of Burlington* was first printed by John Butt [J. B.] in *Pope and His Contemporaries: Essays presented to George Sherburn* (ed. Clifford and Landa, Oxford: Clarendon Press, 1949). It has since been reprinted, in Appendix C of the Twickenham edition of the *Epistles to Several Persons* (TE III ii), by F. W. Bateson [F. W. B.]. The present text follows the first printing, with the kind permission of the Oxford University Press, but, where appropriate, incorporates the notes of both editors, so designated (again with the permission of the Oxford University Press and, in the case of Bateson's notes, Methuen & Co., publishers of the Twickenham edition).

A Master Key to Popery

or

A True and Perfect Key to Pope's Epistle to the Earl of Burlington

I have undertaken at the Request of Several Persons of Quality,[1] the Explanation of a piece very loudly and justly complain'd of; or more properly a Dissection of the Bad Heart of the Author. It cannot be displeasing to any Man of Honour, to see the same Fair Opinions and good Reasons in *Print* which he has vented & propagated in all Conversations.[2] It must be pleasing, to see here the *Proofs* of many Charges against him, which have hitherto been advanc'd without full demonstration: And it must be an additional Satisfaction to find him guilty of many *others,* which I shall prove, upon the *Same Principles.*

The Poet's Design is two-fold, to *affront* all the *Nobility & Gentry,* and to *Starve* all the *Artisans & Workmen* of this Kingdom.[3] Under pretence of destroying the *Vanity* of the former, he aims to ruin the *Support* of the latter; and by rend'ring the Patrons discontented with all such works, put a Stop to the Arts, & obstruct the Circulation of Money, in this Nation,[4] to Send a begging the Industrious Mechanicks we have at home, & introduce Italians, Frenchmen, Papists & Foreigners, in their Stead.

I appeal to all my Superiors, if any thing can be more insolent than thus to Break (as I may say) into their Houses & Gardens, Not, as the Noble Owners might expect, to *Admire,* but to *laugh* at them? or if any thing can be more Grating and vexatious, to a Great Peer or an Opulent Citizen, than to see a Work, of the expence of twenty or thirty thousand pounds, which he thought an Ornament to the Nation, appear only a Monument of his own Folly?[5] Insolent Scribler! that being unable to tax Men of their Rank & Worth with any Vice or Fault beside, is reduced to fall upon their *Taste* in those polite Expences & elegant Structures which are the Envy of all other Nations, and the Delight of our own![6] God forbid, it should hinder any of those Magnificent Persons, from enjoying their Noble Fancies,

& delighting in their own Works! May every Man *Sit peaceably Under his own Vine,*[7] in his own Garden; May every *Man's House be his Castle,*[8] not only against Thieves, but against *Ill Eyes* & Envious Observers; and may those who have succeeded the worst, meet with a better fate than to be at once *Ill-lodg'd* & Ridiculed.

To avoid the imputation of any Envy against this Poet, I shall first confess that I think he has some Genius, and that it is *Only his Morals* that I attack.[9]

But what seems very unaccountable is, that A Man of any *Genius* (which one wou'd think has its foundation in *Comon Sense*) shou'd be the *Greatest Fool* in his age, & constantly choose for the Objects of his Satire, the Best Friends he has? All the Noblemen whom we shall prove him to abuse in this Epistle are such, whose Esteem and Distinction he seem'd most to Court, & to possess; or whose Power and Influence cou'd best protect or credit him: Nay all the Criticks who have been most provok'd at it, are such, as either had been his Friends or call'd themselves so, or had made some pretence to his Acquaintance or Correspondence.

It it [*sic*] to *some* of *these* that I am beholden for many In-lets into his *Meaning & Thoughts*: For a man's meanings & Thoughts lye too remote from any such, as cou'd make the discovery from *Private Conversation,* or some degree of *Confidence,* or *Familiarity.* The Honour & Veracity of such I will not doubt: especially of so honourable Persons as Lord Fanny,[10] Mr Dorimant,[11] the Lady De-la-Wit,[12] the Countess of Methusalem, & others.

I confess further, that I am in many instances, but the Collector of the dispers'd Remarks of his Majesty's Poet Laureat,[13] his Illustrious Associate Sr William Sweet-Lips,[14] the Lady Knaves-acre[15] & Mrs Haywood[16] (those ornaments of their Sex) and Capt. Breval,[17] and James Moore Esqr:[18] and Mr Concanen,[19] & Mr Welsted,[20] and Henry K——y Esqr[21] of the two last of whom I ought in Justice to say, we owe to the one the most *considerable writings,* & to the other the *Longest Discourses* on this Subject.[22]

My First Position is, that this Poet is a man of so *Bad a Heart,* as to stand an Exception to the Rule of Macchiavel,[23] who says 'No Man, in any Nation, was ever Absolutely Wicked, *for nothing.*' Now this Poet being so, it is fair to Suppose, that of *two* or *more* persons whom he may be thought to abuse, we are always to understand it of the Man he is *most oblig'd to*: but in such cases where his obligations seem *equal,* we impartially suppose the Reflection on *both.* Secondly, when so malevolent a man draws any character consisting of *many Circumstances,* it must be apply'd, not to the person with whom *most* but with whom *fewest* of those Circumstances agree:[24] And this for a plain reason, because it is a stronger mark of that Artifice & Cowardice on the one hand, and of that Injustice & Malice on the other, with which such a Writer abounds.

I am nevertheless so reasonable as not to insist as some Criticks on this occasion have done, that when a Circumstance will not suit with a Father, it shou'd be apply'd to a Son or Grandson,[25] but I must insist on my two former Positions, upon which depends all which others have said, & which I shall say on this subject.

To begin with his Title, It was first, of *Taste,* Now 'tis of *false Taste,* to the Earl of Burlington.[26] Is this alteration made to impute False Taste to that Earl? or out of unwillingness to allow that there is any True Taste in the Kingdom?

Nothing is more certain, than that the Person first & principally abus'd is the said Earl of Burlington.[27] He cou'd not well abuse him for *Want* of *Taste,* since the allowing it to him was the only Channel to convey his Malignity to others: But he abuses him for a *worse want,* the want of *Charity* (one from which his Lordship is as free as any man alive). This he tells him directly, without disguise, and in the second person,[28]

> —What thy hard heart denies,
> Thy charitable Vanity supplies.

So much for Malice; now for ill-nature,

> Another age shall see the golden Ear
> Imbrown *thy* Slope, and nod on *thy* Parterre,
> Deep Harvest bury all *thy* Pride has plann'd,
> And laughing Ceres re-assume the Land.[29]

That is, 'My Lord, your Gardens shall soon be Plow'd up, & turned into Corn-fields.'

How he indulges himself in drawing this picture? and with what joy does he afterwards expatiate upon the mortifying Consideration, how all his Lordships labours in Architecture shall be lost, and his Models misapply'd by imitating Fools?

> ——Reverse your Ornaments & hang them all
> On some patch'd Dog-hole &c

This is his Element! this his Pleasure! when he comes at last, with much ado, to com̃end the Noble Lord, how spareing, how short, is he! The whole is but two lines,

> In you, my Lord, Taste Sanctifies Expence,
> For Splendour borrows all her rays from *Sense.*

which amounts just to this, 'My Lord, you are no Fool.' but this we shall see by what follows, he thinks a great distinction for a Lord in these days.

> Oft' have you hinted to your Brother Peer—
> Something there is—'Tis Sense.—Good Sense.[30]

A Hint does he call it? 'tis a very broad one, that there is a Want of Sense in his Brother Peers, that is to say, in the whole House of Lords. Mr Concanen[31] & Mr Theobald[32] (both Lawyers) are of opinion, this may be prosecuted as Scandalum Magnatum on the whole Collective Body. From what we have observ'd of his Prophecy of the Destruction of Chiswick Gardens,[33] it shou'd seem as if this wretch alluded to his Lordships want of a *Male Heir.*[34] If he had one, he had been probably treated like another of his *Friends,* the Lord Bathurst:[35] whose noble Plantations at Cirencester he prophecy's with like Malignity shall be destroy'd & lay'd levell by his Lordships *Son*; for which no doubt, that ingenious and sober young Gentleman is much oblig'd to him.

> Thro' his young Woods how pleas'd Sabinus stray'd,
> Or sate delighted in the thick'ning Shade,
> With annual joy the red'ning shoots to greet,
> And see the stretching branches long to meet.
> His Son's fine Taste an op'ner Vista loves,
> Foe to the Dryads of his Fathers Groves;
> The thriving Plants ignoble Broomsticks made
> Now sweep those Allyes they were born to shade.

I wonder this piece of Malice has escap'd all the Criticks; and I suspect it was to screen this Author, that his gentle Friend Lord Fanny apply'd to this Nobleman the Character of Villario[36]

> His bloomy Beds a waving Glow display,
> Blushing in bright Diversities of Day,
> With silver-quiv'ring Rills mæander'd o'er,
> —Enjoy them you! Villario can no more:
> Tir'd with the Scene Parterre & Fountains yield,
> He finds at last he better likes a Field.

For first, my Lord Bathurst is known to be of the most constant temper in the world in all his Pleasures.[37] Secondly, he never was a *Florist,*[38] is so much an Enemy to *nice Parterres,* that he never mows, but grazes them, & thirdly, has no water at Cirencester to squander away in Mæanders. I should rather think we are still at Chiswick, abusing all my Ld Burlington's Friends & Neighbours. I know such a Garden, which has an Out-let too into the *Fields,* where this Nobleman sometimes takes the Air,[39] the name of Villario shews him to live near the Town; where Flowers & Parterres are most in Vogue; & (which is more with me than all other circumstances) where this very Author has been often receiv'd in a manner far superiour to his deserts.

The Houses of these two Lords have escaped Abuse, for a plain reason; neither of them wou'd be hurt by it—and the latter has by good fortune some Works at present under the direction of the Earl of Burlington.[40]

We have now done with Chiswick, a Soyl so fruitfull of Satyr for the Poet, that I tremble for the *Reverend Vicar* of the *Parish!* not only as he is his *Friend,* but as his eminent Learning, & particularly in the *Greek,* must have made him sorely obnoxious to him.[41]

Being arrived in Town, where should he begin but with the *Best, Good Man* of the City, even the Father of the City, Sir Gilbert![42]

> What brought Sr Shylocks ill-got wealth to waste!

There could not be invented a falser Slander, or one that would *more hurt* this eminent Citizen, than to insinuate that he had *wasted his wealth.* 'Tis true, I think as well as Sir Gilbert, that *every Expence is Some Waste:* yet surely so small a sum, as ten pounds eleven shillings, for Iron Rails to secure his Court-yard, ought never to have been thus pointed out & insulted? But what means he by wealth ill-got? neither Sir G nor I know of any such thing. This is as errant nonsense as what follows—— A *Wealthy Fool.* How can that be? Wealth is the proof of Wisdom, & to say that Sir G——'s wealth is wasted, is to say that his Parts are decay'd.

> See Sportive Fate——Bids Babo build——

Here the Criticks differ. Some read, for Babo, Bubo.[43] Others fix this on a Peer who I confess is noble enough for our Authors abuse; but (what I always take for a cause to doubt it) one to whom he has no sort of Obligation. Tis certain Sh——d is this Nobleman's Builder, but why should he satyrize Sh——d? Sh——d is none of his *Friends.* I am persuaded that by Sh——d he means *Gibs* with whom he is acquainted.[44]

The next we shall take notice of is the only Person he seems willing to praise, & perhaps loves (if he loves anybody) the Lord Cobham.[45] Yet when he speaks of his Gardens or some other of his L^dships personal performances (for I am not clear of which) what a filthy stroke of smut has he bestowed upon him?

> Parts answer'ing Parts, shall slide into a *whole*

As if his L^dsps fine Gardens were to be just such another Scene of Lewdness as Cupids Gardens or Faux-hall.[46]—I ought not to suppress, that I owe this Remark to a Right Honourable Lady.

Here we have a fling at honest Bridgeman.[47] I don't wonder to see his name at length, for he is his particular Acquaintance. What a Malicious Representation of one who lives by his profession, as taking pleasure to destroy and overflow Gentlemens fine Gardens!

> The vast Parterres a thous^d hands shall make
> Lo Bridgeman comes, & floats them with a Lake.[48]

As if he should have the Impudence, when a Gentleman has done a wrong thing at a great Expence, to come & pretend to make it a right one?[49] Is it not his business to please Gentlemen? to execute Gentlemen's will and Pleasure, not his own? is he to set up his own Conceits & Inventions against Gentlemen's fine Taste & Superiour

Genius? Yet is this what the Poet suggests, with intent (doubtless) to take the Bread out of his mouth, & ruin his Wife & Family.

We come now to the Character (or rather Description) of Timon: and it is in this I shall principally labour, as it has chiefly employ'd the pains of all the Criticks. I shall enumerate the several opinions of all others, & shew the Malice & Personal Reflection to extend much farther than has hitherto been imagin'd by any. It is shewing the Author great & undeserv'd Indulgence to confine it to any One, tho' that one were the Best Man in the world: There are so many By-peeps & squinting Glances, besides the main View, that instead of twenty things being aim'd at one, every one Circumstance is aim'd at twenty.[50]

I must first take notice of the greatest Authorities which seem against me, and great ones they are indeed, Sir William Sweet-lips and Mr Dorimant.[51] Equal Genius's! Equal Judges! every way equal Ornaments to their Country! the Mecænas, & the Phoebus of our Age! and to both of whom our Poet has been indebted for as great Commendation & Praise as was consistent with their own Superiority. In order to give due Weight to their several arguments, I must take a View of Timon's character in all its Circumstances.

A Proud, haughty Man, with no other Idea of Greatness but Bulk and Size, but himself a little contemptible Creature. His House consists of Unequal Parts, heap'd one upon another like a Quarry of Stones. His Gardens are choak'd up with Walls, every where in sight, which destroy all Appearance of Natural Beauty. The Form of his Plantation is stiffly regular, & the same repeated. A vast Lake-fall to the North: an immense Parterre with two Small Cupids in it: Trees cut into human figures, & statues as close as Trees: his Fountains without Water: a Terras of Steep Slopes with a Study opening upon it, where he receives his guests with the utmost Affectation: his Books chosen for their Printers or Binders, no good Modern Books, & (to make them perfectly a Show) the upper Shelves only Wooden and painted ones. He has a Chappel, with Musick & Painting in it, but the Musick consists of Jigs and loose Airs, and the painting of indecent or naked figures. He gives Entertainments attended by an hundred Servants, in a Hall paved with Marble; his Bufet is ornamented with Serpents & Tritons; his Dinner is a sol-

emn, formal, troublesome thing, with perpetual rounds of Salvers &
Sweet wine, & upon the whole with so much Pride & affected State,
as to make every man Sick both of his Dinner & of Him.

This is the Character, which Mr Dorimant, M^r K——y,[52] the Lord
Fanny, have imputed to the D. of C.[53] This is what has been affirmed
with Oaths by M^r C——r[54] and very publickly by Mr Theobalds, M^r
Goode,[55] Mr James Moore, the whole Herd of Criticks, & all the
honourable Gentleman of the Dunciad.

I have the greatest temptation imaginable to wish this could be
proved. Nothing would be so high an instance of this Man's
Wickedness as to fix the worst-natured Satire on the best-natured
Man; to tax with Pride the most Affable, with Vanity the most
Charitable, with the worst Choice of Books one of the most Learned
of our Nobility, with the Pride of Prayer one of the sincerest Wor-
shippers of God, and with ill-judged Extravagance one of the most
hospitable and hearty Lovers of his Neighbour.[56]

This would have been such a Pleasure to me, that I thought no
pains too great to procure it; and therefore (out of my great Love
to Truth, & for the same reason that Pythagoras and Plato travel'd
into Ægypt) I took a Journey to C——n——ns.[57] I may venture to
say, few Criticks have been at the trouble: & yet it is impossible to
judge exactly of this Authors Spite & Malice, without being at the
pains, both of knowing the place, & of reading the Poem.

I went first to the Chappel: I ask'd after the *Musick*; they told me
there had been none for several years. I ask'd for the *Dean,* there
was no such Man. I enquir'd for the *hundred servants,* there had been
no such number. There was no *Silver Bell*; no Paintings of Verrio or
La guerre, but of Bellucci or Zeman;[58] no Study opening on a Terras,
but up one pair of stairs; no Books dated on the back or painted,
and as many Modern as Ancient ones. In the Garden, no Walls
crossing the eye, no large Parterre at all, no little Cupids, no Lake
to the North, no cut Trees, no such Statues, no such Terras; in a
word, no one Particular resembling: only what is common to all
great Men, there was a large House, a Garden, a Chappel, a Hall,
and a Dinner.[59]

I must declare Not One of these Circumstances to be True, which
so many Gentlemen have affirm'd upon their own Knowledge. I am sensible

of the Consequence of giving *Gentlemen* the LYE, but it is ever held fair among *Criticks,* practis'd by the *most Learned* and both given & taken reputably by the best Authors.

Yet far be it from me to say, but in spite of the disagreement of All the Particulars, there may yet be Excellent Reasons for fixing the whole on the Duke. However it is but fair to report the Arguments on all sides. Timon (says one) was a Man-Hater, ergo it is not the Duke. But M[r] Moore replys very wittily, Timon lov'd Mankind *before* he hated them, he did not hate men till they had *abus'd* him, and the Duke may now with some cause, for he has been *very much abused.* Timon was famous for Extravagancies, the Duke for well-judg'd Bounties; but Peter W——rs Esq.[60] argues thus. 'He that is bountifull: is not so rich as if he had never been bountifull: whatever a man parts with, he is so much the poorer for; & he that has but a hundred pounds less than he had, is in some decline of Fortune.' This he thinks a plain reason for any body to disesteem, or abuse a Man. And M[r] Dorimant also thinks nothing so natural, as to *Desert* or *fall upon a Great Man* on the *first suspicion* of his *Decline* of *Fortune.* But certainly every Man of Honour who is what another-guess Author than this, in another-guess Epistle than this, describes himself,

In Power a Servant, out of Power a Friend,[61]

must feel the highest Indignation at such a practise. Indeed our Poets Enemies (and to such only I give Credit) have often severely lash'd him in sharp Satyrs & lively Ballads for the Contrary practise: for his adhering to some Folks in their Exile, to some in their disgrace, & others in their Imprisonment.[62] And I do think there is one good reason why he should rather attack a Man in Power, because it were a greater Object of his Envy, and a greater Proof of his Impudence.

Let us then hear Sir William (who thinks in this against the Majority, as he never sides with it, but on cogent reasons.) Why (says he) for God's sake may not this be Sir Robert?[63] are not his works as great as any man's? Who has more Groves nodding at Groves of his own plantation? I cannot say much as to his Chappel; but who has rival'd his Dinners? especially at the Time this Poem was publish'd, when he was splendidly entertaining the Duke of

Lorain?[64] Has he not a Large Bufet? Has he not a hundred, nay near five hundred, Servants? (In power, your Servants) and who oftener drinks the King's Health? How convincing are all these circumstances! I defy the Partizans of the other opinion to match them. And yet there is one which convinces me more than all; the Author never Saw Houghton:[65] and how marvellously does it suit with his Impudence, to abuse the Things he never Saw?

But what principally inclines Sir William to this opinion is, that unless Sir Robert be abus'd here, he is not abus'd in the whole Poem, a thing which he thinks altogether Incredible. And I may add another reason which persuaded Mr Welsted (and doubtless will many others) that the Duke does not take this to himself, therefore it can do the Poet no hurt; unless we can fix it on another.[66]

Furthermore, if (as some have suggested) this Malevolent Writer hates any man for Munificence to his Brethren, certainly Sir Robert of all Mankind must be the Man he hates.[67] Tis true he never endeavour'd to obstruct that Munificence to any of them, but that is to be imputed to his Malice, as he thought those Distinctions would be no Credit to that great Minister.

Be it as it will, this Poet is equally happy when he can abuse either side. To shew his wicked Impartiality, at the same time he is squinting at Sir R. he has not spared his old Friend the Lord Bolingbroke.

> A gaping Triton spews to wash y^r face,

is the exact Description of the bufet at Dawley.[68] Nothing sure can equal the Impudence of such a Guest, except the Indifference of that stupid Lord, who they say is not provok'd at it. I doubt not the Honourable Mr Pulteney wou'd have had his share, but that he, poor Gentleman! has no Villa to abuse.[69]

I return to my first Position. The Extent of this mans malice is beyond being confin'd to any One. Every Thrust of his Satyr, like the Sword of a Giant tranfixes four or five, and serves up spitted Lords and Gentlemen with less ceremony than Skew'r'd Larks at their own Tables.

I am very sure that all he says of the Chappel, its Painting & its Musick, is to be apply'd to his Grace the Duke of R——tl——d's at

Be——ir-Castle.[70] Why not to several other Lords who have Musick in their Chappels, unless Organs be no Musick?

I am as certain that what follows was to ridicule the Dignity & the Dinners, the Solemnity and the Salvers, the numerous attendants & gaudy Sideboard, of a Nobleman (who to inhance the Ill-nature of the Satyr) has lay'd all his Vanities in the Grave. I mean the Companion in arms & Friend of the great Duke of Marleborough.[71]

I know that the Building describ'd to be so huge, so like a Quarry, such a Heap, &c. is the Immortal Castle of Blenheim[72] (to which the Spite of a Papist may well be imagin'd) and I know my Lord F——th[73] will be of my opinion. And possibly had not the Duke of Shrewsbury[74] been once a Papist, he wou'd never have call'd it a *Quarry of Stone above-ground*: That well known saying of his fixes this to Blenheim.

Were it to be apply'd to a House and not a Castle, I should fancy it must be to one in Dorsetshire of the same Architect; It would be like this Poets Injustice, to reflect on a Gentleman's Taste for a thing which he was oblig'd to build on another Man's scheme—But this Gentleman's Taste is since fully vindicated, by what has been built on his own Directions, that most Genteel Pile in Pall-Mall, which is the Admiration of all Beholders.[75]

No, the Greater the Object, the Stronger is his malice. Greatness itself is his Aversion; nay he hates Pride for being only the Shadow of Greatness. From National Works he would proceed to Royal, if he durst. Who but must have observ'd in this light that monstrous Couplet?

> ——Proud Versailles! thy Glory falls,
> And Nero's Terrasses desert their walls.

What an Impudent Reflection on the memory of Lewis the Fourteenth of France, and another Great Prince!

I hope the Zeal which has been shewn hitherto only in general against this Poet, may soon operate farther when the Three Estates are assembled, and Proper Pains and Penalties be found to repress such Insolence.

After all, it would seem unfair not to own, there is something at the end of his Epistle which looks like a Complement to the King:

But sure 'tis a very strange one! just to single out the Only Good & great things which his Majesty has *Not* done for his Subjects. His Majesty may do them yet; but so much as I wish the Publick Good, I can hardly desire it should be just at the Time, when an Impertinent Poet prescribes it. No——may those Usefull and popular Works be first advised by such whose Office and Dignity it better agrees with, by Men less warp'd by Interest than he, less led by Party than he, less affected by Passion than he;[76] in whom, the same suggestions, wch in him are doubtless Dis-affection & Malice, may be look'd upon as Affection & Loyalty: And who (tho' the Things propos'd be the same) may yet be better heard, & therefore may better deserve the Thanks of the Publick.

FINIS

Annotations

(See Note . . . on the Text, p. 409, . . . for the "J. B." and "F. W. B." designations.)

1. Sherburn, in " 'Timon's Villa' and Cannons" (*The Huntington Library Bulletin,* 8 [1935]), conjectures that "The first outcry [against the *Epistle to Burlington*] . . . must have been oral rather than printed, and it may have been voiced by persons of importance, whose opinions are difficult to trace" (pp. 132–33).

2. One of the things that had so disturbed Pope about the Chandos furor was that much of it *was* nebulous gossip: "It's an aukward Thing for a Man to print, in Defence of his own Work, against a Chimaera: You know not who, or what, you fight against: The Objections start up in a new Shape, like the Armies and Phantoms of Magicians, and no Weapon can cut a Mist, or a Shadow." (Pope to Hill, 22 December 1731; *Correspondence,* III, 260.)

3. Pope had obviously been stunned by the reception which greeted his poem—attacks which ignored its basic themes of prodigality, gardening, and architecture, to focus almost exclusively and vitriolically on the Timon portrait. His letter in the *Daily Post-Boy* voiced his dismay and frustration:

> I am *astonished* at the Complaints occasion'd by a late *Epistle* to the *Earl of Burlington.* . . . Had the Writer attacked Vice, at a Time when it is not only tolerated but triumphant. . . . Had he satirized Gamesters of one hundred thousand Pounds Fortune. . . . In any of these Cases, indeed, I might have judged him too presumtuous, and perhaps have trembled for his Rashness.
>
> I could not but hope better for this small and modest Epistle, which

attacks *no one Vice* whatsoever; which deals only in *Folly* and not Folly in general, but a single Species of it; that only Branch, for the opposite Excellency to which, the Noble Lord to whom he writes must necessarily be celebrated, I fancied it might escape Censure, especially seeing how tenderly he treated these Follies, and seemed less to accuse them, than to make their Apology. (*Correspondence,* III, 254–55.)

4. *A Miscellany on Taste* (ascribed to Matthew Concanen, London, 1732) had challenged Pope's lines "At Timon's Villa let us pass a day, / Where all cry out, 'What Sums are thrown away!' " with the argument, "The Publick certainly gathered up as much as he threw away, and this was no more than changing Hands. The whole was undoubtedly given to Stone-Cutters, Carvers, Statuaries, Bricklayers, Carpenters, Joyners, Labourers, &c. All the Materials too were undoubtedly the Produce of our own Island, except a little foreign Marble, and some other Trifles of small Importance. So that such a private Expence is so far from being a Publick Loss, that the Nation would not be one Farthing the poorer, if fifty such Fabricks were erected every ten or a dozen years." ("Remarks," pp. 12–13.) Ironically, this was part of Pope's point; see n. 27. As he himself commented in the *Daily Post-Boy* letter, ". . . *Ill Taste* employs more Hands, and diffuses Expence more than a *Good* one." (*Correspondence,* III, 255.)

5. In sketching Timon (for about one-third of the poem) Pope had had his fun, of course, satirizing the bad taste and pretentiousness of such wealthy noblemen.

6. "Burlington's short preface in Italian to Palladio's *Fabriche Antiche* (1730) includes the claim, advanced in all seriousness, that no other period in history had exhibited 'maggiore disposizione a dispendiose Fabriche'. But no other period had 'più ignoranti Pretenditori che guidano altrui fuor delle vere Traccie di tanto bell' Arte'." [F. W. B., p. 177.]

7. "Cf. *Henry VIII,* v v 34–5:

> every man shall eat in safety
> Under his own vine . . .

The original source is *Micah,* iv 4." [F. W. B., p. 177.]

8. "The proverb appears in this form in John Ray's *English Proverbs* (1670), p. 106." [F. W. B., p. 177.]

9. "Pope was especially sensitive to attacks upon his morals. He told Hill (26 Jan. 1730–1) that he 'never thought any great matters of my poetical capacity; I only thought it a little better, comparatively, than that of some very mean writers, who are too proud. But I do know certainly, my moral life is superior to that of most of the wits of these days.' " [J. B., p. 46.]

10. "Probably Lord Hervey, though Pope's first use of the soubriquet in print, in *Imit.Hor., Sat.,* II i, 6 (February 1732/3), is later than the probable date of

composition of *A Master Key* (February 1731/2.)" [F. W. B., p. 178.] For Pope's relations with Lord Hervey, see *Letter to a Noble Lord*.

11. "Probably George Bubb Dodington. . . . Dorimant is the witty hero of Etherege's *The Man of Mode*, and Dodington was celebrated both for his wit and his magnificent clothes. Pope has a Dorimant again in *Imit. Hor., Ep.*, I i, 88, who may also be Dodington. Cf. Atticus and Addison, Worldly and Wortley, etc." [F. W. B., p. 178.]

12. "Perhaps Mary Howard, Countess of Delorain (1700–44), a mistress of George II whom Pope was to attack in *Imit. Hor., Sat.*, II i, 81 (February 1733). See [TE] vol. IV, p. 365. It is more likely that Lady Mary Wortley Montagu was intended. Butt quotes the MS. variant of *Epistle to Arbuthnot*, 369, 'that dang'rous thing, a female wit'." [F. W. B., p. 178.]

13. "Colley Cibber (1671–1757), appointed Poet Laureate December 1730 and an old enemy of Pope's (see [TE] vol. V, pp. 433–4)." [F. W. B., p. 178.]

14. "Probably Sir William Yonge (d. 1755), the Whig politician, who was often satirized in Pope's later poems. The association with Cibber may allude to Yonge's contributing the songs to *The Jovial Crew*, a successful ballad opera produced by Cibber at Drury Lane in February 1730/1. Hervey's description of Yonge as 'good-natured, never offensive in company' (*Memoirs*, p. 36), suggests that 'Sweet-Lips' was an appropriate name to give him. See also [TE] *E. on Man*, IV 278*n* and [TE] vol. IV, p. 394." [F. W. B., p. 178.]

15. "I do not know who Pope intended Lady Knaves-Acre to represent. Her association with Eliza Haywood suggests that she may have been somebody with literary pretensions." [F. W. B., p. 178.]

16. "Eliza Haywood (1693?–1756), novelist, dramatist, and writer of scandalous memoirs. See [TE] vol. V, p. 443." [F. W. B., p. 178.]

17. "John Durant Breval (1680?–1738), one of the 'dunces'. See [TE] vol. V, pp. 430–1." [F. W. B., p. 178.]

18. "James Moore Smythe. See *To a Lady*, 243–8*n* [TE III ii, 69–70] and [TE] vol. V, p. 455." [F. W. B., p. 178.]

19. "Matthew Concanen (1701–49), a 'dunce' who was suspected of a hand in the retaliatory *A Miscellany on Taste* (1732), ridiculing *To Burlington*. See [TE III ii,] p. 128 . . . and [TE] vol. V, pp. 434–5." [F. W. B., p. 179.]

20. "Leonard Welsted (1688–1747), a 'dunce', who had published on 3 January 1731/2 a poem attacking Pope entitled *Of Dulness and Scandal. Occasion'd by the Character of Lord Timon*, and had followed this up on 10 February with the more offensive *Of False Fame*. See [TE] vol. V, p. 166." [F. W. B., p. 179.]

21. "Probably the 'Kelsey' whose talkativeness is satirized in the later editions of *Dunciad* A, II 382. The MS. of that passage gives 'Kelsall'. Henry Kelsall (d. 1762) was one of the four Chief Clerks to the Treasury. Nothing is known about Kelsall's relations with Pope. He was clearly a staunch Whig, and the fact

that he is always referred to as 'Esquire' indicates that he was of gentle birth."
[F. W. B., p. 179.]

22. Rather than "the two last," Pope undoubtedly meant the two next to last, Concanen and Welsted (see nn. 19 and 20).

23. In *Dulness and Scandal,* Welsted had inveighed,

> Sure, that fam'd MACHIAVIL, what time he drew
> The Soul's dark Workings in the crooked Few,
> The rancour'd Spirit, and malignant Will,
> By *Instinct* base, by *Nature* shap'd to ill,
> An unborn Demon was inspir'd to see,
> And in his Rapture prophesied of Thee.   (P. 6.)

24. In his letter to the *Daily Post-Boy* Pope had protested "But the Application of it to the D. of Ch. is monstrous; to a Person who in *every particular* differs from it" (*Correspondence,* III, 257). And writing to Hill about the matter, "I am certain, if you calmly read every Particular of that Description, you'll find almost all of 'em point-blank the Reverse of that Person's *Villa*" (ibid., III, 260).

25. For example, the *Miscellany on Taste* had identified Sabinus as "The Son of Virro," in turn identified as "Mr. S——es of Hertfordshire." According to Bateson, ". . . Sabinus must therefore be a son of Benjamin Styles of Moor Park, Rickmansworth. I cannot trace any such person and suspect this is a blunder. Sabinus and his son were probably both imaginary." (TE III ii, 146n.)

26. On 17 December Hill had written to Pope, "I ought, sooner, to have thanked you, for the pleasure you have given me, by that excellent letter to Lord *Burlington,*—If the title had been *Of False Taste,* would it not have been properer?" (*Correspondence,* III, 257.) Pope concurred and the next edition was so designated. The opening "Remark" of *A Miscellany on Taste* noted, "Some of our little Second-Hand Smatterers in Criticism, will be apt to imagine our Author ought to have wrote *On Taste,* rather than *Of Taste,* as if *Of* and *On* had two different Significations. But Mr. *Pope* has declar'd himself in favour of *Of,* and thereby clapt a Gag into the Mouths of all Gainsayers. His *hoc volo, sic jubeo* is sufficient to make any Expression pass for Standard, and *stet pro Ratione Voluntas.*"

27. "Cf. Pope to Burlington, 21 Dec. 1731: 'I hope you are not abused too, because I meant just ye contrary; I can't tell, but I fancy your L^dship is not so easy to be persuaded contrary to y^r senses, even tho ye whole Town & Court too should require it.' " [J. B., p. 47.]

28. The passages cited (and in editions after 1731 the second person is changed to third) refer not to Burlington but to Timon. In any case, Pope is ironically commenting on his readers' failure to grasp his point. As he explains to Spence, "As to the general design of Providence, the two extremes of a vice serve like two opposite biases to keep up the balance of things. Avarice lays up (what would be

hurtful); Prodigality scatters abroad (what may be useful in other hands). The middle [is] the point for virtue." (*Anecdotes,* I, 130–31.)

29. Referring to this passage, Bateson notes in his introduction to the Twickenham edition of the *Epistles,* "Indeed, it has only been in our own time that critical tribute [by Empson, Leavis] has been paid to the fine lines in which Pope put into symbolic form the theory of a 'Ballance of things.' " (III ii, xxvi.)

30. With the deletions, some five lines have been compressed into these two.

31. "Matthew Concanen was appointed Attorney-General of Jamaica 30 June 1732." [F. W. B., p. 180.]

32. "Lewis Theobald (1688–1744), the king of the 'dunces', started life as an attorney but soon abandoned the law for literature." [F. W. B., p. 180.]

33. "Burlington's country house was at Chiswick. Gay's *Epistle to Burlington* (before 1720) begins

> While you, my Lord, bid stately piles ascend,
> Or in your *Chiswick* bow'rs enjoy your friend;
> Where *Pope* unloads the boughs within his reach,
> Of purple vine, blue plumb, and blushing peach."

[F. W. B., p. 180.]

34. Burlington left three daughters but no male heir; Bathurst, whom Pope had addressed as "a Patriarch of great Eminence, for getting children, at home & abroad" (*Correspondence,* II, 292), had four legitimate sons and five daughters.

35. Again, Allen Bathurst, to whom the third Epistle, *Of the Use of Riches,* was addressed, was an old, valued friend ("You cannot know, how much I love you, & how gratefully I recollect all the Good & Obligation I owe to you for so many years." Pope to Lord Bathurst, 6 August 1735 [*Correspondence,* III, 480]). An avid gardener, whose country houses Pope often visited and whose garden at Cirencester he helped shape, Bathurst had been heralded in the *Epistle to Burlington*:

> Who then shall grace, or who improve the Soil?
> Who plants like Bathurst, or who build like Boyle.

That Pope should be satirizing him and Burlington in the poem is patently absurd.

36. This suggests that Hervey (Lord Fanny) had spread the unlikely rumor. A *Miscellany on Taste* identifies Villario as "Lord C——le——n": Richard Child, earl Tynley of Castlemaine.

37. Pope is probably being playful here: Bathurst, while having a restless, impetuous personality (one of the "two most impetuous men I know" [*Correspondence,* III, 405–6]), was indeed constant in directing his energies toward new pleasures and amusements. (Peter Quennell, *Alexander Pope* [London: Weidenfeld and Nicolson, 1968], p. 183.)

38. "For Pope's contempt for florists, see *Dunciad,* iv, 403 ff." [J. B., p. 49.]

39. "Possibly the estate adjoining the Burlington estate at Chiswick. It was bought by Sir Stephen Fox in 1682, who built a house there on the site of the present great conservatory of Chiswick House. Pope's acquaintance, Spencer Compton, Earl of Wilmington (1673?–1743), the politician, lived there from 1728 until his death." [F. W. B., p. 181.]

40. "One of Burlington's drawings, dated 1732, for alterations in Wilmington's hall [see n. 39], was published by R. Wittkower in the *Archaeological Journal* (1947)." [J. B., p. 49.] Judging that by the "two Lords" Pope meant Bathurst and Burlington, Bateson notes, "F. Kimball, "Burlington Architectus,' *Journal Royal Institute of British Architects,* 15 October, 12 November 1927, does not record that Burlington ever acted as Bathurst's architect, but it is *a priori* probable. Most of his friends consulted Burlington when they had any building on hand." [F. W. B., p. 182.]

41. "The Vicar of Chiswick at this time was Thomas Wood (1681–1732). *Gent. Mag.,* 1735, V 253, prints an epigram said to have been written by Pope on Wood's presenting Kent, the architect and landscape-gardener protégé of Burlington, with a copy of Evelyn's *Numismata.* [It is reprinted in TE vol. VI, pp. 340–1.] Although Wood had been educated at Wadham College, Oxford, I can find no contemporary confirmation of the depth of his Greek scholarship. The shallowness of Pope's, for a translator of Homer, was an old jibe, of course." [F. W. B., p. 182.]

42. "Sir Gilbert Heathcote (1652–1733), one of the founders of the Bank of England and reputed to be the richest commoner in England. 'Father of the City' is the traditional soubriquet for the Senior Alderman of the City of London. For Heathcote's reputation for parsimony see *To Bathurst,* 101*n.*" [F. W. B., p. 182.] "Pope mentions him again in . . . *Imit. of Hor., Ep. II,* ii, l. 240." [J. B., p. 50.] Shylock (after 1731 changed to Sir Visto) was identified by *A Miscellany of Taste* as "Sir R.—— W——," but, as Bateson argues (TE III ii, 137n), that does not seem applicable; "Pope probably did not mean anybody in particular."

43. "Until 1735 the printed editions of Pope's poem read 'Babo' in l. 20. 'Bubo' is the reading of the Burlington MS. (an early draft of the poem) and all the later editions. According to *A Miscellany on Taste* (1732), Babo was 'Lord C——d——n', i.e., presumably, Charles, second Baron Cadogan (1691–1776). By Bubo Pope undoubtedly meant Bubb Dodington." [F. W. B., p. 182.]

44. "James Gibbs (1682–1754), a distinguished architect; he was probably to have been the architect of the town house that Pope was thinking of building in 1718. 'Sh——d' is Edward Sheppard or Shepherd (d. 1747) who had recently designed Covent Garden Theatre (opened 3 December 1733) and was probably the architect of Cadogan's country seat at Caversham, Oxfordshire, which was built in 1718." [F. W. B., p. 183.]

45. It was to Sir Richard Temple, Lord Viscount Cobham, that Pope addressed

his first Epistle. His house at Stowe in Buckinghamshire was often visited by Pope, who greatly admired the gardens that Bridgman had laid out.

46. " 'Faux-hall' is, of course, Vauxhall. Pope's allusion, however, is not to the famous Gardens of Jonathan Tyers, which were only opened in June 1732, but to their less fashionable precursor on the same site, the old Spring Garden described in *Spectator*, no. 383. 'Cupid's Gardens', *recte* 'Cuper's Gardens' (from Boydell Cuper, who opened them *c.* 1680), were at Lambeth, exactly opposite Somerset House." [F. W. B., p. 183.]

47. Charles Bridgman (or Bridgeman), d. 1738, gardener to George I and George II, was a friend of Pope, whose garden he helped plan as well as that at Marble Hill (DNB Supple.); Sherburn cites Walpole's assertion that Pope's ideas gained currency through Bridgman (*Early Career*, p. 281).

48. In later editions Cobham's name was substituted for Bridgman's, at the gardener's request. According to the DNB he was disturbed over the Timon scandal.

49. Bateson cites Gilpin's comment on the Stowe lake (*A Dialogue upon the Gardens of Viscount Cobham, at Stowe,* 1748) which describes how a marsh had been transformed into "a Noble Piece of Water!" (TE III ii, 144n).

50. In his *Daily Post-Boy* letter Pope had railed, "Why in God's Name, must a *Portrait* apparently collected from twenty different Men, be applied to one only?" (*Correspondence*, III, 256)—a sentiment re-echoed in his letter to Burlington a few days later, ". . . nothing is so evident, to any one who can read the Language, either of English or Poetry, as that Character of Timon is collected from twenty different absurditys & Improprieties: & was never the Picture of any one Human Creature." (Ibid., III, 259.)

51. "Possibly Sir William Yonge and Bubb Dodington [see nn. 11 and 14]. Dodington, the patron of Young, Thomson, Fielding, Glover, and Whitehead, was certainly a 'Mecaenas'; Yonge's claim to being a 'Phoebus' rested on the songs contributed to *The Jovial Crew* and such trifles as 'A Ballad Occasioned by the enlarging of the House of Office at D. of D——'s Seat in Sussex, for the Accommodation of three Ladies at once' (*Gent. Mag.*, *1736*, p. 103)." [F. W. B., p. 184.]

52. "Henry Kelsall [see n. 21]." [F. W. B., p. 184.]

53. James Brydges, first duke of Chandos (1673–1744). Paymaster-general of forces abroad from 1707–12, he amassed a fortune, which he lavished on his residences (Cannons near Edgware and the duke of Ormond's former house in St. James's Square). He was also a patron of the arts, having Handel at Cannons for two years. Although he was in no sense a friend of Pope's, he was a close acquaintance of some of the poet's intimates like Arbuthnot, Bolingbroke, Burlington—making it all the less likely Pope would have made him the focus of his satire. A letter from Chandos to Pope, in answer to what was obviously an

apologetic letter from the poet at the time of the furor, suggests his willingness to believe these protestations: ". . . It would indeed be a real concern to me did I beleive One of your Judgment had designedly given grounds for their imbibing an Opinion, so disadvantageous of me. But as your obliging Letter, is sufficient to free me from this apprehension, I can with great indifference bear the insults they bestow, and not find myself hurt by 'em: nor have I Reason to be much disturb'd, when I consider how many better persons are the daily objects of their unjust censures." (*Correspondence*, III, 262–63).

54. "Colley Cibber." [F. W. B., p. 184.]

55. "Barnham Goode (1674–1739), a master at Eton college and one of Walpole's writers in the *Daily Courant*. Pope believed that 'sneering Goode, half malice and half whim' had written a libel on him called *The Mock Aesop*. [See *Dunciad* (TE V, 441)]." [J. B., p. 52.]

56. In the *Daily Post-Boy* letter, Pope had written, "I am confident the Author is incapable of imputing any such to a Person, whose whole Life (to use his own Expression in Print of him [in the Preface to the *Iliad* Pope had paid a compliment to Brydges, then earl of Carnarvon]) *is a continued Series* of good and generous Actions." (*Correspondence*, III, 256.)

57. Pope's own friends who knew Chandos well—like Arbuthnot and Bolingbroke—could have supplied him with the details that follow.

58. "Antonio Belucci (1654–1726) was 'employed on the chapel of Canons,' according to Horace Walpole (*Anecdotes of Painting*, ed. R. N. Wornum, London, 1888, ii. 283). Enoch Zeeman (d. 1744) was a portrait painter." [J. B., p. 53.] "Laguerre, however, had painted one of the staircases at Cannons as well as the altarpiece in the adjacent church at Whitchurch which Chandos had built" (TE III ii, 151n).

59. In the postscript to the *Daily Post-Boy* letter (which was reprinted as a second letter in the *Daily Journal* the next day) Pope had protested:

> But the Application of it to the D. of Ch. is monstrous; to a Person who in *every particular* differs from it. 'Is his Garden crowded with *Walls*? Are his Trees cut into *Figures of Men*? Do his Basons want *Water*? Are there *ten steep Slopes* of his Terrass? Is he piqued about *Editions of Books*? Does he exclude all *Moderns* from his *Library*? Is the *Musick* of his Chappel bad, or *whimsical*, or *jiggish*? On the contrary, was it not the best composed in the Nation, and most suited to grave Subjects; witness *Nicol. Haym's*, and Mr. *Hendel's* noble *Oratories*? Has it Pictures of naked Women in it? And did ever Dean Ch——w——d preach his Courtly Sermons there? I am sick of such Fool-Applications.' (*Correspondence*, III, 257.)

And as he wrote to Hill, "I am afraid of tiring you, and (what is your best Security) I have not Time to do it. I'll only just tell you, that many Circumstances you have heard, as Resemblances to the Picture of *Timon*, are utterly Inventions of Lyars; the Number of Servants never was an Hundred, the Paintings not of *Venio* [misprint for *Verrio*] or *La Guerre,* but *Belluci* and *Zaman*; no such Buffet, Manner of Reception at the Study, Terras, *&c.* all which, and many more, they have not scrupled to forge, to gain some Credit to the Application: And (which is worse) belyed Testimonies of Noblemen, and of my particular Friends, to condemn me." (Ibid., III, 268.)

60. "Peter Walters or Walter (1664?–1746), the notorious moneylender, who was continually satirized by Pope. See *To Bathurst,* ll. 20n [and 125n]." [F. W. B., p. 185.]

61. "Pope is quoting from Bubb Dodington's *Epistle to The Right Honourable Sir Robert Walpole* (1726), p. 9. The line is also quoted in *To Cobham* [TE III ii, 29n], *Epilogue to Satires,* Dia. II 161, and an undated letter to Fortescue (Sherburn, II 294, V 2)." [F. W. B., p. 186.]

62. "Pope had adhered to Atterbury in exile, to Bolingbroke in disgrace, and to Oxford in imprisonment. Cf. also *Imit. Hor., Sat. II.,* i, l. 125f.; *Epilogue to Satires,* ii. 74 ff., and the 'Epistle to Robert Earl of Oxford,' prefixed to Parnell's poems." [J. B., p. 54.]

63. "Sir William Yonge was one of Walpole's principal lieutenants in the House of Commons." [F. W. B., p. 186.] See also n. 65 below.

64. "Francis, Duke of Lorraine, later Emperor Francis I (1708–65) and husband of Maria Theresa, paid a much-publicized visit to England in the autumn of 1731. On Monday, 15 Nov., the *Daily Journal* reported that His Serene Highness had come to Town 'last Saturday' from Sir Robert Walpole's seat in Norfolk." [J. B., p. 54.]

65. But Kathleen Mahaffey and Maynard Mack contend that Houghton, Walpole's ostentatious seat in Norfolk, *was* the model of Timon's villa and Walpole the object of Pope's satire, an argument rebutted by James Aubrey (see n. 11 to "Introduction," p. 408.)

66. See the duke of Chandos's letter to Pope, 27 December 1731 (*Correspondence,* III, 262–63 and n. 53, above). In the open letter to Burlington prefixed to the third edition of the *Epistle,* Pope had written, "I was too well content with my Knowledge of that noble Person's Opinion in this Affair, to trouble the publick about it. But since Malice and Mistake are so long a dying, I take the opportunity of this Third Edition to declare *His Belief,* not only of *My Innocence,* but of *Their Malignity. . . .*" (*Correspondence,* III, 266.)

67. "Alluding, no doubt, to 'All men have their price,' the notorious perversion of a remark of Walpole." [J. B., p. 55.]

68. "Pope had often stayed with Bolingbroke at Dawley Farm near Uxbridge. He was drinking asses' milk there in May 1731." [F. W. B., p. 187.]

69. "William Pulteney, later Earl of Bath (1684–1764), was notoriously parsimonious. Burlington's design for a 'House with an Arcade' in Kent's *Designs of*

Inigo Jones (1727) was for Pulteney, but apparently was not proceeded with." [F. W. B., p. 187.]

70. John Manners, third duke of Rutland, had his seat at Belvoir Castle.

71. "Probably William, Earl Cadogan (1675–1726), a favourite *bête noire* of Pope's, who was Marlborough's quartermaster-general in the War of the Spanish Succession. See *To Bathurst*, 91, and Spence [*Anecdotes*, I, 101–02.]" [F. W. B., p. 187.]

72. Bateson notes, "One of the houses Pope undoubtedly had in mind in describing Timon's villa . . . , which he had seen (still far from complete) in 1717 (EC, IX 277). In a letter to Martha Bount, 6 August 1718, he calls it, 'the most proud and extravagant Heap of Towers in the nation' (Sherburn, I 480). Letter IX of the 'Letters to Several Ladies' in *Letters of Mr Pope*, 1735 (Sherburn, I 432) contains a long satirical account of Blenheim, parts of which Pope utilized in this passage [*Epistle to Burlington*, ll. 109ff.]: 'I never saw so great a thing with so much littleness in it . . . the Duke of *Shrewsbury* gave a true character of it, when he said, it was a great *Quarry of Stones above ground*.' " (TE III ii, 148n.) (See, also, n. 11 to "Introduction.")

73. "Hugh Boscawen, Viscount Falmouth (1680?–1734), who had married Marlborough's niece." [J. B., p. 56.]

74. "The Duke of Shrewsbury had been brought up a Roman Catholic, but had transferred his allegiance to the Church of England in 1679. For Pope's relations with him, see *Imitations of Horace* . . . [TE IV 388–89]." [J. B., p. 56.]

75. "Vanbrugh, the architect of Blenheim, was also responsible for Bubb Dodington's mansion at Eastbury, Dorset. This was begun by Dodington's uncle and was only half finished when Dodington inherited it. Dodington's town house, in Pall Mall, was an undistinguished affair opposite Carlton House." [F. W. B., p. 188.]

76. It is a dominant refrain in Pope's letters how much he hated the excessive party spirit of his day, the corrupting power of faction, and the debasement by the patronage system. Swift, writing to him in 1728, comments on "your situation, which hath made all parties and interests indifferent to you, who can be under no concern about high and low-church, Whig and Tory, or who is first Minister—" (*Correspondence*, II, 497).

A LETTER to a NOBLE LORD.
On occasion of some Libels
written and propagated
at Court, in the Year 1732–3.

INTRODUCTION

Pope's activities in the 1730s illustrate his characteristic complexity—both as man and artist. The letters, despite the chicanery that led to their publication, are evocative of a warm, generous nature. But it is also the period when he "stoop'd to Truth, and moraliz'd his song," highlighting an equally productive capacity for hatred, whether fired by moral indignation or personal vindication. In both instances, what could have been purely private (and individual) became public (and general) through the transforming art of the writer. How depersonalization is achieved—and yet how uncertain the terrain of aesthetic distance—can be examined in the *Letter to a Noble Lord,* Pope's prose answer to attacks by John, Lord Hervey and, secondarily, by Lady Mary Wortley Montagu, who was the focus of his most intense love-hate relationship.

Both aristocrats had been early acquaintances of Pope.[1] With Lord Hervey it was the easy association of wits and courtiers at St. James's and Leicester House, a heady world for the young country poet who ventured into it in his late twenties, to become a friend of one of the Princess's Maids of Honour, Mary Lepell. She in 1720 would become Lady Hervey. With Lady Mary it was a far different matter: a short-lived (essentially from 1715 to 1721) but passionately felt attachment—on Pope's part—which had a lasting impact as devotion turned to animus once the relationship cooled. With both Hervey and Lady Mary he had been attracted by wit, elegance, and position—bonds which soon drew the two peers together in a permanent friendship of their own, but not ties destined to survive very long the poet's contrasting political and social sympathies, even had a more personal rupture not taken place between him and Lady Mary. Just what occasioned that breach still remains conjectural, but everything points to some emotional rebuff,[2] scarring to a young man painfully sensitive of his "little, tender, and crazy Carcase."[3]

As Pope's friendship with Hervey had been casual, so too were his early satiric thrusts at the man he was beginning to identify as a court type (with foolish poetic pretensions to boot) no longer to be admired; his two-line squib on "Lord Fanny"[4] in *The First Satire of the Second Book of Horace, Imitated* (February 1733) is in that spirit. On the other hand—possibly in the belief that she had been libelling him[5] and probably because he would always overreact to her—his brief allusion to Lady Mary in that same poem is vicious and personal, as were two earlier attacks, in *The Capon's Tale,* published in the Pope-Swift *Miscellanies* of 1728,[6] and in the

Dunciad of that year (TE V, 112). It was when Hervey joined her in the lists, to collaborate on *Verses Address'd to the Imitator of the First Satire of the Second Book of Horace,* that the battleground changed: their attack, extensive and ruthless (and most likely actually written by Lady Mary), invited the warfare that left Hervey damned eternally in the Sporus portrait of the *Epistle to Dr Arbuthnot* and Lady Mary harried through the length and breadth of the Satires.[7] It became Pope's most deeply personal grudge, a rare satiric departure from his more usual missionary vendetta against the dunces and the Walpolian world of town and court.

One chapter less known in the history of this feud is the *Letter to a Noble Lord.* Soon after the *Verses Address'd to the Imitator* (in March 1733) came a further attack, this time by Hervey alone—a long doggerel poem, *An Epistle from a Nobleman to a Doctor of Divinity* (written somewhat condescendingly to a family acquaintance, Dr. Sherwin, who published it anonymously in November), a quarter of which was devoted to a dull diatribe against Pope as satirist and translator. He retaliated swiftly with the *Letter,* which he never published, saving his fire for the *Epistle to Dr. Arbuthnot,* which appeared about a year later, in January 1734/5.

Warburton, who first published the essay, recognized its obvious relationship to the later poem, and in an introductory footnote established certain immediate if superficial differences: the poem is directed against Grub-Street writers, the letter against "Court-Scribblers"; in poetry, the attack is "more grave, moral, and sublime"; in prose, "more lively, critical, and pointed. . . ."[8] The validity of this judgment can be argued; more significant, in any case, are the further distinctions to be drawn, exploring how differing situations and purposes and media (prose vs. verse) lead to differing creative perceptions and projections.

The famous poem, with its acid portrait of Sporus, is a stunning example of poetic transformation. Hervey, the man, is generalized into a type of perverse-pernicious courtier localized in the historical model of Sporus, Nero's male wife. The sketch (just one vignette from a tableau of demeaning, destructive figures) is extravagant, exaggerated, alogical—devastating. If the speaker of the poem wears the mantle of the good man goaded to outrage, the situation is further universalized by the imagery, in which Hervey is made to figure in animal-insect terms and in the symbol of Satan. It is beside the point for Robert Halsband, Hervey's biographer and apologist, to argue the injustice of the picture, assuring us that, in actuality, Hervey was really a fastidious person, not a "painted Child of Dirt that stinks and stings";[9] this is as irrelevant as to argue that Hervey is not the literal insect of the couplet. Poetry—as Halsband finally acknowledges—works on other levels of truth, with its reality not necessarily that of verisimilitude.

In contrast, the largely unfamiliar *Letter to a Noble Lord* is a straight-forward, restrained, personal response to two topical attacks by well-known contemporaries, who are plainly to be recognized as former associates. Just as it was effective in the poem to assume the usual *persona* of the socially concerned satirist and to make of the historical Hervey a concrete universal, so it is important here for Pope to appear as Pope—a distinguished author who is speaking out, with a cool disdainful civility, against adversaries whose historically verifiable behavior ill becomes them: "highborn" enemies, behaving no better than their lowborn brethren of Grub-Street, who, at the best, slighted him as a human being, at worst treated him like a deformed monster.

The prose piece, then, instead of transcending the personal and temporal, bears hard upon it. Exploiting the difference between the crude attacks on his poetry and person and his own elegant rebuttal, Pope focuses on all the implications of Hervey's "nobility," quietly suggesting the discrepancy in "quality" between birth and performance, between the Great World and the learned, artistic one. Hervey's "superiority" is self-depreciated by the baseness of his actions and the vulgarity of his style, while Pope, with a different kind of pride, can point to earned respect, to achieved rather than inherited values, and to a career rooted in talent.

The ironic reversals carry over to the medium too. By presuming to engage Pope poetically, Hervey had ventured into dangerous waters, far beyond his depth—as Pope made clear when he demolished him in the *Epistle to Dr. Arbuthnot.* Here, developing another kind of contrast, he does not deign to meet the "Court-Scribbler" on his own inept terms but instead projects a counter-image of decency and dignity through the balanced measures of his prose:

> I presume you will allow me to take the same liberty, in my answer to so *candid, polite,* and *ingenious* a Nobleman, which your Lordship took in yours, to so *grave, religious,* and *respectable* a Clergyman: As you answered his *Latin* in *English,* permit me to answer your *Verse* in *Prose.* And tho' your Lordship's reasons for not writing in *Latin,* might be stronger than mine for not writing in *Verse,* yet I may plead *Two good* ones, for this conduct: the one that I want the Talent for spinning *a thousand lines in a* Day (which, I think, is as much *Time* as this subject deserves) and the other, that I take your Lordship's *Verse* to be as much *Prose* as this letter. But no doubt it was your choice, in writing to a friend, to renounce all the pomp of Poetry, and give us this excellent model of the familiar.

At the same time, all is not so straightforward as it might at first seem. It is not what the satirist says but what he does not say in the face of what he could say that makes the quiet statements so damning, and against which the taunts of his adversaries echo shrilly or ponderously. To savage allusions to his crippled body, he demurs, "I am persuaded you can reproach me truly with no great *Faults*, except my *natural ones*, which I am as ready to own, as to do all justice to the contrary *Beauties* in you." Reverberating beneath the deceptively bland tone is the reminder that Hervey is good-looking (which makes his cruelty all the more intolerable) but, further, that he is "beautiful" in some sense that is unnatural and unwholesome, so that "contrary" can take on other nuances, reinforced by the rest of the passage:

> It is true, my Lord, I am short, not well shap'd, generally ill-dress'd, if not sometimes dirty: Your Lordship and Ladyship are still in bloom; your Figures such, as rival the *Apollo* of *Belevdere,* and the *Venus* of *Medicis*; and your faces so finish'd, that neither sickness nor passion can deprive them of *Colour*; I will allow your own in particular to be the finest that ever *Man* was blest with: preserve it, my Lord, and reflect, that to be a Critic, would cost it too many *frowns,* and to be a Statesman, too many *wrinkles!*

Considering Hervey's effeteness (with his familiar use of cosmetics), Lady Mary's slovenliness, and the aristocratic stance of indolence, it is all wonderfully sardonic—all the more so for being delivered so dispassionately (and in such contrast to Pope's comparable poetic thrusts). Even his self-disparagement has its satiric aspect, a twist on Hervey's strangely self-depreciating style in his *Epistle.*

Dr. Johnson, in his life of Pope, dismisses the *Letter* for its "tedious malignity."[10] This is a surprising judgment on a document that, however different in tone, resembles in some important respects his own famous letter to Chesterfield. Both are statements by men sensible of their talent and sensitive to the aristocratic rebuffs of an age which overvalued wealth and position—and we need to remind ourselves that the sturdy independence of patronage which Johnson shows in his letter, Pope showed all his life, holding no pension from the state and refusing all solicitations that would have made such support possible. Both letters, too, are couched in a prose style powerfully evocative of dignity, worth, and good sense—Pope's with some accompanying ironies:

> . . . I have but one thing to intreat of your Lordship. It is, that you will not decide of my *Principles* on the same grounds as you have done of my *Learning*: Nor give the same account of my *Want of Grace,* after you have lost all acquaintance with my *Person,* as you do of my *Want of Greek,* after you have confessedly lost all acquaintance with the *Language.*

Here, my Lord, allow me to observe the different proceeding of the *Ignoble* poet, and his *Noble Enemies*. What he has written of *Fanny, Adonis, Sappho,* or who you will, he own'd he publish'd, he set his name to: What they have *publish'd* of him, they have deny'd to have *written*; and what they have *written* of him, they have denied to have *publish'd*.

Though unquestionably Johnson's protest is "nobler," partly because it is terser, "malignity" is hardly an exact, or even imaginable, description of the content of Pope's. He writes with bitterness and sometimes even rancor—perhaps a legacy from his frustrated infatuation with Lady Mary—but the bitterness continually ranges beyond personal affront to the sense of failed responsibility in high places that will permeate the entire body of his Horatian poems:

> I beseech your Lordship to consider, the Injury a Man of your *high Rank* and *Credit* may do to a *private Person*, under *Penal Laws* and many other disadvantages, not for want of *honesty* or *conscience*, but merely perhaps for having too *weak a head* or too *tender a heart*. It is by *these alone* I have hitherto liv'd excluded from all *posts* of *Profit* or *Trust*: As I can interfere with the *Views* of *no man*, do not deny me, my Lord, *all that is left*, a little *Praise*, or the common Encouragement due, if not to my *Genius*, at least to my *Industry*.
>
> Above all, your Lordship will be careful not to wrong my *Moral Character*, with THOSE under whose *Protection* I live, and thro' whose *Lenity* alone I can live with Comfort. Your Lordship, I am confident, upon consideration will think, you inadvertently went a little *too far* when you recommended to THEIR perusal, and strengthened by the weight of your Approbation, a *Libel*, mean in its reflections upon my poor *figure*, and scandalous in those on my *Honour* and *Integrity*: wherein I was represented as "*an Enemy* to Human Race, a *Murderer* of Reputations, and a *Monster* mark'd by God like *Cain*, deserving to wander accurs'd thro' the World."

And the note on which the *Letter* ends—

> *That, while he breathes, no rich or noble knave*
> *Shall walk the world in credit to his grave*—

echoes a couplet in the *First Satire on the Second Book of Horace*, the poem which inaugurates his new creative phase.

Given the care and conviction shown in the writing, why did Pope fail to dispatch the letter to Hervey or make the statement public? Historical reasons are offered: that he owed Walpole a favor—Sir Robert and Horatio Walpole having secured from the French prime minister an abbey for his friend Southcote—or that in deference to the queen he had for the time spared her favorite counselor (strong considerations for one who, as a Roman Catholic, lived on sufferance in his native land). Yet one feels there may have been other considerations equally decisive. For all its satiric perspective, the *Letter* remains a very personal statement, dealing directly with sensitive matters: the aspersions on his family, the insults to his physique from someone to whom he was emotionally vulnerable, and the threats to his reputation and career, especially as has been suggested through the general political pressure to be exerted on a Catholic with suspected Jacobite sympathies. Superior and aloof as Pope may seek to appear in this work, he is from time to time betrayed by his feelings. When he comments,

> I know your Genius and hers so perfectly *tally,* that you cannot but join in admiring each other, and by consequence in the contempt of all such as myself. You have both, in my regard, been like—(your Lordship, I know, loves a *Simile,* and it will be one suitable to your *Quality*) you have been like two *Princes,* and I like a *poor Animal* sacrificed between them to cement a lasting League: I hope I have not bled in vain; but that such an amity may endure for ever!

it is debatable whether the simile does not indeed become Hervey's, with Pope losing control of it as he elicits distress from the reader rather than scorn.

At best the mask of the satirist is not an easy one to wear. When the mask follows too closely the living features, the fit becomes even more crucial: there may not be enough room for artifice, the covering may not sufficiently protect but expose—and this seems to be the case toward the end of the essay, when the tone shifts, becoming more emotional and defensive, less controlled and oblique. In the long passage quoted earlier we experience the tautness of the lines—and, two and a half centuries later, are more moved by them than by all the ironies of the situation.

Pope charges Hervey's *Epistle* with being "a piece not written in *haste,* or in a *passion,* but many months after all pretended provocation; when you was at *full leisure* at Hampton-Court, and I the object *singled,* like a *Deer out of Season,* for so ill-timed, and ill-placed a diversion." His own letter is in some respects and at some points too much the opposite—too responsive, too vulnerable: better to wait to set his sights more coldly on his prey, that "mere white Curd of Ass's milk." The Pope of the *Epistle to Dr. Arbuthnot,* secure behind his satiric mask (or his three "voices" if one follows Maynard Mack's reading),[11] is completely in control: the hand never falters in that relentless exposé. The Sporus portrait is justly famous and will remain Pope's ultimate word on Lord Hervey. Yet for the con-

cerned reader, the *Letter to a Noble Lord* offers its own interest and satisfaction, as it mingles the art of the satirist with the passion of the man.
It is a more human Pope that is exposed, appealing in his outraged pride,
splendid in the essential nobility—personal and artistic—that sustains it.

Notes

1. See the relevant annotations to the *Letter to a Noble Lord*, where Pope traces
the relationships; and the Introduction to *Imitations of Horace* (TE IV, xv–xxiv).

2. John Butt cites the testimony of Lady Mary's granddaughter (TE IV, xvn),
but equally telling are the nature and extent of Pope's anger towards her and of
her own counter-attacks; see annotations 11, 33, 34, 35, 36, 37, 40, 41, 42,
48, 57, 58, 61.

3. Wycherley to Pope, 19 February 1708/9 (*Correspondence, I*, 55).

4. There is an even earlier glancing reference to Lord Fanny in *A Master Key
to Popery*, an anonymous pamphlet of February 1731/2 now attributed to Pope.
See above, pp. 411.

5. Pope had written to Fortescue (13 September [1729?]): "I have seen
Sir R. W. but once since you left. I made him then my confidant in a complaint
against a lady, of his, and once of my, acquaintance, who is libelling me, as she
certainly one day will him, if she has not already. You'll easily guess I am speaking
of Lady Mary. I should be sorry if she had any credit or influence with him, for
she would infallibly use it to bely me; though my only fault towards her was,
leaving off her conversation when I found it dangerous." (*Correspondence*, III, 53.)

6. See annotation 41.

7. See annotation 42.

8. *The Works of Alexander Pope Esq.*, ed. Warburton (London, 1751), VIII,
253n.

9. Robert Halsband, "Sporus, or Lord Hervey," [London] *Times Literary Supplement*, 15 September 1972, pp. 1069–70.

10. Johnson, *Lives*, III, 179.

11. Maynard Mack, "The Muse of Satire," *Yale Review*, 41 (1951), 80–92.

NOTE ON PUBLICATION AND TEXT

Although Pope responded swiftly to *An Epistle from a Nobleman to a Doctor of Divinity* (written, according to Warburton, 28 August 1733,[1] and published anonymously, and probably inadvertently, on 10 November)[2] with the *Letter to a Noble Lord,* which he dated Nov. 30, 1733, the piece was not actually published until 1751, when Warburton included it, the last item among the letters in Volume VIII of *The Works* (pp. 253–80)—though it is not listed in the table of contents to that volume. It was later reprinted in the Elwin/Courthope edition (EC V, Appendix III).

Lord Hervey reported to his friend Henry Fox late in January 1734: ". . . Pope has not written one word but a manuscript in prose never printed, which he has shown to several of his friends, but which I have never seen, and which, I have heard from those who did see it very low and poor, ridiculing only my person, and my being vain of over-rated parts and the undeserved favour of a Court."[3] Pope himself had written to Swift earlier that month: "There is a Woman's war declar'd against me by a certain Lord*, his weapons are the same which women and children use, a pin to scratch, and a squirt to be-spatter. I writ a sort of answer . . . , and after shewing it to some people, supprest it. . . ."[4] If Pope held back his rebuttal[5] (perhaps to repay Walpole for a favor or to please the Queen),[6] others did not, and the following months saw a number of attacks and lampoons: *Tit for Tat: Or An Answer to the Epistle to [sic] a Nobleman; A Tryal of Skill Between a Court Lord and a Twickenham 'Squire; An Epistle from a Gentleman at Twickenham, to a Nobleman at St. James's;* and *An Apology for Printing a Certain Nobleman's Epistle to Dr. S{her}w{i}n.*[7]

The present text follows that of the 1751 edition, with some of Warburton's notes incorporated into the annotations:

1751: *The Works of Alexander Pope Esq.,* ed. Warburton, Vol. VIII, octavo, Griffith 650.

Notes

1. *Works* (1751), VIII, 253n.
2. Robert Halsband, *Lord Hervey* (Oxford: Clarendon Press, 1973), p. 162. In November and December 1733, and early January 1734, there was a run of advertisements, notices, and counter-notices in *The Daily Courant* (20 November,

22 November, 10 December), *The Grub-street Journal* (29 November, 6 December, 13 December, 27 December, 10 January), and *The Craftsman* (15 December, 29 December) about the publication of the *Epistle.* The poem was advertised, then denied, the denial challenged, and the exchange continued with pertinent squibs.

3. Earl of Ilchester, *Lord Hervey and His Friends 1726–38* (London: John Murray, 1950), p. 189; see also Pope's letter to Swift (*Correspondence,* III, 401) cited here after Hervey's comment.

4. *Correspondence,* III, 401.

5. Or, at least, an acknowledged rebuttal; he was most likely responsible for the anonymous pamphlet *A Most Proper Reply to the Nobleman's Epistle to a Doctor of Divinity,* q. v.

6. Ilchester, *Lord Hervey and His Friends,* p. 189n; Halsband, *Lord Hervey,* p. 164.

7. Guerinot, *Pamphlet Attacks,* pp. 339, 340, 332, 341.

A LETTER[1] to a NOBLE LORD.

On occasion of some Libels written and propagated at Court, in the Year 1732–3.[2]

MY LORD,   Nov. 30, 1733.

Your Lordship's Epistle has been publish'd some days,[3] but I had not the pleasure and pain of seeing it till yesterday: Pain, to think your Lordship should attack me at all; Pleasure, to find that you can attack me so weakly.[4] As I want not the humility, to think myself in every way but *one* your inferiour, it seems but reasonable that I should take the only method either of self-defence or retaliation, that is left me, against a person of your quality and power. And as by your choice of this weapon, your pen, you generously (and modestly too, no doubt) meant to put yourself upon a level with me; I will as soon believe that your Lordship would give a wound to a man unarm'd, as that you would deny me the use of it in my own defence.[5]

I presume you will allow me to take the same liberty, in my answer to so *candid, polite,* and *ingenious* a Nobleman, which your Lordship took in yours, to so *grave, religious,* and *respectable* a Clergyman:[6] As you answered his *Latin* in *English,*[7] permit me to answer your *Verse* in *Prose.* And tho' your Lordship's reasons for not writing in *Latin,* might be stronger than mine for not writing in *Verse,* yet I may plead *Two good* ones, for this conduct: the one that I want the Talent of spinning *a thousand lines in a* Day[8] (which, I think, is as much *Time* as this subject deserves) and the other, that I take your Lordship's *Verse* to be as much *Prose* as this letter. But no doubt it was your choice, in writing to a friend, to renounce all the pomp of Poetry, and give us this excellent model of the familiar.[9]

When I consider the *great difference* betwixt the rank your *Lordship* holds in the *World,*[10] and the rank which your *writings* are like to hold in the *learned world,* I presume that distinction of style is but necessary, which you will see observ'd thro' this letter. When I speak of *you,* my Lord, it will be with all the deference due to the inequality which Fortune has made between you and myself:[11] but

442

when I speak of your *writings,* my Lord, I must, I can do nothing but trifle.

I should be obliged indeed to lessen this *Respect,* if all the Nobility (and especially the elder brothers) are but so many hereditary fools,[12] if the privilege of Lords be to want brains,[13] if noblemen can hardly write or read,[14] if all their business is but to dress and vote,[15] and all their employment in court, to tell lies, flatter in public, slander in private, be false to each other, and follow nothing but self-interest.[16] Bless me, my Lord, what an account is this you give of them? and what would have been said of me, had I immolated, in this manner, the whole body of the Nobility, at the stall of a well-fed Prebendary?[17]

Were it the mere *Excess* of your Lordship's *Wit,* that carried you thus triumphantly over all the bounds of decency, I might consider your Lordship on your *Pegasus,* as a sprightly hunter on a mettled horse; and while you were trampling down all our works, patiently suffer the injury, in pure admiration of the *Noble Sport.* But should the case be quite otherwise, should your Lordship be only like a *Boy* that is *run away with*; and run away with by a *Very Foal*; really common charity, as well as respect for a noble family, would oblige me to stop your carreer, and to *help you down* from *this Pegasus.*

Surely the little praise of a *Writer* should be a thing below your ambition:[18] You, who were no sooner born, but in the lap of the Graces;[19] no sooner at school, but in the arms of the Muses;[20] no sooner in the World, but you practis'd all the skill of it;[21] no sooner in the Court, but you possess'd all the art of it![22] Unrivall'd as you are, in making a figure, and in making a speech,[23] methinks, my Lord, you may well give up the poor talent of turning a Distich. And why this fondness for Poetry? Prose admits of the two excellencies you most admire, Diction and Fiction: It admits of the talents you chiefly possess, a most fertile invention, and most florid expression; it is with prose, nay the plainest prose, that you best could teach our nobility to vote, which, you justly observe, is half at least of their business:[24] And, give me leave to prophesy, it is to your talent in prose, and not in verse, to your speaking, not your writing, to your art at court, not your art of poetry, that your Lordship must owe your future figure in the world.[25]

My Lord, whatever you imagine, this is the advice of a Friend, and one who remembers he formerly had the honour of some profession of Friendship from you:[26] Whatever was his *real share* in it, whether small or great, yet as your Lordship could never have had the least *Loss* by continuing it, or the least *Interest* by withdrawing it; the misfortune of losing it, I fear, must have been owing to his own *deficiency* or *neglect*.[27] But as to any *actual fault* which deserved to forfeit it in such a degree, he protests he is to this day guiltless and ignorant.[28] It could at most be but a fault of *omission*; but indeed by omissions, men of your Lordship's uncommon merit may sometimes think themselves so injur'd, as to be capable of an inclination to injure another; who, tho' very much below their quality, may be above the injury.

I never heard of the least displeasure you had conceived against me, till I was told that an imitation I had made of *Horace* had offended some persons, and among them your Lordship.[29] I could not have apprehended that a few *general strokes* about a *Lord scribling carelessly,* a *Pimp,* or a *Spy* at Court, a *Sharper* in a gilded chariot, &c. that these, I say, should be ever applied as they have been,[30] by *any malice* but that which is the greatest in the world, *the Malice of Ill people to themselves*.[31]

Your Lordship so well knows (and the whole Court and town thro' your means so well know) how far the resentment was carried upon that imagination, not only in the *Nature* of the *Libel* you propagated against me, but in the extraordinary *manner, place,* and *presence* in which it was propagated;[32] that I shall only say, it seem'd to me to exceed the bounds of justice, common sense, and decency.[33]

I wonder yet more, how a *Lady,* of great wit, beauty, and fame for her poetry (between whom and your Lordship there is a *natural, a just,* and a *well-grounded esteem*) could be prevail'd upon to take a part in that proceeding.[34] Your resentments against me indeed might be equal, as my offence to you both was the same; for neither had I the least misunderstanding with that Lady, till after I was the *Author* of my own misfortune in discontinuing her acquaintance. I may venture to own a truth, which cannot be unpleasing to either of you; I assure you my reason for so doing, was merely that you had both *too much wit* for me;[35] and that I could not do, with *mine,* many things which you could with *yours*.[36] The injury done you in withdrawing myself could be but small, if the value you had for me was no greater than you have been pleas'd since to profess. But surely, my Lord, one may say, neither the Revenge, nor the Language you held, bore any *proportion* to the pretended offence: The appellations of *Foe* to *humankind,* an *Enemy* like the *Devil* to all that have *Being*; *ungrateful, unjust,* deserving to be *whipt, blanketed, kicked,* nay *killed*; a *Monster,* an *Assassin,* whose conversation every man ought to *shun,* and against whom *all doors* should be shut; I beseech you, my Lord, had you the least right to give, or to encourage or justify any other in giving such language as this to me?[37] Could I be treated in terms more strong or more atrocious, if, during my acquaintance with you, I had been a *Betrayer,* a *Backbiter,* a *Whisperer,* an *Evesdropper,* or an *Informer?*[38] Did I in all that time ever throw *a false Dye,* or palm *a foul Card* upon you?[39] Did I ever *borrow, steal,* or accept, either *Money, Wit,* or *Advice* from you?[40] Had I ever the honour to join with either of you in one *Ballad, Satire, Pamphlet,* or *Epigram,* on any person *living* or *dead*? Did I ever do you so great an injury as to put off *my own Verses* for *yours,* especially on *those Persons* whom they might *most offend?*[41] I am confident you cannot answer in the affirmative; and I can truly affirm, that, ever since I lost the happiness of your conversation I have not published or written, one syllable of, or to either of you; never hitch'd your *names* in a *Verse,* or trifled with your *good names* in *company.*[42] Can I be honestly charged with any other crime but an *Omission* (for the word *Neglect,* which I us'd before, slip'd my pen unguardedly) to continue my admiration of you all my life, and still to contemplate, face to face, your many excellencies and perfections? I am persuaded you can reproach me truly with no great *Faults,* except my *natural ones,* which I am as ready to own, as to do all justice to the contrary *Beauties* in you. It is true, my Lord, I am short, not well shap'd, generally illdress'd, if not sometimes dirty:[43] Your Lordship and Ladyship are still in bloom; your Figures such, as rival the *Apollo* of *Belvedere,* and the *Venus* of *Medicis*;[44] and your faces so finish'd, that neither sickness nor passion can deprive them of *Colour*; I will allow your own in particular to be the finest that ever *Man* was blest with: preserve it, my Lord, and reflect, that to be a Critic, would cost it too many *frowns,* and to be a Statesman, too many *wrinkles*![45] I further confess, I am now somewhat old; but so your Lordship and this excellent Lady, with all your beauty, will (I hope) one day be.[46]

I know your Genius and hers so perfectly *tally,* that you cannot but join in admiring each other, and by consequence in the contempt of all such as myself. You have both, in my regard, been like—(your Lordship, I know, loves a *Simile,* and it will be one suitable to your *Quality*) you have been like *Two Princes,* and I like a *poor Animal* sacrificed between them to cement a lasting League: I hope I have not bled in vain; but that such an amity may endure for ever![47] For tho' it be what common *understandings* would hardly conceive, Two *Wits* however may be persuaded, that it is in Friendship as in Enmity, The more *danger,* the more *honour.*

Give me the liberty, my Lord, to tell you, why I never replied to those *Verses* on the *Imitator* of *Horace?* They regarded nothing but my *Figure,* which I set no value upon; and my *Morals,* which, I knew, needed no defence: Any honest man has the pleasure to be conscious, that it is out of the power of the *Wittiest,* nay the *Greatest Person* in the kingdom, to lessen him *that way,* but at the expence of his own *Truth, Honour,* or *Justice.* [48]

But tho' I declined to explain myself just at the time when I was sillily threaten'd,[49] I shall now give your Lordship a frank account of the offence you imagined to be meant to you. *Fanny* (my Lord) is the plain English of *Fannius,* a real person, who was a foolish Critic, and an enemy of *Horace:*[50] perhaps a Noble one, for so (if your Latin be gone in earnest) I must acquaint you, the word *Beatus* may be construed.

> *Beatus Fannius! ultro*
> *Delatis capsis et* imagine.[51]

This *Fannius* was, it seems, extremely fond both of his *Poetry* and his *Person,* which appears by the pictures and *Statues* he caused to be made of himself, and by his great diligence to propagate *bad Verses* at *Court,* and get them admitted into the library of *Augustus.* He was moreover of a delicate or *effeminate complexion,* and constant at the Assemblies and Opera's of those days, where he took it into his head to *slander poor Horace.*

> *Ineptus*
> Fannius, *Hermogenis* laedat *conviva Tigelli.*[52]

till it provoked him at last just to *name* him, give him a *lash,* and send him whimpering to the *Ladies.*

Discipularum *inter jubeo plorare cathedras.*[53]

So much for *Fanny,* my Lord. The word *spins* (as Dr. *Freind* or even Dr. *Sherwin* could assure you)[54] was the literal translation of *deduci*; a metaphor taken from a *Silk-worm,* my Lord, to signify any *slight, silken,* or (as your Lordship and the Ladies call it)[55] *flimzy* piece of work. I presume your Lordship has enough of this, to convince you there was nothing *personal* but to *that Fannius,* who (with all his fine accomplishments) had never been heard of, but for *that Horace* he injur'd.

In regard to the right honourable Lady, your Lordship's friend, I was far from designing a person of her condition by a name so derogatory to her, as that of *Sappho*; a name prostituted to every infamous Creature that ever wrote Verses or Novels.[56] I protest I never *apply'd* that name to her in any verse of mine, *public* or *private*; and (I firmly believe) not in any *Letter* or *Conversation.*[57] Whoever could invent a Falsehood to support an accusation, I pity; and whoever can believe such a Character to be theirs, I pity still more. God forbid the Court or Town should have the complaisance to *join* in that opinion! Certainly I meant it only of such modern *Sappho's,* as imitate much more the *Lewdness* than the *Genius* of the ancient one;[58] and upon whom their wretched brethren frequently bestow both the *Name* and the *Qualification* there mentioned.

There was another reason why I was silent as to that paper—I took it for a *Lady*'s (on the printer's word in the title page)[59] and thought it too presuming, as well as indecent, to contend with one of that *Sex* in *altercation*: For I never was so mean a creature as to commit my Anger against a *Lady* to *paper,* tho' but in a *private Letter.*[60] But soon after, her denial of it was brought to me by a Noble person of *real Honour* and *Truth.*[61] Your Lordship indeed said you had it from a Lady, and the Lady said it was your Lordship's; some thought the beautiful by-blow had *Two Fathers,* or (if one of them will hardly be allow'd a man) *Two Mothers*; indeed I think *both Sexes* had a share in it,[62] but which was *uppermost,* I know not: I pretend not to determine the exact method of this *Witty Fornication*: and, if

I call it *Yours,* my Lord, 'tis only because, whoever *got* it, you *brought it forth.*[63]

Here, my Lord, allow me to observe the different proceeding of the *Ignoble poet,* and his *Noble Enemies.* What he has written of *Fanny, Adonis, Sappho,* or who you will, he own'd he publish'd, he set his name to: What they have *publish'd* of him, they have deny'd to have *written*; and what they have *written* of him, they have denied to have *publish'd.* One of these was the case in the past Libel, and the other in the present.[64] For tho' the parent has own'd it to a few choice friends, it is such as he has been obliged to deny in the most particular terms, to the great Person whose opinion *concern'd him most.*[65]

Yet, my Lord, this Epistle was a piece not written in *haste,* or in a *passion,* but many months after all pretended provocation; when you was at *full leisure* at Hampton-Court, and I the object *singled,* like a *Deer out of Season,* for so ill-timed, and ill-placed a diversion. It was a *deliberate* work, directed to a *Reverend Person,* of the most *serious* and *sacred* character, with whom you are known to cultivate a *strict correspondence,* and to whom it will not be doubted, but you open your *secret Sentiments,* and deliver your *real judgment* of men and things.[66] This, I say, my Lord, with submission, could not but awaken all my *Reflection* and *Attention.* Your Lordship's opinion of me as a *Poet,* I cannot help; it is yours, my Lord, and that were enough to mortify a poor man; but it is not yours *alone,* you must be content to share it with the *Gentlemen* of the *Dunciad,*[67] and (it may be) with many *more innocent* and *ingenious men.* If your Lordship destroys my *poetical* character, *they* will claim their part in the glory; but, give me leave to say, if my *moral* character be ruin'd, it must be *wholly* the work of *your Lordship*; and will be hard even for you to do, unless I *myself co-operate.*[68]

How can you talk (my most worthy Lord) of all *Pope's* Works as so many *Libels,* affirm, that *he has no invention* but in *Defamation,*[69] and charge him with *selling another man's labours printed with his own name?*[70] Fye, my Lord, you forget yourself. He printed not his name before a line of the person's you mention; that person himself has told you and all the world in the book itself, what part he had in it, as may be seen at the conclusion of his notes to the Odyssey.[71] I can only suppose your Lordship (not having at that time *forgot your*

Greek) despis'd to look upon the *Translation*; and ever since entertain'd too mean an Opinion of the Translator to cast an eye upon
it. Besides, my Lord, when you said he *sold* another man's works,
you ought in justice to have added that he *bought* them, which very
much *alters the Case*. What he gave him was five hundred pounds:[72]
his receipt can be produced to your Lordship. I dare not affirm he
was as *well paid* as *some Writers* (much his inferiors) have been since;
but your Lordship will reflect that I am no man of Quality, either
to *buy* or *sell* scribling so high: and that I have neither *Place, Pension,*
nor Power to reward for *secret Services*.[73] It cannot be, that one of
your rank can have the least *Envy* to such an author as I: but were
that *possible,* it were much better gratify'd by employing *not your
own,* but some of *those low and ignoble pens* to do you this *mean office*.
I dare engage you'll have them for less than I gave Mr. Broom, if
your friends have not rais'd the market: Let them drive the bargain
for you, my Lord; and you may depend on seeing, every day in the
week, as many (and now and then as pretty) Verses, as these of your
Lordship.[74]

And would it not be full as well, that my poor person should be
abus'd by them,[75] as by one of your rank and quality? Cannot *Curl*
do the same? nay has he not done it before your Lordship, in the
same *kind of Language,* and almost the *same words?*[76] I cannot but
think, the worthy and *discreet Clergyman* himself will agree, it is
improper, nay *unchristian,* to expose the *personal* defects of our brother:
that both such perfect forms as yours, and such unfortunate ones as
mine, proceed from the hand of the same *Maker*; who *fashioneth his
Vessels* as he pleaseth, and that it is not from their *shape* we can tell
whether they are made for *honour* or *dishonour.*[77] In a word, he would
teach you Charity to your greatest enemies; of which number, my
Lord, I cannot be reckon'd, since, tho' a Poet, I was never your
flatterer.[78]

Next, my Lord, as to the *Obscurity of my Birth*[79] (a reflection copy'd
also from Mr. *Curl* and his brethren)[80] I am sorry to be obliged to
such a presumption as to name my *Family* in the same leaf with
your Lordship's: but my Father had the honour in one instance to
resemble you, for he was a *younger Brother.*[81] He did not indeed think
it a Happiness to bury his *elder Brother,* tho' he had one, who wanted
some of those good qualities which *yours* possess. How sincerely glad

could I be, to pay to that young Nobleman's memory the debt I ow'd to his friendship, whose early death depriv'd your family of as much *Wit* and *Honour* as he left behind him in any branch of it.[82] But as to my Father, I could assure you, my Lord, that he was no Mechanic (neither a hatter, nor, which might please your Lordship yet better, a Cobler) but in truth, of a very tolerable family: And my Mother of an ancient one,[83] as well born and educated as that *Lady,* whom your Lordship made choice of to be the *Mother of your own Children*; whose merit, beauty, and vivacity (if transmitted to your posterity) will be a *better present* than even the noble blood they derive *only* from *you*.[84] A Mother, on whom I was never oblig'd so far to reflect, as to say, she *spoiled me*.[85] And a Father, who never found himself oblig'd to say of me, that he *diasapprov'd my Conduct*. In a word, my Lord, I think it enough, that my Parents, such as they were, never cost me a *Blush*; and that their Son, such as he is, never cost them a *Tear*.[86]

I have purposely omitted to consider your Lordship's Criticisms on my *Poetry*. As they are exactly the same with those of the *fore-mention'd Authors,* I apprehend they would justly charge me with partiality, if I gave to *you* what belongs to *them*; or paid more distinction to the *same things* when they are in your mouth, than when they were in theirs.[87] It will be shewing both them and you (my Lord) a *more particular respect,* to observe how much they are honour'd by *your Imitation of them,* which indeed is carried thro' your whole Epistle. I have read somewhere at *School* (tho' I make it no *Vanity* to have forgot where) that *Tully* naturaliz'd a few phrases at the instance of some of his friends. Your Lordship has done more in honour of these Gentlemen; you have authoriz'd not only their *Assertions,* but their *Style*.[88] For example, A Flow *that* wants skill *to restrain its* ardour,[89]—*a* Dictionary *that gives us nothing at* its own expence.[90]—As *luxuriant branches* bear *but little fruit, so Wit unprun'd* is *but raw fruit*[91]—*While you* rehearse ignorance, *you still* know enough *to do it in Verse*[92]—*Wits* are *but glittering* ignorance.[93]—The *account of* how *we pass our time*[94]—and, *The weight on Sir R. W——'s* brain.[95] *You can* ever *receive from* no *head more than such a head* (as no head) *has to give*:[96] Your Lordship would have said *never* receive instead of *ever,* and *any head* instead of *no head*: but all this is perfectly new, and has greatly enrich'd our language.

You are merry, my Lord, when you say, *Latin* and *Greek*

> *Have quite deserted your poor* John Trot-head,
> *And left plain native English in their stead.*[97]

for (to do you justice) this is nothing less than *plain English*. And as for your *John Trot-head*, I can't conceive why you should give it that name; for by some papers I have seen sign'd with that name, it is certainly a head *very different* from your Lordship's.[98]

Your Lordship seems determined to fall out with every thing you have learn'd at school: you complain next of a *dull Dictionary,*

> *That gives us nothing at its own expence,*
> *But a few modern words for ancient Sense.*[99]

Your Lordship is the first man that ever carried the love of Wit so far, as to expect a *witty Dictionary*. A Dictionary that gives us *any thing but words,* must not only be an *expensive* but a very *extravagant Dictionary.*[100] But what does your Lordship mean by its giving us but *a few modern words* for *ancient Sense*? If by *Sense* (as I suspect) you mean *words* (*a mistake not unusual*) I must do the Dictonary the justice to say, that it gives us *just as many modern words as ancient ones.*[101] Indeed, my Lord, you have more need to complain of a bad Grammar, than of a dull Dictionary.

Doctor *Freind*, I dare answer for him, never taught you to talk

> *of Sapphic, Lyric, and Iambic Odes.*[102]

Your Lordship might as well bid your present Tutor, your Taylor, make you a *Coat, Suit of Cloaths,* and *Breeches*; for you must have forgot your Logic, as well as Grammar, not to know, that Sapphic and Iambic are both included in Lyric; that being the *Genus,* and those the *Species.*

> *For all cannot* invent *who can* translate,
> *No more than those who* cloath us, *can* create.[103]

Here your Lordship seems in labour for a meaning. Is it that you would have Translations, *Originals*? for 'tis the common opinion, that the *business* of a Translator is to *translate,* and not to *invent,* and of a Taylor to *cloath,* and not to *create*. But why should you, my Lord, of all mankind, abuse a Taylor? not to say *blaspheme* him; if he can (as some think) at least go halves with God Almighty in the formation of a *Beau*. Might not Doctor *Sherwin* rebuke you for this, and bid you *Remember your* Creator *in the days of your Youth?*[104]

From a *Taylor,* your Lordship proceeds (by a beautiful gradation) to a *Silkman.*

> *Thus* P——pe *we find*
> *The Gaudy* Hinchcliff *of a beauteous mind.*[105]

Here too is some ambiguity. Does your Lordship use *Hinchcliff* as a *proper name?* or as the Ladies say a *Hinchcliff* or *Colmar,*[106] for a *Silk* or a *Fan?* I will venture to affirm, no Critic can have a perfect taste of your Lordship's works, who does not understand both your *Male Phrase* and your *Female Phrase.*[107]

Your Lordship, to finish your Climax, advances up to a *Hatter;* a Mechanic, whose Employment, your inform us, is not (as was generally imagined) to *cover people's heads,* but to *dress their brains.*[108] A most useful Mechanic indeed! I can't help wishing to have been one, for some people's sake.——But this too may be only another *Lady-Phrase*: Your Lordship and the Ladies may take a *Head-dress* for a *Head,* and understand, that to *adorn the Head* is the same thing as to *dress the Brains.*

Upon the whole, I may thank your Lordship for this high Panegyric: For if I have but *dress'd* up *Homer,* as your *Taylor, Silkman,* and *Hatter* have *equip'd your Lordship,* I must be own'd to have dress'd him *marvellously indeed,* and no wonder if he is *admir'd by the Ladies.*[109]

After all, my Lord, I really wish you would learn your *Grammar.* What if you put yourself awhile under the Tuition of your Friend W——m?[110] May not I with all respect say to you, what was said to *another Noble Poet* by Mr. Cowley, *Pray, Mr.* Howard, *if you did read your* Grammar, *what harm would it do you?*[111] You yourself wish all Lords would *learn to write;*[112] tho' I don't see of what use it could be, if their whole business is to *give their Votes:*[113] It could only be serviceable in *signing their Protests.*[114] Yet surely this small portion of learning might be indulged to your Lordship, without any Breach of that *Privilege*[115] you so generously assert to all those of your rank, or too great an Infringement of that *Right*[116] which you claim as *Hereditary,* and for which, no doubt, your noble Father will thank you. Surely, my Lord, no Man was ever so bent upon depreciating himself!

All your Readers have observ'd the following Lines:

> *How oft we hear some Witling pert and dull,*
> *By fashion Coxcomb, and by nature Fool,*
> *With hackney Maxims, in dogmatic strain,*
> *Scoffing Religion and the Marriage chain?*
> *Then from his Common-place-book he repeats,*
> *The Lawyers all are rogues, and Parsons cheats,*
> *That Vice and Virtue's nothing but a jest,*
> *And all Morality Deceit well drest;*
> *That Life itself is like a wrangling game, &c.*[117]

The whole Town and Court (my good Lord) have heard *this Witling*; who is so much every body's acquaintance but his own, that I'll engage *they all name* the *same Person.* But to hear *you* say, that this is only—*of whipt Cream a frothy Store,*[118] is a sufficient proof, that never mortal was endued with so humble an opinion both of himself and his own Wit, as your Lordship: For, I do assure you, these are by much the best Verses in your whole Poem.

How unhappy is it for me, that a Person of your Lordship's *Modesty* and *Virtue,* who manifests so tender a regard to *Religion, Matrimony,* and *Morality;*[119] who, tho' an Ornament to the Court, cultivate an exemplary Correspondence with the *Clergy;* nay, who disdain not charitably to converse with, and even assist, some of the very worst of Writers (so far as to cast a few *Conceits,* or drop a few *Antitheses*[120] even among the *Dear Joys* of the *Courant*)[121] that you, I say, should look upon Me alone as reprobate and unamendable! Reflect what *I was,* and what *I am.* I am even *Annihilated* by your Anger: For in these Verses you have robbed me of *all power to think,*[122] and, in your others, of the very *name* of a *Man!*[123] Nay, to shew that this is wholly your own doing, you have told us that before I wrote my *last Epistles* (that is, before I unluckily mention'd *Fanny* and *Adonis,*[124] whom, I protest, I knew not to be your Lordship's Relations) *I might have lived and died in glory.*[125]

What would I not do to be well with your Lordship? Tho', you observe, I am a mere *Imitator* of *Homer, Horace, Boileau, Garth,*[126] &c. (which I have the less cause to be asham'd of, since they were

Imitators of one another) yet what if I should solemnly engage never
to imitate *your* Lordship? May it not be one step towards an accommodation, that while you remark my *Ignorance in Greek,* you are so
good as to say, you have *forgot your own?* What if I should confess I
translated from *D'Acier?*[127] That surely could not but oblige your
Lordship, who are known to prefer *French* to all the learned Languages.[128] But allowing that in the space of *twelve years* acquaintance
with *Homer,* I might unhappily contract as much *Greek,* as your
Lordship did in *Two* at the University, why may I not forget it
again, as happily?[129]

Till such a reconciliation take effect, I have but one thing to
intreat of your Lordship. It is, that you will not decide of my
Principles on the same grounds as you have done of my *Learning:* Nor
give the same account of my *Want of Grace,* after you have lost all
acquaintance with my *Person,* as you do of my *Want of Greek,* after
you have confessedly lost all acquaintance with the *Language.* You
are too generous, my Lord, to follow the *Gentlemen* of the *Dunciad*
quite so far, as to seek my *utter Perdition*; as *Nero* once did *Lucan's,*[130]
merely for presuming to be a *Poet,* while one of so much greater
quality was a *Writer.* I therefore make this humble request to your
Lordship, that the next time you please *to write of me, speak of me,*
or even *whisper of me,*[131] you will recollect it is full *eight Years* since
I had the honour of *any conversation* or *correspondence* with your Lordship, except *just half an hour* in a Lady's Lodgings at Court, and
then I had the happiness of her being present all the time. It would
therefore be difficult even for your Lordship's penetration to tell, to
what, or from what *Principles, Parties,* or *Sentiments,* Moral, Political,
or Theological, I may have been converted, or perverted, in all that
time. I beseech your Lordship to consider, the Injury a Man of your
high Rank and *Credit* may do to a *private Person,* under *Penal Laws*
and many other disadvantages,[132] not for want of *honesty* or *conscience,*
but merely perhaps for having too *weak a head,* or too *tender a heart.*[133]
It is by *these alone* I have hitherto liv'd excluded from all *posts* of
Profit or *Trust:*[134] As I can interfere with the *Views* of *no man,* do not
deny me, my Lord, *all that is left,* a little *Praise,* or the common
Encouragement due, if not to my *Genius,* at least to my *Industry.*

Above all, your Lordship will be careful not to wrong my *Moral Character*, with THOSE under whose *Protection* I live, and thro' whose *Lenity* alone I can live with Comfort.[135] Your Lordship, I am confident, upon consideration will think, you inadvertently went a little *too far* when you recommended to THEIR perusal, and strengthened by the weight of your Approbation, a *Libel*, mean in its reflections upon my poor *figure*, and scandalous in those on my *Honour* and *Integrity*: wherein I was represented as *"an Enemy* to Human Race, a *Murderer* of Reputations, and a *Monster* mark'd by God like *Cain*, deserving to wander accurs'd thro' the World."[136]

A strange Picture of a Man, who had the good fortune to enjoy many friends, who will be always remember'd as the first Ornaments of their Age and Country;[137] and no Enemies that ever contriv'd to be heard of, except Mr. *John Dennis*,[138] and your Lordship: A Man, who never wrote a Line in which the *Religion* or *Government* of his Country, the *Royal Family*, or their *Ministry* were disrespectfully mentioned; the Animosity of any one Party gratify'd at the expence of another; or any Censure past, but upon *known Vice, acknowledg'd Folly*, or *aggressing Impertinence*.[139] It is with infinite pleasure he finds, that *some Men* who seem *asham'd* and *afraid* of *nothing else*, are so very sensible of *his Ridicule*:[140] And 'tis for that very reason he resolves (by the grace of God, and your Lordship's good leave)

> *That, while he breathes, no rich or noble knave*
> *Shall walk the world in credit to his grave.*[141]

This, he thinks, is rendering the best Service he can to the Publick, and even to the good Government of his Country; and for this, at least, he may deserve some Countenance, even from the GREATEST PERSONS in it.[142] Your Lordship knows of WHOM I speak. Their NAMES I should be as sorry, and as much asham'd, to place near *yours*, on such an occasion, as I should be to see *You*, my Lord, placed so near *their* PERSONS, if you could ever make so ill an Use of their Ear[143] as to asperse or misrepresent any one innocent Man.[144]

This is all I shall ever ask of your Lordship, except your pardon for this tedious Letter. I have the honour to be, with equal *Respect* and *Concern,*

My Lord,

Your truly devoted Servant,

A. POPE.

Annotations

1. This Letter bears the same place in our Author's prose that the Epistle to Dr. Arbuthnot does in its poetry. They are both Apologetical, repelling the libelous slanders on his Reputation: with this difference, that the Epistle to Dr. Arbuthnot, his friend, was chiefly directed against *Grub-street Writers,* and this Letter to the Noble Lord, his enemy, against *Court-Scribblers.* For the rest, they are both Master-pieces in their kinds; *That* in verse more grave, moral, and sublime; *This* in prose, more lively, critical, and pointed; but equally conducive to what he had most at heart, the vindication of his Moral Character: the only thing he thought worth his care in literary altercations; and the first thing he would expect from the good offices of a surviving Friend. [Warburton's note (*Works* [1751], VIII, 253); further notes of his will be identified by a "W." in brackets.]

2. In response to Pope's *The First Satire of the Second Book of Horace, Imitated,* published 15 February 1733, Hervey and Lady Mary had collaborated on *Verses Address'd to the Imitator of the First Satire of the Second Book of Horace,* which appeared some three weeks later. Then in November came Hervey's *An Epistle from a Nobleman to a Doctor of Divinity.*

3. "Entitled, *An Epistle to a Doctor of Divinity from a Nobleman at Hampton-Court, Aug.* 28, 1733, and printed the November following for J. Roberts. Fol." [W., p. 253]; for the history of its publication see Note on Publication and Text and Introduction.

4. Although the *Epistle* is largely a mock-autobiographical account of himself, aristocratically self-deprecating and platitudinous, Hervey devoted the last quarter of it to an attack on Pope as translator and satirist:

> Since such you'll find most Men of our Degree,
> Excuse the Ignorance appears in me.
> Nor marvel whilst that Ign'rance I rehearse,
> That still I know enough to do't in Verse:
> Guiltless of Thought, each Blockhead may compose
> This nothing-meaning Verse, as fast as Prose.
> And *P——e* with Justice of such Lines may say,

His Lordship spins a thousand in a Day.
Such P——e himself might write, who ne'er could think:
He who at *Crambo* plays with Pen and Ink;
And is call'd Poet, 'cause in Rhyme he wrote
What Dacier construed, and what *Homer* thought:
But in Reality this Jingler's Claim,
Or to an Author's, or a Poet's Name,
A Judge of writing would no more admit,
Than each dull *Dictionary*'s Claim to Wit;
That nothing gives you at its own Expence,
But a few modern Words for ancient Sense.
'Tis thus, whene'er P——pe writes, he's forced to go
And *beg a little Sense,* as School-boys do.
"For all cannot invent, who can translate;
No more than those who cloath us can create.
When we see *Celia* shining in Brocade,
Who thinks 'tis *Hinchlif* all that Beauty made?
And P——pe, in his best Works, we only find
The gaudy *Hinchlif* of some beauteous Mind.
To bid his Genius work without that Aid,
Would be as much mistaking of his Trade,
As 'twould to bid your *Hatter* made a *Head.*
Since this Mechanic's, like the other's Pains,
Are all for dressing other Peoples Brains.

But had he not, to his eternal Shame,
By trying to deserve a Sat'rist's Name,
Prov'd he can ne'er invent but to defame:
Had not his *Taste* and *Riches* lately shown,
When he would talk of Genius to the Town,
How ill he chuses, if he trusts his own.
He had, in modern Language, only wrote
Those Rules which *Horace,* and which *Vida* taught;
On *Garth* or *Boileau*'s Model built his Fame,
Or sold *Broome*'s Labours printed with P——pe's Name:
Had he ne'er aim'd at any *Work* beside,
In Glory then he might have liv'd and dy'd;
And even been, tho' not with Genius fir'd,
By *School-boys* quoted, and by *Girls* admired.
So much for P——pe. . . .

(Hervey, *Epistle,* pp. 6–8.)

The lines indeed support Pope's assessment of them. Hervey's poetry characteristically lacks the bite and drive of Lady Mary's—one reason that in their collaboration on *To the Imitator of the First Satire of the Second Book of Horace,* the actual
writing is usually ascribed to her. (See, as an example of her style, the concluding
passage cited in n. 37.)

5. The reference to weapons, retaliation, and wounds might well suggest
to contemporary readers, however obliquely, the notorious duel between Hervey
and William Pulteney fought in January 1731 over a pamphlet attack by Pulteney,
A Proper Reply to a Late Scurrilous Libel, Intitled Sedition and Defamation Display'd,
in which Hervey, as "pretty Mr. *Fainlove,*" was damningly characterized as an
effeminate, homosexual courtier. According to Halsband the lampoon and duel
"initiated Hervey's career as an object of satire, a career that would outlast his
life" (Robert Halsband, *Lord Hervey* [Oxford: Clarendon Press, 1973], p. 116).

6. There is irony in this designation too: Canon Sherwin was treated by
Hervey and his friends the Richmonds as a figure of fun (in the summer, for
example, he had been the butt of a widely reported highway robbery hoax staged
by the duke of Richmond [Earl of March, *A Duke and His Friends* (London:
Hutchinson, 1911), I, 264–73]); and even at the same time that Hervey was
addressing his Epistle to him, he was writing for the entertainment of the family
a satire, *Dr. Sherwin's Character, design'd for his Epitaph,* which embarrassingly got
out. As Hervey reported to his good friend Henry Fox, "What vexed me was the
printer's having got a copy of Sherwin's 'Character,' written by me, which they
threatened to print. However I warded this blow, by turning the verses immediately into an 'Epitaph on Ford,' and pretending they were written two years
ago. This, by the Duke of Richmond's good management, passed on Sherwin;
and he is now boasting of being abused with me by the *Craftsman* and says it is
because he and I are known to be such useful and firm friends to the Government."
(Earl of Ilchester, *Lord Hervey and His Friends 1726–38* [London: John Murray,
1950], p. 189.) If Sherwin was easily assuaged, there were others—not so guileless—ready to answer for him. One of them may have been Pope. In the name
of W. SH——W——N, a pamphlet was published early in 1734 (dated from
Chichester on Childermas-Day, 1733), *A Most Proper Reply to a Nobleman's Epistle
to a Doctor of Divinity* (London printed: sold by J. Huggonson, 1734), q. v., which
opens, "I should long ago have answer'd your Lordship's *Epistle* to me, but comparing it with your Lordship's *Character* [*the Character of Dr. Sh—— which
will be printed next week] of me, which I have since received, I found *some Things
hard to be understood,* 2 Pet. iii. 16."

7. To Sherwin's Latin letter, Hervey—who was well versed in Latin—had
replied:

> In the next place, when I declare how long
> I've taken leave of *Greek* or *Latin* Song;

That all I learn'd from *Doctor Freind* at School,
by *Gradus, Lexicon,* or Grammar-Rule;
Of Saphic, Lyric, or Iambic Odes,
Or *Doctor King's* Machinary of Gods,
Has quite deserted this poor *John-Trot* Head,
And left plain native *English* in its stead:
I'm sure your courteous Rev'rence will forgive
The homely Way, in which you now receive
These heart Thanks, from an illiterate Hand,
For Favours which I barely understand.
(Harvey, *Epistle,* p. 4; ll. 7–18.)

8. Reiterated by Hervey in the *Epistle* (see n. 4) this had been the substance of Pope's attack on him in the *First Satire of the Second Book of Horace*:

The Lines are weak, another's please'd to say,
Lord *Fanny* spins a thousand such a Day.
(TE IV, 5.)

9. There is much to suggest that Hervey had not meant the Epistle for general circulation—its style and his own statements to Henry and Stephen Fox as he traced its history: (to Henry Fox, 20 October 1733) "Send me your opinion of the enclosed. They were written to Dr. Sherwin to entertain the Richmond-Caravan in their late progress"; (to Stephen Fox, 6 December 1733) "I send you enclosed some verses, which you have already seen in manuscript, and which were printed without my knowledge. The advertisement you saw was, I fear, for the publication of genuine things; and all the trouble and bustle I have had to prevent their coming out, I shall adjourn the recital of till I see you. Pope is in a most violent fury; and j'en suis ravi." (Ilchester, *Lord Hervey and His Friends,* pp. 179, 183.)

10. Pope himself consistently expressed his indifference to this "great" world: "Courts I see not, Courtiers I know not, Kings I adore not, Queens I compliment not; so I am never like to be in fashion, nor in dependance" (*Correspondence,* II, 469 and III, 367). See also *Correspondence,* IV, 156. On the other hand, for all his disclaimers about his commitment to literature, Pope took very seriously the world of letters and the value of his own talent.

11. His sensitivity on this score is not without basis. Lady Mary, for example, could write to her daughter autocratically, "It is pleasant to consider that had it not been for the good nature of those very mortals they [Pope and Swift] contemn, these two superior beings were entitl'd by their Birth and hereditary Fortune to be only a couple of Link Boys." (*The Complete Letters of Lady Mary Wortley Montagu,* ed. Halsband [Oxford: Clarendon Press, 1967], III, 57 [to Lady Bute, 23 June (1754)].)

12.   *"That to good blood by old prescriptive rules*
         Gives right hereditary to be Fools."
                    [W., p. 255 (Hervey, *Epistle*, p. 4).]

13.   *"Nor wonder that my Brain no more affords,*
         But recollect the privilege of Lords."
                              [W., p. 255 (ibid.).]

14.   *"And when you see me fairly write my name;*
         For England's *sake wish all could do the same."*
                              [W., p. 255 (ibid.).]

15.   *"Whilst all our bus'ness is to dress and vote."*
                              [W., p. 255 (ibid.).]

16.   *"Courts are only larger families,*
         The growth of each, few truths, and many lies:
         *   in private satyrize, in publick flatter.*
         Few to each other, all to one point true;
         Which one I sha'n't, nor need explain. Adieu."
                              [W., p. 255 (ibid., p. 8).]

17. If Pope was not to "immolate" "the whole body of the Nobility" at this point, another, inspired by him, had provided a comparable account of Hervey himself. In this same year, 1733, Paul Whitehead had published, anonymously, *The State Dunces,* "Inscribed to Mr. Pope," with this passage:

> To dance, dress, sing, and serenade the Fair,
> "Conduct a Finger," or reclaim a Hair,
> O'er baleful Tea with Females taught to blame,
> And spread a Slander o'er each Virgin's Fame;
> Form'd for these softer Arts, shall *H——y* strain,
> With stubborn Politicks his tender Brain!
> For Ministers laborious Pamphlets write,
> In Senates prattle, and with Patriots fight!
> Thy fond ambition, *pretty Youth,* give o'er,
> Preside at Balls, old Fashions lost restore;
> So shall each Toilet in thy Cause engage,
> And *H——y* shine a *P——re* of the Age.

(London: Printed for W. Dickenson in Witch-Street, 1733, pp. 15–16.) Interestingly enough some of the phrases of Hervey's original—and Pope's paraphrase here in the *Letter*—are echoed in a lampoon occasioned by Hervey's first speech for the House of Lords on 17 January 1734 (and relayed by him to Henry Fox on 8 February), where he is satirized as being "Created *Lady* of the *Lords*":

To teach hereditary fools,
  And the rude race of elder brothers,
To dress and vote by newer rules,
  And make you gentle as your mothers.

But even more intriguing for students of Pope are the metaphors with which the poem opens:

My Lords,
  Tho' when I stand upright,
    You take me for a skein of silk;
  And think me with a face so white,
    A perfect curd of ass's milk.

According to the earl of Ilchester, who published the verses in his *Lord Hervey and His Friends,* they "are probably by some hack-writer connected with the *Craftsman,* and are disallowed by the experts for various reasons from being part of the output of Pope's own pen." (Pp. 296, 191.)

18. A sentiment voiced by no less a person than the king: "You ought not to write verses; 'tis beneath your rank: leave such work to little Mr. Pope." (Quoted by Halsband, *Lord Hervey,* p. 144.)

19. Born in 1696, Lord Hervey was the second son (the first by a second wife) of a wealthy Suffolk squire, of a family that included a maternal grandfather and a paternal great-uncle who had held court posts under Charles II. His father, who retired to the country to live the life of a country gentleman after nine years as a staunch Hanoverian Whig M.P., was raised to the peerage in 1703 as Baron Hervey of Ickworth and, at the coronation of George I, created earl of Bristol. His mother, an heiress from a Suffolk landed family, remained at court after her husband's retirement, serving for twenty-five years as a Lady of the Bedchamber to Caroline, first when she was Princess of Wales and then when Queen. Always on affectionate terms with his father, Lord Hervey had a less stable relationship with his mother, who doted on him as a child and young man but who became estranged from him after his marriage.

20. Because of ill health, Hervey was pampered as a child by indulgent parents, who kept him with them on visits, travels, and stays at Newmarket for the races. He was educated privately by a tutor until he entered Westminster School at the late age of sixteen, leaving there a year and a half later for the family college, Clare Hall, Cambridge, which had grown fashionable in the early eighteenth century. After taking his M.A. he finished his education with the requisite Grand Tour, though the trip was cut short when, after Paris, he was directed to Hanover by his father and returned home with the king. During this time, "Hervey had shown an alarming zest for writing verse. This worried his father,

who feared that his constant rhyming would stand in the way of his advancement in the world" (Halsband, *Lord Hervey*, p. 37).

21. With his mother appointed a Lady of the Bedchamber in March of 1718, Hervey had entrée into the fashionable world of London and Richmond, where he made a great social success, marrying one of the Princess's most attractive Maids of Honour, Mary Lepell, the handsome couple being heralded in a contemporary ballad:

> Bright Venus yet never saw bedded,
> So perfect a beau and a belle,
> As when Hervey the handsome was wedded,
> To the beautiful Molly L[epe]l.
> (Quoted by Halsband, *Lord Hervey*, p. 44.)

After his brother Carr's death in 1723, Hervey inherited his courtesy title of Lord Hervey and, in 1725, was elected to the family seat in Parliament. In 1733 he was elevated to the House of Lords to strengthen the ministry's position there.

22. For services to Walpole in Commons, Hervey was rewarded in 1731 with the post of Vice-Chamberlain in the King's Household, an office which he held for ten years until he was made Lord Keeper of the Privy Seal. These years at court, where he became a great favorite and intimate of the queen, were the basis for his famous *Memoirs*.

23. When the newly crowned George II opened Parliament in 1728, it was Hervey who was chosen to move the Address of Thanks; it was his maiden speech, the first of many he was to make (first in Commons, later in the House of Lords) for the ministry, which he served also as a pamphleteer. Though Hervey seems to have been a fairly respected speaker, at least in certain quarters (see Halsband, *Lord Hervey*, pp. 94, 166), he remained personally a controversial figure. In February 1734 he sent to Henry Fox a copy of the current lampoon noticed above in n. 17, *The Lord H——R——Y's First Speech in the House of Lords*, which asserts in his name—

> So I, the softest, prettiest thing,
>   This honourable House affords,
> Come here by order of the King,
>   Created *Lady* of the *Lords*.
>
> . . . .
>
> As ev'ry one my talents knows,
>   Observe my Lords how I shall serve you,
> I'll turn Swift's satire into prose
>   It shall be praise from my Lord H——.
> (Ilchester, *Lord Hervey and His Friends*, pp. 296–97.)

24. *"All their bus'ness is to dress, and vote."* [W., p. 257 (Hervey, *Epistle*, p. 4).]

25. Pope was quite right; Hervey was an able prose writer: he was an astute and witty pamphleteer, and his brilliant *Memoirs* has provided his modern reputation with what saving grace it possesses.

26. Pope's early acquaintance with Hervey had been the casual friendship of the fashionable world of wits and courtiers at St. James's and, later, Leicester House, into which he ventured in his late twenties. Much closer had been his relationship with Mary Lepell—to become Hervey's wife in 1720—one of the Princess's Maids of Honour whom Pope celebrated in *The Court Ballad* (1717) and *Epigrams, Occasion'd by an Invitation to Court* (1717). In fact, in March 1720, before her secret marriage to Hervey on 21 April, Mary Lepell had been a house guest of the Popes in Twickenham, recuperating there from an illness. Such was Pope's known relationship at the time with both her and Hervey that Gay included them together among the well-wishers on hand to greet him in "A Welcome from Greece," written to herald the completion of the *Iliad*:

> Now Hervey, fair of face, I mark full well,
> With thee, youth's youngest daughter, sweet Lepell.

27. What caused the relationship to cool is not clear-cut. There was basically the divergency in their personal and political interests; more specifically, Hervey's close association with Lady Mary automatically placed him in the ranks of the enemy when she and Pope parted ways. In 1731, writing to Stephen Fox, Hervey had observed generally:

> I own I have an aversion to those wits by profession, who think it incumbent upon them always to reflect and express themselves differently from the rest of the world; they are a sort of mental poster-masters [self-advertisers?] in company who think they must distort themselves to entertain you, and often give me pain, but never give me pleasure. Pope is the head of this sect. If he had never talked, one should have thought he had more wit than any man that ever lived, and if he had never written he would have talked much better; but the endeavouring to raise his character as a companion up to the point it stands as an author, has sunk it as much below its natural pitch as he has endeavoured to put it above it. But this is a rock many have split upon as well as him. (Ilchester, *Lord Hervey and His Friends*, pp. 83–84.)

Certainly Pope's *Epistle to Burlington* and then the *Epistle to Bathurst* were to cause considerable flutter in the aristocratic dovecotes, and Hervey's own critical remarks might well have antagonized the author. (Ibid., p. 154.)

28. Hervey had commented to Henry Fox about the *Epistle*: "And my answer to Arbuthnot, when he asked me why I had been so very severe on Pope, was,

'Because he was a rascal, had begun with me, and deserved it; and that my only reason for being sorry the verses were printed, which I did not design they should be, was because I thought it below me to enter into a paper-war with one that had made himself by his late works as contemptible as he was odious.' " (Ilchester, *Lord Hervey and His Friends,* p. 189.) Pope, on the other hand, maintained that Lord Hervey was the aggressor, as he wrote to Caryll early in 1734: "You have heard of a poetical war begun upon me by Lord Harvey [*sic*] but it is like to a war only on one side, for I shall not contend with angels either of light or darkness." (*Correspondence,* III, 400.)

29. See n. 8. The allusion to "Lord Fanny" is relatively innocuous when compared to Pope's attack on Lady Mary in the same work:

> From furious *Sappho* scarce a milder Fate,
> P—x'd by her Love, or libell'd by her Hate:
> (TE IV, 13; ll. 83–84.)

30. What, arm'd for *Virtue* when I point the Pen,
> Brand then bold Front of shameless, guilty Men,
> Dash the proud Gamester in his gilded Car,
> Bare the mean Heart that lurks beneath a Star. . . .
> (TE IV, 15; ll. 105–08.)

> *Envy* must own, I live among the Great,
> No Pimp of Pleasure, and no Spy of State. . . .
> (TE IV, 19; ll. 133–34.)

These offhanded allusions (which to contemporaries would certainly suggest Walpole and his associates [see Maynard Mack, *The Garden and the City* (London: Oxford University Press, 1969), pp. 182–84]) recall the reader to a poem whose spirit permeates the letter to Hervey.

> (And I not strip the Gilding off a Knave,
> Un-plac'd, un-pension'd, no Man's Heir, or Slave?
> I will, or perish in the gen'rous Cause.)
> (TE IV, 17; ll. 115–17.)

31. Pope had offered a comparable (if perhaps slightly more acrimonious) "excuse" to Lady Mary through the earl of Peterborow, to whom she had protested the attack; see n. 58.

32. "It was for this reason that this Letter, as soon as it was printed, was communicated to the Q[ueen]." [W., p. 258.] Writing to Swift in April about "Libels" and *Verses Address'd to the Imitator,* Pope mentions that "it was labour'd, corrected, præcommended, and post-disapprov'd. . . ." *Correspondence,* III, 366.)

33. On 9 March 1733, there was published the Lord Hervey-Lady Mary collaboration, *Verses Address'd to the Imitator of the First Satire of the Second Book of*

Horace. By a Lady. London: Printed for A. Dodd, and sold in all the Pamphlet-Shops in Town. A piracy of it—with no mention of the "Lady"—was advertised the same day: *To the Imitator of the Satire of the Second Book of Horace.* London: Printed for J. Roberts, near the Oxford Arms in Warwick-Lane. According to J. V. Guerinot in his study of the pamphlet attacks on Pope, it is "The most famous of the attacks on Pope and perhaps the only one where Pope has found a worthy adversary." He concludes the entry, "In the appalling final lines she [Lady Mary] rises to a full command of the rhetoric of hate. . . ." (Guerinot, pp. 225, 226.) It is a devastating attack, and unlike Hervey's later *Epistle,* brutally personal. (See n. 37.)

34. Pope's friendship with Lady Mary covered only some ten years and in its greatest intensity about five—from 1715 to 1720–21, but she had a lasting emotional impact upon him, whether reflected in his early effusions of devotion or in the later invectives. About the time Pope's infatuation was waning, she had embarked on a more enduring, if also more dispassionate friendship, one of comrade-in-wit, with Hervey. The two acid-tongued aristocrats shared common political and literary interests and, later, even a joint passion, for a young Italian savant, Francesco Algarotti. After Lady Mary's retirement to the Continent, they continued to be close correspondents until Hervey's death.

35.   "Once, and but once, his heedless youth was bit,
       And lik'd that dang'rous thing a female Wit.

See the Letter to Dr. Arbuthnot amongst the Variations." [W., p. 259.] [A MS variant, ll. 368–69; the published lines run "Yet soft by Nature, more a Dupe than Wit, / *Sappho* can tell you how this man was bit. . . ."]

36. What brought about the estrangement in this relationship that had been so important to Pope, still remains conjectural, with theories ranging from borrowed bed linens returned unwashed by Lady Mary to more likely rebuffs on her part. She reported to Spence,

> I got a third person to ask Mr. Pope why he had left [off] visiting me. He answered negligently that he went as often as he used to. I then got Dr. Arbuthnot to ask what Lady Mary had done to him? He said that Lady Mary and Lord Hervey had pressed him once together (and I don't remember that we were ever together with him in our lives) to write a satire on some certain persons, that he refused it, and that this had occasioned the breach between us. (*Anecdotes,* I, 306.)

That the rupture was more personal than this is suggested by the intensity of Pope's later animus. In the ruthless attack of *Verses Address'd to the Imitator,* Lady Mary may have been probing what she knew all too well to be his great vulnerability when she wrote, "But how should'st thou by Beauty's Force be mov'd, / No more for loving made, than to be loved?"

37. As Lady Mary (and Hervey) had put it:

> *Satire* shou'd, like a polish'd Razor keen,
> Wound with a Touch, that's scarcely felt or seen.
> Thine is an Oyster-Knife, that hacks and hews;
> The Rage, but not the Talent of Abuse;
> And is in *Hate,* what *Love* is in the Stews.
> 'Tis the gross *Lust* of Hate, that still annoys,
> Without Distinction, as gross Love enjoys:
> Neither to Folly, nor to Vice confin'd;
> The Object of thy Spleen is Human Kind:
> It preys on all, who yield, or who resist;
> To thee 'tis Provocation to exist.
>
> But if thou see'st a great and gen'rous Heart,
> Thy Bow is doubly bent to force a Dart.
> Nor only Justice vainly we demand,
> But even Benefits can't rein thy Hand:
> To this or that alike in vain we trust,
> Nor find Thee less Ungrateful than Unjust.
>
> . . . .
>
> When God created Thee, one would believe,
> He said the same thing as to *the Snake of Eve*;
> *To human Race Antipathy declare,*
> *'Twixt them and Thee be everlasting War.*
> But oh! the Sequel of the Sentence dread,
> And whilst you *bruise their Heel,* beware your Head.
> Nor think thy Weakness shall be thy Defence;
> The Female Scold's Protection in Offence.
> Sure 'tis as fair to beat who cannot fight,
> As 'tis to libel those who cannot write.
> And if thou drawst thy Pen to aid the Law,
> Others a Cudgel, or a Rod, may draw.
> If none with Vengeance yet thy Crimes pursue,
> Or give thy manifold Affronts their due;
> If Limbs unbroken, Skin without a Stain,
> Unwhipt, unblanketed, unkick'd, unslain;
> That wretched little Carcass you retain:
> The Reason is, not that the World wants Eyes;
> But thou'rt so mean, they see, and they despise.
> When fretful *Porcupines,* with rancorous Will,
> From mounted Backs shoot forth a harmless Quill,

Cool the Spectators stand; and all the while,
Upon the angry little Monster smile.

. . . .

Those, who thy Nature loath'd, yet lov'd thy Art,
Who lik'd thy Head, and yet abhor'd thy Heart;
Chose thee, to read, but never to converse,
And scorned in Prose, him whom they priz'd in Verse.
Even they shall now their partial Error see,
Shall shun thy Writings like thy Company;
And to thy Books shall ope their Eyes no more,
Than to thy Person they wou'd do their Door.
  Nor thou the Justice of the World disown,
That leaves Thee thus an Out-cast, and alone;
For tho' in Law, to murder be to kill,
In Equity the Murder's in the Will:
Then whilst with Coward Hand you stab a Name,
And try at least t'assassinate our Fame;
Like the first bold Assassin's be thy Lot,
Ne'er be thy Guilt forgiven, or forgot. . . .
                              (Pp. 4, 5, 6, 7, 8.)

It must be noted that while Pope's references cover almost all of their attacks on
him, he omits the most direct and painful personal allusions to his deformity:

          Thine is just such an Image of *his* Pen,
          As thou thy self art of the Sons of Men:
          Where our own Species in Burlesque we trace,
          A Sign-Post Likeness of the noble Race;
          That is at once Resemblance and Disgrace.

          . . . .

          Not even Youth and Beauty can controul
          The universal Rancour of thy Soul;
          Charms that might soften Superstition's Rage,
          Might humble Pride, or thaw the Ice of Age.
          But how should'st thou by Beauty's Force be mov'd,
          No more for loving made, than to be lov'd?
          It was the Equity of righteous Heav'n,
          That such a Soul to such a Form was giv'n;
          And shews the uniformity of Fate,
          That one so odious, shou'd be born to hate.

          . . . .

          But as thou hate'st, be hated by Mankind,

> And with the Emblem of thy Crooked Mind,
> Mark'd on thy Back, like *Cain,* by God's own Hand;
> Wander like him, accursed through the Land.

(*Verses Address'd to the Imitator of the First Satire of the Second Book of Horace. By a Lady.* London: Printed for A. Dodd, and sold at all the Pamphlet Shops in Town, pp. 4, 5, 8.)

38. These jibes (which parallel Pulteney's attack in his *Reply to a Late Scurrilous Libel* [See n. 5]: "A circulator of Tittle-Tattle, a Bearer of Tales, a Teller of Fibs, a station's Spy" [p. 7]) are well directed at Lord Hervey, whose position at court, especially as confidant of the queen, placed him at the heart of that world and all its intrigue and gossip. It was in 1733 that he began compiling his memoirs—*Some Materials Toward Memoirs of the Reign of George II*—where he himself describes his activities as damningly as any satirist:

> Sunday and Monday Lord Hervey lay constantly in London; every other morning he used to walk with the Queen and her daughters at Hampton Court. His real business in London was pleasure; but as he always told the King it was to pick up news, to hear what people said, to see how they looked, and to inform Their Majesties what was thought by all the parties of the present posture of affairs, he by these means made his pleasure in town and his interest at Court reciprocally conducive to each other.
>
> These excursions put it also in his power to say things as from other people's mouths, which he did not dare to venture from his own, and often to deliver that as the effect of his observation which in reality flowed only from his opinion. However, that he might not draw on others the anger which by this method he diverted from himself, he used, both to the King and the Queen, to say he would willingly let them know everything he heard, but must beg leave always to be excused from telling where he had it or from whom; and as it was of much more use to Their Majesties to know what was said than by whom, so he hoped they would give him leave whilst for their sakes he communicated the one, for his own to be silent upon the other.

(*Lord Hervey's Memoirs,* ed. Romney Sedgwick [London: William Kimber, 1952], pp. 65–66.)

39. *Dye,* obsolete form of *die,* the singular of *dice.* From his mother, an inveterate card player, Lord Hervey inherited a well-known taste for gaming. (Sedgwick, "Introduction," *Lord Hervey's Memoirs,* pp. 14–15.)

40. The matter of borrowing money seems to have been a sensitive issue for Hervey since he fastened on it as one of Pulteney's imputations in *A Proper Reply* [see n. 5]. (Halsband, *Lord Hervey,* p. 113.) These references are also suggestive of Lady Mary, who, with her husband, had a reputation for miserliness that Pope

was shortly to satirize in *The Second Satire to the Second Book of Horace* (TE IV, 57–59) and *Sober Advice from Horace* (TE IV, 77). More particularly, they could recall the earlier Rémond scandal, when Lady Mary had been accused of financial misdealings by a French acquaintance for whom she had speculated in South Sea stock (TE V, 112). And more recently, in 1731, there had been further contention over the custody of her insane sister, Lady Mar, also with unpleasant financial implications and charges. (TE IV, 306.)

41. In 1716—when Pope's friendship with Lady Mary was flourishing—Curll got hold of and printed a collection of three poems, entitled *Court Poems* and advertised as being by "a Lady of Quality" or by Gay—or by "the Judicious Translator of *Homer.*" While two of the poems are generally recognized to be Lady Mary's, with one perhaps by Gay, Pope gallantly took upon himself the onus of the somewhat discreditable work, and the vengeance for its publication, by punishing Curll with an emetic—the whole episode recorded in *A Full and True Account of a Horrid and Barbarous Revenge by Poison on the Body of Mr. Edmund Curll.* However, ten years later when Lady Mary might have been trying to involve him in the authorship of a ballad attacking his friend Mrs. Joanna Baillie Murray, Pope was looking on matters differently, and in the "Last" volume of the *Miscellanies* (1728) included a coarse poem "The Capon's Tale," which satirized Lady Mary for trying to foist off her "chicks" on others. (*Early Career,* pp. 167–69; 206–7.) There may be some even more recent episode meant here, perhaps involving Lady Mary's access to Walpole; in 1729 Pope was protesting to Fortescue, "I should be sorry if she had any credit or influence with him, for she would infallibly use it to bely me . . ." (*Correspondence,* III, 53).

42. Despite such protestations, Lady Mary had been satirized in "The Capon's Tale" (see above) as well as in a couplet in the *Dunciad* (TE V, 112) before the Sappho allusion in the *First Satire on the Second Book of Horace,* where there is the first acknowledged attack on Lord Hervey as Lord Fanny (the reference itself having appeared a year earlier in the anonymous *A Master Key to Popery,* q.v.). Afterwards would come, of course, *The Epistle to Dr. Arbuthnot*—the ultimate attack on Hervey, with reference too to Lady Mary—and a long series of jibes at both of them, registered under their names in the Biographical Appendix of TE IV.

43. Note TE IV, 291; ll. 161–64:

> You laugh, half Beau half Sloven if I stand,
> My Wig all powder, and all snuff my Band;
> You laugh, if Coat and Breeches strangely vary,
> White Gloves, and Linnen worthy Lady Mary!

But since it *was* Lady Mary who was more memorable for her untidiness, Pope is being ironic here, touching briefly on what must have been the most painful aspect of their attack (see n. 37) only to turn it against them.

44. At the time of his marriage, Hervey was celebrated as handsome (see n. 21) and he is usually described as a man of striking if delicate good looks, rather effeminate in manner. But the ill health from which he suffered all his life must have taken its toll early; by 1737 the antagonistic old duchess of Marlborough was describing him as "a painted face and not a tooth in his head" (though Halsband counters this with a reference to his fine set of false teeth) (Halsband, *Lord Hervey*, p. 188). Lady Mary was a pretty young woman, with notable eyes, until an attack of smallpox in 1715 left her badly scarred and without eyelashes. In his later attacks on her, Pope played on her reputation for slovenly dress and slatternly ways.

45. Halsband reports that on his Grand Tour Hervey would have encountered in Paris women varnished in shining red and beaux painted white. "If Hervey later used white make-up, as satirists charged, it was *à la mode* in Paris; and he preferred to look like a pale Frenchified beau rather than a red-faced English hearty." (Halsband, *Lord Hervey*, pp. 25–26.)

46. In 1733, Pope would have been forty-five years old, Hervey thirty-eight and Lady Mary forty-four. During this contention, Hervey had relayed to Henry Fox, in a letter of 8 February 1734, four lampoons, among them a poem which he attributed to Pope—"to Lord Hervey and Lady Mary Wortley"—with these lines:

> Thanks, dirty Pair! You teach me what to say,
>   When you attack my Morals, Sense, or Truth.
> I answer thus,—poor Sapho you grow grey,
>   And sweet Adonis—you have lost a Tooth.
>   (TE VI, 357.)

47. When Lady Mary's letters to Lord Hervey were returned to her after his death, she commented to his son that they would have revealed how lasting a relationship could exist between two individuals, even of opposite sexes, whose bond was purely that of deep friendship. (Robert Halsband, *The Life of Lady Mary Wortley Montagu* [Oxford: Clarendon Press, 1956], pp. 223–24.) Certainly their early acquaintance had thrived on the comradeship of mutual antagonisms, and they thought of themselves as confrères-in-wit. Pope's simile for their friendship was one he obviously liked: see *Thoughts on Various Subjects,* p. 156.

48. On 18 March 1732/33, Pope had written to Fortescue:

> You may be certain I shall never reply to such a Libel as Lady Mary's. 'Tis a pleasure & a comfort at once to find, that with so much mind, as so much Malice must have to accuse or blacken my character, it can fix upon no one ill or immoral thing in my Life; & must content itself to say my Poetry is dull, & my person ugly. I wish you would take an opportunity to represent to the Person [Walpole probably, who had in-

tervened on Lady Mary's behalf about the Sappho lines] who spoke to you about that Lady, that Her Conduct no way deserves *Encouragement* from him, or any other Great persons: & that the Good name of a Private Subject ought to be as sacred even to the Highest, as His Behaviour toward them is irreproachable, loyal, & respectfull. ——What you writ of his Intimation on that head shall never pass my lips. (*Correspondence*, III, 357.)

49. In its threat of corporal punishment, *Verses Address'd to the Imitator* continued in the spirit of a 1728 lampoon which appeared after the publication of the *Dunciad* and which Pope always attributed to Lady Mary: *A Popp upon Pope: Or a True and Faithful Account Of a late Horrid and Barbarous Whipping, Committed on the Body of A. Pope, a Poet, as he was innocently walking in Ham-Walks, near the River Thames, meditating Verses for the Good of the Publick* (London, 1728). In his letters of the period Lord Hervey echoed the same warning; for example, to Stephen Fox, 21 December 1731: "Everybody concurs in their opinion of Pope's last performance [*On the Use of Riches*], and condemns it as dull and impertinent. . . . It is astonishing to me that he is not afraid this prophecy will be verified, which was told to him a year or two ago,

> 'In black and white whilst satire you pursue,
> Take heed the answer is not black and blue.' "

(Ilchester, *Lord Hervey and His Friends*, pp. 124–25.)

50. Pope would have been familiar with Fannius as a pretentious critic and poet not only through Horace's satires (as he indicates) but also through Ben Jonson's *The Poetaster*. "A Comicall Satyre" (1601). *The Grub-Street Journal* for Thursday, 6 December 1733, printed (under "From Pegasus in Grub-Street") "Advice to a Nobleman, the author of an *Epistle to a Dr. of divinity* from H——ton C——t. ——By Ben Johnson. [in his *Poetaster.* act the 5th, scene the last.]" The scene is all too applicable, with Fannius being punished for his libels against Horace, "*taxing him falsly of* railing, filching by translation, & . . . ." (See also Introduction to *A Most Proper Reply to the Nobleman's Epistle*, pp. 487–88.)

51. *Satires* 1. 4. 21–22: "Happy fellow, Fannius, who has delivered his books and bust unasked." (Loeb [1955], p. 51.)

52. *Satires* 1. 10. 79–80: "[am I to be tortured] because silly Fannius, who sponges on Hermogenes Tigellius girds at me?" (Loeb [1955], p. 122.) Here Horace is contrasting bad writers, like Tigellius, with those like him who belonged to Maecenas's circle.

53. *Satires* 1. 10. 91: "[But you, Demetrius, and you Tigellius] I bid you go whine amidst the easy chairs of your pupils in petticoats." (Loeb [1955], p. 123.)

54. See n. 7; Dr. Freind, the headmaster of Westminster School, was a lifelong friend of Hervey.

55. *"Weak texture of his* flimzy *brain."* [W., p. 263 (Hervey, *Epistle,* p. 6).]

56. An ascription that had become ambiguous in tone. On the one hand there was the classical Sappho, still a symbol of poetry and female attainment (in fact, despite Pope's slanders, Lady Mary seems always to have identified herself with the historic figure and, on her travels, had noted, "I will pass by all the other islands with this general reflection, that 'tis impossible to imagine any thing more agreeable than this journey would have been between two and three thousand years since, when, after drinking a dish of tea with Sappho, I might have gone the same evening to visit the temple of Homer in Chios . . ." [quoted by Halsband, *The Life of Lady Mary,* p. 89]); on the other hand, the allusion had degenerated into a designation for any "literary" lady and Pope's early, self-consciously rakish correspondence is filled with such Sapphos (*Correspondence,* I, 42, 47, 99–100).

57. Pope may have forgotten an early allusion to "sprightly Sappho," who "force[s] our Love & Praise" (*Correspondence,* II, 139), though the reference there is private, unspecific, and perhaps more honorific than pejorative. There is no mistaking the intention and identification in the first imitation of Horace. After that Lady Mary and Sappho are inextricably linked, as Lady Mary complained to Dr. Arbuthnot at the time of the *Epistle to Dr. Arbuthnot*: "but as the Town (except you who know better) generally suppose Pope means me whenever he mentions that name, I cannot help taking Notice of the terrible malice he bears against the Lady signify'd by that name. . . ." (Ibid., III, 448.)

58. When Lady Mary complained to the earl of Peterborow about Pope's attack, he replied in a letter which Sherburn believes to have been dictated or shaped by Pope:

> He said to me what I had taken the Liberty to say to you, that he wondered how the Town could apply those Lines to any but some noted common woeman, that he should yet be more surprised if you should take them to your Self, He named to me fower remarkable poetesses & scribblers, Mrs Centlivre Mrs Haywood Mrs Manly & Mrs Been, Ladies famous indeed in their generation, and some of them Esteemed to have given very unfortunate favours to their Friends, assuring me that Such only were the objects of his satire. (*Correspondence,* III, 352.)

59. See n. 33.

60. Except for Lady Mary—where there seems to have been a deep psychic hurt—Pope's enmities were not with women, towards whom he tended to be sentimental and gallant; though his great hatreds often included personal resentments, they usually involved broader, more significant moral battles as well.

61. As late as 3 January 1735—after the publication of the *Epistle to Dr. Arbuthnot*—Lady Mary was maintaining her innocence in the matter of the *Verses Address'd to the Imitator*; in a letter then to Dr. Arbuthnot, she protested, ". . . now I can assure him they were wrote (without my knowledge) by a Gentleman of great merit, whom I very much esteem, who he will never guess, & who, if he did know he durst not attack; but I own the design was so well meant, & so excellently executed that I cannot be sorry they were written . . ." (*Correspondence*, III, 448).

62. In April, Pope had written to Swift: "Tell me your opinion as to Lady M———'s or Lord H———'s performance? they are certainly the Top wits of the Court, and you may judge by that single piece what can be done against me; for it was labour'd, corrected, præcommended and post-disapprov'd, so far as to be dis-own'd by themselves, after each had highly cry'd it up for the others." (*Correspondence*, III, 366.)

63. It is Halsband's contention that the title page designation of the *Verses Address'd to the Imitator* "By a Lady" is probably accurate, with Hervey assisting in its revision and publication. (*Lord Hervey*, p. 143.)

64. See Note on Publication and Text, n. 2. As Hervey had written to Henry Fox (31 January–11 February 1734): "The jumble of the advertisements in the *Daily Courier* is too long a story for me to enter into the particulars of it. The first of them was owing to a mistake of the Duke of Newcastle, whom I desired to order the printer to say that nothing promised by a former advertisement to be published should come out; and instead of that they said what was come out was not mine, though I had own'd it to every mortal, and to Arbuthnot, who came to me from Pope about it." (Ilchester, *Lord Hervey and His Friends*, p. 189.)

65. Presumably this refers to the king and queen, more probably to Queen Caroline, Hervey's real patron at court. Walpole was also an important figure in his career, but the need for secrecy there seems less likely.

66. Given the real situation of the relationship between Hervey and Dr. Sherwin, these are very sardonic comments; see n. 6.

67. Pope is quite right in his barb: with the exception of Hervey and Lady Mary, and a few figures like Gildon and Dennis, the bulk of Pope's denigrators belonged to Grub Street. As Guerinot describes Pope's attackers, "They are the dunces." (Guerinot, p. xxxvii.) See also n. 87.

68. Although the first major, *collective* attack on Pope had focused on his Homeric translation, the range of abuse had always been broad, and personal as well as aesthetic. Guerinot comments, "It must have seemed to Pope that there was almost nothing his enemies would not say. Or having once said, repeat forever. Nothing in his work, his personal life, or his character was spared." (Guerinot, pp. xxii, xxix.)

69.   *"to his eternal shame,*
          Prov'd he can ne'er invent but to defame."
                    [W., p. 267 (Hervey, *Epistle,* p. 6).]

70. *"And sold* Broom's *labours printed with* Pope's *Name."* [W., p. 267 (ibid., p. 7).]

71. Pope is still perpetuating his deceptive and discreditable version of Broome's collaboration with him on the *Odyssey.* (See TE VII, xliv.)

72. Though detractors have decried the amount—since Pope probably realized some £5,000 on the venture—the profit was earned from the more than 1,000 subscriptions which Pope's reputation and effort gained for him. Sherburn (referring to Broome's lament that hunting with the lion costs the lion's share) puts it neatly: "One doubts if Broome and Fenton were ever better paid for verses than they were when hunting with a lion who was worthy of Phaedrus' fable." (*Early Career,* p. 259.)

73. Although he had been approached first by Lord Halifax and later by Secretary Craggs about a pension, Pope was adamant about his independence; it was always a great source of pride to him that he lived and wrote free of patronage or political bondage. (*Anecdotes,* I, 99–100.) Hervey, on the other hand, pursued a political career based upon reward. In 1728 he had been granted a pension of £1,000 (for services or promises of them), which he later gave up, gambling on the hope of something better: ". . . I must entreat the King, whenever he shall think proper, to consider me in some manner which I shall not be ashamed to own." (Quoted by Halsband, *Lord Hervey,* p. 88.)

74. Hack writers (and detractors of Pope) like Welsted and Concanen were known to be government hirelings; in fact, as Guerinot notes, "Praise of Walpole in a pamphlet prepares you for an attack on Pope . . ." (Guerinot, p. xlv).

75. Guerinot's study of the attacks on Pope reveals how prevalent are the abusive references to his deformity; even as reputable a figure as Dennis "not only seems incapable of writing about Pope without mentioning his deformity; he congratulates himself that he can do it with a clear conscience since Pope's shape is a mark of divine reprobation." (Guerinot, p. xxx.)

76. *The Curliad* (1729) included *"Lord* Bacon's *Essay* on *Deformity*: Or, a *Looking-Glass* for Mr. Pope" with its argument of the relationship between body and soul (" *'Deformed Persons* are commonly *even* with Nature; for as Nature hath done *ill* by them, so *do* they by Nature, being for the most Part (as the Scripture saith) *void of natural Affection,* and so they have Revenge of Nature' ").

77. 2 Timothy 2.20—"But in a great house there are not only vessels of gold and of silver, but also of wood and of earth; and some to honour and some to dishonour." It is a metaphor which had appealed to the Wife of Bath too!

78. A consideration of great general importance to Pope, who mentioned to

Spence, "If I am a good poet . . . , there is one thing I value myself upon and which can scarce be said of any of our good poets—and that is, that 'I have never flattered any man, nor ever received anything of any man for my verses.' " (*Anecdotes*, I, 160.)

79. "*Hard as thy Heart, and as thy Birth obscure.*" [W., p. 269 (*Verses Address'd to the Imitator*, p. 4).]

80. *Codrus: Or, the Dunciad Dissected* (1728), attributed by Pope to Curll and Elizabeth Thomas, contained both a "biography" of the poet ("his Father was but a Husbandman on *Windsor-Forest*") and a poem "Farmer Pope and his Son: Or, the Toad and the Ox, a Fable." Aspersions on his father were a fairly common form of attack on Pope; see n. 83.

81. Alexander Pope, senior, a posthumous child, had an older brother, William, with whom he went into the linen trading business. Little is known of their careers, with Sherburn utilizing these comments of Pope as a source for his information on William's death and possible estrangement from his brother (*Early Career*, pp. 29–30).

82. References to Carr Hervey (who died in 1723) in early letters to Pope suggest their congeniality; for example, Jervas reports, "Lord Hervey has the Homer & Letter, & bids me thank the Author———." (*Correspondence*, I, 295.)

83. Guerinot's index of charges made against Pope includes attacks on his father as a rustic, a bankrupt, a farmer, a hatter, and a mechanic. Pope must have been very sensitive to these denigrations for he was to append a defensive footnote to the *Epistle to Dr. Arbuthnot* on the matter:

> In some of *Curl*'s and other Pamphlets, Mr. *Pope*'s Father was said to be a Mechanic, a Hatter, a Farmer, nay a Bankrupt. But, what is stranger, a *Nobleman* (if such a Reflection can be thought to come from a Nobleman) has dropt an Allusion to this pitiful Untruth, in his *Epistle to a Doctor of Divinity* ["To bid his Genius work without that Aid, / Would be as much mistaking of his Trade, / As 'twould to bid your *Hatter* make a *Head*," p. 7]: And the following line,
>
> > *Hard as thy Heart, and as thy Birth Obscure,*
>
> has fallen from a like Courtly pen, in the *Verses to the Imitator of Horace*. Mr. *Pope*'s Father was of a Gentleman's Family in *Oxfordshire*, the Head of which was the Earl of *Downe*, whose sole Heiress married the Earl of *Lindsey*. —His Mother was the Daughter of *William Turnor*, Esq; of *York*: She had three Brothers, one of whom was kill'd, another died in the Service of King *Charles*, the eldest following his Fortunes, and becoming a General Officer in *Spain*, left her what Estate remain'd after the Sequestrations and Forfeitures of her Family. . . ." (TE IV, 125n.)

But Sherburn notes that however sincere Pope might have been in this belief, the Andover Popes and the Oxfordshire ones were apparently not related (*Early Career,* p. 30).

84. See n. 21 and n. 26. Mary (Molly) Lepell—one of the princess's Maids of Honour much heralded for her youthful charm and beauty (by Pope among others)—was the daughter of a Danish gentleman who had come to England in the retinue of George of Denmark, had become a citizen and made an army career, rising to the rank of brigadier-general, and had married a Suffolk heiress. The future Lady Hervey, according to Halsband, received an education much superior to that of her contemporaries, though her reputation was for civility rather than brilliance. (Halsband, *Lord Hervey,* pp. 39–40.) As the antagonism developed between Pope and her husband, her friendship with the poet cooled too.

85. "*A noble Father's heir spoil'd by his Mother.* His Lordship's account of himself" [W., p. 270 (Hervey, *Epistle,* p. 4)].

86. Pope was indeed an exemplary son, devoted to both his parents. Although Lord Hervey's relationship with his doting mother deteriorated radically after his marriage, he was always a favorite of his father, despite the displeasure caused by his support of a ministry which the earl detested.

87. When the *Dunciad* was revised 1742/43, Pope included Lord Hervey (TE V, 291–92, 351), whose recent death allowed him to make a last minute change in the text from "Impatient waits, till * * grace the quire" to "With Fool of Quality compleats the quire."

88. Hervey's poetic style is generally—the *Epistle* is a case in point—rather insipid. That he was apparently known at the time for bathetic tendencies is seen in the references by William Pulteney to "The little, quaint Antitheses, the labour'd Gingle of the Periods, the great Variety of rhetorical Flourishes, affected Metaphors, and puerile Witticisms" (*A Proper Reply to a Late Scurrilous Libel* [London, 1731], p. 4) and in Pope's own satiric comment in the *Dunciad*:

> And thou! his Aid de camp, lead on thy sons,
> Light-arm'd with Points, Antitheses, and Puns.
>> (TE V, 291–92.)

89. Hervey, talking about himself and "*the Great*":

> That dang'rous Flow of a licentious Brain,
> Which wanting Skill it's Ardour to restrain,
> Converts to Ill, like Nourishment to Pain.
> Perhaps you'll say, to its Excuse inclin'd,
> If 'tis an Ill, 'tis of a pleasing kind.
>> (Hervey, *Epistle,* p. 5.)

90. Referring here to Pope:

> But in Reality this Jingler's Claim,
> Or to an Author's, or a Poet's Name,
> A Judge of writing would no more admit,
> Than each dull *Dictionary*'s Claim to Wit;
> That nothing gives you at its own Expence,
> But a few modern Words for ancient Sense.
>
> (Hervey, *Epistle*, p. 7.)

91. Again, speaking of aristocratic Wits:

> Luxuriant Branches show a fertle Root,
> But unrestrain'd, they bear but little Fruit:
> So Wit unprun'd, and wanting Judgment's Aid,
> Is the crude Fruit of a good useless Head.
>
> (Hervey, *Epistle*, p. 5.)

92. Speaking of himself:

> Nor marvel whilst that Ign'rance I rehearse,
> That still I know enough to do't in Verse:
>
> (Hervey, *Epistle*, p. 6.)

93. Referring to men like him:

> Such Wits are naught but glittering Ignorance:
> What *Monkeys* are to Men, they are to Sense. . . .
>
> (Hervey, *Epistle*, p. 5.)

94. Hervey himself:

> I now would try to jumble into Rhyme,
> Th'Account you ask of how we pass our Time:
>
> (Hervey, *Epistle*, p. 8.)

95. Referring further to some "Witling" like him:

> Thinks he's so wise no *Solomon* knows more:
> That the weak Texture of his flimsy Brain,
> Is fit the Weight of *Walpole's* to sustain. . . .
>
> (Hervey, *Epistle*, p. 6.)

96. Hervey referring again to himself:

> You know the Proverb says, That of a Cat,
> The Creature's Skin is all that you can get;
> So from no Head you ever can receive
> More Wit, than such a Head has got to give:
>
> (Hervey, *Epistle*, p. 4.)

97. Hervey, *Epistle*, p. 4.

98. *John Trot* is an obsolete appellation for bumpkin; it was used, as "John Trot, Yeoman," as a pseudonym of Bolingbroke, who under that name wrote some letters (1728–29) to the *Craftsman*, the Opposition newspaper of which he was a prime mover.

99. Hervey, *Epistle*, p. 7.

100. "Yet we have seen many of these *extravagant* Dictionaries, and are likely to see many more, in an age so abounding in science." [W., p. 272.]

101. Pope seems to be quibbling here: *sense* as in *dictionary meaning* was common enough usage at the time; Dr. Johnson so uses the term in the preface to his Dictionary.

102. Hervey, *Epistle*, p. 4.

103. Ibid., p. 7.

104. Ecclesiastes 12.1. Phrase suggestive of *A Most Proper Reply*, (q.v.).

105. Hervey, *Epistle*, p. 7. The lines actually go:

> And P——pe, in his best Works, we only find
> The gaudy *Hinchlif* of some beautous Mind.

106. The dictionary (for the year 1736) ". . . of the Directors of Companies, Persons in Publick Business, Merchants, and other Eminent Traders in the Cities of *London* and *Westminster*, and Borough of *Southwark*" lists Thomas Hincliff, Mercer, Ludgate Hill, and Thomas Colmore, Merchant, Pudding-Lane, East-cheap.

107. These remarks are suggestive of Hervey's sexual ambiguity. The attack on Hervey as homosexual which Pope alludes to here and develops in the Sporus portrait had been launched by William Pulteney (see n. 5) in *A Proper Reply to a Late Scurrilous Libel*: "But though it would be barbarous to handle such a *delicate Hermophrodite*, such a pretty, little, *Master Miss*, in too rough a Manner; yet you must give me Leave, my Dear, to give you a little, gentle Correction, for your own good"; Hervey's effeminate good looks and manners as well as his intense attachment to Stephen Fox gave credence to the allegation.

108.   *"For this Mechanic's, like the Hatter's pains,*
        Are but for dressing other people's brains."
                                [W., p.274 (Hervey, *Epistle*, p. 7).]

109. *"by Girls admir'd."* [W., p. 274.]

110. Probably William Windham, undertutor to the duke of Cumberland. Thought by Lord Oxford to have collaborated with Hervey and Lady Mary on *Verses to the Imitator*, he may have been the butt of some satiric lines in the *Epistle to Dr. Arbuthnot*. (See Maynard Mack, "Letters to the Editor," [London] *Times Literary Supplement* (1939), p. 515; TE IV, 340.)

111. Edward Howard, one of Dryden's brothers-in-law, was an untalented

dramatist and versifier who inspired many satiric attacks, Dorset heralding him
in a poem entitled "To a Person of Honour, on his Incomparable, Incomprehensible
Poems" and Pope including him in the *Peri Bathous* and the *Dunciad.* Pope's
anecdote is also to be found, more fully, in *The Tatler,* No. 234.

112.   "*And when you see me fairly write my name,*
         For England's sake wish all Lords did the same."
                      [W., p. 274 (Hervey, *Epistle,* p. 4).]

113. "———*All our bus'ness is to dress and vote.*" [W., p. 275 (ibid.).]

114. Hervey's father, the earl of Bristol, as a stalwart opponent of Walpole's
ministry, was a familiar signer of Protests, which his son, as writer for the
ministry, was often called upon to answer. (Halsband, *Lord Hervey,* pp. 92, 134.)

115. "*The want of brains.*" ["Nor wonder that my Brain no more affords, /
But recollect the Privilege of L——ds. . . ."] [W., p. 275 (Hervey, *Epistle,* p. 4).]

116. "*To be fools.*" [W., p. 275 (ibid.).]

117. Hervey, *Epistle,* p. 6. Probably because they are not appropriate to the
point he is pursuing here, Pope leaves out two lines (between ll. 6 and 7 cited—
the original in quotation marks):

> Physicians ignorant, and Courtiers Slaves,
> Great Kings but Actors, and great Statesmen Knaves. . . .

118. Hervey, *Epistle,* p. 6. The passage he has been quoting concludes:

> And when this Catalogue he has run o'er,
> And empty'd of Whipt Cream his frothy Store,
> Thinks he's so wise no *Solomon* knows more:
> That the weak Texture of his flimsy Brain,
> Is fit the Weight on *Walpole's* to sustain;
> In Senates to preside, to mold *the State,*
> And fix in *England's* Services, *Europe's* Fate.

Pope can nicely have it both ways: the lines are damning both as personal and
literary appraisal.

119. Hervey's aspersions—which Pope so sardonically picks up—were actually
characteristic of his attitudes, given his remarks on parsons, marriage, and mortality to be garnered from his letters (see Ilchester, *Lord Hervey and His Friends,*
pp. 209–10, 232–33). As for Hervey's own marriage, even his sympathetic biographer Robert Halsband finds his actions and attitudes toward his exemplary
wife baffling, finally citing a comment by Lady Mary's granddaughter, Lady Louisa
Stuart, that the couple "lived together upon very amicable terms, 'as well-bred
as if not married at all' . . . but without any strong sympathies, and more like

a French couple than an English one." (Halsband, *Lord Hervey*, pp. 305–6 and note.)

120. Obviously a stylistic "trademark" for Hervey; see n. 88.

121. Although at this time the *Daily Courant* (the first successful daily paper begun in Queen Anne's reign) was subsidized by the ministry, whether Hervey actually wrote for it, as Pope imputes, I have not discovered.

122. "P——e, *who ne'er cou'd think.*" [The line has been condensed.] [W., p. 276 (Hervey, *Epistle*, p. 7).]

123. In *Verses Address'd to the Imitator*, he had been castigated as "A little Insect shiv'ring at a Breeze" and, sardonically, as a *"Thing* to keep Mankind in awe. . . ."

124. *Epistle to Bathurst*, ll. 61–62:

> Or soft Adonis, so perfum'd and fine
> Drive to St. James's a whole herd of swine?
> (TE III ii, 91–92.)

125. *"In glory then he might have liv'd and dy'd."* [W., p. 276 (Harvey, *Epistle*, p. 7).]

126. Hervey, *Epistle*, p. 7: [lines preceding that cited in n. 125, just above]

> Had he, in modern Language, only wrote
> Those Rules which *Horace*, and which *Vida* taught;
> On *Garth* or *Boileau*'s Model built his Fame. . . .

Pope's most celebrated predecessors in the mock heroic were Boileau (*Le Lutrin*) and Dr. Samuel Garth (*The Dispensary*). Both Horace and Vida had each written, of course, an *Art of Poetry*.

127. Hervey's lines "And is call'd Poet, 'cause in Rhyme he wrote / What *Dacier* construed, and what *Homer* thought:" (*Epistle*, p. 7) refer to Mme Anne Lefèvre Dacier, a distinguished Homeric scholar on whose translation and commentary Pope had leaned heavily.

128. Hervey was indeed fluent in French (Halsband, *Lord Hervey*, pp. 10, 25–28) and his wife a great Francophile. If Pope meant anything further, it is not clear what he intended.

129. Hervey's course of study at Clare Hall (from 1713–15) would have been essentially classical. As Halsband suggests, "if it was like the curriculum drawn up (in 1707) by a Fellow of Clare, he read the Roman poets and prose writers daily, and each week wrote Latin themes and verses and translated passages from Greek and Latin." (Halsband, *Lord Hervey*, p. 17.)

130. Nero forced Lucan—a Roman poet best known for his epic *Pharsalia* (with a translation by Rowe to which Pope had subscribed)—to commit suicide when the poet conspired against the emperor's tyranny. In a famous letter to Arbuthnot, on 26 July 1734, in which he defended his satires, Pope wrote:

It is certain, much freer Satyrists than I have enjoy'd the encouragement and protection of the Princes under whom they lived. Augustus and Mecoenas made Horace their companion, tho' he had been in arms on the side of Brutus; and allow me to remark it was out of the suff'ring Party too, that they favour'd and distinguish'd Virgil. You will not suspect me of comparing my self with Virgil and Horace, nor even with another Court-favourite, Boileau: I have always been too modest to imagine my Panegyricks were Incense worthy of a Court; and that I hope will be thought the true reason why I have never offr'd any. I would only have observ'd, that it was under the greatest Princes and best Ministers, that moral Satyrists were most encouraged; and that then Poets exercised the same jurisdiction over the Follies, as Historians did over the Vices of men. It may also be worth considering, whether Augustus himself makes the greater figure, in the writings of the former, or of the latter? and whether Nero and Domitian do not appear as ridiculous for their false Taste and Affectation, in Persius and Juvenal, as odious for their bad Government in Tacitus and Suetonius? In the first of these reigns it was, that Horace was protected and caress'd; and in the latter that Lucan was put to death, and Juvenal banish'd. (*Correspondence*, III, 420.)

131. "The *whisper*, that, to greatness still too near / Perhaps yet vibrates on Sov'reign's ear. *Epist. to Dr. Arbuthnot*" [ll. 356–57]. [W., p. 278.]

132. As an avowed Catholic and, at one time, suspected Jacobite, Pope could well feel vulnerable. When in 1723 his good friend the bishop of Rochester was tried for treason and exiled, he too feared for his future, worrying that he might be obliged to leave England to escape persecution for his religious and political sympathies. See *Correspondence*, II, 167.

133. "See Letter to Bishop Atterbury, Lett. iv." [W., p. 278.] Warburton's note is to Pope's letter to Atterbury (20 November 1717) in which he answered the Bishop's suggestion that he change his religion, with the response that such a conversion would distress his mother greatly and, while politic, would be of no ultimate advantage, spiritual or temporal, since he was not a Papist but a Catholic "in the strictest sense of the word" and one "with a dis-relish of all that the world calls Ambition." (*Correspondence*, I, 453–54.) *Verses Address'd to the Imitator* had leveled an attack on him through his readers "Who lik'd thy Head, and yet abhor'd thy Heart" (p. 7).

134. ". . . I take my self to be the only Scribler of my Time, of any degree of distinction, who never receiv'd any Places from the Establishment, any Pension from a Court, or any Presents from a Ministry." (*Correspondence*, II, 160.)

135. In the same letter cited above (n. 134) Pope had also written (to Lord Carteret, 16 February 1722/3): "And I assure your Lordship, tho' the King has

many Subjects much more valuable than my self, he has not one more Quiet; no Man is more Sensible of the Indulgence I enjoy from my Rulers, I mean that which is common to every Subject from the Protection of a Free Government." (*Correspondence*, II, 160.) Halsband records as one possible reason for Pope's withholding *The Letter to a Noble Lord* from publication, his deferring to the Queen's concern for her favorite counselor. (Halsband, *Lord Hervey*, p. 164.)

136. *The Verses Address'd to the Imitator of the First Satire of the Second Book of Horace*, pp. 6, 8 [see n. 37].

137. Although *Verses Address'd to the Imitator* had derided Pope for "thy Readers few, as are thy Friends," the wealth of his friendships were well known and the range of his reading audience attested by the demand for his editions.

138. In reply to a question of Spence's about his minding what angry critics published against him, Pope answered, "Never much: only one or two things at first. When I heard for the first time that Dennis had writ against me, it gave me some pain, but it was quite over as soon as I came to look into his book and found he was in such a passion." (*Anecdotes*, I, 42.)

139. Although many of his friends—like Swift and Bolingbroke—were politically active, Pope was not, for the most part, a party man, and his letters reiterate his political and religious neturality (see, for example, *Correspondence*, III, 401–2). After the publication of *Verses Address'd to the Imitator*, he had written to Swift, "You are sensible with what decency and justice I paid homage to the Royal Family, at the same time that I satirized false Courtiers, and Spies, &c. about 'em." (*Correspondence*, III, 366.) Even the more strongly political emphasis of his Horatian satires seems directed less to current issues and more to a fundamental clash in values, between the luxury and corruption of Court and Parliament and the innocence of Horatian retirement. (See Maynard Mack, *The Garden and the City* [London: Oxford University Press, 1969].)

140. "The only sign by which I found my writings ever did any good, or had any weight, has been that they rais'd the anger of bad men. And my greatest comfort, and encouragement to proceed, has been to see, that those who have no shame, and no fear, of any thing else, have appear'd touch'd by my Satires." (Pope to Dr. Arbuthnot, 26 July 1734 [*Correspondence*, III, 419].)

141. From *The First Satire of the Second Book of Horace, Imitated*, ll. 119–20 (TE IV, 17):

> Yes, while I live, no rich or noble knave
> Shall walk the World, in credit, to his grave.

142. In the same vein Pope had written to Fortescue about Lady Mary and *Verses Address'd to the Imitator* (see n. 48).

143. "Close at the ear of Eve. *Ep. to Dr. Arbuth.*" [W., p. 280.] As Warburton suggests in his note, the phrase anticipates one used in the *Epistle to Dr. Arbuthnot*;

it echoes lines from *The Fourth Satire of Dr. John Donne*, ll. 178–79: "Not *Fannius* self more impudently near, / When half his Nose is in his Patron's Ear" (TE IV, 41); in fact Halsband argues that "the *Epistle from a Nobleman* could perhaps be regarded by its readers as Hervey's retaliation for this contemptuous mention of his friendship with the Queen." (Halsband, *Lord Hervey*, p. 162.)

144. As a great favorite of the queen, Hervey was in a position of influence which he made the most of (see n. 38). Romney Sedgwick, his editor—who refers to him as Queen Caroline's gigolo—describes the situation tellingly: "so long as the Queen lived he was, so to speak, chief eunuch of the Palace with a reasonable possibility of becoming grand vizier." (*Memoirs* [London: Eyre and Spottiswoode, 1931], I, xi, l.)

A MOST
PROPER REPLY
TO THE
Nobleman's EPISTLE
TO A
DOCTOR of DIVINITY.

INTRODUCTION

Writing to Swift in January 1734, Pope commented on his current embroilment with Lord Hervey over *An Epistle from a Nobleman to a Doctor of Divinity,* with its attack upon him as satirist and translator:[1]

> There is a Woman's war declar'd against me by a certain Lord*, his weapons are the same which women and children use, a pin to scratch, and a squirt to bespatter. I writ a sort of answer [*Letter to a Noble Lord,* q. v.], but was ashamed to enter the lists with him, and after shewing it to some people, supprest it: otherwise it was such as was worthy of him and worthy of me.[2]

Included in the earliest printing of the letter (in the 1740–41 "clandestine"/Cooper edition of the Pope-Swift correspondence)[3] was an additional sentence, deleted in all the succeeding texts: "He has been since very well answered by the Parish Bellman's repeating his Verses from door to door and printing them as his own in his paper."[4] Sherburn, who restored the sentence in his printing of the *Correspondence,* notes: "Is it possible that the *Bellman of St James's Verses for the Year 1734* (used and published at the beginning of the year) came from Pope's pen and for that reason were omitted from mention here? The verses were hardly more hostile to Hervey than several other 'answers' that Pope might have mentioned."[5] It is a query that could well be extended to the authorship of the two companion pieces to the *Verses* in the small volume "Sold by J. Huggonson, near *Serjeant's-Inn,* in *Chancery-Lane.* 1734": *A Most Proper Reply to the Nobleman's Epistle to a Doctor of Divinity* and *Horace versus Fannius; or, A Case in Poinct. As Reported by Ben. Johnson.*

All three pieces have similar features. *The Belle-man of St. James's His Verses For the Year 1733. Extracted from the Nobleman's Epistle. As they were spoken every Night of the Holidays by J. Stuart, Beadle and Bellman* is a pastiche of bits,[6] as the title suggests, from Hervey's *Epistle* which needed no change in their doggerel measures to make them more appropriate to "Men of my degree" than to a nobleman; and so Hervey is ludicrously damned out of his own mouth. *Horace versus Fannius* (which first appeared in the *Grub-Street Journal* for 6 December 1733, as "Advice to a Nobleman, the author of an Epistle to a Dr. of Divinity, from H——ton C——t. by Ben Johnson") is an abridged and edited version of the last scene of Ben Jonson's *Poetaster* (itself an indictment of contemporary enemies, in that case Marston and Dekker), doctored to focus on Fannius,[7] whose foolish attack on his poetic superior Horace has its obvious counterpart in the situation at hand. The featured work—which gives the volume its title—is the short prose letter here printed, purportedly by a disgruntled William Sherwin ("W. SH——W——N"), the clergyman to whom Hervey had addressed his *Epistle* at the same time that he was satirizing him in "Dr. Sherwin's Character, design'd for his Epitaph."[8] It is essentially a collection of biblical strictures, wickedly appropriate—both to the hypocritical Hervey and to what one suspects may have been a fairly sanctimonious and platitudinous cleric.[9]

That Pope wrote any or all of these is difficult to prove. Yet there is the fact of that carefully excised statement to Swift; there is the advertisement, ascribed to Pope,[10] in the *Craftsman* of 29 December 1733, which though it may refer to the *Letter to a Noble Lord,* has suggestive phrasing and timing (". . . *This is to certify that unless the said Noble Lord shall, this next Week, in a Manner* as publick as the Injury, *deny the said Poem* [the *Epistle*] *to be his, or contradict the Aspersions, therein contain'd, there will with all Speed be published* A Most Proper Reply *to the same.*"); and there are the works themselves. All can be seen as extensions of points advanced in the unpublished *Letter* but unsuited to that very self-consciously personal work, with its tone of chill contempt moving to righteous indignation. The *Belle-man's Verses* puts Hervey into poetic (and with its pun on *belle,* into personal) place in amusing short order, while the Jonson fragment reinforces the Fanny-Hervey identification which Pope had disavowed in the *Letter,* formally restricting his commentary there to Horatian sources. Most persuasive, though, is *A Proper Reply.* In his *Letter to a Noble Lord,* Pope had taken note of Hervey's condescending and hypocritical tone in addressing his so-called friend.[11] As Robert Halsband comments, "Unwittingly Sherwin had his revenge when a literary prankster published *A Most Proper Reply.* . . ."[12]

"Literary prankster" it may be—a Pope in a jocularly damning mood (as with the Belle-man's *Verses*), but it should be remarked that the fine harangue of scriptural chiding focuses on the image of the Cherubim which "hath two Faces," of the child to be corrupted, of comeliness "turned into Corruption," and of one who "seemed one of the *Daughters of Sion tripping nicely.*" The *Epistle to Dr. Arbuthnot* looms in the offing. In fact, the three works—*The Letter to a Noble Lord,* this little collection, and the *Epistle to Dr. Arbuthnot*—make an interesting study of a range of satiric mood and technique, and we see once again how complex are the masks of the great Augustan satirists.

Notes

1. See *Letter to a Noble Lord,* above, for general background.
2. *Correspondence,* III, 401.

3. See above, pp. 389, 391.

4. In "The First Printing of the Letters of Pope to Swift" (*The Library*, 19 [1939], 465–85), Maynard Mack cited this variant as one of his arguments for relating the 1741 Cooper edition to the "clandestine" volume; it is to him that I am indebted for the suggestion that the SH-W-N letter might also be Pope's.

5. *Correspondence*, III, 401n.

6.   The
                  Belle-Man of St. *James*'s
                        His
                       Verses
                 For the Year 1733.

This *Christmas* time, your pardon I implore,
(My Masters) that I never Rhym'd before.
You know the Proverb says, that, of a Cat,
The Creature's Skin is all that you can get.
Let, for this reason, then, my Learned Friends,
Gracious, accept the All your Bellman sends.
Since such you'll find most Men of my degree,
Excuse the ignorance appears in me.
Because, when thus I write, I'm forc'd to go,
And beg a little Sense, as School Boys do.
No *Greek,* or *Latin,* has my *John-Trot* Head,
But brings plain native *English* in its stead.
My Master's courteous Rev'rence will forgive
The homely way in which you these receive.
And when you see me fairly write my Name,
For *England*'s sake, wish all could do the same:
Nay I, my self, could not so much have done,
Had I been bred, and born, an Eldest Son.
But ev'n as those may write, who ne'er can think,
So I, at *Crambo* play, with Pen and Ink,
And am call'd Poet, 'cause I write, in Rhyme,
Th' Account of, how, to pass our *Christmas* time.
So much for this,—but I am sore afraid,
Tho' I wrote more, that you no more would read.
So Masters to My Mistresses be true:
I say no more.—Past Twelve o'Clock,—adieu.

(See *Letter to a Noble Lord,* annotations 4 (pp. 556–57) and 7 (pp. 458–59).

7. See *Letter to a Noble Lord*, p. 446, and n. 50 to that text.

8. See *Letter to a Noble Lord*, p. 442, and n. 6 to that text.

9. See *Letter to a Noble Lord*, p. 452.

10. Robert Halsband, *Lord Hervey* (Oxford: Clarendon Press, 1973), p. 163. The whole advertisement ran:

> *Whereas a great Demand hath been made for an* Answer *to a certain, scurrilous* Epistle from a Nobleman to Dr. Sh——r——n; *This is to acquaint the Publick that it hath been hitherto hindered by what* seemed *a* Denial of that Epistle *by the Noble Lord, in the* Daily Courant *of* Nov. 22, *affirming that* no such Epistle was written by Him. *But whereas that Declaration hath since been* un-de-clared *by the* Courant, *This is to certify that unless the said Noble Lord shall, this next Week, in a Manner* as publick as the Injury, *deny the said Poem to be his, or contradict the Aspersions, therein contain'd, there will with all Speed be published* A Most Proper Reply *to the same.* [*Craftsman*, 29 December 1733, No. 391.]

The publication of Hervey's *Epistle* had been marked by a series of advertisements, denials, challenges, etc.; see *Letter to a Noble Lord,* Note on the Text, n. 2. See also annotation 64 to the text (p. 473).

11. See *Letter to a Noble Lord,* pp. 442, 448; also Halsband, *Lord Hervey,* pp. 158–59.

12. Halsband, *Lord Hervey,* p. 164.

NOTE ON PUBLICATION AND TEXT

The anonymous *A Most Proper Reply to the Nobleman's Epistle to a Doctor of Divinity*, bearing the name "W. SH——W——N" and dated from Chichester on "Childermas Day" (28 December) 1733, was published, along with *Horace versus Fannius* and *The Belle-Man of St. James's Verses*, in London in a small quarto and "Sold by J. Huggonson, near *Serjeant's-Inn, in Chancery-Lane*, 1734." It is from this sole printing that the present text is taken. (It carries as heading the slightly different caption title of the original text, and the notes of that text are here identified by letters of the alphabet rather than the asterisks and daggers to be found there.)

A
PROPER REPLY
TO THE
NOBLEMAN's Epistle
TO A
Doctor of Divinity

MY LORD,

I should long ago have answer'd your Lordship's *Epistle*[1] to me; but comparing it with your Lordship's [a]*Character* of me, which I have since received,[2] I found *some Things hard to be understood,* 2 *Pet.* iii.16.[3] Indeed, your Lordship verifies the Scripture, which saith, *Every* Cherubim *hath two Faces.*[4] *Ez.* xli. 18. I am sorry, after having *weighed thee in* these *Balances, to find thee so wanting.*[5] *Dan.* v. 27. But being of a tender Disposition, and observing your Epistle to begin with *Dear Doctor,*[6] (which also marks a Tenderness on your Part,)[7] I could not but reflect, *Is not* Cherubim *my dear Son? Is not he a* pleasant Child? *I do earnestly remember him still; therefore my Bowels are troubled for him,*[8] *Jer.* xxxi. 20. Tell me therefore, *if I give thee Counsel, wilt thou not hearken unto me? Jer.* xxxviii. 15. *He that hearkeneth to Counsel, is wise. Prov.* xii. 15. Now (under Correction, my good Lord,) this is my Counsel, *Never to open thy Mouth any more.*[9] *Ez.* xvi. 63. and not to *write,* at least, till you know how to *handle the Pen of the Writer.*[10] *Judg.* v. 14. For it is said, *Woe to the Writers that write grievously.*[11] *Isa.* x. 1. In Truth, my good Lord, these Verses are such, as *even a Child may write them. Isa.* x. 19. Not only a *Child* who had *continued in the Things he had learn'd, knowing of whom he learn'd them.*[12] 2 *Tim.* iii. 14. but even a Child like you, *spoiled by his Mother;*[b] and who hath *forgot all the Things he learn'd* of Doctor

[a] The CHARACTER of Dr. Sh—— which will be printed next Week.

[b] A noble Father's Heir, spoil'd by his Mother. *Nobleman's Epistle,* pag. 2.

Friend at School.^c Most certainly, if the MASTER[13] you now have, will not order you some Correction, he will (as saith *Solomon,*) *Spare the Rod, and spoil the Child.*[14]

You say, you are always imploy'd in *Business,* or *Sport;*^d but, under Favour, you have no Notion of either. Pray, my Lord, what is your *Business? You have no Business with any Man, Judg.* xviii. 7. *Your Office is to wait in the Courts,* 1 *Chron.* xxiii. 28. But, alas! if real *Business* was to be transacted by such as you, you would render it *a Court for Owls, Isa.* xxxiv. 13. Therefore I say, as to *Business,* content your self with what you are, a *Shrub growing in the Court.*[15] 1 *Mac.* iv. 38. And as to *Sport, it is as Sport to a Fool, to do Mischief, Prov.* x. 23. You are the *Man that deceiveth his* Neighbour, *and saith, Am not I in* Sport? *Prov.* xxvi. 19. But such Sport, my Lord, will ruin your *Interest; He that loveth* Sport, *shall be a* Poor Man.[16] *Prov.* xxi. 17. And you should take care (my Dear Lord) not to call forth your *Betters* to make you Merriment; least it befal you, as it befel the silly Lords of the *Philistines*; who said, *Call* Sampson, *that he may make us Sport*: And he pulled the WHOLE HOUSE on their Head. *Judg.* xvi. 23.[17] For certain it is, *The Lords favour thee not.* 1 *Sam* xxix. 6.

Your Lordship maketh much Mention of your *Head;*^e You call it a ^f*John-Trot-Head:*[19] but might not you better have said, with 2 *Sam.* iii. 8. *I am a Dog's Head;*[20] or one whose *Head is sick, Isa.* i. 5. or, *whose Plague is in his Head, Lev.* xiii. 44.

It is true, you have buried an *Elder Brother,*[21] and are become *a Lord over thy Brethren, Gen.* xxiv. 29.[22] Yet do not therefore insult and despise all Elder Brothers; nor stand up, and cry (like *another* Angel,) *I will* smite *all the* First-born, *Exod.* xii. 12. Take heed rather, that *you displease not the Lords,*[23] 1 *Sam* xxix. 7. no, not even

---

^c ——All I learnt from Doctor *Friend* at School
   Has quite deserted this poor *John Trot-Head. Ibid.*
^d ——Amidst our *Business* and our *Sport,*
   There's scarce one Moment passes unemploy'd. *Pag.* 1.
^e In *Page* 2.[18]
^f *Ibid.*

those who *want Brains,* and are *hereditary Fools;*[g] lest you chance to receive a Kick even from *every Firstling of an Ass, Exod.* xxxiv. 20.[24]

I REMEMBER when *thou wast a witty* Child, *and hadst a good Spirit.*[25] *Wisd.* viii. 19. *beautiful in thy Countenance, and witty in thy Words, Jud.* xi. 23. I well hoped, You were one of *those Children that will not lye, Isa.* lxiii. 8. But pray, my good Lord, is it not pity you should pass your time, (as you gallantly declare at the End of this glorious Epistle) in [h]Flattering, Slandering, and Lying? *Nay, my Lord, do not lye.* 2 *K.* iv. 6.[26] Much better would it be, that you imitated *Great Lords, and renown'd, riding on Horses,*[27] *Ezech.* xxiii. 6. than as you now do, Walk *with the* Spirit of Falshood, *and Lye. Mic.* ii. 11. And albeit, that *Courtiers* may have some cause to lye to the World in general, yet it is written, *Lye not* one *to* another. *Col.* iii. 9. When your Lordship told *Fibs* to the Publick, it was said by the Booksellers and Advertisers,[28] *Shall thy Lyes make Men hold their Peace? Job.* xi. 3. nay they will continue, untill the *Mouth of him that speaketh Lyes shall be stopped. Psal.* lxiii. 11. But pray, my good Lord, *Of whom hast thou been* afraid, *that thou hast lyed? Isa.* v. 11.[29] Was it of *Pope,* or of thy *Peers?* or of thy MASTER WHO HATETH A LYE? Thou should'st *be ashamed of a Lye before a* Prince, *Eccles.* xli. 17. Yet art thou known to be of those, who if not admitted any where else, can still *speak Lyes at* ONE TABLE.[30] *Dan.* xi. 27. Thou hast need to *tread warily,* though thou seemest one of the *Daughters of Sion tripping nicely.*[31] *Isa.* iii. 16. *Thou hast made thy Beauty to be abhorred. Ez.* xxv.[32] Verily, verily *thou art a Nointed Cherub!*[33] *Ez.* xxviii. 14. And if thou art, as thou sayest, *only to* [i]*one Point true,*[34]

---

[g] No Wonder, that my Brain no more affords
But recollect the Privilege of Lords.
That to good Blood by old prescriptive Rules,
Gives Right hereditary to be Fools. *Pag.* 2.

[h] For Courts are only larger Families,
The Growth of each, few Truths, and many Lyes——
In private, satirize, in publick, flatter.——*&c.*

[*viz. Interest,*] what else can be said of thee, but that *thy* COMELINESS *is turned into* CORRUPTION? *Dan.* x. 8.[35]

I am (my good Lord)
Your Faithful Monitor,

Chichester,[36] *Childermas-*   W. SH——W——N.
Day,[37] 1733.

ⁱ See the last Verses of the Epistle.

Annotations

1. *An Epistle from a Nobleman to a Doctor of Divinity: In Answer to a* Latin *Letter in Verse. Written from* H——n C——t, *Aug. 28. 1733.* See *Letter to a Noble Lord,* above, for a full account of this work and its attack on Pope (with its autobiographical section "such as one might send to thank a donnish friend for a [fulsomely] flattering letter" [Halsband, *Lord Hervey* (Oxford: Clarendon Press, 1973), p. 162]).

2. That Canon Sherwin was treated by Hervey and his friends as a figure of fun (see annotation 6 to *Letter to a Noble Lord*) was further evidenced by a satiric "character" ("Dr. Sherwin's Character design'd for his Epitaph") that Hervey had composed at the same time as the *Epistle* and which also to his embarrassment "got out"). In a letter to Henry Fox, Hervey had written: "I forgot to tell you that the printer of the *Craftsman* wrote to Sherwin, and sent him enclosed his own 'Character' as written by me, desiring him to sign a certificate, that a *Letter from a Nobleman* was written by me." (Halsband, *Lord Hervey,* p. 191.)

3. The biblical quotations which comprise the bulk of the letter are "essentially" accurate, though the original is often adapted to syntax and/or content, sometimes rather freely; more often than not, the author's concern is with the phrase itself, not with the actual reference. There are also errors or slips in citation which suggest that the work was not carefully printed or checked. Where extensive or significant variations appear, they are noted. Guerinot, in his *Pamphlet Attacks,* refers to the *Proper Reply* as a "tasteless jumble of scriptural passages" (p. 337). Given the purported speaker and the text to which he is replying, this is perhaps not an inappropriate condemnation.

4. ". . . every cherub has two faces:" There are references in the *Proper Reply* which anticipate some of Pope's brilliant sallies in the Sporus portrait, as in this instance—

Eve's Tempter thus the Rabbins have exprest,
A Cherub's face, a Reptile all the rest. . . .
(TE IV, 119–20; ll. 330–31.)

5. ". . . thou art weighed in the balance, and art found wanting."

6.   Suppliant your Pardon first I must implore,
(Dear Doctor!) that I've never wrote before. . . .

7. If Sherwin was completely guileless and imperceptive, Pope certainly was not, and his *Letter to a Noble Lord* seized on Hervey's hypocrisy and condescension.

8. "Is Ephraim my dear son? is he a pleasant child? for since I spake against him, I do earnestly remember. . . ."

9. ". . . never open thy mouth any more because of thy shame. . . ."

10. Hervey's lack of poetic ability constitutes an important theme in Pope's *Letter to a Noble Lord,* which picks up many other of Hervey's weaknesses and disclaimers (his being a spoiled son, etc.) as does SH——W——N's *Reply.*

11. "Woe unto them that decree unrighteous decrees, and that write grievousness which they have prescribed. . . ."

12. "But continue thou in the things which thou hast learned and hast been assured of, knowing of whom thou hast learned them. . . ."

13. Probably Walpole, implying Hervey's minion role in the Ministry ("and, as the Prompter breathes, the Puppet squeaks" [TE IV, 118; l. 318]).

14. See Proverbs 13.24—"He that spareth his rod hateth his son: but he that loveth him chasteneth him betimes," and 29.15—"The rod and reproof give wisdom: but a child left to himself bringeth his mother to shame."

15. "And when they saw the sanctuary desolate . . . and shrubs growing in the courts as in a forest. . . ."

16. "He that loveth pleasure. . . ."

17. Judges 16.25.

18.   So from no Head you ever can receive
More Wit, than such a Head has got to give. . . .

Hervey's *Epistle* also has a later reference, in the section castigating Pope, on heads and hatters; see annnotation 83 to *Letter to a Noble Lord.*

19. Ibid., annotation 98.

20. ". . . Am I a dog's head . . . ?"

21. At the death of his half-brother Carr, John Hervey inherited his courtesy title and became his father's heir. In the *Epistle* he had written jocularly—

> Nay, I perhaps could not as much have done,
> Had I been bred and born an eldest Son.
>
> . . . .
>
> The very Moment therefore I grew Great,
> A lazy, titled Heir to an Estate . . .
> I streight began upon a quite new Score,
> Neglected all that I had learn'd before. . . .

22. Genesis 27.29.

23. "Wherefore now return, and go in peace, that thou displease not the lords of the Philistines."

24. "But the firstling of an ass thou shalt redeem with a lamb. . . ."

25. "For I was a witty child, and had a good spirit."

26. 2 Kings 4.16—". . . Nay, my lord, thou man of God, do not lie unto thine handmaid."

27. "Which [the Assyrians] were clothed with blue, captains and rulers, all of them desirable young men, horsemen riding upon horses." Hervey, himself, in his *Memoirs*, had commented on his lack of interest in riding and hunting, a situation he turned to his own advantage:

This summer [1733] Lord Hervey had more frequent opportunities than any other person about the Court of learning the Queen's sentiments in these affairs, and conveying to her his own. Wednesdays and Saturdays, which were the King's days for hunting, he had her to himself for four or five hours, her Majesty always hunting in a chaise, and she neither saw nor cared to see much of the chase, she had undertaken to mount Lord Hervey the whole summer (who loved hunting as little as she did) so that he might ride constantly by the side of her chaise, and entertain her whilst other people were entertaining themselves with hearing dogs bark and seeing crowds gallop. (*Lord Hervey's Memoirs*, ed. Romney Sedgwick [London: William Kimber, 1952], p. 65.)

28. The publication of the *Epistle from a Nobleman* was heralded by advertisements, disavowals, counteradvertisements, summarized in part by Hervey himself in a letter to Henry Fox (see annotation 64 to *Letter to a Noble Lord.*)

29. Isaiah 57.11.

30. Evidently an allusion to Hervey's well-known influence with the queen: "Or at the Ear of *Eve*, familiar Toad, / Half Froth, half Venom, spits himself abroad, / In Puns, or Politicks, or Tales, or Lyes" or perhaps another little anticipation of the *Epistle to Dr. Arbuthnot*: "Does not one Table Bavius still admit?" (TE IV, 118; ll. 319–21 and TE IV, 102; l. 99.)

31. "Moreover the Lord saith, Because the daughters of Zion are haughty, and walk with stretched forth necks and wanton eyes, walking and mincing as they go, and making a tinkling with their feet. . . ." The author's modification of the biblical phrasing here (*tripping* for *mincing*) seems particularly significant because of the famous line in the portrait of Sporus: "Now trips a Lady, and now struts a Lord." (TE IV, 119; l. 329.)

32. Ezekiel 16.25.

33. The verse that follows ties in well with the rest of this section: "Thou

wast perfect in thy ways from the day that thou wast created, till iniquity was found in thee." Ezekiel 28.15.

34. Hervey's *Epistle* had concluded:

> For C——ts are only larger Families,
> The Growth of each, few Truths, and many Lies:
> Like you we *lounge,* and feast, and play, and chatter;
> In private satirize, in publick flatter.
> Few to each other, all to one Point true;
> Which one I sha'n't, nor need explain. Adieu.

35. The basic theme of the Sporus passage.

36. Dr. Sherwin was a canon of Chichester Cathedral.

37. 28 December.

THE
LAST WILL
AND
TESTAMENT
OF
ALEXANDER POPE,
of TWICKENHAM, Esq;

To WHICH IS ADDED,
An INSCRIPTION wrote by HIMSELF.

INTRODUCTION

Spence's simple account of Pope's death—by asthmatical dropsy—inevitably calls to mind the opening simile of Donne's "A Valediction: forbidding mourning": "Mr. Pope died the thirtieth of May [1744], in the evening, but they did not know the exact time, for his departure was so easy that it was imperceptible even to the standers-by. May our end be like his!"[1]

"Virtuous men pass mildly away." So it is in poetry—but when, in real life, they leave wills, matters seldom remain so serene. The probation of Pope's will brought reverberations both private and public, with a contemporary jibe summarizing the clamor—" 'the public said . . . that Mr. Pope had divided his fortune without any other regard than to his fame and his mistress.' "[2] That the poet had made Martha Blount his principal legatee was cause for malicious gossip, never long dormant during his lifetime,[3] and for legal action on the part of his relatives. His half-sister, Magdalen Rackett (in whose financial problems Pope had been involved since the death of her husband in 1728), entered a caveat against the will in Doctors' Commons and, according to Courthope, appeared to have undertaken proceedings, though the matter was subsequently dropped.[4] Her indignation is understandable given her financial difficulties, but over the years Pope had been generous of his time and money in behalf of the family,[5] and Martha Blount, to whom he had long been devoted, was also beset with money worries.

In any case the inheritance was not so sizable as rumor—which had generously endowed old Mrs. Pope[6]—might have it. Martha Blount reported to Spence:

> Everybody thought Mr. Pope worth a great deal more than he left behind him. What was over, after paying legacies, etc. did not amount to £2,000 (besides the thousand turned to her [Mrs. Blount] in the will).

> He [Pope] did not know anything of the value of money, and his greatest delight was in doing good offices for friends. I used to know by his particular vivacity, and the pleasure that appeared in his looks, when he came to town on such errands or whilst he was employed in them, which was very often.[7]

As her comments suggest, Pope's wealth lay elsewhere. In 1736 he had written to Swift, "I am a man of desperate fortunes, that is a man whose friends are dead: for I never aimed at any other fortune than in friends"[8]—a cry that was to be re-echoed as the years took more and more of his companions, an inevitable occurrence since so many of his associations had been formed, precociously, with older men. Later, however, he was to write again to his old friend, extolling a recent acquaintance as "one of those whom his own merit has forced me to contract an intimacy with, after I had sworn never to love a man more, since the sorrow it cost me to have loved so many, now dead, banished, or unfortunate,"[9] and there were others, bringing to his middle age a fresh resource of invigorating friendships. The will, then, serves as roster of these old and new ties—a testimonial to the strength and vitality of his attachments.

The literary legacies had more lasting repercussions. By placing his works in the hands of the two rivals for his greatest friendship, Bolingbroke and Warburton, Pope no doubt thought he had protected his remains. But, as Dr. Johnson was to comment in the *Idler,* "The performances of Pope were burnt by those whom he had perhaps selected from all mankind as most likely to publish them."[10] Dr. Johnson implies, in the *Lives,* that Bolingbroke withheld papers that had been left him;[11] and it is certainly a fact that, antagonized by the discovery of Pope's secret printing of his *Patriot King,* he was instrumental in the suppression of the deathbed edition of the four moral essays, because of what, in the portrait of Atossa, he took to be an attack on the dowager duchess of Marlborough.[12] As for Warburton (who was also a party to that suppression, since it was a printed work), a truculent and insensitive editor, a do-nothing biographer, he left only a questionable text and commentary for what Pope meant to be the definitive edition of his works, and discouraged Spence from undertaking what could have been a definitive "Life." For good or bad, Pope's friends left their marks upon him.

Notes

1. *Anecdotes* I, 269.

2. Cited by Owen Ruffhead, *The Life of Alexander Pope . . .* (London, 1769), p. 426n.

3. See *Early Career,* p. 191ff.; also see text, annotation 28.

4. EC, V, 345.

5. *Correspondence,* II, 429 et passim.

6. "On Monday Night last was bury'd at Twickenham, the Mother of Alexander Pope, Esq. who died very rich. . . ." (*The Universal Spectator,* 16 June 1733.)

7. *Anecdotes,* I, 158; also, Pope had invested heavily in annuities.

8. 25 March 1736: *Correspondence,* IV, 6.

9. 12 October 1738: *Correspondence,* IV, 134; the next spring (17–19 May;

Correspondence, IV, 178) he added: "Yet I cultivate some Young people's friendship, because they may be honest men. . . ."

10. *The Idler,* No. 65 (14 July 1759).

11. "After a decent time Dodsley the bookseller went to solicit preference as the publisher, and was told the parcel had not been yet inspected; and whatever was the reason the world has been disappointed of what was 'reserved for the next age.' " (Johnson, *Lives,* III, 192.)

12. See F. W. Bateson, "Introduction," *Epistles to Several Persons* (TE III ii, xiiff.).

NOTE ON PUBLICATION AND TEXT

In March of 1743 Pope wrote to Hugh Bethel commenting on an "Asthmatical Complaint" which had been bothering him for the prior three months,[1] and which, as asthmatical dropsy, was finally to cause his death little over a year later. Although he was encouraged to report the following February that "I live like an Insect, in hope of reviving with the Spring,"[2] his condition that winter had been so grave that on 12 December he had executed his *Last Will and Testament.*

The will was published by A. Dodd, probably in June, after his death on 30 May 1744, and from that publication (Griffith 593) the present text is taken (with the original caption title used as heading). The piece was subsequently reprinted in the two anonymous pamphlet "Lives" of the poet which followed fast on his death (one printed for Charles Corbett and one for Weaver Bickerton),[3] in various current periodicals, and finally—for our purposes—in the 1751 Warburton edition. The only significant difference in these later printings was the omission of an English translation of Pope's inscription for the family monument which was included with the first publication,[4] and the addition, in some instances, of a note on the probation of the will:

> This Will was proved at *London,* before the Worshipful *George Lee,* Doctor of Laws and Surrogate, on the 14th day of *June* 1744, by the Oaths of the Right Honourable *Allen* Lord *Bathurst,* the Right Honourable *Hugh* Earl of *Marchmont, the Hon. William Murray,* Esq., his Majesty's Solicitor General, and *George Arbuthnot,* Esq; the Executors to whom Administration was granted, being first sworn duly to administer.

William Legard,   ⎫
Peter St. Eloy,   ⎬   Deputy Registers.[5]
Henry Stevens,   ⎭

1744: *The Last Will and Testament,* sm. octavo, Griffith 593.

[1744: *Life* [with Will], Griffith 594 [Corbett].
1744: *Life* [and Will], Griffith 595 [Bickerton].
1744: Will [in *The Gentleman's Mag.*], Griffith 597.
1744: Will [in *The London Magazine*], Griffith 598.
1744: Will [in *The Scots Magazine*], Griffith 602.
1751: *Works,* ed. Warburton, Vol. IX, Griffith 651.]

Notes

1. *Correspondence,* IV, 445.

2. Ibid., IV, 499.

3. Griffith lists—and questions—another of these pamphlet lives (596): The Life of Alexander Pope, Esq; with remarks on his works; to which is added, his last will . . . [printed for W. Pinkerton], for which he cites a copy in the British Library. His suspicions were correct: the BL copy proves to be printed for Bickerton and to be identical with 595, the Bickerton entry (represented by a volume in the Boston Public Library), the correct title of the volume, though, being that listed under 596.

4. Which bore the full title: The Last Will and Testament of Alexander Pope, of Twickenham, Esq; To Which is Added, An Inscription wrote by Himself. The inscription:

> To God the Creator and best of Beings,
> To *Alexander Pope,* a Gentleman of Honesty, Probity and
>   Piety, who liv'd LXXV. Years, died M.DCC.XVII.
> And to *Editha,* his Excellent and truely Pious Wife,
>   who lived XCIII. Years, died M.DCC.XXXIII.
> To his well-deserving Parents the Son erected this,
>   and to himself.

is a translation of the Latin memorial that Pope had erected to the memory of his parents in Twickenham Church (to which was subsequently added the date of his own death and his age). See also annotation 2, p. 509.

5. Taken from the Bickerton "Life"; the Corbett does not include the citation of the Deputy Registers, and the entire notation is lacking in Warburton.

THE
LAST WILL, &c.

IN THE NAME OF GOD, AMEN. I *Alexander Pope, of Twick-enham,* in the County of *Middlesex,* make this my last Will and Testament. I resign my Soul to it's Creator in all humble Hope of it's future Happiness, as in the Disposal of a Being infinitely Good. [1] As to my Body, my Will is, That it be buried near the Monument of my dear Parents at *Twickenham,*[2] with the Addition, after the words *filius fecit*—of these only, *Et sibi: Qui obiit Anno* 17. *Ætatis*— and that it be carried to the Grave by six of the poorest Men of the Parish, to each of whom I order a Suit of Grey course Cloth, as Mourning.[3] If I happen to die at any inconvenient Distance, let the same be done in any other Parish, and the Inscription be added on the Monument at *Twickenham.* I hereby make and appoint my particular Friends, *Allen* Lord *Bathurst*;[4] *Hugh* Earl of *Marchmont*;[5] the Honourable *William Murray,*[6] his Majesty's Solicitor General; and *George Arbuthnot,*[7] of the Court of *Exchequer,* Esq; the Survivors or Survivor of them, Executors of this my last Will and Testament.

But all the Manuscript and unprinted Papers which I shall leave at my Decease, I desire may be delivered to my Noble Friend, *Henry St. John,* Lord *Bolingbroke,*[8] to whose sole Care and Judgment I commit them, either to be preserved or destroyed;[9] or in the case he shall not survive me, to the abovesaid Earl of *Marchmont.* These, who in the Course of my Life have done me all other good Offices, will not refuse me this last after my Death: I leave them therefore this Trouble, as a Mark of my Trust and Friendship; only desiring them each to accept of some small Memorial of me: That my Lord *Bolingbroke* will add to his Library all the Volumes of my Works and Translations of *Homer,* bound in red Morocco, and the Eleven Volumes of those of *Erasmus*: That my Lord *Marchmont* will take the large Paper Edition of *Thuanus,* by *Buckley*;[10] and that Portrait of Lord *Bolingbroke,* by *Richardson*;[11] which he shall prefer: That my Lord *Bathurst* will find a Place for the three Statues of the *Hercules* of *Furnese,* the *Venus* of *Medicis,* and the *Apollo* in *Chiaro oscuro,* done by *Kneller*:[12] That Mr. *Murray* will accept of the Marble Head of

Homer, by *Bernini*; and of Sir *Isaac Newton*, by *Guelfi*;[13] and that Mr. *Arbuthnot* will take the Watch I commonly wore, which the King of *Sardinia* gave to the late Earl of *Peterborow*, and he to me on his Death-Bed;[14] together with one of the Pictures of Lord *Bolingbroke*.

Item, I desire Mr. *Lyttleton*[15] to accept of the Busts of *Spencer*, *Shakespear*, *Milton*, and *Dryden*, in Marble, which his Royal Master the Prince, was pleased to give me.[16] I give and devise my Library of printed Books to *Ralph Allen*,[17] of *Widcombe*, Esq; and to the Reverend Mr. *William Warburton*,[18] or to the Survivor of them (when those belonging to Lord *Bolingbroke* are taken out, and when Mrs. *Martha Blount* has chosen Threescore out of the Number) I also give and bequeath to the said Mr. *Warburton* the Property of all such of my Works already Printed, as he hath written, or shall write Commentaries or Notes upon, and which I have not otherwise disposed of, or alienated; and all the Profits which shall arise after my Death from such Editions as he shall publish without future Alterations.[19]

Item, In case *Ralph Allen*, Esq; abovesaid, shall survive me, I order my Executors to pay him the Sum of One hundred and fifty Pounds; being, to the best of my Calculation, the Account of what I have received from him; partly for my own, and partly for Charitable Uses.[20] If he refuse to take this himself, I desire him to employ it in a Way I am persuaded he will not dislike, to the Benefit of the *Bath*-Hospital.

I give and devise to my Sister-in-law, Mrs. *Magdalen Racket*,[21] the Sum of Three hundred Pounds; and to her Sons, *Henry*, and *Robert Racket*,[22] One hundred Pounds each. I also release, and give to her all my Right and Interest in and upon a Bond of Five hundred Pounds due to me from her Son *Michael*.[23] I also give her the Family Pictures of my Father, Mother and Aunts,[24] and the Diamond Ring my Mother wore, and her Golden Watch. I give to *Erasmus Lewis*, *Gilbert West*, Sir *Clement Cotterell*, *William Rollinson*, *Nathaniel Hook*, Esqs; and to Mrs. *Anne Arbuthnot*,[25] to each the Sum of Five Pounds, to be laid out in a Ring, or any Memorial of me; and to my Servant, *John Searl*,[26] who has faithfully and ably served me many Years, I give, and devise the Sum of One hundred Pounds over and above a Year's Wages to himself, and his Wife; and to the Poor of the Parish of *Twickenham,* Twenty Pounds to be divided among them by the said *John Searl*; and it is my Will, if the said *John Searl,* die before me, that the said Sum of One hundred Pounds go to his Wife or Children.

Item, I give, and devise to Mrs. *Martha Blount,* younger Daughter of Mrs. *Martha Blount,* late of *Welbeck-Street Cavendish-Square,*[27] the Sum of One thousand Pounds immediately on my Decease; and all the Furniture of my Grotto, Urns in my Garden, Household Goods, Chattels, Plate, or whatever is not otherwise disposed of in this my Will, I give and devise to the said Mrs. *Martha Blount,* out of a sincere Regard, and long Friendship for her:[28] And it is my Will, that my abovesaid Executors, the Survivors or Survivor of them, shall take an Account of all my Estate, Money, or Bonds, *&c.* and after paying my Debts and Legacies, shall place out all the Residue upon Government, or other Securities, according to their best Judgment; and pay the Produce thereof, half-yearly, to the said Mrs. *Martha Blount,* during her natural Life:[29] And after her Decease, I give the Sum of One thousand Pounds to Mrs. *Magdalen Racket,* and her Sons *Robert, Henry,* and *John,* to be divided equally among them, or to the Survivors or Survivor of them; and after the Decease of the said Mrs. *Martha Blount,*[30] I give the Sum of Two hundred Pounds to the abovesaid *Gilbert West*; two hundred to Mr. *George Arbuthnot*; two hundred to his Sister, Mrs. *Anne Arbuthnot*; and One Hundred to my Servant, *John Searl,* to which soever of these shall be then living: And all the Residue and Remainder to be considered as undisposed of, and go to my next of Kin. This is my last Will and Testament, written with my own Hand, and sealed with my Seal, this Twelfth Day of *December,* in the Year of our Lord, One thousand, seven hundred and forty-three.

ALEX. POPE.

Signed, Sealed, and De-
clared by the Testator,
as his last Will and
Testament, and Pre-
sence of us,

    Radnor,[31]

Stephen Hales,[32] *Minister of* Teddington,
Joseph Spence,[33] *Professor of History, in*
the University of Oxford.

Annotations

1. According to Spence, a short time before his death, Pope commented, "I am so certain of the soul's being immortal that I seem even to feel it within me, as it were by intuition." (*Anecdotes*, I, 268.) Spence also reported that when Pope was asked "whether he would not die as his father and mother had done, and whether he should send for a priest, he said, 'I do not suppose that is essential, but it will be right, and I heartily thank you for putting me in mind of it'." (ibid.). But Warton related, "Such was the fervour of his devotion, that . . . he exerted all his strength to throw himself out of his bed, that he might receive the last sacrament kneeling on the floor." (Joseph Warton, "The Life of Alexander Pope, Esq," *The Works of Alexander Pope*, 1797, I, lxv–vi.) Pope lived and died a Roman Catholic though his religious concerns were always more a matter of ethics than dogma. His attitude toward Catholicism and his reasons for remaining in the faith are set forth in a letter to Atterbury, 20 November 1717. (*Correspondence*, I, 453–54.)

2. To his father (d. 23 October 1717 at Chiswick) and to his mother (d. 7 June 1733 at Twickenham) Pope had erected a monument in Twickenham Church:

D. O. M.

ALEXANDRO. POPE. VIRO. INNOCUO. PROBO. PIO.

QUI VIXIT. ANNOS. LXXV. OB. MDCCXVII.

ET. EDITAE. CONIUGI. INCULPABILI.

PIENTISSIMAE. QUAE. VIXIT. ANNOS.

XCIII. OB. MDCCXXXIII.

PARENTIBUS. BENEMERENTIBUS. FILIUS. FECIT.

ET. SIBI.

In the summer of 1725 Pope became involved in a controversy with Lady Kneller over her efforts to acquire the location of the Pope monument for a memorial for Sir Godfrey. While the affair was distressing, with Lady Kneller taking the issue to the ecclesiastical courts—where she lost her battle—some of Pope's correspondence at the time is not without its humor. Lady Kneller's insistence upon making room for a sizable tomb and her own apparently generous proportions proved irresistible subject for an "epitaph":

> One day I mean to Fill Sir Godfry's tomb,
> If for my body all this Church has room.
> Down with more Monuments! More room! (she cryd)
> For I am very large, & very wide.
> (*Correspondence*, II, 309.)

3. Cf. the account of the funeral of Pope's mother—"On Monday Night last was bury'd at Twickenham, the Mother of Alexander Pope, Esq., who died very

rich; the Supporters of the Pall were six of the poorest and oldest Women in the Parish, and six of the poorest and oldest Men to carry her Corpse; they all had Mourning except Gloves or Hatbands, which were not allow'd to the Minister, nor any Body to follow the Corpse. (*The Universal Spectator,* 16 June 1733.)

4. Allen, Baron later Earl Bathurst, a lifelong friend of Pope (and described by him, in "Sober Advice from Horace," as "Philosopher and Rake"), to whom the poet dedicated the third moral essay and one of the prominent men to whom he assigned the copyright of the *Dunciad Variorum.*

5. Hugh Hume, Lord Polwarth, third earl of Marchmont, active member of Parliament and one of the group of younger men with whom Pope associated later in his life (in 1739 Pope had written to Swift:

> Yet I cultivate some Young people's friendship, because they may be honest men, whereas the Old ones, Experience too often proves not to be so. I have droppd ten, where I have taken up one, & hope to play the better with fewer in my hand: There is a Lord Cornbury, a Lord Polwarth, a Mr Murray, & one or two more, with whom I would never fear to hold out against all the Corruption of the world." [*Correspondence,* IV, 178.])

6. William Murray, later first earl of Mansfield, another of Pope's younger acquaintances (see n. 5), to whom he had addressed his imitation of the sixth epistle of the first book of Horace. Famous as an orator, Murray was supposed to have been coached by Pope in elocution. (DNB.)

7. George Arbuthnot, son of Dr. John, and a close friend of Pope from 1735, when his father died. At that time Pope had offered (*Correspondence,* III, 452) every assistance to him and the rest of the family—which included his sister Anne, soon to become a great favorite of the poet and to be remembered also in his will.

8. Henry St. John, viscount Bolingbroke, Pope's "greatest man in the world" (*Correspondence,* IV, 6, 153, etc.), whose influence on the poet's thought and production is seen in the imitations of Horace, the moral epistles, and the *Essay on Man.* Although Pope was early acquainted with Bolingbroke (Spence, *Anecdotes,* I, 32, 150), it was not until after his return from exile in 1723 and his subsequent establishment nearby at Dawley, that Bolingbroke assumed his influential role as mentor and friend.

9. Almost immediately an issue arose over an edition of the four Epistles (Moral Essays) corrected and prepared for the press by Pope just before his death. Since this involved or was thought to involve the dowager duchess of Marlborough, who had written to Marchmont in anticipation of any such material detrimental to herself or the Duke, there was soon a wrangle between Bolingbroke and Warburton over the edition, which was eventually suppressed—although the matter was far from finished. (See TE III ii, xiiff.) Soon after, Bolingbroke was to burn

an edition of his *Patriot King*, which Pope had secretly edited and printed, not at all to the author's pleasure. (EC V, 346–47.)

10. Samuel Buckley, printer and bookseller, publisher of the *Daily Courant* and *London Gazette*, where the proposals for the *Odyssey* were printed. His great edition of Thuanus [de Thou, sixteenth-century French historian], brought out in seven folio volumes in 1733, had utilized the ornaments from Pope's Homer, for which the poet—an old friend—was handsomely acknowledged.

11. Richardson had done several portraits of Bolingbroke, references to which may be found in Pope's correspondence. This may be the painting he is speaking of in a letter to Richardson in 1738[?]: "I desire you will cause mine of him [Bolingbroke], to be framed in the manner you best approve, for which I'll be in your debt." (*Correspondence*, IV, 148.)

12. The subject of Pope's little poem *To Sir Godfrey Kneller, on his painting for me the Statues of Apollo, Venus, and Hercules*:

> What God, what Genius did the Pencil move
>   When KNELLER painted These?
> Twas Friendship—warm as *Phoebus*, kind as Love,
>   And strong as *Hercules*.

Sherburn reported that the pictures are still to be seen at Cirencester, the seat of Lord Bathurst. (*Correspondence*, II, 18n.)

13. Giovanni Battista Guelfi, Italian sculptor, protégé in England of Lord Burlington, who had been commissioned to do the funeral monument for Secretary Craggs, which Pope supervised.

14. Pope had written to Swift in November 1735:

> Poor Lord Peterborow! there is another string lost, that wou'd have help'd to draw you hither! He order'd on his death-bed his Watch to be given me (that which had accompanied him in all his travels) with this reason, 'That I might have something to put me every day in mind of him.' It was a present to him from the King of Sicily, whose arms and *Insignia* are graved on the inner-case; on the outer, I have put this inscription. *Victor Amadeus, Rex Sicilae, Dux Sabaudiae, &c.&c., Carolo Mordaunt, Comiti de Peterborow, D.D. Car. Mor. Com. de Pet. Alexandro Pope moriens legavit. 1735.* (*Correspondence*, III, 509.)

Victor Amadeus II was given the title of King of Sicily, but in 1720 he exchanged that domain for Sardinia; in Spence's *Anecdotes* there are several complimentary references to him.

15. George Lyttelton, later Lord Lyttelton, nephew of Lord Cobham, and another of the group of young politicians whom Pope cultivated in his middle age. A writer himself (poems, *Letters from a Persian in England . . . ,* etc.) as well as a patron of writers (Mallet, Thomson, Fielding), he had written a verse epistle

to Pope from Rome in 1730, about the time their friendship began. For Pope's comment on him to Swift, see above, Introduction, p. 502.

16. Lyttleton, as secretary to the Prince of Wales, had arranged the gift (*Correspondence*, IV, 170, 178). Although Pope was very proud of his independence ("Courts I see not, Courtiers I know not, Kings I adore not, Queens I compliment not; so am never like to be in fashion, nor in dependance" [*Correspondence*, II, 469]), he did enjoy his intimacy with the prince, who visited Twickenham and whom he met on other occasions.

17. Ralph Allen, leading citizen of Bath, whose fortune, derived from a system of crossposts for the Post Office, was used so generously that he became the prototype for Squire Allworthy in *Tom Jones*. His friendship with Pope dated from the 1735 publication of the letters, which so delighted him that he offered to underwrite the authorized edition. Although a visit of Martha Blount and Pope to the Allens in 1743 resulted in some unpleasantness between Martha and Mrs. Allen, Pope was reconciled to Allen before long and Dr. Johnson's representation of Pope's bequest as "contemptuous mention" and "affected repayment of his benefactions" (*Lives*, III, 195) seems unwarranted.

18. Pope's celebrated friendship with Warburton began with the latter's defense of the *Essay on Man* against Crousaz. Judging Warburton "the greatest general critic I ever knew" (*Anecdotes*, I, 217), Pope became more and more dependent on him as a commentator until he soon rivaled Bolingbroke as "guide, philosopher, and friend." The association proved particularly valuable for Warburton, who received from it not only the post of official editor to a distinguished contemporary author—with copyright interests which would be worth £4,000 (Johnson, *Lives*, III, 190n)—but also such influential friends as Allen, who as Dr. Johnson so nicely put it, "gave him his niece and his estate, and by consequence a bishoprick." (*Lives*, III, 169.)

19. Pope had written to Warburton not long before his death, "I own the late Encroachments upon my Constitution make me willing to see the End of all further Care about *Me* or my *Works*. I would rest, for the one, in a full Resignation of my Being to be disposd of by the Father of all Mercy; & for the other (tho indeed a Triffle, yet a Triffle may be some Example) I would commit them to the Candor of a sensible & reflecting Judge, rather than to the Malice of every short-sighted, & malevolent Critic or inadvertent & censorious reader; And no hand can set them in so good a Light, or so well turn their best side to the day, as your own." (Correspondence, IV, 500–1.) However much he esteemed Warburton's services—"those Garlands which a Commentator weaves to hang about his Poet, & which are Flowers both of his own gathering & Painting too, not Blossomes springing from the dry Author" (ibid., IV, 399–400)—Pope obviously sought to protect his work against "future alteration," but without, for a time, entire success, since Warburton's liberties under this restriction have been the despair of modern editors.

20. The loan from Allen (see *Correspondence,* IV, 217) was probably made for his nephew Michael Rackett, to enable him to purchase a commission in the army (see also ibid., IV, 161, 215). Dr. Johnson noted (*Lives,* III, 196; see also n. 17 above): "Allen accepted the legacy, which he gave to the Hospital at Bath, observing that Pope was always a bad accomptant, and if to 150 *l.* he had put a cypher more he had come nearer to the truth." Johnson's account probably came from Owen Ruffhead (*The Life of Alexander Pope* [London, 1769], pp. 425–26n), who includes the detail in some references to the Allen-Martha Blount hostilities, of which Ruffhead, writing under the direction of Warburton, took of course a partisan view.

21. Magdalen was Pope's half sister, by his father's first wife, a Magdalen also, who had died in 1678. Her marriage to Charles Rackett took her to Hall Grove near Bagshot, within close visiting distance of Binfield; on his death, in 1728, she became involved in legal and financial difficulties which were to plague Pope for over a decade. In spite of his various efforts on her behalf and on that of his nephews, she was understandably indignant when it was made known that Martha Blount was his principal legatee (see above, Introduction, p. 501).

22. Information about the Rackett children is scant. Pope mentions by name in his correspondence only Michael, the eldest; Henry, the lawyer—confused by EC with Robert (VI, 325); and John, the sailor. Why the latter is not recognized in this part of the will I do not know, though it is apparent from the letters that Henry was the most responsible of these three. Robert might well have been a younger child since his obituary in the *Gentleman's Magazine* of 1780 lists him as the only surviving nephew of the poet. (See n. 30.)

23. Michael Rackett, Pope's eldest nephew, like his brother John, seems to have been constantly faced with debts (see n. 20.) Pope in a letter to him of 22 January 1738 (*Correspondence,* IV, 160–61) reviewed the Rackett family finances, which were indeed in a precarious state.

24. Pope's mother had fourteen sisters, one of whom married the painter Samuel Cooper and another of whom, Elizabeth, taught the poet to read. (*Early Career,* p. 33.)

25. Except for Gilbert West, who was Lyttleton's cousin and also a nephew of Lord Cobham (whose gardens at Stowe he celebrated in a poem of 1732 addressed to Pope), and Anne Arbuthnot, herself the daughter of an old acquaintance (see n. 7), all these were friends of long standing: Erasmus Lewis, a close friend of Swift, one of his Tory circle, was a Scriblerian; Sir Clement Cotterell, court Master of Ceremonies, as the brother-in-law of Sir William Trumbull must have met Pope early in his Binfield days; William Rollinson, retired wine merchant and companion too of Swift and Bolingbroke, was writing the poet as early as 1714 (*Correspondence,* I, 240); Nathaniel Hooke, translator, editor, and friend of many of the great, may have been able to claim an association which stretched

from Pope's boyhood, when he may have been a schoomate at Twyford School (DNB), to his death, when he provided the priest for the last rites. What is certain, is that by 1731 Pope called him "my particular friend" and was involved in the subscriptions for his *Roman History,* the first volume of which was dedicated to the poet (*Correspondence,* III, 185; IV, 31, etc.).

26. John Searle, Pope's gardener, 1724–44, guardian of his pineapples and custodian of his little estate. Although his *Plan of Mr. Pope's Garden* did not appear until 1745, Pope wrote playfully to Marchmont in 1743: "He [Chesterfield] tells me your Lordship is got a-head of all the Gardening Lords, that you have distanc'd Lord Burlington & Lord Cobham in the true scientific part; but he is studying after you, & has here lying before him those Thesaurus's from which he affirms you draw all your knowledge, Millers Dictionaryes. But I informed him better, & told him your chief lights were from Joannes Serlius; whose Books he is now enquiring for, of Leake the Bookseller, who had writ for them to his Correspondents." (*Correspondence,* IV, 459.) Ruffhead reported (*Life,* p. 426n) that Allen doubled the legacy to Searle and took him and his family under his wing.

27. Mrs. Blount had died not too long before, on 31 March 1743. Pope worried about what would happen to Martha, who might continue to live with her sister, an unhappy situation even before their mother's death. The problem was solved by his bequest, which left her a house on Berkeley Row, where she lived until her death in 1763. (*Correspondence,* IV, 450, 508n.)

28. When, specifically, the long friendship began is not clear. As Sherburn has summarized the problem, "Martha Blount told Spence she met Pope after the appearance of the *Essay on Criticism* (1711) and before that of the *Iliad* (1715). She also remarked that it was when she was 'a very little girl,' and since she was born in 1690, her statements leave us guessing." (*Early Career,* p. 49.) In any case, despite subsequent opposition by her family, it was a lasting association and Pope was obviously very devoted to her, whatever exactly their relationship may have been. There was much gossip of a secret marriage or of an illicit alliance (*Early Career,* 292ff.) and the matter is still debatable, but there is no existing evidence to prove that the relation was not the intimate yet innocent friendship that Pope described it to be (*Correspondence,* II, 353–54). Many accounts of Martha's appearance and personality and of her behavior, especially during the poet's last illness (see, for example, Johnson, *Lives,* III, 275), are colored by the hostility of the speakers. The Allens—hence Warburton and Ruffhead—as well as Bolingbroke and Marchmont disliked her, though even Warburton admitted (*Anecdotes,* I, 264) that "Mrs. Blount's coming in gave a new turn of spirits or a temporary strength to him, very agreeable to what we saw of him in his last month."

29. See Introduction, p. 501.

30. Martha Blount died in 1763; her will (proved 18 July 1763) made small bequests to her goddaughter, to her sister, to a Matthew Swinborne, to her

servants, and to her nephew, whom she made her executor. As for Pope's reversionary legacy: Magdalen Rackett had died in 1747 or 1748. She left most of her property to her son Robert ("assigning as her reason for this preference, that she had not done so much for him as for her other children" [*The Athenaeum,* 30 May 1857]); and we know, from the announcement in the *Gentleman's Magazine,* that Robert died in 1780, the last surviving nephew of the poet. By 1763 Gilbert West also was dead (1756), though George Arbuthnot was not to die until 1779. I do not know about Anne Arbuthnot or John Searle.

31. Henry Robartes, third earl of Radnor, Pope's next door neighbor.

32. Stephen Hales, physiologist and inventor, as well as parish priest in nearby Teddington. Pope apparently valued him as a friend rather than scientist: " 'I shall be glad to see Dr. Hales, and always love to see him; he is so worthy and good a man' [said Spence]. Yes he is a very good man, only—I'm sorry—he has his hands imbrued with blood [Pope replied]. 'What, he cuts up rats?' Aye, and dogs too! (and with what emphasis and concern he spoke it.) Indeed, he commits most of these barbarities, with the thought of being of use to man. But how do we know that we have a right to kill creatures that we are so little above as dogs, for our curiosity, or even for some use to us?" (*Anecdotes,* I, 118.) As Osborn notes, "Pope called him 'plain Parson Hale' (Twickenham, III. ii. 64) and alluded in the *Epistle to Cobham* (ll. 39–40) to Hale's experiments on animals. . . ." (*Anecdotes,* I, 118n.)

33. What Sherburn describes as "one of Pope's most satisfactory friendships" (*Early Career,* p. 265) began with Spence's unsolicited essay on Pope's translation of the *Odyssey.* In the words of Dr. Johnson (*Lives,* III, 143), "With this criticism Pope was so little offended, that he sought the acquaintance of the writer, who lived with him from that time in great familiarity, attended him in his last hours, and compiled memorials of his conversation." Indeed he became Pope's own self-effacing Boswell.

BIBLIOGRAPHY

Arbuthnot, Dr. John. *The Miscellaneous Works of the Late Dr. Arbuthnot.* 2 vols. Glasgow, 1751.

Audra, E. *L'Influence française dans l'oeuvre de Pope.* Paris: H. Champion, 1931.

Ault, Norman. *New Light on Pope.* London: Methuen, 1949.

Avery, Emmett Langdon. *The London Stage 1660–1800.* Part II. Carbondale: Southern Illinois University Press, 1960.

Blackmore, Sir Richard. "An essay upon Epick Poetry." *Essays upon Several Subjects.* London, 1716.

———. *A Paraphrase on the Book of Job; as likewise on the Songs of Moses, Deborah, David; on four select Psalms; some chapters of Isaiah, and the third chapter of Habakuk.* 2d ed. London, 1716.

Boileau-Despreaux, Nicolas. *The Works of Mons' Boileau Despreaux.* [Translated by Ozell.] Vol. II. London, 1711.

[Le] Bossu, René. *Monsieur Bossu's Treatise of the Epick Poem. . . . "Done into* English *from the* French, *with a new Original* Preface *upon the same Subject, by* W. J." London, 1695.

Burnet, Gilbert. *Bishop Burnet's History of His Own Time.* 6 vols. Oxford: Clarendon Press, 1823.

Characters of the Times; or An Impartial Account of the Writings, Characters, Education, &c. of several Noblemen and Gentlemen, libell'd in a Preface to a late Miscellany Publish'd by P–pe and S–ft. . . . . London, 1728.

Clark, A. F. B. *Boileau and the French Classical Critics in England (1660–1830).* Paris: H. Champion, 1931.

Clifford, James L. and Landa, Louis A., eds. *Pope and His Contemporaries: Essays Presented to George Sherburn.* Oxford: Clarendon Press, 1949.

A Compleat Collection of All the Verses, Essays, Letters and Advertisements which have been occasioned by the Publication of Three Volumes of Miscellanies, by Pope and Company. To which is added an Exact List of the Lords, Ladies, Gentlemen and others, who have been abused in those Volumes. . . . London, 1728.

[Cooke, Thomas.] *Tales, Epistles, Odes, Fables, &c.* London, 1729.

Curll, Edmund. "The Initial Correspondence." In *Mr. Pope's Literary Correspondence.* Vol. II. London, 1735.

Dacier, Anne Lefèvre. "Preface." *L'Odyssée d'Homere,* traduite en françois, avec des remarques. Vol. I. Paris, 1716.

———. "Reflexions sur la première Partie de la Preface de M. Pope." *L'Iliade d'Homere,* traduite en françois, avec des remarques. 2d ed. Vol. III. Paris, 1719.

Dearing, Vinton A. "Pope, Theobold, and Wycherley's *Posthumous Works.*" *PMLA,* 60 (1953), 223–36.

Dennis, John. *The Critical Works of John Dennis.* Edited by Edward Hooker. 2 vols. Baltimore: Johns Hopkins Press, 1939, 1943.

Dictionary of National Biography. Edited by Leslie Stephen and Sidney Lee. 21 vols. with supplement. London: Oxford University Press.

Dixon, Peter. "Pope's Shakespeare." *Journal of English and German Philology,* 58 (1964), 191–203.

Douglas, Loyd. " 'A severe animadversion on Bossu.' " *PMLA,* 62 (1947), 690–706.

Dryden, John. *Essays of John Dryden.* Edited by W. P. Ker. 2 vols. Oxford: Clarendon Press, 1900.

———. *The Works of John Dryden.* General editors, Alan Roper and H. T. Swedenberg, Jr. 20 projected vols. Berkeley and Los Angeles: University of California Press, 1956–.

Durham, W. H. *Critical Essays of the Eighteenth Century.* New Haven: Yale University Press, 1915.

Farquhar, George. "A Discourse upon Comedy." *The Works of . . . Mr. George Farquhar.* 2d ed. London, [1711?].

Foxcroft, H. C. *A Life of Gilbert Burnet.* Cambridge: Cambridge University Press, 1907.

Foxon, David. "Pope and the Early Eighteenth-Century Book Trade." 1975. Typescript. British Library, London.

[Gildon, Charles]. "An Essay on the Art, Rise, and Progress of the Stage." *The Works of Mr. William Shakespear.* Vol. VII. London, 1710.

Griffith, Reginald Harvey. *Alexander Pope: A Bibliography.* 1 vol. in two parts. Austin: University of Texas Press, 1922, 1927.

Guerinot, J. V. *Pamphlet Attacks on Alexander Pope, 1711–1744.* London: Methuen, 1969.

Halsband, Robert. *The Life of Lady Mary Wortley Montagu.* Oxford: Clarendon Press, 1956.

———. *Lord Hervey.* Oxford: Clarendon Press, 1973.

Hart, John A. "Pope as Scholar-Editor." *Studies in Bibliography,* 23 (1970), 45–59.

Hervey, John, Lord. *An Epistle from a Nobleman to a Doctor of Divinity.* London, 1733.

Ilchester, Earl of [Giles S. H. F. Strangways]. *Lord Hervey and His Friends 1726–38.* London: John Murray, 1950.

Jacob, Giles. *A Law Grammar.* In the Savoy, 1749.

Johnson, Samuel. *Lives of the English Poets.* Edited by George Birbeck Hill. 3 vols. Oxford: Clarendon Press, 1905.

Laprevotte, Guy. "Notes sur le *Peri Bathous* d'Alexander Pope." *Revue des langues vivantes,* 39 (1973), 325–45.

Lounsbury, T. R. *The Text of Shakespeare.* New York: Scribner's, 1906.

Mack, Maynard. "The First Printing of the Letters of Swift and Pope." *The Library,* 19 (1939), 465–85.

———. *The Garden and the City.* London: Oxford University Press, 1969.

McKerrow, Ronald B. *The Treatment of Shakespeare's Text by his Earlier Editors, 1709– 1768.* Proceedings of the British Academy, No. 19. London, 1933.

A Miscellany on Taste. [By Matthew Concanen?] London, 1732.

Oxford English Dictionary. Edited by A. H. Murray, et al. 13 vols. with supplement. Oxford: Clarendon Press.

Philips, Ambrose. *The Poems of Ambrose Philips.* Edited by M. G. Segar. Oxford: Basil Blackwell, 1937.

Pope, Alexander. *The Art of Sinking in Poetry.* [See Steeves, Edna Leake.]

———. *"A Master Key to Popery."* Edited by John Butt. In *Pope and His Contemporaries,* edited by James L. Clifford and Louis A. Landa. Oxford: Clarendon Press, 1949.

———. *The Correspondence of Alexander Pope.* Edited by George Sherburn. 5 vols. Oxford: Clarendon Press, 1956.

———. *Epistles to Several Persons.* Edited by F. W. Bateson. *The Twickenham Edition of the Poems of Alexander Pope.* Vol. IIIii. London: Methuen, 1961.

———. *Memoirs of the Extraordinary Life, Works, and Discoveries of Martinus Scriblerus.* Edited by Charles Kerby-Miller. New Haven: Yale University Press, 1950.

———. *The Prose Works of Alexander Pope.* Vol. I. Edited by Norman Ault. Oxford: Basil Blackwell, 1936.

———. *The Twickenham Edition of the Poems of Alexander Pope.* General editor, John Butt. 10 vols. London: Methuen, 1938–67.

———. *The Works of Alexander Pope.* Edited by Whitwell Elwin and William John Courthope. 10 vols. London: John Murray, 1871–89.

———. *The Works of Alexander Pope Esq.* Edited by [William] Warburton, 9 vols. London, 1751.

Rapin, René. *Reflections on Aristotle's Treatise of Poesie.* London, 1674.

Roberts, W. Rhys, trans. *Longinus on the Sublime.* 2d ed. Cambridge: Cambridge University Press, 1907.

Rowe, N[icholas]. "Some Account of the Life &c. of Mr. William Shakespear." *The Works of Mr. William Shakespear.* Vol. I. London, 1709.

Ruffhead, Owen. *The Life of Alexander Pope, Esq.* London, 1769.

Rymer, Thomas. *A Short View of Tragedy.* London, 1693.

Seary, Peter. "Language versus Design in Drama: A Background to the Pope-Theobold Controversy." *University of Toronto Quarterly,* 42 (1972), 40–63.

Sherburn, George. *The Early Career of Alexander Pope.* Oxford: Clarendon Press, 1934.

[Smedley, Jonathan.] *Gulliveriana: Or, as Fourth Volume of Miscellanies. Being a Sequel to the Three Volumes, published by Pope and Swift.* London, 1728.

Smith, David Nichol. *Eighteenth Century Essays on Shakespeare.* Glasgow: James MacLehose, 1903.

————. *Shakespearian Criticism.* London: World Classics, 1923.

————. *Shakespeare in the Eighteenth Century.* Oxford: Clarendon Press, 1928.

Spence, Joseph. *Observations, Anecdotes, and Characters of Books and Men.* Edited by James M. Osborn. 2 vols. Oxford: Clarendon Press, 1966.

Spingarn, J. E., ed. *Critical Essays of the Seventeenth Century.* 3 vols. Oxford: Clarendon Press, 1908.

Steeves, Edna Leake, ed. *The Art of Sinking in Poetry.* New York: King's Crown Press, 1952; reprinted, Atheneum Press, 1968.

Straus, Ralph. *The Unspeakable Curll.* London: Chapman and Hall, 1927.

Swedenberg, H. T., Jr. *The Theory of the Epic in England 1650–1800.* Berkeley and Los Angeles: University of California Press, 1944.

Swift, Jonathan. *The Correspondence of Jonathan Swift.* Edited by Harold Williams. 5 vols. Oxford: Clarendon Press, 1963–65.

————. *Journal to Stella.* Edited by Harold Williams. 2 vols. Oxford: Clarendon Press, 1948.

————. *A Proposal for Correcting the English Tongue, Polite Conversation,* Etc. Edited by Herbert Davis with Louis Landa. Oxford: Basil Blackwell, 1964.

————. *A Tale of a Tub* with Other Early Works. Edited by Herbert Davis. Oxford: Basil Blackwell, 1965.

Teerink, H[erman] and Scouten, Arthur H. *A Bibliography of the Writings of Jonathan Swift.* 2d. ed. Philadelphia: University of Pennsylvania Press, 1963.

Theobald, Lewis. *Shakespeare Restored: or, a Specimen of the Many Errors, as well Committed, as Unamended, by Mr. Pope in his Late Edition of this Poet.* London, 1726.

Tyson, Dr. Edward. *Orang-Outang, sive Homo Sylvestris: or, the Anatomy of a Pygmie compared with that of a monkey, an ape, and a man. To which is added a Philological Essay Concerning the Pygmies, the cynocephali, the satyrs, and sphinges of the ancients, etc.* London, 1699.

Verses Address'd to the Imitator of the First Satire of the Second Book of Horace. By a Lady. By Lady Mary Wortley Montagu and Lord Hervey. London, 1733.

Warren, Austin. *Alexander Pope as Critic and Humanist.* Princeton: Princeton University Press, 1929.

Warton, Joseph. *Essay on the Genius and Writings of Pope.* 2 vols. London, 1782, 1806.

Welsted, Leonard. "A Dissertation concerning the Perfection of the *English* Lan-

guage, the State of Poetry, &c." *Epistles, Odes, &c. Written on Several Subjects.*
  London, 1724.
Winn, James. *A Window in the Bosom.* Hamden, Connecticut: Archon Books,
  1977.
Wycherley, William. *The Posthumous Works of William Wycherley Esq; in Prose and
  Verse. Faithfully publish'd from His Original Manuscripts, by Mr. Theobald.*
  London, 1728.

INDEX

[The works edited in this volume are listed by short titles and each is provided with a table of contents. Pope's name is abbreviated to "P." for the sake of brevity.]